SAINTS & SINNERS OF THE MARCHES

Saints & Sinners of the Marches

Michael Tavinor

with illustrations by

Sandy Elliott

Logaston Press

LOGASTON PRESS
Little Logaston Woonton Almeley
Herefordshire HR3 6QH
logastonpress.co.uk

First published by Logaston Press 2012

ISBN 978 1 906663 61 2

Typeset by Logaston Press
and printed in China by Everbest

Jacket design: Dominic Harbour
Cover illustrations:
Front: 'Saint and Sinner' – icons of St Ethelbert and King Offa
from the Shrine of St Ethelbert in Hereford Cathedral (Peter Murphy, 2007)
Inside front: 'The saints of Hereford' – icon on Shrine of St Thomas of Hereford (Peter Murphy, 2008)
Rear: 'You are as prone to love as the sun to shine' and 'The corn was orient and immortal wheat' from
windows commemorating Thomas Traherne in the Audley Chapel of Hereford Cathedral
(stained glass by Tom Denny, 2007)
Inside rear: Photographs by Gordon Taylor and Dominic Harbour

PRIVATEJonesWilliamPennyBrookesOFFARevWilliamGilpinCYNDIR

EdwardElgarOldTomPARRBlancheParryTarletonBISHOPBrownBerylReidRichardATKINS

DavidStirlingBRILLIANAHarleyJohnJebbStDavidDameLauraKnight

Fr.IgnatiusDEINIOLPuttaSirThomasEytonAdmiralLordNELSONBrianHattonStDOMINIC

To the Friends of Hereford Cathedral
on their 80th anniversary
1932–2012

Contents

Foreword

Some years ago I was asked to deliver an oration in Durham Cathedral on a topic of my own choosing. It turned out to be an unforgettable occasion, not on account of anything I said but because I found that it was a part of what was, in effect, an annual celebration of the great saints of the North. Everyone came together, civil and ecclesiastical dignitaries, representatives of the university, of the trades unions and of numberless local organisations and charities. The culmination was a huge procession in which everyone took part, circling the interior of the building to place wreaths and posies of flowers on the tombs of St Cuthbert and the Venerable Bede and others who had done good in the area. The prayers embraced all sorts and conditions of people from those who founded almshouses and hospitals to those who tended the sick and the poverty-stricken of our own age. I was deeply moved by what we would now categorise as an expression of localism, a pride in those who had contributed to life in the North, in terms of holiness and self-sacrifice. I recall describing the experience to the dean and saying 'Wouldn't it be wonderful if Hereford Cathedral could have just such an annual day?' Well, we haven't got that, but instead it triggered him to compile this delightful book, a cross between John Aubrey's famous *Brief Lives*, Thomas Fuller's *The Worthies of England* and an ecclesiastical calendar of local saints and, from time to time, villains. Its pages are full of people and things upon which to ponder and reflect, but equally, to fill us with grateful surprise that this ancient area of the Marches succeeded in producing, over the centuries, so many extraordinary saints and sinners.

Sir Roy Strong
The Laskett
February 2012

Acknowledgements

It was Sir Roy Strong who, almost four years ago, while approving of the idea of developing our celebration of the saints of Hereford, suggested that there was an even bigger project to be explored, including the lesser known 'saints and sinners' of our region. Roy has continued that encouragement and I'm grateful indeed that he agreed to write the Foreword for this volume.

This book has only been made possible through the generous financial help of those who have 'caught the vision' and have enabled costs to be covered. This will now allow all proceeds of the book to be directed towards the cathedral, its ministry and upkeep. Special thanks for such help to Nan Copp, Monique Heijn, Ken Weaver and the Friends of Hereford Cathedral, who have generously supported the book as part of the celebrations for their 80th anniversary in 2012.

With such a large number of entries to research, I have relied on the ideas of others. The calendar for the diocese of Gloucester, *Companions in the Faith*, gave me the original idea, but it has only expanded to 366 entries through the patient contributions of many people. I am especially grateful for the work of Dr Stella Rogers in her booklet *Remembering our Bishops*. Grateful thanks for ideas, information and material to Kate Andrew, Sarah Arrowsmith, Kirsty Clarke, Henry Connor, Timothy Day, Michael Evans, Rosemary Firman, Faith Ford, Walter Gould, Norman Morris, the late Paddy Morrow, Richard and Fiona Mynors, Liz Pitman, Guy Rawlinson, Averil Taylor, Rory Turnbull, Esther de Waal, David Whitehead, Michael Whittock and Jonathan Wooding.

The layout and type-setting of this volume is key to its usefulness to the reader and I'm grateful to Tim Symons for his guidance in these areas. Thanks, too, to Dominic Harbour for his splendid book jacket design and to Steve Kent and Josie Owen for their help in marketing the book.

The checking and proof-reading of the text has been a great task and has been made possible through the patience and hard work of good friends. Joy and Thomas Roderick and Valerie Vaughan Williams checked for infelicities in punctuation, while Howard Tomlinson read through the whole text, giving invaluable guidance on local entries. Similarly, Rosalind Caird ensured that cathedral-related entries were as accurate as possible. Tim Bridges spent much time reading through the text and giving me the benefit of his very wide local knowledge. A book of this length is bound to contain some inaccuracies and these are entirely my own. Perhaps we can incorporate corrections in a future edition?

Thanks, too, to my colleagues at the cathedral, who, perhaps unknowingly, have given me time and space to work on this project, not least during my study leave in Spring 2010. Special thanks to Christine Davies and Julie Anscomb in the cathedral office for their never-ending patience.

I have mentioned elsewhere my debt of gratitude to Sandy Elliott for her superb illustrations – but thanks are due, also, for her constant encouragement for the project, right from the time I first broached the idea three years ago.

My warmest thanks to Andy and Karen Johnson of Logaston Press. No author could receive a higher level of help and support. At every stage of the project, Andy and Karen have had a 'can do' approach and have been determined to translate my sometimes unfocused thoughts into what is practicable and achievable.

Last but not least, grateful thanks to all the 'saints and sinners' – the people – of the various communities who focus on Hereford Cathedral and make it the special place it is. You all continue to be an enormous inspiration to me.

Michael Tavinor
The Deanery, Hereford
New Year's Day 2012

Acknowledgements for the inclusion of copyright material

We are very grateful for permission to include the following:

W H Auden: for 'Summer Nights', to Curtis Brown Ltd. John Betjeman: for 'Blame the Vicar', 'Saint Cadoc' and 'A Shropshire Lad', to John Murray (Publishers) Ltd. Ruth Bidgood, 'Cwm Pennant: Patron Saint', to Canterbury Press. Charles Causley: for 'Mary, Mary Magdalene', to David Higham Associates. C Day Lewis: for 'Walking Away', to Peters, Fraser & Dunlop. Laurie Lee: for 'Apples', to United Agents. Walter de la Mare: for 'Motley' and 'Fare Well', to the Society of Authors. Michael Flanders & Donald Swann: for 'Misalliance', to Leon Berger, the Estates of Michael Flanders & Donald Swann. Faith Ford: 'It was hugely powerful'. Robert Graves: for 'A Pinch of Salt', to Carcanet Press Ltd. Elizabeth Jennings: for 'The Thinker', to David Higham Associates. Kirsty Clarke: 'Gethsemane'. Edwin Muir: 'The Heart Could Never Speak', to Faber & Faber Ltd. Siegfried Sassoon: 'Suicide in the Trenches', to Barbara Levy Literary Agency. David Scott: for 'The Priest in the Pulpit' and 'Piecing Together', to Bloodaxe Books. Stephen Spender: for 'I think continually of those who were truly great', to Ed Victor Ltd. Lindsay Staniforth: for 'Lord of Creation, may my every guest'. Rowan Williams: for translations 'After Silent Centuries' and 'I Saw him Standing', to the Perpetua Press.

Introduction

Saints in Sunday School?

Saints weren't much in evidence at the Baptist Sunday School I attended as a boy – at least not the official, fully paid-up ones. True, there was the saintly Mrs Emmett, who taught us all to sing 'Tell me the old, old story' and other choruses and who came round to our house if I was absent! And there was little Mr Coutts who played the harmonium in the service; he was always in competition with the adjacent piano, played loudly and enthusiastically by Mrs Scott, in her hat and fox fur. Mrs Scott always won, for you could never hear poor Mr Coutts on his wheezy instrument. I'm sure *he* was a saint! But, apart from hearing about the twelve disciples in bible readings, there was little about saints. To discover them I had to go with schoolfriend John and his parents when they occasionally took me with them to the local Roman Catholic church, the 'Immaculate Heart of Mary' in Hayes, Middlesex. In 1960 the church had been recently completed and, on the eve of Vatican Two, was full of the most exotic things. There was a huge painting of Mary by Pietro Annigoni – Mary pointing to her flaming heart; there was a painting of St Jude, patron of lost causes; and there was a statue which I later came to expect in every single French church I visited – a statue of St Thérèse of Lisieux, as always clutching her bouquet of pink roses.

Other saints appeared on my horizon. In 1965 my father resumed his duties as a church organist and so I left the Baptist Church and went with him to the fold of the Church of England. Our church at Harlington was dedicated to St Peter and St Paul, and there were statues of them in the sanctuary holding crossed keys and sword. Thus I came to realise that saints had their own symbols. Being part of the Anglican Church made me realise that there were quite a few saints in our own locality. I had been baptized at St Mary's church, Hayes, and on being taken there saw the huge and magnificent 15th-century wall painting of St Christopher, the Christ-child on his back as he waded through fish-laden waters. And just down the road from there, yet another saint – a church dedicated to St Anselm, that great 12th-century archbishop of Canterbury. Rumour had it that, although it was an Anglican church, the vicar conducted services in Latin! Even rarer birds appeared, for on going on holiday with my parents to Cornwall I discovered saints I had never heard of. The church at Tintagel, standing on a cliff and bravely facing the Atlantic, was dedicated to St Materiana, and we went to a concert at St Endellion. There was certainly nothing like this at Hayes, within a mile of Heathrow airport!

From Durham to Rome

Next stop was university and three years at Durham under the shadow of that great Norman cathedral. One didn't have to be there long to be aware of a whole new company of saints, especially Cuthbert and the Venerable Bede. Not only were they remembered with fondness by the people of the North; their very bodies were still entombed in the cathedral.

Ordination training at Cuddesdon concluded in 1982 with an exchange visit to the English College in Rome. This ancient Catholic seminary welcomed two Anglican students each year, and my four month stay there proved the richest of experiences. Not only did it give me a lifelong love of the Eternal City, but it introduced me to yet more saints! Rome, of course, has a wealth of them – Peter and Paul, Cosmas and Damian, Cecilia – many of them enshrined in the city's great churches. The Venerable English College has its own roll of saints – several martyred in penal times in England. Men would come to the College for training, then be infiltrated back into England for mission work, often to meet their deaths at Tyburn. The earliest of these martyrs was St Ralph Sherwin in 1582, and the martyrdoms went on until the late 1670s, when hysteria surrounding the Popish Plot gripped the nation. The martyrdoms of these saints were graphically portrayed in murals high up in the tribune of the college church, and playing the organ in the gallery I saw, almost daily, the terrible torture that Christian inflicted on Christian in the name of truth.

It was at the English College that I first beheld the relics of saints. The college had many relics of its martyrs and when, on 1 December 1981, the college church was consecrated, I saw these relics borne in solemn procession to a new resting place in a bronze reliquary beneath the new marble altar. On the front of the reliquary is engraved the words 'Blessed are those called to the supper of the lamb' – words which we used, years later, on the shrine canopy of St Thomas of Hereford.

Saints and sinners in the parish

I was ordained deacon in June 1982, and my title parish in Ealing returned me to the mainstream of saints and to St Peter. Here the chief of the apostles was celebrated by statue and symbol. There were crossed keys everywhere; even the youth group was called the 'Keys Club'! I have always maintained a particular affection for St Peter, not least as I celebrated my first Eucharist on his feast day in 1983.

It was at Ealing that I found new saints. These were, of course, the people of the parish. Every newly ordained priest soon discovers them – they are the parishioners who, in unsung ways, work for the kingdom. They are the ones to whom we take Holy Communion at home; they are the ones, often housebound, who say 'I'll pray for you' and really mean it. And as a new priest I came into contact not only with saints but also with many sinners. It is the priest's privilege to hear the confessions of others and to assure them of God's forgiveness, and in this action, above all others, we are reminded that the saint and the sinner are not very far apart – that both rely on God's mercy. Indeed, whenever I hear a confession, after giving absolution I always end with those wonderful words, 'Go in peace: the Lord has put away your sin – and pray for me, a sinner also.'

Ely Cathedral – built by saints?

Ely Cathedral is most certainly 'built upon the saints', and at this great church I spent five years as Precentor. The 'Ship of the Fens', seen for miles from the surrounding flatlands, was founded by the doughty St Etheldreda, who presided over her double monastery of monks and nuns with sanctity and strictness. At her death she was buried in the monastery alongside her saintly sisters with their wonderful names – Withburga, Sexburga and Ermenilda. Etheldreda was 'translated' on several occasions to new and more glorious burial accommodation, and each time her body was said to be incorrupt – a frequent occurrence with saintly remains in earlier centuries. Etheldreda's influence lives on, her life carved in 14th-century reliefs around the magnificent Octagon, her feast and translation observed with great solemnity each year, and the site of her shrine (destroyed along with many others at the Dissolution) clearly marked and celebrated in front of the High Altar of the cathedral.

The Roman Catholic church in Ely is also dedicated to Etheldreda and in it, in a reliquary, is preserved the hand of the saint – a reminder that in the 19th century, when Catholic churches were built in cathedral cities, they often took on the local saint's cult, at a time when the cathedral itself was rather nervous of reviving pre-Reformation practices which many saw as popish. Only in the second half of the 20th century did cathedrals begin to celebrate their local saints with anything like confidence and enthusiasm. Years later, when at Hereford, I was to discover that Etheldreda's influence wasn't limited to East Anglia, but that she has a church dedicated to her in the Marches (see 23 June).

Tewkesbury Abbey – built by sinners?

If Ely Cathedral was firmly founded on the saints of the past, Tewkesbury Abbey, where I spent the next 12 years, most definitely juggled with saints and sinners in its distinguished history. Saints there certainly were. It was said, in legend, to have been founded by two saintly noblemen of Mercia – Oddo and Doddo – but its true foundation was by Robert Fitzhamon, a Norman warlord, who tempted the Benedictine community at Cranborne to come to his new and splendid monastery in 1102. Over the years, many saints certainly gained honour at Tewkesbury – the magnificent chevet of chapels at the east end of the abbey contains chapels to St Faith, St Dunstan, St Edmund, St Catherine, St John the Baptist and St James. The latter's chapel is now the abbey shop, where the reredos jostles with books, postcards and souvenirs, and to me this juxtaposition of sacred and secular always seemed a contemporary symbol of the paradox which is at the heart of Tewkesbury's history. Unlike Ely, with its many saintly shrines, Tewkesbury has no indigenous saint. There were several 'near misses'. The tomb of Abbot Robert Forthington (abbot 1232–54) was the scene of many recorded miracles of healing, and in a nearby tomb is interred Abbot Alan (abbot 1186–1202) who certainly had a brush with sainthood, being prior at Canterbury when Thomas Becket was martyred there in 1170. We know, too, that Tewkesbury had its own 'feast of relics', when the relics of saints were displayed, so there was clearly a great devotion in the abbey. But Tewkesbury is essentially a great church built on the resources of the great and the good of the Middle Ages. Members of the powerful families of the period – the de Clares, the Despensers, the Beauchamps – are all buried here, and they saw the abbey as their mausoleum. Indeed, Tewkesbury Abbey has sometimes been called 'The Westminster Abbey of the Feudal Baronage'. Those buried in the abbey were warlords, rich in lands and influence and often brutal in their gaining of such influence. Among them, perhaps the most notorious sinner was Hugh Despenser, husband of Eleanor de Clare and favourite of Edward II, who, on 24 November 1326, persecuted by Roger Mortimer and other warlords, was dragged through the streets of Hereford, hanged, drawn and quartered. Only through the pleadings of his widow were his remains returned to his family church and mausoleum and, by a twist of fate, his tomb recess is now shared with a later abbot of Tewkesbury – saint and sinner coexisting even in death! Another famous sinner is supposedly interred in the abbey. East of the High Altar is the so-called Clarence vault, for many years thought to contain the remains of George, duke of Clarence –

the 'false, fleeting, perjur'd Clarence' of Shakespeare's *Richard III*. Later research, however, concluded that the bones in the vault were those of an 18th-century alderman who requisitioned the vault for himself and his family! Near to the Clarence vault is the so-called Wakeman Cenotaph, which depicts a decaying cadaver in an open shroud, covered with vermin. This monument has always been associated with John Wakeman, abbot at the time of the Dissolution. He was rewarded for his co-operation by being made bishop of the newly formed diocese of Gloucester. Now, was he a saint or a sinner? An abbot who sensibly embraced the new religion, or a 'turncoat' who betrayed his monastery? If the monument really is Wakeman's own cenotaph, then the grim image of mortality – a *memento mori* – suggests that he had a sober estimate of his life and destiny.

The lordly sinners of Tewkesbury were certainly intent on making their achievements known – the wonderful 14th-century stained glass in the chancel shows them all, resplendent in their tabards with their own heraldic devices proudly worn. Yet these sinners did have an eye to faith and eternity. When they were buried, they gave instructions that they should be commemorated by chantry chapels where masses would be said for their souls. The chapels crowd around the High Altar, each chapel and tomb jostling for space and influence. There is Lord Edward Despenser, the 'kneeling knight', in a niche above his own Trinity Chapel in an attitude of prayer and perpetually looking toward the High Altar as the source of his salvation. One of the chapels, too, is dedicated to St Margaret of Scotland, chosen, we believe, as she was herself an ancestor of the Despenser family – saints and sinners sharing the same family tree.

So, Tewkesbury Abbey began to show me that saints and sinners were not so far apart – the dividing line was often quite blurred. Also at Tewkesbury, I began to see that often we don't pay enough regard to those who, while not being actual saints, were people of courage and vision who made a difference to their age in all sorts of ways. In Tewkesbury is a memorial tablet to Victoria Woodhull Martin, the first woman presidential candidate in the USA. She was never elected, of course, but she stands here as a woman of courage and inspiration to many others, not least those who have pressed the cause of women's rights and who have worked for justice in the world. I began to see that 'Saints and Sinners' encompassed a great company – and that our churches contained both categories in full measure.

Hereford Cathedral – *Celebrating the Saints*

And so to Hereford, in May 2002. Here I found, to my delight, two important saints – Ethelbert the King and Thomas of Hereford. Each is an example of different ways of saint-making in their time – Ethelbert, the Saxon king, made a saint by acclaim, or the common consent of the people, and Thomas Cantilupe, the medieval bishop, canonized only after over 30 years of exhaustive enquiry. Each saint was certainly revered in the cathedral – one could spot images of both in wood, stone and glass, and their memory was perpetuated through the cathedral seal, coats of arms, St Ethelbert's Hospital, and the local Thomas Cantilupe primary school. Indeed, Hereford Cathedral's full title is 'The Cathedral Church of the Blessed Virgin Mary and St Ethelbert the King'. There had been a major Cantilupe festival in 1982, the 700th anniversary of his death, and a similar festival in 1994, the 1,200th anniversary of the death of Ethelbert. And yet I felt that there could be much more in the cathedral to celebrate the lives and influence of these saints now, and that through them we could enrich our liturgical life.

To these two saints we added a third – Thomas Traherne, the 17th-century visionary priest and poet who spent nearly all his life in Hereford and its environs and who is now remembered in the Calendar of the Church of England as a holy person worthy of national commemoration.

And so, with these three holy men, the project *Celebrating the Saints* was conceived – a project to use and develop what remained in the cathedral of their earlier cults, and to adapt all this to the needs of a 21st-century cathedral.

The first of the saints to be tackled was Thomas Traherne. The Traherne Association had been formed in 1990 under the leadership of Richard Birt, and much had been discovered about Traherne's unique influence on the life and literature of the 17th-century church. But little mention was made of him in the cathedral he must have known so well. We decided to fill the windows in the 16th-century Audley Chapel on the south side of the Lady Chapel with glass commemorating Traherne. We approached several scholars – Denise Inge, Donald Allchin and Julia Smith – asking them to suggest images from Traherne's writings which might 'translate' well into stained glass. From these conversations emerged a brief, containing texts and focusing on four key areas of Traherne's thinking – his love of the Herefordshire countryside, his emphasis on the importance of the Cross of Christ, his insistence that 'You are as prone to love as the sun to shine', and his love of the city of Hereford. This brief was given to artist Tom Denny, who created a magnificent design for the stained glass, weaving together so many texts and allusions. I had known Tom's work at Tewkesbury and in other churches and was convinced that he was exactly the right artist to undertake the project, and this proved to be the case. Tom's work here, as in so many of his commissions, may be seen on several levels. The glass makes an immediate impact of glorious colour and yet repays closer and more frequent inspection, as details emerge, unseen at first. In this way, Tom's interpretation exactly matches Traherne's own work, which is also able to be understood on many different levels. The glass is placed in the Audley Chapel, its internal wall in the Lady Chapel a magnificent riot of colour with its 16th-century screen of painted saints. Through this screen a narrow aperture enables us to glimpse the wonderful colour of the windows – symbol, perhaps, of the glimpses of God's glory which we are (perhaps all too infrequently) granted. The chapel is now a place of beauty and prayer and visitors and pilgrims are often seen there, just sitting and gazing at these windows and discovering more and more in them.

The windows were dedicated by Anthony, bishop of Hereford, on 25 March 2007. The work was made possible through the generosity of many donors, including members of the Traherne Association and the Jerwood Foundation.

The next saint to be celebrated was Hereford's own Ethelbert, king and martyr. He was born in East Anglia in the late 8th century. He journeyed to Mercia to seek marriage and was caught up in political intrigue at the court of King Offa, who had the young king beheaded (traditionally on 20 May) at Marden, five miles north of Hereford. To this bare fact must be added more elaborate stories of his life and death which have been passed down to us through several medieval writers. It is these moving and miraculous stories that we wished to communicate in Hereford today. And so we decided to commemorate Ethelbert by telling his story in 12 episodes portrayed through the vivid medium of the icon. For a site we chose the space immediately east of the High Altar, as this was traditionally the place where saints were enshrined. We can still see this arrangement today in many cathedrals – Chichester (St Richard), Durham (St Cuthbert), Winchester (St Swithin), and many more. It seemed logical to place any new 'shrine' in the traditional place, especially as the retro-choir in Hereford had a well-placed pillar, which seemed ideal for the purpose. The pillar is encircled by a wooden structure, designed by Robert Kilgour, cathedral architect, and made by Stephen Florence, furniture maker and designer to HRH The Prince of Wales. The icons were created by Peter Murphy, a Roman Catholic icon writer whose work I had known and admired for years. The structure is gilded and painted to match the glorious colour seen in the nearby Lady Chapel reredos and to reflect the glowing colours of the recently restored Audley Chapel. The structure is seven-sided and on two carved bands encircling the structure are some of Our Lord's words:

> Jesus said: All who want to be followers of mine must renounce self.
> Day after day they must take up their cross and follow me. (Luke 9:23)

The gospel verse puts into context the suffering at the heart of Ethelbert's story and marks the saint as one who, by his death, followed Christ in his Passion. It reminds us, too, that Ethelbert's story of suffering is one that is experienced by so many people in the world today, and underlines the Christian vocation of following our Lord Jesus in joy and in sorrow.

The new shrine of St Ethelbert was dedicated by Anthony, bishop of Hereford, on 9 June 2007 and was made possible through the generosity of many individual donors and by the Friends of Hereford Cathedral.

The final part of *Celebrating the Saints* was completed in 2008. The cathedral is fortunate in possessing substantial remains of the base of the medieval shrine of Thomas of Hereford. This survived the destruction of the later Lady Chapel shrine and is one of the few such bases remaining in England. The impetus to restore the shrine came partly as a result of the pilgrimages made by the Friends of Hereford Cathedral in the steps of the saint between 2002 and 2005. In 1999 a manuscript was discovered in the cathedral library which was found to be the household roll of Thomas Cantilupe and his entourage when he journeyed from Hereford to Orvieto in 1282 to seek release from the excommunication placed on him by Archbishop John Peckham. The manuscript contained details of all the places Thomas had stopped *en route* and gave a fascinating glimpse into the last days of the saint's life. The Friends decided to recreate this journey and, in four stages, (Hereford to Paris, Paris to Nîmes, Nîmes to Genoa and Genoa to Rome), a group made these journeys and ended in Rome, with a mass of thanksgiving in the Catacombs and an evensong in the Venerable English College. We returned from pilgrimage determined to find a way of commemorating 'our Thomas' today.

The stonework of the shrine base itself had been restored during the 1990s and we were left with a beautiful example of medieval stonemasons' art. The area in the north transept seemed to me, however, in much need of colour and narrative. And so fabrics were created telling the story of Thomas Cantilupe in 12 episodes. These were designed by Terry Hamaton and embroidered by Croft Design of Much Wenlock. The shrine base itself is now surmounted by a gilded and painted canopy, giving a glimpse of how the shrine might have looked before the Reformation. The shrine canopy has in its apex an icon of saints associated with Hereford – The Blessed Virgin Mary, St John the Baptist (the parish patron), Ethelbert, Thomas of Hereford and Thomas of Canterbury (on whose cult Hereford's was based). Within the canopy is seen a reliquary containing a small relic of Thomas of Hereford. The relic had been in the care of Stonyhurst College since the 1830s, and is now on loan to the cathedral. The shrine area has been a place of prayer and intercession since the 13th century, and now new stands were made for the candles of pilgrims, who can leave their own prayers on the intercession board. On the board itself are inscribed words from *In memoriam* by Alfred, Lord Tennyson: 'More things are wrought by prayer that this world dreams of'.

And so, on 8 November 2008, in the presence of a great company, including the abbots of Downside and Belmont and the parish priest of St Francis Xavier, Hereford, Fr Michael Evans, the relic was placed in the shrine – the presence of the Roman Catholic clergy seen as a powerful ecumenical gesture. The shrine itself was re-dedicated by Anthony, bishop of Hereford, as a symbol of prayer and devotion for all at the heart of the cathedral. Many took part in the service, including those who had been on the Cantilupe pilgrimage and had completed all four stages. They felt that the journey had brought them very close to St Thomas and that the saint celebrated by us was indeed one who knew what it was to be treated as a sinner and whose humanity now shone through for them. Many who went on the journey donated to the project themselves, and their initials are woven into the fabric panels on either side of the shrine telling the story of St Thomas. Perhaps in this way the present generation is woven into the story and thus transforms it from a medieval narrative into one of real relevance to life and spirituality today. Indeed, if pilgrims squeeze between the shrine and the east wall of the transept, they will see representations of modern-day pilgrims – Sir Roy Strong and his late wife, Julia – offering up the shrine canopy as a gift, with other representatives of contemporary Hereford life looking on. Even the present bishop and dean make an appearance. A varied cast indeed!

What difference has *Celebrating the Saints* made to the life of Hereford Cathedral?

Each project has certainly brought colour back into the building. We tend to forget that the pink sandstone with which we are familiar would have been completely unknown to our medieval forebears. In their day every possible surface in churches would have been painted in the brightest colours. So much was scraped off at the Reformation or during the Civil War or subsequent years of neglect or restoration. We can still glimpse earlier glories in Hereford in the brightly coloured screen of the Audley Chapel, but apart from this little has survived. The new Traherne glass and the two shrines have certainly added 21st-century colour. Celebrating our three saints has encouraged us in our prayer – so many more now leave their intercessions at the shrine of St Thomas, and each Friday we have prayers at St Ethelbert's shrine, when we pray for peace and justice in the world. We use the three focuses of prayer liturgically. In evening pilgrimages we celebrate a Eucharist 'on the move', using each saint to guide us in a particular part of the service, and by interpreting each saint for our visitors, we encourage them to make their own personal pilgrimage around the cathedral, 'translating' these saints and their message into our own day.

The shrines have given us renewed inspiration to celebrate the saints' festivals. St Ethelbert's day is celebrated with a five-mile walk from Marden, site of his martyrdom, to the cathedral and a Eucharist which begins at St Ethelbert's Well on Castle Green, where we are sprinkled with water. On the feast of St Thomas, in October, we process to the shrine, cense it and make our intercessions there. Not everybody will approve! One prayer left at the shrine of St Thomas said 'Whatever happened to the Reformation?' Not all are comfortable with devotion to the saints – and the possession of a relic may seem very un-Anglican. But should not devotions which have helped people in the past help them again today? Is not our church today happy to embrace a much wider range of devotion, confident that these need not be limited to one denomination but that rather we are led to God by any number of means? I hope so. Didn't John Wesley use a rosary?

***Celebrating the Saints* – enlarging the picture**

It crossed my mind that we know a great deal about the cult of the saints, especially in Hereford, in pre-Reformation times, and we are rediscovering their powerful influence in spirituality today. But what of the 'hidden years', that is, the period between the 16th and the 19th centuries? Did the Church of England give up on them?

It was partly to answer this question that I undertook a course of study with Lampeter University which led, eventually, to a Master of Theology degree. The title of my thesis was: *A survey of Cathedral Shrines which escaped destruction at the Reformation – to analyse attitudes towards these survivals in terms of conservation and cultic significance during the period 1550-1850.* In this, I looked at shrines which had, somehow, survived the Reformation – St Edward the Confessor at Westminster Abbey, St Werburgh at Chester and St Thomas Cantilupe at Hereford – and tried to discover why each had survived. Clearly, Westminster's shrine survived because of royal links and it remains one of the very few shrines where the saint's body has remained intact. Chester's shrine base survived through being made into a bishop's throne during the Laudian remodelling of the cathedral during the early 17th century, and Hereford's Cantilupe shrine seems to have survived through ignorance as well as local antiquarian interest.

But, in all three cases, it seems that no amount of official disapproval could completely destroy a devotion which spoke so powerfully to ordinary people. Indeed, one of the great sadnesses of post-Reformation cathedrals was that, while their lives continued on similar lines to those before the Reformation (places where music and learning were important), the links with cathedrals for ordinary people were all but lost as they became enclaves of elitism and privilege. The saints had always brought sinners into cathedrals – to pray at their shrines, and to seek healing, reassurance and encouragement in an often violent and confusing world. Now that link was seemingly gone. Or was it? There is evidence that, at Hereford, the embattled and defaced shrine still had links with people's prayers and devotion. In the guide book by J Price of 1797 we read:

> Many miracles were said to have been wrought at the place of his (Cantilupe's) burial, and his tomb is frequented by Roman Catholics.

And only a few years later, writing in another guide book of 1827, W T Rees observes:

> ... the reputed sanctity of this prelate occasioned his tomb to be visited by pilgrims and travellers from all parts of Europe, and is still regarded with veneration by those who hold the tenets of the Catholics.

In other words, the link of saint and sinner seen in our cathedral churches and especially at the shrines of the saints is a very strong one – one which seems to survive turmoil and upheaval in the church. Far from being exclusive, the saints 'gave permission' for ordinary people – saints and sinners alike – to be in these great buildings.

My researches have shown that, over the last century, cathedrals regained their confidence in celebrating the saints in their midst. Thus shrines at St Albans, Oxford, Winchester and, as we have seen, at our own Hereford, were restored and their significance re-established. And people are drawn to these sites in huge numbers. Is there, I wonder, any link between what went on – and what goes on – at shrines in cathedrals and what happens today at 'roadside shrines' with the leaving of flowers and tributes at scenes of tragedy? And might these be connected with the so-called 'Diana phenomenon'? Are they both ways in which sinners and saints – medieval and modern – are seeking to deal with the unspeakable and unknowable in society and in their lives through being in touch with those they see as saints? It is a study well beyond the scope of this introduction, but it reminds us, once again, that those dividing lines between ordinary and extraordinary, saint and sinner, sacred and secular, are thin indeed.

Saints and Sinners – finding them in the locality

Anthologies have always had a fascination for me. Perhaps it is my limited attention span, or perhaps it is my growing realisation that people often learn more when the material is in 'thin slices', but certainly, several anthologies have had a great influence on me. Alan Ecclestone's *Gather the Fragments* (1993) is a wonderful *tour de force* – a lifetime's squirreling away of poems and prose from an astonishing breadth of literature. Similarly *Sacred and Secular*, by Adam Fox, Gareth and Georgina Keene (1975) impressed me by its ability to draw from a vast range of sources – from classical, medieval and contemporary writings. It struck me that there was a place for an anthology of local 'saints and sinners' – men and women who had made a difference to the Marches for better or, sometimes, for worse, and whose lives deserved to be better known. Far from reinforcing our notions that saints and sinners were another breed, it seemed creative to discover them out on our own back doorsteps. And so the idea of *Saints and Sinners of the Marches* came into being.

But how to choose them? I decided upon the target of one person each day for a whole year – that is, 366 people. The names came from a variety of sources – the *Oxford National Dictionary of Biography* proved invaluable. Arthur Mee's *King's England* histories of Herefordshire and Shropshire contain wonderful vignettes of towns and villages which always mention famous sons and daughters of the places described. Local historian David Whitehead was most generous in suggesting names which might be followed up. When the 366 names had been assembled, they had to be fitted into a whole year! Date of birth, date of death – these were obvious starting points. But it was not that easy – some dates (27 August sticks in my mind) claimed six or seven characters and so there had to be some re-distribution. Sometimes the date of baptism might come to the rescue, sometimes a significant date in a person's life and, in the case of a jester to Elizabeth I, Condover's Richard Tarlton, April 1 seemed the ideal date for commemoration!

Who is in? Who is out?

While writing the book, people have sometimes asked me – 'How do you decide who are saints and who are sinners?' The answer is that I would rather leave this to the reader! Some of those included are most certainly saints. None, presumably, would argue with the inclusion of the Blessed Virgin Mary, patron of Hereford Cathedral and of many churches in the diocese. Similarly, great saints and apostles are sometimes included because of a great local devotion to them. Local saints are obvious candidates – Clydog, Dubricius – these are heroes who brought the faith to the Marches and who deserve to be better known.

Some sinners are fairly clear cut. Few would argue with the inclusion of Roger Mortimer, brutal warlord of the Marches, or that of Hugh Despenser, ambitious and scheming favourite of Edward II. But dividing lines are often unclear. It might be thought that convicted and executed criminals would be placed firmly in the 'sinners' category – and this might well be true of Major Armstrong, the 'Hay Murderer' – but what of Mary Morgan, executed in 1805 in Presteigne for the murder of her new-born child? Later evidence suggests that she would have been suffering from chronic post-natal depression. She received harsh justice rather than the help she desperately needed. Was Mary Morgan just a sinner?

The truth is that most people in the book are 'somewhere in between'. There are musicians, poets, artists, those committed to the abolition of the slave trade, actors, philanthropists and benefactors; there are television celebrities like Gilbert Harding; there is 'Old Parr', who is said to have lived to the age of 152; there is Sergeant Hugh Carter, Herefordshire policeman, killed by a sniper's bullet in the Cyprus troubles of 1956. The list is extensive and varies hugely. What we can say is that all of them have made a difference to our part of God's world. Nobody in the anthology is living – the latest death date is 1996 (Beryl Reid).

What area is covered?

The core of the area covered is the diocese of Hereford – that is, Herefordshire and Shropshire south of Shrewsbury – an area associated with the diocese since the 7th century. To this we add border areas of Wales, remembering that the diocese contains 15 parishes in the principality as well as three in Worcestershire. There are nods towards our neighbouring dioceses – Worcester, Gloucester, Lichfield, St Asaph, Monmouth, Swansea and Brecon. We remember areas of the world with which we have special links as a diocese – Bavaria in Germany and Tanzania. In other words, 'the Marches' of this book's title is an area which has been generously interpreted!

How to use the book

Each saint or sinner commemorated has a page devoted to him or her. Half the page consists of a biographical note, then a connecting passage, sometimes with some personal reflections, which leads into a poem or piece of prose associated with the person commemorated. This might be by the saint herself or the sinner himself. I might choose a passage which suggests what the person 'stood for' – truth, justice, suffering. The emphasis is on 'lateral thinking' – using a local character to expand our thinking, then lead from the local to the national and even international and allow who and what is on our doorstep to broaden our horizons. Perhaps the theme might even lead us into prayer and reflection on what this person, with their joys and sorrows, might be saying to us today. Sometimes the passages chosen will be serious and might be used in worship, at other times the theme is more secular, and occasionally a passage may be included for no other reason than to raise a laugh! The breadth of them – sacred and secular – reflects, I hope, the breadth of sainthood and 'sinner-dom' reflected in the book. A reader might choose to use the book day by day, others may prefer to dip into it at random.

The book might, I suppose, be used by teachers and lecturers who could value being able to use this anthology to introduce students to some of the people who have made the Marches the wonderful place it is.

One thing is certain. I won't have included everybody's saints or sinners in this anthology. People have expressed amazement that I've discovered 366 people on whom to write. But the truth is that there are hundreds more. Some will be known by many, others by the reader alone. We all have our own saints and sinners – those who have made a difference to our own lives, and who have helped us to become better and more rounded people.

The illustrations

Whatever the value or otherwise of the text, what is written is immeasurably enlivened by the illustrations by Sandy Elliott. Sandy and I worked for two years on this project and she always succeeded in capturing what I had in mind for each character. She brings each to life in a stylish, whimsical, serious, humorous way and I know that all who read the book will immediately identify with them. I owe Sandy a huge debt of gratitude for her inspiration, hard work and constant encouragement.

January

1

The Blessed Virgin Mary, Mother of God

Patron of Hereford Cathedral

Although we may debate whether many in this anthology are 'saints' or 'sinners', the Church is united in its tradition not only that Mary is pre-eminent among the saints but also that she shares the state of her son, Jesus Christ, as being without sin. Mary exceeds all other saints in the number of church dedications. In Herefordshire alone, there are over 50 such dedications to which we must add nearly 40 in south Shropshire, Worcestershire and parts of Wales in the diocese of Hereford. Sometimes dedications are more specific and will be celebrated on different days – the Nativity of the Blessed Virgin at Madley (8 September) – the Assumption at Eardisland (15 August). 1 January is kept in the Roman Catholic church as 'Mary, Mother of God' and we rightly begin a new year celebrating her honour. Mary is principal patron of Hereford Cathedral and in the Lady Chapel is an icon by Aidan Hart of Mary 'who points the way'. Mary points to her son – Jesus points to his mother. There is a mutuality and reciprocal love in their relationship, a giving and receiving which we pray will be at the heart of our lives in the coming year.

Mary has been honoured in prose and poetry throughout the centuries. In this meditation, the 17th-century Herefordshire poet Thomas Traherne offers praise:

And first O Lord I praise and magnify thy Name
For the Most Holy Virgin-Mother of God, who is the Highest of Holy Saints.
The most glorious of all thy Creatures.
The most Perfect of all thy Works.
The nearest unto Thee, in the Throne of God.
Whom Thou didst please to make
Daughter of the Eternal Father.
Mother of the Eternal Son.
Spouse of the Eternal Spirit.
Tabernacle of the most Glorious Trinity.
Mother of Jesus.
Mother of the Messiah.
Mother of him that was the Desire of all Nations.
Mother of the Prince of Peace.
Mother of the King of Heaven.
Mother of our Creator.
Mother of our Redeemer.
Mirror of Wisdom and Devotion.
Mirror of Sweetness and Resignation.
Mirror of Sanctity.
Mirror of all Virtues.
The most unworthy of all thy Servants falleth down to worship
Thee for thine own Excellencies; even thee, O Lord, for thine own Perfection,
and for all those Glorious Graces, given and imparted to this Holy Virgin,
and to all thy Saints.

Thomas Traherne *c.*1636–74, *Church's Year-Book*

Merewahl fl.660

Convert to Christianity & founder of Leominster Priory

Leominster Priory claims to be older than Hereford Cathedral. Merewahl (or Merewald) was a son of Penda, king of Mercia. Converted to Christianity by Edfrith of Northumbria, he was the first Anglo-Saxon ruler to become a Christian. Married to Eafe, a Kentish princess, Merewahl and his wife had three daughters, the most famous of whom was Milburga (see 23 February). It is from later legendary material about St Milburga that we have knowledge of Merewahl's conversion and his subsequent gift of land to found the early monastery at Leominster. Merewahl continued to be honoured in Leominster as an important part of the town and priory's early history. The 16th-century historian Leland claimed that Leominster had 'the skulls of Merewald and Ethelmund, kings of the Marches'.

From The Legend of St Etfrid of Leominster, *we have this passage, which speaks of Merewahl's conversion and Leominster's symbol of the lion:*

> Now, six centuries and six decades had run their course from the time of Our Lord's incarnation when Merewald, King of Mercians, was baptized by Etfrid the priest. See how the king, represented as the lion up to now, the lion mentioned earlier, is not now fierce as a lion, but meeker than a lamb. By making clear his condemnation of his own error and his belief in the truth, he escaped from the mire. He adopted the faith of truth, he received from a guest at his own table the bread of life, that is to say the teachings of faith and of life. The place where the conversion of the king through the agency of a lion, as the Lord, was divinely foretold to the man of God. That was chosen as the site for buildings dedicated to the royal deliverer, the gatekeeper of the kingdom of heaven. Consequently that very place was afterwards converted into the Monastery of the Lion.

Another, more famous conversion is that of St Paul, celebrated later this month. This hymn reminds us of the power of 'dramatic conversion' – although this doesn't happen to all, by any means!

We sing the glorious conquest
Before Damascus' gate,
When Saul, the Church's spoiler,
Came breathing threats and hate;
The ravening wolf rushed forward
Full early to the pray;
But lo! The Shepherd met him
And bound him fast today!

O Glory most excelling
That smote across his path!
O Light that pierced and blinded
The zealot in his wrath!
O Voice that spake within him
The calm reproving word!
O Love that sought and held him
The bondman of his Lord!

John Ellerton 1826–93

JOHN WEBB 1776–1869
Civil War historian

IN THE YEAR 1999, a household roll from the time of Bishop Thomas Cantilupe was discovered in Hereford Cathedral Library, the itinerary of which provided a glimpse into Cantilupe's last journey in 1282 to seek the lifting of his excommunication. A similar, more detailed roll, for Cantilupe's successor as bishop (see 15 March), was studied and edited by the cleric we commemorate today. Ordained in 1800, John Webb served clerical posts in Worcester and Ross before becoming rector of Tretire with Michaelchurch in 1812. He rebuilt the church at Tretire at his own expense. In 1819 he became a Fellow of the Society of Antiquaries and promoted Herefordshire to a wider audience through his researches. His most important work was an edition of *A Roll of the Household Expenses of Richard de Swinfield*, and at his death he left unfinished an edition of *Military Memorials of Colonel John Birch* as well as extensive writings on the Civil War in Herefordshire. He was also a poet, writing in the style of Tudor forebears, and as a librettist, he wrote texts for an oratorio, *David*, set to music by a friend, Chevalier Newkomm, in 1834. He died in 1869 at Hardwicke Rectory, near Hay, where his son was incumbent.

The Roundheads in the Civil War, as described by John Webb, wrought huge damage to church interiors. I can recall several windows made up of fragments of stained glass – hacked out during the Civil War and afterwards painstakingly put together, though often as a jumble of coloured glass. Fine examples are the west window of Winchester Cathedral, in the sacristy at Tewkesbury Abbey and in the south aisle at Hereford Cathedral. Even in their jumbled form, these windows can give us a wonderful image of 'flakes of glory', as the 17th-century poet Edward Taylor puts it. Here, George Herbert uses the image of glass to represent human life and our relationship with God:

Lord, how can man preach thy eternal word?
He is a brittle crazy glass:
Yet in thy temple thou dost him afford
This glorious and transcendent place,
To be a window, through thy grace.

But when thou dost anneal in glass thy story,
Making thy life to shine within
The holy Preacher's; then the light and glory
More rev'rend grows, and more doth win:
Which else shows wat'rish, bleak, and thin.

Doctrine and life, colours and light, in one
When they combine and mingle, bring
A strong regard and awe: but speech alone
Doth vanish like a flaring thing,
And in the ear, not conscience ring.

George Herbert 1593–1633, 'The Windows'

Joseph Corbett (Plymley) 1759–1838

Archdeacon & opponent of transatlantic slave trade

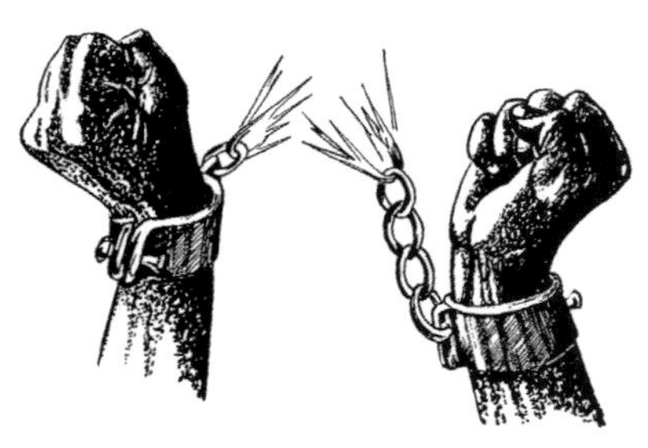

When we think of the abolition of slavery in the British Empire we always think of William Wilberforce. He was a vital force for change, of course, but he was supported by a key group of like-minded individuals in the provinces, and the archdeacon we remember today was an important example. Born in 1759 to an apothecary father who had married into the wealthy Corbett family in south Shropshire, Joseph Plymley was destined for the Church from an early age. In 1792 he became archdeacon of Salop (in Hereford diocese) and proved an energetic and effective pastor, encouraging the rebuilding and repair of church buildings and setting high standards among the clergy. As a magistrate, Plymley used his powers to improve the county's infrastructure of roads and bridges; he promoted the work of the local Bible Society and, because of his deep commitment to Shropshire and its inhabitants, as well as his proven administrative capacity, he was asked by the Board of Agriculture to produce a report on the state of agriculture in Shropshire. This report led Plymley to become the principal link between a number of scientists and intellectuals in what has become termed 'The Shropshire Enlightenment' – an atmosphere of scientific enquiry into which Charles Darwin was born. Plymley came to national prominence as a key supporter of the anti-slave trade movement in the late 1700s, becoming a friend of Wilberforce and a close associate of Thomas Clarkson. He worked tirelessly in Shropshire to encourage those with influence in the county to support abolition. A family man – he married twice (and changed his name to Corbett as a condition of receiving the family inheritance) – his life and character are described in detail by his sister, Katherine, in a long series of diaries.

Some of the most powerful speeches of the age were made by abolitionists – perhaps the most famous of all by William Wilberforce. Here, he reminds his listeners that the freedom which he champions is at the very heart of God:

When I was persuaded of the frequent commission of the crimes mentioned, I found myself impelled to go boldly forward, and had before I had time to reflect, proceeded so far that I could not recede; but had I deserted the great and important undertaking, I should have considered myself wanting in that necessary portion of duty which I owed to my constituents and to my county. There is no accusation made against the gentlemen of the West India trade; but by bringing forward the consideration of such a mighty object, we unite with the person of sensibility, that the measure is necessary and founded in rectitude and universal benevolence.

The great cause, it has been stated, of mortality in the West Indies, is that the slaves are very profligate and dissolute in manners; but the principal cause, however, is ill treatment; for the agents squeeze as much as possible from their exertions. Here a divine doctrine is contradicted by the reverse action – that Sympathy is the great source of humanity.

William Wilberforce 1759–1833, Abolition Speech, House of Commons, Tuesday 12 May 1789

ARTHUR HERBERT TENNYSON SOMERS COCKS 1887–1944

Chief Scout for Great Britain & the Commonwealth

ALFRED LORD TENNYSON was his godfather – hence one of his Christian names – and from an early age he was in contact with famous literary and artistic figures. He succeeded his great uncle as Baron Somers in 1899 at the age of 12. A great athlete, he played cricket for his school, Charterhouse, and for Worcestershire, and in later life became President of the MCC. After serving in the First World War, he inherited the Eastnor estates and became one of the first landowners to offer to the National Trust permanent rights over some of his property. Continuing his spirit of public access, Eastnor Castle estate remains a favourite draw to the public for sightseeing and walking. He served in public office, not least as Lord Lieutenant for Herefordshire in 1933. From 1920 he took an active part in the Boy Scout movement, and succeeded Lord Baden-Powell as Chief Scout of the British Empire in 1941. With his flair for working with young people it is not surprising that the camps he set up in Victoria, during a period of public service in Australia, were a great success and were eventually named 'Lord Somers Camps' after him – they continue to this day. His public service led him to travel widely – to Egypt as Commissioner for the Red Cross and in the Middle East for the St John Ambulance.

Perhaps the Malvern Hills and valleys around Eastnor would have drawn Somers Cocks to this poem by his godfather:

All along the valley, stream that flashest white,
Deepening thy voice with the deepening of the night,
All along the valley, where thy waters flow,
I walked with one I loved two and thirty years ago.
All along the valley while I walked today,
The two and thirty years were a mist that rolled away;
For all along the valley, down thy rocky bed,
Thy living voice to me was as the voice of the dead,
And all along the valley, by rock and cave and tree,
The voice of the dead was a living voice to me.

Alfred Lord Tennyson 1809–92, 'In the Valley of Cauteretz'

Based on the prayer of St Ignatius of Loyola, this prayer was adapted by Baden-Powell for the use of the Rover Scout Section

By the Spirits of the Just,
Made perfect in their suffering,
Teach us in our turn, O Lord,
To serve thee as we ought,
To give and not to count the cost,
To fight and not to heed the wounds,
To toil and not to seek for rest,
To labour and not seek any reward
Save that of knowing that we do thy will.

James Brydges, 1st Duke of Chandos 1674–1744

Generous duke

The leafy suburbs of north London may seem far from the rolling countryside of south Herefordshire, but they are linked in the life of James Brydges. He was born on this day in 1674 at Dewsall in Herefordshire, the eldest son of James Brydges (1642–1714), 8th Baron Chandos, who held estates in Herefordshire and Radnorshire. He grew up at Dewsall and in London; he was educated at Westminster and later at New College, Oxford. In 1696 he married Mary Lake of Cannons in Middlesex; her wealth combined with his progressed his career and in 1698 he was elected MP for Herefordshire. He held various government posts including that of paymaster to the queen's forces. The links he developed in Germany bore fruit on the accession of George I in 1714, when Brydges secured an earldom for his father, inheriting it on the latter's death in 1714. Five years later, he became 1st duke of Chandos. At Cannons, he built a fine house and rebuilt the adjacent church of St Lawrence, Little Stanmore in high baroque style, with an organ said to have been played by Handel. He maintained his Herefordshire links, becoming Lord Lieutenant of the county and of Radnorshire. However, despite his wealth, he was not always astute with money, and a fellow peer, Lord Onslow, spoke of him as a 'bubble to every project and a dupe to men that nobody else almost would keep company with'. Indeed, he incurred heavy losses in the South Sea Bubble of 1720. For all this, he was a man of great generosity and gentleness of spirit. It is said that when anger at an insult to his father led him to fight a duel, he disarmed his opponent and then offered apologies himself and an invitation to dine that evening!

For all his faults, Brydges was a man of great generosity. How we use our possessions and material resources says a lot about our attitude to life. An early Greek Christian speaks of the right use of wealth:

This then is the way in which the Lord sets before us the use of external things, bidding us lay aside, not the means of livelihood, but the things which use these badly; these we have seen to be the infirmities and passions of the soul. For he who considers possessions and gold and silver and houses as God's gifts, and by using them to further men's salvation renders service also to God Who gave them, not being the slave of what he possesses; who does not bear these things about in his soul, nor bind and circumscribe his own life in them, but is always working out some noble and divine work; who is able if ever he must be deprived of these things, to endure the loss of them as contentedly as superabundance: this is he who is called *Blessed* by the Lord, and *Poor In Spirit* (Matt. 5:3), ready to be an heir of the kingdom of heaven. But the man who bears his wealth in his soul, and instead of God's spirit bears in his heart gold or an estate, and is always preoccupied in rendering his possessions unlimited; who on every occasion looks for more with head bent down, shackled by the snares of the world; who is earth, and to earth will return: whence can this man have a wish or thought of the kingdom of heaven?

Clement of Alexandria 155–220

John Jebb 1805–86

Champion of cathedrals

Today we are used to cathedrals being centres of excellence, but it was not always so. In the early 19th century, cathedral music, the care of the building and congregational attendances were in a poor state. That this parlous state of affairs changed was very much due to the energy of John Jebb. Born in Dublin, and educated at Trinity College, Jebb was ordained and spent several years ministering in parishes in Ireland. In 1843, he was appointed rector of Peterstow, near Ross, and prebendary of Hereford Cathedral, becoming canon residentiary in 1870. He was a prolific writer and his *Literal Translation of the Book of Psalms* brought him to the attention of the revisers of the Old Testament, as an able Hebrew scholar. However, his work in translation was short-lived, as he resigned due to his belief that the plan proposed by his colleagues involved unwarranted changes to the text of the *Authorised Version*. As early as 1841, Jebb was acknowledged as 'one of the greatest authorities on liturgy and music' when he arranged services for the consecration of the new Leeds parish church, and he enhanced this reputation through his writings. In 1843 he published *The Choral Service of the United Church of England and Ireland – an enquiry into the poor standard of worship in our cathedrals*, while in 1847 he published *The Choral Responses and Litanies of the United Church of England and Ireland*, with its encouragement of the editing of music from earlier periods, especially the 17th century. Jebb's high standards were observed at the re-openings, in 1863, of Hereford Cathedral, after its major restoration, and of his own parish church of Peterstow in 1866. At the opening service of the Hereford Three Choirs Festival in 1870, Jebb preached on the benefits of excellent choral music – '... a recreation, like those we rejoice to derive from contemplating the works of God; a sober and intelligent and thankful, and healthful enjoyment of one of God's great gifts, perfectly consistent with this great truth, that God's worship is not only a duty *but a pleasure*'. A principal interest of the last years of Jebb's life was St Michael's College, Tenbury and it was perhaps fitting that on his death on 9 January 1886, his friend and colleague Frederick Gore Ouseley (see 6 April), founder of St Michael's, should succeed him as canon residentiary at Hereford Cathedral. Jebb is commemorated by stained glass windows in Hereford Cathedral and in Peterstow church.

One hundred and fifty years after Jebb's enquiry into the state of cathedral music, a new report was published. While saluting the advances in musical standards, this nevertheless encourages a flexibility of approach:

We belong to a generation which has grown up knowing little of the language of religion, or of the basic doctrines and faith of Christianity. Our culture is fragmented and secular, and for most people Choral Evensong, for example, has little to offer except beautiful music. This is true even for many younger Christians. The cathedral tradition is an undoubted musical gem. But a more truly popular liturgy is also required which will combine the demand of St Teresa of Avila for something 'plain and homely' with that which has majesty, poetry, otherness and a power to communicate. A cathedral is in a particularly good situation to give the Church a lead in this area, and to offer an inspiring vision for the future. It has fewer constraints and more resources than the average parish, and as the mother church of the diocese and focus of the bishop's ministry, it should be expected to show the way.

The cathedral's greatest advantage is in its recognition that worship is the well-spring of all else. This is expressed by the daily services said or sung, morning and evening, every day of the year. From so solid a base, it should not be difficult or daunting to make experiments.

In Tune with Heaven – The Report of the Archbishops' Commission on Church Music (1992)

Alfred Russel Wallace 1823–1913

Naturalist, evolutionary theorist & social critic

Although most of his ground-breaking work (which made him, next to Darwin, one of the chief exponents of natural selection) took place outside the county, it was in Herefordshire that Wallace gained much of his early experience. He worked for his brother in Hereford as a surveyor and, from 1841, became associated with the newly formed Kington Mechanics' Institute, for which he wrote several papers. In 1848 an opportunity came for him to pursue his interests in natural history, and he took part in an expedition to the Amazon, during which visit he collected thousands of specimens and was able to come into contact with native peoples unaffected by European influence. Later visits to the Malay archipelago (1854–62) led to his work on natural selection. Similar to Darwin in many ways, he differed from the latter in drawing more attention to the moral and ethical problems involved in applying natural selection to man, and disagreed with Darwin on the origin of humankind's moral and intellectual faculties. His prolific writing in natural history, zoology and anthropology led to his being hailed as the 'Grand Old Man of Science'. In addition his interests were broad. He was something of an historian and a philosopher, and in his book *Man's Place in the Universe,* he argued for the uniqueness of advanced life on earth and its centrality of location in the universe. He became a socialist and was first President of the Land Nationalisation Society, also supporting legislation for the formation of what became 'green belt' land. Although for most of his life an agnostic, he amazed all by becoming a Spiritualist and wrote on the subject. A protester against colonial imperialism, he supported reform of the House of Lords and the Church of England and was a fervent supporter of women's suffrage. A contemporary spoke of him as 'a man conscious of superior powers of sound and solid reasoning ... with a moral sense ... which will not allow him to approve anything illogical or wrong, though it be upon his own side of a question'.

A contemporary novelist uses the theories of Wallace in words spoken by one of the characters, Thomas, a doctor. He is, during the 1860s, researching into the causes of mental illness, and is himself struggling to come to terms with the mental illness of a friend's brother, Olivier:

'I think what they suffer from is a problem in awareness and making connections in the brain. Mr Darwin's great collaborator Alfred Russel Wallace believes that God has been present at various moments in human development, principally the one at which we gained this consciousness of being alive. I strongly sense that at that crucial chemical moment, when one mutation was 'selected' and the first Homo Sapiens was born, a certain instability came into the neuronal circuits of the brain. If God was present, you might argue that He was also for a moment absent. Homer nods. One day, this instability may regulate itself through successful transmutation. Until then, I do not see men like Olivier as being degenerate or retarded; I see them rather as at the forefront, in the vanguard of what it means to be a human.'

'But they suffer,' said Franz.

'My God, they suffer. I think they suffer for all of us. It is almost as if they bear the burden of our sins. It is scarcely too much to say that they pay the price for the rest of us to be human.'

Sebastian Faulks b.1953, *Human Traces* (2005)

Aethelmod 8th century

Leominster's martyr

Although little is known of this saint, he certainly followed his master, Jesus Christ, in the way of suffering. The 11th-century *List of Saints' Resting Places* states that 'St Ethelred rests at Leominster, near the river Lugg'. 'Ethelred' is probably a scribal error, and this entry would seem to commemorate Aethelmod, thought by some to have been a bishop of Sherborne, who ministered in these parts. Little is known of this shadowy figure, but a clue may be found in his name. The Old English word for Aethelmod incorporates the word *treow*, a tree or 'wooden cross'. Could it be that Aethelmod suffered the same fate as his master? Some have noted, in Herefordshire folklore, the presence of a gospel oak at the meeting point of the parishes of Aymestrey, Kingsland, Lucton and Shobdon. Might this have been the place of Aethelmod's martyrdom? We simply don't know, but certainly by 1433 Aethelmod's name appears in the Leominster Priory and Reading Abbey lists of relics possessed by these churches. Leominster had a particularly fine collection of relics. Robert Bethune, bishop of Hereford declared: 'We know and have learned by undoubted proofs that this church is loved of God for in it are contained relics of the saints in greater and more precious quantity then we can find words to express.' Reading, too, celebrated St Aethelmod and in the Dissolution inventory of 1539 we read of 'a chawbone of saynt Ethelmod'.

Did Aethelmod die on a cross? On a tree like his Saviour? The words of the Anglo-Saxon poem The Dream of the Rood *focus on the tree as place of execution for Christ – and for many since:*

Many years ago – the memory abides –
I was felled to the ground at the forest's edge,
Severed from my roots. Enemies seized me,
Made of me a mark of scorn for criminals to mount on;
Shoulder-high they carried me and set me on a hill.
Many foes made me fast there. Far off then I saw
The King of all mankind coming in great haste,
With courage keen, eager to climb me.
I did not dare, against my Lord's dictate,
To bow down or break, though I beheld tremble
The earth's four corners. I could easily
Have felled his foes; yet fixed and form I stood.
Then the young hero – it was God Almighty –
Strong and steadfast, stripped himself for battle;
He climbed up on the high gallows, constant in his purpose,
Mounted it in sight of many, mankind to ransom.
Horror seized me when the Hero clasped me,
But I dared not bow or bend down to earth,
Not falter, nor fall, firm I needs must stand.
I was raised up a Rood, a royal King I bore,
The High King of Heaven: hold firm I must.
They drove dark nails through me, the dire wounds still show,
They taunted the two of us; I was wet with teeming blood,
Streaming from the warrior's side when he sent forth his spirit.

? Caedmon fl.658–80, or Cynewulf *c.*770–840

William Laud 1573–1645

Dean of Gloucester, archbishop of Canterbury

Born in 1573, the son of a clothier in Reading, Laud was educated at Oxford and became leader of the High Church or 'Arminian' party of the Church of England. He became dean of Gloucester in 1616 and, after periods as bishop of St Davids, Bath and Wells and London, was made archbishop of Canterbury by Charles I. Laud and his followers believed that the beauty and majesty of God should be reflected in the liturgy of the Church, and he rigorously set about ensuring change. At Gloucester Cathedral and many other churches, Laud insisted on the erection of altar rails to protect the holy table, and with his encouragement many new churches were consecrated. In Herefordshire, we have a fine example of a Laudian church in Abbey Dore, where Viscount Scudamore (see 4 July), a friend and supporter of Laud, restored the ruined Cistercian church and endowed it with fine woodwork and magnificent decorations. Laud appears in a stained glass window in the ambulatory of the church. However, Laud was uncompromising in his dealings with the Puritan party, which had the upper hand in Parliament, and he was eventually impeached and imprisoned in the Tower of London. The king did not, or could not, come to his assistance and he was beheaded on this day in 1645.

An historian ponders on parallels between Cromwell and Laud – opposite ends of the religious spectrum, but alike in their insistence on a standard which many felt too high to countenance:

(Cromwell's) failure to establish a permanent Government was not due merely to his deficiency in constructive imagination. It was due rather to two causes: the umbrage taken at his position as head of the army whose interference in political affairs gave even more offence than taxation; and the reaction which set in against the spiritual claims of that Puritanism of which he had become the mouthpiece. The first cause of offence requires no further comment. As for the second, it is necessary to lay aside all sectarian preoccupations, if ever a true historic judgement is to be formed. It was no reaction against the religious doctrines or ecclesiastical institutions upheld by the Protector that brought about the destruction of his system of government. It is in the highest degree unlikely that a revolution would ever have taken place merely to restore episcopacy or the Book of Common Prayer. So far as the reaction was not directed against militarism, it was directed against the introduction into the political world of what appeared to be too high a standard of morality, a reaction which struck specially upon Puritanism, but which would have struck with as much force upon any other form of religion which, like that upheld by Laud, called in the power of the State to enforce its claims.

Nor is that all that can be said. Even though Oliver was in his own person no sour fanatic, as Royalist pamphleteers after the Restoration falsely asserted, it is impossible to deny that he strove by acts of government to lead men into the paths of morality and religion beyond the limit which average human nature had fixed for itself.

S R Gardiner 1829–1902, *Oliver Cromwell* (1901)

Laud's last words, preached on the scaffold

Therefore, since we are surrounded by so great a cloud of witnesses, let us also lay aside every weight, and the sin which clings so closely, and let us run with perseverance the race that is set before us.

Hebrews 12:1

Sophia Lane Poole 1804–91

Travel writer

Those of us used to package tours will be thankful for this intrepid traveller! The youngest child of a Herefordshire clergyman, Sophia was born in Hereford. Her elder brothers were Richard James Lane, the engraver, and Edward William Lane (see 11 August), the Egyptian scholar. In 1829 she married Edward Richard Poole, a clergyman, but lived apart from him – drink and debt are suggested as possible reasons for this. In 1842, Sophia, with her two sons, accompanied her brother Richard to Egypt and lived in Cairo for seven years. She wrote an account of her experiences in *The Englishwoman in Egypt* – the first book in English to describe the life of Egyptian women, whose daily life was still hardly affected by western influences. In her book she describes how she herself, in order to be closer to her subjects, dressed in Turkish trousers, took Turkish baths with the locals and visited some of the local harems – details of which shocked her readership.

After her return to England in 1849, she collaborated with her younger son, Reginald Stuart Poole, in a series of descriptions of Francis Frith's *Photographic Views of Egypt, Sinai and Palestine* (1860–1). Her elder son, (Edward) Stanley Poole (1830–67) was an Arabic scholar, writing many articles for Smith's *Dictionary of the Bible* and contributing to the 8th edition of *Encyclopaedia Britannica.*

One of the earliest women to engage in foreign travel was Egeria, who made visits to holy places in Jerusalem in the late 4th century. Her descriptions are key in our understanding of early Christian worship. In this passage, she reflects on her discoveries about the keeping of Easter:

Sunday is the beginning of the Easter week or, as they call it here [Jerusalem], 'The Great Week'. [Sunday] the bishop and all the people rise from their places, and start off on foot down from the summit of the Mount of Olives. All the people go before him with psalms and antiphons, all the time repeating, 'Blessed is he that cometh in the name of the Lord.'

Wednesday is exactly like Monday and Tuesday ... but at night ... a presbyter ... reads the passage about Judas Iscariot going to the Jews and fixing what they must pay him to betray the Lord. The people groan and lament at this reading in a way that would make you weep to hear them ...

Thursday ... everyone receives Communion ...When the cocks begin to crow, everyone leaves the Imbomon [place of the Ascension], and come down with singing to the place where the Lord prayed ... From there all of them including the smallest children, now go down with singing and conduct the bishop to Gethsemane ...

[Friday] The bishop's chair is placed on Golgotha. Behind the Cross he takes his seat. A table is placed before him with a cloth on it, and the deacons stand round, and there is brought to him a gold and silver box containing the holy Wood of the cross, It is opened, and the Wood of the Cross, and the title [inscription] are taken out and placed on the table ... all the people, catechumens as well as faithful, come up one by one to the table. They stoop down over it, kiss the Wood, and move on.

Saturday ... they keep their paschal vigil like us.

Egeria *Travels* (*c.*384)

ALFRED WATKINS 1855–1935

Pioneer photographer & antiquarian

HEREFORD'S OWN modern polymath. Alfred was born on 27 January 1855 at the Imperial Hotel in Widemarsh Street, Hereford, the third of ten children born to Charles and Ann Watkins – his father being a prosperous local businessman. Self-taught, Alfred worked first in his father's brewing and flour-milling businesses. His involvement with photography began with a primitive pinhole camera but he became famous with the development of the exposure meter. These were produced commercially in Hereford and Watkins wrote about their use in the *British Journal of Photography*. Achieving fame for his invention, he went on to write manuals for amateur photographers. He was not a believer in expensive equipment and used suitable everyday materials for his darkrooms. In addition, Watkins continued his father's business interests, inventing a flour to make a perfect brown bread, which was named the 'Vagos' or 'Wandering Maiden' from 'Vaga', the Roman name for the river Wye. The loaf soon became popular and Watkins promoted it at the Bakers' Exhibition in London. As an antiquarian and archaeologist, Watkins became a leading member of the Woolhope Club and gave frequent lectures, often illustrated with his own slides. His report for the *Royal Archaeological Journal* of 1889 surveyed all the pigeon-houses of the county, while another exhaustive survey necessitated the photographing and measurement of 120 church and market crosses in the county. Today, Watkins is best remembered for his controversial studies of ley lines, and his suggestion that a series of straight lines could link all the various landmarks into a series of ancient tracks. He believed that this alignment could not be due to mere chance, and that prehistoric man had deliberately made the tracks. His best known book on the subject is *The Old Straight Track*, published in 1925. On his death in 1925, an obituary in the *Daily Express* spoke well of the respect felt for this extraordinary man:

> He was a scholar, miller, farmer, archaeologist, naturalist, inventor, magistrate, county councillor, politician and leader of public opinion. He was full of years and honour.

In one of Watkins' books we find this moving passage which seems to combine his interests in photography, history, ancient sites and his love of Herefordshire:

Almost every war memorial is at the traditional spot – the cross-road or junction and, quite undesignedly, the fine cross which is the County War Memorial occupies the exact site of St Peter's Cross, one of the two ancient town crosses. A renewed respect for the cross came with the Great War, and our thoughts drift from mere structure to recollection of facts like that at Monet de Cats, described in *The Times* for Sept. 7, 1918: 'Between the remnant of a windmill and the battered walls on which it is difficult to find one square foot which is not pitted with shell-markings, there stands, absolutely untouched, a great tall crucifix, with a figure of our Saviour, with wide-stretched arms, as if still offering his bare breast to the guns, which could not harm him, while everything else was swept out of existence.'

I was giving a photograph of Old Gore Cross to the wife of a country vicar, when she said, quietly: 'The names of my three brothers are on that cross.' On the base of another War Memorial Cross at Cradley are cut four names from one family, three brothers and their sister's husband, young officers in various services. We read and are silent.

The Old Standing Crosses of Herefordshire (1930)

Henry Scott Holland 1847–1918

Theologian & social reformer

The hymn *Judge eternal, throned in splendour* is typical of a new type of hymn, popularised by *The English Hymnal* and *Songs of Praise* in the early 20th century – hymns emphasising social justice. The author of *Judge eternal,* Henry Scott Holland, was born on 27 January 1847 in Ledbury. He showed an artistic imagination from an early age and this was to affect all his preaching and writing in later years. At Oxford, under the influence of new ideas propounded by Charles Darwin, J S Mill and John Ruskin, he became a radical and liberal thinker. As an academic in Oxford, he lectured on biblical and literary topics and showed his practical Christianity in the founding of the Church of England Purity Society, the Christ Church Mission and the Oxford Mission to Calcutta. He extended this work to London, where he formed 'settlements' for young men in poor areas as a preparation for ordination. In 1884, Gladstone nominated him to a canonry at St Paul's Cathedral and he immersed himself in the social problems of London's East End. In 1889 he founded the Christian Social Union and expounded his work through the pulpit and through *Commonwealth,* a monthly periodical, which he edited. He continued his writing and contributed to *Lux Mundi,* a controversial series of essays. He was much in demand as a preacher, his oratory being much admired. On hearing him, a little girl is said to have remarked, 'My, what a lot of adjectives that man knows.' He died in 1918, shocked and disillusioned by the waste and carnage of the Great War.

Just before he died, Scott Holland is said to have recited Wordsworth's poem 'Yarrow re-visited':

And what, for this frail world, were all
That mortals do or suffer,
Did no responsive harp, no pen,
Memorial tribute offer?
Yea, what were mighty Nature's self?
Her features, could they win us,
Unhelped by the poetic voice
That hourly speaks within us?

Flow on for ever, Yarrow Stream!
Fulfil thy pensive duty,
Well pleased that future Bards should chant
For simple hearts thy beauty;
To dream-light dear while yet unseen,
Dear to the common sunshine,
And dearer still, as now I feel,
To memory's shadowy moonshine!

From Scott Holland's most famous hymn:

Judge eternal, throned in splendour,
Lord of Lords and King of Kings,
With thy living fire of judgement,
Purge this realm of bitter things:
Solace all its wide dominion
With the healing of thy wings.

Thomas Faulkner 1707–84

Jesuit missionary in South America

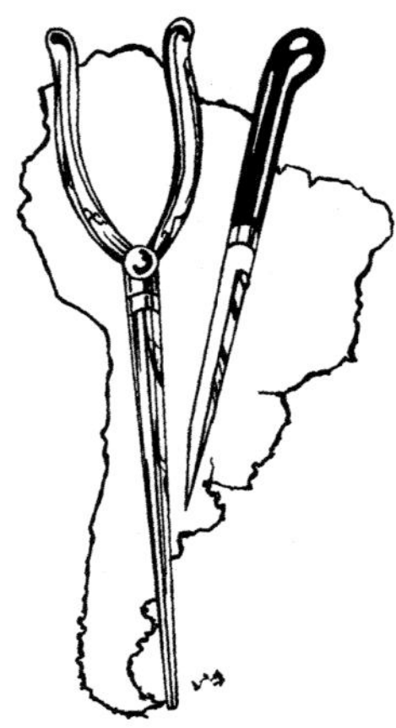

Faulkner's links with our area came at the end of his life, when he became chaplain at Plowden Hall, where he died on 30 January 1784. He is buried at Lydbury North. This quiet end to his days is in great contrast to his earlier life of adventure. He studied mathematics under Isaac Newton as well as medicine and, after practising as a surgeon, joined a slave ship to South America. After a serious illness he became a Jesuit in the Paraguay province where he went on to spend 38 years as a missionary, working as priest and doctor, and becoming involved in the 'Reductions' – collaborations between the Jesuit and local Indian tribes, providing education and work for thousands of native South Americans. He went on expeditions as far as the Rio Negro, using his medical knowledge and studying Indian dialects. In the 1750s, European settlers clashed with the Jesuits and native tribes – the 1986 film *The Mission* being based on these events – and in 1767, all Jesuits were expelled from South America. Faulkner returned to England, and worked on his memoirs, *A Description of Patagonia* (1774), while a further book, *Of the Patagonians*, was published after his death. Those who knew him remarked that his long involvement with the Patagonian Indians had made him lose all European guile and acquire the simplicity and honesty of that people.

A contemporary account reflecting on the legacy of the Jesuits in the 'Reductions':

Still, in America, and most of all in Paraguay, I hope to show the Order did much good, and worked amongst the Indians like apostles, receiving an apostle's true reward of calumny, of stripes, of blows, and journeying hungry, athirst, on foot, in perils oft, from the great cataract of the Parana to the recesses of the Tarumensian woods ... my only interest is how the Jesuits' rule acted upon the Indians themselves, and if it made them happy – more happy or less happy then those Indians who were directly ruled from Spain or through the Spanish Governors of the viceroyalities ... All that I know is I myself, in the deserted missions, five-and-twenty years ago often have met old men who spoke regretfully of Jesuit times, who cherished all the customs left by the company and ... kept the illusion that the mission in the Jesuits' time had been a paradise.

R Cunninghame-Graham, *A Vanished Arcadia, Being Some Account of the Jesuits in Paraguay 1607–1767*

A prayer of Ignatius of Loyola, founder of the Society of Jesus

Lord Jesus Christ,
Take all my freedom,
My memory, my understanding, and my will.
All that I have and cherish,
You have given me.
I surrender it all to be guided by your will.
Your grace and your love are wealth enough for me.
Give me these, Lord Jesus,
And I ask nothing more.

Henry Graves Bull 1818–85

Hereford physician & polymath

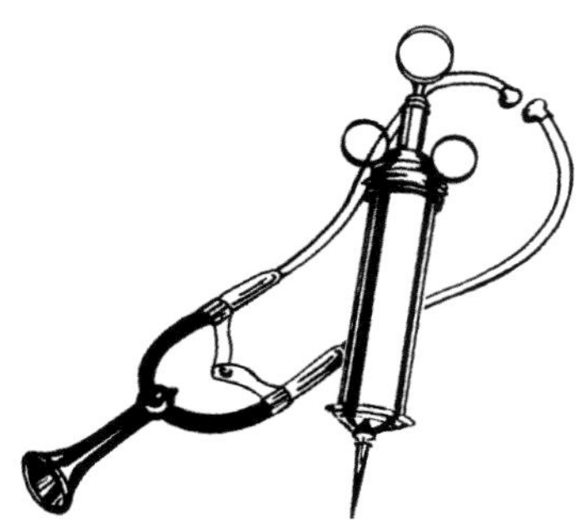

Today we may think it unusual for a doctor to be interested in – and a known writer about – architecture, natural history, ancient history, ornithology and botany. Yet Henry Graves Bull, born on this day in 1818, was exactly this, having a breathtaking range of interests in addition to his life's work as a physician. Graduating in medicine at Edinburgh University, he moved to Hereford in 1841, eventually setting up practice at 1, St John Street, where he lived from 1851. He achieved a high reputation as a doctor and became attached to the Hereford Dispensary, being also a founder member of the Herefordshire Medical Association. Bull's concern for the health of local residents extended to his becoming a champion of reforms in public health. Hereford at that time had very poor sanitary conditions (and a mortality rate of 27 per 1,000 – above the national average). Bull led improvements in sewage, housing conditions and water supply and spoke out against the inadequacy of local burial grounds. As a result, Hereford became one of the first corporations to adopt the new combined system of waterworks and sewage works. As a founder member of the Woolhope Club, Bull wrote articles on many subjects. He was an expert in mycology, or the study of mushrooms, and led annual 'fungus forays' into the local countryside, identifying new species. He was a keen exponent of pomology, or the study of apples, and with his daughter Edith assisted in the production of *The Herefordshire Pomona*, published in 1884 – a lavishly illustrated book describing 432 local varieties of apples and pears. This interest took him to Rouen, where Bull exhibited 248 varieties of local fruit and, with colleagues, won six medals and a Diplome d'Honneur. In addition to all this, Bull encouraged local charities and promoted two libraries in Hereford. Living in St John Street, he was a regular worshipper in the Cathedral Lady Chapel – then functioning as the parish church of St John the Baptist – and in the chapel there is a memorial tablet to him.

Bull's wide interests were always subservient to his profession as a doctor – duties he took seriously, often giving his services free to those unable to pay. No doubt he had read these words from the Apocrypha, *extolling the ideal doctor:*

Honour the doctor with the honour that is his due in return for his services;
for he too has been created by the Lord.
Healing itself comes from the Most High,
like a gift from a king.
The doctor's learning keeps his head high,
he is regarded with awe by potentates.
The Lord has brought medicines into existence from the earth,
and the sensible man will not despise them.
Did not a piece of wood once sweeten the water,
thus giving proof of its virtue?
He has also given men learning
so that they may glory in his mighty works.
He uses them to heal and relieve pain,
the chemist makes up a mixture from them.
Thus there is no end to his activities,
and through him health extends across the world.

Ecclesiasticus 38: 1–8

Joseph Berington 1743–1827

Roman Catholic radical & reformer

The great hall at Stonyhurst College proudly displays portraits of its seven holders of the Victoria Cross, gained during the First World War – proof, if it was needed, that Roman Catholics could be as patriotic as any other Englishmen. This insistence on the compatibility of Catholicism with being British can be traced, in part, to the influence of the priest we commemorate today. Born on this day in 1743 at Winsley, Hope-under-Dinmore, Herefordshire, Joseph Berington was ordained priest and served at the English College in Douai. From an early stage of his career, he courted controversy and embraced the philosophy of the Enlightenment. In his quest for social reform he came into contact with prominent scientists and industrialists, including Joseph Priestley, Matthew Boulton and James Watt. At one meeting with them, a contemporary described him as:

> A finished gentleman of the old school, and a model of the ecclesiastical decorum of the church of ancient monuments and memories; his cold, stern eye instantly silenced any unbecoming levity either on religion or morality. His voice was deep and majestic, like the baying of a bloodhound; and when he intoned Mass, every action seemed to thrill through the soul.

But it is as a radical reformer that he is best remembered, arguing for the 'reasonableness' so often opposed in the Roman Catholic church of his time. He encouraged universal toleration, and insisted that Catholicism was quite capable of being reconciled with the British Constitution. He saw the need for reform of the Roman church through a vernacular liturgy and a change in the discipline of a celibate priesthood.

A contemporary writer sees a lack of reason and a failure to insist on the priority of goodness as causes for religious strife:

Christ's reference to his own blood occurred at the supper which celebrated the Passover, normally a feast of thanksgiving for deliverance. For two centuries after his death, the Eucharist was celebrated as an Agapé, or Love-Feast. However much Christ's view of the Last Supper was dominated by his premonition of his own death, we may reasonably conclude that the more positive and living symbolism of the Bread and Wine, the idea of sharing one's substance with the brothers and the beloved, was not obliterated from his mind any more than from those of his disciples. Such a poetic awareness of life continuing and circulating is more in consonance with the gospel of love than later interpretations have been, however orthodox.

The efforts of Reformers of religion have usually been directed towards recovering the truth of Christianity, the actual meaning of Christ's words behind the current theological misinterpretations. But they have repeatedly failed and have stopped short at some new justification of the hatred of opponents, in their more abstract theory, and some rationalization of their own guilt, as far as their practical precepts are concerned.

The most unarguable meaning that Christ's words have is the biological observation that 'We must love one another or die', but this is seldom marked in any new outbreak of orthodoxy. As I continue to point out, our most recent orthodox are far more concerned with establishing codes of behaviour and belief than with helping any of us to live in the actual world around us. It may be that they know, as we all do, that to love one another at present, as heretofore, appears impossible. But it may still be necessary for survival that we should learn to do so and it serves nothing to offer people instead mere talismans of salvation.

Kathleen Nott 1905–99, *The Emperor's New Clothes* (1953)

Charles Wallwyn Radcliffe Cooke 1840–1911

Politician & promoter of cider-making

We know about the health-giving properties ascribed to Guinness. Less well-known is one man's insistence on the healthy qualities of Herefordshire cider. Born on 16 January at Hellens in Much Marcle, Radcliffe Cooke was educated at Cambridge where, in addition to academic success, he showed his keen sense of humour by publishing a spoof undergraduate diary, purportedly by Samuel Pepys. Entering politics, he founded the Constitutional Union, which aimed to bring together a younger generation of Conservatives, and it was as a Conservative that he won the election of 1893 when he became MP for Hereford, and, on a national level, became a fierce opponent of women's suffrage. As a farmer and landowner in Herefordshire, he founded the Herefordshire Cattle Breeders' Association and, most important of all, encouraged the cider industry, earning himself the title 'Member for Cider'. Founding in 1894 the National Association of English Cider Makers, he aimed to place cider-making on the same scientific basis as brewing. In his *Book about Cider and Perry* (1898) he insisted on the importance of quality in cider-making, deploring the existing practice of using inferior varieties and damaged fruit. He urged the county gentry to serve cider at their tables, and ensured that Herefordshire cider was stocked in the bars at the Houses of Parliament. To him, cider had health-giving properties, and he pointed out that Herefordshire had experienced no recorded cases of Asiatic cholera, though whether today we could support his recommendation of six unpeeled apples and a pint of cider nightly before bed is debatable!

The wine they drink in Paradise
They make in Haute Lorraine;
God brought it burning from the sod
To be a sign and signal rod
That they that drink the blood of God
Shall never thirst again.

The wine they praise in Paradise
They make in Ponterey,
The purple wine of Paradise,
But we have better at the price;
It's wine they praise in Paradise,
It's cider that they pray.

The wine they want in Paradise
They find in Plodder's End,
The apple wine of Hereford,
Of Hafod Hill and Hereford,
Where woods went down to Hereford,
And there I had a friend.

The soft feet of the blessed go
In the soft western vales,
The road of the silent saints accord,
The road from Heaven to Hereford,
Where the apple wood of Hereford
Goes all the way to Wales.

G K Chesterton 1874–1936, 'A Cider Song'

General Sir William Forbes Gatacre 1843–1906

Courageous Shropshire army officer

We associate the British Raj with luxury and class distinction, but the man we commemorate today is famed for his compassion to all classes in the India of his day. Though born in Scotland, William Gatacre had important connections with Shropshire, where his family had held the manor of Claverley for centuries. Educated at Sandhurst, William served much of his military career in India, commanding the Bombay district, where he showed great enthusiasm and endurance. At one stage he was greatly involved in fighting the plague in Bombay – at a time when there were over 300 deaths each day, Gatacre not only took care of his troops, but was chairman of the plague committee and repeatedly visited the houses of plague victims to ensure their removal to hospital. For his courage, he was awarded, in 1900, the gold medal of the Kaisar-i-Hind order. He was greatly admired by contemporaries and Conan Doyle wrote of 'his gaunt Don-Quixote face, and his aggressive jaw'. His later career was dogged by misfortune. In 1898, Gatacre went to Egypt, to command the British brigade in Kitchener's advance up the Nile to re-conquer the Sudan. He was criticised for driving his men too hard, and they nicknamed him 'General Backacher'. Later, in the Boer War, a series of mistakes in the capture of Stormberg railway junction and the resulting defeat led to fierce criticism, and his commander-in-chief wrote that he had shown 'a want of care, judgement and even of ordinary military precautions'. Nor did he retrieve his earlier reputation when serving in the Boer War, and he was ordered back to England. On retiring from the army, he engaged in business interests and joined the board of the Kordofan Trading Company. In 1905 he went to explore the rubber forests in Abyssinia, where he caught fever, apparently from camping in a swamp, and died at Ideni on this day in 1906. He was buried in the Abyssinian Christian cemetery at Gambela.

Gatacre's career in India points us to that vast Subcontinent with its many religions and its wisdom seen in the writings of holy men of all faiths – as in this Hindu parable:

An ageing master grew tired of his apprentice complaining, and so, one morning, sent him for some salt. When the apprentice returned, the master instructed the unhappy young man to put a handful of salt in a glass of water and then to drink it. 'How does it taste?' the master asked. 'Bitter,' spat the apprentice.

The master chuckled and then asked the young man to take the same handful of salt and put it in the lake. The two walked in silence to the nearby lake, and once the apprentice had swirled his handful of salt into the water, the old man said, 'Now drink from the lake.'

As the water dripped down the young man's chin, the master asked, 'How does it taste?' 'Fresh,' remarked the apprentice. 'Do you taste the salt?' asked the master. 'No,' replied the young man.

At this, the master sat beside the serious young man who so reminded him of himself and took his hands, saying, 'The pain of life is pure salt; no more, no less. The amount of pain in life remains the same, exactly the same. But the amount of bitterness we taste depends on the container we put the pain in. So when you are in pain, the only thing you can do is to enlarge your sense of things. Stop being a glass – become a lake.'

Wulfstan *c.*1008–95

Eleventh-century bishop of Worcester

A LINK WITH our sister diocese of Worcester. A priest and Benedictine monk, Wulfstan served most of his life in Worcester, becoming bishop in 1062. He is the first English bishop known to have made systematic visitation of his diocese. He encouraged the building of churches and rebuilt his cathedral, of which his crypt remains today, although somewhat altered. During his episcopate, Worcester became a great centre for English literature and culture, Wulfstan being devoted to the works of Bede and to Oswald (see 29 February), his predecessor as bishop, whose abstinence and generosity to the poor he imitated and surpassed. After the Norman Conquest, he was one of the first bishops to submit to William the Conqueror and was one of the few Englishmen to retain high office to the end of the Conqueror's reign. He was a fierce critic of the trade in slaves from Bristol to Viking islands and encouraged its abolition. After his death, on this day in 1095, a cult began almost at once and cures were reported at his tomb. King John (see 11 June) held his memory in special esteem and was buried close beside him.

'Wolf' (Lat. lupus) was a pen-name used on several occasions by Wulfstan. The author of at least 21 homilies, this passage comes from The Institutes of Polity, *representing the summary of his experience as a jurist. In it, Wulfstan speaks of the virtues necessary in the good king:*

There are eight columns which firmly support lawful kingship: truth, patience, liberality, good counsel: formidableness, helpfulness, moderation, righteousness. And seven things befit a righteous king: first that he have a very great awe of God; and second that he always cherish righteousness; and third that he be humble before God; and fourth that he be resolute against evil; and fifth that he comfort and feed God's poor; and sixth that he advance and protect the Church of God; and seventh that he order correct judgement for friend and stranger alike.

In a sermon, Wulfstan preaches against false gods:

Many other heathen gods also were devised in various ways, and heathen goddesses likewise held in great honour throughout the world to the ruin of mankind; but these, though, are reckoned the most important in paganism, although they lived foully in the world. But blessed is he who completely scorns such affairs and loves and honours the true God who created and fashioned all things. Almighty God is one in three persons, that is Father and Son and Holy Spirit. All three names encompass one divine power and one eternal God, ruler and maker of all creation. To him for ever be praise and honour in all worlds, world without end. Amen.

A prayer such as this, by the great liturgist, Alcuin,
will have inspired clergy and laity alike in Anglo-Saxon times

O King of glory and Lord of valours, who hast said, 'Be of good cheer, I have overcome the world': be thou victorious in us thy servants, for without thee we can do nothing. Grant thy compassion to go before us, thy compassion to come behind us: before us in our undertakings, behind us in our ending. And what more shall we say but that thy will be done; for thy will is our salvation, our glory, and our joy.

Alcuin 735–804

Winifred Wigmore 1585–1657

Roman Catholic religious sister & schoolmistress

Born at Lucton, Winifred was a pious child, from an early age speaking and writing in five languages, including Latin. In 1605, while visiting her Catholic cousins at Coughton in Warwickshire, Winifred met her contemporary, Mary Ward, shortly to become a nun at St Omer. Following Mary's return to London in 1609, Winifred joined her as part of a group living in London, working with persecuted Catholic women. These 'companions' remained with Mary, and were known as the 'English ladies' or 'Mary Ward's Institute'. Winifred accompanied Mary Ward on many journeys across Europe, where her linguistic skills were particularly valued, and in 1622–3, she became headmistress of schools, first in Rome then in Naples. By the 1620s, there was pressure on the papacy to enclose Mary and her followers; the resulting disagreements led to the suppression of the institute and Winifred was temporarily imprisoned. However, the 'English ladies' were able to continue their work, discreetly, in Munich and in Rome. Later, Winifred accompanied Mary on her last journey to England in 1637, remaining with her, in London and Yorkshire, until Mary's death, on this day in 1645. After the execution of Charles I, Catholic allegiance seemed even more precarious and Winifred moved to Paris, where she established a school for English girls. She was co-author of a biography of Mary Ward and chose the subjects for the 'Painted Life', a series of 50 oils with captions, giving an account of Mary's life. The Mary Ward sisters are today known as the Congregation of Jesus.

Winifred's devotion to the Blessed Virgin Mary is reflected in this passage in which the author speaks of the strength of Mary, seen so powerfully in Magnificat:

It has always seemed to me that every conception is immaculate and that this dogma concerning the Mother of God expresses the idea of all motherhood. At the moment of childbirth, every woman has the same aura of isolation, as though she were abandoned, alone. At this vital moment the man's part is as irrelevant as if he had never had anything to do with it, as though the whole thing was gratuitous.

It is the woman, by herself, who brings forth her progeny, and carries it off upstairs, to some top storey of life, a quiet, safe place for a cradle. Alone, in silence and humility, she feeds and rears the child.

The Mother of God is asked to 'pray zealously to her Son and her God', and the words of the psalm are put into her mouth: 'My soul doth magnify the Lord and my spirit hath rejoiced in God my Saviour'. It is because of her child that she says this. He will magnify her. He is her glory.

Any woman could say it. For every one of them, God is in her child. Mothers of great men must have this feeling particularly, but then, at the beginning, all women are mothers of great men – it isn't their fault if life disappoints them later.

Boris Pasternak 1899–1960, *Dr Zhivago* (1957)

Matthew Webb 1848–83

Cross-Channel swimmer

As a particularly poor swimmer, I have great admiration for today's commemoration! Born in Dawley, now part of Telford, on 19 January 1848, Webb had learned to swim by the age of eight in the river Severn below Ironbridge. His prowess in swimming was put to good use at this early age, when he saved the life of his younger brother, who almost drowned when attempting to cross the river. Matthew joined the Merchant Navy and became famous for his amazing feats of swimming. He abandoned the Navy and concentrated on swimming, setting himself the target to swim the English Channel. After an unsuccessful attempt, he eventually swam it in August 1875, the varying currents forcing him to swim over 40 miles. He quickly recovered and merely felt a sensation in his limbs 'similar to that after the first day of the cricket season'. He returned in triumph to London, and in Shropshire bonfires illuminated the valleys. He continued to swim in order to raise money and in various feats of endurance appeared before hordes of spectators. Finally, in order to avoid poverty for himself and his family, Webb resolved to swim downwater below the Niagara Falls, perhaps the most dangerous stretch of water in the world – a feat for which he reckoned $10,000 was at stake. On 24 July 1883, he made the attempt, but was gripped by the force of the current, and his body was discovered some days later by fishermen. He was buried at the edge of the falls, in a heart-shaped plot of ground known as the 'Stranger's Rest', and there is a memorial brass plaque to him in Coalbrookdale church.

Captain Webb's story of courage and recklessness has inspired generations of writers and poets:

The gas was on in the Institute,
The flare was up in the gym,
A man was running a mineral line,
A lass was singing a hymn,
When Captain Webb the Dawley man,
Captain Webb from Dawley,
Came swimming along the old canal
That carried the bricks to Lawley.
Swimming along – Swimming along –
Swimming along from Severn,
And paying a call at Dawley Bank while swimming along to Heaven.

The sun shone low on the railway line
And over the bricks and stacks,
And in the upstairs windows
Of the Dawley houses' backs,
When we saw the ghost of Captain Webb,
Webb in a water sheeting,
Come dripping along in a bathing dress
To the Saturday evening meeting.
Dripping along – Dripping along –
To the Congregational Hall;
Dripping and still he rose over the sill and faded away in a wall.

John Betjeman 1906–84, 'A Shropshire Lad'

John Philips 1676–1709

Herefordshire poet & aesthete

Of a long line of Herefordshire ancestors (his father was a canon of Hereford and vicar of Lugwardine, his great-grandfather a clothier at Ledbury), John Philips was educated at Winchester. Remembered there for his 'tender constitution', he was excused from sport and loved to spend time in his room, 'where he procured a person to attend him, and comb his hair, of which he had a very handsome flow'. At Oxford, although he studied natural history it was as a poet that he achieved some fame. His first poem, *Splendid Shilling*, in Miltonic verse, was hailed by Joseph Addison in *Tatler* as 'the finest Burlesque Poem in the *British* language'. Other poems followed, praising well-known figures of the age, many in imitation of Milton. Perhaps his greatest poem is the two-book *Cyder* (1708), begun at Oxford, which celebrates his native Herefordshire with a combination of accurate knowledge of apples and cider and a 'sketch of our national history'. The botanist Philip Miller told Johnson that 'there were many books written on the same subject in prose, which do not contain so much truth as that poem'. On his death, Philips was buried in Hereford Cathedral, under a stone in the north transept with a Latin inscription commissioned by his mother. In 1710 a white marble monument was erected in Poets' Corner in Westminster Abbey, between monuments to Chaucer and Drayton. Little of his work was published – he wrote entirely for his own pleasure and that of his friends. He seems also to have been a man of reconciliation, commending in his poetry both Charles I and Milton, both Bolingbroke and Marlborough – all examples of extremes on the political and religious scale.

The apple has been at the heart of theology about the Fall and Original Sin since earliest times – a symbol of the felix culpa *or 'happy sin' which led to the world's rescue by Jesus Christ:*

Adam lay y-bounden,
Bounden in a bond;
Four thousand winter
Thought he not too long.
And all was for an apple,
An apple that he took,
As clerkes finden
Written in their book.
Ne had the apple taken been,
The apple taken been,
Ne had never our lady
A been heavenè queen.
Blessed be the time
That apple taken was.
Therefore we moun singen
Deo gratias!

Anon. 15th century

Sir Banastre Tarleton 1754–1833
An inglorious link with the United States

The years that led up to the American Declaration of Independence were one of the least glorious phases of British history, and the character we commemorate today did little to improve Britain's poor reputation. Born and educated in Liverpool, Tarleton purchased a commission in the Dragoon guards and volunteered for service in America. Over the next three years, he took part in all the major engagements of the American War of Independence in New Jersey, Pennsylvania and New York. He became a captain and was admired by many for his vigour and daring. He also gained an unenviable reputation for ruthlessness and brutality, seeming to regard pillage and plunder as an acceptable weapon against insurgents. 'Nothing will secure these People but Fire & Sword,' he is said to have announced.

After 1780, his fortunes in battle waned. In one battle in the invasion of North Carolina, over 800 of his 1,100 men were either killed or captured. On returning to England he became a friend of the Prince of Wales and was well known for his gambling and a long-running affair with Mary Robinson, actress and poet. His published *History of the Campaigns of 1780 and 1781 in the Southern Provinces of North America* (1787) sought to justify his military career but provoked a hostile response. He went into politics, becoming MP for Liverpool, speaking mainly on military matters and in defence of the slave trade, in which Liverpool had a special interest. He died at Leintwardine on this day in 1833, and there is a memorial to him in Leintwardine church.

Tarleton's reputation did little to further Anglo-American relationships. A great contrast to his character is seen in this poem, by an American writer, in which poverty and freedom from dependence on possessions are seen as key to life:

Afoot and light-hearted I take to the open road,
Healthy, free, the world before me,
The long brown path before me leading wherever I choose.

Henceforth I ask not good-fortune, I myself am good-fortune,
Henceforth I whimper no more, postpone no more, need nothing,
Done with indoor complaints, libraries, querulous criticisms,
Strong and content I travel the open road.

The earth, that is sufficient,
I do not want the constellations any nearer,
I know they are very well where they are,
I know they suffice for those who belong to them ...

You road I enter upon and look around, I believe you are not all that is here,
I believe that much unseen is also here.

Walt Whitman 1819–92, 'Song of the Open Road' in *Leaves of Grass* (1856)

Cadoc *c.*497–577
Abbot

A LINK WITH our neighbouring diocese of Swansea and Brecon. Born of royal parentage in about the year 497, Cadoc was educated in the monastic school at Caerwent. He established a monastery at Llancarfan, in the Vale of Glamorgan and this soon became famous. We are told in the 12th-century *Life of St Cadoc*:

> '... there eagerly flowed together from various districts of the whole of Britannia very many Clerics to Saint Cadoc like rivers to the sea, that they might imitate his wisdom and practice; for he always welcomed eagerly all who steadily toiled in the services of God and paid heed to the divine scriptures'.

Cadoc made visits to Ireland to study in the monastery of Lismore, and there was a frequent interchange between Llancarfan and Irish monasteries. When plague threatened the monastery, Cadoc fled to Brittany and established churches there. He returned to Llancarfan and, in old age retired to Beneventum, probably near Brecon. There, in the year 577, he was murdered by a soldier entering the church. In 1022, to avoid destruction by the Danes, Cadoc's shrine was moved to Mamhilad, near Abergavenny.

Surely one of the great delights of Wales is its language – hearing it spoken is a musical experience! In this passage Sir Walter Scott (1771–1832) writes, in 1820, to his son, Charles in Lampeter:

You hear the Welsh spoken much about you, and if you can pick it up without interfering with more important labours, it will be worthwhile. I suppose you can easily get a grammar and dictionary. It is, you know, the language spoken by the Britons before the invasion of the Anglo-Saxons, who brought in the principal ingredients of our present language, called from thence English. It was afterwards, however, much mingled with Norman French, the language of William the Conqueror and his followers; so if you can pick up a little of the Cambro-British speech, it will qualify you hereafter to be a good philologist, should your genius turn towards languages. Pray, have you yet learned who Howel Dha was? – Glendower you are well acquainted with by reading Shakespeare. The wild mysterious barbaric grandeur with which he has invested that chieftain has often struck me as very fine. I wish we had some more of him.

A prayer composed by a Welsh dean

Set before our minds and hearts, O heavenly Father, the example of our Lord Jesus Christ, who, when he was upon earth, found his refreshment in doing the will of him that sent him, and in finishing his work. When many are coming and going, and there is little leisure, give us grace to remember him who knew neither impatience of spirit nor confusion of work, but in the midst of all his labours held communion with thee, and even upon earth was still in heaven; where now he reigneth with thee and the Holy Spirit, world without end.

Charles J Vaughan 1816–97

James Wentworth Leigh 1838–1923

'Builder' dean keen on Temperance

The handsome portrait of Dean Leigh graces the Masonic Hall in Hereford and reminds us of a dean who not only added to the cathedral's buildings, but who was also a prominent Freemason, a teetotaller and a devotee of the 'Deep South' of the United States. After education at Harrow and Trinity College, Cambridge, James was ordained and appointed to the family living of Stoneleigh in Warwickshire. In visiting the United States and New York, he met and fell in love with Frances Butler, daughter of Pierce Butler and his wife 'Fanny Kemble', of the famous Hereford theatrical family (see 3 April). Frances had managed her father's plantation in Georgia, single-handed and now, after the marriage, they ran the estate together, returning to England in 1877. James became vicar of Leamington and, in 1894, dean of Hereford. During his period of office he took a leading role in the architectural development of the cathedral – the cathedral library was moved in 1897 to a new building on the west side of the Lady Arbour and a new west window was dedicated in 1902 to the memory of Queen Victoria. In addition, in 1908, the new west front was dedicated – it replaced that by Wyatt, was designed by Oldrid Scott and was given by Herefordshire Freemasons. Frances Leigh died in 1910 and her memorial is a window in the south aisle. At the top of the window there is a representation of three children – one a black child, reminiscent of Frances' days in Georgia and the great help she gave there in education. Leigh and his wife were instrumental in setting up the Temperance canteen in Hereford Market – thus providing an alternative to the many public houses in the city on market days! Dean Leigh retired in 1919 and died on this day in 1923.

Although Dean Leigh's preoccupation with Temperance suggests that he was an austere man, his description of the conclusion of a peace mission to Germany in 1906 shows a lighter side:

We concluded our journey at Southampton on the evening of June 20th. On board we had many yarns contributed by various passengers: here is one told me by a prominent Roman Catholic: 'A man was making his confession and when he had concluded, the priest asked him what was his profession – he said he was an acrobat. He was asked what that was, and he proceeded to give a demonstration outside. A stout old woman was waiting to make her confession, and when she had finished, she said: 'I do hope your Reverence will not impose the same penance on me as you have on that poor man.'

Autobiography, Other days (1921)

A hymn used in Hereford Cathedral when the Provincial Grand Lodge of Herefordshire attends Evensong

Now the evening shadows closing,
Warn from toil to peaceful rest;
Mystic arts and rites reposing,
Sacred in each faithful breast.

Humbly now we bow before thee,
Grateful for thine aid divine;
Everlasting power and glory,
Mighty architect be thine.

Charles Anthony 1802–85

Founder of The Hereford Times *& father of modern Hereford*

A man of vision, enterprise and moral courage, Charles Anthony held the office of mayor of Hereford six times between 1836 and 1885, and, at the end of his life was hailed 'Father of modern Hereford'. During his periods of office he renamed many of the city's streets, oversaw the installation of the first iron bridge over the Wye at Hunderton, supported new drainage systems, saw the arrival of the railways and presided over the building of the new railway station. He piloted a scheme for a new cattle market and was influential in the opening of new butter, poultry and meat markets. The *Hereford Times* office opened in 1838 in Maylord Street, with Anthony as first editor. In those days, the cover price was seven pence, at a time when the average farmworker's wage was £20 a year. Of the cost, fourpence went on government tax and the remaining threepence on the production of the four-page newspaper.

The Hereford Times *today does much to open the eyes of those of us who live in this county to the beauties around us. Regular features on the countryside, farming and walks rightly take their place with up-to-the minute news. This love of our county is reflected in a poem by a former archdeacon of Hereford:*

Herefordshire Place-names

In Much and Little Dewchurch, St David's praise is sung
For all the land of Archenfield has Welsh for mother tongue.
But Ewias Harold marks the time when Norman Lords were here,
As witness Mansel Lacy and Tedstone Delamere.
When peace came to the Border, religion grew once more,
The nuns of Aconbury greet the monks of Abbeydore.
Rich pasture lands and orchards fair along the valley lie,
Where Sellack sees the Wye go by and Leintwardine the Teme,
And Leominster shears here 'golden ore'* by many a pleasant stream.
Let others sing the praises of their counties by the sea,
The Herefordshire place-names are the fairest names to me.

*The wool by which Leominster merchants grew rich

Arthur Winnington-Ingram, archdeacon of Hereford 1942–58, *Various Verses* (1990)

The Journalist's Prayer

Almighty God, strengthen and direct, we pray, the will of all whose work it is to write what many read, and to speak where many listen. May we be bold to confront evil and injustice: understanding and compassionate of human weakness; rejecting alike the half-truth which deceives and the slanted word which corrupts. May the power which is ours, for good or ill, always be used with honesty and courage, with respect and integrity, so that, when all here has been written, said and done, we may, unashamed, meet Thee face to face, through Jesus Christ our Lord.

From St Bride's Church, Fleet Street, London

Henry Hickman 1800–30

Promoter of anaesthesia before Lister

We associate Joseph Lister with the invention of anaesthesia, but others must be given credit too. Born at Bromfield on this day in the year 1800, Henry Hickman studied medicine in London and Edinburgh and joined the Royal Medical Society, becoming a Member of the Royal College of Surgeons in 1820 (the College's symbol is shown) and setting up practice as a surgeon in Ludlow. He is best known for his experiments in anaesthesia whereby he suggested the use of suspended animation to tranquillize fear and relieve suffering during operations. He conducted experiments on animals, rendering them unconscious by denying air or by administering carbon dioxide and then amputating limbs, apparently without pain. He wrote papers on his work, but was roundly criticised in *The Lancet* for his 'Surgical Humbug' – in a letter which was signed 'Antiquack'. Unperturbed, Hickman appealed to Charles x, king of France, for the collaboration of the king's medical schools with his experiments – but here he received the same ridicule as in England. On his return to England, he set up practice in Tenbury Wells, where he died in 1830 and was buried at Bromfield, where there is a memorial to him. His work, though perhaps misguided, has been reappraised in recent years and he is regarded as 'The Father of Anaesthesia'.

Hickman worked for the lessening of pain in medical procedures. Here, a poet speaks of the inevitability of pain in this life and of the vital importance of weaving it into the experience of our lives:

And a woman spoke, saying, Tell us of Pain.
And he said:
Your pain is the breaking of the shell that encloses your understanding.
Even as the stone of the fruit must break, that its heart may stand in the sun, so must you know pain.
And could you keep your heart in wonder at the daily miracles of your life, your pain would not seem less wondrous than your joy;
And you would accept the seasons of your heart, even as you have always accepted the seasons that pass over your fields.
And you would watch with serenity through the winters of your grief.
Much of your pain is self-chosen.
It is the bitter potion by which the physician within you heals your sick self.
Therefore trust the physician, and drink his remedy in silence and tranquillity:
For his hand, though heavy and hard, is guided by the tender hand of the Unseen,
And the cup he brings, though it burn your lips, has been fashioned of the clay which the Potter has moistened with His own sacred tears.

Kahlil Gibran 1883–1931, *The Prophet* (1926)

Henry Percival Bulmer 1867–1919

Maker & promoter of Herefordshire cider

The woodpecker carved on the organ case in Hereford Cathedral reminds us of famous cider associations in our county. Percy Bulmer was born on this day in the year 1867, the son of the rector of Credenhill. His father, himself the son and grandson of Hereford wine merchants and cider makers, had won prizes for his own bottled cider and perry. Percy, although educated at Hereford Cathedral School, did not continue his studies but began to make cider out of the apples grown in his father's glebe orchard. At this time, most cider was made to be stored in barrels, and bottled cider was a rarity; it was this market that Percy exploited and developed. With his elder brother Frederick, he built up the business, their cider winning prizes in Paris in 1888 and at the Royal Agricultural Show in 1889. Together, the brothers bought land, erected buildings and invested in machinery. Percy developed his knowledge of cider-making techniques, visiting Rheims to learn the techniques of champagne-making, while Frederick took on purchase and marketing. With their own laboratory, they developed a high-quality product and their evocative brand names – *Pomagne, Woodpecker* and *Strongbow* – became household words. The Bulmer firm ran its business on paternalistic lines, instituting a superannuation scheme in 1898 and family allowances in 1938. The firm's housing schemes and charitable trusts continue to benefit the people of Hereford, and they left to the community a product which put Hereford 'on the map' throughout the world.

In Hereford's celebrated fruit – in the crop of apples – a poet sees an image of the variety of life itself:

Behold the apples' rounded worlds:
juice-green of July rain,
the black polestar of flowers, the rind
mapped with its crimson stain.

The russet, crab and cottage red
burn to the sun's hot brass,
then drop like sweat from every branch
and bubble in the grass.

They lie as wanton as they fall
and when they fall and break,
the stallion clamps his crunching jaws,
the starling stabs his beak.

In each plump gourd the cidery bite
of boys' teeth tears the skin;
the waltzing wasp consumes his share,
the bent worm enters in.

I, with as easy hunger, take
entire my season's dole;
welcome the ripe, the sweet, the sour,
the hollow and the whole.

Laurie Lee 1914–97, 'Apples'

Francis Moore 1657–1714

Astrologer & medical practitioner

Horoscopes in the tabloid newspapers may be a 'bit of fun' but they are a pale reflection of horoscopes which employ serious astrology. Born on this day in 1657 in Bridgnorth, Francis Moore is recorded as an astrologer in London from 1698, advertising himself as a 'Licensed Physician and Student in Astrology ... who gives Judgement by Urine or the Astrological way, which is surest, without seeing the Patient'. This would have meant a diagnosis from a horoscope, based on the moment the physician received a sample of the patient's urine. Moore is best known for his annual almanac, entitled *Vox stellarum* (renamed in the 19th century *Old Moore's Almanac*). The first edition, for 1700, was dedicated to Sir Edward Acton, MP for Bridgnorth. It consisted of a daily list, with signs of the zodiac, together with other astronomical information (lunar quarters, information on the planets), lists of fairs, tides and a chronology of important dates and historical events. Future events were predicted through a mysterious code. In many ways, *Old Moore's Almanac* fulfilled an important educational role, bringing to many a simplified introduction to astronomy and medicine. The almanac's readership continued after Moore's death and peaked in 1839 with a print-run of 560,000. The reformer Charles Knight stated: 'There was scarcely a house in southern England in which this two shillings worth of imposture was not to be found.' *Old Moore's Almanac* is still in circulation, with new predictions added each year.

A church historian writes on the Christian adoption of the signs of the zodiac in art and theology:

The Christian literary allegorization of the zodiac in the early Church is confined to two contexts: that of Christian baptism and that of discussions of the functions of the Twelve Apostles, particularly with regard to their preaching. There is, so far as I know, only one early Christian text which allegorizes the zodiacal signs directly, that to be found in an Easter-night sermon of the fourth century bishop Zeno of Verona, on the occasion of the baptism of the neophytes. Zeno expounds for them the horoscope of their new birth in Christ. Since, as he says, he knows their curiosity about such things in their former way of life, he gives each of the twelve signs, save Capricorn, a specifically Christian meaning. His text refers to the use of the zodiac in a non-iconographical form, that of horoscopes, but he is relevant for us in that he demonstrates that a link was made at the level of popular preaching between the zodiac and the sacrament of baptism.

Mary Charles Murray, *The Church and the Arts* (1995)

A prayer which reminds us of the importance of 'the star' at this season of Epiphany

Lord Jesus, our Master, go with us
While we travel to the heavenly country;
That, following your star,
We may not walk in the darkness of this world's night,
While you, who are our Way, and Truth, and Life,
Shine within us to our journey's end.

Charles i 1600–49

King & martyr

Charles succeeded to the throne in 1625, when he encountered the increasing power of an antagonistic Parliament. This he resisted, together with the development of religious Puritanism. He frequently dismissed sittings of Parliament and tried to enforce high-church Anglican practice on all, both in England and in Scotland. Opposition resulted in Civil War. During the war, Hereford was besieged by 14,000 Scots under Lord Leven, but the siege was abandoned and, on 4 September 1645, Charles rode in triumph into Hereford. A window in the south aisle in Hereford Cathedral commemorates this visit, depicting the king standing beneath a canopy in High Town handing a charter to the mayor, augmenting the arms of the city. With the mayor is Lord Scudamore (see 4 July), a friend of the king and of Archbishop Laud (see 10 January), and collaborator with Laud in the introduction of high-church practices in the county. However, such victories were short-lived. Royalist defeats, here and in other parts of the kingdom, led to Charles' imprisonment and trial, and he was put to death by beheading at Whitehall on this day in 1649. A faithful member of the Church of England, catholic and reformed, he suffered for what he believed in.

Eikon Basilike (The Royal Image) *is a book of prayers and meditations of King Charles' last months. Said to have been compiled by the king himself, they are more likely to have been written by Dr John Gauden, from the king's papers. First published in February 1649, the book proved extremely popular and ran to 36 editions. The work presents Charles as a victim of tyranny and as a Christian martyr, his sufferings parallel to those of Christ. This section is entitled 'Meditations upon Death, after … imprisonment in Carisbrooke Castle':*

Though they think my kingdoms on earth too little to entertain at once both them and me, yet let the capacious Kingdom of thy infinite mercy at last receive both me and my enemies. When being reconciled to thee in the blood of the same Redeemer, we shall live far above these ambitious desires, which beget such mortal enmities.

When their hands shall be heaviest and cruellest upon me, O let me fall into the arms of thy tender and eternal mercies.

That what is cut off of my life in this miserable moment, may be repaid in thy ever blessed eternity.

Lord, let thy servant depart in peace, for my eyes have seen thy salvation.

Vota dabunt, quae bella negarunt.

A prayer of Charles i

Almighty and most merciful Father, look down upon us thy unworthy servants through the mediation and merits of Jesus Christ, in whom only thou art well pleased. Purify our hearts by thy Holy Spirit, and as thou dost add days to our lives, so good Lord, we beseech thee to add repentance to our days; that when we have passed through this mortal life we may be partakers of thine everlasting kingdom; through the merits of Jesus Christ our Lord.

John Abel 1579–1675

Master carpenter

JOHN ABEL was born and lived at Sarnesfield. A recusant, he is best known for his skills in fine carpentry. His first documented commission was at Kington in 1625, where he assisted in the building of Lady Hawkins School. His best known work can be seen at Abbey Dore, where he was employed by John, Viscount Scudamore (see 4 July) during the 1630s to assist in the refurbishing of that great church. The famous screen in Abbey Dore, with its renaissance detail, is his greatest testament. Abel also built market halls at Brecon, Kington and Leominster, of which the latter survives as Grange Court, next to the priory church. He was clearly a man of great versatility. Thomas Blount, the antiquary, describes an incident during the Civil War when Abel:

Being in Hereford City when the Scots besieged it ... made Mills to grind corn which were of great use to the besieged ... for which King Charles the first did afterwards honour him with the title of one of his Master Carpenters. *(History of Herefordshire, 56)*

Abel was buried in Sarnesfield churchyard on this day in 1675 – at the age of 97.

The image of the carpenter is a rich seam in the Bible. We see it used by the prophet Isaiah as a warning against idolatry:

The carpenter stretches a line, he marks it out with a pencil; he fashions it with planes, and marks it with a compass; he shapes it into the figure of a man, with the beauty of a man, to dwell in a house. He cuts down cedars; or he chooses a holm tree or an oak and lets it grow strong among the trees of the forest; he plants a cedar and the rain nourishes it. Then it becomes fuel for a man; he takes a part of it and warms himself, he kindles a fire and bakes bread; also he makes a god and worships it, he makes it a graven image and falls down before it. Half of it he burns in the fire; over the half he eats flesh, he roasts meat and is satisfied; also he warms himself and says, 'Aha, I am warm, I have seen the fire!' And the rest of it he makes into a god, his idol; and falls down to it and worships it; he prays to it and says, 'Deliver me, for thou art my god!'

Isaiah 44:13-17

And yet, beautiful craftsmanship in wood, stone, metal and glass can put us in touch with God:

Things men have made with wakened hands, and put soft life into, are awake through years with transferred touch, and go on glowing for long years. And for this reason, some old things are lovely, warm still with the life of forgotten men who made them.

D H Lawrence 1885–1930, *Pansies* (1929)

The Carpenter's Prayer

O Christ, the Master Carpenter of Nazareth, on a cross through wood and nails you have wrought our salvation; wield well your tools in the workshop of your world, so that we who come to you rough-hewn, may by you be fashioned according to your will; for the sake of your tender mercy.

CITC Schools Prayer, Nairobi

February

Bridget of Kildare *c.*453–523
Abbess

A favourite Irish saint. She is said to have been baptized by St Patrick and later founded many convents, of which that at Kildare is the most famous. Legends surrounding her life suggest her to have been a person of great compassion; there are many examples of the multiplication of food for the poor, and even her cows gave milk three times the same day to enable some visiting bishops to have enough to drink! Other legends make her a personification of the Blessed Virgin ('Mary of the Gael'). 20 churches were dedicated to her in Wales (including nearby Skenfrith), and 20 in England, perhaps the most famous being St Bride, Fleet Street. The sole Herefordshire dedication is at Bridstow. She is patron of poets, blacksmiths and healers. Her most usual symbol is a cow lying at her feet, which recalls her phase as a nun-cowgirl. Gerald of Wales (see 28 March) described her cult and the story of a fire being kept burning at her shrine for centuries, tended by the 20 nuns of her community.

Our illustration shows a St Bridget Cross, said to have been made by the saint from rushes she found beside a dying man, using the cross to convert him. It is like a plaited corn dolly – in Irish homes a new cross is made each St Bridget's Day, and the old one burned to keep the home from fire in the coming year.

A hymn in honour of St Bridget by the Celtic saint Brogan-Cloen, said to have been written by him at the request of St Ultan of Ardbraccan (d. c.657). It portrays Bridget as a glorious saint, rivalling the Blessed Virgin Mary in splendour:

Bridget, noble woman,
A flame, golden, beautiful,
A sun, dazzling splendid!
May she bear us to the eternal kingdom.
May Bridget save us,
Despite the throngs of demons,
May she overthrow before us
The battle-hosts of every disetie.
May she destroy within us
Our flesh's taxes [sins].
Mother of Jesus!
The Pure Virgin, dear to us,
Grant her dignity.
May we be always safe
With thy saints.
She is a pillar of the kingdom,
With Patrick the pre-eminent,
The garment of garments,
The Queen of queens.
When in our old age
Our bodies are laid in sackcloth,
May Bridget shower her blessings on us,
May Bridget save us.

Herbert Hensley Henson 1863–1947

Controversial bishop of Hereford

When Lloyd George nominated Henson as bishop of Hereford in 1917, there was an immediate outcry because of his perceived heretical views. At his election, several prebendaries absented themselves or voted against and the resulting unpleasantness caused Henson much grief – he looked back to this day, 2 February, the day of his consecration in Westminster Abbey, with some sadness. In fact, although he was a theological liberal, he was only concerned, as his biographer Owen Chadwick states, 'to restate the doctrines of the Church of England in such a way that they will not offend intelligent men'. He stood for the right of Christians to profess their faith, while remaining agnostic about miracles. When he came to Hereford, he was immediately seen as a pastoral bishop – the first to drive round his diocese in a motor car – one which, apparently, regularly broke down!

After only two years at Hereford, Lloyd George translated Henson to Durham, where he became a powerful voice, both locally and nationally, showing his strong opinions on all subjects; for example, he was a critic, on moral grounds, of the behaviour of the Trades Unions. While loved by ordinary people, he came into fierce controversy with the miners' leaders. He strenuously defended the Establishment of the Church of England, but after the 1927 Prayer Book fiasco in Parliament, he became its most vocal assailant.

Henson published many charges to clergy, prior to their ordination. Full of good practical advice, they can sound stern, yet they contain much truth:

Be very careful about paying your debts. Young men are often careless in these matters. To the poor especially, and to the best kind of tradesmen, punctuality in payment is a proof of character, and they suspect irregularity. You may have a comparatively small income: but you must live within it. This is, of course, the tritest of counsels. Nevertheless it is too often neglected.

Yet this rather stern approach could melt at times, as in this letter, written in 1919, when Henson was bishop of Hereford:

Last Wednesday I had to go into Shropshire, and there I was taken to see a tiny Norman Church – 1,000 feet up in the hills – which was a gem of architecture. The parson told me that last Spring when he was ministering at the altar, when he turned to pronounce the blessing, he found 3 lambs who had strolled in through the open door and were standing at the communion rail! They walked in front of him down the church like choirboys in procession!

And what bishop would write thus to clergy today? Henson had no hesitation!

My dear Rector,

I note with considerable surprise that only two girls were presented for Confirmation from your parish, and I think there must be some circumstance unknown to me which can do something to explain so disconcerting a fact. When I was myself a parish priest, it was commonly accepted that 20 persons reached the age of 14 every year in a thousand people, and this was held to be an indication of what we had to undertake.

The population of ------- is stated to be 2,304, which would suggest that not less than 45 persons arrived at the age for Confirmation during the year. Making large allowances for Roman Catholics and Non-conformists, it seems difficult to believe that there were no more than two girls to be brought to the Bishop for Confirmation.

I should like to hear from you what explanation occurs to you as adequate ...

John Miles 1620/21–1683

Founder of Baptist movement in South Wales

Although most of my life has been spent as an Anglican, I attended a Baptist Sunday School in my earliest years and have never forgotten my debt for what I learned then. And how the Baptist congregation *sang* – they put many Anglicans to shame! Today we remember a distinguished local Baptist who did much to establish the movement in Wales. Born at Newton, in the parish of Clifford, near Hay-on-Wye, John Miles followed his father to Brasenose College, Oxford, where he matriculated in 1636. We next hear of him in London, attending a meeting of Dissenters. Miles and his friend Thomas Proud were baptized by total immersion and returned to Wales to evangelize. Miles established a Baptist church at Ilston on the Gower, but soon fell foul of local Independents over the question of believers' baptism by immersion. The local population having been won over, new meetings were established and Miles became incumbent of Ilston. In answer to a growing threat from Quakers, he published in 1656 *An Antidote Against the Infection of the Times* – a stern affirmation of strict Calvinist doctrine. At the Restoration, Miles was ejected from the living of Ilston and the Baptist church moved, for three years, to the secluded ruins of the chapel of St Cenydd in the parish. Sometime after 1665, he and his family emigrated to Massachusetts, where they established a church at Rehoboth. Later they moved and founded the town of Swansey (renamed Swansea in 1903), where Miles served as minster and schoolmaster until his death. He died on this day in 1683 and was buried at Barrington, Rhode Island. A memorial enclosure of the ruins of the chapel at St Cenydd, Ilston, dedicated to the memory of Miles and his church there, was unveiled by Lloyd George on 13 June 1928.

The early Puritans emigrated to America to find freedom of religion and politics, and freedom has always been at the heart of the way life is seen by the American people. Two passages from different traditions – one from a Russian Orthodox writer and one from a Christian philosopher of the Enlightenment – both speak of freedom:

God can do everything, except compel a man to love him.
Man is free, for he is in the image of divine liberty; and that is why he has the power to choose.

Paul Evdokimov 1901–70

It was only when the idea of human freedom developed and was brought into relation with divine providence that the doctrine of predestination arose, and had to arise in trying to solve this problem. It solves the riddle by denying one of the concepts and consequently explains nothing.

The most tremendous thing granted to man is choice, freedom. And if you want to save it and keep it, there is only one way: in the very same second to give it back to God, and yourself with it. If the sight of what is granted to you tempts you, and you give way to the temptation and look with desire of your own on your freedom to choose, you lose your freedom.

Soren Kierkegaard 1815–55

Nell Gwyn 1650–87

Hereford's own renowned actress?

Three cities make claim to being birthplace of the celebrated Nell Gwyn – London, Oxford and Hereford. Dispute as to the place there may be, but there seems to be agreement on the time of her birth from her horoscope – Saturday 2 February 1650 at 6 o'clock in the morning! The Hereford tradition suggests that Nell was born in a house in Pipe Well Lane, later named Gwynne Street, near the cathedral. Her grandfather, who is said to have come from Hereford, was a churchman who became a canon of Christchurch, Oxford, while her father, leaving the army, is said to have returned to Hereford to become a brewer. Nell and her sister went to London and found work in Covent Garden, selling fruit and vegetables. Nell continued her selling career at the Theatre Royal, Covent Garden and later went on stage there; at the age of 15 she played the role of Cydaria in Dryden's *The Indian Emperor*. Samuel Pepys was highly taken with Nell and speaks of her in his diaries. Nell came to the attention of Charles II in 1667, becoming one of his mistresses. Her first son by the king was named Charles Beauclerk and he was later created Duke of St Albans. A grandson, James – also a Beauclerk (see 20 October) – was later to become bishop of Hereford – another local link! Tradition has it that Nell persuaded the king to set up the Royal Hospital at Chelsea, with its uniforms modelled on those of Coningsby Hospital (also for old soldiers) in Hereford.

Nell Gwyn, for all her royal connections, knew what it was to be ostracised from respectable society and the life of the Church. Many years later, the novelist Jeanette Winterson experienced extreme disapproval from her highly religious parents:

My mother wanted me to move out, and she had the backing of the pastor and most of the congregation, or so she said. I made her ill, made the house ill, brought evil into the church. There was no escaping this time. I was in trouble. Picking up my Bible, the hill seemed to be the only place to go just then. On the top of the hill is a stone mound to hide behind when the wind blows. The dog never worked it out; used it to pee against, or to play hide and seek with me, but still stood ears flattened and water-eyed till I slung her up in my jacket, warming both of us. The dog was a tiny and foolhardy Lancashire heeler, brown and black with pointy ears. She slept in an Alsatians' basket which might have been her problem. She didn't show that she knew what size she really was, she fought with every other dog we met, and snapped at passers by. Once, trying to reach a huge icicle, I fell down on to a quarry ledge and couldn't climb back again; the earth kept crumbling away. She barked and spluttered and then ran off to help me. Now, here we were, on a different edge.

It all seemed to hinge around the fact that I loved the wrong sort of people. Right sort of people in every respect except this one; romantic love for another woman was a sin.

'Aping men,' my mother had said with disgust.

Jeanette Winterson b.1959, *Oranges are not the Only Fruit* (1985)

Nell Gwyn's funeral took place at St Martin-in-the-Fields and the service was taken by the vicar, Thomas Tenison, later archbishop of Canterbury. He took as his text words from St Luke's Gospel:

Just so, I tell you, there will be more joy in heaven over one sinner that repenteth than over ninety and nine just persons that need no repentance.

Luke 15:7

Violette Szabo 1921–45

Victim of Nazi persecution

When Hereford Cathedral hosted the Anne Frank exhibition in 2002, there was much local interest in another heroine of the Second World War, this one with Herefordshire connections. Born in Paris, Violette came to England with her family in 1932 and settled in Brixton. On leaving school, she worked as a shop assistant and spent time on her uncle's farm in Wormelow near Hereford. In 1940, Violette married Etienne Szabo, a Frenchman who had fought in Norway with the French Foreign Legion and elected to join General de Gaulle's Free French forces. Etienne was posted to North Africa and died there of wounds in 1942. To avenge him, his widow joined the independent French section of the Social Operations Executive. She proved herself an excellent shot and twice parachuted into occupied France. With Philippe Liewer she set up new groups of resisters. Once, on being challenged in a German road block, Violette is said to have covered her companions' retreat through standing corn for twenty minutes, armed only with a sub-machine gun, She was taken prisoner and put in Ravensbruck concentration camp. For some misdemeanour, she and friends were sent to a punishment camp, 60 miles east. Here, even Violette's normally high sprits were crushed by the regime. On 27 January, 1945, on her return to Ravensbruck, Violette was shot dead. She was awarded a French *Croix de Guerre* in 1944 and a posthumous George Cross – this was presented to her four-year-old daughter, Tania in 1946. Violette's wartime exploits were immortalized in 1958 in a film, *Carve her Name with Pride* (from the book of that name by R J Minney). The role of Violette was taken by Virginia McKenna. A commemorative blue plaque was placed on her home in Brixton and in 2000 a museum about her was opened at Cartref, her uncle's home in Wormelow near Hereford.

Where is God in suffering? This question has been asked for centuries as men and women have struggled to come to terms with human cruelty and the seeming arbitrariness of Creation. These words of W H Vanstone, although applying to a tragedy very different from that experienced by Violette Szabo, rightly place God at the very heart of the suffering:

We do not believe, of the children who died at Aberfan, that God willed their death as a means to some greater good. If we so believed, we should find that alleged 'good' tainted, compromised and unacceptable: like Ivan Karamazov, we would have no part in it and would 'hand in our ticket'. We believe that, at the moment when the mountain of Aberfan slipped, 'something went wrong': the step of creative risk was the step of disaster: the creative process passed out of control. Our faith is in a Creator Who does not abandon even this, nor those who suffered, wept and died in it, but Who so gives Himself that He finds, for the redeeming of this, yet more to give, and knows no respite until the slag-heap has become a fair hillside, and the hearts of the parents have been enlarged by sorrow, and the children themselves understand and are glad to have so feared and wept and died. Our preaching on the Sunday after the tragedy was not of a God Who, from the top of the mountain, caused or permitted, for His own inscrutable reasons, its disruption and descent; but of One Who received, at the foot of the mountain, its appalling impact, and Who, in the extremity of endeavour, will find yet new resource to restore and to redeem.

W H Vanstone, 1923–77, *Love's Endeavour, Love's Expense* (1977)

Reginald Waterfield 1868–1967

Dean of Hereford & prominent Freemason

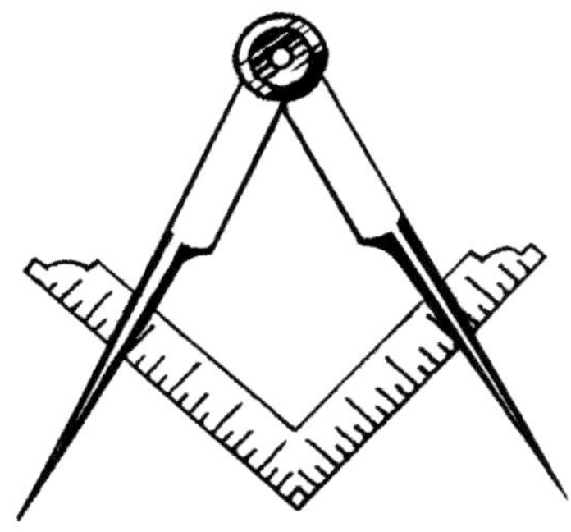

Dean Waterfield's handsome portrait graces the hall of the Masonic Lodge in Hereford. With his apron and other regalia there is no mistaking that he was a high-ranking Freemason! After Oxford, the young Reginald was ordained and became assistant master at Rugby and later, principal of Cheltenham College and archdeacon of Cheltenham. During his time as dean, from 1919, he was much involved in work on the cathedral fabric, with the rebuilding of the cathedral organ in 1933 and the vacation of the deanery. This vast residence had become a headquarters for troops stationed in Hereford during the First World War. The dean reclaimed it at the conclusion of the war, but by the end of the Second World War, during which it was used for housing American troops, the building was felt to be too big and was given over to the Cathedral School as a boarding house, the dean taking up residence in College Cloisters. Outside cathedral life, Dean Waterfield was a member of the Cathedrals Commission, president of the Woolhope Naturalists Field Club and founder-president of the Hereford Rotary Club. He was a distinguished Freemason, and served for many years as Provincial Grand Master of Herefordshire. On his retirement in 1946, the dean continued his love of classics and, even at the age of 90, during sleepless nights delighted to turn nursery rhymes into Latin hexameters which he published. He died in 1967 in his one hundredth year. The date chosen for his commemoration is the date of the foundation, in 1966, of the Waterfield Lodge in Hereford, named after the dean.

Freemasonry has often found itself in conflict with Christianity and churches have forbidden their members to become involved with 'the Craft'. Others have taken a more liberal approach; Archbishop Geoffrey Fisher, and many members of the bench of bishops during his time in office, were Freemasons. In the following passage, Samuel Seabury, first Anglican bishop in North America, preaches to a large gathering of Freemasons:

The honourable fraternity to which I have the pleasure of addressing myself, make it their professed principle to cultivate the humane and sociable propensities of the heart, and to diffuse the blessings of unity, concord and peace, through the world. And may God, the God of unity and concord, bless and prosper their endeavours! Permit me, however, to observe, that the dictates of reason, of humanity and of our holy religion, all concur to give a sanction to your efforts, and to excite you to persist in the well-meant undertaking, of spreading the blessings of benevolence and mutual love over the whole earth. Your society is not confined to parties and sects; it admits not of the local distinctions of nations and countries: Mankind is the object of its attention, their happiness the end of its pursuit; and this end it aims to accomplish, by the most reasonable means, the culture of the benign and friendly propensities of our nature; by promoting peace and unity, benevolence and affection among all the individuals of the human species. This also is one grand design of the religion of the holy Jesus. His gospel proclaims peace and good will to mankind; and endeavours to promote their happiness by promoting unity, concord and benevolence among them. It confines not its attention to particular sects, and parties of men, to particular nations, countries, states or kingdoms. It aims to connect the whole human race together by love and benevolence, and to make them all happy in this world by the mutual intercourse of goodwill and affection; and by cultivating the tender, benign and amiable propensities of the human heart, to fit and prepare them for perfect, never-ceasing happiness in the kingdom of God our creator.

A discourse on brotherly love, preached before the Honourable Fraternity of Free and Accepted Masons of Zion Lodge at St Paul's Chapel in New York, 24 June, 1777 by Samuel Seabury, MA

George Robertson Sinclair 1863–1917

Master of 'Dan the dog'

From the Deanery garden, on the opposite bank of the river Wye, I can see the outline of one of Hereford's endearing features – a wooden statue of a small bulldog. This is 'Dan', once faithful friend of his master, the cathedral organist George Robertson Sinclair. Dan may be one of the most famous dogs in history, with his own musical reference and anecdote. Educated at St Michael's College, Tenbury and the Royal Irish Academy of Music in Dublin, in 1879 Sinclair became assistant organist of Gloucester Cathedral and organist of St Mary de Crypt church in the city. In 1880 he moved to Truro as the organist of the newly-built cathedral and in 1889 came to Hereford Cathedral. He was a much-loved conductor of the Three Choirs Festival, in which he worked with Elgar (see 1 July) and many of the leading musicians of the day. Sinclair's impetuous character, his skilful organ pedalling and the barking of Dan and his falling into the river are, famously, subjects in the 11th of Elgar's *Enigma Variations*. Sinclair died on this day in the year 1917, and his handsome art nouveau memorial, with its enamel portrait, is seen in the south choir aisle of Hereford Cathedral.

Elgar's music, so well promoted by Sinclair, has inspired poets and writers as well as musicians:

So quietly he sleeps upon the hill
That sees the seasons go by Severn tide,
He who by music manifested still
Across the earth the ancient English pride –
This Worcester man who out of little lanes
Of whitethorn bud, Evesham orchards bright
In harvest, made a magic that disdains
That easy summons of the lesser light.

Lyric of England, sturdy yet so sweet
As cider-presses give their well-begot,
Symphonic master that the crowded street
Of Chaucer knew by gospel scot and lot,
Your music rhymes upon the large unrest
That is our time and, blessing us, is blest.

Because of you we heard tonight the note
That once in Worcester fields he newly found,
And put into the minstrelsy that wrote
A later epic of the Malvern ground
That Langland in an age beyond our ken
Made one with these our living Englishmen.

John Drinkwater 1882–1937

Ada Ellen Bayley 1857–1903

Novelist & Unitarian

A NOVELIST we remember today had radical ideas that were admired by Gladstone and also had a great love of Herefordshire. Born in Sussex, Ada was a firm supporter of political and social liberalism and a firm encourager of women's suffrage. But it is as a novelist that she is chiefly known, writing under the pseudonym of Edna Lyall. She published her first book, *Won by Waiting*, in 1879, while her second novel, *Donovan, a Modern Englishman*, won the admiration of Gladstone, who wrote to her describing its first volume as 'a very delicate and refined work of art'. She espoused the cause of Charles Bradlaugh, a liberal free-thinker, whose views led to his exclusion from the House of Commons. On his death, she published an appeal for a memorial fund and based her novel *We Two* (1884) on notes supplied by Bradlaugh. Later novels led to more fame and wealth. In 1886, a stranger falsely claimed in public to be Edna Lyall and a report claimed that the author was in a lunatic asylum. Bayley met the falsehood by announcing her identity and the experience led to her *Autobiography of a Slander* (1887), which was hugely popular and was translated into French, German and Norwegian. Later novels espoused political causes – an ardent supporter of Home Rule for Ireland, in *Doreen* (1894) she presented the Irish revolutionary leader Michael Davitt in the guise of her hero, Donal Moore. Gladstone, writing to her, commended 'the singular courage with which you stake your wide public reputation in the Irish cause'. She supported the Armenian cause in *The Autobiography of a Truth* (1896), and gave the profits to the Armenian Relief Fund, while *The Hinderers* (1902) was a veiled criticism of the South African War. She died on 3 February 1903 and her ashes were buried at the foot of the old cross in Bosbury churchyard, near Bosbury Hill, a place which figures in her novel *In Spite of All,* and of which her brother, the Reverend R Burges Bayley, was vicar. She was a Unitarian, the symbol of which organization is seen here.

Edna Lyall's sympathy for the cause of Irish Home Rule is reflected in this poem by W B Yeats. His reference to 'A terrible beauty' in the last line takes us to the Easter Rising of 1916 and its place in the passage to an independent Ireland:

I have met them at the close of day
Coming with vivid faces
From counter or desk among grey
Eighteenth-century houses.
I have passed with a nod of the head
Or polite meaningless words,
Or have lingered before I had done
Of a mocking tale or gibe
To please a companion
Around the fire at the club,
Being certain that they and I
But lived where motley is worn:
All changed, changed utterly:
A terrible beauty is born.

W B Yeats 1865–1939, 'Easter 1916'

TEILO 6th century

Patron saint of Llandaff

ONE OF HEREFORDSHIRE'S WELSH SAINTS, reminding us of the close links between our county and diocese and the Principality. Born at Penally, near Tenby, Teilo studied with David (see 1 March) at Paulinus' school at Llanddeusant, near Llandovery. Legend has it that Teilo, along with David and Padarn, went on pilgrimage to Jerusalem, where, it is said, all three were consecrated bishops. Teilo certainly had oversight of a number of monasteries in west Wales, the chief being at Llandeilo Fawr. With the coming of the yellow plague in 547, Teilo fled to Brittany, staying with Samson at Dol for seven years and founding a number of churches. Soon after his return to Llandeilo Fawr, Teilo died and a dispute arose between Llandeilo, Penally and Llandaff as to which should have his body. It was miraculously multiplied during the night so that each could have it! Eventually, according to the 12th-century *Book of Llandaff*, 'miracles proved that Teilo's body was undoubtedly brought to Llandaff' and his shrine on the south side of the high altar became a place of pilgrimage. When his tomb was opened in 1736, his crozier, a pewter 'crotcher' and a large cup were discovered. Teilo is said to be a patron of apples and horse, so a worthy saint for our county! Churches dedicated to him are found at Llanwarne and Hentland (see also 14 November).

A medieval Life of Teilo *attributes to him many miracles, including the following:*

Now it came to pass that a certain friend of his, named Geren, whom he had beyond the sea, who rested after a spiritual manner in his love, had departed this life; and one day, when the blessed Teilo was, with the clergy and people, carrying crosses in a procession, the saint lifted up his eyes and saw his soul being borne by angels, who were surrounded by malignant spirits. Calling for silence, he said: 'Pray, all of you, to the Lord for my friend, because I see him being borne by angels, and enemies following him.' And when they had all prayed the demons were driven away from that soul. Then they launched a vessel in the sea, with the aid of sailors, to find out the truth about the miracles, and in the middle of the sea they met men who brought the news of the death of the friend of the man of God.

Another prayer by the 19th-century dean of Llandaff, Charles J Vaughan

Give us, O Lord God, a deep sense of Thy wonderful love towards us; how Thou wouldst not let us alone in our ruin, but didst come after us, in the Person of Thy Son Jesus Christ to bring us back to our true home with thee.

Quicken in us, O Lord, the Spirit of gratitude, of loyalty and of sacrifice, that we may seek in all things to please Him who humbled himself for us, even to the death of the Cross, by dying unto sin and living unto righteousness; through the same Jesus Christ our Lord.

Athelstan d.1056

Bishop of Hereford & possessor of the Hereford Gospels

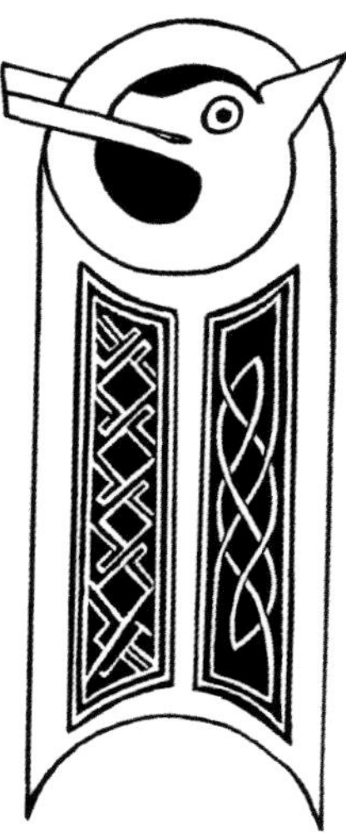

When swearing the oath on my installation as dean, I placed my hand (on this occasion permitted to do so without the customary protective white glove!) on one of the greatest of the cathedral's treasures: the Hereford Gospels. That this volume survives is much due to the man we remember today. Athelstan became bishop of Hereford in 1012. In the early years of his episcopate he rebuilt much of the cathedral, finishing in about 1040. In 1055, Elfgar, earl of Mercia was outlawed by King Edward the Confessor (see 13 October). In anger he went to Ireland for help and returned via Wales, bringing with him a strong combined force. He marched on Hereford, because it was held by Earl Ralph, nephew of Edward the Confessor. Ralph failed to defend the city and Hereford was captured and plundered, the cathedral destroyed and relics and vestments stolen, although seven canons of the cathedral, in a spirited but futile defence, attempted to hold the great west door. Athelstan retired, blind and broken, to his manor at Bosbury and died on this day in the year 1056. He was buried somewhere in his devastated cathedral. No trace of this building remains, but tradition has it that his most treasured possession now belongs to the present cathedral. This is the Hereford Gospels mentioned above – the four gospels in Latin, with illuminated titles to each gospel (one is now missing).

We can only imagine Athelstan's grief as he beheld his cathedral destroyed in 1055. Similar grief is expressed in this Anglo-Saxon poem as the anonymous author walks about the overgrown and stricken streets of a city – possibly Aquae Sulis, the Roman Bath:

Well-wrought this wall: Wierds broke it.
The stronghold burst ...

Snapped rooftrees, towers fallen,
the work of the Giants, the stonesmiths,
mouldereth.
Rime scoureth gatetowers
rime on mortar.

Shattered the showershields, roofs ruined,
age under-ate them.
And the wielders and wrights?
Earthgrip holds them – gone, long gone,
fast in gravesgrasp while fifty fathers
And sons have passed.
        Wall stood,
grey lichen, red stone, kings fell often,
stood under storms, high arch crashed –
stands yet the wallstone, hacked by weapons,
By files grim-ground ...
... shone the old skilled work
... sank to loam-crust.

M Alexander (trans.), 'The Ruin', from *The Earliest English Poems* (1966)

Richard Payne Knight 1751–1824

Scholar, art collector & writer

The riches of the British Museum in London owe much to the generosity of this tireless collector and dilettante. Richard Knight was born on this day in 1751 at Wormsley Grange. He came of a privileged background and gained his education from journeying on the Grand Tour. His first such visit was made in 1772, when he travelled to Florence, Rome and Naples, and gained his fascination with classical architecture. On returning to England he put this enthusiasm into practice with the building of Downton Castle on his estate. This realised not only his love of the classical but also his passion for the Picturesque – seen especially in Downton's site overlooking the wooded valley of the river Teme. Knight also journeyed to Sicily and Greece and here he found his lifelong love of all forms of Greek culture. Indeed, he regarded 5th-century Greece as the culmination of civil society, linking its success to the political and personal freedom enjoyed by its citizens. This freedom he contrasted with that of all forms of religion, which he caricatured as 'priestcraft' and superstition. He certainly offended the Church by his first publication – *An Account of the Remains of the Worship of Priapus,* published in 1786. In this, he suggested that sexual symbolism lay at the basis of all religions, and for this he was roundly criticised by all polite society! A similar reaction resulted when in a poem, *The Progress of Civil Society* (1796), he gave an enthusiastic endorsement of the French Revolution.

He is best known as a collector of Greek objects – coins, bronzes, gems and cameos – and his vast collection was bequeathed to the British Museum at his death. He served the local community and was MP for Leominster and then for Ludlow, but here again he attracted controversy when, in his capacity as a magistrate, he ordered the cavalry to break up a demonstration by the colliers at his mines at Clee Hill. Despite his damaged reputation, he became known as an arbiter of the nation's taste and was elected vice-president of the Society of Antiquaries in 1819. He died on 23 April 1824 and is buried at Wormsley church. His brother, Thomas Andrew Knight (see 22 May) is also buried there.

Many churchmen have seen in classical pagan religion, at its best, a foreshadowing of the good moral life. Indeed, if God is God of all, then we should be open to glimpses of goodness in all:

Seneca, Epictetus, [Marcus] Aurelius, are among the truest and loftiest of Pagan moralists, yet Seneca ignored the Christians, Epictetus despised, and Aurelius persecuted them. All three, so far as they knew anything about the Christians at all, had unhappily been taught to look upon them as the most degraded and the most detestable sect of what they had long regarded as the most degraded and the most detestable of religions.

There is something very touching in this fact; but, if there be something very touching, there is also something very encouraging. God was their God as well as ours – their Creator, their Preserver, who left not Himself without witness among them; who, as they blindly felt after Him, suffered their groping hands to grasp the hem of His robe. And His Spirit was with them, dwelling in them, though unseen and unknown, purifying and sanctifying the temple of their hearts, sending gleams of illuminating light through the gross darkness which encompassed them, comforting their uncertainties, making intercession for them with groanings which cannot be uttered. And, more than all, *our* Saviour was *their* Saviour too. Yes, they too were all His offspring.

F W Farrar 1831–1903, *Seekers after God* (1868)

Blanche Parry *c.*1508–90

Courtier, friend & carer to Elizabeth I

When I watch the television series 'Blackadder' starring Rowan Atkinson, I sometimes wonder whether the character 'Nursie' is based on this real-life – and rather terrifying – figure! Born at Newcourt, Bacton, Blanche Parry spent most of her life in service at Court. She nursed the infant Princess Elizabeth 'whose cradell saw I rockte' (as her monument in Bacton Church has it) and was a lady-in-waiting by the time Elizabeth was three years old. Blanche became a gentlewoman of the privy chamber and eventually chief gentlewoman, the queen entrusting to her the custody of her personal jewellery as well as her personal collection of books. She may also have had literary interests of her own, and a contemporary acknowledges that he received material for a book from Blanche – 'a singular well willer and furtherer of the weale publike of Wales'. Certainly she had huge influence, described by one as 'our best friend of the privy chamber', and was able to gain favours for family, friends and the city of Hereford. She may well have wielded some political power and certainly her power in her own family was legendary. A relative asserted, 'My spirit being too tender to indure the bitterness of her humour, I was by her careful (though crabbed) austerity forced unto the Irish wars.' Like her mistress, the queen, Blanche was attached to conservative religious ceremonies, and in her effigy in Bacton church she is depicted wearing a pectoral cross. She died on this day in the year 1590 and was buried at St Margaret's, Westminster. The monument there records her charity and that she was 'never no man's wife'. The monument to her in Bacton church is of stone and alabaster and displays figures of Queen Elizabeth and, kneeling beside her, Blanche Parry, clasping a book. Pevsner noted that 'the idea is really a secular version of the medieval motif of the worshipper on his monument kneeling before the Virgin – only it is the Virgin Queen here'.

Words attributed to Elizabeth I:

To be a King and wear a crown is a thing more glorious to them that see it, than it is pleasant to them that bear it ...

There is no jewel, be it of never so rich a price, which I set before this jewel: I mean your love ... Though God hath raised me high, yet this I count the glory of my crown, that I have reigned with your loves.

Golden Speech, 30 November 1601

Elizabeth to the French Ambassador after he had praised her linguistic skills:

There is no marvel in a woman learning to speak, but there would be in teaching her to hold her tongue.

A prayer of Elizabeth I

I acknowledge, O my King, without Thee my throne is unstable, my seat unsure, my kingdom totter-ing, my life uncertain. I see all things in this life subject to mutability, nothing to continue still at one stay. Create therefore in me, O Lord, a new heart, and so renew my spirit that Thy law may be my study, Thy truth my delight, Thy Church my care, Thy people my crown, Thy righteousness my pleasure, Thy service my government; so shall this my kingdom through Thee be established with peace.

Sir Richard Croft 1762–1818

Tragic physician & man-midwife

A tragic story of the dangers of medicine in the past and of the perils of public fame and reputation. Richard Croft came of the ancient family of Croft Castle and after schooling, he went into medicine, receiving his training at St Bartholomew's Hospital, London. He continued his studies with Thomas Denman, who wrote extensively on obstetrics, deploring unnecessary interference in the normal course of labour, and especially discouraging the use of forceps. Partly through his influence, Croft rose in his profession and in 1817, he was appointed surgeon-in-ordinary to the Prince of Wales. Because of the disastrous marriage between the prince and Princess Caroline of Brunswick, their daughter, Charlotte, grew up rather isolated and lonely, but enjoyed much public affection. At the age of 18 she married Prince Leopold of Saxe-Coburg, and Croft was nominated to attend her confinement. Charlotte's labour was long and tedious, and Croft felt that some interference might become necessary, but colleagues dissuaded him. In the end, a still-born baby was delivered and five hours later, Charlotte herself died, There was great public sorrow, not least as hopes for the succession to the throne were dashed. Soon, public grief turned to anger and Croft was accused in the press of ignorance, neglect and mismanagement, although medical opinion was very divided and Croft himself received sympathy and consideration from the royal family and most of the members of his own profession. Croft continued in practice but never managed to throw off the depression and despair which overtook him after the tragedy. After three months, while attending another patient whose labour was proceeding as had that of the princess, he retired to an adjoining room and shot himself – on this day in the year 1818. At the coroner's inquest, it was disclosed that in the room to which Croft retired, a copy of Shakespeare's *Love's Labour's Lost* lay open at these words: 'Fair Sir, God save you! Where's the princess?' By a quirk of history, had Charlotte's child lived, he would have succeeded George IV and Victoria would probably never have become queen.

Suicide brings with it guilt, confusion, regret, grief. All these are brought together in this poem by one of the great poets of the First World War:

I know a simple soldier boy
Who grinned at life in empty joy,
Slept soundly through the lonesome dark,
And whistled early with the lark.

In winter trenches, cowed and glum,
With crumps and lice and lack of rum,
He put a bullet through his brain,
No one spoke of him again.

You smug-faced crowd with kindling eye
Who cheer when soldier lads march by,
Sneak home and pray you'll never know
The hell where youth and laughter go.

Siegfried Sassoon 1886–1967, 'Suicide in the Trenches' (1918)

Edward Marston 1825–1914

Publisher, writer, angler

THOSE OF US who enjoyed *Lorna Doone* and *Little Women* in childhood owe much to this energetic publisher. Edward Marston was born on this day in 1825 in Lydbury North in Shropshire. He attended Lucton School and was apprenticed to a local bookseller, moving to Liverpool for his first job with a publisher specialising in the export trade. This international element of publishing was to prove of the greatest significance for Marston. He set up an Australian import-export business in London in 1852 and later went into partnership with a colleague, Sampson Low. Between them they cornered the publishing markets in the United States and Australia, specialising in books of a geographical nature. Marston corresponded with Henry Martin Stanley and met with him in Egypt to bring home part of the manuscript of Stanley's *In Darkest Africa*. He had a substantial list of American writers, including Louisa May Alcott and Harriet Beecher Stowe, and he was close to famous European writers. His firm published at least 55 works by Jules Verne, starting with *Twenty-Thousand Leagues under the Sea* (1871), and he secured the rights to Victor Hugo and other French authors. British writers held him in high esteem, among them Thomas Hardy and Charles Reade. A grateful R D Blackmore wrote to him: 'But for you, *Lorna Doone* might never have seen the light.' With his worldwide contacts he became an expert on international law regarding intellectual property, and his work in encouraging works on world geography earned him a Fellowship of the Royal Geographical Society. Marston had been fond of fishing as a boy and returned to it in the 1880s, acquiring some fame with his book *An Amateur Angler's Days in Dove Dale* (1884), which paid homage to Izaak Walton.

This passage from Lorna Doone *contains delicious references to worship in a country church and also an example of one of those most unsettling moments – a disturbance in church:*

We heard of it first in church, on Sunday the eighth day of February, 1684–5, from a cousin of John Fry, who had ridden over on purpose from Porlock. He came in just before the anthem, splashed and heated from his ride, so that everyone turned and looked at him. He wanted to create a stir (knowing how much would be made of him), and he took the best way to do it. For he let the anthem go by very quietly – or rather, I should say, very pleasingly, for our choir was exceedingly proud of itself, and I sang bass twice as loud as a bull, to beat the clerk with the clarionet – and just as Parson Bowden, with a look of pride at his minstrels, was kneeling down to begin the prayer for the King's Most Excellent Majesty (for he never read the litany, except upon Easter Sunday), up jumps young Sam Fry and shouts:

'I forbid that there prai-er.'

'What!' cried the parson, rising slowly, and looking for someone to shut the door, 'have we a rebel in the congregation?' For the parson was growing short-sighted now and knew not Sam Fry at that distance.

'No,' replied Sam, not a whit abashed by the staring of the parish; 'no rebel, parson; but a man who mislaiketh popery and murder. That there prai-er be a prai-er for the dead.'

R D Blackmore 1825–1900, *Lorna Doone* (1869)

James Hill 1697–1727

Antiquary

Collecting coins is a minor interest of mine – it's possible, without being wealthy, to possess a small piece of history from many periods. The local numismatist James Hill was born in February 1697 in the parish of St Nicholas, Hereford. After Oxford and a legal training he began a lifelong passion for history, especially of the Hereford area. In 1717 he issued proposals for a two-volume history of the city and county, although the work was unfinished at his death. He became a Fellow of the Society of Antiquaries and used his vast collection of drawings and observations in lectures to the society. When the society resolved to attempt a complete history of British coins, Hill undertook to describe the Saxon coins in Lord Oxford's collection, and his own collection provided a substantial element in the study. In the Hereford area, he worked on a survey of the Roman settlement Ariconium (near Weston under Penyard), and made many drawings of ancient remains in the locality. Perhaps the most famous was of Tintern Abbey, included in John Stevens' famous *History of Antient Abbeys* in 1723. He was a friend of other notable antiquaries, among them William Stukeley and Roger Gales and, under the Celtic name Caradoc, was a member of their Society of Roman Knights, which met to study Roman remains.

Hill died in August 1727 and was buried in Hereford Cathedral.

Coins, particularly those from ancient Greece and Rome, have the power to reflect the personalities of those depicted. In this poem, the meaning of a Greek coin is explored:

Make sure the engraving is done skilfully.
The expression serious, majestic.
The diadem preferably somewhat narrow:
I don't like that broad kind the Parthians wear.
The inscription, as usual, in Greek:
nothing excessive or pompous –
we don't want the proconsul to take it the wrong way;
he's always smelling things out and reporting back to Rome –
but of course giving me due honour.
Something very special on the other side:
perhaps a discus-thrower, young, good-looking.
Above all I urge you to see to it
(Sithaspis, for God's sake don't let them forget)
that after "King" and "Saviour",
they add "Philhellene" in elegant characters.
Now don't try to be clever
with your "where are the Greeks?" and "what Hellenism
here behind Zagros, out beyond Phraata?"
Since so many others more barbarian than ourselves
Choose to inscribe it, we'll inscribe it too.
And besides, don't forget that sometimes
Sophists do come to us from Syria,
and versifiers, and other triflers of that kind.
So we're not, I think, un-Hellenized.

C P Cavafy 1863–1933, 'Philhellene', *Collected Poems*

Stephen of Thiers d.1124

Founder of Grandmontine Order

A few years ago, I joined in a pilgrimage from Abbey Dore to the scattered remains of Craswall Priory, in the shadow of the Black Mountains. These ruins are all that survive of one of the three English monastic houses in the Marches, belonging to a now little-known order, the Grandmontines. Their founder, Stephen of Muret or Thiers, was so impressed by the lives of the hermits he saw in Calabria, that he determined to form his own hermitage and lived a life of solitude in the valley of Muret, near Limoges. There he was joined by disciples, and with them he developed an austere life of prayer. Stephen left no writings, but his maxim was 'There is no rule save the Gospel of Christ'. Although the order was eventually claimed by both Benedictines and Canons Regular, it had an independent existence and, under Stephen's successor, Etienne de Luciac, had over 60 houses, mainly in Normandy, Anjou and Aquitaine. However, after initial success, the order descended into disputes and quarrels, and it suffered greatly during the Hundred Years War. Eventually, it was suppressed, just before the French Revolution. Three medieval Grandmontine houses were established at Alberbury, Grosmont and Craswall.

Stephen of Thiers emphasises the importance of solitude and of simplicity – elements of the spiritual life so prized by the Desert Fathers, from the earliest years of the Church. In their writings is great wisdom:

A hunter in the desert saw Abba Anthony enjoying himself with the brethren and he was shocked. Wanting to show him that it was necessary sometimes to meet the needs of the brethren the old man said to him, 'Put an arrow in your bow and shoot it.' So he did. The old man then said, 'Shoot another,' and he did so. Then the old man said, 'Shoot yet again,' and the hunter replied, 'If I bend my bow so much I will break it.' Then the old man said to him, 'It is the same with the work of God. If we stretch the brethren beyond measure they will soon break.'

An elder said: 'The reason why we do not get anywhere is that we do not know our limits, and we are not patient in carrying on the work we have begun. But without any labour at all we want to gain possession of virtue.'

A certain philosopher asked St Anthony: 'Father, how can you be so happy when you are deprived of the consolation of books?' Anthony replied: 'My book, O philosopher, is the nature of created things, and at any time I want to read the words of God, the book is before me.'

Anthony the Great *c.*251–356, *Sayings of the Desert Fathers*

The same theme of solitude is reflected in words by a mystic hundreds of years later:

He who is 'in Christ', is never solitary in the sense of being isolated from others. He cannot be unalive to that ultimate, triumphant sense of unity with his brother whom he sees in the place where every man stands before God. He can have no sense of antagonism or indifference towards any human being, for though there are those who are not yet reborn, yet he sees in every man a potential child of God, a potential brother in Christ, a potential member of the same heavenly family in union with which he rejoices. Those who love solitude rejoice in it, rejoice in that condition which alone can make them conscious of the 'great multitude which no man can number of every nation and kindred and tongue which stand before the throne and before the Lamb'.

Shirley Carter Hughson 1867–1949, *The Spiritual Letters of Father Hughson* (1953)

James Cowles Prichard 1786–1848

Physician & ethnologist

As a boy, I remember the fear (and often ridicule) associated with the local mental hospital. With its high walls and bleak buildings, it was a symbol of outmoded attitudes to mental illness. Indeed, many still called it the 'lunatic asylum', continuing, unknowingly, the cruel link between mental illness and the phases of the moon. But when these places were built in the 19th century they were thought enlightened establishments, compared to what had gone before. Many institutions like them owe their philosophy to forward-thinkers like the doctor we remember today. Born in February 1786 in Ross-on-Wye, James Prichard came of a well-established Quaker family and his religious background was to underpin all his future work in medicine and psychiatry. He trained in London and Edinburgh and first worked as a physician in Bristol, in a combined poorhouse and lunatic asylum. In Bristol, he was a leading spirit in setting up a college for scientific education which would admit dissenters. Many of his medical views were conservative – he still advocated blood-letting and trepanning. A frightened patient wrote in verse:

> Dr Prichard do appear, with his attendance and his care,
> He fills his patients full of sorrow – you must be bled today and cupped tomorrow.

He became an expert in ethnology, aiming to prove the unity of mankind and justifying the anthropological order laid down in Genesis. To Prichard, all mankind belonged to one species, views he expounded in *The Natural History of Man* (1843). He extended this notion of shared origin to the realm of languages and published his theories, insisting that Celtic was the connecting link between ancient Sanskrit and Hebrew.

His enlightened attitude towards mental illness suggested that mental disease was part of the make-up of human nature, common to primitive and civilized people alike. In an age when madness was often defined as lunacy and as a moral affliction, his views, which he expounded in *A Treatise on Insanity, and other Disorders affecting the Mind* (1835) were ground-breaking and were part of an important transition to developments in the 19th century. Prichard died in 1848 and was buried in Sellack by his son-in-law, William Henry Ley, the local vicar.

Gerard Manley Hopkins, the 19th-century poet, knew much about darkness and depression. Here, in one of his so-called 'Dreadful Sonnets', he articulates his own sense of isolation:

> No worst, there is none. Pitched past pitch of grief,
> More pangs will, schooled at forepangs, wilder wring.
> Comforter, where, where is your comforting?
> Mary, mother of us, where is your relief?
> My cries heave, herds-long; huddle in a main, a chief
> Woe, world-sorrow; on an age-old anvil wince and sing –
> Then lull, then leave off. Fury had shrieked 'No ling-
> ering! Let me be fell: force I must be brief'.
>
> O the mind, mind has mountains; cliffs of fall
> Frightful, sheer, no-man-fathomed. Hold them cheap
> May who ne'er hung there. Not does long our small
> Durance deal with that steep or deep. Here! creep,
> Wretch, under a comfort serves in a whirlwind: all
> Life death does end and each day dies with sleep.

Sir Henry Williams Baker 1831–77

Priest & hymn writer

Many of us will have been brought up on *Hymns Ancient and Modern Standard*, with its black covers, hymns whose texts were peppered with dynamic markings and whose numbers, even now, I can remember clearly (59 always 'O come, all ye faithful'). The leading light in the development of this ground-breaking book lived in our midst. After ordination in 1846, Henry Williams Baker was presented to the living of Monkland near Leominster, where he remained until his death in 1877. In 1859, he succeeded his father as 3rd baronet. While at Monkland, Baker published several volumes of devotional writing but was chiefly known for his work as a hymn writer. His greatest achievement was *Hymns Ancient and Modern,* first published in 1861. This went on to become one of the most widely-accepted and best-selling hymnals of the period. Baker's own Tractarian or high-church enthusiasm comes through in the book but its appeal is wide-ranging, with texts and tunes ranging from plainsong to contemporary contributions. As chairman of the hymnal's proprietors, Baker showed his musical experience by recruiting W H Monk as musical editor and his business acumen by insisting that copyright be claimed by the proprietors to protect and promote their work. He was also a contributor himself, with 30 of his own texts, among them *O praise ye the Lord!*, *We love the place*, *Praise, O praise our God and king* (drawing upon Milton) and, perhaps most famous of all, *Lord, thy word abideth.* He died on 12 February 1877 and is buried in the churchyard at Monkland.

Baker's most popular hymn, The King of love my Shepherd is, *leads us to a reflection on the image of shepherd, so often used of Christ and of those in pastoral ministry:*

The bishop's works must surpass other men's works as much as the shepherd's life is superior to that of the flock. It behoves him to think and carefully consider how very necessary it is for him to be bound to righteousness with the rope of understanding through whose dignity the people is called flock; it befits the shepherd to be lofty in works, profitable in words, and discreet in silence; he must grieve for the troubles of others as if he suffered equally with them; he must care and provide for all; through humility he must be the equal of all well-doers; he must be stern with sinners, and through righteousness he must feel indignation at their ill deeds; and yet in his care of them he is not to neglect the obedient; nor also in his love of the latter is he to neglect the disobedient.

Pope Gregory the Great 540–604, *Regula Pastoralis*

Part of one of Baker's most famous hymns

We love the place, O God,
 Wherein thine honour dwells;
The joy of thine abode
 All earthly joy excels.

It is the house of prayer
 Wherein thy servants meet;
And thou, O Lord, art there
 Thy chosen flock to greet.

February

David Garrick 1717–89

Hereford's renowned actor

It was by a quirk of fate that David Garrick was born in Hereford. His father, an army officer, was on a recruiting mission in the city and the family stayed at the Angel Inn (in Maylord Street), where the baby was born. Garrick's early connections were with another cathedral city, Lichfield, where his grandfather was a vicar choral. Garrick is, however, claimed by the city of his birth, proud to acknowledge the greatest actor and playwright of his time. His fame rests on his changing the acting style of the nation, and engineering a shift in the expectations of audiences. In place of accuracy, Garrick worked for energy and personal interpretation, and his portrayal of Shakespearean characters was legendary. He did much to promote William Shakespeare as national poet and icon – indeed, much of the bard's huge reputation may be attributed to Garrick's energy and enthusiasm. He was the first theatre manager to set about mastering public relations, especially at Drury Lane, and he surrounded the acting profession with convivial activity – many pubs and streets bear his name. Hereford's former theatre was named after Garrick, and the Garrick Club (1831) is a famed meeting place for the literary world.

At first sight, the following passage seems a rather spiteful resumé of Garrick's life, yet the poet sees beyond Garrick's faults. Would that we could all see beyond others' faults in that way!

Here lies David Garrick. Describe him who can,
An abridgement of all that was pleasant in man;
As an actor, confest without rival to shine,
As a wit, if not first, in the very first line.
Yet with talents like these, and an excellent heart,
The man had his failings, a dupe to his art ...
He cast off his friends as a huntsman his pack,
For he knew when he pleased he could whistle them back.
Of praise a mere glutton, he swallowed what came,
And the puff of a dunce, he mistook it for fame ...
But peace to his spirit, wherever it flies,
To act as an angel and mix with the skies;
Those poets, who owe their best fame to his skill,
Shall still be his flatterers, go where he will;
Old Shakespeare receive him, with praise and with love
And Beaumonts and Bens be his Kellys above.

Oliver Goldsmith 1728–74, 'Retaliation'

W H Auden 1907–73

Twentieth-century writer of renown

Auden is considered one of the 20th century's finest poets and writers – his work is of huge virtuosity, with a vast range of verse form, experience and emotion. While much of his work dates from periods spent in the United States, Italy and Austria, he spent three years in Herefordshire, from the autumn of 1932, as a teacher at the Downs School in Colwall. By all accounts he was a popular and imaginative teacher, indulging his theatrical interest in revues for the whole school and in a production of *The Deluge* from the Chester Mystery Plays. It was in June 1933, sitting on the school lawn with three other teachers, that he experienced what he called a 'Vision of Agape', in which:

> 'I felt myself invaded by a power which, though I consented to it, was irresistible and certainly not mine. For the first time in my life I knew exactly – because, thanks to the power, I was doing it – what it means to love one's neighbour as oneself.'

Auden's 'moment of revelation' is surely reflected in our own lives – glimpses of God which, although they may come infrequently, nevertheless go on sustaining us, sometimes years after the moment:

A Summer Night

Out on the lawn I lie in bed,
Vega conspicuous overhead
In the windless nights of June,
As congregated leaves complete
Their day's activity; my feet
Point to the rising moon.

Lucky, this point in time and space
Is chosen as my working-place,
Where the sexy airs of summer,
The bathing hours and the bare arms,
The leisured drives through a land of farms
Are good to a newcomer.

Equal with colleagues in a ring
I sit on each calm evening
Enchanted as the flowers
The opening light draws out of hiding
With all its gradual dove-like pleading,
Its logic and its powers.

That later we, though parted then,
May still recall those evenings when
Fear gave his watch no look;
The lion griefs loped from the shade
And on our knees their muzzles laid,
And Death put down his book.

Humphrey Smith bapt.1624 d.1663

Quaker preacher

We revere the Society of Friends today for their liberal thinking, their espousal of social issues and their quiet worship, but the life of a Quaker in the 17th century was not all peace. Born possibly at Stoke Bliss in Worcestershire, Humphrey Smith was baptized there on this day in 1624, and, although he had religious leanings from an early age, became, like his immediate family, a farmer at Little Cowarne. At the outbreak of the Civil War, with the collapse of church discipline, Smith began to preach in his native county and became involved with the emerging Quaker movement. George Fox called him 'a former priest' although there is no evidence that he was ever ordained – he was simply a local preacher. After a period of inner crisis, he left Herefordshire and travelled from town to town, encouraging Quaker meetings. At Evesham he had the first of many clashes with authority, which often led to his imprisonment or whipping. He travelled into Dorset and Hampshire, nearly always being abused by the townspeople because of his views, and often inflaming the situation through the propagation of his views through printed tracts. Smith was one of the earliest 'Sufferers', as the early Quakers called them, and he exercised a prophetic ministry; in 1660 he wrote a work about London which foretold the Great Fire and the Dutch attack on the Royal Navy in the Medway. His own spirituality was intense – he confided to friends that 'he had a narrow path to pass through, and more than once signified, he saw he should be imprisoned and that it might cost him his life'. In the end he did die in gaol, in Winchester, and was buried there. Those who saw him in his last days noted that 'he continued sweetly still and sensible unto the end, and died in perfect peace'.

The hardships endured by early Friends are captured in this passage by Joseph Besse from A Collection of the Sufferings of the People called Quakers (1737)*:*

Anno 1676
On the 20th of the month called August this year, Henry Caldicott, Mayor of Hereford with his officers, came to the Meeting there and warned the assembly not to meet any more, telling them, if they did, let it be at their peril. This threat of the Mayor was followed for many weeks after with outrageous insults and abuses from the populace, for on the 27th many boys of the city threw stones and dirt into the Meeting. On the 3rd September a rude rabble, with confused noise and shouting, beset the Meeting-House; some broke the glass windows, others with staves beat the hats off the men's heads, threw stones among them, and stuck burrs in their hair, and one of them, said to be the Mayor's son, broke the head of John Rea with a stone. On the 17th, the outrageous mob, part of which were choristers or singing boys of the Cathedral, encouraged by their superiors, broke in pieces the reminder of the glass windows with the window frames, and some of the walls of the house. After Meeting they pursued the country Friends, pelting them with stones, about a quarter of a mile.

The Peace Testimony *is probably the best known and best loved of the Quaker testimonies. Here, the great 17th-century Quaker William Penn speaks eloquently:*

A good end cannot sanctify evil means; nor must we ever do evil, that good may come of it. It is as great presumption to send our passions upon God's errands, as it is to palliate them with God's name. We are too ready to retaliate, rather than forgive, or gain by love and information. And yet we could hurt no man that we believe loves us. Let us then try what Love will do: for if men did once see we love them, we should soon find they would not harm us. Force may subdue, but Love gains: and he that forgives first, wins the laurel.

William Penn 1644–1718, from *Quaker Faith and Practice*

Thomas Winter / Tom Spring 1795–1851

Prize-fighter

In the 1960s, I can remember the family gathering round the television on a Saturday afternoon as the icons of the wrestling world of their day (Mick McManus, Jackie Pallo) grunted and preened their way to fame. Watching people fight has long lost its appeal for me, but it has often been a popular pastime, as today's character reminds us. Born at Witchend, near Fownhope, on this day in the year 1795, Thomas Winter was baptized at Fownhope church on 6 April that year. After serving an apprenticeship in his father's butchery business, he discovered his talent as a boxer in a local fight against a well-known bully and this led to his lifelong fame. Known by his new name – Tom Spring – he went to London, where he gained not only fame but also prize money for his victories. His technique used science rather than brute force and this gained him nicknames from disgruntled opponents, who called him 'Lady's Maid', 'Powder-Puff fighter' and 'The Light Tapper'. In 1821 he became Champion of All England and retired from fighting for a while in order to keep a tavern in London. He married and settled down but the lure of the fight brought him back to the ring and in 1823 he was back fighting on Hinckley Down, near Andover, before a crowd of 35,000. He rarely lost a fight (in the one he did lose, he also lost an eye) and his fame became legendary. Spring finally retired from the ring and from 1824 until 1828 kept the Booth Hall tavern in Hereford. In 1823 he received from the people of Hereford a handsome vase as a testimonial, while a weekly newspaper, *Tom Spring's Life in London* and *Sporting Chronicle* (1841–4), took his name. Despite his love of the fight, he had a high reputation for honesty and humanity and on his death in 1851 he received generous obituaries in the *Gentleman's Magazine* and the *Annual Register.*

The Bible's great fighter, Samson has inspired numerous poets and composers. Here, John Milton sees Samson at the end of his life, his strength spent:

Come, come, no time for lamentation now,
Nor much more cause. *Samson* hath quit himself
Like *Samson,* and heroickly hath finish'd
A life Heroick, on his Enemies
Fully reveng'd ...
To *Israel*
Honour hath left, and freedom, let but them
Find courage to lay hold on this occasion,
To himself and Father's house eternal fame;
And which is best and happiest yet, all this
With God not parted from him, as was fear'd,
But favouring and assisting to the end.

John Milton 1608–74, 'Samson Agonistes' (1671)

Milburga d.715
Abbess of Wenlock

On a long and tiring walk through Shropshire in 2007, at the end of the day I arrived at the pretty village of Stoke St Milborough, and there, nestled in the cleft of the hill, was the medieval church of St Milburga. Close to the church is St Milburga's Well, from which I was offered some of the most delicious and cooling water I have ever tasted! Its relationship to one of Shropshire's foremost holy women reminds us of the web of fact, legend and geographical feature that surrounds some of our early saints. Daughter of Merewahl, king of Mercia (see 2 January), Milburga became second abbess of the nunnery of Wenlock, which had been founded by her father in *c.*670. She was consecrated as a nun by Theodore, and had miraculous healing powers. After her death, her tomb was venerated but after the abbey's destruction, its site was forgotten and was unknown when Cluniac monks re-founded Wenlock in 1079. However, by 1101, the site had been discovered and had been described by Otto, Cardinal-bishop of Ostia, who also described miracles at Milburga's tomb – the healing of lepers and the blind and the vomiting of an extraordinary worm, which had caused a wasting disease locally. These miracles helped to make her cult more popular, and five ancient churches were dedicated to her. Many legends are associated with Milburga – it is said she had great power over birds, persuading them not to devour crops in local fields, while other sources credit her with the power of levitation. In common with many saintly virgins of the Saxon period, Milburga was troubled with an unwanted and over-enthusiastic suitor, who pursued her with an armed force. Milburga, it is said, crossed a river, which immediately swelled into a flood impassable by the suitor and his henchmen. St Milburga's Well was first mentioned in 1321 and is said to have particular healing powers to assist those with sore eyes.

Holy wells are powerful places. Perhaps the most famous in Britain was – and is – St Winefrede's Well in North Wales. Winefrede's story isn't dissimilar to that of Milburga (a fleeing virgin, a series of miracles, a springing well) and devotion at St Winefrede's Well attracted king and commoner alike. Even the rigours of the Reformation and repeated prohibitions could not prevent pilgrims seeking healing at the well and the site was greatly revered by the 19th-century poet, Gerard Manley Hopkins, who wrote a short play on the subject of the saint's life and suffering. Here, her uncle, St Beuno, in words from the play, speaks of the miracles surrounding the well, as Winefrede is raised from the dead:

O now while skies are blue, now while seas are salt,
While rushy rains shall fall or brooks shall fleet from fountains,
While sick men shall cast sighs, of sweet health all despairing,
While blind men's eyes shall thirst after daylight, draughts of daylight,
Or deaf ears shall desire that lipmusic that's lost upon them,
While cripples are, while lepers, dancers in dismal limb-dance,
Fallers in dreadful frothpits, waterfearers wild,
Stone, palsy, cancer, cough, lung-wasting, womb-not-bearing,
Rupture, running sores, what more? In brief, in burden,
As long as men are mortal and God merciful,
So long to this sweet spot, this leafy lean-over,
This Dry Dene, now no longer dry, nor dumb, but moist and musical
With the uproll and the downcarol of day and night delivering
Water, which keeps thy name, for not in rock written,
But in pale water, frail water, wild rash and reeling water ...

Stringer Lawrence 1697–1775

Army officer in the East India Company

Such was the contribution made by this man to the development of British Rule in India that he was honoured, on his death, with a commemoration in Westminster Abbey. Born in Hereford on this day in the year 1697, Stringer Lawrence was baptized on 27 February in All Saints church. In his military career he saw service in Gibraltar, Spain and Flanders and took part in the suppression of the Jacobite rising of 1745, when he fought at Culloden. In 1746 he began what was to be his major work in India. He was given a major's commission by the East India Company, to command its forces at Madras, and to make them more professional. His success in this led to his later being hailed as 'the Father of the Indian army', and certainly, under his direction, the company's soldiers at Madras were transformed from being mere garrison guards into a small, professional army. For almost 20 years Lawrence served in India, also helping to manage the East India Company's political affairs at Madras. During this time, the company changed from being a large trading concern into a major political power in India and Lawrence contributed greatly to this. However, he viewed British domination in India with caution (unlike his successor, Clive), and insisted, 'All the Rights that we [should] demand or any Europeans ought to have, are a few Settlements with a little country for their Bounds allotted to them, and a Liberty for a free Trade.' History was to prove the wisdom of this balanced view.

On his retirement, he lived in Devon, where a memorial was erected to him near Exeter. Sir Joshua Reynolds painted his portrait and the directors of the East India Company placed a monument, with a bust, in Westminster Abbey, inscribed: 'For Discipline established, Fortresses protected, Settlements extended, French and Indian armies defeated, and Peace restored in the Carnatic'.

Just as Lawrence helped to bridge the gap between British and Indian culture, so the 20th-century writer Rabindranath Tagore (1861–1941) helped introduce the west to Bengali culture. Most of his poetry invokes a universal God. This poem, The Son of Man, *is rare in being inspired particularly by Christ – and His Passion:*

From his eternal seat Christ comes down to this earth, where, ages ago, in the bitter cup of death He poured his deathless life for those who came to the call and those who remained away.

He looks about Him, and sees the weapons of evil that wounded his own age.

The arrogant spikes and spears, the slim, sly knives, the scimitar in diplomatic sheath, crooked and cruel, are hissing and raining sparks as they are sharpened on monster wheels.

But the most fearful of them all, at the hands of the slaughterers, are those on which has been engraved His own name, that are fashioned from the texts of His own words fused in the fire of hatred and hammered by hypocritical greed.

He presses His hand upon His heart; He feels that the age-long moment of His death has not yet ended, that new nails, turned out in countless numbers by those who are learned in cunning craftsmanship, pierce Him in every joint.

They had hurt Him once, standing at the shadow of their temple; they are born anew in crowds.
From before their sacred altar they shout to the soldiers, 'Strike!'

And the Son of Man in agony cried, 'My God, My God, why hast Thou forsaken me?'

Malcolm Saville 1901–82

Children's writer

The majestic scenery of the Shropshire hills has inspired many writers, and their mystery and sense of adventure is nowhere better evoked than in the work of Malcolm Saville. Born in Hastings on 21 February 1901, he started his career in publishing at Oxford University Press and went on to work for Cassell and George Newnes. A later autobiographical note tells us of his first introduction to Shropshire in 1936:

> I remember that it was a fine, clear summer afternoon when we first saw the lower, rolling contours of the majestic Long Mynd rising out of the plain on our right. Then, from the other side of the carriage we saw the rock-crowned Caradoc guarding the vale like a crouching lion.

During the Second World War, Saville's wife and children were evacuated to a farmhouse at Cwm Head, while he himself worked in London, and to alleviate the lonely separation he began to write his first children's book. *Mystery at Witchend* marked the beginning of a part-time writing career that was to produce 89 children's books over the next 38 years. The *Lone Pine Adventures* were his enduring creation, many inspired by the Shropshire hills – books with titles such as *The Neglected Mountain*, *Seven White Gates* and *The Secret of Grey Walls*. He always researched the local area for geography and history and only then began to plan the storyline, following one golden rule above all others: 'Have a curtain to every chapter. They must read on. I've failed unless a child wants to read on.' On retirement, Saville moved to Sussex, where he died on 30 June 1982 and is buried in the churchyard at Winchelsea.

Malcolm Saville has a rare gift for conjuring up the unique nature of the Shropshire countryside. In this passage, he writes of the folklore surrounding the Shropshire hills:

'See they take care,' he went on, 'for the Mynd is a mountain of moods – not black and cruel like the Stiperstones ...'

'Tell us about them. Talk about the Stiperstones.'

'Well, they're different. The Long Mynd is smooth and rolling. It's wild and lonesome, as I say, but the Stiperstones, way over the other side, are rugged and cruel, and those who live near 'em know they're evil too.'

'Gosh!' said Richard. 'Go on. Tell us more.'

'At the top of the Stiperstones is the Devil's Chair – a big outcrop of shining black rock. My father told me once that these rocks are the oldest in England and that long ago, when all this part of the country under sixteen hundred feet was buried under a sheet of ice, the Devil's Chair stood up like a black island. But that's as may be. What we do know is that one day Satan came with giant strides out of the west, and you can still see the imprint of his foot on a stone in the brook which he crossed in the valley below. He was on his way to the Long Mynd to fill one of the valleys – we call 'em gutters – with stones which he was carrying in his apron. We reckon the old devil was a bad walker, for they say he picked up a stone in his shoe and sat down in his chair to rest. He undid his shoe and flicked out a pebble which landed nine miles away in a field near Bishop's Castle. Some say this great stone turns round when the church clock strikes thirteen!'

'Go on!' said Mary, 'tell us more!'

'Well, he rested on his chair a bit, but when at last he got up to step across the Mynd his apron string broke and all the stones dropped out, and you can see 'em there today.'

From *Mystery at Witchend* (1943)

Simund de Freine d. before 1228

Medieval poet & philosopher

"La nus doinst le joie fine
Qui nul jour de l'an ne fine
Joie e permenable vie
Amen! Amen! chescun die"

Many of us who live in Herefordshire need no persuasion to stay in our county, with its magnificent scenery and timeless atmosphere. Young people, however, often wish to move away to what they see as more exciting places. A young person in the 12th century faced a similar dilemma. The family of Simund de Freine was connected with Sutton Freen (Sutton St Michael) in Herefordshire and by 1190 he was a canon of Hereford, bearing the title 'magister'. Two poems were addressed by him to Gerald of Wales (see 28 March) during the period 1194–7. One poem urges Gerald to stay in Hereford, commending the extensive studies of its cathedral school.

You are the flower and star of the clergy: transfer yourself to our city,
where there are philosophers. You are sure to be reckoned the greatest among them.
The city of Hereford is ideal for you: here
the *trivium* and the *quadrivium* have their proper place.
Respect for the seven-fold art has flourished and continues to flourish here;
in this city especially it rules supreme.
Instruction in *Grammar* teaches about correct sentence construction,
without which no-one is able to speak correctly.
The art of *Logic* enables one to tell the difference
between inductions, enthymemes, maxims and commonplaces.
The *Rhetorician* is distinguished by filling his words with such charm
that he can move everybody by his eloquence.
The art of *Arithmetic* teaches about numbers:
which numbers are integers, which squares and which cubes.
The *Geometer*, looking through the two holes of his surveying device,
calculates accurately by his art the height of a tower.
The *Musician* teaches about the right proportions of intervals
and how to join different notes together.
Astronomy explains the movement of the sun and the moon,
and predicts by its art the day for an eclipse of the sun.
Here in Hereford the *Astrologer* notes the hours and the arc of the day,
at what time the day is short and at what time long.
When Aries or Libra receive the sun, he discovers by his art
that the day is equal in length to the night under those signs.
Here in Hereford the *Geomancer* draws the fifteen shapes
by whose guidance he sees all the future.
He makes all the necessary distinctions, and finally he declares
whether people can have their wish granted, be they male or female.
Here in Hereford the *Physic* discloses the elements, the humours
and the underlying cause of an illness.

Since you are the star of the arts, you are rightly considered
to love this place of art where so many arts shine.
Please therefore come here: you will be lord over the whole city,
the whole city will bend the knee and serve you.

A simplified translation by Guy Rawlinson (2011)

February

George Moffatt 1806–78

Tea broker & politician

Behind even the humble tea bag there is a story – and it has a local relevance too! George Moffatt came of a family of tea-brokers and entered the family business. He had a sharp business acumen from early in his career and insisted on selling his tea at the average daily market rate plus ½d per pound. His business skills brought him to the attention of the government and he served as treasurer of the Mercantile Committee. He entered Parliament, representing first Ashburton in Devon and later Honiton. In politics he was a free-trader and something of a liberal, advocating the total abolition of church rates, and was also in favour of a large extension of voting rights. However, his parliamentary career received a setback when he unsuccessfully contested several seats, and for the remaining years of his life he lived the life of a country gentleman at Goodrich Court, near Ross-on-Wye, where he filled his gothic mansion with a collection of armour. He was a Justice of the Peace and a deputy lieutenant for Herefordshire. Small of stature, he could be domineering, and was caricatured in the novel *Beauchamp's Career* (1876) by George Meredith, in which he figures as the long-winded Mr Cougham. He was buried in Goodrich churchyard on this day in 1878.

The passions that drinking tea can arouse are well described here:

Johnson's defence of tea against Mr Jonas Hanway's violent attack upon that elegant and popular beverage, shews how very well a man of genius can write upon the slightest subject, when he writes, as the Italians say, *con amore*. I suppose no person ever enjoyed with more relish the infusion of that fragrant leaf than Johnson. The quantities which he drank of it at all hours were so great, that his nerves must have been uncommonly strong, not to have been extremely relaxed by such an intemperate use of it. He assured me, that he never felt the least inconvenience from it; which is a proof that the fault of his constitution was rather a too great tension of fibres, than the contrary. Mr Hanway wrote an angry answer to Johnson's review of his *Essay on Tea*, and Johnson, after a full and deliberate pause, made a reply to it; the only instance, I believe, in the whole course of his life when he condescended to oppose anything that was written against him.

James Boswell 1740–95, *The Life of Dr Johnson*

While in British culture drinking tea is often associated with 'comfort in adversity' or as a symbol of opposition to alcohol, in some cultures drinking tea takes on an almost mystical and contemplative significance, as seen in the Japanese Tea Ceremony:

The practice of the tea ceremony in Japan shows the sensitive feeling of respect and reverence towards both people and things which has so much in common with Benedictine awareness. Each individual is greeted with courtesy, each object (the small hearth, the charcoal fire, the tea utensils laid out in order, above all the specially chosen pottery bowls) will be handled in such a way as to pay homage to their particular material and shape, and to the specific contribution they make to the whole occasion. Each guest, before he or she drinks, takes the bowl in both hands, turns it and raises it, out of respect and thankfulness for all that went into the making of the bowl and of the tea: the earth, the clay, the potter's skill, the sun, the fire, the water, the tea plants. The most ordinary action and the most prosaic substance have become in that moment an act of worship.

Esther de Waal, *Seeking God – the Way of St Benedict* (1984)

Robert Burhill bapt.1572 d.1641

Herefordshire & Shropshire cleric & scholar

LAUS
ΔΟΞΑ
GLORIA
ΑΙΝΕΣΙΣ

Great men have often relied on their 'ghost-writers', and the best speeches often bear the marks of those whose names we will never know. Here is one whose learning was sought out by the best minds of the day, but whose own ecclesiastical rewards were modest. Burhill was baptized on this day in 1573 at Dymock, Gloucestershire. He came of a Herefordshire family from Thinghill, and after ordination became a canon of Hereford, also holding livings at Peterstow near Ross and Holdgate in Shropshire. Esteemed for his Greek and Hebrew scholarship, Burhill was consulted by Sir Walter Raleigh when he was writing *The History of the World.* He wrote Latin tracts defending the Protestant cause, one supporting Lancelot Andrewes, bishop of Ely and another supporting John Buckeridge, bishop of Rochester – both tracts raging against the Jesuits. He wrote a preface to *A Learned and Godly Sermon* by Miles Smith, bishop of Gloucester, and in other works wrote passionately in favour of episcopacy and monarchy. Burhill was a candidate for the presidency of his old college, Corpus Christi, Cambridge, but he failed at the final vote and had to be content with modest parochial preferment, which came in the form of livings at Snailwell in Cambridgeshire and Northwold in Norfolk, where he died in October 1641 and was buried in the chancel.

Robert Burhill may not have achieved the preferment he deserved or sought but he nevertheless found fulfilment in perhaps the greatest privilege of any priest – that is, preaching and ministering the sacraments to his congregation. Did the long spell in his country parish nurture his soul and enable him to keep inspired in his ministry? This poem by a contemporary writer imagines a priest questioning how his message may nowadays be received:

The Priest in the Pulpit

Will it last, this opening of the heart
to the Word, or will the new ways,
the film, the television, the e-mail,
dislodge us from the art of oratory?
Climbing the steps, taking off the paper clip,
remembering not to put it in my mouth,
the text, the Greek, the joke, the text again,
all this, O God, you know, as well as asking you
to make all things, especially the haste,
respectable. As the spiral notebooks rust
along the shelves, who knows how a word
in the thickest of the sermon's stickiest part,
might just have winged its way into the heart
of one young stranger there, and taken roost.

David Scott b.1947, *Piecing Together* (2005)

Oswald d.992
Benedictine monk & bishop of Worcester

Today, we remember a saint associated with our sister cathedral at Worcester. We can see the Saxon Oswald's figure, with that of his famous successor, Wulfstan (see 19 January), on the tomb of King John, before the high altar at Worcester. King John (see 11 June) revered them both, and on his tomb their tiny figures appear to whisper in his ear! Of Danish parentage, Oswald received his early training as a monk in France and, on taking up residence in England, became bishop of Worcester. He founded monasteries at Westbury-on-Trym and Ramsey in the Fens and obtained for these monasteries and for his bishopric large quantities of land. He was appointed archbishop of York, a post which he held in plurality with Worcester. He ruled both dioceses with wisdom, founding churches, acting as judge and visiting monasteries. In his final year, he lived at Worcester and began Lent with his usual ascetic practices, which included washing the feet of 12 poor men each day. As he completed this task on 28 February 992, he died, reciting the psalms. Oswald's memory and example lived on at Worcester, inspiring his successors, especially Wulfstan, who translated his body to a new shrine *c.*1086.

Wulfstan, Oswald's successor as bishop of Worcester wrote The Institutes of Polity *as a summary of his experience as politician and churchman. They are words of wise guidance for those who take up the ministry of a bishop:*

The daily work of a bishop is rightly: his prayers first and then his book-work, reading or writing, teaching or learning, and his Church hours at the correct time, always together with those things which pertain to it, and washing the feet of the poor and his distribution of alms and the direction of works where it be necessary. Good manual crafts befit him also, and that those in his household cultivate crafts, so that at any rate no one too idle dwell there, and it also befits him well that in a meeting he over and again disseminate divine teaching to the people with whom he then is.

Wisdom and prudence always befit bishops, and that those that attend them have honourable ways, and that they practise some special craft also. Nothing useless ever befits bishops: not folly nor stupidity, nor too much drinking, nor childishness in speech, nor idle buffoonery of any kind, not at home nor on a journey, nor in any place. But wisdom and prudence are appropriate to their rank, and gravity befits those that attend them.

A prayer seeking the humility that was shown by Jesus Christ

Jesus, Lord and Master, who served your disciples
in washing their feet; serve us often, serve us daily,
in washing our motives, our ambitions, our actions;
that we may share with you and in your mission to the
world and serve others gladly for your sake; to
whom be glory for ever.

Michael Ramsey 1904–88

David d.*c*.601

Patron saint of Wales

With 15 Welsh parishes in the diocese of Hereford it is surely right today to celebrate David or Dewi. We know little about his life – most comes from medieval sources and may be legendary. All agree that he was highly regarded for his kindness and compassion to others, especially the poor and the sick. He was a champion of the ascetic, spiritual life and is thought to have founded several monasteries, among them that at Menevia, now St Davids. He is thought to have based the Rule for his monasteries on that of the Egyptian desert monks, with a regime of heavy manual work, sustained by a diet of bread, vegetables and water. By the 12th century his cult had spread across South Wales, with other church dedications to him in Brittany, Cornwall and Herefordshire. He is the only Welsh saint to be canonized and honoured throughout the western church – Pope Callistus approved his cult in 1120, with the prestigious proclamation that two pilgrimages to St Davids were worth one to Rome.

The 19th-century poet Shelley speaks of the wonders of Wales:

Hail to thee, Cambria! For the unfettered wind,
Which from thy wilds even now methinks I feel,
Chasing the clouds that roll in wrath behind,
And tightening the soul's laxest nerves to steel;
True mountain Liberty alone may heal
The pain which custom's obduracies bring,
And he who dares in fancy even to steal
One draught from Snowdon's ever sacred spring
Blots out the unholiest rede of worldly witnessing.

And shall that soul, to selfish peace resigned,
So soon forget the woe its fellows share?
Can Snowdon's Lethe from the free-born mind
So soon the page of injured penury tear?
Does this fine mass of human passion dare
To sleep, unhonouring the patriot's fall,
Or life's sweet load in quietude to bear
While millions famish even in Luxury's hall,
And Tyranny, high raised, stern lowers on all?

No, Cambria! Never may thy matchless vales
A heart so false to hope and virtue shield;
Nor ever may thy spirit-breathing gales
Waft freshness to the slaves who dare to yield.
For me! ... the weapons that I burn to wield
I seek amid thy rocks to ruin hurled,
That Reason's flag may over Freedom's field,
Symbol of bloodless victory, wave unfurled,
A meteor-sign of love effulgent o'er the world.

Percy Bysshe Shelley 1792–1822, 'On leaving London for Wales'

March

CHAD d.672

Bishop of Lichfield

THE DIOCESES of Hereford and Lichfield share Shropshire so it is right that today we should celebrate Lichfield's founding saint. Chad was born in Northumbria, the youngest of four sons, all of whom became priests and monks. They entered the monastery on the Isle of Lindisfarne and were taught by St Aidan. Chad's brother Cedd had founded the abbey at Lastingham, Yorkshire, and on his brother's death, Chad was elected abbot. During the confusion between Celtic and Roman disciplines, Chad had become bishop of York for a time, but he graciously stepped aside when Theodore, Rome's choice, arrived in Britain. Eventually, Chad again became a bishop, this time of Mercia – a huge diocese, the centre of which he moved from Repton, Derbyshire to Lichfield. Chad travelled extensively and was much loved for his wisdom and gentleness. On his death, on this day in the year 672, he was immediately revered as a saint. His relics were moved to the Lady Chapel of Lichfield Cathedral in 1296 and an even more splendid shrine was built by Bishop Robert Stretton in the 14th century.

At the Reformation the shrine was destroyed but Chad's relics were claimed and preserved by recusant Roman Catholic families. Four bones, believed to be those of Chad, are now in the Roman Catholic cathedral of St Chad in Birmingham. The 8th-century illuminated *Gospels of St Chad* were associated with his shrine and are now in Lichfield Cathedral library.

The Venerable Bede is one of the great sources of information about the life of our early saints:

Chad died on the second of March [672], and was first buried close by Saint Mary's church; but when a church of the most blessed Peter, Prince of the Apostles, was built there later, his body was transferred to it. In both of these places, frequent miracles of healing attested to his virtues. More recently, a madman wandering at large arrived there one evening, and passed the night in church unnoticed and unheeded by the watchmen. And in the morning, to the amazement and delight of all, he left the place in his right mind, showing clearly what healing he had been granted there by the goodness of God. Chad's burial place is covered by a wooden tomb made in the form of a little house with an aperture in the wall through which those who visit it out of devotion may insert their hand and take out some of the dust. They mix this in water and give it to sick men or beasts to drink, by which means their ailment is quickly relieved and they are restored to the longed for joys of health.

Venerable Bede 672/3–735, *Ecclesiastical History of the English People*

Dr Samuel Johnson (1709–84), man of letters and lexicographer, was Lichfield's most famous son. Included in his literary output are many prayers, including this one for blessing on our studies

O God, who hast ordained that whatever is to be desired, should be sought by labour, and who, by thy blessing, bringest honest labour to good effect, look with mercy upon my studies and endeavours. Grant me, O Lord, to design only what is lawful and right; and afford me calmness of mind, and steadiness of purpose, that I may so do thy will in this short life, as to obtain happiness in the world to come; for the sake of Jesus Christ our Lord.

Edward Herbert, 1st Baron Herbert of Cherbury 1582–1648

Philosopher & free-thinker

The beautiful countryside on the borders of Shropshire and Montgomeryshire produced one of the great thinkers of the early 17th century – one who was ahead of his time and whose liberal thinking has much to teach us today. Of noble birth, as a boy, Edward Herbert studied Greek and logic with 'one Mr Newton at Diddlebury in Shropshire', and went on to study in Oxford. He was introduced to the court of the ageing Elizabeth I, who is said to have remarked, 'It is a pity he was married so young.' Herbert became MP for Montgomeryshire and travelled widely in France, Germany and Italy. While in Rome, he visited the Roman Catholic English College, insisting that he came in peace and not to quarrel. His words were prophetic of his later generosity of spirit:

> I conceived the points agreed upon both sides were greater bonds of amity between us than that the points disagreed could break them, that for my part I loved every body that was for a pious and virtuous life.

Herbert became a respected diplomat, as ambassador to Paris, and was something of a polymath, being also a writer, a poet and an historian. But it is as a philosopher that he is chiefly remembered. He insisted that too much energy was spent in proving religious revelation – much more was to be gained by an understanding of God's gracious activity in each person. To him, divine salvation was open to all, through repentance, through prayer and through common-sense virtue. He is considered 'the Father of Deism in England', perhaps looking towards the great figures of the Enlightenment a hundred years later. His work *De religione gentilium* is probably the first study of comparative religion.

Rodin's The Thinker *may seem a world away from a 16th-century polymath like Edward Herbert, and yet this sculpture seems to reflect Herbert's ideas, exhibiting elements of a quality so much needed in the world today – that of quiet and deep thought.*

He is mild-mannered and some people say
'He's in another world.' They are quite wrong,
He is in now and here, and every day
He thinks of plans to which we all belong.

He's read past notions. In his mind he holds
A shape, a purpose, meaning written live.
Night and day he watches now our world's
Behaving wildly. He wants it to thrive.

He wants all men to share his appetite
For truth. It is a way of life, a choice
Of how to be and know. He claims no right
But tries to be a civilised, true voice.

Elizabeth Jennings 1926–2001, 'The Thinker', *Timely Issues* (2001)

John Duncumb 1765–1839

Herefordshire historian

Writing county histories became a popular occupation during the 18th century, especially with clergy, and today we remember one whose work, though incomplete, led to Herefordshire becoming better known for its history and traditions. Born the son of a clergyman at Shere, in Surrey, John Duncumb attended Guildford Grammar School and Trinity College, Cambridge. He moved to Hereford and became editor and printer of the *British Chronicle* or *Pugh's Hereford Journal* – the city's first real organ of news and comment. Securing the patronage of the duke of Norfolk, he set out to compile and edit a history of the county, supported by two guineas a week from the duke. Adopting the standard practice of distributing printed lists of queries to the clergy and others, asking for historical information about each parish, he embarked on the long process. In 1791 he was ordained and held livings first in Talachddu, near Brecon, then in Berkshire and Sussex. He was, however, a non-resident parson of these parishes, making his home in Herefordshire and holding the livings of Abbey Dore and Mansell Lacy. Duncumb was also interested in agricultural improvement and served as Secretary of the Herefordshire Agricultural Society from 1797 until just before his death, publishing in 1803 a *Sketch of the Rural Economy of Herefordshire*. At last, in 1804, the first volume of *Collections towards the History and Antiquities of the County of Hereford* was published, with the first part of the second volume in 1812. However, the death of the duke of Norfolk led to the abandonment of the project.

In addition to historical information, Duncumb includes fascinating insights into contemporary rural customs:

Visiting Wells

The heathens are known to have paid adoration to wells and fountains: the Roman Catholic church also adopted this practice, and hence many wells are still termed *Holy Wells* or retain the name of some saint to whom they were dedicated. St Ethelbert's Well in the city of Hereford, and many others in different parts of the county are still in some repute for their supposed medicinal qualities. A well in the parish of Dinedor excites much emulation on each New-Year's Day, in a contest for the first pail-full of water, which is termed *the cream of the well*, and is presented to some neighbour as a mark of respect or as a pledge of good fortune; a pecuniary compliment is expected in return. This custom appears harmless but it would be difficult, perhaps, to point out any useful or laudable purpose resulting from it.

John Duncumb, *Collections towards the History and Antiquities of the County of Hereford* (1804)

A prayer seeking the stability of God's grace through the turbulence of history

O Almighty God, who alone canst order the unruly wills and affections of sinful men; Grant unto thy people, that they may love the thing which thou commandest, and desire that which thou dost promise; that so, among the sundry and manifold changes of the world, our hearts may surely there be fixed, where true joys are to be found; through Jesus Christ our Lord.

Book of Common Prayer, Collect for the Fourth Sunday after Easter.

William Henry Purchas 1823–1903

Botanist

We wouldn't dare indulge in this man's passion for collecting wild flowers, although when I was a boy, this was actively encouraged in schools and I still have albums full of dried and pressed specimens! Purchas was born in Ross-on-Wye, but spent most of his career as a clergyman in Staffordshire, where he was vicar of Alstonefield. On his annual holidays to Herefordshire he studied the flora of the county, giving lectures to the Hereford Literary and Philosophical Society in 1852 and to the Woolhope Club in 1866. He published many articles in national botanical journals and finally, with the Reverend Augustin Ley, vicar of Sellack and King's Caple, published *A Flora of Herefordshire* (1889).

Purchas identified different kinds of bramble – hence our illustration and hence this passage from the book of Judges, where the bramble is a symbol of the perfidious rule of Abimilech, in contrast to the gentler symbolism of other trees and shrubs:

Listen to me, you men of Shechem, that God may listen to you. The trees once went forth to anoint a king over them; and they said to the olive tree, 'Reign over us.' But the olive tree said to them, 'Shall I leave my fatness, by which gods and men are honoured, and go to sway over the trees?' And the trees said to the fig tree, 'Come you, and reign over us.' But the fig tree said to them, 'Shall I leave my sweetness and my good fruit, and go to sway over the trees?' And the trees said to the vine, 'Come you, and reign over us.' But the vine said to them, 'Shall I leave my wine which cheers gods and men, and go to sway over the trees?' Then all the trees said to the bramble, 'Come you and reign over us.' And the bramble said to the trees, 'If in good faith you are anointing me king over you, then come and take refuge in my shade; but if not, let fire come out of the bramble and devour the cedars of Lebanon.'

Judges 9:7–15

A prayer of thanksgiving for nature

O God, we thank you for this earth, our home; for the wide sky and the blessed sun, for the salt sea and the running water, for the everlasting hills and the never-resting winds, for trees and the common grass underfoot.
We thank you for our senses by which we hear the songs of birds, and see the splendour of the summer fields, and taste of the autumn fruits, and rejoice in the feel of the snow, and smell the breath of the spring.
Grant us a heart wide open to all this beauty; and save our souls from being so blind that we pass unseeing when even the common thorn bush is aflame with your glory, O God our creator, who lives and reigns for ever and ever.

Walter Rauschembusch 1861–1918

ELIZABETH BARRETT BROWNING 1806–61

Poet

ELIZABETH BARRETT was born near Durham on this day in 1806, the eldest of 12 children. Three years later, the family moved to Hope End, near Ledbury, where they were to live for the next 23 years. The beautiful setting near the Malvern Hills was reflected in Elizabeth's poetry throughout her life. In *The Lost Bower,* published in 1844, she recalls

> Green the land is where my daily
> Steps in jocund childhood played,
> Dimpled close with hill and valley,
> Dappled very close with shade.

Elizabeth was a studious child, learning Greek and Latin, and she wrote verses at an early age. An epic poem, *The Battle of Marathon*, in the style of Pope, was privately printed by her father for her 14th birthday. From the age of 20, Elizabeth began to battle with a lifelong illness which caused her to be frail and weak, necessitating her prolific writing being done mainly in her home. In 1828 her mother died and was buried in the parish church of St Michael and All Angels in Ledbury. This was followed by a decline in family fortunes, caused by a downturn in profits from the Jamaican sugar plantations from which her father had grown rich. Leaving Hope End, the family moved first to Devon and then to London. Elizabeth's verse and prose drew the attention of fellow poet Robert Browning, eventually leading to a secret marriage in 1846, and the couple's leaving for Italy. There, Elizabeth continued her poetry, dying in Florence on 29 June 1861. Much of her poetry has religious significance. She believed that 'Christ's religion is essentially poetry – poetry glorified' – and certainly in the poem *Aurora Leigh* there is much religious imagery and the poem also has allusions to images in the apocalypse. During her time in Italy she became a devotee of spiritualism and a supporter of socialist and humanitarian causes. More recently, her poems have found a new resonance with the feminist movement.

Elizabeth Barrett Browning knew tragedy and the shattering of dreams. Perhaps that wistful disappointment is reflected in her interpretation of Peter's denial of Jesus:

> I think that look of Christ might seem to say,
> 'Thou Peter! Art thou, then, a common stone
> Which I at last must break my heart upon,
> For all God's charge to His high angels may
> Guard my foot better? Did I yesterday
> Wash thy feet, my beloved, that they should run
> Quick to deny me 'neath the morning sun?
> And do thy kisses, like the rest, betray?
> The cock crows coldly. – Go, and manifest
> A late contrition, but no bootless fear!
> For when thy final need is dreariest,
> Thou shalt not be denied, as I am here:
> My voice to God and angels shall attest,
> *Because I KNOW this man, let him be clear.'*

'The Meaning of the Look', from *The Poems of Elizabeth Barrett Browning* (1853)

Herbert Westfaling 1532–1601

'Unsmiling' bishop of Hereford?

Where would we be without laughter in the church? Yes, there is much to cause sorrow in our world, but far too often the church itself takes life far too seriously. The bishop we remember today may have needed his leg pulling now and again. Westfaling's family came from Germany (hence the name) and he had a distinguished academic background at Oxford. While there, he served on a commission investigating complaints against the dean and chapter of Gloucester, who had been criticised for their neglect of duties. For such investigations, Westfaling gained the reputation (probably unjustified) of being of unsmiling gravity, as well as for being upright and impartial and given to excessively long speeches and sermons. In Hereford diocese, his strongly Protestant views were not always readily accepted in an area where opinions among the clergy were conservative. His survey of the morals and education of the clergy revealed that many had no academic qualifications, and a low level of preaching skills. His four attempts to conduct a Visitation at the cathedral were resisted on the basis that while the bishop might correct heretical views, all other matters should be dealt with by the canons themselves. In any case, he sent a warning about suspect religious views, images and pictures to the vicars choral in 1586. Westfaling died on this day in the year 1601 and his effigy, with long beard and folded robes, lies under the north window in the north transept of the cathedral. He looks so uncomfortable there – perhaps this contributes to his lack of humour ...?

Westfaling's portrait in the Great Hall of the Bishop's Palace reinforces the view of this bishop as rather humourless. But portraits can sometimes get it wrong.

Bishop Hensley Henson, when bishop of Durham, went to see Cosmo Gordon Lang, who was then archbishop of York. When he arrived at Bishopthorpe he was shown a newly painted portrait of the archbishop, resplendent in episcopal robes. Lang asked Henson: 'What do you think of it?'

'What do *you* think of it?' Henson answered.

'I don't like it,' the archbishop replied. 'They say it makes me too proud, pompous and prelatical.'

'And to *which* of these adjectives,' Henson answered, 'does Your Grace object?'

On walking the Pilgrims' Way from Winchester to Canterbury in 2010, I visited the tiny church at Easton, in the Itchen Valley, just outside Winchester. There, in the chancel, was a memorial to Agatha Barlow, late wife of William Barlow, bishop of Chichester in the 17th century. She produced five daughters:

Margaret, wife unto William Overton, Bishop of Lichfield and Coventry
Anne, wife unto Herbert Westfayling, Bishop of Hereford
... Wife unto William Day, now Bishop of Winchester
Frances, Wife unto Toby Mathew, Bishop of Durham
Antonine, late wife unto William Wickam, disceased Bishop of Winchester.
She being a woman godly, wise and discreete from her youthe,
Most faithful unto her husband, both in prosperite and adversite and
A companion with him in banishment for the gospel.

She was also clearly a woman of high ambition for her daughters – all of whom she married off to bishops. Alas, even the lovely Anne doesn't seem to have brought a smile to the face of Bishop Westfaling!

Abraham Darby 1678–1717

Ironmaster

The great industrial inventions of the later 18th and 19th centuries relied on new technology, especially the development of iron and steel. Today we remember a family in which successive generations made a huge impact on the industrial life of our region and country. Abraham Darby senior was apprenticed to a malt-mill maker in Birmingham but went on to make his name in brass and iron foundry work. In 1706 he set up his works near Coalbrookdale and this became the scene of huge advances in iron-making processes – in 1709/10 he used coke in the blast furnaces for the first time. In an age of experiment in industrial management and technology, his firm became the symbol of British industrial success. Abraham died in 1717 and was buried in the Quaker burial ground at Broseley. He was succeeded by his son Abraham (1711–63), who commercially developed the iron-making processes, extending the use of coal and marketing it. He was also involved in brick making and lime burning as well as in the construction of primitive railways. His grandson, also Abraham (1750–89), built the Iron Bridge over the Severn near Coalbrookdale, universally acknowledged in the 18th century as the first of its kind.

Part of Darby's success lay in the enlightened way in which he dealt with his workforce. This theme is found time and again in the work of enlightened thinkers, who saw the worst excesses of the Industrial Revolution in its lack of humanity and in its failure to find a place for good relationships in the world of industry and commerce. A later writer, John Ruskin, put this well:

We shall find the best and simplest illustration of the relations of master and operative in the position of domestic servants ... It may indeed happen, and does happen often, that if the master is a man of sense and energy, a large quantity of material work may be done under mechanical pressure, enforced by strong will and guided by wise method; also it may happen, and does happen often, that if the master is indolent and weak (however good-natured), a very small quantity of work, and that bad, may be produced by the servant's undirected strength, and contemptuous gratitude. But the universal law of the matter is that, assuming any given quantity of energy and sense in master and servant, the greatest material result obtainable by them will be, not through antagonism to each other, but through affection for each other; and that if the master, instead of endeavouring to get as much work as possible from the servant, seeks rather to render his appointed and necessary work beneficial to him, and to forward his interests in all just and wholesome ways, the real amount of work ultimately done, or of good rendered, by the person so cared for, will indeed be the greatest possible.

John Ruskin 1819–1900, *Unto this Last* (1860)

God of creation, the earth is yours
with all its beauty and goodness,
its rich and overflowing provision.
But we have claimed it for our own,
plundered its beauty for profit,
grabbed its resources for ourselves.
God of creation, forgive us.
May we no longer abuse your trust,
but care gently and with justice for your earth.

Jan Berry

Constantine 6th century

Cornwall in Herefordshire

There is just one dedication to this British saint in Herefordshire, but it is a timely reminder that there are clear links between Cornwall, with its many Celtic saints, and the Celtic tradition which spread as far as what we now call Herefordshire. Tradition has it that Constantine was converted by Petroc, became a monk and founded churches in Devon and Cornwall. These are recalled by two places in Cornwall called Constantine: one near Padstow, the other on the banks of the Helford river in south-west Cornwall. The ruined chapel at Constantine Bay also has a nearby holy well – 'taking the waters' there was said to bring rain during dry weather. This chapel survived as a monastery until the 11th century. The church at Welsh Bicknor beside the river Wye has connections with this obscure Cornish saint. By 1144, we read that Constantine was patron saint of the church, but in time, this dedication was superseded by the patronage of St Margaret. But Constantine is still remembered on the banks of the Wye and we are proud of our connection with Cornwall!

Herefordshire is proud to give 'refuge' to a Cornish saint – a reminder that Celtic influence was strong throughout western England. Here we are introduced to another Cornish saint and his spirituality:

A flame of rushlight in the cell
On holy walls and holy well
And to the west the thundering bay
With soaking seaweed, sand and spray,
Oh good St Cadoc pray for me
Here in your cell beside the sea.

Somewhere the tree, the yellowing oak,
Is waiting for the woodman's stroke,
Waits for the chisel saw and plane
To prime it for the earth again
And in the earth, for me inside,
The generous oak tree will have died.

St Cadoc, when the wind was high,
Saw angels in the Cornish sky
As ocean rollers curled and poured
Their loud Hosannas to the Lord,
His little cell was not too small
For that great Lord who made them all.

Here where St Cadoc sheltered God
The archaeologist has trod,
Yet death is now the gentle shore
With land upon the cliffs before
And in his cell beside the sea
The Celtic saint has prayed for me.

John Betjeman 1906–84, 'Saint Cadoc' (1940)

Richard Dawes 1793–1867
Educational reformer & dean of Hereford

Deans are sometimes remembered for skills and talents outside the pulpit! Here is one who made a huge difference to the standard of education in the 19th century. Richard Dawes' mathematical skills were recognised when he became bursar of the newly-founded Downing College in Cambridge – he was a man of many parts. Influenced by a contemporary circle of scientists, including Adam Sedgwick, he saw the vital need for the improvement of science education, especially in schools. He put this into practice during the 1840s when, as newly appointed incumbent of King's Somborne in Hampshire, he developed applied science at the local school, encouraging rudimentary laboratory experiments – unheard of in the early 19th century. He made the school a model of efficient management and radical curriculum, broadening pupils' horizons through secular reading and opening the school to children from different social classes. He believed in the necessity of education for all and was an articulate supporter of the removal of barriers preventing Dissenters from entering universities. Dawes recognised the importance of good teacher training and his pioneering manual, *Suggestive Hints towards Improved Instruction, making it Bear upon Practical Life* (1849), became a prescribed text and ran to seven editions.

In 1850 he became dean of Hereford, and put his skills and energies into working with Scott in the continuing restoration of the cathedral, seeing it opened for worship again in 1863. In Hereford he continued to take a keen interest in education and science through the Bluecoat and Foundation schools and through Ledbury's National Schools. He was a much-loved priest and George Eliot described his face as 'so intelligent and benignant that children might grow good by looking at it'. Dawes died on this day in the year 1867.

Richard Dawes made a great impression on all – those he taught and those to whom he ministered as dean. On his death, a pupil at the Cathedral School, Fred Weatherly (who went on to become a well-known song-writer – see 7 September) wrote this poem in the dean's memory:

Yes, he is gone, the Husband, Pastor, Friend,
To those pure realms where Time shall have no end.
Burst from the shackles of this mortal clay,
Upwards his spirit wings its blissful way
To those bright golden mansions of the blest
Where sorrows cease, and all the weary rest.
We know his value, know his native worth,
Now that he sleeps beneath his kindred earth,
Now that his place is desolate and lone,
We know him truly as he should be known.
All straitened thoughts, ruffling the selfish breast,
All narrow minded jealousies have rest.
While Envy folds her drooping wings for shame,
And pales before his bright and honoured bane.

Hereford Cathedral School, 16 March 1867

James Davies (Banks) 1820–82

Classical scholar

Caesar adsum iam forte, Pompey aderat
Caesar sic in omnibus, Pompey in is at.

So goes the old schoolboy Latin joke. I wonder if this famous Latin scholar would have found it as amusing as I did at school? James Banks was born at Kington, the son of Richard Banks of Moor Court. After ordination, he became incumbent in the Forest of Dean and, from 1852, headmaster of Ludlow Grammar School. He changed his name to Davies on succeeding to his uncle's property at Moor Court, where he subsequently resided, now combining the roles of squire, clergyman and financier and becoming a partner in his brother's bank. He erected a church in his own grounds for the convenience of neighbours for whom the parish church was too remote. Davies became a prebendary of Hereford Cathedral in 1875.

He is best known as a classical scholar and for many years wrote articles on classical themes for the *Saturday Review.* In 1860 he published a metrical version of the *Fables of Babrius* from the text of his friend, Sir George Cornewall Lewis (see 15 April) and translated volumes of Catullus and other Roman poets for popular editions. Davies was in many ways a 19th-century polymath, and in addition to his classical interests wrote on architecture, archaeology, topography and horticulture.

W R Inge, dean of St.Paul's, a great philosopher, saw the classical tradition as having a place in the development of a reasonable religion which might draw together different traditions and break down denominational barriers:

My contention is that besides the combative Catholic and Protestant elements in the Churches, there has always been a third element, with very honourable traditions, which came to life again at the Renaissance, but really reaches back to the Greek Fathers, to St Paul and St John, and further back still. The characteristics of this type of Christianity are – a spiritual religion, based on a firm belief in absolute and eternal values as the most real things in the universe – a confidence that these things are knowable by man – a belief that they can nevertheless be known only by whole-hearted consecration of the intellect, will, and affections to the great quest – an entirely open mind towards the discoveries of science – a reverent and receptive attitude to the beauty, sublimity, and wisdom of the creation, as a revelation of the mind and character of the Creator – a complete indifference to the current valuations of the worldling.

W R Inge 1860–1954, *The Platonic Tradition in English Religious Thought* (1926)

We often associate the religion of Greek and Roman civilisation with pagan sacrifice and in opposition to the Christian faith, but its prayers and religious observances often have a strong ethical dimension:

May I be no man's enemy, and may I be the friend of that which is eternal and abides. May I never quarrel with those nearest to me; and if I do, may I be reconciled quickly. May I love, seek, and attain only that which is good. May I wish for all men's happiness and envy none. May I never rejoice in the ill-fortune of one who has wronged me ...When I have done or said what is wrong, may I never wait for the rebuke of others, but always rebuke myself until I make amends ... May I win no victory that harms either me or my opponent ... May I reconcile friends who are wroth with one another.

Eusebius 263–339

Arthur Keysall Yapp 1869–1936

National promoter of YMCA

The Young Men's Christian Association (YMCA) has had an influence on millions of young lives, especially in our cities. One of its leading lights lived and died in our midst. Born on this day in the year 1869, Arthur Yapp came from a farming family, and throughout his life he never forgot his roots and his love of the countryside. He was educated at Hereford County College and entered a local firm of agricultural engineers. His mother had been the daughter of a Congregational minister and religion played a vital part in his life; at this time he devoted much of his spare time to temperance and mission work. At the age of 21 he became involved in the YMCA, first as a volunteer and later as an employee in the north of England. In 1907 the Manchester branch invited him to superintend its new building work and he became the branch's General Secretary, extending this work in 1912 when he became Secretary for the National Council in London. With the outbreak of the First World War, the YMCA was called upon to provide emergency service on the Front and Yapp was heavily involved in this – in 1914 there were 250 centres of rest and recreation at the Front and by the end of the war this number had risen to 10,000. At this time, Yapp introduced the YMCA's symbol – a red triangle, symbolising spirit, mind and body. He was knighted in 1917 and later invited by Lloyd George to take charge of the food economy campaign – a task which involved much travelling and public speaking. His Christian faith was an integral part of this work and he was a regular preacher in churches and chapels throughout the land – the first layman to occupy the pulpit in Canterbury Cathedral. Yapp died in 1936 and was buried at Orleton.

The YMCA did and does much to encourage and support young people leaving home for the first time – an independence often experienced with mixed emotions by them and their parents alike:

It is eighteen years ago, almost to the day –
A sunny day with the leaves just turning,
The touch-lines new ruled – since I watched you play
Your first game of football, then like a satellite
Wrenched from its orbit, go drifting away

Behind a scatter of boys. I can see
You walking away from me towards the school
With the pathos of a half-fledged thing set free
Into a wilderness, the gait of one
Who finds no path where the path should be.

That hesitant figure, eddying away
Like a winged seed loosened from its parent stem,
Has something I never quite grasp to convey
About nature's give-and-take – the small, the scorching
Ordeals which fire one's irresolute clay.

I have had worse partings, but none that so
Gnaws at my mind still. Perhaps it is roughly
Saying what God alone could perfectly show –
How selfhood begins with a walking away,
And love is proved in the letting go.

C Day-Lewis 1904–72, 'Walking Away'

John Bull 1563–1628

Musician & keyboard composer

I wonder why the lovely church of St Stephen, Old Radnor has such a wonderful organ case? Some say it is one of the oldest in the country. Might it be that one of the most famous composers of the 16th century hailed from this area, and found some way of repaying his debt to the area of his birth? John Bull was almost certainly born in Herefordshire or, more likely, Radnorshire. He was certainly in the choir of Hereford Cathedral as a boy, and returned to the cathedral as assistant organist in 1582 after a period of service in the Chapel Royal. In 1589, he became cathedral organist, a post he shared at first with John Hodges, who had held the post since 1538. When Bull assumed the post of Master of the Choristers, his skill was apparent to all, but so was his difficult character – he was, on several occasions, chastised for absence without leave and for being impudent to the Precentor! When he returned to the Chapel Royal, he maintained his links with Hereford, being granted rooms in the College of the vicars choral in 1587 and again in 1591. At court, he became the first organist to be remunerated as such, and in addition to this work, he became first Reader of the newly-formed Gresham College. He was popular at the court of James I and taught the king's daughter, the young Princess Elizabeth, to play the virginals. Scandal struck in 1613, when he was charged with adultery and with being a Papist, and he had no option but to flee from England to the Netherlands. Here he held several posts at Antwerp, most importantly at the cathedral. Much of his best music is for keyboard – 'a most prodigious hand on the organ' – and the collection *Parthenia* contains not only his own compositions but also those of Byrd and Gibbons. He also wrote a small amount of church music. He died on 12 or 13 March 1628 and is buried near Antwerp Cathedral.

Words by Bull's contemporary, William Byrd (1542–1623) on the benefits of singing:

1. Reasons briefly set down by the author to persuade every one to learn to sing.
First, it is a knowledge easily taught, and quickly learned, where there is a good Master, and an apt Scholar.
2. The exercise of singing is delightful to Nature and good to preserve the health of Man.
3. It doth strengthen all parts of the breast and doth open the pipes.
4. It is a singular good remedy for a stuttering and stammering of the speech.
5. It is the best means to procure a perfect pronunciation, and to make a good Orator.
6. It is the only way to know where Nature hath bestowed the benefit of a good voice: which gift is so rare, as there is not one among a thousand, that hath it: and in many, that excellent gift is lost, because they want Art to express Nature.
7. There is not any Musick of Instruments whatsoever, comparable to that which is made of the voices of Men, where the voices are good, and the same well sorted and ordered.
8. The better the voice is, the meeter it is to honour and serve God there-with: and the voice of man is chiefly to be employed to that end. *Omnis spiritus laudet Dominum.*

Since singing is so good a thing,
I wish all men would learn to sing.

Psalmes, Sonnets, & Songs of Sadness and Pietie (1588)

John Salisbury 1576–1626

Jesuit teacher

The quiet valley of the Monnow near Monmouth was the scene of much quiet courage in the 17th century, as the Catholic community sought to work and study in this area. Today we remember a leading light in this episode of our religious history. A native of Merioneth, John Salisbury seems to have been taken to Ireland at an early age and there persuaded to become a Catholic. He studied at St Albans College, Valladolid in Spain and was ordained priest in 1600. Newly ordained priests were often immediately sent back to England to engage in Catholic missionary work in the now Protestant country and the government were always on the look-out for such movements. In 1602 the Privy Council had been warned of such a mission from Spain and knew about John Salisbury. He was said to be 'yellow haired, sanguine and short of stature, about the age of 26 and never will have a beard'. This seems to fit in with other contemporary descriptions of him as 'pulchellus admodus puer' ('a very pretty boy'). In 1613 Salisbury was sent to the English College at Douai and subsequently returned again to England, this time using the *alias* John Parry. He became a member of the Society of Jesus in 1604 and took the four vows in 1618. At that time, England and Wales were divided into districts for the training of would-be Catholic clergy, and Salisbury became superior of the united district for North and South Wales, also residing at Raglan Castle as chaplain to Lady Frances Somerset. At this time he translated several works into Welsh, among them those of the Jesuit saint, Robert Bellarmine. In 1622, he established the College of St Francis Xavier, based at the Cwm at Llanrothal near Monmouth, and became rector in 1623. He died on this day in the year 1626, while preparing to journey to Rome.

The Spiritual Exercises *of St Ignatius Loyola (1491–1556), one of the founders of the Society of Jesus, would have been at the heart of John Salisbury's learning and teaching. The* Exercises *are still of great value in spiritual direction and are used by Christians of all denominations. Several excerpts give their flavour:*

A person who is in consolation ought to think of how she will conduct herself during a future desolation and thus build up a new strength for that time. A person who is in consolation should also take care to humble and abase himself as much as possible. He should recall how little he felt he was worth in the previous time of desolation when he was without such grace or consolation. On the other hand, a person who is in desolation should recall that she can do much to withstand all of her enemies by using the sufficient grace that she had and taking strength in her Creator and Lord.

Thoughts on Predestination:

Although it is very true that no one can be saved without being predestined, we must speak with great circumspection on this matter, for fear that, giving too much to grace, we should appear to destroy man's free will and the merit of good works; or that giving too much to free will we should weaken the power and efficacy of grace.

The final prayer at the end of the Exercises:

Take, Lord, and receive my entire liberty, my memory, my understanding and my whole will. All that I am, all that I have, you have given me, and I give it back again to be at your disposal, according to your good pleasure. Give me only your love and your grace; with them I am rich enough.

Bishop Richard Swinfield d.1317

Man of perseverance

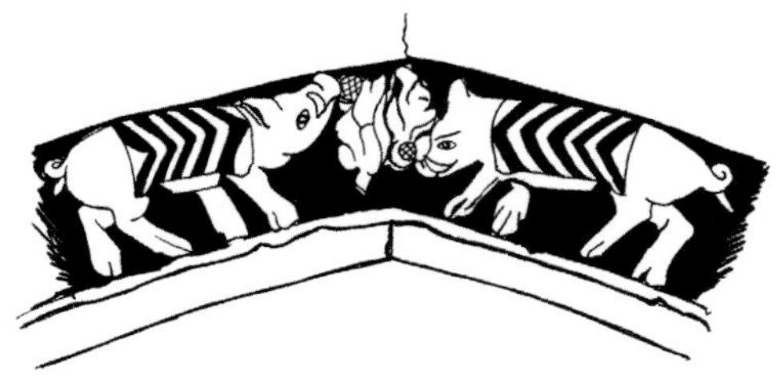

'Patience is a virtue, possess it if you can'

So goes the old saying. The bishop we remember today was tireless in his own patience, determined that his mentor and guide over many years should be accorded the honour of sainthood. He refused to give up, despite all the red tape that the 14th century could produce! After Thomas Cantilupe's death in Italy (see 25 August), in 1282, Swinfield had his bones and heart brought back to England. The heart was entrusted to a community of canons at Ashridge in Hertfordshire, while the bones were buried in the north transept of Hereford Cathedral. From 1287, many miracles and healings at the tomb were recorded and a Papal Commission was sent in 1307 to investigate the petition for Cantilupe's canonisation. All this was driven by Swinfield, but despite the encouragement of royalty and a huge body of evidence, the canonisation process dragged on and he did not live to see his mentor being declared a saint. This had to wait until 1320 – three years after Swinfield died on this day in the year 1317. As a bishop, he was exemplary in his administration and he made many visitations to parishes and monasteries. In Hereford's Lady Chapel, look out for the piglets on the tomb of a relative of his, with its pun or *rebus* on the name of Swinfield.

Jesus often urges his disciples to persevere. In this passage, he reminds them that prayer is often rewarded when we persist against all the odds:

He told them a parable, to the effect that they ought always to pray and not lose heart. He said, 'In a certain city there was a judge who neither feared God nor regarded man; and there was a widow in that city who kept coming to him and saying, "Vindicate me against my adversary." For a while he refused; but afterwards he said to himself, "Though I neither fear God nor regard man, yet because this widow bothers me, I will vindicate her, or she will wear me out by her continual coming."' And the Lord said, 'Hear what the unrighteous judge says. And will not God vindicate his elect, who cry to him day and night? Will he delay long over them? I tell you, he will vindicate them speedily. Nevertheless, when the Son of man comes, will he find faith on earth?'

Luke 18:1-8

Perseverance is seen as part of the pilgrimage of faith, in the words of this New Testament author:

These all died in faith, not having received what was promised, but having seen it and greeted it from afar, and having acknowledged that they were strangers and exiles on the earth. For people who speak thus make it clear that they are seeking a homeland. If they had been thinking of that land from which they had gone out, they would have had opportunity to return. But as it is, they desire a better country, that is, a heavenly one. Therefore God is not ashamed to be called their God, for he has prepared for them a city.

Hebrews 11:13-16

O Lord God, when thou givest to thy servants to endeavour any great matter, grant us also to know that it is not the beginning, but the continuing of the same to the end, until it be thoroughly finished, which yieldeth the true glory; through him who for the finishing of thy work laid down his life, our Redeemer, Jesus Christ.

Sir Francis Drake 1540–96

John Cuthbert Hedley 1837–1915

Benedictine monk & Roman Catholic bishop of Newport

Those who enjoy a meal or stay at Hedley Lodge at Belmont may not be aware why these splendid facilities are so named. Behind the name is the life and character of a priest and bishop who contributed greatly to the church of his day – in this area and far beyond.

In 1854 the young Hedley joined the Benedictine community at Ampleforth in Yorkshire and on ordination he was sent to Belmont, the house of studies and novitiate for English Benedictines, where he taught philosophy and theology. He had a reputation as 'an inspirer and guide in all studious pursuits'. In 1873 he was consecrated bishop and in 1881 became bishop of Newport. At that time, Belmont Abbey was the cathedral church of the diocese and Hedley was instrumental in moving the cathedral dignity to Cardiff, which in 1915 became an archdiocese. The whole of Herefordshire remains in the archdiocese of Cardiff.

The 1880s were years of turbulence in the Benedictine community. There were two schools of thought; some placed greater emphasis on the monastic life centred in English monasteries, while others favoured the continuation of the mission system, with monks living away from their monasteries in Benedictine missions – a system dating back to the 17th century and penal times. Hedley's work at Belmont favoured the first model, although he did not favour wholesale change, but saw that each model had different aims and should pursue its own course. In the end, Pope Leo XIII decided in favour of the first model and the missions were placed under the control of the monasteries, many of which were raised to the status of abbey.

Hedley was an energetic and well-loved bishop. In 1881 there were just 13 diocesan priests in Wales – by 1915 there were 54. He was keen to be engaged in contemporary issues, writing on these regularly in *The Dublin Review*. His gift, according to a contemporary, was a 'great unity and great mellowness of intellect' which enabled him to be 'keenly alive to modern needs ... seeing that human nature is ever the same and that much that is modern is a recurrence of older ways of thinking'. He was much involved in debates concerning Roman Catholics in higher education and he encouraged changes that would permit Roman Catholics to attend Oxford and Cambridge – until his time, most had attended 'secular' universities like London, rather than the more ancient foundations with their Anglican background. In 1895, Leo XIII honoured Hedley by making him an 'assistant at the pontifical throne'.

In his Rule, St Benedict has clear instructions as to the discernment of vocation in the monastic life:

Do not grant newcomers to the monastic life an easy entry, but, as the Apostle says, Test the spirits to see if they are from God (1 John 4:1). Therefore, if someone comes and keeps knocking at the door, and if at the end of four or five days he has shown himself patient in bearing his harsh treatment and difficulty of entry, and has persisted in his request, then he should be allowed to enter and stay in the guest quarters for a few days. After that, he should live in the novitiate, where the novices study, eat and sleep.

A senior monk chosen for his skill in winning souls should be appointed to look after them with careful attention. The concern must be whether the novice truly seeks God and whether he shows eagerness for the Work of God, for obedience and for trials. The novice should be clearly told all the hardships and difficulties that will lead him to God.

Rule of St Benedict, chapter 58

William Waterworth 1811–82

Jesuit historian & early ecumenist

When we understand something about our own history, and about the histories of those with whom we differ, then we begin to understand just a little more of 'what makes us tick'. This is especially true when it comes to ecumenical matters, and today we remember one whose historical studies helped pave the way for greater understanding between Anglicans and Roman Catholics.

Educated at the Jesuit College at Stonyhurst, William Waterworth became a Jesuit in 1829 and after ordination taught dogmatic theology there. He served as a priest at Hereford until 1854, where he wrote a number of historical and apologetic works, including *The Jesuits or An Examination of the origins, progress, principles and practices of the Society of Jesus* (1852). He was also interested in the history of Christianity in England and in 1854 wrote *England and Rome* or *The history of religious connexion between England and the Holy See from 179 to the Anglican Reformation in 1534.* In 1854 Waterworth moved to London, to be rector of the church of the Immaculate Conception in Farm Street, Mayfair, and in 1857 moved back to Worcester to head the mission there. His last works were a history of the Church in Ireland and a survey of the history of the *Book of Common Prayer.* Waterworth died in Bournemouth on this day in the year 1882.

While Waterworth could be critical of ways in which Anglican liturgy had developed, he was in Hereford at a time of development in ecumenical partnership. In 1829 Catholic Emancipation lifted many restrictions on Roman Catholics and many new churches were built, including St Francis Xavier, in Broad Street, Hereford. At the laying of the foundation stone on 19 September 1837, the High Sheriff attended. Contemporary sources point out that this was 'the first time for three hundred years the monarch's representative graced a catholic function'. During the sermon, given by the Reverend R Boyle, the preacher celebrated the presence of Anglican friends at the ceremony:

There might, he observed, be differences in points of faith or doctrine, but this need not prevent men from living together in peace and amity, as trusting in one common Redeemer, cleansed by the purifying waters of the same baptism, and journeying onward, they trusted to the same realms of heavenly bliss; there was nothing throughout the whole Scriptures which authorised anyone to anathematise or curse his brother. Life was too short, and the real troubles and calamities in it too numerous to render it prudent for them to spend their time in wrangling. Let, then, each one attend to his own concerns, and examine his own motives and conduct, being most anxious about that in which he was most interested, his own eternal salvation.

Words which, over 150 years later, have not lost their relevance!

Teach us, good Lord, to serve you as you deserve; to give and not to count the cost; to fight and not to heed the wounds; to toil and not to seek for rest; to labour and not to ask for any reward, save that of knowing that we do your will; through Jesus Christ our Lord.

St Ignatius Loyola 1491–1556

Jacob Tonson 1656–1736

Bookseller & publisher of Milton

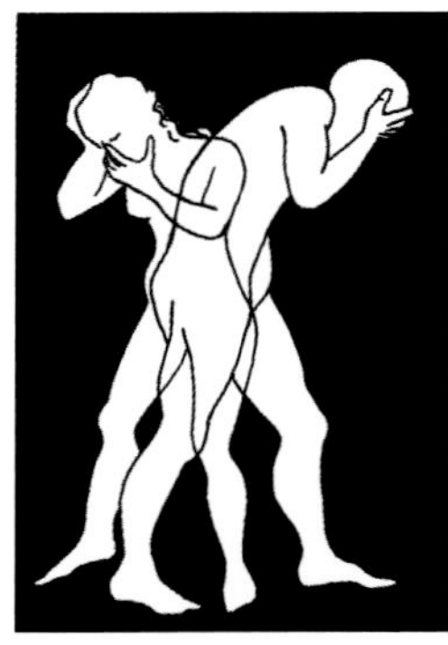

We often read Milton at school, and perhaps know short sections of his poetry by heart, but often this great poet is taken for granted. Today we remember one whose enthusiasm and skills led to Milton's fame being established for posterity. Apprenticed to a London stationer, Jacob Tonson developed a lifelong love of books. By 1679 he had become the exclusive publisher of the works of John Dryden. Part of his success was his courting of publicity – indeed, he was the first bookseller to advertise in newspapers. But it was Tonson's love of the works of Milton which became his abiding interest. As an apprentice, he had, on Milton's death, walked to Milton's house in Chalfont St Giles, Buckinghamshire in the hope of buying some books from the great poet's library. In 1689 he purchased half the rights to *Paradise Lost* and he bought the other half in 1690. In many ways, Tonson was responsible for the fame and reputation of Milton's great poem and for keeping Milton's reputation alive at a time when poetic styles were changing. In 1688, Tonson published the first edition of *Paradise Lost,* with its careful editing and illustrations making the work more accessible to the public. However, Tonson had his critics. Although he worked with Dryden, the latter could be acerbic about him:

With leering look, bull faced and freckled fair
With frowsy pores poisoning the ambient air,
With two left leggs and Judas coloured hair.

The 'two left leggs' apparently refers to Tonson's rather eccentric way of walking!

He was a Whig in politics, and a founder member of the Kit-cat club (an exclusive club, many of whose members had been instrumental in establishing the Hanoverian dynasty and succession). Tonson handed on his business to a nephew and died on this day in 1736, at The Vineyard, his estate between Gloucester and Ledbury. In the Kneller portrait of him, he is shown holding his folio edition of Milton's *Paradise Lost.*

Milton's incomparable words on the expulsion of Adam and Eve from the Garden of Eden:

So spake our mother Eve, and Adam heard,
Well pleased, but answered not; for now too nigh
The archangel stood, and from the other hill
To their fixed station, all in bright array,
The cherubim descended; on the ground,
Gliding meteorous, as evening mist,
Risen from a river, o'er the marish glides,
And gathers ground fast at the labourer's heel,
Homeward returning. High in front advanced,
The brandished sword of God before them blazed,
Fierce as a comet which with torrid heat
And vapour as the Libyan air adust
Began to parch that temperate climate; whereat
In either hand the hastening angel caught
Our lingering parents, and to the eastern gate
Led them direct, and down the cliff as fast
To the subjected plain; then disappeared.

John Milton 1608–74, *Paradise Lost* Book XII

Alkmund born *c.*774

Local saint & martyr

Just one dedication to this saint in Herefordshire – but why is he here at all, when he clearly has allegiance to other parts of the country? Alkmund was the son of Alchred, king of Northumbria. The kingdom was seized by Eardwulf, who pursued Alkmund to Lilleshall in Shropshire, where he had taken refuge, and had him murdered there. Another source says he was killed in battle near Cricklade in Wiltshire. He was certainly claimed as a martyr and miracles were reported at his tomb in Lilleshall. His body was later transferred to Derby and his shrine and holy well became a place of pilgrimage. Several churches were dedicated to him in Derbyshire and Shropshire. Aymestrey is the sole dedication in Herefordshire.

The tombs and shrines of saints have always drawn pilgrims, seeking healing and close knowledge of God's presence. In a passage about Canterbury Cathedral, a 19th-century dean speaks of their power, and the importance of their preservation:

Round it [the shrine of St Thomas] still lie the tombs of King, and Prince, and Archbishop; the worn marks on the stones show the reverence of former ages. But the place itself is vacant, and the lessons which that vacancy has to teach us must now take the place of the lessons of the ancient Shrine.

There are very few probably at the present time, in whom, as they look round on the desolate pavement, the first feeling that arises is not one of disappointment and regret, that a monument of past times so costly and curious should have been thus entirely obliterated.

There is probably no one, who, if the Shrine were now standing, would dream of removing it. One such tomb, as has been said, still remains in Westminster Abbey: the very notion of destroying it would call out a general outcry from all educated men throughout the kingdom. Why is it that this feeling, so familiar and so natural to us, should then have been so completely overruled? The answer to this question is doubly instructive. First, it reveals to us one great difference between our age and the time, not only of the Reformation, but of many preceding ages. In our time, there has sprung up, to a degree hitherto unprecedented, a love of what is old, of what is beautiful, of what is venerable – a desire to cherish the memorials of the past, and to keep before our eyes the vestiges of times, which are brought so vividly before us in no other way. It is, as it were, God's compensation to the world for its advancing years. Earlier ages care but little for these relics of antiquity; one is swept away after another to make room for what is yet to come; precious works of art, precious recollections, are trampled under foot; the very abundance in which they exist seems to beget an indifference towards them. But in proportion as they become fewer and fewer, the affection for them grows stronger and stronger; and the further we recede from the past, the more eager now seems our craving to attach ourselves to it by every link that remains. Such a feeling it is, which most of us would entertain towards this ancient Shrine – such a feeling as, in the mass of men, hardly existed at the time of its destruction. In this respect at least we are richer than were our fathers; other gifts they had which we have not: this gift of insight into the past, of loving it for its own sake, of retaining around us as much as we can of its grace and beauty – we have, as they had not. It is true that reverence for the dead ought never to stand in the way of the living – that when any great evil is avoided, or any great good attained, by destroying old recollections, no historical or antiquarian tenderness can be pleaded for their preservation: but where no such reason exists, let us keep them as best we can, and as we stand on the vacant space of Becket's shrine, let us be thankful that we have retained what we have, and cherish it accordingly.

Arthur Stanley 1815–81, *Historical Memorials of Canterbury Cathedral* (1883)

Cuthbert *c.*634–87

Monk & bishop of Lindisfarne

It may seem strange to be celebrating a northern saint in the Marches! No fewer than 83 churches are dedicated to Cuthbert – 66 in England, with some as far afield as Cornwall, Somerset and East Anglia. In our own area, two churches, Clungunford and Holme Lacy, have Cuthbert as patron. As a shepherd he is said to have seen one night a dazzling light in the sky and angels carrying to heaven a soul which he later interpreted as the saintly Aidan. After this vision, he resolved to dedicate his life to God. Some years later, he came to Melrose Abbey, asking to be admitted as a monk. It was from here that he began his missionary work, becoming prior of Lindisfarne.

Consecrated bishop in 685, he became a tireless preacher, travelling all over his diocese, withdrawing for months to the Farne Islands, to live in complete solitude. Here, it is said, he lived an ascetic life, bathing daily in the ice-cold sea water, with the sea otters coming to him, to warm him with their breath! He died on this day in 687 on Inner Farne and was buried at Lindisfarne, where his body became the focus of great veneration. After the Danes destroyed Lindisfarne in 875, several members of its community travelled round northern England and south-west Scotland with his relics, seeking a safe home for them. Eventually, they reached Durham in 995; a Saxon church was built over the shrine there and Cuthbert's relics were translated into it in 999. The great Durham Cathedral still houses Cuthbert's relics and his own pectoral cross (pictured here). The famous Lindisfarne Gospels remind us of the great artistic legacy left us by Cuthbert and his contemporaries.

The Venerable Bede describes Cuthbert's missionary activity in Northumberland:

It was then the custom of the English people, that when a cleric or priest came into a town they all, at his command, flocked to hear the word, willingly heard what was said, and more willingly practised what they could hear and understand. But Cuthbert was so skilful a speaker, so fond of making his point, and had so much brightness showing in his angelic face, that no one present tried to conceal from him the most hidden secrets of his heart, but all openly confessed what they had done; because they thought the guilt of this could not be hidden from him. They wiped away the guilt that they had confessed with worthy fruits of penance, as he commanded.

He was accustomed especially to reach those places, and preach in those villages, as are high up among the crags and moorland, inaccessible because of their poverty and wildness, which nevertheless he, in his entire devotion to duty, would seek industriously to polish with his teaching. When he left the monastery he would often stay a week, sometimes two or three, and sometimes a whole month, before he returned home, continuing in the mountains to allure the rustics to heavenly employments by preaching and example.

The prayers of the Venerable Bede so often encapsulate the prayer and devotion of early saints like Cuthbert

Remain, O Christ, in the hearts you have redeemed. You who are perfect love, pour into our words sincere repentance. We raise our prayer to you, O Jesus, with faith; pardon the sin we have committed. By the holy sign of the cross, by your tortured body, defend us constantly as your children.

Philip Wilson Steer 1860–1942

Landscape artist

Sometimes, when we hear a piece of music or see a painting we are moved to exclaim, 'That's so English!' It's a hard concept to define but we know it when we see or hear it. Today we remember one whose artistic style and landscapes led to his being hailed an 'icon of Englishness'.

In boyhood, Philip Steer's family moved to Whitchurch, near Ross-on-Wye, and the young Philip attended Hereford Cathedral School from 1875 until 1877. He showed great artistic skill from an early age and trained at Gloucester School of Art and later in Paris under Cabanal. His early work showed much influence of the impressionist school of Monet, although as a founder member of the New English Art Club in 1886, he allied himself more with the work of Walter Sickert and the so-called 'London Impressionists'. From 1893 he taught at the Slade School of Fine Art where his work developed – and was also criticised for what others saw as jarring colour relationships. Steer was unrepentant. 'A true impressionist,' he maintained, 'is a poet and not a journalist and is not destined simply to record facts.' English landscapes became his forte and he revisited the countryside of his youth, especially around Ludlow and the Wye valley, seeking subject matter. In some circles he was spoken of as a successor to Constable, sharing that artist's love of changeable, stormy skies and broad, distant prospects. Steer was certainly influenced by Constable and, to a lesser extent, by Turner, and he emerged a champion of Englishness in an age desperate to assert the idea of cultural unity in art. In 1918 he became an official war artist and produced paintings of the British fleet. After the war, he turned more to watercolour, but the onset of blindness threatened and he was forced to retire. He was appointed to the Order of Merit in 1931 and died on this day in the year 1942.

Steer's philosophy of art is reflected in this piece, which powerfully describes ways in which a painting can speak to the beholder:

All art re-presents. I have hyphenated re-presents for a good reason, but must now show the reason. If I wrote, for example, of Hogarth's highly realistic painting called 'The Shrimp Girl' that it 'represented such and such', I should not convey at all what that work in fact is. If I wrote 're-presented such and such' there is a slight gain, and 're-presented such and such under other forms' is still more a gain, but much more amplification is required to cover fully what is indicated under the shorthand hyphenated term 're-present'. I shall therefore attempt a fuller statement, sticking to Hogarth's 'Shrimp Girl' as my example partly because it is a picture of which I am fond, also because no one can cavil as to its merits; but more because it is highly visual, and, as they say, 'faithful to the appearance of nature'. It is a charming record of an apparently charming subject, so all that could be desired by the most popular and sophisticated standards. My fuller statement of what that painting is and does might read somewhat as follows: It is a 'thing', an object contrived of various materials and so ordered by Hogarth's muse as to show forth, recall and re-present, strictly within the conditions of a given art and under another mode, such and such a reality. It is a signum of that reality and it makes a kind of anamnesis of that reality.

David Jones 1895–1974, *Epoch and Artist* (1973)

Harry Marshall Ward 1854–1906

Hereford's plant doctor

For gardeners among us, here is one to celebrate! Harry Marshall Ward was a scientist whose studies led to greater understanding of plant diseases and their treatment. His work on bacteriology, however, may make us cautious when we drink a glass of water! Ward was born on 21 March 1854 in Victoria Street, Hereford. He was educated at the Cathedral School in Lincoln and later at Cambridge, studying botany and physiology. His career was established after he spent two years in Ceylon, investigating coffee-leaf diseases ravaging the island – a success which led to a distinguished academic career as professor at the Royal Indian Engineering College and later at Cambridge. Under Ward, the university erected a new and well-equipped botanical centre in 1904. He published more than 50 reports, papers and books on morphology and the development of fungi and plant diseases. In 1892–3, at the request of the Royal Society, he conducted a series of investigations on the bacteriology of water and identified 80 species of bacteria in the water of the river Thames – a conclusion which caused some public alarm at the time! He was honoured for his work by being made a Fellow of the Royal Society in 1888.

Plants and trees are surely a parable of Resurrection in their yearly death and rebirth, and those who work closely with them observe the most subtle changes in them. Here, a writer speaks of his sense of wonder in nature:

I never exhaust the beauty of trees and woods. Careless of their species, I observe them as patterns against the sky, perhaps most beautiful when leafless. But though leafless they are never lifeless. The leaves are scarcely fallen when the new buds begin shyly to press through the tender bark, like dark blebs of blood. There are 365 days in a year and a tree has the same number of faces, or rather facets, for it is a composite picture of many minute changes. Perhaps only once or twice a year there is a chance to wander in these woods when sunlight has succeeded hoar frost or a light fall of snow, and the whole scene scintillates in electric brilliance. Very rarely such an event takes place in April, when the first pale green leaves have already unfolded, and the undergrowth is starred with primroses and violets. I am then reminded of something very unnatural but still poetic. Those crystallised fruits we sometimes eat at Christmas; but these are clumsy compared with a frosted veil of snowflakes on a bed of violets.

Herbert Read 1893–1968, *The Contrary Experience* (1963)

The return of new life in the spring, seen in plants and flowers, is hailed as a sign of Resurrection:

Now the green blade riseth from the buried grain,
Wheat that in dark earth many days has lain;
Love lives again, that with the dead has been:
Love is come again, like wheat that springeth green.

Forth he came at Easter, like the risen grain,
He that for three days in the grave had lain,
Quick from the dead my risen Lord is seen:
Love is come again, like wheat that springeth green.

J M C Crum 1872–1958

Richard Hawes 1604–68
Persecuted Dissenter

This clergyman was something of a 'Vicar of Bray' who changed with the times and whose often stormy life belies the myth that church life in Herefordshire is always quiet! Born in East Anglia, Hawes attended Corpus Christi College in Cambridge and on ordination became rector of Humber near Leominster. His later movements become unclear but we know that from this day in 1638 he was rector of Kenderchurch in the Golden Valley. He may well have been a faithful priest but we learn that 'for many years after he entered the ministry, he continued much addicted to vain company and was sometimes guilty of excessive drinking'. When Hereford was garrisoned by the Royalists he was imprisoned for a time, and the experience seems to have changed him for, on release, he turned to nonconformity and 'became a plain, earnest and useful preacher'. From 1651 we find him preaching in his old patch, at Llangua and Kenderchurch, but with a new denominational allegiance. Apparently, he found his old stamping ground 'a paganish and brutish place'. A step up the ecclesiastical ladder was offered to him by Sir Edward Harley in 1659 and he became minister at Leintwardine. However, the Restoration of Charles II turned all this upside down and he found himself imprisoned again 'upon the noise of plots'. He refused to conform to the Prayer Book in 1661 and Bishop Herbert Croft (see 18 May) ejected him, whereupon he went to live with his daughter and her husband, Nicholas Billingsley, vicar of Weobley (see 29 May) and, while the bishop of Hereford refused to license him, the bishops of Gloucester and Monmouth apparently did! He expressed 'in his last hours, great satisfaction with his nonconformity'.

'Never be afraid of throwing away what you have' is a key phrase in the following passage. Its wise counsel was followed by Richard Hawes in his 'living for the moment'. Being a 'hoarder' by nature, myself, I find this rather more difficult!

The greatest mistake that we make with our own lives is to *snatch* at the particular objects we desire. If we realized the riches that lie within every one of us we should know that we can afford to be spendthrift of nine-tenths of the possessions which we treasure; success, praise, and good opinion among men, achievements and still more material well-being. Never be afraid of throwing away what you have. If you *can* throw it away it is not really yours. If it is really yours you cannot throw it away. And you may be certain that if you throw it away, whatever in you is greater than you will produce something in its place. Never be afraid of pruning your branches. Trust the future and take risks. In moral, as in economic affairs, the rash man is he who does not speculate.

R H Tawney 1880–1962, *Diary, 30 June 1912*

A song I often taught and sang in primary school assemblies:

Love is something, if you give it away
You end up having more.
It's just like a magic penny,
Hold it tight, and you won't have any,
Give it, share it, you'll have so many
They'll roll all over the floor.
Love is something, if you give it away,
You end up having more.

Samuel Croxall 1689–1752

Poet & pluralist

Here is a clergyman who seemed to collect clerical positions like postage stamps. Did he do a good job in all of them? Who can tell? Samuel Croxall, like many clergy of his time, was something of a poet and famously wrote a florid ode celebrating the arrival of George I in England. He was a classical scholar and made translations of Ovid and other Latin poets. His most famous work was a translation of the *Fables of Aesop and others, with applications and useful Observations* (1722), dedicated to Lord Sunbury – a book which enjoyed reprints well into the 20th century. It is said to have been one of the first books to influence the poet Robert Browning. When his friend Henry Egerton was consecrated bishop of Hereford in 1724, Croxall's career in the church, until then quite modest, took off. He preached at the consecration service and Egerton made him, successively, a prebend of the cathedral (1727), then treasurer, then archdeacon of Shropshire, incumbent of Bromyard and finally, in 1740, chancellor. For good measure, Bishop Egerton presented him to two livings in the City of London. However, his rise to fame seemed to stop there, for Walpole, the prime minister, is said to have remembered a sermon preached in 1730 in which Croxall attacked him, and he certainly never became a bishop or dean. But life at Hereford seems to have occupied him, and as Bishop Egerton grew older, Croxall took over much of the running of the diocese. He also had time to write, and his last work was *Scripture Politics – a prose treatise on the political and social organization of the Israelites* (illustrated here).

One particular sermon is remembered. Preached for the meeting of the Three Choirs at Hereford in September 1741, it was entitled 'The Antiquity, Dignity and Advantages of Music'. On his death Croxall was buried in the north transept of Hereford Cathedral.

Aesop's Fables, *so beloved of Samuel Croxall, have a timeless quality, with down-to-earth common sense which has endured for centuries. These two fables combine Croxall's love of antiquity with his interest in music:*

Kites originally had singing voices as clear as any swan. But when they heard horses neighing they were envious and did their best to imitate them. In trying to acquire this new trick, they lost the ability they already had: they could not learn to neigh and they forgot how to sing.

Moral: The desire for imaginary benefits often involves the loss of present blessings.

A man who had heard that swans had very beautiful voices bought one which he happened to see exposed for sale. One day when he was giving a dinner party he went out and asked the swan to sing to his guests as they sat over their wine. But not a note could he get out of it. Some time afterwards, however, when it felt that it was going to die, it began to sing a dirge over its approaching end; for it is said that swans sing when they are at the point of death. When its owner heard it he said: 'If you sing only when you are dying, I was a fool to ask you for a song the other day. I'd have done better to prepare you for sacrifice.'

Moral: When people will not do a thing as a favour, they are sometimes made to do it against their will.

Aethelflaed d.918

The 'Lady of the Mercians'

Today is a day when we remember the Annunciation to Mary – a reminder of Mary's strength and determination and her part in our salvation. Many famous women have, in their own day, played vital parts in preserving their communities, and today we recall one who, in this part of the world, did much to preserve the people from the onslaught of marauding Vikings. She was Aethelflaed, daughter of Alfred the Great. She married Aethelred, a Mercian nobleman, and she supported him in his rule over the English half of the Mercian kingdom. Aethelflaed was clearly a woman of faith, and founded a new minster at Gloucester in 911, to which she brought relics of Oswald, the 7th-century Northumbrian saint. On the death of her husband, Aethelflaed was accepted as ruler in his stead and, with her brother Edward, fortified with 'burhs' many communities in this area against the Danes, including Bridgnorth, Chirbury, Gloucester and Hereford. This action provided the basis for the successes of 917 against the Vikings. Her courage made a great impression on her own generation and for many years after. Writing in *c.*1130, Henry of Huntingdon declared her 'to have been so powerful that in praise and exultation of her wonderful gifts, some call her not only lady or queen, but even king', and followed this with a poem describing her as 'worthy of a man's name' and 'more illustrious than Caesar'.

The strength and courage of Aethelflaed reminds us of Mary, mother of Jesus Christ. On this day we remember her joy and the angel's greeting. Perhaps, too, we should remember her own courage and strength at the end of her son's life as he hung upon the cross. These words are attributed to a 13th-century Franciscan writer:

His mother stood there by the cross
Where her son was hanging,
His anguish sharing.
A sword pierced through her heart.

Though blessed and set apart
As mother of God's son,
Yet how great her painful sighing
To watch her child's slow dying.

Can there be one so cold
Who, seeing Christ's mother standing there,
Could watch her unconcernedly?
Not sorrowful himself, but hard and bold?

Not sharing her grief
To see him sliced by whips,
Split by nails,
In torment for our own sins and ills?
Her sweet son,
Abandoned, alone?

attrib. Jacapone da Todi *c.*1230–1306, 'Stabat Mater'

Francis Biddulph bapt.1734 d.1800

Discreet financier

I can remember, as a boy, trailing with my mother into the Midland Bank, and there queuing for her to do business with the clerk – the surroundings always hushed and mahogany-lined, the clerk always in a grey suit, speaking in hushed tones, always discreet. The financier we remember today was famed for his own discretion. Baptized at Ledbury in March 1734, from 1750 Francis Biddulph was apprenticed to a goldsmith and later set up a banking business in St Paul's Churchyard in London. By 1757 he had the confidence to set up a new and independent banking house, and asked an old Hereford neighbour, Sir Charles Cocks of Eastnor, to help with this new venture. Cocks sent his sons, James and Thomas Somers Cocks, and the firm of Cocks, Biddulph & Co became a leading bank in the city, numbering dukes, bishops and Oxbridge dons among its clients, all of them impressed by the discreet service they received in this delicate area! The firm also became London agent to several cathedrals, among them Hereford and St Davids. For all his care with money in his lifetime, Biddulph died intestate and much of his considerable fortune passed to his nephew, Robert Biddulph, MP for Hereford.

Charles Dickens writes amusingly of what we might call the 'nouveau-riche':

Mr and Mrs Veneering were bran-new people in a bran-new house in a bran-new quarter of London. Everything about the Veneerings was spick and span new. All their furniture was new, all their friends were new, all their servants were new, their plate was new, their carriage was new, their harness was new, their horses were new, their pictures were new, they themselves were new, they were as newly married as was lawfully compatible with their having a bran-new baby, and if they had set up a great grandfather, he would have come home in matting from the Pantechnicon, without a scratch upon him, French-polished to the crown of his head.

For, in the Veneering establishment, from the hall-chairs with the new coat of arms, to the grand piano-forte with the new action, and upstairs again to the new fire-escape, all things were in a state of high varnish and polish. And what was observable in the furniture was observable in the Veneerings – the surface smelt a little too much of the workshop and was a trifle sticky.

Charles Dickens 1812–70, *Our Mutual Friend*

A prayer for the spirit of generosity

Spirit of God, brooding over the waters of our chaos,
inspire us to generous living.
Wind of God, dancing over the desert of our reluctance,
lead us to the oasis of celebration.
Breath of God, inspiring communication among strangers,
make us channels of your peace,
That we may give in deep thankfulness,
placing the overflowing basket of our gifts
on the table of rejoicing.

Kate McIlhagga

John Malvern d.1422

Physician & heresy seeker

With a name like that, he may have been born near Malvern. Perhaps the health-giving waters of the hills encouraged him in what was to be his life work – that of a physician to the great and the good. He served as a chaplain at Balliol College, Oxford, where he may have obtained a doctorate in medicine, as mentioned in a later tract, *Contra Pestilentiam.*

John Malvern's fame as a physician received a boost from his links with Henry Bolingbroke, later King Henry IV. Bolingbroke used him as one of his domestic physicians in 1395 – but a question mark must be placed over his loyalty, for in 1405 there is some suggestion that he was attending rebel forces rather than the king.

Malvern was said to be one of the last bystanders to whom Richard Scrope, archbishop of York spoke when, on 8 June 1405, he was awaiting his execution outside the walls of York. In resigned mode he remarked that not even Malvern's battery of cures could save the life of one who was now beyond earthly medicine – and so the archbishop insisted that he had no further need of physic. Malvern had other distinguished clients, among them Richard Mitford, bishop of Salisbury, who employed him at considerable expense during his final illness in 1407. Various honours came Malvern's way – in 1408 he became a canon of St George's, Windsor and nearer home, master of St Katherine's Hospital at Ledbury from 1398. It seems an unlikely sideline for a doctor that he should have taken part in heresy trials but this seems to have been Malvern's other 'day job' – in 1393 he was present at heresy trials against two Lollards, William Swinderby and Walter Brut.

Medieval physicians were certainly adaptable! At his death, he left various books, including collections of sermons and volumes by Seneca and Aristotle.

Many years after John Malvern, a Welsh country doctor is described by an eminent politician:

Anyone who has lived in these mountain regions knows what sickness means there. There are miles of track, broken and rutted by the winter rains, before you even reach the high road. The people there never send for medical aid for petty ailments. The doctor is not even summoned for important family events. He is only called when life is in jeopardy. Here in this district you have fifty square miles without a doctor. Ask anybody who has lived on a wayside farm in these districts or in the villages in the valleys, and they will tell you that one of the most vivid memories of their youth was to be wakened up in the dead of the night by hearing the clatter of a horse ridden furiously past in the dark, and everyone knew there was a dire struggle for life going on in the hills.

David Lloyd George 1863–1945, *House of Commons Speech, 1912, on Disestablishment and Disendowment of the Church in Wales*

Gerald of Wales *c.*1146–*c.*1223

Priest, chronicler, travel writer

Gerald of Wales is the medieval predecessor of modern travel writers like Bill Bryson – authors who bring to life, with wit and perception, the customs and peculiarities of countries and their inhabitants. Of Welsh stock, Gerald was educated in Gloucester and in Paris and was appointed archdeacon of Brecon. On the death of his uncle, the bishop of St David's, Gerald was considered as his successor, but was rejected in this by King Henry II. He became a royal clerk and chaplain to the king – a post which involved him in much travel. Such journeying appealed to him and in 1188 he was selected to accompany the archbishop of Canterbury, Baldwin of Exeter, on a tour of Wales – the object being a recruitment campaign for the Third Crusade. Gerald left Hereford at the beginning of March, travelling 500 miles and returning to Hereford by the end of April. His *Itinerarium Cambriae* (1191) was followed by the *Descriptio Cambriae* in 1194. These two works remain valuable historical documents. They tell us much about Welsh history and geography and reflect on the cultural relationship between the Welsh and the English. His descriptions of contemporary music give much pride to Welsh singers today:

> In their musical concerts they do not sing in unison like the inhabitants of other countries, but in many different parts ... You hear as many different parts and voices as there are performers who all at length unite with organic melody.

In 1198 Gerald was nominated again for the bishopric of St David's, but Hubert Walter, archbishop of Canterbury, refused the nomination. Despite petitions from the chapter and eminent Welsh support, he was resisted by King John (see 11 June) and was obliged to leave Wales, fleeing to Rome. He famously complained, in a letter to Pope Innocent III:

> Because I am a Welshman am I to be debarred from all preferments in Wales? On the same reasoning so would an Englishman in England, a Frenchman in France, and Italian in Italy. But I am sprung from the Princes of Wales and the Barons of the Marches and when I see injustice in either race I hate it.

He spent the remainder of his life in academic study and died in about 1223 in his 77th year. His death was attested by the then dean of Hereford, and it is generally thought that he died in the city – a place which he clearly knew well and to which he was encouraged to come, in a poem by Simund de Freine (see 26 February).

Gerald's Itinerary through Wales *is a delightful mixture of fact, miracle and legend. Here, we cannot help but notice that not even Welsh literature could hold a candle to the power of the Gospels!*

> It is worthy of observation that there lived in the neighbourhood of this City of Legions in our time, a Welshman named Melerius, who ... acquired the knowledge of future and occult events ... If the evil spirits oppressed him too much, the Gospel of St John was placed on his bosom, when, like birds, they immediately vanished; but when that book was removed, and the History of the Britons, by Geoffrey Arthur *(i.e.* Geoffrey of Monmouth) was substituted in its place, they instantly reappeared in greater numbers, and remained a longer time than usual on his body and on the book.

Woolos 6th century
Monk, father of Cadoc

A LINK WITH our neighbouring diocese of Monmouth. Woolos or Gwynllyw and his wife Gwladys were traditionally the parents of St Cadoc (see 24 January), who, it is said, converted his parents from a life of violence to one of devotion and peace. Woolos and Gwladys settled at Stow Hill, near Newport, where they lived austerely like monks. They had unusual ascetic practices – bathing in cold water in the Usk, summer and winter alike, preceded and followed, it appears, by a mile-long walk in the nude. These pursuits were brought to an end by the seemingly prudish Cadoc, who persuaded his parents to separate. The stories come from a 12th-century *Life* of the saints, and, as always, such delicious details sometimes have to be taken with a pinch of salt. Woolos built a church on the site where the cathedral bearing his name now stands. Legend has it that he chose that particular place because he found there a white ox with a black spot on his forehead. Another source tells us that Woolos and Gwladys settled together in a nearby hill-fort, where they spent their days devoutly 'enjoying the fruits of their labour, and taking nothing which belonged to other persons'. We should expect nothing less of them!

An anonymous writer of the 4th century speaks of the importance of co-operation and mutual understanding of others' gifts in community:

Whatever they may be doing, the brothers should bear themselves lovingly and happily with one another. Then one who is working will speak thus of another who is praying: 'The treasure which my brother has is mine too, since we hold all things in common.' On his part, one who is praying will say of another who is reading: 'The profit which he derives from his reading will enrich me too.' And again, a brother who is working will say: 'This is for the community.' The one who prays shall not judge another who is working, for not praying. One who is working shall not judge one who is praying, and say: 'Look at that loiterer, while as for me, I'm working!' A worker must not judge the others. On the contrary, everyone, whatever he does, shall do it for the glory of God. A brother who is reading shall think lovingly of one who is praying, and say to himself, 'He is praying for me too.' And a brother who is praying shall think thus of one who is working: 'He is doing that for the benefit of the whole community.'

The need to find simple contentment has been at the heart of Christian faith for centuries. It was something for which Woolos and the early Celtic saints strove, and we see a similar spiritual strand in the worlds of later writers, of different Christian traditions:

He that is down needs fear no fall,
    He that is low, no pride:
He that is humble ever shall
    Have God to be his guide.

I am content with what I have,
    Little be it or much:
And, Lord, contentment still I crave;
    Because thou savest such.

John Bunyan 1628–88

March

Henry Hall c.1656–1707

Vicar choral & composer

Henry Hall was one of the more famous vicars choral at Hereford Cathedral during the 17th century. While not a household name today, he was greatly esteemed in his time as a singer and composer. As a boy in the choir of the Chapel Royal, Hall studied under Henry Cooke and Pelham Humphrey. A contemporary of Henry Purcell, he paid tribute to his more famous friend in a verse tribute, printed in Purcell's posthumous *Orpheus Britannica*. In this, the modest Hall describes how he and Purcell were jointly taught composition by John Blow:

Apollo's Harp at once our souls did strike
We learnt together, but not learnt alike,
Though equal care our Master might bestow,
Yet only Purcell e'er shall equal Blow:
For Thou by Heaven for wondrous things design'd,
Left's thy Companion lagging far behind.

After service at Wells and Exeter Cathedrals, Hall was appointed assistant organist at Hereford Cathedral in 1679 and became a vicar choral – a position he held until his death.

He was an esteemed composer of church music but is better known for his secular music – songs, glees and catches (drinking and love songs, based on local and national events, often with rather racy vocabulary). His satirical pieces are often acerbic and show his staunch Jacobite tendencies. He wrote one piece, 'Haste, Charon, haste' as a slur against Oliver Cromwell, and yet, while other pieces covertly attacked William and Mary, urging the return of James II, he could also 'change his tune' when required, and composed an ode, 'Bless, Albion, bless thy stars above' on the accession of Queen Anne. Hall died on this day in the year 1707 and was buried in Hereford Cathedral.

Some of Hall's older contemporaries as vicars choral may well have known the cathedral's music before the Commonwealth and would have known the pain of the choir's disbanding during the 1640s. Many years before, that same grief at remembering former glory was felt by the Israelites who returned to rebuild the Temple after the Exile:

And when the builders laid the foundation of the temple of the Lord, the priests in their vestments came forward with trumpets, and the Levites, the sons of Asaph, with cymbals, to praise the Lord, according to the directions of David king of Israel; and they sang responsively, praising and giving thanks to the Lord,

For he is good, for his steadfast love endures for ever towards Israel.

And all the people shouted with a great shout, when they praised the Lord, because the foundation of the house of the Lord was laid. But many of the priests and Levites and heads of fathers' houses, old men who had seen the first house, wept with a loud voice when they saw the foundation of this house being laid, though many shouted aloud for joy; so that the people could not distinguish the sound of the joyful shout from the sound of the people's weeping, for the people shouted with a great shout, and the shout was heard afar.

Ezra 3:10–13

Dora de Houghton Carrington 1893–1923

Tragic artist

The 1995 film *Carrington,* written and directed by Christopher Hampton, starred Emma Thompson in the title role and brought to the attention of a new generation a talented artist whose often bohemian life caused sensation and scandal in her own day. Born in Hereford on 29 March 1893, Dora was encouraged by her father to attend art school, and in 1910 she became a student at the Slade under Henry Tonks. Lady Ottoline Morrell, who knew her at this time, described her as a 'wild moorland pony'. Her paintings at this period, with their three-dimensional effect and dense, rich colour, were influenced by her contemporary Mark Gertler. After leaving the Slade, she obtained commissions from the great and the good – woodcuts for Virginia and Leonard Woolf – and Aldous Huxley characterised her in one of his novels. Her life changed on meeting Lytton Strachey and, despite his homosexuality, the couple set up home together at Tidmarsh Mill, Pangbourne, Berkshire. Eventually, Dora married Reginald Sherring Partridge (Ralph) and he joined the *ménage à trois.* Ralph and Strachey bought Ham Spray House in Wiltshire in 1924, with a studio for Dora and a library for Lytton Strachey. In 1931, Strachey became ill and he died of cancer in January 1932. His many friends were distraught at his death, not least Dora, who shot herself at Ham Spray House on 11 March 1932.

A moving poem, perhaps reflecting on suicide and sudden grief?

Let us go hence, my songs; she will not hear.
Let us go hence together without fear.
    Keep silence now, for singing-time is over,
And over all old things and all things dear.
    She loves not you nor me as all we love her.
Yes, though we sang as angels in her ear,
    She would not hear.

Let us rise up and part; she will not know,
Let us go seaward as the great winds go,
    Full of blown sand and foam. What help is there?
There is no help, for all these things are so.
    And all the world is bitter as a tear.
And how these things are, tho' ye strive to show,
    She would not know.

Let us go hence, go hence, she will not see.
Sing all once more together. Surely she,
    She too, remembering days and words that were,
Will turn a little towards us, sighing. But we,
    We are hence, we are gone. As though we had not been there.
Nay, and though all men seeing had pity on me,
    She would not see.

A C Swinburne 1837–1909, *A Leave-Taking* (1866)

April

Richard Tarlton d.1588

Royal jester

April Fools' Day seems an ideal day on which to remember one of the most famous jesters of the Elizabethan age. Richard Tarlton, according to the 17th-century historian Thomas Fuller, was born in Condover in Shropshire and:

> was in the field, keeping his Father's Swine, when a servant of Robert Earl of Leicester ... was so pleased with his happy, unhappy answers, that he brought him to Court, where he became the most famous Jester to Queen Elizabeth.

Certainly, Tarlton had natural talent for repartee, comic acting and impromptu verse, and in 1583 he was invited to be a member of the *Twelve Queen's Players,* a group to which Shakespeare later belonged. Some Shakespearean scholars are convinced that he was the 'poor Yorick' whose disinterred skull provoked Hamlet's musings and certainly the role of Dericke in *Henry V* is generally assigned to him. In addition, Tarlton kept taverns in London and became a freeman of the Company of Vintners. His comic writings were published posthumously as *Tarlton's Jests* and throughout the country, inns were named after him, with his familiar portrait, with clay pipe and tabor, on the signboard. Tarlton is said to have died in poverty in London and is buried at St Leonard's church, Shoreditch.

Wit and humour are surely an essential ingredient of church life and some of our seemingly most serious-minded bishops have had a wry sense of humour:

William Boyd-Carpenter, who was bishop of Ripon between 1884 and 1911, was once heckled by a man who shouted, 'Do you really believe that Jonah was swallowed by a whale?'

'When I get to heaven I will ask him,' the bishop said.

'And suppose he isn't there?' his questioner persisted.

'In that case,' the bishop answered, 'you will have to ask him yourself.'

Dr Potter, the Episcopalian bishop of New York, was once asked by a lady at a dinner party why in pictures and statues of angels they are always women or young men without beards or moustaches. He answered: 'Everyone knows that women naturally inherit the Kingdom of Heaven, but men only get in by a very close shave.'

I am sure that God has a keen sense of humour and appreciates this in prayer

Lord of Creation, may my every guest
By all my kitchen skill be much impressed.
I know you were content with loaves and fishes,
But these days they expect less homely dishes.
May they not spot the traps I've set for mice,
But be beguiled by scents and bread and spice;
Let meals run smoothly from the rough terrine
To summer pudding with sauce mousseline.
And please, Lord, let them never ever guess
It's mostly been acquired at M and S.

Lindsay Staniforth, 'The Cook's Prayer'

Arthur, Prince of Wales 1486–1502

Royal death at Ludlow

The eldest son of Henry vii and his wife, Elizabeth of York, Arthur was baptized in Winchester Cathedral and named after the famous British hero, King Arthur. He was a bright child, and at the time of his untimely death was said to be familiar with the works of 24 classical authors in Latin. By 1490, his father had set up a Council for the prince, to act as a focus for royal authority in Wales and in the Marches. Arthur's marriage was under discussion as early as 1488, when it was suggested he should marry Catherine of Aragon. Two proxy marriages took place, in 1499 and 1500, before Catherine finally arrived in England, landing at Plymouth in October 1501. The couple were married in St Paul's Cathedral on 14 November. The following month they left for the Marches of Wales, where they established their household at Ludlow. Arthur died there on 2 April 1502.

His body lay in state for three weeks before being taken in procession to Worcester Cathedral. There he is buried in a sumptuous chantry chapel on the south side of the sanctuary. He is also commemorated in stained glass in a transept window in Malvern Priory. One of the most important consequences of Arthur's early death was the remarriage of his widow to the prince's younger brother, the future Henry viii. The controversy to which that later gave rise concerned the consummation or otherwise of Catherine's first marriage – vital evidence, as Henry viii saw it, in his seeking a divorce from Catherine.

Wife to both Arthur and Henry, Catherine of Aragon was clearly a woman who was noble in the face of pain and adversity. Shakespeare gives her a moving speech, as she addresses her second husband:

Sir, I desire you do me right and justice,
And to bestow your pity on me; for
I am a most poor woman, and a stranger,
Born out of your dominions, having here
No judge indifferent, nor no more assurance
Of equal friendship and proceeding. Alas, sir,
In what have I offended you? What cause
Hath my behaviour given to your displeasure,
That thus you should proceed to put me off,
And take your good grace from me?
If in the course
And process of this time you can report,
And prove it too, against my honour aught,
My bond to wedlock, or my love and duty
Against your sacred person; in God's name
Turn me away, and let the foul'st contempt
Shut door upon me, and so give me up
To the sharp'st kind of justice.

William Shakespeare 1564–1616, *Henry VIII,* Act iv, Scene 2

Stephen Kemble 1758–1822
Shakespearean actor

Hereford's Kemble Theatre (demolished in 1970) reminded the city's inhabitants of a famous theatrical dynasty which had its roots in their county. The most famous member of the family, Stephen, was born on this day in 1758 in Kington. Originally apprenticed to a chemist in Coventry, Stephen soon followed his brothers and sisters into an acting career, making his debut as Othello at Covent Garden in 1783. He married Elizabeth Satchell in the same year, and the Kembles toured the provinces, appearing in Shakespearean roles and later opening their own theatres in Newcastle, Edinburgh and Aberdeen. By all accounts, he was neither an efficient manager nor a great actor, but he made several roles his own, including that of Falstaff. In this he was helped by his enormous size – by the 1790s he weighed 18 stone. Returning to Drury Lane in 1802 in the character of Falstaff, he composed a poem to mark his arrival:

> ... all good honest flesh, and blood, and bone,
> And weighing, more or less, some thirty stone!
> Upon the northern coast by chance we caught him,
> And hither in a broad-wheeled wagon brought him;
> ... Blest with unwieldiness – at least his size
> Will favour find in every critic's eyes.

Kemble was also known for his writing. In 1809 he brought out *Odes, Lyrical Ballads and Poems,* a collection of his songs, addresses and miscellaneous poems which included an intriguing pair: the pro-trade 'On the Slave Trade' (1784) and the counter-poem of 1808, 'Being fully convinced of my former errors'.

Kemble died in 1822 near Durham and is buried in the Chapel of Nine Altars in Durham Cathedral. His family had a later Hereford link through Frances Butler, daughter of Pierce Butler and his wife 'Fanny Kemble'. Frances became wife to James Leigh, dean of Hereford 1894–1919 (see 25 January).

Falstaff's endless ability for self-deception and moral cowardice is well noted in these words:

Counterfeit? I lie, I am no counterfeit; to die is to be a counterfeit; for he is but the counterfeit of a man who hath not the life of a man; but to counterfeit dying, when a man thereby liveth, is to be no counterfeit, but the true and perfect image of life indeed. The better part of valour is discretion; in the which better part I have saved my life.

William Shakespeare 1564–1616, *Henry IV, Part One*, Act v, Scene 4

A prayer for truthfulness

Almighty God, who hast sent the Spirit of truth unto us to guide us into all truth: so rule our lives by thy power that we may be truthful in thought and word and deed. May no fear or hope ever make us false in act or speech; cast out from us whatsoever loveth or maketh a lie, and bring us all into the perfect freedom of thy truth; through Jesus Christ our Lord.

Brooke Foss Westcott 1825–1901

John Merewether 1797–1850

Dean & cathedral restorer

HEREFORD CATHEDRAL owes much to certain bishops and deans during its history – not least those who made a priority of caring for its fabric and restoration. John Merewether was one of Hereford's great Victorian restorers. Ordained in 1819, he soon attracted royal attention and became chaplain to the duchess of Clarence, later Queen Adelaide. He became incumbent of New Radnor in 1828 and four years later was made dean of Hereford, a post he held with that of the incumbency of Madeley in Shropshire. He made strenuous attempts to reform the cathedral, instituting weekly rather than monthly chapter meetings and attempting to make the vicars choral more regular in attendance at services. In 1837 he began a long feud with the chapter about custody and use of the chapter seal. Merewether objected to its use in his absence – while the chapter objected to his long absences. An appeal to the bishop led to Merewether backing down. In 1847, the dean was a vociferous opponent of the election of Renn Dickson Hampden as bishop of Hereford, regarding some of Hampden's opinions as dangerous (see 24 April). He even petitioned the queen and announced to Lord John Russell, the prime minister, in a lengthy letter, his intention of voting against Hampden's election. He received a terse response from the prime minister: 'Sir, I had the honour to receive your letter of the 22nd inst. in which you intimate to me your intention of violating the law.' Eventually, when the bishop's election was confirmed, he refused to affix the chapter's seal to formal documents, and refused to attend the enthronement. Merewether had a great interest in architecture and in 1842 wrote *Statement on the Condition and Circumstances of the Cathedral Church of Hereford,* describing its parlous state at that time. He engaged Lewis Cottingham as architect and many parts of the building were restored under his direction.

Merewether died at Madeley on this day in 1850 and was buried in the Lady Chapel at Hereford Cathedral, where the five lancet windows at the east end of the chapel were filled with stained glass in his memory.

In his Statement, *Merewether makes a moving summary in his long plea to the 'great and the good' of the county:*

> If personal entreaty, as its Dean, can have any weight, I do beseech you let the sacred principle on which I have based my appeal, have its perfect work. I ask not of you what I am not ready and zealous to do myself, – I can sincerely aver that I have ever looked upon my connection with this cathedral church as a matter of trust, – I have ever been ready to sacrifice self considerations cheerfully, to make it what it ought to be, – I have already made sacrifices for its sake, perhaps more, and greater that might ever appear, and I am ready to do so again, to the utmost of my ability ... but when your sons, and your son's sons, shall tread these courts of the Lord's house, and mark the spot where then shall my remains be crumbling with their kindred dust; oh, I do hope and trust, that I have precluded the possibility of their complaint, their accusation that I had been supine and listless, deficient in my bounded endeavours to have justice done to such a monument of early piety and splendid liberality.

A prayer that our churches and cathedrals may be places of welcome

> O God, make the door of this church wide enough to receive all who need human love and fellowship, and a heavenly Father's care; and narrow enough to shut out all envy, pride and hate. Make its threshold smooth enough to be no stumbling-block to children, nor to straying feet, but rugged enough to turn back the tempter's power: make it a gateway to thine eternal kingdom.
>
> Bishop Thomas Ken 1637–1711

Albert Walter Gamage 1855–1930

Retail entrepreneur & department store owner

Those of us brought up with the joys of visits to London department stores may not realise that one of the most famous – Gamages – had a connection to Hereford through its founder. Born in the city in 1855, Albert Walter Gamage was educated locally, but left the area and was apprenticed as a draper. In 1878, he went into partnership, leasing a small hosiery shop in Holborn. He soon expanded his horizons and became known as a shrewd entrepreneur, travelling throughout Europe and North America to seek out new goods. Gamage opened his department store in the early 1900s, and there he sold a huge range of goods exploiting popular crazes, first for cycling and then for the newly-invented motor car. Gamage made a lot of effort to market his goods – his thousand-page mail-order catalogue was one of the first of its kind and he was the first to take out a full-page newspaper advertisement to announce enlargements to his store, which he named the 'People's Popular Emporium'. Gamages was loved by generations of children, and here the famous 'Steiff' teddy bears were first sold – hence our illustration. By 1920, Gamages had a turnover of over £1 million per year and employed over 2,000 people. Gamage himself died on this day in 1930. He 'lay in state' in the store's motor department with his staff standing guard, encouraged to do so by the unprecedented offer of a Saturday afternoon holiday.

Department stores like Gamages were wonderful in bringing together people of all classes. Here, in a letter to his sister Elsie, Rudyard Kipling describes a visit to the store in 1912:

Then Mom to Bayswater on the Eternal Quest and I to Gamages in Holborn where, with everything else, they sell gold-fish. A stern woman at a counter who said she liked 'Nat'ral 'Ist'ry', led me off to a pool and a fountain near the grocery department and in the presence of a thick ring of spectators fished out for me, with a small green net, six minnow-like things at a bob each and three portly papas (and I hope a mamma) at five bob. It reminds me of catching our trouts at the place behind Cannes. I bore them all off in a perforated shiny tin, with a squirt to aerate it with. They are now in a pond and very happy, thank you.

Christ in Woolworth's

I did not think to find you there –
Crucifixes, large and small,
Sixpence and threepence, on a tray.
Among the artificial pearls,
Paste rings, tin watches, beads of glass.
It seemed so strange to find you there
Fingered by people coarse and crass,
Who had no reverence at all.
Yet – what is it you would say?
'For these I hang upon my cross,
For these the agony and loss,
Though heedlessly they pass me by.'
Dear Lord forgive such fools as I
Who thought it strange to find you there
When you are with us everywhere.

Teresa Hooley 1888–1973

Sir Frederick Arthur Gore Ouseley, Baronet 1825–89

Priest & church musician

St Michael's Church and College, near Tenbury, Worcestershire were major influences in the raising of standards of church music during the 19th century and many eminent church and cathedral musicians received their education there before its closure during the 1980s. The founder and builder of church and college, Frederick Gore Ouseley was born into a wealthy family and from an early age displayed signs of prodigious musical talent. Following ordination, Ouseley saw it as his vocation 'to do something to raise the music of the sanctuary'. This quest he put into practice while curate in the parish of St Paul, Knightsbridge in London, but it came to full flowering at Tenbury, where he built a church (consecrated 1856) and college mainly at his own expense. This foundation he intended to 'form a model for the choral service of the Church in these realms'.

Ouseley also raised the standard of music as an academic subject at Oxford University, where he had received degrees of bachelor and doctor of music. He became professor of music and instituted music examinations for music degrees. He was a prolific composer, having great skills in counterpoint and writing cantatas and anthems. Few of these are sung today although his *O Saviour of the World* still finds a place in the repertoire of many parish choirs. He encouraged the study of early music, himself editing works by the 17th-century composer, Orlando Gibbons. He was an assiduous collector of antiquarian music and manuscripts and most of these, on the closure of the college, passed to the Bodleian Library. In 1886 Ouseley became also a canon of Hereford Cathedral, having held the titular dignity of precentor since 1855, and it was at Hereford, during a period of canonical residence, that he died, on this day in 1889.

A theologian sees parallels between the work of the singer and that of the priest:

What is true of the singer we see as true also of the priest. Her pastoral ministry, out among people, takes her to 'the cross roads of human experience'. The priest's theology, in Scripture and in liturgy, is to her what the score, a contrived pattern of dots and lines, is to the singer: it embodies that experience, that common property of all mankind, in a pattern of words and actions which she is educated, or ought to be, to interpret, to articulate, with the musician's fidelity.

It is the priest's office so to read the words before him that they awaken in those for whom he ministers an awareness of those theological truths which form the substance of the Christian faith; that they evoke a response to those truths of a sort which might, perhaps would, lie dormant, were it not for his ministry. Good liturgy, like the Bible itself, cannot be read without effort, without a determined study to find the meaning of the words, to make that meaning one's own, and then to convey it so that others are seized of it; the priest's task is no less demanding than the singer's.

Gordon Dunstan 1917–2004, *Theology* (1973)

The Choristers' Prayer

Bless, O Lord, us thy servants who minister in thy Temple.
Grant that what we sing with our lips we may believe in
our hearts and what we believe in our hearts, we may
shew forth in our lives; through Jesus Christ our Lord.

William Wordsworth 1770–1850

Romantic poet

William Wordsworth, the great poet, was born on this day in 1770. With Samuel Taylor Coleridge, he helped to launch the Romantic Age in English literature in 1798 with their joint publication, *Lyrical Ballads*. Wordsworth's *magnum opus* is generally reckoned to be *The Prelude* – a semi-autobiographical poem describing his early years, revised and expanded a number of times.

We often associate Wordsworth with the Lake District, where with Coleridge and Southey he is known as one of the 'Lake poets', his poems here focusing on themes of endurance, separation and death; but this great Romantic poet also has close associations with Herefordshire and the Marches. He often stayed, with his wife Dorothy, at the moated Brinsop Court. Indeed, there are windows in Brinsop church commemorating the family. It is said that on a journey from Brinsop he wrote his sonnet inspired by the legend of Katherine of Ledbury (see 7 October). In the poem, he tells how the saintly Katherine heard how the Ledbury bells:

> Broke forth in concert flung adown the dells
> And upward, high as Malvern's cloudy crest.

There are associations with Wordsworth at Leysters, near Leominster, where the poet visited friends and admired the magnificent views. 'Wordsworth's Stone', set in a clearing of the wooded hillside, bears the initials of the poet and his wife. But it was Wordsworth's tour of the Wye valley in 1798 which gave rise to what is arguably his most famous poem, with its wonderful evocation of the beauties of hill and river.

The Picturesque movement, with many of its roots in the Wye valley, is well reflected in these words:

> that blessed mood
> In which the burthen of the mystery,
> In which the heavy and the weary weight
> Of all this unintelligible world,
> Is lightened – that serene and blessed mood,
> In which the affections gently lead us on –
> Until, the breath of this corporeal frame
> And even the motion of our human blood
> Almost suspended, we are laid asleep
> In body, and become a living soul:
> While with an eye made quiet by the power
> Of harmony, and the deep power of joy,
> We see into the life of things.

William Wordsworth,
'Lines composed a few miles above Tintern Abbey, on revisiting the banks of the Wye during a tour. 13 July 1798'

John Prophete *c.*1350–1416

Reformer & benefactor of St Katherine's Hospital, Ledbury

Welsh by birth, John Prophete spent much of his life in the civil service of his day, serving three kings and acting as registrar to the Provincial Court at Canterbury and later as a kind of watchdog to supervise the constraints placed upon Richard II. On Richard's return to power, Prophete was dismissed and spent much of his time in Hereford, where he became dean, holding his deanery with as many as 12 additional benefices! With his legal background, he was the ideal person to effect reforms in various areas of church life. He was dean at the time of the granting of a charter to endow a 'college of vicars in the choir of the cathedral', which enabled the vicars to have their own seal and appoint their own custos or warden but to remain under the jurisdiction of the dean and chapter. At this time there were 27 vicars living in Castle Street, where they had their own chapel, hall, common room and dormitory, and there they remained until their move to the present cloister in 1473–5. In Ledbury, Prophete set about the reform of St Katherine's Hospital by his *Ordinances* of 1398, appointing the outstanding John Malvern as Master (see 27 March). He became dean of York in 1406 but still had great affection for Hereford, petitioning the king in 1414 to allow him to build a chapel of St John the Baptist in the south part of the cathedral church, 'on account of his affection for Hereford Cathedral where he had been prebendary and dean'. The chapel was never built, but Prophete showed his generosity in other ways, not least to St Katherine's Hospital, and he made his will on this day in the year 1416.

St Katherine's Hospital, Ledbury with its Master surely bears some similarities to another such institution in fiction! But, whether fact or fiction, there is little doubt that generous benefactions, to church and charitable institutions, played – and continue to play – a vital part in their ongoing life:

In the year 1434, there died at Barchester one John Hiram, who had made money in the town as a woolstapler, and in his will he left the house in which he died and certain meadows and closes near the town, still called Hiram's Butts, and Hiram's Patch, for the support of twelve superannuated wool-carders, all of whom should have been born and bred and spent their days in Barchester; he also appointed that an almshouse should be built for their abode, with a fitting residence for a warden, which warden was also to receive a certain sum annually out of the rents of the said butts and patches. He, moreover, willed, having had a soul alive to harmony, that the precentor of the cathedral should have the option of being also warden of the almshouses, if the bishop in each case approved.

From that day to this the charity had gone on and prospered – at least, the charity had gone on, and the estates had prospered. Wool-carding in Barchester there was no longer any; so the bishop, dean and warden, who took it in turns to put in the old men, generally appointed some hangers-on of their own; worn-out gardeners, decrepit grave-diggers, or octogenarian sextons, who thankfully received a comfortable lodging and one shilling and fourpence a day, such being the stipend to which, under the will of John Hiram, they were declared to be entitled.

Such was the condition of Hiram's twelve old men when Mr. Harding was appointed warden.

Anthony Trollope 1815–82, *The Warden* (1855)

April

Dietrich Bonhoeffer 1906–45

Lutheran pastor

The diocese of Hereford established its Hereford/Nuremberg link in 1982, with the purpose of fostering ecumenical relationship with our Lutheran partners in Kirchenkreis Nürnberg. Although they are different in population and character, Nuremberg and the diocese of Hereford cover an almost identical land area and share similar tasks in rural ministry. It seems particularly appropriate that, on this day when he suffered, we should remember Dietrich Bonhoeffer, the brave and defiant Lutheran Pastor. He has become such a symbol of fortitude to our generation – for all denominations. Born into an academic family, and ordained in the Lutheran Church, Bonhoeffer's theology was influenced by Karl Barth and he became a lecturer – in Spain and the USA and, in 1931, back in Berlin. Opposed to the philosophy of Nazism, he was one of the leaders of the Confessing Church, a movement which broke away from the Nazi-dominated Lutherans in 1934. Banned from teaching and persecuted by Hitler's regime, he bravely returned to Germany at the outbreak of war in 1939. His experiences led him to propose a more radical theology in his later works, which have been influential among post-war theologians. His defiant opposition to the Nazis led to his arrest in 1943 and he was murdered by the Nazi police in Flossenburg concentration camp on this day in 1945.

Bonhoeffer speaks of the cost of discipleship:

Cheap grace is the deadly enemy of our Church. We are fighting today for costly grace. Cheap grace means grace sold on the market like cheapjack's wares. The sacraments, the forgiveness of sin and the consolations of religion are thrown away at cut prices ... Cheap grace is the preaching of forgiveness without requiring repentance, baptism without church discipline, communion without confession, absolution without personal confession. Cheap grace is grace without discipleship, grace without the Cross, grace without Jesus Christ, living and incarnate. Costly grace is the treasure hidden in the field; for the sake of it a man will gladly go and sell all that he has. It is the pearl of great price to buy which the merchant will sell all his goods ... Such grace is costly because it calls us to follow, and it is grace because it calls us to follow Jesus Christ. It is costly because it cost a man his life, and it is grace because it gives a man the only true life.

An evening reflection by Bonhoeffer

O Lord my God, I thank thee that thou hast brought this day to a close; I thank thee for giving me rest in body and soul. Thy hand has been over me and has guarded and preserved me. Forgive my lack of faith and any wrong that I have done today, and help me to forgive all who have wronged me. Let me sleep in peace under thy protection, and keep me from all the temptations of darkness. Into thy hands I commend my loved ones and all who dwell in this house; I commend to thee my body and soul. O God, thy holy name be praised.

Thomas Hildeyard 1690–1746

Jesuit engineer & clock maker

The Roman Catholic chapel at Rotherwas, near Hereford, amidst industrial surroundings, is an unexpected survival of a place of worship in Catholic hands throughout the times of persecution. On this day we remember a priest who had long dealings with the chapel here and who was an expert in areas other than religion.

Thomas Hildeyard was born in London and educated at the English College at St Omer in France. He entered the Society of Jesus and was ordained priest in 1725. After teaching philosophy, theology and mathematics at Liege, he was sent to the English mission and by 1726 had become chaplain to the Bodenham family at Rotherwas. In 1743 he was declared rector of the college of St Francis Xavier – a geographical area which included the counties of Hereford, Monmouth, Gloucester and Somerset and the whole of South Wales. Hildeyard was also an accomplished engineer. In 1720 he was probably the first person in continental Europe successfully to build a steam engine after the designs of Thomas Newcomen. He was also noted for creating a number of innovative clocks. One of them was described in the *Chronometrum mirabile Leodiense* as 'being a most curious clock'. This was an ingenious table clock giving time of day, information from the calendar, dates of moveable feasts and all kinds of astronomical details, such as the movement of constellations. His 'Lectures on Penance' were preserved in a manuscript at the presbytery at St George's Roman Catholic church in Worcester. He died on this day in 1746 at Rotherwas and was buried in the family chapel.

As we remember Hildeyard and his clocks, well-known words on Time by an Old Testament writer:

For everything there is a season, and a time for every matter under heaven:
A time to be born, and a time to die;
A time to plant, and a time to pluck up what is planted;
A time to kill, and a time to heal;
A time to break down and a time to build up;
A time to weep and a time to laugh;
A time to mourn and a time to dance;
A time to cast away stones and a time to gather them;
A time to embrace and a time to refrain from embracing;
A time to seek and a time to lose;
A time to keep and a time to cast away;
A time to rend and a time to sew;
A time to keep silence and a time to speak;
A time to love and a time to hate;
A time for war and a time for peace.

Ecclesiastes 3:1–8

Guthlac 7th century
Hermit

Some saints associated with Hereford never came near our city! Guthlac was a hermit in 7th-century East Anglia, but his fame led to churches and monastic foundations in his honour being built far from his native Lincolnshire. Of royal blood, Guthlac trained as a soldier, but gave up warfare to be a monk at Repton, Derbyshire. In 701, he became a hermit at Crowland in Lincolnshire – a site accessible only by boat. Here his life resembled that of the Desert Fathers such as St Anthony of Egypt and he became known for his harsh, ascetic life. Like Anthony, he was greatly troubled by demons; indeed, his symbol is a scourge – not for self-flagellation but for use as a defensive weapon against diabolical attacks. The great and the good came to Guthlac to seek his wisdom and guidance, including Aethelbald, king of the Mercians. After Guthlac's death, on this day in 714, it is said that Aethelbald returned to Crowland and stayed in the hut 'where he used to stay when Guthlac was alive'. There he received a vision of reassurance from the saint. Not only did the king embellish Guthlac's shrine at Crowland; it has been argued that it was he who was responsible for introducing the saint's cult, with relics, into Hereford, where, by the 10th century, a church had been dedicated to Guthlac. Later, the Benedictine community at Hereford was moved to a new site outside the city walls, to a building known as the priory of St Guthlac, subject to St Peter's Abbey at Gloucester. This was destroyed at the Dissolution, but its magnificent carved stalls, with canopies and misericords, may still be seen in St Peter's Church, Hereford.

Much of what we know about St Guthlac comes from the work of contemporary Anglo-Saxon writings, including one, c.740, by the learned East Anglican monk, Felix. In this passage we read about Guthlac's mercy and sense of humour:

At one time there came to him two brethren from a certain monastery. While they journeyed there they had with them two flagons filled with beer. Then it was agreed between them that they should hide them under a turf so that they should have them again when they journeyed home. Then, when they came to Guthlac, he strengthened them with his instruction and edified their hearts with his exhortation. When they had spoken about many things between them, then with cheerful face and laughing voice the blessed Guthlac said to them: 'Why did you hide the flagons under a turf, and why did you not bring them with you?' Then they greatly marvelled at the words of the holy man, and bowed to him begging his blessing. And he blessed them and then they journeyed home again.

A prayer for humour

Dear Lord, I thank you for calling me to share with others your precious gift of laughter. May I never forget that it is your gift and my privilege. As your children are rebuked in their self-importance and cheered in their sadness, help me to remember that your foolishness is wiser than our wisdom.

'The Clown's Prayer'

Thomas Joseph Brown 1796–1880

Bishop of Menevia & founder of Belmont

By the mid 19th century, Belmont Abbey had become an important influence in the developing monastic and educational life of the Roman Catholic church, as it re-emerged from the shadows of earlier discrimination. Its vital role owes much to Bishop Thomas Joseph Brown, whom we commemorate today and who died on this day in 1880. 40 years earlier, as Benedictine prior of Downside, he had been consecrated bishop of Apollaria and vicar apostolic of the newly formed Welsh district – which included Herefordshire and Monmouthshire.

Brown found he had an uphill task – the area had scant financial resources with only 5,000 practising Catholics and a mere three chapels at Hereford, Weobley and Courtfield – but through his influence the Catholic population increased and prospered. Brown became bishop of Newport and Menevia in 1850, on the restoration of the Catholic hierarchy, and he wrote to the English Benedictines asking them to make Wales a special sphere of work. Plans were laid for the formation of a diocese whose cathedral chapter consisted of monks, as in many pre-Reformation cathedrals, and in 1853, with the offer of land by Mr Wegg-Prosser, the dream of a cathedral for the new diocese began to achieve reality. The architect of the new church was E W Pugin, son of A W N Pugin, and the new building, in opulent 14th-century style, was consecrated by Bishop Brown in 1860. As well as its uniqueness as a cathedral priory, Belmont developed an important role in the training and formation of monks, acting as the mother house of a common novitiate – novices being sent from other English houses to Belmont for at least three years of their training. The new church, with its imposing tower, quickly became part of the Hereford landscape, although in the community's early years it was necessary to station a policeman outside the priory church during vespers on Sundays to prevent brawlers from the city making a disturbance. In his last year, Bishop Brown lived at Bullingham Manor; it is said that, when he was over 80, his episcopal ring fell into the river, and he waded waist-deep into the water to recover it!

Bishop Brown helped to bring the re-emerging Roman Catholic church into English society. Similarly, Cardinal Newman, through his writings, has given us passages which transcend denominational boundaries. The meeting of the soul with God in The Dream of Gerontius, *with its music by Elgar, is unforgettable:*

Angel Thy judgement now is near, for we are come
Into the veiled presence of our God.
Soul I hear the voices that I left on earth.
Angel It is the voice of friends around thy bed,
Who say the 'subvenite' with the priest.
Hither the echoes come; before the Throne
Stands the great Angel of the Agony,
The same who strengthened Him, what time He knelt
Lone in the garden shade, bedewed with blood.
That Angel best can plead with Him for all
Tormented souls, the dying and the dead ...
Soul I go before my judge. Ah! ...
Angel Praise to his Name!

John Henry Newman 1801–90

Mary Morgan 1788–1805

Victim of injustice

A POIGNANT GRAVESTONE in the churchyard of St Andrew's, Presteigne bears witness to a terrible event in the town's history. Mary Morgan, from Glasbury, was employed as an undercook at Maesllwch Castle, the seat of Walter Wilkins, MP for Radnorshire. In September 1804, she was accused by the cook of having given birth to a baby, and later, she herself confessed that she had not only given birth, but had killed the child with a knife. An inquest found this to be so, and Mary Morgan was committed for trial. Too ill to travel to Presteigne, where the Assizes were held, her trial eventually began in April 1805 before Mr Justice Hardinge, concluding on 11 April, when the jury found her guilty of murdering her child. On this day, 13 April, she was hanged – though said to be almost unconscious when brought to the gallows. It is also said that no farmer could be found to lend a cart to bring Mary from the gaol to the execution at Gallows Lane. She was buried later that day in what was then unconsecrated ground near the church.

For some time after the execution, it was claimed that the father of the murdered child was the son of her employer, who himself was a member of the jury which found that Mary had a case to answer. Although this theory is discredited today, it has been an important element in the popular characterisation of Mary Morgan as the helpless victim of an unscrupulous aristocrat. Her case became a *cause célèbre* for feminists, who have presented her trial as a miscarriage of justice and one displaying ignorance of the traumas surrounding what may have been a nervous breakdown or some other cause of diminished responsibility.

Mary Morgan has two gravestones. One of them, erected by the earl of Aylesbury, a friend of the judge, has a sanctimonious epitaph, describing Mary as:

Young, beautiful, endowed with a good understanding and disposition, but unenlightened by the sacred truths of Christianity became the victim of sin and shame and was condemned to an ignominious death on 11 April 1805, for the murder of her bastard child. Rous'd to a first sense of guilt and remorse by the eloquent and humane exertions of her benevolent judge, Mr Justice Hardinge, she underwent the sentence of the Law on the following Thursday with unfeigned repentance and a fervent hope of forgiveness through the merits of a redeeming intercessor. This stone is erected not merely to perpetuate the remembrance of a departed penitent, but to remind the living of the frailty of human nature when unsupported by religion.

The second gravestone is more compassionate and has, simply, words from St John's Gospel:

He that is without sin among you, let him first cast a stone at her.

Archbishop Temple reflects on these startling and challenging words:

The story carries its own meaning. These odious ecclesiastics are so set upon their barren controversy that they will use a woman's shame as a chance to score a point. Now, will this mercy-loving teacher, who is so lax about the law of the Church, openly express dissent from Moses? If He does, He is trapped ... He alone was entitled to condemn; and He did not condemn. But neither did He condone. He said 'From now on do not sin any more'. May this at least be so with us. May the Wrath of the Lamb against our combination of impurity and complacency quicken our slow consciences, and may his cleansing glance so penetrate us that from now on we do not sin any more!

William Temple 1881–1944, *Readings in St John's Gospel* (1939)

Thomas Percy 1729–1811

Writer of Reliques of Ancient English Poetry

In the 18th century, clergy were often experts in fields far removed from theology, and many had leisure to pursue literary and scientific pursuits. Thomas Percy, who rose to become a bishop on the Irish bench, was a prolific writer and collector of verse. Born in Bridgnorth on 13 April 1729, he spent his early years in Shropshire, went to Oxford and was ordained, serving several curacies in his home area. It was when visiting a friend at Shifnal in 1753 that he noticed a battered volume 'lying dirty on the floor, under a bureau in the parlour ... being used by the maids to light the fire'. It proved to be a 17th-century collection, and he persuaded his friend to reprieve it from the flames. In due course it provided the basis for Percy's anthology *Reliques of Ancient English Poetry*, for which he is best known. When the book was published, the *Gentleman's Magazine* commented that Percy 'has with great judgement selected such specimens [of ballads] as either show the gradation of our language, exhibit the progress of popular opinion ... or throw light on our early classical poets'. The work, containing ballads from the late medieval period to the early 18th century, includes verses on popular themes such as St George and Robin Hood, and is generally reckoned to be a work with great influence on the Romantic movement. Percy was appointed dean of Carlisle in 1778 and in 1782 became bishop of Dromore in Northern Ireland. He immersed himself in his pastoral duties and on his death was affectionately remembered:

> Promoting the instruction and comfort of the poor with unremitting attention, and superintending the sacred and civil interests of the diocese, with vigilance and assiduity; revered and loved for his piety, liberality, benevolence and hospitality, by persons of every rank and religious denomination.

To Thomas Percy we owe much of the increased fervour surrounding St George as patron saint of England:

Mark our father Abraham, when first he rescued Lot
Only with his household, what conquest there he got.
David was elected a prophet and a king,
He slew the great Goliath, with a stone within a sling.
Yet these were not knights of the table round;
Nor St George, St George who the dragon did confound.
St George he was for England; St Dennis was for France;
Sing, *Honi soit qui mal y pense.*

Jephthah and Gideon did lead their men to fight,
They conquered the Amorites and put them all to flight.
Hercules his labours were on the plaines of Basse.
And Samson slew a thousand with the jawbone of an ass,
And eke he threw a temple down, and did a mighty spoil.
But St George, St George he did the dragon foil.
St George he was for England; St Dennis was for France;
Sing, *Honi soit qui mal y pense.*

'St George for England', *Reliques* (1765)

George Cornewall Lewis 1806–63

Politician & author

A wise and honest statesman – *a profound scholar – a kind and firm friend.* The statue of George Cornewall Lewis, with its inscription, outside the Shire Hall in Hereford breathes an air of authority and wisdom. It celebrates a man who represented a notable combination of politics and literary pursuits in the mid-Victorian era.

Born in Old Radnor, Lewis was educated at Eton and Oxford, where he studied classics and mathematics and was originally set on a career in the law. Instead, he became involved in the politics of newly-passed legislation introducing the Poor Law, and became a commissioner in similar government research in Ireland. After his marriage he became more involved in main-stream politics and became member for Herefordshire in 1847. His career advanced under Lord John Russell and he supported the prime minister in his denunciation of 'papal aggression', with the restoration of the Catholic hierarchy in 1850. Losing his seat in 1850, he turned more to literary interests, becoming editor of the *Edinburgh Review*, and contributing essays on politics and early Roman history. His reputation as a classical scholar, however, experienced a major reverse in 1859, when a work he was editing was proved to be a forgery. On his father's death in 1855, Lewis inherited the title of baronet and succeeded to his father's seat for the Radnorshire boroughs. The prime minister, Palmerston, made him chancellor of the exchequer, a post he found challenging, not only because his predecessor was the brilliant Gladstone but also because of the severe crisis in the nation's finances brought on by the Crimean War.

In the 1859 Palmerston administration, Lewis became home secretary and later war secretary. In the latter role, he sowed the seeds of late Victorian 'splendid isolation', and bitterly opposed Russell's and Gladstone's pressure for British intervention in the American Civil War. In character, Lewis was laconic and opposed to 'enthusiasm', seen in his oft-quoted remark, 'Life would be tolerable were it not for its amusements'. Indeed, in his final work, describing a debate among classical thinkers, he opines, with breathtaking moderation, that 'it is the part of wisdom and prudence to acquiesce in any form of government which is tolerably well administered, and affords tolerable security to person and property'. Lewis died on 13 April 1863 and is buried in the family vault at Old Radnor parish church.

A poet of the 20th century speaks of those whose greatness endures:

I think continually of those who were truly great.
Who, from the womb, remembered the soul's history
Through corridors of light where the hours are suns,
Endless and singing. Whose lovely ambition
Was that their lips, still touched with fire,
Should tell of the Spirit, clothed from head to foot in song.
And who hoarded from the Spring branches
The desires falling across their bodies like blossoms.

What is precious is never to forget
The essential delight of the blood drawn from ageless springs
Breaking through rocks in worlds before our earth.
Never to deny its pleasure in the morning simple light
Nor its grave evening demand for love.
Never to allow gradually the traffic to smother
With noise and fog the flowering of the Spirit.

Stephen Spender 1909–95, *Poems* (1934)

Robert Bethune d.1148

Nearly a saint

Robert de Bethune was a native of Flanders and came to England, helping to build the priory of Llanthony under Augustinian rule, in the lonely mountains of Wales. He was made its first prior and always loved that remote spot. It was only with great reluctance that he was persuaded by the Pope, in 1131, to accept the bishopric of Hereford, and he retained his affection for Llanthony, granting prebendal rights when the priory was transferred to Gloucester, and offering the Llanthony canons rights of sanctuary in the episcopal palace at Hereford. Bethune was the first bishop to encourage the Hereford canons to act as a distinct chapter, and the term *capitulum* first occurs in 1134. He seems, though, to have had a stormy relationship with Ralph, generally reckoned to be Hereford's first dean, and Bethune travelled to Pisa to obtain an injunction from the Pope ordering obedience from the dean and chapter. He became involved in the conflict between Stephen (see 23 October) and Matilda, siding first with the king. In 1141, Matilda's forces occupied the cathedral – the clergy were expelled and the nave used as stables. Bethune eventually cleansed the cathedral, recalled the clergy and restored the services. He went on to complete the building of the nave and held a dedication service in 1148. In that year, he attended a council at Châlons, but was taken ill there and died on this day. The Pope directed that his body be taken back to Hereford for burial. It was enclosed for protection in the hide of an ox and buried in the south choir aisle. On his death-bed he is said to have confessed his failings – an undue affection for his storks, his peacocks and his black dog with white legs! By the early 14th century there was an attempt to press for his canonisation and a collecting box appeared by his tomb, suggesting that devotions were being made there. Indeed, there is a space carved into the bishop's crozier on the effigy on his tomb which looks very much as if the collecting box was originally placed here. At least one of the miracles attributed to Cantilupe was also ascribed to Bethune.

The see-saw of relationships between Stephen and Matilda, with its farcical and tragic elements, is described in this well-known historical satire:

The Dreadful Story of Stephen and his Aunt Matilda (or Maud)

The moment Stephen came to the throne it was realized that he was a mistake and had been christened wrong; thus everything was thrown into confusion.

Stephen himself felt quite uncalled for, and even his Aunt Matilda was able to take him in when she began announcing that she was the real King. Stephen, however, soon discovered that she had been malchristened, too, and was unable to say for certain whether her name was Matilda or Maud.

After this Stephen and Matilda (or Maud) spent the reign escaping from each other over the snow in nightgowns while 'God and His Angels slept'.

Taking advantage of this lax state of affairs, the Barons built a surfeit of romantic castles, into which they lured everybody and then put them to the torture; nor is it recorded that the Sword was once sheathed, right to the bottom, during the whole of this dreadful reign. Hence the memorable greeting so common among the Barons of the time – 'Merrie Englande!'

W C Sellar and R J Yeatman, *1066 and all that* (1930)

April

Nathan Wetherell 1726–1808

Dean when the west front collapsed

While we remember some deans for their positive work on the fabric of Hereford Cathedral, we remember this one for quite the opposite! Like several 18th-century deans, Wetherell was also a head of house at Oxford – he was master of University College and only came to Hereford for two months during the summer. The chapter had often been warned during the 18th century of the parlous state of the cathedral fabric, and disaster finally struck on this day in 1786 – Easter Monday that year – when the great west tower collapsed, demolishing half the nave and leaving it open to the sky. The dean was in Oxford, as usual, but hurried back at once; stories that he was not told of the calamity by his butler until he had finished his dessert are probably apocryphal! Certainly the chapter was blamed for the neglect and the *Gentleman's Magazine* railed against 'the barbarous indolence of the chapter'. The cathedral carpenter was ordered to erect a wooden screen at the west end so that services could continue, but it was two years before the architect James Wyatt was called in. He supervised the restoration, rebuilding the nave one bay shorter than it was before the collapse. The whole restoration cost nearly £20,000 – not finally paid until 20 years later. Wetherell died on 29 December 1808 and is buried in the chapel of University College, Oxford, where there is a memorial to him.

William Golding's The Spire *is a salutary warning of the hubris which can consume one building a great cathedral. Dean Jocelin builds his cathedral and its enormous spire without foundations, and against the anxious advice of clergy and masons alike. It all ends in disaster as the spire collapses and the dean himself is destroyed:*

He came up out of a deep well. There was a flat noise at the top like a cover; but this was not what drew him up. There were other noises, thin screams, bird noises, almost. Suddenly he was wide awake, knowing where he was, in the dimmest of grey lights. He could hear their clamour on the stairs.

He rolled off the bed and went quickly to the door.

'I'm here. You must be brave, my children!'

But the voices shrieked and sobbed.

'– now and in the hour of –'

'– Father!'

He shouted down the stairs.

'No harm is coming to you!'

There were hands at his feet, and pulling at his gown.

'The city's being destroyed!'

'– the whole thatch of a house lying in the graveyard and beating to pieces.'

He shouted down at them.

'What's happened to the spire?'

Hands crawled up his body, and a beard thrust into his face.

'It's falling, Reverend Father. There were stones falling from the parapet even before dark –'

He pulled himself away and went to the window and rubbed at the dullness with foolish fingers as though he could smear it away like paint. He hurried back to the stairs.

'Satan is loose. But no harm shall come to you. I swear it.'

'Help us, Reverend Father! Pray for us!'

William Golding 1911–93, *The Spire* (1964)

Richard Mayhew 1440–1516

Bishop of Hereford & first president of Magdalen College, Oxford

In his will, Richard Mayhew directed that he should be buried in Hereford Cathedral 'near the effigy of the holy and glorious Ethelbert, King and Martyr', and there we see his tomb today. Symbols of lilies on the tomb indicate that Mayhew was much connected with Magdalen College, Oxford – indeed, he was its first President, appointed by the college's founder, William Waynflete, in 1480, and he laid the foundation of the college's great tower. Mayhew attended the coronation of Henry VII in 1485 and in 1501 was an envoy to Spain to negotiate the marriage of Prince Arthur with Catherine of Aragon (see 8 May), escorting the bride to England. In 1504 he became bishop of Hereford, but for several years conducted most diocesan business from Oxford. On relinquishing the presidency of Magdalen College, he became an assiduous diocesan bishop, consecrating the church at Croft, dedicated to St Michael, in the grounds of the castle. In the cathedral, he began work on an extension to the north porch – work completed by Bishop Booth, his successor. He died on this day in 1516. In addition to directions for burial in his will, he left a silver-gilt holy water sprinkler, the gift of Catherine of Aragon and, for the chapel of the Blessed Virgin Mary and St Thomas Cantilupe, he bequeathed 'my lately purchased organs to be placed in the chapel of the same' for use in the daily mass of Our Lady. His tomb is overlooked by the crest of Magdalen College, Oxford, featured in the top of a stained glass window in the south choir aisle.

One of the most famous churches dedicated to St Mary Magdalen is at Launceston, in Cornwall. There, the granite parish church has a medieval statue of the saint, and by tradition, people throw stones at the statue, making wishes – often for a successful marriage!

Mary, Mary Magdalene, lying on a wall,
I throw a pebble on your back, will it lie or fall?
Send me down for Christmas,
Some stockings or some hose,
And send, before the winter's end,
A brand new set of clothes.
Mary, Mary Magdalene, under a stony tree,
I throw a pebble on your back, what will you bring me?

Charles Causley 1917–2003, 'Mary, Mary Magdalene', *Collected Poems* (1975)

From the School Hymn of Magdalen College School, Oxford

The lilies bloomed in Galilee,
 Where once the Saviour trod;
The earth with fairest flowers was strewn
 About the feet of God.
And He to whom the lords of earth
 Their adoration yield,
O'er all the pride of kings did praise
 The lilies of the field.

The lilies in the fields that grow,
 They know not toil nor care,
Yet God doth clothe them year by year
 In glowing raiment fair.
Much more shall He who loveth us
 Our lives from evil shield,
And make us in His grace to grow
 Like lilies of the field.

John Beale bapt.1637 d.1683

Clergyman, writer on agriculture & natural philosophy

There is not the like man in the whole island, nor in the continent beyond the seas, so far as I know it ... that could be made more universally use of, to do good to all, as I in some measure know and could direct.

So wrote a 17th-century scientist of a Herefordshire man who left a lasting mark on the county's agriculture and whose interests made him one of the great polymaths of the age. Born into an agricultural family (his father cultivated the famous redstreak apples on their estate), he was baptized at Yarkhill on 17 April 1608. Educated at Worcester Cathedral School and King's College, Cambridge, he had a photographic memory, relating candidly: 'Thus I oft-times saved my purse by looking over books in stationers' shops.' After ordination, he became vicar of a Somerset village, but was ejected, returned to Herefordshire and took on the living of Stretton Grandison, later becoming, for a short period, master of St Katherine's Hospital, Ledbury. Beale continued his practical pursuits, encouraging local production of cider. In 1653 he published *A Treatise on Fruit Trees* and in 1657, *Herefordshire Orchards – a Pattern for All England*, a work which brought him to the attention of Oliver Cromwell. On becoming a Fellow of the Royal Society, he wrote papers on successful production of cider orchards and collaborated with Evelyn in the preparation of *Pomona* in 1664. At his own expense he distributed 20,000 grafts of Herefordshire genet moyle and redstreak apples to Somerset, Devon and Dorset. As a scientist, he encouraged the use of optical instruments, thermometers and barometers, and he made many observations on unusual natural phenomena – these he said provided 'more ... valuable truth in one houre than a carte loade of monckish philosophy'. In religion he was an independent, with loyalty to the established church and yet with a tolerant attitude to Dissenters. He was greatly interested in millenarianism, and had a lifelong belief in prophetic dreams.

John Beale's broadminded approach to matters of faith and religion mark him out in an age not always noted for its comprehensiveness. In our own day, Christians work together so much more, preferring to emphasize what unites them rather than to dwell on what divides them. Churches Together in Hereford joined together for the Feast of Pentecost in 2009 and at the end of a service in Hereford Cathedral enjoyed refreshments and fellowship in the Chapter House garden. Local poet Faith Ford, was moved to record the event in a poem:

It was hugely powerful.
To leave the building – the Cathedral –
and to come into the garden.
Suddenly we were the Church,
together, together in that place.
A straggling, untidy group – just a rag and tag,
stripped of the beautiful medieval structure,
the stone and carvings, the artefacts, icons, stained-glass pictures,
candles, tapestries; and now out on our own?
No, not alone.
Blessed still by the beauty and hush of a perfect Spring evening,
bathed in warmth and evening sunlight,
mature trees and Spring blossoms to colour, adorn,
and the solitary song of a blackbird –
more heavenly than all the rest – calling us to worship and be blessed.

Ralph Baldock d.1313

Commissioner into case for Cantilupe's canonisation

Until the 12th century, many saints were 'acclaimed' by popular accord – a person showed him or herself holy or saintly and was recognised as such by the community. With the centralisation of papal power, searching enquiries were now made into candidates for sainthood. Sometimes these enquiries could be concluded swiftly – Thomas Becket was declared a saint after due process in less than three years. With Hereford's own Thomas Cantilupe, the process was much longer (see 2 October), and today we commemorate one who was at the centre of this enquiry. Ralph Baldock became, successively, archdeacon of Middlesex, dean of St Paul's and bishop of London, being consecrated at Lyons in 1306. The following year he was commissioned by Pope Clement v to conduct, along with other eminent churchmen, the enquiry at Hereford into the miracles attributed to Thomas Cantilupe.

The commissioners heard not only about the miracles which occurred after Cantilupe's death but also about the intimate details and saintliness of his life, making records which were sent to the papal court for consideration. These records are preserved in the Vatican, beautifully written in medieval Latin, and from them we are able to learn much about daily life in rural England six centuries ago, the medical problems of the time and the framework of thought which could include miraculous cures as frequent events.

The commissioners spent five months in London and Hereford and interviewed 181 witnesses. There were 470 miracles to be catalogued and we must have sympathy with the committee who by the last day of their enquiry had dealt with only 17 of them in detail. The remaining evidence was submitted in a rush of witnesses and paperwork.

Baldock himself made a name as a scholar, writing on natural science, medicine and history while his codification of the customs and statutes for St Paul's Cathedral is unrivalled among medieval English cathedral codes for its comprehensiveness and logical arrangement. At St Paul's, he rebuilt the Lady Chapel. He died on 24 July 1313 and is buried at Stepney.

At its heart, the enquiry into Cantilupe's miracles was the age-old challenge of faith and doubt. In medieval times, much of the population looked to the supernatural for help and reassurance in dark and uncertain times and perhaps faith played a greater part in the lives of all. Yet doubt is always the obverse of faith, and the struggle between them often creative:

Faith and Doubt

We too often forget that Christian faith is a principle of questioning and struggle before it becomes a principle of certitude and of peace. One has to doubt and reject everything else in order to believe firmly in Christ, and after one has begun to believe, one's faith itself must be tested and purified. Christianity is not merely a set of foregone conclusions. The Christian mind is a mind that risks intolerable purifications, and sometimes, indeed very often, the risk turns out to be too great to be tolerated. Faith tends to be defeated by the burning presence of God in mystery, and seeks refuge from him, flying to comfortable social forms and safe conventions in which purification is no longer an inner battle but a matter of outward gesture.

Thomas Merton 1915–68, *Conjectures of a Guilty Bystander* (1968)

April

Beuno 6th century
Abbot in North Wales

The beautiful church of Llanveynoe, in the Olchon Valley, is dedicated to this saint, said to have been born and educated in Herefordshire. The main centre of his work was, however, at Clynnog Fawr (Gwynedd), where he founded his principal monastery. Some of his many dedications may reflect his foundations, while others are doubtless those of his disciples. They are found in central east Wales and in Clwyd, but the largest number is in the extreme north-west, including Anglesey and the Lleyn peninsula. Beuno died and was buried at Clynnog Fawr, where a stone oratory was built over his tomb. The relics were later translated to a new church (Eglwys y Bedd), where miracles were reported. He is often considered the most important saint of North Wales, and his miracles are famous. Many legends and stories concern those in which he brings back to life those who had been beheaded, the most famous example being his niece, Winifrede or Gwenfrewi. His cult survived the Reformation and in the reign of Elizabeth I (1589) there were complaints that lambs and calves offered at the saint's tomb were later brought back and were highly esteemed because Beuno's cattle 'prospered marvellous well'. In 1770 this custom still survived. Sick children were bathed in his holy well and left all night at his tomb, to encourage healing.

Beuno died on Low Sunday and it is said that on his deathbed he had a vision of Heaven and the Risen Christ. A later mystic, Richard Rolle, speaks of a similar vision of glory as death approaches:

I seek that face of beauty past belief;
Only immortal love can ease my grief;
To see him, or to know him, ends all pain,
Turns mourning song to brightest glad refrain.

They live in joy who love that sweetest Child:
Jesu, it is, of all most meek and mild.
Though sinful, one who loves him shall not fear;
Evil and wrath of God shall not come near.

I love to speak of him whose sweetest charms
My heart till it must burst, and cures all harms;
Whose unforgettable love snares all my thought,
Whose bleeding hands and feet my soul have bought.

Love's sweetness is beyond man's power to tell;
Who loves with longing, God protects from hell.
O endless joy, that those who dwell in love
Shall from their foes be saved by God above!

Jesu, who makes the day from darkness spring,
Guard us, for we acknowledge you as King.
O everlasting love whom we adore,
Give us grace to love you evermore!

Richard Rolle *c.*1300–49, 'Love made firm in Christ'

Thomas Bisse 1675–1731

Founder of the Three Choirs Festival

The oldest music festival in Europe – and indeed the world – owes its inception to a desire for convivial music-making and support for those in need. Those early aspirations are still at the heart of the Three Choirs Festival. Today we commemorate one of the festival's founding fathers. Educated at Oxford, Thomas Bisse held parochial offices in Herefordshire – Cradley and later Weston under Penyard – as well as being chancellor of Hereford Cathedral. With his brother Philip as bishop of Hereford (see 6 September), Bisse was well placed to introduce new ideas. Before moving to Herefordshire he had been much impressed by the annual charity services for the Corporation of the Sons of the Clergy in London (founded in 1655). These took the form of a choral service and an appropriate sermon, one of which Bisse had preached at St Paul's. On his arrival in Hereford, he became an enthusiastic supporter of the existing occasional meetings of the three cathedral choirs of Hereford, Gloucester and Worcester, and at Bisse's suggestion, these meetings were put on a regular footing, possibly in 1716 or 1717, and certainly by 1724. Each cathedral took a turn every three years and there was a sermon in support of orphans of clergy in the three dioceses. Bisse himself was regarded as an eloquent preacher. Among the subjects of his published sermons are a defence of episcopacy and charity schools, but perhaps the most important are those which deal with the place of music in worship, among them *The Beauty of Holiness in the Common Prayer* (1716), *A Rationale on Cathedral Worship or Choir-Service* (1720) and *Musick the Delight of the Sons of Men* (preached at the Three Choirs Festival in 1726). Bisse died on this day in 1731.

The sermon preached at the opening of the Three Choirs Festival today still focuses on ways in which music may lift us to God. Archbishop Rowan Williams, when bishop of Monmouth, preaching this sermon in 1988, focuses on the importance of time in our music and worship. The sermon ends with these words:

The authority of music, what silences and holds us, is, then, one of the fullest parables we have of the authority of God; not in commanding and imposing from outside, but in asking for our time, so that it can become a time of mending and building. In that double gift – time given away, time given back – we are taken more deeply into the wisdom of God, and freed from the destructive illusion that we are supposed to be God. There is no wisdom for us if we cannot receive it as a gift; because the beginning of wisdom is to know we must come to the reality around us and the reality that sustains us in expectancy, with open hands, not with the lust for domination.

We open ourselves to the gift, yet it doesn't make us passive; it draws out our most strenuous energy. What we learn, in music as in the contemplative faith of which music is a part and also a symbol, is what it is to work with the grain of things, to work in the stream of God's wisdom. That is why contemplative faith makes us more not less human, human with the humanity of Jesus, in whom wisdom built a house in our midst; human in patience and expectant attentions, free to give because we have taken time to receive. Our busy ambition and our yearning for control are brought to judgement. The time we wanted to save for our obsessive busyness becomes the time in which grace brings us to our maturity – towards the fullness of Christ's stature and the liberty of God's wisdom.

George 4th century
Patron saint of England

With four dedications in Herefordshire (Brinsop, Burrington, Orleton, Woolhope) and two in Shropshire's part of the diocese (Clun and Pontesbury), St George is a popular dedication, although little is known about him. Probably a soldier living in Palestine at the beginning of the 4th century, he was martyred at Lydda about the year 304, the beginning of the Diocletian persecution, and he became known throughout the East as 'The Great Martyr'.

There were churches dedicated to St George before the Norman Conquest. The story of his slaying the dragon is probably due to his being mistaken in iconography for St Michael, who is also usually depicted wearing armour. In any case, George replaced Edward the Confessor (see 13 October) as patron saint of England following the Crusades, when returning soldiers brought back with them a renewed cult of St George. Edward III made St George patron of the Order of the Garter, and this seems finally to have confirmed his position. There are other links with Hereford, not least through the Audley Chapel in Hereford Cathedral. Here, the blue vault above the chapel is very similar indeed to that in St George's Chapel, Windsor. Perhaps this is hardly surprising – Edmund Audley (see 22 June) had the chapel built before his death and he was also a canon of Windsor. Indeed, Edward III himself, St George's great Windsor champion, stood in the Lady Chapel on 25 October 1349, when the body of St Thomas of Hereford was 'translated' to this spot (see 25 October).

St George is often associated with nationhood and patriotism. Two passages which ask us to look carefully what we mean by this:

Nationhood as a gift from God

In recent times it has been fashionable to talk of the levelling of nations, of the disappearance of different races in the melting-pot of contemporary civilisation. I do not agree with this opinion ... The disappearance of nations would have impoverished us no less than if all men had become alike, with one personality and one face.

Nations are the wealth of mankind, its collective personalities; the very least of them wears its own special colours and bears within itself a special facet of divine intention.

Alexander Solzhenitsyn 1918–2008

The paradox in patriotism

There is an ethical paradox which defies every but the most astute and sophisticated analysis. The paradox is that patriotism transmutes individual unselfishness into national egoism. Loyalty to the nation is a high form of altruism when compared with lesser loyalties and more parochial interests. It therefore becomes the vehicle of all the altruistic impulses and expresses itself, on occasion, with such fervour that the critical attitude of the individual towards the nation and its enterprises is almost completely destroyed ...

Unquestionably there is an alloy of projected self-interest in patriotic altruism. The man in the street, with his lust for power and prestige thwarted by his own limitations and the necessities of social life, projects his ego upon his nation and indulges his anarchic lusts vicariously. So the nation is at one and the same time a check upon, and a final vent for, the expression of individual egoism.

Reinhold Niebuhr 1892–1970

Renn Dickson Hampden 1793–1868

A doctrinal heretic?

It is sometimes said that the diocese of Hereford is a sleepy backwater of rural charm. That may be so, but at least two of its bishops in the last 150 years have caused seismic ripples throughout the Church of England, and Hereford has become, for a while, synonymous with radical heresy! Renn Dickson Hampden was, twice in his career, vilified for his perceived unorthodoxy. At Oxford he was one of the Noetic theologians, insisting that scriptural revelation was rightly supplemented by evidence of divine dispensation in the natural world, and that both were properly understood in the context of human reason. In 1834 he became professor of moral philosophy at Oxford and in 1836 he was nominated by Lord Melbourne as Regius Professor. This caused a storm of protest, not least from Pusey and other Oxford dons, who opposed his liberal views on the admission of Dissenters to the University. The controversy marked the emergence of parties within the Church of England, separating high-churchmen from liberal Anglicans. Hampden was greatly hurt by the controversy, which became personal – some even suggested that his Bampton Lectures were substantially the work of Joseph Blanco White, the lapsed Spanish Catholic. The criticism was such that he lost confidence in his work and thereafter published little. He did, however, do much to reform the teaching of theology at Oxford. In 1847 Lord John Russell offered Hampden the see of Hereford. Again, there was much protest, and 13 bishops remonstrated with the prime minister. At Hampden's election as bishop, several prebendaries absented themselves and Dean John Merewether (see 4 April) voted against the new appointment. When he arrived at Hereford, Hampden threw himself into his diocesan duties; he founded the Diocesan Education Society in 1849 and encouraged church building, also securing the reopening of the cathedral after its restoration. As he grew older, his orthodoxy became more pronounced and he was a critic of the liberal-minded book *Essays and Reviews* following its publication in 1860. Hampden died in London on 23 April 1868 and is buried in Kensal Green Cemetery.

For all the furore of his appointment, Hampden turned out to be an able and pastorally minded bishop in his diocese. Perhaps he fell in love with the 'understated' nature of our diocese, with its self-effacing beauty. A Diocesan History, *written in 1888 by Henry Wright Phillott, ends with a charming summary of what successive bishops, clergy and people have loved about this place:*

The diocese of Hereford has seldom held, and is never likely to hold, a very conspicuous place among the dioceses of the Church of England, but it has a claim to represent that unobtrusive phase of life which is expressed to us in the notion of family rather than of a great community. Wide in extent, comparatively scanty in population, not reaching in this respect the amount of many of our larger towns, the diocese of Hereford is nevertheless, nay, for this very reason, within reach of influences to which such as are more populous and busy must be in great measure strangers. These are of a more personal and domestic kind, not so heroic and impressive as elsewhere, perhaps, not so fruitful in good deeds as is sometimes the case, but containing elements more amenable to kindly personal influence, and more favourable to individual direction of character. Let us hope that while in the course of God's good providence the faults incidental to such a population may be corrected, and the standard of their character raised, of which there is only too much need, these favourable elements may not be crushed or frittered away by the hungry tide of modern civilisation.

Thomas Symonds *c.*1735–91

Architect blamed for the collapse of the cathedral's west front

The 18th century tells a story of woe in the chapter's handling of the cathedral's fragile fabric. In 1777, following many warnings (see Nathan Wetherell, 17 April), Thomas Symonds, a local mason, was appointed as Surveyor of the Fabric. His early training provided him with design skills and he did important work for Richard Knight at Downton Castle (see 11 February), with major schemes at the county gaol, the infirmary and Allensmore Court. Symonds did his best to repair the ailing cathedral. In 1777 he raised scaffolding to 'repair the Pannels of the Groins of the Roof of the Nave' and in the following spring he delivered a 'memorial of repairs necessary to be done to the West Tower', but time passed and it was not until 1781 that the chapter made a determined effort to save the building. Symonds repaired the west tower with local stone but did not get to the root of the problem, being criticised as 'injudicious and unskilful'. After the fall of the west tower and part of the nave, the dean and chapter were roundly criticised, one critic attributing the blame to 'the woeful idleness and neglect of the canons of the see'. The chapter, in turn, blamed the hapless Symonds and he was asked to resign – and therefore the guiding hand of the man most familiar with the quirks of the ancient cathedral was removed.

Thomas Symonds was victim of a culture of blame which permeated the cathedral community at the end of the 18th century. To blame another is one of the less attractive sides of human nature, but it can have a humorous side, as this poem makes clear:

When things go wrong it's rather tame
To find we are ourselves to blame,
It gets the trouble over quicker
To go and blame things on the Vicar.
The Vicar, after all, is paid
To keep us bright and undismayed.
The Vicar is more virtuous too
Than lay folks such as me and you.
He never swears, he never drinks,
He never *should* say what he thinks.
His collar is the wrong way round,
And that is why he's simply bound
To be the sort of person who
Has nothing very much to do
But take the blame for what goes wrong
And sing in tune at Evensong.

John Betjeman 1906–84, 'Blame the Vicar', *Church Poems* (1981)

Richard Delamaine the Younger 1627–57

Seventeenth-century 'firebrand'

Here's a complicated character if ever there was one! Baptized at St Andrew's Holborn in March 1627, we first hear of Delamaine when he claimed to have attended Oxford University. When challenged as to which college, he brazenly replied: 'Emmanuel' (of course, a *Cambridge* college). He had an eye for publicity and made a first 'public appearance' with a presentation to the House of Lords in 1642, of a tabulated ready-reckoner, setting out the rates at which investments might be made in the provinces of Ireland. By 1648 he had become established as a parliamentarian preacher in Hereford, but he soon made enemies, one writing a pamphlet which criticised Delamaine's 'notional frenzy' and 'familistical carriages'. In Hereford he became an intimate of the governor, Lieutenant-Colonel Wroth Rogers, and was given responsibility for the castle; at the same time he secured the benefices of Aymestrey, Little Hereford and Longtown. In 1652, he secured, with the help of Wroth Rogers, the mastership of St Ethelbert's Hospital in Hereford, and became manager of Tomson's Charity. He gained a position of responsibility in the cathedral itself and painted titles on the cathedral stalls – 'Taurus' on the Governor's seat, 'Gemini' on the seats of the mayor and aldermen and 'Aries' on those of the garrison officers. Delamaine married a woman called Mary, described as a serving woman to the wife of Wroth Rogers, and indeed, their son was christened Wroth. Delamaine made his will on this day in 1657 and died some time between then and 14 August when the document was proved. Although most thought of him as an ignorant and immoral man, his friends thought differently and he was buried in the cathedral, a monument in the bishop's cloister describing him as 'a minister of the gospel'.

One of the criticisms of Richard Delamaine was that he was sparing with the truth – whether it be regarding his university education or his ability to serve as a minister of religion. In this passage, the vital importance of truth is emphasised:

The theological quest for truth involves us first in the discipline of being true to ourselves, of maintaining intellectual honesty and integrity; it involves us next in the discipline of being true to our neighbour, in the openness and reciprocity of our common quest for the truth; it involves us finally in being true to truth, to that living truth that is already there ahead of us and that we could not find unless it drew us to itself. Certainly, when we use the name 'God', one thing we must mean by that name is truth, the final reality that is uncovered when all illusions and errors have been stripped away. The desire for truth implanted in us is the desire to know the real, and 'God' is our name for that which is most real. The desire for truth is the desire for God. St Augustine wrote: 'where I found truth, there found I my God, who is the truth itself. And thus since the time I learned thee, thou abidest in my memory; and there do I find thee whensoever I call thee to remembrance, and delight in thee.'

John Macquarrie 1919–2007, *Paths in Spirituality* (1972)

A prayer for truth

Dear Lord, give me the truths which are veiled by the doctrines and articles of faith, which are masked by the pious words of sermons and books. Let my eyes penetrate the veil, and tear off the mask, that I can see your truth face to face.

John of the Cross 1542–91

DOROTHY CONSTANCE BAYLIFF PEEL 1868–1934

Herefordshire's own Mrs Beeton

THE GLORIOUS CAVALCADE of celebrity cookery presenters takes us back through Jamie Oliver, Gary Rhodes, 'The Galloping Gourmet', Fanny Craddock, Philip Harben, and ultimately to Mrs Beeton herself. A lesser known though no less influential character was born on this day in 1868 at Ganarew, between Ross and Monmouth. Constance Bayliff had a frugal upbringing and moved to London where she entered the world of journalism, writing for *The Queen*. In 1894 she married Charles Peel and the couple moved to Dewsbury, Yorkshire. There she drew on her experience of setting up home in her first book, *The new home: treating of the arrangement, decoration and furnishing of a house of moderate size to be maintained by moderate income* (1898). She later became editor and director of *Hearth and Home, Woman* and *Myra's Journal*, published a series of popular cookery books and was managing director of Beeton & Co from 1903 to 1906. Other interests included setting up a fashion business (which boasted famous clients such as Ellen Terry) and writing novels – her first, *The Hat Shop*, was published in 1914. Constance later became editor of the *Daily Mail* women's page and continued to write books on household management – *Marriage on Small Means* (1914) and *The Labour Saving House* (1917). During the First World War she organized various clubs for the troops and worked with Maud Pember Reeves as co-director of women's services for the Ministry of Food, delivering 176 addresses promoting the economical use of food. Above all, she is remembered as one who furthered the cause of women's independence, not least their right to work, and insisted that she worked out of necessity as well as pleasure, to provide for her two children, to support an aunt and to save for her old age.

Mrs Peel followed in the footsteps of the more famous Mrs Beeton. The latter is sometimes criticised for her class-conscious writings, but as this passage shows, much of her fretting was to ensure that everybody was given his or her due honour and that all should feel included and at ease:

Provided care has been taken in choosing congenial guests, and that in a mixed party one sex does not preponderate, a well arranged picnic is one of the pleasantest forms of entertainment.

Watch carefully not to provide too much of one thing and too little of another: avoid serving plenty of salad and no dressing; two or three legs of lamb and no mint sauce; an abundance of wine and no corkscrew; and suchlike little mistakes. Given a happy party of young people bent on enjoyment, these are trifles light as air, which serve rather to increase the fun than diminish it; but, on the other hand, the party may not all be young and merry – it may be very distasteful to some to have to suffer these inconveniences.

The easiest way to arrange that there should be nothing wanting, is to make out a menu, adding all the little etceteras. It is advisable to estimate quantities extravagantly, for nothing is more annoying that to find everything exhausted and guests hungry. Following is a list of articles that should be provided in addition to the repast:

Wines, bottled beer, soda-water, lemonade, plates, knives, forks, spoons, glasses, tumblers, table-cloths, serviettes, glass cloths, pepper, cayenne, salt, mustard, oil, vinegar, caster sugar, corkscrews, and champagne-opener. A chafing dish and accessories are very useful accompaniments to a picnic.

Isabella Beeton 1836–65, *Beeton's Book of Household Management* (1861)

Florence Wallace Pomeroy 1843/4–1911

Dress reform campaigner

Women wearing trousers today raise few eyebrows, but it was a different matter in the late 19th century. More liberal attitudes were encouraged by the woman we remember today. By marrying James Spencer Pomeroy, Florence Pomeroy became Viscountess Harberton and she used her influence to change attitudes. An article in *The Queen* described her divided skirts, an enthusiasm which she commended to the National Health Society in 1882. Her passion for 'divided' garments extended to 'The Harberton' – patented divided petticoats – while, more daringly, in 1893, according to the *Manchester Guardian,* members of Lady Harberton's 'Short skirt League' pledged to wear walking dresses at least five inches above the ground! Her daring knew no bounds. In 1899, while out with the Cyclists' Touring Club, and wearing her customary dress of flat shoes, voluminous knickerbockers and big hat, she was refused entry to the coffee room of the Hautboy Hotel in Ockham, Surrey. The club sued the landlady, a Mrs Sprague, who was found not guilty as Lady Harberton had declined the offer of a meal in the bar-parlour. The press had a field day and the episode did much to raise awareness of dress reform. It became a test case on the rights of travellers, and cycle enthusiasts still meet in her memory at the Hautboy. She certainly did much for the cause of women; she was an ardent suffragist and constantly drove home her key message – that female clothing devalued women. She wrote in the *Rational Dress Gazette* for 1889: 'no one is free who is unable at least to have the unrestricted use of her own limbs, and woman's present appearance is the perpetual expression of this fact, and of her abject acquiescence in a humiliating position'. The Harbertons spent much time in Herefordshire, renting Lyston Court, Ross and, in later years, houses in the Malvern area. Lady Harberton died on 30 April 1911 and was buried at Brookwood Cemetery, Surrey.

A fashion art historian reflects on changes in fundamental principles with regard to women's clothing in the early 20th century:

The search for new, rational clothing led to harsh criticism of prevailing fashions. Ladies' clothing 'attested to intellectual and spiritual incapacity', thundered the painter and architect Paul Schultze-Naumburg, and made 'an unsightly blemish on our culture and irreconcilable with 20th-century intellectual enlightenment'. Although this meant that clothing reformers of both sexes saw a fundamental contradiction in terms between women's situation and enlightenment, they also scornfully condemned women who wore corsets: 'If women had so much as a smattering of real taste for all their vanity, they would never look at corsets again.' Fashion, they maintained, was a 'sin', a strategy for making 'method out of madness', sniffed Pudor, for whom clothing represented 'human incarceration', 'something unnatural' and 'negation of life itself'. Maria van Halde, who joined forces with her husband, Henry van de Velde, to create clothes which were presented to the public at the most important exhibitions mounted by the clothing reform movement, regarded fashion as 'led greatly astray, to a great extent guilty of all the ugliest things the century had accumulated'.

Elke Gaugele, *Femme Fashion 1780–2004*

Francis Godwin 1562–1633

Hereford's 17th-century Jules Verne

If we think Jules Verne was ahead of his time in his *Journey to the Centre of the Earth*, we can marvel still more that such 'science-fiction' was available 300 years before Verne – and from the pen of a learned bishop of Hereford! Francis Godwin first came to prominence through his interest in historical and antiquarian studies. In 1590, he accompanied William Camden into Wales in search of antiquities for his revised edition of *Britannia*. Godwin's most important work was *A catalogue of the bishops of England, since the first planting of Christian religion in this island* and the work led to his appointment as bishop of Llandaff in 1602. The catalogue was translated into Latin and this achievement earned Godwin promotion to the wealthier see of Hereford in 1617. As a diocesan bishop he was criticised for neglecting visitations – indeed he spent much time on his own writing, advocating the need for a definitive national history. *The Man in the Moone* is probably an early work, describing Gonsales, a Spaniard, who trains large swans, or gansas, to carry an 'engine' to the moon, where he meets with all kinds of adventures. Godwin had far-sighted views on gravity and what it requires to launch a machine into space. He also discussed the motions of the planets, using views developed from those of Copernicus. It seems that Herefordshire was home to several famous explorers in the 16th century. Some had sailed with Thomas Cavendish on his voyage around the world between 1586 and 1588. One Herefordian, Robert Hues (see 21 May), may even have written one of the accounts of the voyage, and he was certainly at Oxford at the same time as Godwin. All these were influences on Godwin and helped to form his world view, encouraging him to write a remarkable book which is both a cover for scientific debate and a political call for greater seaborne exploration. Godwin died at the bishop of Hereford's palace at Whitbourne and was buried on this day in 1633, in the chancel of the church there.

Godwin's description of Gonsales' arrival on the moon is remarkable for its assumptions about extra-terrestrial beings. To Godwin, these creatures were not 'little green men' or 'daleks' but simply extraordinary versions of humanity – who had naturally heard of the Christian faith, and recognised it, as this excerpt makes clear:

It remaineth now that I speake of the Demeanure of this people, who presenting themselves unto me upon the sudden and that in such extraordinary fashion as I have declared; being struck with great amasement, I crossed my selfe, and cried out Jesus Maria.

No sooner was the word Jesus out of my mouth, but young and old, fell all downe upon their knees, (at which I not a little rejoyced) holding up both their hands on high, and repeating all certaine words which I understood not. Then presently they all arising, one that was farre the tallest of them came unto me, and embraced me, with great kindnesse, and giving order (as I partly perceived) unto some of the rest to stay by my Birds, he tooke me by the hand, and leading me toward the foote of the hill, brought me to his dwelling, being more than half a league from the place where I first alighted.

It was such a building for beauty and hugenesse, as all our world cannot shew any neere comparable to it. Yet such I saw afterwards elsewhere, as this might seeme but a Cottage in respect of them. There was not a doore about the house, that was not 30 foote high, and twelve in breadth. The rooms were betweene 40 and 50 foote in height, and so all other proportions answerable.

Francis Godwin, *The Man in the Moone* (publ. 1638)

Alfred Edward Housman 1859–1936

Poet & classical scholar

The name of A E Housman will forever be associated with his great work *A Shropshire Lad*. In fact, in childhood, he rarely visited the county from his home town of Bromsgrove, Worcestershire but insisted that 'its hills were our western horizon'. After Bromsgrove School, Housman attended St John's College, Oxford, but failed to distinguish himself academically, partly, perhaps, as his attentions were focused on his love for a college contemporary, Moses Jackson – a love, unrequited, that consumed him throughout his life. Housman worked for ten years as a higher division clerk in the trade marks registry of the Patents Office. At the same time, however, he was studying in the evenings at the British Museum library and by 1882 had begun to publish papers on textual criticism of Greek and Latin authors. This was to prove his life's work, and, on the strength of his published work, he applied for, and was offered, the professorial chair of Latin at University College, London, where he stayed for 19 years. At this time he turned to poetry and in 1896 published *A Shropshire Lad* – 63 lyrics which soon won universal admiration through their poignant themes of nature, love, war and death, and the directness of their language and rhythms. Meanwhile, his academic work continued and he became professor of Latin at Cambridge in 1910, as well as being a fellow of Trinity College.

Although a bachelor don with a reputation for being 'distant', he nevertheless was known as a raconteur and loved to travel to France for holidays, one Paris restaurant naming a dish after him (*barbue Housman*). After *A Shropshire Lad,* he was reluctant to write more, but did write the defiantly titled *Last Poems* in 1920. He died on this day in 1936 and his ashes were interred against the north wall of St Laurence's Church, Ludlow. In 1985 a statue of him was unveiled at Bromsgrove and in 1996 a memorial was erected in Poets' Corner, Westminster Abbey. His poetry has an enduring appeal, made even more famous by its setting to music by early 20th-century composers such as Butterworth and Somervell.

Housman's themes of deep pessimism and preoccupation with death, as well as his magical descriptive powers, are well seen in this poem:

White in the moon the long road lies,
The moon stands blank above;
White in the moon the long road lies
That leads me from my love.

Still hangs the hedge without a gust,
Still, still the shadows stay:
My feet upon the moonlit dust
Pursue the ceaseless way.

The world is round, so travellers tell,
And straight though reach the track,
Trudge on, trudge on, 'twill all be well,
The way will guide one back.

But 'ere the circle homeward hies,
Far, far must it remove:
White in the moon the long road lies
That leads me from my love.

A E Housman, *A Shropshire Lad* (1896)

1

May

William de Wicumbe and William de Winton late 13th century

Leominster monks & composers

The arrival of Spring is traditionally heralded on May Day and has been celebrated in poetry and music from time immemorial. One of the most famous pieces greeting Spring possibly had its roots in Leominster Priory.

Sumer is icumen in
Loudly sing cuckoo
Groweth seed and bloweth mead
And springs the wood anew
Sing cuckoo!

It is a canon or round in six parts, having not only an English but also a Latin text. Research suggests that it was written during the period 1261–5. Two names are associated with the canon – both named William and both monks of Reading Abbey, who spent time at Leominster Priory. William de Wicumbe seems to have spent several years at Leominster as precentor and was viewed there as a troublesome monk. He was employed mainly in copying manuscripts, and his asides and margin notes give glimpses of the petty squabbles and rivalries in the small and enclosed community. One piece of copying work was apparently halted because of 'malicious tongues'. But he was more than a mere copyist, and there are several examples of his work as a composer. William de Winton (or Winchester) was, like Wicumbe, often in trouble with the authorities. On a visit to Leominster Priory during the 1270s, he was brought before the bishop of Hereford for incontinence with a number of women, including a nun of Limebrook Priory. Despite all this he became sub-prior in 1282. He was a man of wide interests, writing treatises on theology, arithmetic, geometry and astronomy. He was certainly a composer of polyphonic alleluias and there are 40 settings identified in various sources, though only one is restored completely. Some of his works appear in the *Worcester Fragments* – a collection of 59 manuscript leaves, representing about one third of the total surviving polyphony of the 13th century. Recent research suggests that, if Wicumbe copied *Sumer is icumen in*, Winton may well have composed it.

Spring has always inspired poets and composers. Here, Gerard Manley Hopkins writes ecstatically of the wonder of nature as it breaks into new life after the winter, and sees in the new season a glimpse of a world unsullied by the sin of humankind:

Nothing is so beautiful as Spring –
When weeds, in wheels, shoot long and lovely and lush;
Thrush's eggs look little low heavens, and thrush
Through the echoing timber does so rinse and wring
The ear, it strikes like lightnings to hear him sing;
The glassy peartree leaves and blooms, they brush
The descending blue; that blue is all in a rush
With richness; the racing lambs too have fair their fling.

What is all this juice and all this joy?
A strain of the earth's sweet being in the beginning
In Eden garden. – Have, get, before it cloy,
Before it cloud, Christ, lord, and sour with sinning,
Innocent mind and Mayday in girl and boy,
Most, O maid's child, thy choice and worthy the winning.

Gerard Manley Hopkins 1844–89, 'Spring'

May 2

Thomas Bray 1658–1730

Founder of SPCK

Many of our cathedral cities had, until recently, SPCK bookshops which provided religious and educational material of all kinds. Less well-known is the fact that the leading light behind the society which inspired them was born in our midst. Baptized on this day in 1658, at the parish church of Marton near Chirbury in Shropshire, Thomas Bray attended Oswestry Grammar School and Oxford University, and was ordained, becoming curate near Bridgnorth. Early on in his ministry, he became concerned at the lack of Anglican religious education among young people, not least with the challenges the church faced from both Roman Catholics and Nonconformists. Through Bray's enthusiasm, parish libraries were founded both in this country and in Maryland in America, with which colony he had become connected. From these beginnings, a larger enterprise was begun and the Society for Promoting Christian Knowledge was founded in 1698. SPCK distributed religious literature not only in parishes but also in prisons and workhouses, and supported the establishment of hospitals and infirmaries. Overseas missionary work was extended with Bray's foundation, in 1701, of the Society for the Propagation of the Gospel in Foreign Parts (SPG), with the archbishop of Canterbury becoming its president.

Bray continued his parochial ministry in London as rector of St Botolph's, Aldgate, where he was famed for his generosity to the poor. He was also a prolific writer and historian. A fellow writer described him as 'So great a master of the Papal history, that few authors could be presum'd with equal accuracy and learning to trace the origin and growth of those exorbitant powers which are claimed by the See of Rome'. Bray died in 1730 and was buried at St Botolph's. Without doubt, he had a powerful influence on the Church of England's role in education and social welfare.

Attitudes towards missionary work have changed greatly in the 200 years since Bray's death. Here we see two very contrasting pieces of writing – one proclaiming an uncompromising Christian message, and the other showing a greater sensitivity towards adherents of other faiths:

Founding the Society for the Propagation of the Gospel in Foreign Parts

1. That the design of propagating the Gospel in foreign parts does chiefly and principally relate to the conversion of heathens and infidels, and therefore that branch of it ought to be prosecuted preferably to all others.

2. That, in consequence thereof, immediate care be taken to send itinerant missionaries to preach the Gospel among the Six Nations of the Indians according to the primary intentions of the late King William of glorious memory.

Two resolutions of the SPG, 20 April 1710

To deny religious pluralism and to affirm the centrality, the decisiveness, the absoluteness of this one name [Jesus Christ], is to affirm that – in the last analysis – the human story is one story, not a medley of different stories. It is to affirm that we belong together in one history and that this history has a shape, a meaning, and a goal. But that affirmation can be made without incurring the accusation of imperialism only because it is made, not in the name of the Christian church, but in the name of the one who reigns from the tree, the one who has made peace by the blood of the cross, the one who has alone broken the power of sin and death and pierced that barrier that divides the time of our human history from the eternal of God in whom is our home.

Lesslie Newbigin 1909–98

Joshua Thomas 1719–97

Particular Baptist minister & historian

Born in Carmarthenshire, Joshua Thomas received a rudimentary education in his home parish, then left for Hereford in 1739 to pursue an apprenticeship, possibly as a mercer. Very soon, he had become a Baptist and was baptized by total immersion at Leominster in May 1740. On his return from Herefordshire to his native Wales, Thomas became closely involved with local Baptist churches and began a preaching ministry in the Olchon Valley and at Capel-y-ffin. In 1754, after ordination, he accepted a call to the ministry of the Baptist congregation at Leominster, where he stayed for the rest of his life. It is as an historian of the Baptist movement that Thomas is particularly remembered. His *Brief History of the Baptist Church at Leominster* led to what was probably his most accomplished work, *A History of the Baptists among the Welsh* (1778). This work had involved travelling through Wales in 1776 and, with its 468 pages, it became the principal source for early Welsh Baptist historians for generations to come. His next work, the two-volume manuscript *Ecclesiastical History of Wales*, described the legends which accompanied the coming of Christianity to Wales and its subsequent history up to the Puritan ascendancy. Along with his contribution as denominational historian, Thomas was a key figure in 18th-century Baptist life in the east Midlands as well as in Wales. His long correspondence with his close friend and colleague, Benjamin Francis, another expatriate Welshman, affords a fascinating glimpse of mid 18th-century Dissenting life. He was a powerful writer, arguing for doctrinal orthodoxy, and his own translation of the London Baptists' 1689 Confession was widely used. His family continued in the Baptist tradition and one son, Timothy Thomas (1752–1821), became chairman of the Particular Baptist Fund which eventually became Regent's Park College in Oxford.

Joshua Thomas himself died on 25 August 1797 and is buried in the Etnam Street churchyard in Leominster.

Joshua Thomas' survey of Baptist history and writings would no doubt have included reference to what has become the most popular writing of a 17th-century Baptist:

After this, it was noised abroad, that Mr *Valiant-for-truth* was taken with a Summons by the same Post as the other; and had this for a Token that the Summons was true, *That his Pitcher was broken at the Fountain* [Ecclesiastes 12:6]. When he understood it, he called for his Friends, and told them of it. Then said he, I am going to my Fathers, and tho' with great Difficulty I am got hither, yet now I do not repent me of all the Trouble I have been at to arrive where I am. *My Sword,* I give to him that shall Succeed me in my Pilgrimage; and my *Courage* and *Skill,* to him that can get it. My *Marks* and *Scars* I carry with me, to be a Witness for me, that I have fought his Battles who now will be my Rewarder. When the Day that he must go hence was come, many accompanied him to the River-side, into which as he went, he said *Death, where is thy Sting?* And as he went down deeper, he said *Grave, where is thy Victory?* So he passed over, and all the Trumpets sounded for him on the other side.

John Bunyan 1628–88, *Pilgrim's Progress* (1678)

Sir Robert Smirke 1780–1867

Architect of Eastnor Castle

Two of Herefordshire's great early 19th-century buildings, Eastnor Castle and the Shire Hall, Hereford, were designed by a great architect of the period – one whose Greek Revival style and love of the monumental scale placed him in the forefront of the architectural world for decades. Apprenticed to the architect John Soane, the young Smirke gained a taste for the classical tradition – a taste fed by his taking the Grand Tour in 1802. On this journey he visited Athens and was outraged by Lord Elgin's removal of the Parthenon friezes. Back in England, his architectural practice developed – his genial manner and reliability ensuring that he was never short of wealthy clients. His Shire Hall at Hereford (1815–17) makes great use of the Doric portico, while Eastnor Castle (1812–20) made use of contemporary building features – cast-iron stanchions, beams and girders, previously used only in industrial buildings. Smirke spent three weeks in February 1812 with Lord Somers, discussing plans for Eastnor, which cost a staggering £100,000 to build. On the death of James Wyatt in 1813, Smirke became part of the establishment with contemporaries Nash and Soane and was appointed as joint surveyor of the Office of Works. His new eminence led to even greater commissions in London – the General Post Office, St Martin-le-Grand (1824–9) and the British Museum (1823–46). He was certainly one of the most successful of 19th-century architects, though some have criticised his arguably small repertoire of classical motifs as dull. One critic found him not only complacent but an 'Architectural manufacturer ... a mechanic with no feeling for art, but working for money'. Others found him 'serene, friendly, communicative' and 'provokingly rational'.

Smirke's fame came to a climax with his completion of the British Museum. A few years earlier, he had enhanced his reputation with the designing of temporary rooms (1815–16) for the housing of the Elgin Marbles at the Museum. It was perhaps ironic that Smirke, who had been so outraged by the removal of the Marbles, should in time have so compromised his principles as to design a London home for them! He was not the only one to be outraged by their removal from Athens. The poet Byron had this to say:

'Mortal!' –'twas thus she spake – 'that blush of shame
Proclaims thee Briton, once a noble name;
First of the mighty, foremost of the free,
Now honour'd less by all, and least by me;
Chief of thy foes shall Pallas still be found.
Seek'st thou the cause of loathing? Look around.
Lo! here, despite of war and wasting fire,
I saw successive tyrannies expire.
'Scaped from the ravage of the Turk and Goth,
Thy country sends a spoiler worse than both.
Survey this vacant, violated fane;
Recount the relics torn that yet remain:
These Cecrops placed, this Pericles adorn'd,
That Adrian rear'd when drooping Science mourn'd.
What more I owe let gratitude attest –
Know, Alaric and Elgin did the rest.
That all may learn from whence the plunderer came,
The insulted wall sustains his hated name.'

Lord Byron 1788–1824, 'The Curse of Minerva' (1811)

Asaph early 7th century

Bishop in North Wales

The diocese of Hereford borders three Welsh dioceses – Monmouth, Swansea and Brecon, and St Asaph. Today we remember Asaph, a disciple of St Kentigern, who founded a monastic settlement on the banks of the river Elwy. Asaph is reputed to have brought his master live coals in his apron, without its being burnt or damaged in any way. He worked principally in Flintshire with Llanasa as his centre. When Kentigern was recalled to Strathclyde to become bishop of Glasgow, Asaph was unanimously appointed bishop of Llanelwy (which later became known as St Asaph). There, he endowed the cathedral, and there, centuries later, the Normans established a territorial see. Several churches and a few wells (including the second largest in Wales, called Ffynnon Asa) are dedicated to Asaph, and for many years a fair was held on his feast in his cathedral town.

Here, Gerard Manley Hopkins speaks of the beauty of the valley of the river Elwy, where Asaph made his home:

I remember a house where all were good
To me, God knows, deserving no such thing:
Comforting smell breathed at very entering,
Fetched fresh, as I suppose, off some sweet wood.
That cordial air made those kind people a hood
All over, as a bevy of eggs the mothering wing
Will, or mild nights the new morsels of Spring:
Why, it seemed of course; seemed of right it should.

Lovely the woods, waters, meadows, combes, vales,
All the air things wear that build this world of Wales;
Only the inmate does not correspond:
God, lover of souls, swaying considerate scales,
Complete thy creature dear O where it fails,
Being mighty a master, being a father and fond.

Gerard Manley Hopkins 1844–89,' In the Valley of the Elwy'

Asaph reminds us of the importance of fire as a symbol in our faith:

You are the fire that ever burns without being consumed; you consume in your heat all the soul's self-love; you are the fire which takes away cold; with your light you illuminate me so that I may know all your truth. Clothe me, clothe me with yourself, eternal truth, so that I may run this mortal life with true obedience, and with the light of your most holy faith.

St Catherine of Siena 1347–80

William Langland c.1332–99

Poet & visionary

Two places in our area claim William Langland as a son of their community – Cleobury Mortimer and Ledbury. It is true that in 1550, when Robert Crowley published the first printed edition of Langland's works, he mentions 'Cleybirie' as the birthplace, but his statement that it is 8 miles from the Malvern Hills (Cleobury is 23 miles away) suggests that 'Cleybirie' had become substituted for Ledbury. William probably attended the priory school at Great Malvern or Little Malvern. His home was at Langland in Colwall parish on the Ledbury boundary, where he possibly lived with relations. On 20 December 1348 he was ordained an acolyte in the parish church of Bromyard when he was 16 or 17 years old. He is sometimes called Robert, but never used the name himself, calling himself Will or Long Will. He lived in the frugal and perilous times of the Black Death and the years of repression and poverty of the labourers which preceded the Peasants' Revolt. In his poetry he wrote about the lower orders while his contemporary Chaucer wrote of those in higher places, and his greatest work, *Piers the Plowman*, reflects his sympathy for the under-privileged. Later in his life William went to London. He had no reputation and could not advance in the church because of his illegitimacy. He adopted the family name of Langland or Longland from the place where he had spent many years of his life. He mentioned Malvern only four times in his writings, but there is considerable significance on each occasion and in his old age his mind no doubt reverted to the scenes of his youth on the Malvern Hills.

The Vision of Piers Plowman *tells how William, weary of wandering, sleeps under a broad bank beside a little stream on the Malvern Hills one May morning and how he has a marvellous dream. In his account of it he gives a rich picture of 14th-century life, work and characters. Ploughmen, bishops, lawyers, burgesses, cooks and taverners are all in the tapestry created by Langland:*

In a summer season when the sun was warm,
I dressed myself in the garb of a shepherd,
In the dress of a hermit without holy works,
Went abroad in the world to hear of new wonders.
But on a May morning on Malvern Hills
A wonder befell me; it seemed of fairyland,
I was weary with wandering and sought out my rest
Beneath a broad bank by the side of a stream.
And as I lay and leaned and gazed in the waters
I fell unto a slumber for beauty of the sound –
There I dreamed a marvellous dream
That I was in a wilderness, I knew not where.
And as I looked to the East, to the sun in the heavens
I saw a tower on a mound skilfully formed,
Beneath it a deep valley with a dungeon inside;
Ditches deep and dark and dreadful to see.
Between them I saw a fair field of folk
Of all classes of men, the lowly and the rich
Working and wandering as the world demands.

Thomas Dingley d.1695

Antiquary & artist

Some of the most fascinating glimpses into Hereford Cathedral's past come from the pen of this man. Sometimes called Dineley, he was born in Southampton, became a student at Gray's Inn in London and later joined the household of Sir George Downing, on his appointment as ambassador to the States General of the United Provinces (now the Netherlands). Dingley travelled extensively in the British Isles and on the Continent, recording his journeys with pen-and-ink drawings and with terse comments. First came *Travails through the Low Countreys* in 1674 and then *Observations in a Voyage in the Kingdom of France* in 1675. None of these works was published during his lifetime. His journey to Ireland in 1680 records what he considered to be the outlandish customs and behaviour of its inhabitants! More 'archaeological' in its approach is the account he wrote of Wales as he accompanied Henry Somerset, duke of Beaufort, on his 1684 tour through the principality as Lord President of the Council in the Marches of Wales.

From Herefordshire's point of view, most interesting is his *History from Marble: being Ancient and Modern Funerall Monuments in England and Wales,* the last observation of which is dated 30 April 1684. Dingley records many Herefordshire churches, not least Dilwyn, where he lived, and there are descriptions of tombs and memorials as well as accounts of local customs and cider-making. From Dingley we discover what has long disappeared from Hereford Cathedral: the original memorial which surrounded the now stranded recumbent effigy of Bishop Westfaling (see 7 March) in the north transept; the paintings of both St Thomas of Hereford and St Thomas of Canterbury which flanked the Cantilupe tomb in the north transept; and the structure which covered St Ethelbert's Well on Castle Green. Wonderful to see is Dingley's sketch of the silver verger's mace, new when he drew it in the 1680s, and still used daily in cathedral services today. Most delightful of all is a sketch of the cloister of the vicars choral with a tree and a stag grazing nearby – not a beast we are accustomed to seeing there today! Dingley died at Louvain in Flanders in May 1695.

Tombs and memorials were of especial interest to Dingley. I find them fascinating myself. I recall, as a small choirboy at Harlington in Middlesex, gazing, week by week, from my choir-stall at a monument opposite me. It was in memory of a famous former rector, Joseph Trapp, who was also professor of poetry at Oxford and who was buried in the church in 1747. Apparently, Joseph Trapp's translations of various Latin and Greek authors were not universally praised. A contemporary, Abel Evans wrote the rather cutting epigram:

'Keep the Commandments, Trapp, and go no further
For it is written that thou shalt not murther'.

Whether good poetry or not, the verse on his tomb is touching and strikes several chords with Dingley and his fascination with funerary monuments and their message for us:

Death, Judgement, Heaven and Hell! Think, Christian, think!
You stand on Vast Eternity's dread Brink!
Faith and Repentance! Piety and Pray'r!
Despise this world, the next be all your Care:
Thus, while my tomb the solemn Silence breaks,
And to the Eye this cold dumb Marble speaks;
Tho' dead I preach: if e'er with ill success,
Living I strove th' important Truths to press;
Your precious, your immortal Souls to save;
Hear me at least, O hear me, from the grave.

Charles Booth d.1535

Builder of the cathedral's 'Booth Porch'

The remarkable outer north porch of Hereford Cathedral is a tour-de-force of late gothic architecture – completed just years before the onset of the Reformation. Booth became bishop of Hereford in 1516 and, like his predecessor, Richard Mayhew (see 18 April), he had much to do with Henry VIII's first wife, Catherine of Aragon. In 1520 he was one of three bishops chosen to accompany the queen to the Field of the Cloth of Gold near Calais. Here, a dazzling display of pageantry failed in its real purpose, which was to cement a friendship between the kings of England and France. Booth appears to have been a supporter of Queen Catherine in her appeal against the annulment wished for by the king, although Henry's order to Cromwell 'to make processe and to prosecute against Charles, bishop of Hereford, according to the laws, with all spede, if he do not agree' seems to have brought him into line. Back in his diocese, Booth held a synod, or convocation of clergy on 5 May 1519. In this, after processions around the city, citations were read to all 'in the vulgar tongue for their better understanding' on the behaviour of the clergy and on the life and morals of ordinands. In the same year, Booth completed the extension to the outer north porch, begun by his predecessor. The porch consisted of two storeys, the upper forming a chapel with an altar dedicated to the Blessed Virgin Mary. It is flanked by twin staircase turrets, one for ascent to the chapel, the other for descent. Adjoining the porch stands a doorway – now ruined – all that was built of the proposed oratory of the Good Shepherd, with the date 1519 inscribed on the lintel. The oratory was intended to be a place where worshippers might say a prayer before attending mass upstairs, but it was never completed. Booth died on 5 May 1535 and in his will directed that he should be buried at the north door, close to the porch which he constructed. He also made generous provision for a funeral feast – 'Let there be a good dinner for the ministry and for the mayor and townsmen, ten fat oxen, thirty fat sheep, ten calves, etc, if funds permit'. His personal bequests included a black gown and a year's wages to his household servants, to his nephew a feather bed and books of grammar, and his best gold ring to adorn the shrine of St Thomas of Hereford. He left a Netherlands tapestry depicting David and Nabal for the High Altar and 27 works to the cathedral.

One of the most evocative figures on Bishop Booth's sumptuous porch is of a pilgrim – an appropriate figure to welcome visitors as they enter the cathedral by its main door:

It was a friar of orders grey
Walked forth to tell his beads;
And he met with a lady fair
Clad in a pilgrim's weeds.

Now Christ thee save, thou reverend friar
I pray thee tell to me,
If ever at yon holy shrine
My true love thou didst see.

And how should I know your true love
From many another one?
Oh by his cockle hat and staff
And by his sandal shoon.

Anonymous medieval ballad

Sir William Gregory 1625–96

Judge & Speaker of the House of Commons

The magnificent refurbishment of How Caple church owes much to this man. Born near Fownhope, at his father's vicarage, he was educated at Hereford Cathedral School and was admitted to Gray's Inn in London. Returning to Herefordshire, he became steward to several manors, including Holme Lacy, and was later deputy steward of Hereford City. By 1660 he was among Hereford's ruling gentry and purchased the manor of How Caple as well as lands in Woolhope and Fownhope. His parliamentary career began as member for Weobley and in 1679 he became Speaker of the House of Commons. Although no forceful orator, it was during Gregory's tenure that the Habeas Corpus Act was passed. Some contemporaries insisted that he was 'firm, temperate, and impartial' while others saw him as 'inept in controlling the House'. Later, Gregory became a judge and presided at the trial of Sir Miles Stapleton for high treason. He continued his association with Hereford and in February 1682, with two other local squires, went to Whitehall, to present to Charles II 'the Humble Address of Hereford'. Removed from office during the reign of the Catholic James II, he returned after the Glorious Revolution, having subscribed £30 for Prince William of Orange. During the 1690s he refurbished the church at How Caple, and was buried there, having died in London in May 1696.

Gregory was part of a noble tradition of democratic government in this land. This passage reminds us of one of the most significant moments in our constitutional history:

It is a curious fact that the most important debate in English political history took place not in the House of Commons but in the fifteenth century parish church of St Mary in Putney. There, on 28th October 1647, and for the next two weeks, a group of about forty men met in informal conclave, and proceeded to invent modern politics – to invent, in fact, the public framework of the world in which nearly 3,000 million now live. There was no significance in the choice of the church; it was simply convenient. The men sat or stood around the bare communion table and kept their hats on, as Englishmen had learnt to do in the Commons House. The meeting was officially styled the General Council of the New Model Army, the force which had recently annihilated the armies of King Charles and was now the effective master of the whole country. It was a very representative gathering of Englishmen, covering all classes save the highest, and a wide variety of peace-time trades and callings. Every major political concept known to us today, all the assumptions which underlie the thoughts of men in the White House, or the Kremlin, or Downing Street, or in presidential mansions or senates or parliaments through five continents, were expressed or adumbrated in the little church of St Mary.

Paul Johnson b.1928, *The Offshore Islanders* (1972)

Prayers began to be said in the House of Commons in the early 16th century and were common practice by 1567. The present prayer, used daily, appears to date from the reign of Charles II.

Lord, the God of righteousness and truth, grant to our Queen and her government, to Members of Parliament and all in positions of responsibility, the guidance of your Spirit. May they never lead the nation wrongly through love of power, desire to please, or unworthy ideals, but laying aside all private interests and prejudices keep in mind their responsibility to seek to improve the condition of all mankind, so may your kingdom come and your name be hallowed.

John Birch 1615–91

Parliamentary army officer & politician

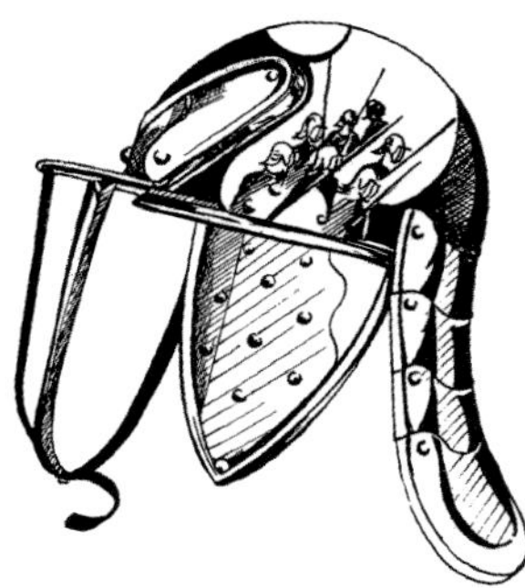

The figure of this man in Weobley church is a well-known memorial to one of the great military and political figures of the mid to late 17th century in Herefordshire. Beginning his career as a wine merchant in Bristol, Birch joined the Parliamentarian army and by 1644 had been given command of a regiment which helped the New Model Army to capture Bridgwater and Bristol. He won glory in the siege of Hereford on 18 December 1645, when he infiltrated the city with help from malcontents from the Hereford royalist garrison. He was appointed Governor of Hereford Castle, but earned the displeasure of the dean, Herbert Croft, for opening the cloister of the vicars choral to those made homeless by his men's attack. He became MP for Leominster in 1646 and purchased the Homme, where his family lived until 1661. Birch had a reputation for feathering his own nest and bought church lands in Herefordshire, notably the bishop's palace at Whitbourne – indeed, by 1670, Herbert Croft (see 18 May), now promoted from dean to bishop of Hereford, calculated that he had paid £2000 to Birch, whom he described as 'the greedy harpy'. In 1661 he purchased the Garnstone estate outside Weobley, and continued life as a politician and landowner.

His interests were wide – he oversaw attempts to implement the act for river Wye navigation and was a great supporter of religious comprehension, seeking to include moderate Nonconformists within the established church. He was, however, fiercely anti-papist and on 15 April 1678 he reported to the Commons upon the mood of Herefordshire where 'they are in fear of Popery and worse'. Birch was happy to change his political allegiances and gladly supported William of Orange, presenting him with £40 from the Herefordshire gentry.

He died on this day in 1691 at Garnstone and was buried at Weobley church. Even in death he stirred up controversy, for he had arranged for a monument to himself in the church in full military gear, which not only over-emphasized his military service but was also so built that its railings extended into the raised altar area. In 1694 Bishop Gilbert Ironside went personally to Weobley to deface the monument. It remains to this day with its inscription, but so also do the holes where the railings were ripped out!

Birch, with his fellow Parliamentarians, would no doubt have participated in the destruction of Popish adornments in many contemporary churches, including stained glass with its images. Here, a contemporary poet describes a window in Ely Cathedral where the shards of glass have been pieced together, thus making a parable of the fragmentary nature of life. A similar collection of stained glass fragments may be seen in the south aisle of Hereford Cathedral:

I am a window full of glass
pieced together from fragments blown apart in wars
where old conjunctions and a random placing
are lit just where the sun decides to pause.

A leering bit of face with twisted lips,
a bit of bread, and letters almost spelling 'holy',
a sheaf of corn, a leaf, and then the sun dips,
lighting Mary in her simple glory.

The misplaced jigsaw rearranged in parts
slips at the edges into bits of dream.
The sun is patient, and its darts
redeem my war-torn lack of scheme.

David Scott b.1947, *Piecing Together* (2005)

John Stanbury d.1474

Hereford's link with Eton

Bishop Stanbury's chapel on the north side of the cathedral is, for many, one of the most beautiful examples of perpendicular architecture in the land. It celebrates one of Hereford's most distinguished bishops. A Cornishman and a Carmelite friar, John Stanbury became confessor to Henry VI. As a result of the Wars of the Roses, Henry retained his title to the throne, but had little power, and instead devoted himself to religion and education. He founded King's College, Cambridge and Eton College and, while the tradition that Stanbury was first provost of Eton is unfounded, as his confessor he doubtless advised the king. He became bishop of Hereford in 1453 and was enthroned on 25 April. Stanbury did much to assist the vicars choral, who complained that their accommodation in Castle Street was unsatisfactory and that, 'through fear of evil-doers and inclemency of weather, many cannot go to celebrate divine service'. Stanbury provided a range of buildings to accommodate the 27 vicars, with a chapel, hall and kitchen. The cloisters remain one of the finest survivals of 15th-century domestic architecture in the country. Stanbury died on this day in 1474 in the Carmelite house at Ludlow and was buried in Hereford Cathedral. He had directed in his will that his body be buried 'on one side or the other of the high altar at the discretion of my executors' and a beautifully carved alabaster tomb, with weepers, was erected over the grave. Opposite the tomb, the Stanbury chantry chapel was built in about 1480, with fan-vaulting and stone panelling with emblematic shields. The chantry was refurbished in 1924 and glass by the Bromsgrove Guild of craftsmen was installed, depicting scenes from Stanbury's life, including his advice to Henry VI on the building of Eton College (see 14 December).

An 18th-century poet writes rhapsodically about the glories of life at Eton and reflects on human life:

Ye distant spires, ye antique towers
  That crown the watery glade,
Where grateful science still adores
  Her Henry's holy shade;
And ye, that from the stately brow
Of Windsor's heights th'expanse below
Of grove, of lawn, or mead survey,
Whose turf, whose shade, whose towers among
Wanders the hoary Thames along
  His silver-winding way:

To each his sufferings: all are men,
  Condemn'd alike to groan;
The tender for another's pain,
  Th'unfeeling for his own.
Yet ah! Why should they know their fate,
Since sorrow never comes too late,
And happiness too swiftly flies?
Thought would destroy their paradise.
No more; – where ignorance is bliss,
  'Tis folly to be wise.

Thomas Gray 1716–71, 'Ode on a distant Prospect of Eton College'

John Venn 1802–90

Friend to Hereford's poor

Si monumentum requiris, circumspice – 'if you seek his memorial, look around you'. The famous phrase on the tomb of Sir Christopher Wren in St Paul's Cathedral reminds us that while sometimes memorials may be made of marble, those which reflect a person's life and achievement are often expressed and remembered in human terms. This is certainly true of the Reverend John Venn. Buildings founded through Venn's influence still stand: the Working Boys' Home, the former soup kitchen, farm buildings, affordable housing, former washing baths. These are his most lasting monuments, reflecting one whose care for the poor and those on the margins is legendary. Born into a clerical family, which included in its circle William Wilberforce and members of the Clapham Sect, the young John embarked on a career in the East India Company. Ill-health forced his return home, and he trained as an Anglican priest. He became incumbent at St Peter's, Hereford in 1833 and never left the parish again, apart from the occasional visit to London and one overseas trip. Part of his parish included the area of St Owen's, one of the poorest parts of the city. In the terrible winters of the early 1840s, Venn organised a soup kitchen to help keep people alive and healthy. Realising that this was only dealing with the symptoms of poverty, he set about more radical work and established the Society for Aiding the Industrious. This soon created many activities in the Portfields area of Hereford, between what is now Bath Street and the hospital. The society built and ran a steam corn mill, producing corn at a cheaper rate than was charged elsewhere. There was a baths complex, heated by waste energy from the mill, and allotments, a model farm and gardens, and a coal store, where coal was bought in bulk and the cheaper prices were passed on to the poor in winter. Venn created a whole mixed welfare system for the poor of Hereford and he helped promote health and cleanliness, provided jobs and gave sound financial advice. In all this he was helped by his sister, Emelia, who died in 1881. A poor woman who stood at her graveside is quoted as saying, 'Well, she always had a smile ready for everyone!' John himself died on this day in 1890, and was buried alongside Emelia in the family grave in the burial ground off Commercial Road. He was 88 years old, and for 55 of those years he had carried his evangelism in practical ways to the people of Hereford, including the foundation and building of St James' church.

John Venn's influence continued after his death. The Society for Aiding the Industrious continued and bought land on which it built 'garden suburb' housing during the 1920s, with the Venn Close development of almshouses in the late 1930s and the Venn Memorial Homes, Friar Street, in the 1950s.

There is perhaps no better passage of scripture to reflect John Venn's following of his master, Jesus Christ, in practical love and compassion:

Jesus said: When the Son of man comes in his glory, and all the angels with him, then he will sit on his glorious throne. Before him will be gathered all the nations and he will separate them one from another as a shepherd separates the sheep from the goats and he will place the sheep at his right hand, but the goats at the left. Then the King will say to those at his right hand, 'Come, O blessed of my Father, inherit the kingdom prepared for you from the foundation of the world; for I was hungry and you gave me food, I was thirsty and you gave me drink, I was a stranger and you welcomed me, I was naked and you clothed me, I was sick and you visited me, I was in prison and you came to me.' Then the righteous will answer him, 'Lord, when did we see thee hungry and feed thee, or thirsty and give thee drink? And when did we see thee a stranger and welcome thee, or naked and clothe thee? And when did we see thee sick or in prison and visit thee?' And the King will answer them, 'Truly, I say to you, as you did it to one of the least of these my brethren, you did it to me.'

Matthew 25:31–40

Edward John Rapson 1861–1937
Sanskrit scholar

Edward Rapson was one of the finest scholars to have been educated at Hereford Cathedral School. Born on 12 May 1861, his father was a clergyman who later opened a school at Ledbury. He gained a Somerset award at the Cathedral School (scholarships endowed by the duchess of Somerset in the late 17th century for Old Herefordians at Brasenose College, Oxford and St John's College, Cambridge) and he went on to Cambridge, gaining a first in the classical tripos and in Indian languages and philology. In 1887, after a short spell as assistant librarian at the newly founded Indian Institute at Oxford, Rapson was appointed assistant keeper in the department of coins and medals at the British Museum, where he soon established himself as a leading authority on Indian numismatics, and published substantial works on the subject. He became professor of Sanskrit at University College, London, in 1903 and held the chair of Sanskrit at Cambridge from 1906 until just a year before his death, 30 years later. At Cambridge, he continued his scholarly work, publishing in 1914 *Ancient India from the Earliest Times to the First Century AD*, which provided a summary of all that was then known about early Indian history and culture. His second important undertaking at this time was editing the first two volumes of the *Cambridge History of India*, the first volume of which was published in 1922. Rapson is held to have been 'a scholar ... distinguished by great thoroughness and strict adherence to scientific method' – qualities that were no doubt initiated during his early years of classical training at Hereford.

Sanskrit takes us back to the very earliest language forms and to the very cradle of civilisation and yet, the themes that are found in these earliest poems are timeless – love, loss, life, death. Every generation has sought to interpret these, as we see in these two very ancient writings:

Blow, wind, to where my loved one is,
Touch her, and come and touch me soon:
I'll feel her gentle touch through you
And meet her beauty in the moon.
These things are much for one who loves –
A man can live by them alone –
That she and I breathe the same air
And the earth we tread is one. (From the *Ramayana*)

Look to this day – for it is life
the very life of life.
In its brief course lie all
the realities and truths of existence
the joys of growth
the splendour of action
the glory of power.
For yesterday is but a memory
and tomorrow is only a vision
but today well lived
makes every yesterday a memory of happiness
and every tomorrow a vision of hope.
Look well, therefore, to this day. (By Kalidasa)

Samuel Lee 1783–1852

Orientalist

हिन्दुस्तानी

ہندوستانی

One of the most prodigious scholars in eastern languages was born on this day in 1783 in Longnor, in the shadow of the Long Mynd. Samuel Lee was the youngest of eleven children. After elementary education at the charity school at Longnor, he was apprenticed at the age of 12 to a Shrewsbury carpenter and joiner. He was bright and enjoyed reading, and with his modest wages would buy books, sell them and buy others. Thus he read all the standard Latin authors, learnt Greek and Hebrew, and before the age of 25 had mastered Chaldee, Syriac, Samaritan, Persian and Hindustani. With the help of Archdeacon Corbett (see 4 January), he became a teacher at Bowdler's School, Shrewsbury and gave lessons in Persian and Hindustani. He was spotted by the Church Missionary Society, and with its support he studied at Cambridge, continuing his linguistic studies. It is said that eventually he mastered 18 languages. In 1819 he became professor of Arabic in the university, in 1823 chaplain of Cambridge gaol, and in 1825 rector of Bilton-with-Harrogate in Yorkshire. Honours were showered on him, and in 1831 he was appointed Regius Professor of Hebrew in the university, a post he retained until 1848. As was common in the 19th century, he was able to combine his academic and scholarly interests with parochial work, and he also held livings in Somerset and Hertfordshire. His output of publications is extraordinary – the New Testament in Syriac (1816), the Old Testament in Malay (1817–18) and in Syriac (1823), and later translations of the scriptures into Arabic, Coptic and Persian. He supervised the translation of the prayer book into Hindustani as well as Persian and Hebrew grammars and he helped to create the first dictionary of Reo, the Maori language – altogether a person with an extraordinary interest in and grasp of language.

H G Wells describes another character who has a great interest in language, albeit of a rather lower order than that showed by Samuel Lee!

Mr Polly specialised in slang and the misuse of English, and he played the role of an appreciative stimulant to Parsons. Words attracted him curiously, words rich in suggestion and he loved a novel and striking phrase, His school training had given him little or no mastery of the mysterious pronunciation of English, and no confidence in himself. His schoolmaster indeed had been both unsound and variable. New words had terror and fascination for him; he did not acquire them, he could not avoid them, and so he plunged into them. His only rule was not to be misled by the spelling. That was no guide anyhow. He avoided every recognised phrase in the language, and mispronounced everything in order that he should be suspected of whim rather than ignorance.

'Sesquippledan!' he would say. 'Sesquippledan verboojuice.'

'Eh?' said Platt.

'Eloquent Rapsodooce.'

'Where?' asked Platt.

'In the warehouse, O'Man. All among the tablecloths and blankets.'

H G Wells 1866–1946, *A History of Mr. Polly* (1910)

Cyril Alington 1871–1955

Dean of Durham with Treago connections

Our collection of 'Saints and Sinners' includes not only those who were born here, but also those who made this part of the world their home – even for a short time. This was true of the churchman we celebrate today, who spent his final years in our midst. Cyril Alington taught at Shrewsbury and Eton, eventually becoming headmaster at the latter in 1916. He became dean of Durham in 1933 and, despite being a 'southerner' found his way into the hearts of the city's and county's residents. On his retirement in 1951, Cyril and Hester Alington retired to Treago, at St Weonards, where they took up residence in the 14th-century manor house owned by Sir Roger Mynors and the Alingtons' daughter, Lavinia. There the dean and his wife became familiar figures in the village.

Deans have a reputation for being scholarly, interested in history and sometimes even witty! Cyril Alington had a great talent for verse, which we see in several hymns which have stood the test of time:

Tell the praise of him who called you
  Out of darkness into light,
Broke the fetters that enthralled you,
  Gave you freedom, peace and sight:
Tell the tale of sins forgiven,
  Strength renewed and hope restored,
Till the earth, in tune with heaven,
  Praise and magnify the Lord.

Alington's wit could be matched by others, as in this reply, by the Roman Catholic Monsignor, Ronald Knox, to a letter of congratulation, in verse by Dean Alington:

I'm the sort of man they make an Apostolic Protonotary –
I've written reams and reams of prose, and quite a lot of poetry;
To walk on garden-rollers, is among my minor glories,
And I used to be prevailed upon to write detective stories;
I can also punt canoes (or, as they say in Greenland) kayaks,
And had quite a flair at one time for composing elegiacs;
I can look up trains in Bradshaw, on occasions locomotory,
As undoubtedly becomes an Apostolic Protonotary.
In short, when I've unravelled all the complicated mystery
About what the Holy Office does, the Rota, the Consistory;
When I've studied more theology, and don't get quite so drowsy
  On
Attending learned lectures which discuss the Homoousion;
When I've somehow put behind me (with my poor command of
  French) a list
Of authors whose philosophy is known as Existentialist,
When my learning on a multitude of themes is less bucolic –
There's ne'er a Protonotary will be so Apostolic.

Ronald Knox 1888–1957, from *In Three Tongues* (1959)

Edmund Frocester d.1529

Dean 'known throughout the world for his virtue'

Dean Edmund Frocester died on this day in 1529. His memorial brass, originally in the south choir aisle, is now in the north transept, close to the shrine of St Thomas of Hereford. It depicts the dean vested in a cope decorated with pomegranates. Also on the brass are images of St Ethelbert, St John, St Katherine, St Thomas and St Peter with emblems of the evangelists, and the coat-of-arms of the dean and of the see. A 12-line Latin inscription extols him as 'father of fair counsel, known throughout the world for his virtue' and continues: 'this spot rejoices in his body, his spirit rejoices in its heavenly home'. Frocester was clearly a man trusted by his superiors. Much happened in the cathedral during his period of office: Bishop Mayhew's tomb was erected on the south side of the high altar, Mayhew's organ, left in his will, was most likely placed in the upper storey of the Audley Chapel, and the north porch was extended, through the generosity of Bishop Booth (see 8 May). In addition, during his time, St Ethelbert's Hospital became too impoverished to support a warden or master and it was suggested that it should be united with the cathedral treasurership – a union ratified in 1525. Frocester himself was a man of generosity and left bequests for many, including two of the most promising choristers.

The pomegranate, seen on Edmund Frocester's cope, is a frequent symbol in Christian iconography, seen famously in the works of Botticelli and Leonardo da Vinci. The rich red fruit, bursting open to reveal its seeds, is often seen in the hands of the Virgin Mary or the infant Christ – a symbol of Christ's saving blood. This poem, written around the time of Frocester, vividly portrays Christ's passion:

Woefully arrayed,
My blood, man,
For thee ran,
It may not be nayed:
My body blue and wan,
Woefully arrayed.
Thus naked am I nailed, O man, for thy sake.
I love thee, then love me. Why sleepest thou? Awake!
Remember my tender heart-root for thee brake,
With pains my veins constrained to crack.
Thus was I defaced,
Thus was my flesh raced,
And I to death chased,
Like a lamb led unto sacrifice,
Slain I was in most cruel wise.
Of sharp thorn I have worn a crown on my head,
So rubbed, so bobbed, so rueful, so red;
Sore pained, sore strained, and for thy love dead,
Unfeigned, not deemed, my blood for thee shed;
My feet and hands sore
With sturdy nails bore.
What might I suffer more
Than I have suffered, man, for thee.
Come when thou wilt and welcome to me!

Archibald Alison 1757–1839

Cleric & writer on aesthetics

How often do we hear the phrase 'It's a matter of taste', and how many discussions around additions to church architecture and furnishings have stumbled on this hurdle? Archibald Alison was born in Edinburgh, and educated at Glasgow University and later at Oxford. After ordination, he became a lowly paid curate at Brancepeth in County Durham, but on marriage to Dorothea Gregory in 1784 his prospects improved and he secured the more wealthy curacy of Sudborough in Northamptonshire. Regular visitors included the engineer Thomas Telford (see 2 September), who carried out repairs on his parsonage. In 1790, Alison wrote a study of aesthetics, *Essays on the Nature and Principles of Taste*, for which he is best known. For Alison, the aesthetic quality of an art work, a music composition, an architectural or natural form was the result of a complex 'emotion of taste' – more a case of personal association than a quality integral to the studied object. The success of his book led to ecclesiastical preferment – first the curacy of Kenley in Shropshire. Here, Alison enjoyed the happiest period of his life, dedicated to a combination of 'literary study with active beneficence and easy independence'. In addition to writing his essays on taste, Alison studied botany, zoology and ornithology, and while at Kenley he advocated the development of an allotment system for impoverished parishioners, a project he later emphasised in a sermon, 'On summer'. In this he identified land ownership as the 'most honourable, the most important and the most fruitful' task of society. In 1794 he became vicar of another Shropshire parish, High Ercall, to which he added the parish of Roddington in 1797. In 1800, Alison and his family returned to Edinburgh, where he became minister of the episcopal church near the city's Cowgate. Here he published a number of new works and collections of sermons.

A clerical poet of the 1950s writes amusingly of a clergyman whose exquisite taste is manifested in his passion for correct and elegant deportment in church:

Of variegated clergymen, we had a queer assortment,
But now we have a parson who's a wizard in deportment.
He moves with lofty dignity in grandeur unapproachable,
With manners indefectible and gestures irreproachable.

His stern dislike of levity would credit Queen Victoria,
Nor will you ever meet him in the 'help-yourself' emporia:
It's certainly a sight that you will wish to see again
When he elevates the alms-dish with superlative disdain.

In tones of rich sonority, replete with prunes and prisms,
He deprecates the vanity of heresies and schisms;
Embellishes the ritual with dignified improvements,
And pays a choreographer to regulate his movement.

He rectifies his carriage by the plumb-line and the ruler,
And limbers up his midriff with a hoop (but not a 'hula'!)
And students of eurhythmics would give anything to see
His mobile little finger when he drinks a cup of tea.

S J Forrest *Chapter and Verse* (1959)

Herbert Croft 1603–91

Bishop with gift of friendship

Brought up as a Jesuit at Douai, Herbert Croft returned to the Anglican church under the influence of Bishop Morton of Durham. Ordained deacon and priest in 1638, he became dean of Hereford at the height of the Civil War in 1644. When the city was taken by Colonel Birch's Roundheads (see 10 May), he preached bravely from the pulpit against sacrilege and wanton destruction – his pulpit still stands in the cathedral and a roundel showing the scene appears on the west front. During the Commonwealth he was dispossessed but returned as dean at the Restoration of Charles II being consecrated bishop of Hereford in 1661. He was a man of great piety, conscientious in his duties. A contemporary correspondent wrote that 'the bishop hath won the hearts of all sorts of people, and yesterday at least five hundred persons came to be confirmed to their great joy and comfort'. He was generous, providing a weekly dole at the palace gate for 60 poor people. Although brought up a Roman Catholic, he dealt harshly with the Jesuit College at the Cwm in the south of the diocese, confiscating its library – which is still in the possession of the cathedral. At the same time he worked tirelessly to heal divisions among the Protestant churches and to encourage the return of Nonconformists to the established church. His tomb-slab in the south-east transept is alongside that of his dean, George Benson. Engraved hands are joined across the black slabs – a great symbol of friendship, with the inscription 'In vita coniuncti, in morte non divisi' – 'united in life, not divided by death'.

The gift of friendship so valued by Croft is reflected in these words by George Herbert:

Lord, thou art mine, and I am thine,
If mine I am: and thine much more,
Than I or ought, or can be mine.
Yet to be thine, doth me restore;
So that again I now am mine,
And with advantage mine the more,
Since this being mine, brings with it thine,
And thou with me dost thee restore.
    If I without thee would be mine,
    I neither should be mine nor thine.

Lord, I am thine, and thou art mine:
So mine thou art, that something more
I may presume thee mine, then thine.
For thou didst suffer to restore
Not thee, but me, and to be mine:
And with advantage mine the more,
Since thou in death wast none of thine,
Yet then as mine didst me restore
    O be mine still! still make me thine!
    O rather make no Thine and Mine!

George Herbert 1593–1623, 'Clasping of Hands'

Samuel Clark 1810–75

Educationalist & local parson

The transformation of elementary education from a church-based to a more liberal curriculum owes much to Samuel Clark, born in Southampton on this day in 1810. Brought up a strict Quaker, one of his earliest recollections was of being patted on the head by Tsar Alexander I of Russia, who had expressed a wish, while on his visit to England in 1814, to meet a typical English middle-class family! Withdrawn from education to assist his father in his brush-making business, Clark nevertheless continued his studies and soon became proficient in Latin, Greek, Hebrew, French and German, with a great knowledge of geography and chemistry. Clark struck up a friendship with the liberal theologian F D Maurice, and through his influence was baptized. Now an Anglican, he continued his studies at Oxford, was ordained and began his main career of training teachers in London – first as vice-principal of St Mark's Training College for Schoolmasters at Chelsea and later as principal of the training college at Battersea. He revolutionized the curriculum taught and raised the standard of training given to teachers at all levels. His special interest in geography bore fruit in his superlative maps – in 1849 he published *Maps Illustrative of the Physical and Political History of the British Empire* and later, in 1868, compiled the large *Bible Atlas*, published by the Christian Knowledge Society. Ill health led to the end of his teaching career and in 1862 he accepted the living of Bredwardine, where he was a conscientious pastor and continued his educational work as a diocesan inspector of schools. His biblical scholarship came to the fore with the publication of commentaries on Leviticus, Exodus and Micah for the *Speaker's Commentary on the Bible*, and he was chosen as one of the editors to work on the Revised Version of the Old Testament, eventually published in 1881. Finally, in 1871 he became incumbent at Eaton Bishop, but his last years were dogged by ill health and he died and was buried in Hampshire in 1875.

Clark became an Anglican priest, but perhaps his early Quaker principles never left him. Members of the Society of Friends place great emphasis on education. Here, in an excerpt from a document of the 1980s, we see their emphasis on peace and individuality:

The Quaker emphasis in education probably lies in non-violence, in participation, and in caring. Not only to run the school without violence, but to produce young people who will feel a concern to reduce the level of violence in the world. Not to impose the aims of the school on the pupils, but to lead them to their own acceptance of these aims, to a share (however small) in its running, and a pleasure in its successes. To find that of God in every pupil.

'This is the true ground of love and unity,' wrote Isaac Penington in 1659, 'not that such a man walks and does just as I do, but because I feel the same Spirit and life in him, and that he walks in his rank, in his own order, in his proper way.' This marvellous statement by an early Friend of the value of individualism surely commands our assent today. The school which respects every pupil as an individual will try to teach each one what he (or she) needs to learn, to draw out his unique talents, to understand his proper way, whether he is studying or misbehaving. 'This is far more pleasing to me,' Penington continues, 'than if he walked just in that track wherein I walk.'

Quaker Faith & Practice (1994)

ETHELBERT, KING AND MARTYR d.794

Patron saint of Hereford Cathedral

HEREFORD CATHEDRAL'S ancient dedication is to St Ethelbert the King – a saint not to be confused with Canterbury's Ethelbert of Kent, who was the first Christian Anglo-Saxon king. Hereford's Ethelbert was born in East Anglia in the late 8th century. He journeyed to Mercia to seek the hand of Aelfrytha, the daughter of King Offa of Mercia (see 29 July). For political reasons, Offa had the young King Ethelbert murdered (traditionally on this day in 794) at Marden, five miles north of Hereford. To this bare outline must be added more elaborate stories or legends of his life, which have passed down to us through several medieval writers. These weave together traditions associated with Ethelbert's life and death: a spring rose at the site of his beheading – the body was taken by ox-cart to what is now Hereford – on the journey the head fell from the cart – it was rescued by a blind man, whose sight was restored. Certainly, Ethelbert's body was buried at Hereford Cathedral and became the centre of a thriving pilgrimage cult until the 14th century, when it was eclipsed by the newer cult of St Thomas Cantilupe (see 2 October). Little is heard of Ethelbert's relics until after the 12th century but it is known than that his head was a focus of devotion at Westminster Abbey until the Dissolution. Representations of Ethelbert may be found in several places in Hereford Cathedral – a defaced 14th-century statue is placed near the high altar; there are images of him in several stained glass windows and there is a 19th-century marble representation of Ethelbert's beheading in the pavement in the chancel. In addition, Ethelbert is commemorated on the cathedral seal and by an ancient stone structure near the cathedral, known as 'St Ethelbert's Well'. The cathedral is responsible for the care of the ancient almshouses – St Ethelbert's Hospital in Castle Street. Our saint is also remembered at Marden, where he died, and where, within the church itself, is 'St Ethelbert's Well'. In 2007 a new shrine-like structure was placed in the retro-choir of Hereford Cathedral, on the site generally associated with Ethelbert's original shrine. It is inscribed with words from St Luke's gospel (9:23), linking Ethelbert's own suffering with that of Jesus Christ:

> Jesus said: All who want to be followers of mine must renounce self.
> Day after day they must take up their cross and follow me.

Ethelbert was celebrated with great splendour in the medieval Hereford Missal. These words, taken from the Sequence for the Mass of St Ethelbert, and translated from the Latin, remind us that Ethelbert attained a more than local significance

Lift we now on high our voice
And in Christ our Lord rejoice
  Who his saints upraiseth.

By whose will the king once slain
Ethelbert, in heaven doth reign,
  And his glory praiseth.

Thou, O king, with grace divine
Didst a bright example shine
  When a monarch reigning:

As a sun thou didst illume
Britain's land else sunk in gloom,
  Waiting for the morning.

By thy birth the east was blest
By thy holy death the West,
  Both alike adorning.

Great in life 'ere thou wast slain,
Great in death thou dost remain
  King, by God elected.

Ever may God hear thy prayer
And our sinful ways repair
  That we may be accepted.

ROBERT HUES 1553–1632

Round-the-world sailor

BORN AT Little Hereford, Robert Hues attended Brasenose College, Oxford and numbered among his friends the geographer, Richard Hakluyt (see 23 August), who drew Hues into Raleigh's circle of navigators and explorers in the 1580s. Certainly, by 1585 he was taking part in explorations off the coast of Newfoundland, and making observations of compass variations there. He struck up a friendship with Thomas Cavendish, and both men circumnavigated the world between 1586 and 1588, 'purposely for taking the true latitude of places'. In 1589 Hues accompanied Edward Wright on a voyage to the Azores, and two years later he set out on a second round-the-globe exploration with Cavendish. The latter died in the attempt, but Hues returned and continued with further voyages, including ones to the South Atlantic. He wrote his findings in a treatise *Tractatus de globis et eorum usu* (1594). Dedicated to Raleigh, it was intended to encourage practical astronomy by English seamen, being translated into several languages. Hues worked with several noblemen, including Thomas Grey, Lord Wilton and the earl of Northumberland, accompanying them during periods of imprisonment in the Tower of London. He passed his final years in Oxford, writing on mathematics and preparing the papers of contemporaries for publication.

350 years after Hues' circumnavigation, records were still being attempted and broken. As a boy, I remember following with fascination Sir Francis Chichester's circling of the world in 1967 – in a record-shattering 226 days. In his book Gipsy Moth Circles the World*, Chichester describes many of his adventures:*

Twice I entered the Forties, and was driven out by a gale. A 50-knot squall going through was like the infernal regions with great white monsters bearing down out of a black void, picking up the boat and dashing it about. I hated the feeling of being out of control. Once a wave broke over the cockpit, not seriously, but the immense power it showed was frightening. I wrote, 'It requires a Dr Johnson to describe this life. I should add that the cabin floor is all running wet, and my clothes are beginning to get pretty wet too. Vive le yachting!'

Francis Chichester 1901–72, *Gipsy Moth Circles the World* (1967)

In reviewing Francis Chichester's book Mark Lewis suggests that its style is 'repetitive and flat in the telling' and 'not poetic or particularly evocative', but he more than balances these criticisms by saying:

It was not the sort of journey you and I would depart on. You or I do not have the resources to commission a 53 foot long boat. You or I do not suffer from life-long myopia or from a diagnosis of terminal cancer. You or I do not have the will (or hubris) to set off, not on a leisurely sight-seeing tour of the seven oceans, but a pell-mell race against the clock. You and I are normal. Francis Chichester taught what it is to be more than that.

Thomas Andrew Knight 1759–1838

Horticulturalist & plant physiologist

One of my childhood chores was to sit on the backdoor step shelling peas – a lowly task, but one with an unexpectedly academic background, as today's character will prove! Born at Wormsley Grange, Thomas Knight was educated at Ludlow School and Balliol College, Oxford. Although wealthy enough not to need to work, he began a career in farming, experimenting with new varieties of fruit and vegetables. Encouraged by Sir Joseph Banks, he wrote extensively on Herefordshire agriculture, produced papers for the Royal Society on grafting and diseases in fruit trees, and was elected Fellow of the Royal Society in 1805. In his work he set out his ideas about the movement of sap in plants and the effects of gravity, moisture and sunlight on roots and leaves. His lasting work was in the Horticultural Society – from 1811 till his death in 1838 he was president and greatly expanded the work of the society, with the introduction of exhibitions, medals and the publication of transactions. In 1808/9, Knight moved into Downton Castle, Herefordshire, a castellated house and 10,000–acre estate, built and owned by his brother (Richard Payne Knight, see 11 February). Knight developed his ideas here, and his horticultural and agricultural experiments brought him into contact with other physiologists such as Dutrochet and Sir Humphrey Davy, who, when visiting Downton, praised the quality of the fishing there in his *Salmonia.* Knight encouraged the development of a wide variety of traditional varieties of fruit, grew specialist varieties himself and gave his name to a variety of garden pea! He also looked into meat production in sheep, breeding from a Merino ram given to him by George III. Enjoying company and entertaining, Knight would amuse his friends by reciting huge tracts of obscure poetry by heart. He died in May 1838 and is buried at Wormsley.

Thomas Knight's love of plants, fruit and flowers is well reflected in this poem by an 18th-century writer:

Flowers to the fair: to you these flowers I bring,
And strive to greet you with an earlier spring.
Flowers, sweet and gay and delicate like you,
Emblems of innocence and beauty too.
With flowers the Graces bind their yellow hair,
And flowery wreaths consenting lovers wear.
Flowers, the sole luxury which nature knew,
In Eden's pure and guiltless garden grew.
To loftier forms are rougher tasks assigned;
The sheltering oak resists the stormy wind,
The tougher yew repels invading foes,
And the tall pine for future navies grows;
But this soft family, to cares unknown,
Were born for pleasure and delight alone;
Gay without toil, and lovely without art,
They spring to cheer the sense, and glad the heart
Not blush, my fair, to own you copy these,
Your best, your sweetest empire is – to please.

Anna Laetitia Barbauld 1743–1825, 'To a Lady, with some Painted Flowers'

Ralph d.*c.*1158

First dean of Hereford

Of the 'Three Choirs' cathedrals, Hereford has had deans for longest! Before the Reformation, Worcester, being a monastic cathedral, had a prior as head of the cathedral establishment, while Gloucester's prior had no cathedral duties, as St Peter's was solely an abbey. Cathedrals like Hereford, of the 'old foundation', were staffed by secular priests, who provided the bishop's *familia* or close community, and under the Normans these groups of priests began to take more formal shape. Certainly, the term *capitulum* first occurs under Robert de Bethune (see 16 April) in 1134 and it was he who encouraged the canons to act as a clearly defined body, consisting of dean, treasurer, chancellor, precentor and canons. Dean Ralph appears to have been a rebellious priest – when he disagreed with Bishop Bethune, the latter went to Pisa to obtain a papal privilege which ordered the dean and canons to be obedient to their bishop. Ralph certainly gets a bad press from Robert's biographer, William de Wycombe, but by the 1140s he and Robert appear to have been reconciled, and there is evidence of a happy association between them when they united the two churches of St Peter and St Guthlac in Hereford. From the 1140s, Dean Ralph and the chapter started to issue their own charters and use their own communal seal, an important step towards independence from the bishop. As in other cathedrals, the dean and chapter steadily built up rights of jurisdiction, and the dean had the rights of archdeacon within the city of Hereford.

Dean Ralph is associated with the stormy times that befell Hereford during the reign of King Stephen (see 23 October) – he was dean when the king attended mass on Whitsunday in 1138 in celebration of the capture of Hereford Castle from his cousin Matilda, rival for the throne. Tradition has it that the king sat in the ancient wooden chair now in the sanctuary, wore his crown and received homage, an unreliable tradition as the chair is unlikely to date from before 1200. The civil unrest of the period put a stop to building work at the cathedral, but on its resumption the Norman cathedral was completed, and dedicated in 1148, shortly before the death of Bishop Bethune.

Of the many Whitsunday hymns, the following dates from before the 10th century and may well have been sung in Hereford Cathedral when Dean Ralph received King Stephen at mass:

Come, O Creator Spirit, come,
And make within our hearts thy home;
To us thy grace celestial give,
Who of thy breathing move and live.

O Comforter, that name is thine,
Of God most high the gift divine;
The well of life, the fire of love,
Our souls' anointing from above.

Thou dost appear in sevenfold dower
The sign of God's almighty power;
The father's promise, making rich
With saving truth our earthly speech.

Our senses with thy light inflame,
Our hearts to heavenly love reclaim;
Our bodies' poor infirmity
With strength perpetual fortify.

Latin, 10th century, trans. R Bridges (1899)

Aaron le Bund 1266–90

The Jew of Hereford

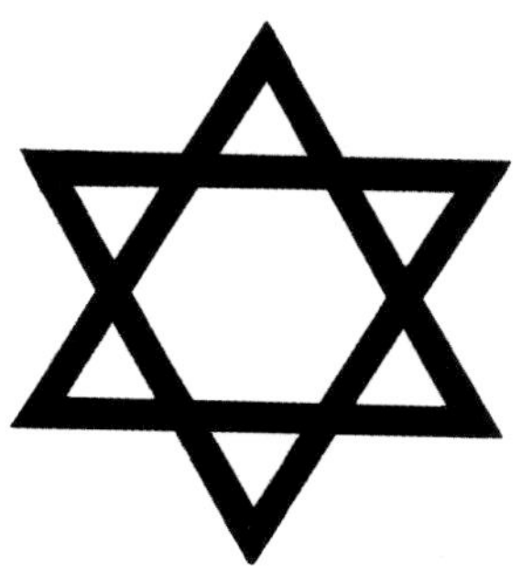

As in many medieval English cities, Hereford's Jewish population was very powerful. There is evidence of a community from 1179, and it greatly flourished from 1218 under a Jew named Hamo, who founded a synagogue in the city. From 1260, the Jews were led by Aaron le Bund, who had come to the city from London. He was very wealthy and had provided funds for the nobility in various military campaigns. The Jews, however, had many enemies – in 1275 fellow Jews from Gloucester and Worcester were deported to Hereford, while individual Jews felt the scourge of persecution from the church itself. Thomas Cantilupe himself (see 25 August), so revered, was manifestly anti-Semitic; it is said that when a Jewish convert was proposed for appointment as a commissioner to investigate criminal charges, Cantilupe petitioned King Edward I to prevent such an action – in the bishop's view it was unthinkable that a Jew should testify against a Christian. In 1290 Edward I gave orders to the sheriff that all Jews, with their wives, children and chattels, should be expelled from Hereford and quit the realm by 1 November, All Saints Day, that year – any who refused to leave faced death. The date of the announcement of the expulsion, 18 April, is poignant as, in that year, it fell on the 9th day of the month of Av in the Jewish calendar, and the 9th day of Av is *Tisha Baav*, a day of fasting and the date of the destruction of both the first and second Temples. Aaron le Bund was exiled to France and died there.

The Jewish community, dispersed throughout the medieval world, was nurtured by the scriptures and by additional writings such as the Talmud. *While basically a legal book, the* Talmud *provided its rabbinic authors with opportunities to expound on many topics, from astrology to medicine and it helped to provide the transition of Judaism from its ancient life around temple and political nation to its later life as a dispersed minority, engaged in the study and practice of the rabbinic law in synagogue and home. Excerpts from the* Talmud:

Rabbi Chonan, of Zepora, said, 'The study of the law may be compared to a huge heap of dust that is to be cleared away. The foolish man says, "It is impossible that I should be able to remove this immense heap. I will not attempt it", but the wise man says, "I will remove a little today, some more tomorrow, and more the day after, and thus in time I shall have removed it all."'

In Proverbs 24:7, we find this sentence: 'Wisdom is too high for a fool'.
Rabbi Jochanan illustrates this verse with an apple depending from the ceiling. The foolish man says, 'I cannot reach the fruit, it is too high;' but the wise man says, 'It may be readily obtained by placing one step upon another until thy arm is brought within reach of it.' The foolish man says, 'Only a wise man can study the entire law,' but the wise man replies, 'It is not incumbent upon thee to acquire the whole.'

A prayer on the Sabbath

Our God and God of our fathers, may our rest be pleasing to You. Make us holy by doing Your commands and let us share in the work of Your Torah. Make us content with Your goodness and let our souls know the joy of Your salvation. Purify our hearts to serve You in truth. In Your love and goodwill let us inherit Your holy Sabbath and may all Israel who seek holiness find in it their rest. Blessed are You Lord, who makes the Sabbath holy.

Haemma fl.7th century

First abbot of Leominster

By the 11th century, the nuns of Leominster were celebrating the memory of Haemma as first abbot of Leominster with a feast on this day. A source includes a short prayer of intercession to Haemma, 'to succour and preserve me from all my adversaries'. Haemma's relics are mentioned in Bishop Swinfield's list of 1286 and the Reading Abbey list of 1190 records 'one large bone and two ribs of St Haemma, first abbot of Leominster'. But who was the first abbot? This accolade had previously been awarded to the 7th-century monk, Edfrith (see 26 October). We must assume that Haemma became first abbot of the monastery when it changed from Celtic to Roman use in later Saxon times. Perhaps initially the Benedictine abbey and convent of Reading were reluctant to acknowledge Edfrith's part in the foundation of the minster, now the Priory Church, and preferred to celebrate one of their own. However, the people of Leominster would have none of this and still remembered Edfrith. Indeed, in 1290 the abbot of Reading accepted the transfer of Leominster's great autumn fair to the feast of St Edfrith on 26 October, and by 1433 the list of principal feasts at Leominster included Edfrith on 26 October, but omitted all reference to poor Haemma!

One of the earliest monastic rules comes from the area of Leominster. Ancrene Wisse *is a 12th- or 13th-century rule for anchoresses – for three 'sisters' who chose to lead the contemplative life. It is in a Middle English dialect and belongs to a group of writings probably composed at Wigmore Abbey. The author was clearly a scholar and a rhetorician, steeped in scripture and powerful in idiomatic phrases:*

For what is it that makes us strong to suffer hardship in God's service and to wrestle valiantly in times of temptation against the Devil's assaults, but the hope of a high reward? Hope keeps the heart in health, whatever the flesh suffers; as they say, 'If hope were not, heart would break.' But Jesu, mercy! How stands it with those who are in the place of all grief and misery with no hope of escape, and yet heart cannot burst?

The heart's guardians are the five senses: sight and hearing, tasting and smelling and each limb's feeling. And we shall speak of all of them, for whosoever guards these well, he does Solomon's commandments: he guards well his heart and his soul's salvation. The heart is a very wild beast and makes many a wanton leap. Therefore, my dear sisters, love your windows as little as you possibly can. Let them be small and let the parlour's window be least and narrowest ...

Ancrene Wisse, pt.2, trans. Robert Hasefratz (2000)

A 20th-century writer speaks of the qualities of holiness in the saints:

As we call him the Saviour we must remember that God is the Saviour through him, and that there are a host of liberators and healers, including ourselves, through whom the divine salvation works in all mankind. God does not leave the world at any place, in any time, without saviours – without healing power.

Paul Tillich 1886–1965, *The Eternal Now* (1963)

Augustine of Canterbury d.*c.*604

First archbishop of Canterbury

In the little church of Stanford Bishop, near Bromyard is what Pevsner describes as a 'very simple medieval armchair'. Traditionally, this is known as 'St Augustine's Chair', used by Augustine at a conference in 603 with the British bishops when the question of allegiance to Rome was being discussed. Whether this really is the actual chair is far from certain, yet the story of the meeting of Celtic and western Christianity is one which was of huge importance in 7th-century England. Christianity had been part of British culture from the end of the 3rd century, and the faith had claimed its first martyr with the death of Alban in *c.*254. But it is to Augustine that we look as having been sent by Pope Gregory to re-evangelize the English Church. Augustine and his monks finally landed in Kent in 597, where they were well received by King Ethelbert, whose wife, Bertha, was a Christian. Once established, Augustine returned temporarily to Gaul to receive ordination as a bishop. Pope Gregory would have preferred London to have become the primatial see, but Canterbury was chosen and Augustine became first archbishop of Canterbury. He did much to bring Roman rule to the church and, in his policy of infiltration, took over innocent pagan feasts and made them Christian. Augustine helped King Ethelbert to draft the earliest Anglo-Saxon written laws to survive. He founded a school at Canterbury, which both received and produced books. A 6th-century manuscript called the *Gospels of St Augustine* could well have been brought to England by him; it is now at Corpus Christi College, Cambridge and is used at the enthronement of archbishops of Canterbury.

The Venerable Bede writes of the important meeting between Augustine and the British bishops:

Meanwhile, with the aid of King Ethelbert, Augustine summoned the bishops and teachers of the nearest province to a conference at a place still known to the English as Augustine's Oak, which lies on the border between the Hwiccas and the West Saxons. He began by urging them to establish brotherly relations with him in Catholic unity, and to join with him in God's work of preaching the Gospel to the heathen ... the Britons declared that, while they had learnt that what Augustine taught was the true way of righteousness, they could not abandon their ancient customs without the consent and approval of their own people, and therefore asked that a second and fuller conference might be held.

This was arranged, and seven British bishops and many very learned men are said to have attended. Those summoned to this council first visited a wise and prudent hermit, and enquired of him whether they should abandon their own traditions at Augustine's demand. He answered: 'If he is a man of God, follow him.' 'But how can we be sure of this?' they asked. 'Our Lord says, Take my yoke upon you and learn of Me, for I am meek and lowly in heart,' he replied. 'Therefore if Augustine is meek and lowly in heart, it shows that he bears the yoke of Christ himself, and offers it to you. But if he is haughty and unbending, then he is not of God, and we should not listen to him.' Then they asked, 'But how can we know even this?' 'Arrange that he and his followers arrive first at the place appointed for the conference,' answered the hermit. 'If he rises courteously as you approach, rest assured that he is the servant of Christ and do as he asks. But if ignores you and does not rise, then, since you are in the majority, do not comply with his demands.'

The British bishops carried out his suggestion, and it happened that Augustine remained seated in his chair. Seeing this, they became angry, accusing him of pride and taking pains to contradict all he said.

Bede, *Ecclesiastical History of the English People*

Gibbons Bagnall 1719–1800

Church of England cleric & poet

Eighteenth-century parsons often had the time and leisure to pursue many other interests, not connected with the church. With a poorly paid curate doing much of the pastoral work, incumbents could indulge their passion for writing or collecting. One such was Gibbons Bagnall, who, after taking holy orders, became vicar of Holme Lacy and headmaster of the Cathedral School in Hereford. In 1760 he became prebend of Piona Parva in Hereford Cathedral and seven years later he took on another prebendal stall, that of Bartonsham. For some time he was also rector of Upton Bishop and finally, in 1783, he was presented to the living of nearby Sellack. His writings were mainly in verse. The first was *Education: an Essay* (1765), while a more ambitious literary work was a verse translation of Fenelon's account of the adventures of Telemachus, son of Ulysses.

The parish priest – learned, yet poor – is well reflected in a poem of the 17th century:

A Parish-Priest was of the Pilgrim-Train;
An Awful, Reverend, and Religious Man,
His Eyes diffus'd a venerable Grace,
And Charity itself was in his Face.
Rich was his Soul, though his Attire was poor;
(As God had cloath'd his own Embassador;)
For such, on Earth, his bless'd Redeemer bore...
Yet, had his Aspect nothing of severe,
But such a face as promis'd him sincere.
Nothing reserv'd or sullen was to see,
But sweet Regards; and pleasing Sanctity ...
   The tythes, his parish Freely paid, he took;
But never Su'd; or Curs'd with Bell and Book ...
   Yet, of his little, he had some to spare,
To feed the Famish'd and to cloath the Bare:
For Mortify'd he was to that degree,
A poorer than himself, he wou'd not see.
True Priests, he said, and Preachers of the Word,
Were only Stewards of their Soveraign Lord,
Nothing was theirs; but all the publick Store,
Intrusted Riches to relieve the Poor.
Who, shou'd they steal, for want of his Relief,
He judg'd himself Accomplice with the Thief.
   Wide was his Parish; not contracted close
In streets, but here and there a straggling House;
Yet still he was at Hand, without Request
To serve the Sick, to succor the Distredd's;
Tempting, on Foot alone, without affright,
The Dangers of a dark, tempestuous Night...
His Preaching much, but more his Practice wrought;
A living Sermon of the Truths he taught.

John Dryden 1631–1700, 'The Character of a good Parson'

Melangell 7th century

Abbess & protector of the hare

A link with our neighbouring diocese of St Asaph. When the shrine of St Thomas of Hereford was being restored in 2007–8, the ancient shrine at Pennant Melangell, in a remote part of Montgomeryshire, provided a model for us – one of the few remaining early medieval shrines. At Pennant, it marks the site of the tomb of Melangell or Monacella. She lived in the 7th century, the daughter of an Irish king. In order to avoid an arranged marriage she fled to Wales, hiding in the valley of Pennant, deep in the Berwyn Hills. There Melangell lived a life of quiet prayer, which was interrupted one day by Brochwel Ysgiroth, prince of Powys. He was hunting a hare, which took refuge under the folds of Melangell's cloak. Melangell made such an impression on Brochwel that once he had heard her story, he gave her the valley of Pennant to be a sanctuary for ever. There she gathered around her a community of holy women. Hares in the valley became known as 'wyn Melangell' ('Melangell's lambs') and were specially protected there.

St Melangell's church is sited in a round churchyard, once a Bronze Age site, ringed by ancient yew trees. Within the church is a 15th-century screen, carved with the story of Melangell and Prince Brochwel. The shrine itself was dismantled at the Reformation, reassembled in the 19th century and now re-erected in the chancel, where it is a focus for prayer and devotion. Near to the church is a healing centre, continuing the ancient tradition of prayer and healing on this holy site.

A contemporary poet, Ruth Bidgood write on aspects of Melangell. Here, a meditation on the saint's church – a haven of peace:

Within the girdle of her care she keeps
the farms of her narrow valley. Far upstream
one house is new, foursquare, boldly red,
others insubstantial grey,
across fields, at the foot of hills.
A stranger on the road has to peer
To catch the dark of windows without glass.

Within the girdle of her care she keeps her church,
its ancient round of holy land
under hanging woods, in sight
of wilder heights beyond;
its intricate gnarl, dark spread of yews
over tip-tilt slabs of lettered stone.
At her May festival one bell sounds.
Her people have got up early, and press in
to pray, generation on generation
with never a jostle, while small warm rain
gentles their waiting homes.

Ruth Bidgood b.1922, 'Cwm Pennant: Patron Saint' in *Symbols of Plenty* (2006)

Nicholas Billingsley *c.*1633–1709

Religious poet & Presbyterian minister

Early ill health led Billingsley to dedicate his first published work to the Bristol physician who he believed had saved his life. This was a calendar of poems to the saints and martyrs – in effect selections from *Foxe's book of Martyrs* in rhyming couplets. On 28 May 1657 Billingsley was admitted vicar of Weobley – he was, at this period of the Commonwealth, a Presbyterian. At the Restoration he was ejected from his parish and settled with his family near Abergavenny, where he kept a school. He did, however, 'hedge his bets' by subscribing to the Thirty-nine Articles in order to become a schoolmaster, and was ordained deacon in the Church of England in 1664. Later, he became incumbent of Blakeney, in Gloucestershire. He explained his reconciliation to the Church of England in a poem:

> True, I was one of Levi's turn'd out Tribe,
> Who never durst against my conscience sin,
> Not claw Church-livings with an unjust bribe,
> And stoutly swear I honestly came in.

Billingsley might be described as a 'precarious conformist'. He made his own interpolations in the prayer book service and, only just conforming to the canons of the church, wore his surplice across his shoulders. His Non-conformist preference seems clear in his composition and encouragement of some of the earliest hymns regularly sung in churches. Billingsley was persecuted by successive bishops of Gloucester for his lack of discipline, and by 1689 he had again resigned from the Church of England and become an itinerant preacher.

When I was a boy in Harlington Parish Church, near Heathrow Airport, we welcomed to the parish an elderly retired priest, William Rowland Jones. He preached marvellous sermons. Later, I read his autobiography and discovered that this gentle and scholarly man had, in fact, had a most turbulent ministry – involved in radical ecumenical experiments at the King's Weigh House in Mayfair during the 1920s and, as an Anglican priest, often, like Billingsley many years before him, in trouble with his bishop! He ends his book with a plea for real reunion, not held back by traditions and forms:

Whilst we should all admit that much has been done to cleanse and reform the Church of England since the early nineteenth century, much still remains to be done, and much more has to be done to the episcopacy of the Church of England. It is the tardiness of these reforms which keeps up the persistent protests of the Nonconformists. If the claims to authority and to historical traditions could be so enunciated that they did not brand all other Churches as mere imitations, as wilfully schismatic bodies, dead branches of the true vine, but as brethren whose separation was due to misunderstandings on both sides, then the cause of reunion would be hastened, and the hope of one united Church of all the faithful might speedily be fulfilled.

But even if the Church does not recognize the seriousness of the situation; and if as a result humanity turns away into the wrong direction, we can still believe that God will never leave Himself without witness, and in the midnight hour of darkness Christ will manifest Himself in glory, and the earthly career of His Church and of humanity will be brought to judgement. Whatever be the final issue, beyond all earthly failure and human infidelity, there remains the heavenly triumph and the faithfulness of God. If the cause of Christ and of His Church be defeated on earth, it shall have its triumph in heaven. God has other worlds than this, and His ultimate victory is assured.

W Rowland Jones, *Diary of a Misfit Priest* (1960)

Thomas Coningsby 1550–1625

Soldier & benefactor

One of the most attractive survivals of Hereford's past – Coningsby Hospital – owes its foundation to this generous benefactor. Born at Hampton Court, near Leominster, Coningsby became wealthy on the death of his parents and entered the court of Elizabeth I. With the support of the earl of Leicester and later of the earl of Essex, he achieved considerable power in the county and became steward of Herefordshire and Leominster. He joined Essex's expedition to Normandy and for his courage was knighted in 1591. In 1593 and 1597, Thomas was elected to parliament as senior knight for Herefordshire, but his monopoly of power in the city was increasingly challenged, not least by the Scudamore and Croft families and by the middle of the reign of James I, Coningsby's influence had all but waned. Instead, he turned to charitable causes and, in 1614, established Coningsby's hospital for worn-out old soldiers and serving men, on the site of the Blackfriars community in Hereford. The new ensemble consisted of 12 cottages, a hall and chapel, and was built with stone from the existing structure and from the adjacent Blackfriars. The leader of these servitors was 'to be called Corporal Coningsby and by no other surname'. Coningsby's religious bias is shown by his regulations for the hospital of July 1617, which stipulated that the chaplain (always to be an Oxford man) must be a preacher and that the company of inmates must march to the cathedral in file behind the chaplain, carrying the Bible. The servitors received free food, fuel, clothing and a small weekly allowance, paid to them weekly after prayers on Monday morning. Each was to wear a uniform, with a 'seemely gowne of red cloth reaching downe to the ankle, lined likewise with red baise'. It is said that a version of this uniform was later adopted by the pensioners of the Royal Hospital at Chelsea.

Coningsby's military exploits took him to Normandy, where no doubt he looked back with nostalgia to his homeland, where he eventually retired in peace. It has not been so for many soldiers serving abroad – many died on foreign soil and were buried there. Many years after Coningsby, another soldier looked wistfully over the Channel to the land of his birth:

If I should die, think only this of me:
That there's some corner of a foreign field
That is for ever England. There shall be
In that rich earth a richer dust concealed;
A dust whom England bore, shaped, made aware,
Gave, once, her flowers to love, her ways to roam,
A body of England's, breathing English air,
Washed by the rivers, blest by the suns of home.

And think, this heart, all evil shed away,
A pulse in the eternal mind, no less
Gives somewhere back the thoughts by England given,
Her sights and sounds; dreams happy as her day;
And laughter, learnt of friends; and gentleness,
In hearts at peace, under an English heaven.

Rupert Brooke 1887–1915, 'The Soldier', *Collected Poems*

Herbert Rowse Armstrong 1869–1922

Hay solicitor executed for murder

Herbert Rowse Armstrong is said to have been the only solicitor in Britain to have been hanged for murder. He was born in Devon and studied law at Cambridge. Initially practising in Newton Abbot and Liverpool, he came to Hay-on-Wye in 1906. He married Katherine Mary Friend in 1907 and the couple had three children. Armstrong was a hard-working man and rose in the social community of the town, being a leading Freemason and Clerk to the Justices. He fought in the First World War and gained the rank of Major. In 1919, his wife's health deteriorated and she died on 22 February 1921. Difficult professional relationships with a rival solicitor set in train a series of circumstances which led to Armstrong's being accused of attempted murder of the rival and, subsequently of the murder of his late wife – both through poisoning. Armstrong was arrested on 31 December 1921 and he was brought to trial at Hereford. At the trial, Armstrong had to explain his habits with arsenic – the poison discovered when his late wife's body was exhumed – and he claimed that he kept it for his garden to treat patches of dandelions (hence our illustration). His defence was not accepted and, in April 1922, he was found guilty of murdering his wife. On 16 May the Court of Criminal Appeal dismissed Armstrong's appeal and he was hanged at Gloucester Prison on this day in 1922. The case encouraged a large number of media adaptations, including a BBC radio series in 1952 under the title *The Champagne Glass* and a TV series in 1994 entitled *Dandelion Dead.*

Without doubt the Armstrong case shocked the county and far beyond. Today, living in a country where there is no capital punishment, we cannot feel the terrible effect that such judicial death will have had on a community, but writers of previous generations have written eloquently on the subject and of the great diminishment it caused in society.

Blood demands blood. Does it? The system of compensation might be carried on *ad infinitum* – an eye for an eye and a tooth for a tooth, as by the old Mosaic Law. Why, because you lose your eye, is that of your opponent to be extracted? Where is the reason for the practice? Knowing that revenge is not only evil but useless we have given it up on minor points. Only to the last we stick firm. I came away from Snow Hill that morning with a disgust for murder, but it was for the murder I saw done. I pray to Almighty God to cause this disgraceful sin to pass from among us, and to cleanse our land of blood.

William Thackeray 1811–63, *On Going to See a Man Hanged*

Immediately below the reading-desk [in the prison chapel], on the floor of the chapel, and forming the most conspicuous object in its little area, is the condemned pew; a huge black pen, in which the wretched men who are singled out for death are placed, on the Sunday preceding their execution, in sight of all their fellow-prisoners ... At one time – and at no distant period either – the coffins of the men about to be executed were placed in that pew, upon the seat by their side, during the whole service. It may seem incredible, but it is strictly true. Let us hope that the increased spirit of civilization and humanity which abolished this frightful and degrading custom may extend itself to other usages equally barbarous; usages which have not even the plea of utility in their defence, as every year's experience has shown them to be more and more inefficacious.

Charles Dickens 1812–70, *Sketches by Boz* (1836–7)

Wistan d.850

Martyr with Shropshire link?

Several places claim this saint! There are ancient dedications to Wistan in Leicestershire and in our area, in the village of Wistanstow, near Craven Arms, he is also remembered. He was grandson of Wiglaf, king of Mercia 827–40, and was chosen as king on his grandfather's death. According to legend, he asked his mother to act as regent. Berhtric, Wistan's cousin, wished to marry her, but Wistan refused to allow the marriage, which he regarded as incestuous. Berhtric then murdered him at a place called Wistanstow (generally thought to be the Leicestershire location) – but three of his friends followed him and rescued the body, which was subsequently buried in the royal monastery of Repton in Derbyshire, with his father and grandfather.

In 1019 Alfwaerd, abbot of Evesham, asked King Cnut to give him Wistan's relics, and from then on Evesham became the centre of a cult, where many miracles are said to have taken place. Apparently, some of these were doubted and had to be verified twice over. Later in the 11th century, Walter of Cerisy became abbot of Evesham and subjected Wistan's skull to ordeal by fire – from which it emerged unscathed. Over a century later, according to Thomas of Marleberge, the miracle of 'hair' growing at Wistanstow on the ground where the martyr fell, each year on his feast day, was verified by a commission sent by Baldwin, archbishop of Canterbury. Whatever the truth of the miracles, the devotion to Wistan was real and lasted throughout the medieval period.

Many of the cults of the saints are surrounded by stories of miracles and healing. Were they real? Did they actually happen? People were, of course, more open to the supernatural and would have interpreted as miraculous many things for which we, today, might have a more logical and scientific explanation. Perhaps in our day we need to have a broad understanding of the miraculous and to be open to the very many ways God comes to us. This passage, from a book by John V Taylor, former bishop of Winchester, relates how he and his wife, journeying in dangerous terrain in East Africa, became hopelessly lost:

I looked in all directions with no idea where the hut lay, and an appalled realization of what I had done. In a very small voice Peggy said, 'We're lost, aren't we?' I said, 'Yes, I'm dreadfully sorry, it's my fault.' She said, her voice quite steady, 'I'm frightened, John.' 'So am I,' was all I could answer. And then she said, 'Well, it is Whitsunday,' and at that instant a beam of sunlight struck through the cloud and shone for a few seconds on the hut about two miles away, reflected dazzlingly from its aluminium roof, giving us our bearings. It was the most direct act of God I have personally experienced, but the miracle did not happen up there in the grey sky. The break in the cloud was going to happen anyway. What I know for certain is that, had I been characteristically protesting that we could still find our way, and had Peggy retorted, with justice, 'how could you be such a fool?' we would have been glaring at each other and would never have seen that pointing shaft of light. The miracle was in us, as they almost always are.

John V Taylor 1914–2001, *The Christlike God* (1992)

John Masefield 1874–1967

Herefordshire's Poet Laureate

I can still remember learning poems by heart in primary school, and several by John Masefield stick in the memory – not least 'Cargoes' and 'Sea Fever'. These timeless poems were typical of Masefield's crafted tradition and although they may have gone out of fashion they have helped to earn him a venerated place in 20th-century literature. He was born on 1 June 1874 at The Knapp in Ledbury and he often spoke warmly of his Herefordshire childhood. His parents died when he was young and he was brought up by an aunt and uncle who tried to suppress his love of reading. After Warwick School, he became a merchant marine and his travels took him to Chile, an experience which eventually provided material for his great poem *Dauber* (1913). He travelled in the United States, there discovering Chaucer, Malory and the Romantic poets. He returned to England 'with £6 and a revolver', determined to become a professional poet. There followed *Salt-water Ballads* (1902) and many others in which he came across clearly, like Kipling, as the 'common man'. In 1900 he met W B Yeats and this introduced him to the literary world. Further great poems followed, including *The Everlasting Mercy* (1911). The First World War saw him working with the Red Cross in the Dardanelles, and his *Gallipoli* (1916) was a major account of modern warfare. Masefield not only worked in poetry but wrote plays, including *The Tragedy of Nan* (1909, and championed live poetry reading. He was an obvious choice to become Poet Laureate in 1930 and was showered with honours, and while he refused a knighthood several times, he was appointed to the Order of Merit in 1935. On his death in 1967, his ashes were buried in Poets' Corner in Westminster Abbey, next to the memorial to Robert Browning.

When the Freedom of the City of Hereford was bestowed on Masefield in October 1930, he responded with this wonderful piece of prose, extolling the beauty of the county where he had spent so much of his childhood:

I am linked to this county by subtle ties, deeper than I can explain: they are ties of beauty. Whenever I think of Paradise, I think of parts of this County. Whenever I think of a perfect Human State, I think of parts of this County. Whenever I think of the bounty and beauty of God, I think of parts of this County.

I know no land more full of bounty and beauty than this red land, so good for corn and hops and roses. I am glad to have lived in a country where nearly every one lived on and by the land, singing as they carried the harvest home, and taking such pride in the horses, and in the great cattle, and in the cider trees. It will be a happy day for England when she realises that those things and the men who care for them are the real wealth of a land: the beauty and the bounty of earth being the shadow of Heaven.

Formerly, when men lived in the beauty and bounty of Earth, the reality of Heaven was very near; every brook and grove and hill was holy, and men out of their beauty and bounty built shrines so lovely that the spirits which inhabit Heaven came down and dwelt in them and were companions to men and women, and men listen'd to divine speech. All up and down this county are those lovely shrines, all of the old time.

I was born in this County, where there are so many of those shrines, the still living evidence that men here can enter Paradise. I passed my childhood looking out on these red ploughlands and woodland and pasture and lovely brooks, knowing that Paradise was just behind them. I have passed long years thinking on them, hoping that by the miracle of poetry the thought of them would get me into Paradise, so that I might tell people of Paradise, in the words learned there, and that people would then know and be happy.

Skeffington Dodgson 1837–1919

Echoes of Alice *in Vowchurch*

Known, perhaps to his irritation, as 'the brother of Lewis Carroll', Skeffington Dodgson pursued a career as a country parson rather than that of college don and author, paths chosen by his more famous brother. Born into a clerical family, Skeffington followed his father and elder brother to Christchurch, Oxford. While elder brother Charles was lecturing in mathematics and writing *Alice in Wonderland*, Skeffington had become ordained and held a large number of curacies in various parts of England, some obtained for him through the influence of his brother. He was clearly a man of integrity and holiness – his father, who became an archdeacon in Ripon diocese, wrote thus of Skeffington in a letter to his sister: 'He carries into his profession all the earnest patient diligence and perseverance which has always been his characteristic and in which he rises so much above all his more talented brothers.' Eventually, in 1895, at the age of 58, he obtained his own living and became incumbent at Vowchurch in the Golden Valley. The bishop of Worcester wrote to him from the Hotel Continental in Cannes saying: 'The living of Vowchurch in Herefordshire in my gift is vacant and I have much pleasure in offering it to you. The income I am sorry to say is small – I believe it is only £160 a year, but I believe I am right in supposing that you have some private means and I hope you may see your way to accept this living.' Skeffington, it seems, had no such private means, but served faithfully as parish priest in Vowchurch for 15 years. His daughter Irene later wrote of him: ' Father disapproved of hymns sung during collection because he thought it was a distraction from the words being sung. He always read the texts above the hymns – which after all would seem to be the most important part.' Skeffington and his wife retired to Ewyas Harold in 1910 and he died in 1919, being buried in the churchyard at Vowchurch on 6 May.

Alice in Wonderland *may not been influenced by life in Vowchurch, but early editions of the book will most surely have been avidly read in the vicarage by Skeffington and his family. For all its fairy-tale qualities,* Alice *has some timeless things to say about human life and our perception of it. It asks questions that we rarely ask as we feel that the asking might reveal our stupidity ...*

She was a little startled by seeing the Cheshire Cat sitting on a bough of a tree a few yards off. The Cat only grinned when it saw Alice. It looked good-natured, she thought; still, it had very long claws and a great many teeth, so she felt that it ought to be treated with respect.

'Cheshire-Puss,' she began, rather timidly, as she did not know whether it would like the name: however, it only grinned a little wider.

'Come, it's pleased so far,' thought Alice, and she went on. 'Would you tell me, please, which way I ought to go from here?'

'That depends a good deal on where you want to get to,' said the Cat.

'I don't much care where' – said Alice.

Then it doesn't matter which way you go,' said the Cat.

' – so long as I get *somewhere*,' Alice added as an explanation.

'Oh, you're sure to do that,' said the Cat, 'If you only walk long enough.'

Alice felt that this could not be denied, so she tried another question.

'What sort of people live about here?'

'In that direction,' the Cat said, waving its right paw round, 'lives a Hatter: and in that direction,' waving the other paw, 'lives a March Hare. Visit either if you like: they're both mad.'

Lewis Carroll 1832–98, *Alice in Wonderland*

James Cranston 1748–1835
Nurseryman

Those of us who stock our gardens with plants from Wyevale may not realise that the nursery is on the site of a much older establishment, begun by the man we celebrate today. James Cranston was apprenticed to a famous nurseryman, James Lee of Hammersmith. Cranston came to Hereford as Uvedale Price's gardener in about 1770. He became a practitioner of the Picturesque style and his services were recommended by Price to his friends as a cheaper version of Humphrey Repton. 'Cranny', as he became known, was employed by Sir George Beaumont at Coleorton in Leicestershire and by Lord Musgrave at Lowther Castle in Westmorland. He founded a nursery at King's Acre in 1764 and became involved in the planting of many Herefordshire estates – Moccas, Stoke Edith, Garnons, Allensmore Court. As an enclosure surveyor/commissioner he provided hundreds of miles of hedging and thus transformed the Herefordshire countryside. He is buried in Breinton churchyard – the church there restored in the 1860s at the initiative of James Cranston, a descendant of 'Cranny'.

Gardeners can teach us so much about God and Creation, about the transitory nature of life and our place in the world – as in these timeless words:

Gardener
Go, bind up yon dangling apricocks,
Which, like unruly children, make their sire
Stoop with oppression of their prodigal weight:
Give some supportance to the bending twigs.
Go thou, and, like an executioner,
Cut off the heads of too-fast-growing sprays,
That look too lofty in our commonwealth:
All must be even in our government.
You thus employ'd I will go root away
The noisome weeds, that without profit suck
The soil's fertility from wholesome flowers

First servant
Why should we, in the compass of a pale,
Keep law and form and due proportion,
Showing, as in a model, our firm estate,
When our sea-walled garden, the whole land,
Is full of weeds; her fairest flowers choked up,
Her fruit-trees all unpruned, her hedges ruin'd,
Her knots disorder'd, and her wholesome herbs
Swarming with caterpillars?

Gardener
Hold thy peace:
He that hath suffer'd this disorder'd spring
Hath now himself met with the fall of leaf.

William Shakespeare 1564–1616, *Richard II*, Act III, Scene 4

GILBERT HARDING 1907–60
Radio & television broadcaster

I REMEMBER the first television we had at home – a tiny screen round which we gathered to watch *Blue Peter* and the like! My parents occasionally allowed me to stay up for later programmes and I can just remember *What's my Line?* Its presenter was Gilbert Harding, born on this day in 1907. His parents were officials at Hereford workhouse, and Harding often boasted of his workhouse background! After Cambridge, he went to theological college at Mirfield to train for the Anglican priesthood. Although he left there in 1929 to become a Roman Catholic, his love and respect for the Church of England never left him. After some years teaching in Canada he started other careers – in the police force, then as a lawyer – but the outbreak of war led him to join the BBC monitoring service, in which he served in Canada. Back in England after the war, he became quizmaster in the *Round Britain Quiz* and he soon became a household name in radio programmes such as *The Brains Trust* and *Twenty Questions* and on television in *What's my Line?* He was a popular yet outspoken figure and never suffered fools gladly. In many ways, he regretted his media fame, thinking that he would have made a better academic. In politics he was always very much to the left and he believed, even in his prosperity, in the need for more equal distribution of wealth. For much of his adult life, Harding was in bad health, suffering from asthma, and he died suddenly on 16 November 1960. His requiem took place at Westminster Cathedral.

In his autobiography, Gilbert Harding speaks of his religious background and of the riches of the Church of England which he continued to value after his conversion to Roman Catholicism:

At the Community of the Resurrection (Mirfield), each night after Compline, we observed the Greater Silence. I am a man who delights in talk and finds a certain pleasure in the sound of my own voice: I cannot, however, convey to you how exquisite, how peaceful, was that truce from all talk:

'They never taste who always drink;
They always talk who never think.'

At Mirfield I still said too much at the wrong time. It was there that I was made to hang a text over my bed: 'I will give heed unto my ways that I offend not with my tongue'.

But at Mirfield I did find time for thinking. The result was that I became a Roman Catholic and went to the Benedictine Abbey of St Michael the Archangel and All the Holy Angels at Belmont, outside Hereford, where I became a lay schoolmaster,

I rejoice, with a sense of unbounded relief, at my escape from becoming a parson. I should, I am sure, have found peace and profound pleasure in my parish church if I had become a country parson and my church happened to be a noble and ancient one. The Devil, they say, has all the best tunes; the Church of England has, without question, the best churches, and the finest and the oldest of them were built by men of my Faith.

Yes, the musty-mushroom, old-cushions-and-candles smell of an ancient church has always delighted me. I can always find peace beneath old window-glass, glowing with rich purples, unbelievable blues, crimson, more crimson than any rose. And it goes without saying that I would have delighted in my old, stone pulpit and been ever conscious of the long line of incumbents, eloquent or sleep-producing, who had occupied it before me and worn smooth the rails and steps with their now dead hands and feet.

Gilbert Harding, *Master of None* (1958)

Ella Mary Leather 1874–1928

Champion of Hereford's folk tradition

When the centenary of the English Hymnal was celebrated in 2006, we discovered afresh the great influence of folk song in providing us with some our of best melodies. The rediscovery of folk song owes much to the composer Ralph Vaughan Williams, but he in turn was introduced to the subject by a Herefordshire woman, Ella Mary Leather. Born in Dilwyn, she was educated at the old Hereford High School for Girls and spent most of her life in Weobley. In 1905, Leather contributed a chapter, 'The folk lore of the shire', to a book titled *Memorials of Old Herefordshire* and this encouraged her enthusiasm as an ardent folklorist, conscious that many old country customs were dying out. Further books followed – *The Folk-Lore of Herefordshire* continued in print until the 1990s. Meeting Vaughan Williams at the Three Choirs Festival in Hereford in 1908, she took him (and Cecil Sharp, who also admired her work) to local gypsies and hop-pickers, from whom he was able to hear traditional folk songs. During the course of visits every year from 1909 to 1913 and again in 1922, Vaughan Williams took down from dictation over 80 songs, and in 1920 he collaborated with Leather in the publication of his *Twelve Traditional Carols from Herefordshire*. He especially admired 'The truth from above' and used it in the opening theme of his *Fantasia on Christmas Carols*. Ella Leather became an authority on folklore and was much sought after as a speaker, not least by the Women's Institute, of which she was Herefordshire president in 1928. She also wrote on local timber-framed houses and was an enthusiast for the collecting of folk-dances. She copied down the dance of the last group of Herefordshire Morris men at Bromfield in 1909, and in 1925 established the Herefordshire branch of the Folk Dance Society. A dance called 'Haste to the Wedding' collected by her was performed at the first National Festival of Folk Dance in the Albert Hall in 1926. Ella Leather died in Weobley on this day in 1928 and was buried in Weobley churchyard. Her obituary celebrated her unique role, not only in encouraging Vaughan Williams and Sharp in their own fields but also in finding culture in the so-called 'uncultured' and in showing folk song to be an important part of the English musical scene.

Folk song is timeless. It speaks of very human emotions – love, rejection, grief, sadness, joy – but in a way which is not compromised by sophistication or modern development. Ella Mary Leather wrote: 'It is difficult to convey to those who have never known it the joy of hearing folk songs as we have heard that pathetic ballad [Cold Blows the Wind]; the difference between hearing it there and in a drawing room or concert hall is just that between discovering a wild flower growing in its native habitat and admiring it when transplanted to a botanic garden.' This is seen so clearly in the ballad she mentions:

Cold blows the wind on my true love,
And a few small drops of rain.
I never had but one true love;
In a greenwood he was slain.

'I'd do as much for my true love
As any young girl may.
I'd sit and weep all on his grave
For a twelvemonth and a day.'

When twelve months and a day were gone
This young man he arose:
'Why do you weep down by my grave,
That I can take no repose?'

David Cox 1783–1859
Hereford's Turner & Constable

The cottage orné in Venns Lane, Hereford, with its rustic timberwork and thatched roof, is a lasting reminder of one of the great artists of the 19th century – one who spent an important part of his life in our midst. David Cox was born on the industrial edge of Birmingham and showed talent as an artist at an early age. Unsuited to follow his father as a smith, he was apprenticed to a miniature painter and then to a scene painter at the Theatre Royal, Birmingham – work which eventually took him to London. Later journeys in Wales encouraged him to paint landscapes, and through these he soon became a renowned watercolourist. He was a keen teacher and published several manuals – these are seen as having trained a whole generation of amateurs to imitate his style. He exhibited at the Royal Academy and became a member of the Society of Painters in Water Colours – for which group he exhibited nearly every year of his life – a total of 849 works. In 1814, Cox became drawing-master to a girls' school in Hereford run by a Miss Croucher in the Gate House, Widemarsh Street, and he taught here until 1819. He was also drawing-master of Hereford Cathedral School, 1817–27. In Hereford he found his best pupil, Joseph Murray Ince (see 24 September). After living in several homes in the city, he finally built his new home, the cottage orné, Ash Tree House, in 1824. The Hereford years saw a maturing of his style, and the start of large landscape watercolours. Only in his last years did he receive wider recognition. A contemporary review mused on some unjust criticism of Cox:

> ... a pity that they could not inhale the sweet breath of his hayfields and purple heaths, not see the rushing of his summer showers, nor repose with him under the shadows of his thick umbrageous elms and his graceful ash-trees. Not understand Cox? Why there is hardly a peasant in the land who goes to his daily toil by the hedgerows, or in the fields, who could not thoroughly feel the truth and beauty of his landscapes.

Cox died on this day in 1859 and was buried in Harborne churchyard in Birmingham, alongside his late wife. After his death, his name was often linked with those of Turner and Constable, the popularity of his work being reflected in prices achieved on the art market. The 4500 guineas achieved by *The Vale of Clwyd* in 1892 marked the peak of interest in his work, and was a sum exceeded by only a few British paintings in the whole of the century.

The landscapes of David Cox were particularly admired. Perhaps he exhibits in his work a great understanding of the English countryside and the ways in which it opens for us the greatness of God. Thomas Traherne, in his writings, often sees God in the Herefordshire landscape and in this passage sees parallels between the artist and God himself:

To sit in the Throne of God is to inhabit eternity. To reign there is to be pleased with all Things in Heaven and Earth from Everlasting to Everlasting, as if we had the Sovereign Disposal of them. For He is to Dwell in us, and We in Him, because He liveth in our Knowledge and We in His. His Will is to be in our Will, since our Will is to be in His Will, so that both being joyned and becoming one, we are pleased in all His Works as He is, and herein the Image of God perfectly consisteth. No Artist maketh a throne too wide for the Person. God is the Greatest and Divinest Artist.

Thomas Traherne *c.*1636–74, *Centuries of Meditation*

William Edward Evans 1801–69

Clerical fisherman

Before I set out for my walk along the Pilgrims' Way in 2010, I attended Holy Communion in Winchester Cathedral. There, in Prior Silkstede's chapel, is the memorial window to Izaak Walton, the great 17th-century exponent of angling and champion of the priest and poet, George Herbert. The Marches have their own version of Izaak Walton, though less well known. William Edward Evans was born in Shrewsbury, where he attended Shrewsbury School, and proceeded to Clare College, Cambridge. He was ordained and served curacies in Wales at Llanymynech and Criggion in Montgomeryshire. He moved to Herefordshire when his wife inherited Burton Court, near Leominster and he became incumbent of Monkland (1832–50). In 1841 Evans was appointed prebendary of Hereford and prelector of the cathedral. He is said to have been a fine preacher, a keen naturalist and an excellent angler. His chief work is *The Song of the Birds* or *Analogies of Animal and Spiritual Life* (1845), in which the habits of birds were shown to offer spiritual lessons. In this work, the 22 chapters on British songbirds revealed the accuracy of Evans' observations. Other books include *The First Revelation of God to Man* (1849) and a series of sermons on Genesis. After holding the living of Monkland for 18 years, he moved to the parishes of Madley and Tyberton and in 1861 became a canon of Hereford Cathedral. On his death in 1869, he was remembered by a memorial window in Llanymynech church.

Just as Evans saw in birdsong a reflection of life itself, so Izaak Walton, two centuries earlier, saw in angling – with its necessity of patience, watching and waiting – a means of coming closer to God. Here, he expands on his understanding of this art:

O, Sir, doubt not but that Angling is an art; is it not an art to deceive a Trout with an artificial fly? A Trout! that is more sharp-sighted than any Hawk you have named, and more watchful and timorous that your high-mettled Merlin is bold? And yet, I doubt not to catch a brace or two tomorrow, for a friend's breakfast: doubt not therefore, Sir, but that angling is an art, and an art worth your learning: the question is rather, whether you be capable of learning it? For angling is somewhat like poetry, men are to be born so: I mean, with inclinations to it, though both may be heightened by discourse and practice; but he that hopes to be a good angler, must not only bring an inquiring, searching, observing wit; but he must bring a large measure of hope and patience, and a love and propensity to the art itself; but having once got and practised it, then doubt not but angling will prove to be so pleasant, that it will prove to be, like virtue, a reward to itself.

Izaak Walton 1593–1683, *The Compleat Angler*

The Fisherman's Prayer

God grant that I may learn to fish
Until my dying day,
And when it comes to my last cast
I then most humbly pray,
When in the Lord's safe landing net
I'm peacefully asleep
That in his mercy I be judged
As good enough to keep.

Anon.

Eric Gill 1882–1940

Sculptor, stonecutter, typeface designer, printmaker

The great sculpture *Ariel* on Broadcasting House is admired as the work of one of the greatest artists in stone of the 20th century. Trained as an architect under W D Caröe, doyen of the Arts and Crafts movement, Eric Gill gave up architecture to become a calligrapher, letter cutter and monumental mason. After a period in Sussex, he moved in 1924 to Capel-y-ffin, on the Welsh border, where he and a group of friends took up residence in the former monastery set up by Father Ignatius in the late 19th century (see 15 October). With Gill was the poet and artist David Jones, who painted local scenery. While at Capel-y-ffin, Gill perfected his famous type-faces *Perpetua* and *Gill Sans*. In 1928, he and his family moved to Buckinghamshire, and at this time he produced some of his most famous commissions, including the *Stations of the Cross* in Westminster Cathedral. He was a deeply religious man, a Roman Catholic, and he wrote widely on the place of art in faith, including his book *Christianity and Art.*

Recent biographical information suggests that Gill led a personal life of some notoriety or chaos, his abuse extending even to his own family. Some have suggested that such a person's artistic work should find no place in a Christian church, and point to the Stations of the Cross *in Westminster Cathedral. But surely the work of many of our great artists has come from the hands of flawed individuals – and does this necessarily render the results of their genius unacceptable? Perhaps in Gill's case his own* Stations of the Cross *can speak powerfully to victims of abuse of whatever generation, who, young or old, tread the same* via dolorosa*?*

Look at every vice, pain, and disorder in human nature; it is in itself nothing else but the spirit of the creature turned from the universality of love to some self-seeking or own will in created things. So that love alone is, and only can be, the cure of every evil, and he that lives in the purity of love is risen out of the power of evil into the freedom of the one spirit of heaven. The schools have given us very accurate definitions of every vice, whether it be covetousness, pride, wrath, envy, etc., and shown us how to conceive them as notionally distinguished from one another. But the Christian has a much shorter way of knowing their nature and power and what they all are and do in and to himself. For call them by what names you will, or distinguish them with ever so much exactness, they are all, separately and jointly, just that same one thing, and all do that same one work as the scribes, the Pharisees, hypocrites, and rabble of the Jews who crucified Christ were all but one and the same thing and all did one and the same work, however different they were in outward names. If you would therefore have a true sense of the nature and power of pride, wrath, covetousness, envy, etc., they are in their whole nature nothing else but the murderers and crucifiers of the true Christ of God; not as the High Priests did many hundreds of years ago, nailing His outward humanity to an outward cross, but crucifying afresh the Son of God, the holy Immanuel, who is the Christ that every man crucifies as often as he gives way to wrath, envy, or covetousness etc. For every temper or passion that is contrary to the new birth of Christ and keeps the holy Immanuel from coming to life in the soul is, in the strictest truth of the words, a murderer and killer of the Lord of life. And where pride and envy and hatred, etc., are suffered to live, there the same thing is done as when Christ was killed and Barabbas was saved alive.

William Law 1686–1761, *The Spirit of Love*

Lord Byron 1788–1824

Romantic poet

We tend to associate Byron with the high life in London or on the Continent, but some of his happiest days were spent in Herefordshire. Born in 1788, he was ten when he inherited the title from his uncle and became Lord Byron. After Harrow and Cambridge he travelled in Europe, developing his poetic skills and becoming involved in all manner of romantic entanglements. It was in 1812–13 that he lived at Kinsham Court as the lover of Lady Oxford. There, it is said, his great work *Childe Harold* was inspired. It is a poetic travelogue of picturesque lands, giving vent to the melancholy and disillusion of the post-Revolution and Napoleonic eras. Byron married Annabella Millbanke in 1814, but the marriage dissolved in scandal and Byron fled the country, never to return. He spent his last years in Switzerland and Italy, met with other poets like Shelley, and wrote his great epic poem *Don Juan*. In his final years, he became involved in the Greek struggle for independence from the Turks and on his death in 1824 he was greatly mourned by the Greeks. He was refused burial in Westminster Abbey, the dean, Herbert Ryle, writing sternly: 'Byron, partly by his own openly dissolute life and partly by the influence of licentious verse, earned a worldwide reputation for immorality among English-speaking people. A man who outraged the laws of our Divine Lord and whose treatment of women violated the Christian principles of purity and honour should not be commemorated in Westminster Abbey.' However, in 1969 the Abbey authorities relented and a memorial was placed in Poets' Corner.

In his day, Byron was often shunned by respectable society, but behind this moral indignation was a great deal of hypocrisy. It was always so, and remains so today. These words by a 19th-century historian have a curiously contemporary ring:

We know no spectacle so ridiculous as the British public in one of its periodical fits of morality. In general, elopements, divorces, and family quarrels, pass with little notice. We read the scandal, talk about it for a day, and forget it. But once in six or seven years, our virtue becomes outrageous. We cannot suffer the laws of religion and decency to be violated. We must take a stand against vice. ... Accordingly, some unfortunate man, in no respect more depraved than hundreds whose offences have been treated with leniency, is singled out as an expiatory sacrifice. If he has children, they are to be taken from him. If he has a profession, he is to be driven from it. He is cut by the higher orders and hissed at by the lower. He is, in truth, a sort of whipping-boy, by whose vicarious agonies all the other transgressors of the same class are, it is supposed, sufficiently chastised. We reflect very complacently on our own severity, and compare with great pride the high standard of morals established in England, with the Parisian laxity. At length our anger is satiated. Our victim is ruined and heart-broken. And our virtue goes quietly to sleep for seven years more.

It is clear that those vices which destroy domestic happiness ought to be as much as possible repressed. It is equally clear that they cannot be repressed by penal legislation. It is therefore right and desirable that public opinion should be directed against them. But it should be directed against them uniformly, steadily, and temperately, not by sudden fits and starts. There should be one weight and one measure. Decimation is always an objectionable mode of punishment. ... When adopted by the tribunal of public opinion, it is infinitely more irrational. It is good that a certain portion of disgrace should constantly attend on certain bad actions. But it is not good that the offenders should merely have to stand the risks of a lottery of infamy, that ninety-nine out of every hundred should escape; and that the hundredth, perhaps the most innocent of the hundred, should pay for all.

Lord Macaulay 1800–1859, *Essays: Moore's Life of Byron*

King John 1167–1216

'Wicked king' with Hereford & Worcester links

King John is especially associated with Worcester, where his tomb is set in the midst of the quire of the Cathedral. His effigy is set between smaller images of saints he admired – Oswald and Wulfstan (see 29 February and 19 January), both of whom wave censers in his ears. However, Hereford also has its links to this much maligned monarch, and he is said to have visited the city in each year of his reign. The youngest of the five sons of Henry II and Eleanor of Aquitaine, John succeeded his brother Richard I as king. His reign is often characterised as disastrous for the realm – he did indeed lose Normandy to France and in 1213 made England a papal fiefdom to resolve conflict with the Catholic church. However, he is best known for acquiescing to the sealing of Magna Carta in June 1215, a document which limited kingly power in England and which was certainly an enormously important step in the evolution of government. Hereford Cathedral possesses a copy of the 1217 revision of Magna Carta, issued by Henry III, one of only four surviving, and also a unique letter, from King John to the sheriff of Gloucester, relating to the issue of Magna Carta in 1215. John is surrounded by popular legend – that he was the enemy of Robin Hood, that he lost the Crown Jewels in the Wash in Lincolnshire, and that he died of a 'surfeit of peaches'. Perhaps Winston Churchill offers a more generous assessment of his reign when he writes:

> When the tally is added, it will be seen that the British nation and the English-speaking world owes far more to the vices of John than to the labours of virtuous sovereigns.

A 19th-century historian speaks of the importance of King John's Magna Carta – words with which many will identify when they look at Hereford's own copy of this great document:

It is impossible to gaze without reverence on the earliest monument of English freedom which we can see with our own eyes and touch with our own hands, the great Charter to which from age to age patriots have looked back as the basis of English liberty. But in itself the Charter was no novelty, nor did it claim to establish any new constitutional principles. The Charter of Henry the First formed the basis of the whole, and the additions to it are for the most part formal recognitions of the judicial and administrative changes introduced by Henry the Second. But the vague expressions of the older charter were now exchanged for precise and elaborate provisions. The bonds of unwritten custom which the older grant did little more than recognize had proved too weak to hold the Angevins; and the baronage now threw them aside for the restraints of written law.

It is in this way that the Great Charter marks the transition from the age of traditional rights, preserved in the nation's memory and officially declared by the Primate, to the age of written legislation, of Parliaments and Statutes, which was soon to come. The Church had shown its power of self-defence in the struggle over the interdict, and the clause which recognised its rights alone retained the older and general form. But all vagueness ceases when the Charter passes on to deal with the rights of Englishmen at large, their right to justice, to security of person and property, to good government. 'No freeman,' ran the memorable article that lies at the base of our whole judicial system, 'shall be seized or imprisoned, or dispossessed, or outlawed, or in any way brought to ruin: we will not go against any man nor send against him, save by legal judgement of his peers or by the law of the land.' 'To no man will we sell,' runs another, 'or deny, or delay, right or justice.'

J R Green 1837–83, *A Short History of the English People* (1874)

Stephen Ballard 1804–90

Civil engineer

The great railway viaduct outside Ledbury is lasting testimony to one of the great civil engineers of the 19th century. Born in Malvern in 1804, Stephen Ballard was employed by the Gloucester and Hereford Canal Company, first as its clerk and then its engineer. The canal project needed new impetus and Ballard provided this, resurveying the remaining course of the canal and securing a new Act of Parliament. The canal's final 18 miles into Hereford were completed in 1845. Ballard then became resident engineer of a large project to drain areas of the Fens. His skill earned him membership of the Institution of Civil Engineers in 1846. His experience in canal engineering now moved to the world of the railways and he became involved in major projects, all of which involved work in difficult terrain. Ballard served as contractor of the Worcester and Hereford railway. This involved tunnelling through the very hard rock of the Malvern Hills, a major feat of engineering for which he used a steam drill. The Ledbury viaduct on this line, with its 31 arches and elegant, tapering brick piers was finished on this day in 1861. The project required some five million bricks, which were made on site by his brother. Several men died during the construction of the Malvern tunnel. Ballard married in 1854 and had eight children, the youngest of whom was the horticulturalist, Ernest Ballard (see 30 September).

During my five years as precentor of Ely Cathedral, I daily entered the cathedral by the south door. There, in the cloister, was affixed a memorial to two victims of an accident on the Norwich to Ely railway line in 1845. Pevsner finds it 'eminently characteristic of the earnestness with which this new triumph of human ingenuity was still regarded'.

The line to Heaven by Christ was made,
With heavenly truth the Rails are laid,
From Earth to Heaven the Line extends,
To Life Eternal where it ends.
Repentance is the Station then,
Where Passengers are taken in;
No Fee for them is there to pay,
For Jesus is himself the way.
God's Word is the first Engineer,
It points the way to Heaven so clear,
Through tunnels dark and dreary here,
It does the way to Glory steer.
God's Love the Fire, his Truth the Steam
Which drives the Engine and the Train;
All you who would to Glory ride,
Must come to Christ, in him abide.
In First, and Second, and Third Class,
Repentance, Faith and Holiness,
You must the way to Glory gain,
Or you with Christ will not remain.
Come then, poor Sinners, now's the time,
At any Station on the Line,
If you'll repent, and turn from Sin,
The train will stop and take you in.

William Lambe 1765–1847

Physician & vegetarian

We tend to think of vegetarianism as a modern fashion, but one Herefordshire man proclaimed its health-giving virtues much earlier. Lambe was born in St Peter's parish in Hereford and was educated at Hereford Cathedral School and at St John's College, Cambridge, where he studied medicine. Following his marriage, he moved to Warwick, where he entered general practice and published papers on the health-giving qualities of Leamington spring water. Moving to London in 1803, Lambe became a Fellow of the Royal College of Physicians and practised medicine in Kentish Town. Many of his patients were poor people from whom he would accept no fees. He also taught botany at the Aldersgate School of Medicine and was appointed physician there in 1810. Lambe's poor health encouraged him to become a vegetarian at the age of 41. He also preferred to drink only distilled water. His enthusiasm for this diet led him to publish several papers, including *A medical and experimental enquiry into the origin, symptoms and cure of constitutional diseases* (1805) and *Reports on the effect of a peculiar regimen on schirrhous tumours and cancerous ulcers* (1809). His ideas were embraced by the poet Shelley, with whom he was acquainted. Later in life, Lambe became a zealot in the cause of vegetarianism. It is said that 'he carried his convictions about vegetable diet to such an extent that it well-nigh became a religious belief and he its despotic high priest'. One of Lambe's grandsons later recalled:

> The old man's sudden appearance at the garden gate while the family were breakfasting off (among other things) a ham, great commotion was caused, the ham being thrust into a cupboard and all stray pieces heaped on the plate of a carnivorous governess, who, being ignorant of the reason, looked in bewildered amazement.

Shelley's biographer, Jefferson Hogg, wrote that the last time he met Lambe 'he told me he had breakfasted on one cauliflower and was just about to dine on another'. Lambe retired from medical practice in 1840 and died at Dilwyn on 11 June 1847. He is buried in Dilwyn churchyard in the family vault.

Even two thousand years before William Lambe, the virtues of eating only vegetables was being extolled by that great oriental philosopher, Pythagoras:

Now (lest I stray too far off course, my horses forgetting to aim towards their goal), the heavens, and whatever is under them, change their form, and the earth, and whatever is within it. We, as well, who are a part of the universe, because we are not merely flesh, but in truth, winged spirits, and can enter into the family of wild creatures, and be imprisoned in the minds of animals. We should allow those beings to live in safety, and honour, that the spirits of our parents, or brothers, or those joined to us by some other bond, certainly human, might have inhabited: and not fill our bellies as if at a Thyestean feast! What evil they contrive, how impiously they prepare to shed human blood itself, who rip at a calf's throat with the knife, and listen unmoved to its bleating, or can kill a kid to eat, that cries like a child, or feed on a bird, that they themselves have fed! How far does that fall short of actual murder? Where does the way lead on from there? Let the ox plough, or owe his death to old age: let the sheep yield wool, to protect against the chill north wind: let the she-goats give you full udders for milking! Have done with nets and traps, snares and the arts of deception! Do not trick the birds with limed twigs, or imprison the deer, scaring them with barbed feathered ropes, or hide hooks in treacherous bait. Kill them, if they harm you, but even then let killing be enough. Let your mouth be free of their blood, enjoy milder food!

Richard Baxter 1615–91

He refused to be a bishop

Richard Baxter is Hereford's bishop that never was! Born at Rowton, in Shropshire, he is said to have spent his boyhood at Eaton Constantine, near the Wrekin Hill. He became attached to the court of King James I but was so disgusted with the low moral standards there that he returned home in order to study divinity, He was ordained but after the confirmation of an infamous oath in 1640, which required obedience to a string of persons ending in the trivial phrase 'et cetera', he rejected hierarchical forms and status and went as curate to Kidderminster in Worcestershire. He opposed the Civil War and played a prominent part in the recall of Charles II from exile, but his continued dissatisfaction with the way episcopacy was practised led him to decline the see of Hereford when it was offered to him. This refusal led him to be debarred from further office in the Church, though he continued to contribute to its life as a prolific hymn writer.

Baxter's brave stand against the standards of his time led to his being discriminated against. Here he expands on his dissatisfaction:

When I was a schoolboy of about fifteen years of age, the Bishop coming into the country, many went to be confirmed. We that were boys ran out to see the Bishop among the rest, not knowing anything of the meaning of the business. When we came thither, we met about thirty or forty in all, of our own stature and temper, that had come for us to be 'bishopped', as then it was called. The Bishop examined us not at all in one article of the Faith; but in a churchyard in haste we were set in rank, and he passed hastily over us, laying his hands on our head, and saying a few words, which neither I nor any that I spoke with, understood; so hastily were they uttered and a very short prayer recited, and there was an end. But whether we were Christians or infidels, or knew as much as that there was a God, the Bishop little knew or inquired. And yet he was esteemed one of the best Bishops in England. And though the Canons require that the curate or minister send a certificate that children have learned the Catechism, yet there was no such thing done, but we ran of our own accord to see the Bishop only; and almost all the rest of this country had not this much. This was the old careless practice of this excellent duty of Confirmation.

Richard Baxter, *Works* (ed. W Orme, 1830)

Prayers of Richard Baxter – for unity and for readiness to meet God

Grant more of thy Spirit to all thy churches and servants in the world: that as their darkness and selfishness and imperfections have defiled and divided and weakened them, and made them scandalous and harsh towards unbelievers, so their knowledge, self-denial and impartial love may truly reform, unite and strengthen them: that the glory of their holiness may win an unbelieving world to Christ.

Keep us, O Lord, while we tarry on this earth, in a serious seeking after thee, and in an affectionate walking with thee, every day of our lives; that when thou comest, we may be found not hiding our talent, nor serving the flesh, nor yet asleep with our lamp unfurnished, but waiting and longing for our Lord, our glorious King, for ever and ever.

Henry Rogers 1584–1658

Controversial cleric

Herbert Croft (see 18 May), dean of Hereford during the Civil War, is famously depicted standing in the pulpit, preaching against the excesses of the Parliamentarians. He was not the only one to have preached so provocatively from the pulpit of Hereford Cathedral. Born in the county, Rogers was educated at Jesus College, Oxford and was ordained. He was appointed to a prebendal stall at Hereford Cathedral and held a number of Herefordshire livings – Dorstone, Moccas, Stoke Edith and Foy. He clearly had a feisty personality and this led to trouble with his fellow prebendaries, but in spite of this, in 1637 he became lecturer at Hereford Cathedral, largely through the influence of the secretary of state, Sir John Coke and George Coke, bishop of Hereford (see 10 December). Even Archbishop Laud (see 10 January) gave testimony that Rogers was 'of good learning and conformable', and, despite his frequent skirmishes with authority it was later recalled that he 'showed himself an undaunted champion for the Rights of the King and of the Church of England'. During the Civil War, he became a strong partisan for the Royalist cause, attacking Parliament from the pulpit and thereby attracting condemnation from the Roundheads, who thought him one of 'the devil's orators'. On Hereford's attack by Parliamentary forces in 1643, Rogers was captured. He was deprived of his livings in 1646 and subsequently endured great poverty, although he was 'sometimes comforted by the secret munificence' of Viscount Scudamore (see 4 July), 'and the slenderer gifts of other loyall gentry'. Although the date of Roger's death is unknown, he was buried on this date in 1658 under the parson's seat in Wellington church, Herefordshire.

Henry Roger's courageous preaching is reflected in this passage by George Herbert – words which, though written in the 17th century, clearly have continuing relevance for preaching today:

When he preacheth, he procures attention by all possible art, both by earnestness of speech, it being natural for men to think, that where is much earnestness, there is somewhat worth hearing: and by a diligent and busy cast of his eye on his auditors, with letting them know that he observes who marks, and who not; and with particularising of his speech now to the younger sort, then to the elder, now to the poor, and now to the rich. This is for you, and this is for you; for particulars ever touch, and awake more than generals. Herein also he serves himself of the judgments of God, as of those of ancient times, so especially of the late ones; and those most, which are nearest to his parish; for people are very attentive at such discourses, and think it behoves them to be so, when God is so near them, and even over their heads. Sometimes he tells them stories, and sayings of others, according as his text invites him; for them also men heed, and remember better than exhortations; which though earnest, yet often die with the Sermon, especially with Country people; which are thick, and heavy, and hard to raise to a point of Zeal, and fervency, and need a mountain of fire to kindle them; but stories and sayings they will well remember. He often tells them, that Sermons are dangerous things, that none goes out of Church as he came in, but either better or worse; that none is careless before the Judge, and that the Word of God shall judge us. By these and other means the Parson procures attention; but the character of his Sermon is Holiness; he is not witty, or learned, or eloquent, but Holy.

George Herbert, *A Priest to the Temple*

Briavel (date unknown)

Celtic hermit in the Forest of Dean

The diocese of Hereford included the Forest of Dean until the Reformation settlement, when it was handed over to the new diocese of Gloucester. Deep in the forest is the settlement of St Briavels, with its medieval church and castle, named after a saint about whom little is known. The first record of him appears in about 1130, but his cell or hermitage can be traced back to the middle of the 7th century. One theory suggests that he was among those royal saints of Celtic origin who flourished at that period, while another theory is to identify him with his French contemporary, St Elbrulfus, the well-known abbot of Ouche in Normandy, more generally known as St Evroul, in the diocese of Gloucester St Briavel's feast day is kept on 17 June. Our illustration shows Briavel at prayer in the forest – the canopy of trees making pointed 'gothic' arches, reminding us that so much church architecture is based on natural forms and design.

Briavel's association with the Forest of Dean reminds us of the love of and regard for nature – hallmarks of Celtic Christianity. Seeing God in the world of nature is an approach to the divine with which many, through the centuries have been able to identify. Here, Bishop Edward King, writing over 1,500 years after St Briavel, marvels at God's gifts:

I will thank him for the pleasures given me through my senses, for the glory of the thunder, for the mystery of music, the singing of birds and the laughter of children. I will thank him for the pleasures of seeing, for the delights through colour, for the awe of the sunset, the beauty of flowers, the smile of friendship and the look of love; for the changing beauty of the clouds, for the wild roses in the hedges, for the form and beauty of birds, for the leaves on the trees in spring and autumn, for the witness of the leafless trees through the winter, teaching us that death is sleep and not destruction, for the sweetness of flowers and the scent of hay. Truly, O Lord, the earth is full of thy riches!

And yet, how much more will I thank and praise God for the strength of my body enabling me to work, for the refreshment of sleep, for my daily bread, for the days of painless health, for the gift of my mind and the gift of my conscience, for his loving guidance of my mind ever since it first began to think, and of my heart ever since it first began to love. Oh, from what unknown errors has he guarded me, from what beginnings of sins has he kept me back. I will praise him for my family, my father and my mother, my brothers and sisters, my home, for my husband, for my wife, for the kindness of servants and the love of children.

These are but a few things we can call to mind instantly when we think attentively and reverently of our creation and preservation and of the blessings of this life. Let us resolve each of us to make the text our own today. 'I will extol thee, my God, O King, and I will bless thy name for ever and ever. Every day will I bless thee; and I will praise thy name for ever and ever.'

Edward King 1829–1910, *Sermons and Addresses*

Beryl Reid 1919–96

Actress & comedienne

The ability to present comedy and tragedy on stage and in film is the mark of a great actor, and the woman we celebrate today could make people both laugh and cry. Beryl Reid was born on this day in 1919 at 8 St Olave's, St Owen Street, Hereford. She was educated in Manchester, where she began dancing lessons at the age of three. She made her acting debut in 1936 at Bridlington, as an impressionist and soubrette. She used her comic skills in pantomime, working with famed performers like Max Miller and Will Fyffe. Her wireless breakthrough came in comedy sketches for the radio in Scotland, in which she perfected the comedy character Monica, the wicked, posh-voiced schoolgirl. Beryl was well known for her monologues (much in the style of Joyce Grenfell) and she appeared on the London stage, especially at the London Palladium. Another turning point came in 1965 when she made her 'straight' West End debut in Frank Marcus's *The Killing of Sister George*, playing a hard-drinking, lesbian soap actress. Other successes at this time included Joe Orton's *Entertaining Mr Sloane* (1969) and *Spring Awakening* (1973). On television, she made a great impact in the cameo role of Connie Sachs in John le Carré's *Tinker, Tailor, Soldier, Spy* (1979) and *Smiley's People* (1982), for which she received a BAFTA award. On and off stage, Beryl Reid was an exceptionally funny woman, highly intelligent, always eager to learn new skills and roles. She loved her friends, but also had a reclusive side, happy to be alone with her many cats in her riverside home at Wraysbury in Buckinghamshire.

Beryl Reid used her appearance – small, neat, bright-eyed, with a wide mouth, dimples and tilted nose – to good effect in portraying mischievous characters. Famous roles included that of the Nurse in Romeo and Juliet *– an ideal part, with its gossipy, garrulous, relentless character. Here, Lady Capulet and Juliet try in vain to stop the endless chatter of the Nurse:*

Lady C.	Enough of this; I pray thee hold thy peace.
Nurse.	Yes, madam. Yet I cannot choose but laugh To think it should leave crying and say 'Ay' ...
Juliet.	And stint thou too, I pray thee, nurse, say I!
Nurse.	Peace, I have done. God mark thee to his grace! Thou was the prettiest babe that e'er I nurs'd; And I might live to see thee married once, I have my wish.
Lady C.	Marry, that 'marry' is the very theme I came to talk of, Tell me, daughter Juliet, How stands your disposition to be married?
Juliet.	It is an honour that I dream not of.
Nurse.	An honour! Were not I thine only nurse, I would say thou hadst suck'd wisdom from thy teat.

William Shakespeare 1564–1616, *Romeo and Juliet*, Act 1, Scene 3

Joan de Clifford *c.*1134–91

'Fair Rosamund'

The roses of June are a reminder of a character well-known in fact and in legend. Born Joan de Clifford, she was a native of Herefordshire – her father, Walter, was Lord of the Castle of Clifford, near Hay-on-Wye. Tradition has it that Joan is identified with the story of Fair Rosamund, the tale recorded in an old ballad bearing this title. According to this, Joan (Rosamund) captivated the affections of Henry II, then a young king and married to a wife eleven years his senior – a woman of jealous temper. To keep the intrigue secret from the queen and to protect his favourite from her vengeance, should the secret become known to her, Henry constructed the famous 'bower' at Woodstock in Oxfordshire, which had 'a hundred and fifty doors'. There the king placed 'his love, so faire and bright'. But, during the king's absence in France, the queen, now aware of the secret, gained admittance to the bower. Finding Rosamund, where she 'was like an angel sette', in spite of tears and entreaties, she compelled her to drink a cup of poison. There is certainly some truth in the story. It is mentioned in the chronicles of Roger de Hoveden, but he relates that Rosamund was not poisoned but, on being discovered by the queen, retired to the nunnery at Godstow, where she died a penitent. He also relates that Hugh, bishop of Lincoln, came to Godstow nunnery in 1191, and finding her body, prepared for its requiem mass, ordered it to be taken away and buried outside the church. The nuns agreed to do this, but as soon as Hugh had departed, they buried the body of their beloved, though fallen, sister, within the nunnery church. At the Dissolution of the monasteries, the antiquary, Leland, informs us that the tomb was opened and that 'when it was opened, there came out a very sweet smell'.

The story of Joan (Rosamund) is bitter-sweet – a tale of love and deceit, of forgiveness and retribution. Perhaps the rose is the best flower to represent this – not only because of the heroine's name but because as a flower it combines sweetness and beauty with an often vicious thorn:

For Zeus chose us a King of the flowers in his mirth,
He would call to the rose, and would royally crown it:
For the rose, ho, the rose! is the grace of the earth,
Is the light of the plants that are growing upon it.

For the rose, ho, the rose! is the eye of the flowers,
Is the blush of the meadows that feel themselves fair,
Is the lightning of beauty that strikes through the bowers,
On pale lovers that sit in the glow unaware.

Ho, the rose breathes of love! ho, the rose lifts the cup
To the red lips of Cypris invoked for a guest!
Ho, the rose having curled its sweet leaves for the world
Takes delight in the motion its petals keep up
As they laugh to the wind as it laughs from the west.

Sappho *c.* BC 615–550, 'Song of the Rose'

Thomas William Webb 1807–85

Priest & astronomer

His obituary in the *Hereford Times* of 11 June 1885 states that Thomas Webb had 'probably induced more amateurs to interest themselves in the study of astronomy then any other man of his generation'. His father was a priest and Thomas was educated at the vicarage in Tretire before studying mathematics at Oxford. After ordination in Hereford Cathedral, he served in several parishes, becoming a minor canon and librarian of Gloucester Cathedral from 1844 to 1849 and, later, a prebendary of Hereford Cathedral. In 1856 he became vicar of Hardwicke, near Hay-on-Wye, a parish which he served until his death. As a young man, Webb spent many hours making specula for his home-made telescopes and he became an expert in optics, being elected to the Royal Astronomical Society in 1852. His observational work was chiefly concerned with the moon, double stars, nebulae, meteors and comets, all meticulously recorded in a series of notebooks, covering periods from 1825 to 1874. He served on the British Association's Moon Committee and was active in the Selenographical Society. He encouraged younger astronomers, not least through his *Celestial Objects for Common Telescopes* (1859) – a book which was reprinted as late as 1962. Through this, Webb enabled amateur astronomers to observe double stars and nebulae through a portable (and inexpensive) 3½ inch telescope.

In addition to his interest in astronomy, Webb was very musical and installed the first organ at St Weonards in 1840. He edited and completed his father's books on the Civil War in Herefordshire and wrote articles in several popular periodicals, including *Nature, Knowledge* and *The English Mechanic.*

An interest in the stars leads not only to scientific exploration but also to wonder at the vastness and mystery of the universe. In this poem, Keats sees the stars as informing him of his mortality – and of his ability to love and admire:

Bright star, would I were steadfast as thou art –
   Not in lone splendour hung aloft the night
And watching, with eternal lids apart,
   Like Nature's patient, sleepless Eremite,
The moving waters at their priestlike task
   Of pure ablution round earth's human shores,
Or gazing on the new soft-fallen mask
   Of snow upon the mountains and the moors –
No – yet still steadfast, still unchangeable,
   Pillow'd upon my fair love's ripening breast,
To feel for ever its soft fall and swell,
   Awake for ever in a sweet unrest,
Still, still to hear her tender-taken breath,
   And so live ever – or else swoon to death.

John Keats 1795–1821, 'Written on a Blank Page in Shakespeare's Poems'

Frederick Kempson 1838–1923

Hereford's pre-eminent Gothic architect

Often when we see a famous building, we fail to look up to observe its rooflines and gables. Looking up towards the roof of Hereford's City Museum and Library will reveal a remarkable series of animal carvings – monkeys, lions, dogs. The library is possibly the most original design of the architect we celebrate today. Frederick Kempson was a clergy son – his father was rector of Stoke Lacy and the family lived at Birchfield, Bromyard. He was apprenticed to Philip Hardwick, surveyor to Hereford Cathedral during the 19th century, and later became assistant to John Pritchard, diocesan architect for Llandaff. In an era when many churches were being restored after years of neglect, Kempson played a full part in this process, being responsible for the restoration or rebuilding of 19 Herefordshire churches, 18 in Glamorgan and 11 in Pembrokeshire, as well as 16 secular buildings. A friend of the architect, J P Seddon and of the Hereford historian F T Havergal, he had a great antiquarian interest in churches and his drawings survive in early transactions of the Woolhope Club. In contrast to many brutal restorations, he was sensitive to medieval work – as seen at Pipe-cum-Lyde (1875), Breinton (1866) and Tarrington (1882). Kempson also designed and built new churches – St Paul, Tupsley (1865) and Holy Trinity, Hereford (1882) – and he was renowned as a spire builder in South Wales, his masterpiece, St Peter, Pentre, acknowledged as 'the Cathedral of Rhondda'.

It falls to the ministry of archdeacons in their annual visitations to comment upon the state and repair of churches in their jurisdiction. Some themes constantly recur, and in this passage from the published charges of Archdeacon Richard Lane Freer, these familiar themes are touched upon. Later charges from the same archdeacon reported progress and Frederick Kempson was involved in many of these restorations:

But let me proceed. You, Gentlemen Churchwardens, will not expect me, at this early stage of my office, to enter into your duties respecting the particular ecclesiastical edifices which are severally under your care, and which, with the exception of those within the Rural Deanery I lately held, are at present but little known to me. Generally speaking, I am aware that much has been done in late years towards the decent reparation and the restoration of our Parish Churches. It is much to be regretted, and it falls heavily on the present generation, that during preceding centuries the guardians of those consecrated fabrics appear to have slumbered on their posts. Damp and rot – the exclusion of circulating air, because windows were never opened – and the gradual admission of rain through neglected roofs – has assimilated many of our Churches more to the receptacles of the last remnants of mortality, than the temples where the living meet to celebrate the Lord of life; and later times have been called on, at great expense, and with no little difficulty, to renovate that which a moderate outlay and only ordinary care would have preserved for ages.

Richard Lane Freer, *Charges delivered to the clergy of the Archdeaconry of Hereford* (1863)

Lady Courtney of Penwith 1847–1929

Social worker & internationalist

When we think of suffragettes, we immediately think of Emmeline Pankhurst and similarly famous names. But behind these more prominent leaders of the movement were a large number of provincial supporters, of whom Catherine Courtney was one. Born in April 1847 at Gayton Hall, Upton Bishop, Herefordshire, Catherine came of a privileged background but wished to break away from the world her parents had prepared for her – that of a socialite and debutante. Instead, she left Herefordshire for London, and joined Octavia Hill, then Samuel and Henrietta Barnett, in work for the poor of the East End. On her marriage to the Liberal cabinet minister, Leonard Courtney, she entered the political world and, with her influence, was able to bring to reality many of her dreams for a fairer, more just world. She became a suffragist and a leader of the Women's Liberal Unionist Association. Both the Courtneys were deeply committed to international peace and they spoke out for peace and justice at the outbreak of the South African War. They both became notorious as alleged 'pro-Boers' and both criticised the British for what they saw as uncivilized methods of warfare, with the introduction of concentration camps at Bloemfontein. When the First World War broke out, Lady Courtney (her husband was raised to a peerage in 1906) persisted in her humane pacifism. She refused to become involved in the war and instead helped to found a committee to relieve destitute German civilians who had become stranded in Britain at the outbreak of war. On the international scene, she supported the American progressive Jane Addams in her frustrated attempts in 1915 to organise a negotiated end to the war brokered by neutral nations. Kate Courtney's *Extracts from a Diary* (1927) and her letters to the press in 1919–20 testify to her insight into the fatal consequences of righteous hatred and militarism, such as was found at the end of the Great War. The popular press dubbed her as 'pro-Hun' but she was without doubt a powerful and prophetic voice. Her more famous sister, Beatrice Webb wrote of her, when she died: 'Kate was the most beneficent of my sisters ... she was in a sense faultless – she had no malice, no envy, little egotism.' She died in February 1929 and is buried at Chelsea Old Church.

Words by the more famous Emmeline Pankhurst share many of the principles espoused by Kate Courtney and her generation. These were spoken by Mrs Pankhurst in November 1913 in Hartford, Connecticut, USA. However, Mrs Pankhurst was much happier in using the language of military encounter to achieve her ends than was Kate Courtney:

I am here as a soldier who has temporarily left the field of battle in order to explain – it seems strange it should have to be explained – what civil war is like when civil war is waged by women. I am not only here as a soldier temporarily absent from the field of battle; I am here – and that, I think, is the strangest part of my coming – I am here as a person who, according to the law courts of my country, it has been decided, is of no value to the community at all: and I am adjudged because of my life to be a dangerous person, under sentence of penal servitude in a convict prison. So you see there is some special interest in hearing so unusual a person address you. I dare say, in the minds of many of you – you will perhaps forgive me this personal touch – that I do not look either very like a soldier or very like a convict, yet I am both.

We felt we had to rouse the public to such a point that they would say to the government, 'you must give women the vote.' We had to get the electors, we had to get the business interests, we had to get the professional interests, we had to get the men of leisure all unitedly saying to the government, 'relieve the strain of this situation and give women the vote'; ... We have done it; we are doing it every day; and I think when you take the fact into consideration, you will realise why we have been attacking private property. There is a homely English proverb which may help to clear the situation which is this: 'You cannot rouse the Britisher unless you touch his pocket'.

Edmund Audley *c.*1439–1524

Bishop of Hereford not in his tomb ...

Edmund Audley gave to Hereford Cathedral one of its most beautiful chapels – the chantry on the south side of the Lady Chapel. He studied at Lincoln College, Oxford and in 1464 was presented to the prebend of Colwall in Hereford diocese. This was only the beginning of his collection of ecclesiastical dignities, for he soon held canonries or prebends at Lincoln, Salisbury, Lichfield, Wells, St Paul's and York as well as being archdeacon of the East Riding and of Essex. All these he gave up when he became bishop of Rochester in 1480. He was translated to Hereford in 1492, and ten years later became bishop of Salisbury. In Salisbury he became feared for his zealous persecution of heretics, especially of Lollards, and he gave orders for many to be burned at the stake. For all this, he was also a generous man, leaving Greek manuscripts to Oxford University, a silver shrine to Hereford Cathedral and a pulpit to St Mary's, Oxford.

His magnificent chantry in Hereford Cathedral has two storeys – the upper storey possibly once used as a choir gallery or a watching chamber to guard the shrine of St Thomas of Hereford (at that period in the Lady Chapel). The lower chapel has two windows, now filled with glass commemorating the 17th-century priest-poet, Thomas Traherne (see 10 October). The magnificent stone screen separating the chantry from the Lady Chapel, with its rows of saints, gives a wonderful impression of the brilliant colour with which the whole cathedral would have been painted.

In the apex of the vault is a boss of the Blessed Virgin Mary, very similar to one in Audley's other chantry in Salisbury Cathedral, and we may also note other tiny details – the lock of the door to the staircase has the letters E A, the bishop's initials, and on the stonework outside the chapel there are dragonflies and golden combs.

Edmund Audley prepared his beautiful chantry to receive his body when he died, but he didn't die! No, he became bishop of Salisbury in 1502, and there, in Salisbury Cathedral, is another 'Audley Chapel', rather similar in style to that at Hereford, where his body is buried. But rather than feel cheated by the bishop, should we not see this chapel as a wonderful 16th-century version of 'the empty tomb', celebrated by Christians each Sunday and especially on Easter Day? The Resurrection of Jesus Christ is a multi-faceted jewel, capable of many interpretations, but it has sometimes perplexed Christians, as the following passage makes clear:

If my mind can't quite take certain things – such as the physical Resurrection – does it matter, so long as it doesn't get in the way of belief in Christ as master and saviour and helper, to be sought and served? I know it mattered to the early church, and was perhaps the only way in which they could be convinced – but should one try to force or persuade one's mind to it, if one feels one doesn't need it? You say 'we cannot be expected to do more than yield to God the minds which we actually possess', so I suppose God takes them and does what he can with them. And of course in time they might develop new powers of faith; as you say, it depends on what happens to make connections. He keeps showing us new things, new light on the past, new roads for the future, and one hopes for new powers. But what moors, fens, crags and torrents lie all about.

Rose Macaulay 1881–1958, *Letter to a Friend*

Etheldreda d.679

Ely's saint in the Marches?

Ethelbert's linking East Anglia and Hereford is easily explained, but why does Etheldreda, saint and patron of the great 'Ship of the Fens', Ely Cathedral, have a dedication in our midst – at Hyssington, Montgomeryshire one of the 15 Welsh parishes in the diocese of Hereford? Her story is an inspiring one. Born in Suffolk in the 7th century, a daughter of the king, she desired to commit her life to prayer and chastity. After two arranged and unconsummated marriages, she founded a religious house at Ely for both men and women, over which she ruled as abbess. The pattern of a Saxon princess fleeing from an over-enthusiastic suitor is common and one we have already seen in the story of our own saint, Milburga (see 23 February). Certainly, Etheldreda became famed for her holiness, austerity and prophecy, and many miracles were performed at her shrine. At successive exhumations of her body, to rehouse it in more glorious surroundings, her remains were found to be incorrupt and sweet-smelling. Her shrine attracted many pilgrims, many of whom returned home with souvenirs of their visit, purchased from stalls around the cathedral. The quality of these was often poor, hence the term 'tawdry' (Audrey is the alternative name for Etheldreda).

The Venerable Bede speaks of Etheldreda's holiness:

For a long time Etheldreda begged the king to allow her to retire from worldly affairs and serve Christ, the only true King, in a convent. And having at length obtained his reluctant consent, she entered the convent of the abbess Ebba, King Egfrid's aunt, at Coldingham, where she received the veil and clothing of a nun from the hands of Bishop Wilfrid. A year later she was made Abbess in the district called Ely ... it is said that from the time of her entry into the convent she never wore linen but only woollen garments, and that she would seldom wash in hot water except on the eve of the greater festivals such as Easter, Pentecost, and the Epiphany, and then only after she and her assistants had helped the other handmaids of Christ to wash. She seldom had more than one meal a day except at the greater festivals or under urgent necessity, and she always remained at prayer in the church from the hour of Matins until dawn unless prevented by serious illness.

Bede *Ecclesiastical History of the English People*

Later, Ely became a monastery, famed for its music and liturgy. Legend has it that King Canute once made his way to Ely by boat. As he approached the city he began to hear sweet music on all sides and realised it was the sound of the monks singing the Divine Office in the monastery. A 12th-century account takes up the story:

Canute urged others who were present in the boats to come round about him and sing, joining him in jubilation. Expressing with his own mouth his joyfulness of heart, he composed aloud a song in English the beginning of which runs as follows:

The monks in Ely sweetly sang
When nigh rowed Cnut the King.
Knights, row closer to the land
And let's hear these monks sing!

Liber Eliensis II, 85

John the Baptist

Patron saint of Hereford Cathedral's parish

In the crypt of Hereford Cathedral is a late medieval statue of St John the Baptist – his garment of camel's hair clearly depicted and a book with a headless 'Lamb of God' in his hand. This is a reminder of close links between this saint and the cathedral. Unlike many cathedrals, Hereford Cathedral has no large geographical parish, but from time immemorial there has been a small parish adjacent to the cathedral, dedicated to John the Baptist, which, having no church of its own, has always found a place to worship in the cathedral itself – sometimes in the Lady Chapel, sometimes in the north transept. One of the cathedral clergy has often functioned as 'priest-in-charge' of the parish. The biblical story of John the Baptist, the son of Elizabeth and Zechariah, begins even before his birth. His leaping in his mother's womb is seen as a great sign of welcome to the Christ, and John is always seen as forerunner of the Messiah. He has a role similar to that of the Old Testament prophets, in encouraging the people of God to live lives worthy of the Kingdom and helping all to welcome the coming of the Anointed One. John the Baptist's links with the Cathedral have recently been emphasised by his inclusion as one of the 'Saints of Hereford' in the icon on the canopy surmounting the shrine of St Thomas of Hereford.

John's feast day is surrounded by miraculous happenings. Indeed, in the tradition of the early Fathers, he was seen as one endowed with grace from before his birth, and consequently the Church has always kept his feast day with greater solemnity than that of his death. Perhaps, too, the miracles of nature conspire together with the miracles of grace, as today we also celebrate Midsummer Day. Here, an anonymous Anglo-Saxon writer sees the day as one of miraculous meaning – one which will not go unnoticed in Hereford, as we daily see Jerusalem as the centre of the world on Mappa Mundi*:*

On the same day [the twenty-fourth of the month] is Solstitia, that is in our language the station of the sun, because the sun stands in the middle of the sky. As St Arculf says, he saw in Jerusalem a certain pillar in the middle of the city, which was set up on the place where the dead man came to life when they placed the Lord's cross over him. Then it happens wonderfully in the summer station of the sun at midday: when the sun is in the middle of the heavens, the pillar doesn't have any shadow. When that station of the sun has run on three days, and the day is somewhat shorter, then the pillar has a little shadow; and as the days go on shortening, so the pillar's shadow is longer. This pillar proves that the city of Jerusalem is set in the centre of the earth, because in the middle of the summer at midday the sun shines from the middle of the heavens alike on either side of the pillar which stands in the centre of the earth.

Collect for the feast of St John the Baptist

Almighty God,
by whose providence your servant John the Baptist
was wonderfully born,
and sent to prepare the way of your Son our Saviour
by the preaching of repentance:
lead us to repent according to his preaching
and, after his example,
constantly speak the truth, boldly rebuke vice,
and patiently suffer for the truth's sake;
through Jesus Christ your Son our Lord.

Kyneburga of Gloucester 8th century

Founder of the first religious community in Gloucester, 710

A LINK with our sister diocese of Gloucester (see also 15 July). The monastery Osric founded at Gloucester in about 679 was dedicated in honour of St Peter and was designed to house a community of both men and women in separate enclosures, but within one compound, following the model in Gaul. Osric's sister Kyneburga (or Cyniburg) was the first abbess of the Saxon monastery in Gloucester, and she ruled the convent for 29 years. Other traditions suggest there was another Kyneburga, again linked to Gloucester, with a chapel dedicated to her in Gloucester Abbey in 1147. Legend has it that she was a princess who fled to escape marriage and took employment as a baker's servant. The baker's wife, motivated by jealousy, murdered her and threw her body into a well. She was taken up and buried nearby; a church was built and miracles were reported. For a long time, however, miracles ceased, supposedly because of the custodian's irreverence. Archbishop Courtenay ordered a fresh translation of her body in 1390, and this took place on 10 April that year, with Henry of Wakefield, bishop of Worcester, officiating. Whatever the truth of the real Kyneburga, her name is one revered in Gloucester and it takes us back to the very roots of religious devotion there.

One tradition linked with Kyneburga is that she was a great encourager and benefactor. If this is so, it links her splendidly to that other great abbess of Saxon times, St Hilda, who encouraged the tone-deaf cowherd, Caedmon. The Venerable Bede describes how Caedmon received musical and poetic gifts:

He [Caedmon] had followed a secular occupation until well advanced in years without ever learning anything about poetry. Indeed it sometimes happened at a feast that all the guests in turn would be invited to sing and entertain the company; then, when he saw the harp coming his way, he would get up from the table and go home.

On one such occasion he had left the house in which the entertainment was being held and went out to the stable, where it was his duty that night to look after the beasts. There, when the time came, he settled down to sleep. Suddenly in a dream he saw a man standing beside him who called him by name. 'Caedmon,' he said, 'sing me a song.' 'I don't know how to sing,' he replied. 'It is because I cannot sing that I left the feast and came here.' The man who addressed him then said: 'But you shall sing to me.' 'What should I sing about?' he replied. 'Sing about the Creation of all things,' the other answered. And Caedmon immediately began to sing verses in praise of God the Creator that he had never heard before, and their theme ran thus:

Praise we the fashioner now of Heaven's fabric,
The majesty of his might and his mind's wisdom,
Work of the world-warden, worker of all wonders,
How he the Lord of Glory everlasting,
Wrought first for the race of men Heaven as a rooftree,
Then made he Middle Earth to be their mansions.

Bede, *Ecclesiastical History of the English People*

Robert Losinga d.1095

Norman 'builder' bishop

The remains of the former chapel in the Bishop's Palace bear witness to the energy and skill of one of Hereford's great Norman bishops. Robert de Losinga (or Robert the Lotharingian) probably came from Liège, continuing a tradition begun by Edward the Confessor, of encouraging Lotharingian clergy to serve him at court. With William the Conqueror as his patron, Robert came to England and was ordained priest by Wulfstan (see 19 January), bishop of Worcester, who became a close friend. Consecrated bishop of Hereford on 29 December 1079, Robert swiftly began building work on the episcopal palace, using Norman architects and craftsmen. The bishop's chapel was designed with two storeys, with parallels to the imperial chapel at Aachen, while Robert's choice of patron saints, St Catherine and St Mary Magdalen, reflects Lotharingian interest in the saints of the eastern Mediterranean. The chapel was staffed by four chaplains, who also formed part of the cathedral community. In Robert's time, the cathedral chapter was established and he appointed the first known archdeacon of Hereford, and possibly also the first dean.

Robert was a great administrator and may have been one of the Commissioners for the Domesday Book. Certainly his interest and skill in mathematics and his knowledge of how to use the abacus would have been of great value to both William I and William II, not least in the keeping of episcopal accounts. His links with the diocese of Worcester were close, and Robert was chosen to lay the first stone of the new church of St Peter's Abbey, Gloucester on 29 June 1089. He also attended the translation of the relics of St Oswald of Worcester (see 29 February) into the new cathedral there in 1089. Later, he presided over Wulfstan's funeral and, in a vision of his mentor and friend, was told of his own approaching death, which occurred on this day in the year 1095. His memorial, dated *c.*1300, is in the south choir aisle, where Robert is shown holding a model of a church, possibly the cathedral which he did so much to rebuild and restore.

Robert is said to have received a vision of his death and through it to have found reassurance and a realisation that death is not to be feared when we see it in the context of life and Christian hope. Here, a contemporary spiritual writer gives words of encouragement:

Yet death is but a transition. We pass through a door from one space to another. It is a moment of nature, so that we would do better to use the present participle, 'dying'. We die but to be reborn. And exactly how we go through that last door, how we die, will depend on how we respond to the many hourly, daily, yearly experiences of dying that we encounter in our lives, how we respond to the dying of a hope, a dream, a friendship, an ambition, a passion. If we learn how to live through each of these miniature deaths, each lessening of the ego, then each of them will become a resurrection, and so we shall come at last to those ten thousand several doors with joy and gratitude, humility and trust. If, on our journey down the years, we do this, then we shall also hear, increasingly nearer, that music from another room which is the life that is beyond and yet is all about us even now. And if, continually, hourly, daily, yearly, we learn how to die and be reborn, then we shall find that after long searching a door opens and there is a way ahead when we had thought no door would ever open for us. It may not be the door we expected, nor the door we would have chosen for ourselves but it has opened and we have but to enter.

James Roose-Evans, *Passages of the Soul: Ritual today* (1994)

Alice Foster 1863–1932

Benefactor of All Saints church, Brockhampton

The unique thatched church of All Saints, Brockhampton, is said by Pevsner to be 'one of the most convincing and most impressive churches of its date in any country'. It is the result of the generosity and vision of Alice Foster, wealthy American heiress and wife of Yorkshire mill owner Arthur Wellesley Foster. Alice determined to build a church in the grounds of their home, Brockhampton Court, in memory of her parents, Ebenezer and Julia Jordan. She chose as architect W R Lethaby, the doyen of the Arts and Crafts movement and a follower of William Morris. This commission enabled him to put into practice his own theories of design without financial constraint. The foundation stone was laid on 25 June, 1901 and only 16 months later, the bishop of Hereford consecrated All Saints church in October 1902. It is certainly Lethaby's masterpiece. With its roof thatched with Norfolk reed and its buff stone tower and walls, its traditional aspect belies the use of modern materials, especially reinforced concrete. Inside, there are many examples of Arts and Crafts decoration: wild flowers of Herefordshire, carved on the 48 panels of the choir stalls, tapestries made in the William Morris workshop from designs by Burne-Jones and stained glass made in the studios of Christopher Wall. The south window is a memorial to Alice's father – an angel choir reminds us that 'for ever music found an echo in his heart'. The west window is dedicated to Lethaby's own father, and features St Cecilia, the patron saint of music.

Alice Foster's great benefaction to the community of Brockhampton and to the county of Herefordshire was inspired by her wish to give honour to those who had gone before her and who had influenced her for good. Indeed, her lovely church has given inspiration to many generations of worshippers. The dedication to All Saints is particularly fitting and is summed up well in these words by the 17th-century Anglican divine, Joseph Hall, successively bishop of Exeter and Norwich, who suffered greatly in his old age in the Civil War:

Let no man think that because those blessed souls are out of sight, far distant in another world, and we are here toiling in a vale of tears, we have therefore lost all mutual regard to each other. No; there is still, and ever will be, a secret but unfailing correspondence between heaven and earth. The present happiness of those heavenly citizens cannot have abated ought of their knowledge and charity, but must needs have raised them to a higher pitch of both. They, in a generality, retain the notice of the sad condition of us poor travellers here below. As for us wretched pilgrims that are yet left here below to tug with many difficulties, we cannot forget that better half of us that is now triumphant in glory. It is abundant comfort to us that some part of us is in the fruition of that glory, whereto we, the other poor labouring part, desire and strive to aspire; that our head and shoulders are above water, while the other limbs are yet wading through the stream.

Joseph Hall 1574–1656, *A Treatise of Christ Mystical*

John Ross 1719–92

Herefordshire boy who became bishop of Exeter

His surname was also the place of his birth. John Ross was born in Ross-on-Wye on 24 or 25 June 1719. He was baptized at St Mary's church and educated at Hereford Cathedral School and St John's College, Cambridge, where he was a Somerset scholar and became a fellow. He was ordained priest on Christmas Day 1746 and preferment led to his becoming bishop of Exeter in 1778. Ross was a classic 'Whig' churchman, setting the highest value on the establishment of religion that derives its authority from reason and the gospel and working 'hand in hand' with the government of the day. As a diocesan bishop, he was popular and received the freedom of the city of Plymouth in 1779. Unlike many contemporaries, he regularly toured his diocese and officiated at triennial confirmations. At Barnstaple, on 25 June 1779 he confirmed 4,016 people drawn from 39 parishes. He personally examined all candidates for deacons' orders and sought to know his clergy personally. He was clearly a person of broadminded sympathies – he encouraged his fellow bishops to accept the Dissenters Relief Bill of 1779, which allowed a limited extension of toleration to Nonconformists. Again, unlike many of his fellow bishops, he was friendly towards John Wesley and dined with him at the bishop's palace in 1782. Ross was a learned bishop with a reputation for classical scholarship and edited an edition of Cicero's letter *ad familiares* in 1749. On his death, he left his substantial library to the chapter of Exeter Cathedral and provided liberally for Exeter Hospital in his will.

Ross's reputation for scholarship, generosity and diligence is summed up in these words, written about a bishop of an earlier generation, Lancelot Andrewes:

Upon Bishop Andrewes his Picture before his sermons

This reverend shadow cast that setting Sun,
Whose glorious course through our Horizon run,
Left the dimme face of this dull Hemisphere,
All one great eye, all drown'd in one great Tear.
Whose faire illustrious soule, led his free thought
Through Learnings Universe, and (vainely) sought
Roome for her spatious selfe, until at length
Shee found the way home, with an holy strength
Snatch't her self hence, to Heaven: fill'd a bright place,
Mongst those immortall fires, and on the face
Of her great maker fixt her flaming eye
There still to read true pure divinity.
And now that grave aspect hath deign'd to shrinke
Into this lesse appearance; If you thinke,
'Tis but a dead face, art doth here bequeath:
Looke on the following leaves, and see him breathe.

Richard Crashaw *c.*1613–49, *The Delights of the Muses* (1646)

Peter, Prince of the Apostles

Popular church patron

Over 1,000 churches were dedicated to Peter in England, with 19 in Herefordshire and 12 in our part of Shropshire. Indeed, in Herefordshire, Peter's total is surpassed only by St Mary, St Michael and St John Baptist. Simon, son of Zebedee and brother of Andrew, was given by Christ the nickname 'the Rock' (*Cephas* in Greek, *Petros* in Latin) and became a leader among the disciples. He appears frequently in the gospels, but less so in narratives of the early church, being eclipsed by Paul. An early tradition speaks of Peter becoming bishop of the church in Rome, and suffering persecution with Paul in Nero's persecution of AD 64. It is said that he chose to be crucified head downwards, as a mark of humility towards his Lord. Peter's emblem is that of crossed keys – a reference to Christ's entrusting him with the keys of the kingdom of Heaven. In England there were important dedications to Peter from early times – monasteries such as Glastonbury, Peterborough, Whitby, Wearmouth, Gloucester and especially Westminster celebrate him, while cathedrals at York, Lichfield, Worcester and Selsey had early dedications to Peter. His chief feast is on this day but there is a subsidiary feast on 1 August – St Peter in Chains, which commemorates his escape from prison.

Peter's role in the Passion of Christ is seen in his denial of Jesus when the cock crowed and of his part in the washing of feet at the Last Supper. The 19th-century poet Christina Rossetti uses both these scenes as inspiration for a poem seeking the opening of the heart to God:

St Peter once: 'Lord, dost Thou wash my feet?' –
Much more I say: Lord, dost Thou stand and knock
At my closed heart more rugged than a rock,
Bolted and barred, for Thy soft touch unmeet,
Nor garnished nor in any wise made sweet?
Owls roost within and dancing satyrs mock.
Lord, I have heard the crowing of the cock
And have not wept: ah, Lord, Thou knowest it.

Yet still I hear Thee knocking, still I hear:
'Open to Me, Look on Me, eye to eye,
That I may wring thy heart and make it whole;
And teach thee love because I hold thee dear
And sup with thee in gladness soul with soul,
And sup with thee in glory by and by.'

Christina Rossetti 1830–94, 'St Peter'

John Roger of Hereford late 12th century

Astronomer & mathematician

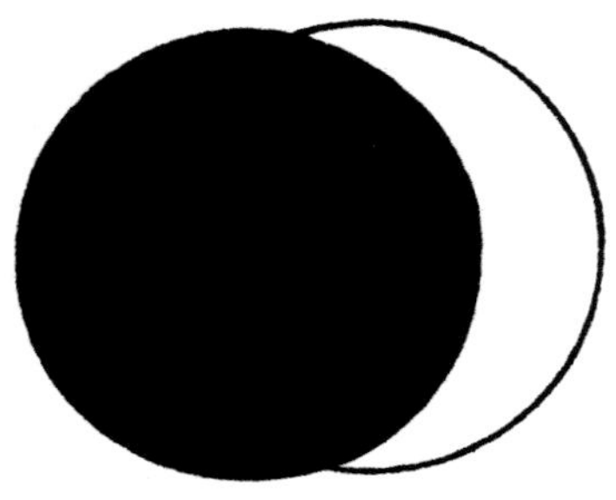

We know from other sources that Hereford, with its library and school, was a place of great learning in the arts during the Middle Ages. Roger of Hereford, whom we commemorate today, put Hereford on the map as regards science and astronomy. It is said that he was born 'apud Herefordiam in confinibus Cambriae' – 'in Hereford and not far from Wales'. His date of birth is uncertain, but we know that he flourished during the reign of Henry II – in the late 12th century. The 17th-century antiquary Thomas Fuller tells us that he was connected with the University of Cambridge – a strange assertion, when we know that the university was founded towards the end of the 13th century. There was, however, an ancient and legendary tradition that Cambridge was founded by Sigbert, King of the East Angles, and 'refounded' by Joffred, abbot of Crowland in the late 11th century – it is to this tradition that Roger possibly belongs. All his treatises relate to mathematics, astronomy and astrology and he is said to have been one of the greatest experimenters in metals of his time. Perhaps most relevant to us is a manuscript in the British Museum of a treatise containing an 'Astronomical Table, composed for midnight at Hereford in 1178, after the eclipse which happened in that year'. An eclipse of the sun, in any age, is a remarkable happening. We can but imagine the consternation it caused in a small provincial community in the 12th century! A 17th-century writer said of him that 'he was so devoted to his studies that if he were asked of what things a man never had enough', he would reply, not as the miser, 'of riches', but as the philosopher, 'of knowledge', and thus, as far as his ordinary occupations would permit, he never allowed one moment of his life to pass by unimproved.

Roger of Hereford clearly had a mind open to the mysteries of the heavens and enabled others to share this wonder. Many centuries later, the poet Gerard Manley Hopkins was similarly overcome by the mystery of the universe – a wonder which helps him to perceive wonders of the terrestrial too:

Look at the stars! Look, look up at the skies!
  O look at all the fire-folk sitting in the air!
  The bright boroughs, the circle-citadels there!
Down in dim woods the diamond delves! The elves'-eyes!
The grey lawns cold where gold, where quickgold lies!
  Wind-beat whitebeam! airy abeles set on a flare!
  Flake-doves sent floating forth at a farmyard scare!
Ah well! It is all a purchase, all is a prize.
Buy then! bid then! –What? – Prayer, patience, alms, vows,
Look, look: a May-mess, like on orchard boughs!
  Look! March-bloom, like on mealed-with-yellow sallows!
These are indeed the barn; withindoors house
The shocks. The piece-bright paling shuts the spouse
  Christ home, Christ and his mother and all his hallows.

Gerard Manley Hopkins 1844–89, 'The Starlight Night'

Edward Elgar 1857–1934

Composer with many local links

Elgar is claimed by Worcester, Hereford and Malvern. Each place has a statue of him, and the different style of each reminds us of the breadth and variety of this great man's music. Worcester's statue depicts Elgar standing, facing towards the cathedral, hands clasped behind his back, wearing the robes of a doctor of music. This is the Elgar beloved of the establishment – the Master of the King's Musick, the Elgar of *Pomp and Circumstance* and the *Coronation Ode*. His statue in Malvern shows him at the foot of the hills he loved, surrounded by flowing water – watching and wondering. This is the mystic Elgar – the Elgar of the Cello Concerto – the one who said 'If ever, after I'm dead, you hear someone whistling this tune on the Malvern Hills, don't be alarmed, it's only me.' The Hereford statue, in the Cathedral Close, by Jemma Pearson, unveiled in 2004, depicts Elgar with the bicycle on which he loved to explore the lanes of this county. The Elgars lived in Hereford between 1904 and 1911, indeed they moved to Plas Gwyn in Hampton Park Road on this day in 1904, just after Elgar had been knighted. He sometimes spoke of this period as containing some of his happiest days – certainly from this period come great works: *The Kingdom* (1906), the First Symphony (1908) and the Violin Concerto (1910). The Hereford statue depicts a human Elgar – the composer full of emotion, one who could be struck silent by the death of his wife, and one who could weave the humour of 'Dan the bulldog' into *Enigma Variations* (see 7 February). As Elgar himself said, when referring to this very human side of his character, 'I am still at heart the dreamy child who used to be found in the reed beds by Severn side, with a sheet of paper, trying to fix the sounds and longing for something very great.'

Although a staunch Roman Catholic, Elgar was open to the influences of the Church of England and his texts often have a solid biblical base. A letter written by Elgar to Randall Davidson on the 25th anniversary of his becoming archbishop of Canterbury, reveals a generosity of spirit and a willingness to see in music an art which breaks down barriers of creed and culture:

Feb. 22, 1927

My Lord Archbishop,

Although your Grace has been so kind to me on every occasion on which I have had the honour to meet you I should not have had the temerity to address a letter to you on any ordinary occasion; but the anniversary occurring this year is unique: and so important that I venture to send respectful congratulations & deeply felt good wishes.

Bred in another form of religious observance I stand aside, unbiased, from the trivialities with which controversies are mostly informed; whatever differences exist there remains the clear, wide and refreshing Christianity, desired by all men, but obscured by the little darkness of their own imperfect vision. To the better understanding of such broad Christian feeling I am thankful to have been permitted, in a small way it is true, to exercise my art; in this spirit and in a spirit of humble fellowship I offer this tribute of deep respect – to an ideal great churchman, a staunch friend, and an embodiment of all that is good and true in Christianity past mere forms and observances.

With every respect
Believe me to be
Very sincerely & affectionately
Your Grace's obedient servant
EDWARD ELGAR

Cewydd 7th century

Welsh hermit & Herefordshire version of St Swithin

This obscure Radnorshire saint is said to have lived as a hermit in a cave at Aberedw Rocks, near Builth Wells. In his native county, two churches – Aberedw and Disserth – are dedicated to him. His chief claim to fame is as the Celtic equivalent of St Swithin. According to tradition, if it rains on Cewydd's feast day (2 July) it will rain for the next 40 days; hence he was known as *Gewydd Gwylaw* (Old Cewydd of the Rain). He is associated locally with the parish of Cusop where it is assumed that he founded the church – it is very likely that it was originally dedicated to him, for the parish feast was always held on the second Sunday in July. Today, Cusop church is dedicated to St Mary, a patronage possibly dating from Norman times, when many local saints' dedications were replaced by more 'mainstream' ones.

There will have been much more to Cewydd's life than simply a memory of an invoker of rain – just as St Swithin should be remembered for more than a gloomy prophecy of rain for 40 days and 40 nights! A story of St Swithin, told by the medieval chronicler William of Malmesbury, gives a more rounded picture of the saint. No doubt St Cewydd was a man of compassion, too!

There was in him [Swithin] a store of all virtues, but he excelled especially in two, humility and clemency. Let my pen provide instances of both. Once upon a time he was standing where workmen were making a bridge on the east side of the city, so that the sight of his presence might keep up the energies of those who were disposed to slack. And, as it happened, a woman came walking over the bridge into the city, carrying a basket of eggs for sale. They jostled her on both sides in the manner of that sort of men, and in their petulant rudeness, broke all the eggs at once. This seemed no light matter for men of gravity, and was reported to the lord bishop. He listened to her complaint as she was brought before him, elderly and slovenly in dress, and deplored the damage. The compassion of his mind overcame his hesitation to work a miracle, and making the sign of the cross he consolidated the fractures of all the eggs.

In the sickness at the end of his life he commanded that his body should be buried outside the church, where it would be trodden by the feet of passers-by and made wet by rain that falls from heaven.

William of Malmesbury *c.*1090–1143, *Gesta Pontificum*

When I was a parish priest, when the time for the annual summer fête came round, and the weather was fine, people would often say, 'You've been saying your prayers, vicar' – and the opposite if the weather was inclement! Of course it is theological nonsense to expect God to respond to requests for this or that particular weather over this or that particular spot, but the Church has sometimes encouraged this, as we find in this collect.

> O God, heavenly Father, which by thy son Jesus Christ hast promised to all them that seek thy kingdom, and the righteousness thereof, all things necessary to their bodily sustenance: send us, we beseech thee, in this our necessity, such moderate rain and showers, that we may receive the fruits of the earth, to our comfort and to thy honour: through Jesus Christ our Lord.
>
> *First Prayer Book of King Edward VI, 1549*

Silas Taylor 1624–78

Seventeenth-century polymath

Before the scientific revolution and Age of Enlightenment it was very possible to know a remarkable amount about many subjects; the age of specialisation had not yet dawned. Silas Taylor, whom we remember today, was a scholar in many fields and also a politician and soldier – a rare combination today! Born in Much Wenlock, after education at Shrewsbury and Oxford, and at the outbreak of Civil War, he joined the Parliamentary army, becoming a captain and garrison commander in the Marches. He achieved high office in the 'civil service' of Herefordshire, being appointed sequestration officer with powerful influence over the ownership of lands in the county. He took his religion seriously, was known to hold Presbyterian views and spoke out fiercely against the 'enthusiasm' of certain contemporaries (among them Richard Delamaine, see 26 April). As a scholar he is said to have been learned in 'Mathematics and Tongues' and was no mean musician, being noted as a composer by Samuel Pepys. The latter's views on Taylor's compositions were less than flattering, for on hearing one of his compositions, Pepys declared it:

> A dull old-fashioned thing of six and seven parts, that nobody could understand: and the duke of York, when he came out, told me that he was a better store-keeper than anthem-maker, and that was bad enough too.

Pepys' reference to 'store-keeper' refers to Taylor's 'day job' after the Restoration as commissioner for the Westminster militia, with responsibilities for supplies. This presumably provided him with the means to indulge his various scholarly interests. While at Hereford he had become embroiled in a controversy concerning the cathedral library. Some contemporaries noted that he found the library 'uncouth and unkiss' after the Commonwealth and that Taylor 'ransacked' it. Other evidence suggests that, far from looting it, he used its contents wisely, especially the bishop's registers, and prepared a *History of the County of Hereford*, combining topography, local and national archive material and personal observations. Certainly, Taylor's work provided a basis for the early 19th-century historian John Duncumb and his *Collections towards the History and Antiquities of the County of Hereford* (1804) (see 4 March). Other scholarly interests gave him respite from his work with the military and his *The History of Gavelkind* (1663) set out to prove the tradition that in certain regions of England land tenure was pre-feudal. All in all, a most remarkable man, with a huge breadth of knowledge.

References to books and their use in the Bible are quite few, but the following two passages always strike me as both moving and true!

The sayings of the wise are like goads, and like nails firmly fixed are the collected sayings which are given by one Shepherd. My son, beware of anything beyond these. Of making many books there is no end, and much study is a wearisome of the flesh. The end of the matter; all has been heard. Fear God, and keep his commandments; for this is the whole duty of man. For God will bring every deed into judgement, with every secret thing, whether good or evil.

Ecclesiastes 12:11–14

There are also many other things which Jesus did; were every one of them to be written, I suppose that the world itself could not contain the books that would be written.

John 21:25

John Scudamore, First Viscount 1601–71

Saviour of Dore Abbey

The remarkable restoration and Laudian interior of Dore Abbey owes much to the vision and generosity of this man. Born into a distinguished Herefordshire family, John Scudamore studied at Oxford, was trained in law, and like many wealthy young men of his era travelled throughout Europe. The death of his father brought him back to England, where he inherited a baronetcy and assumed a seat in Parliament. The early death of his first three children turned him to religion and he struck up a friendship with William Laud, then dean of Gloucester and later archbishop of Canterbury (see 10 January), pledging himself, with Laud's guidance, to use his considerable resources at the service of the Church. The Civil War threw his influence into disarray and, after the capitulation of Hereford in 1643, Scudamore was sent to London and placed under house arrest – he was not released until 1647.

It is as restorer of Dore Abbey that Scudamore is best remembered in Herefordshire. By the early 17th century, the former Cistercian abbey was badly in need of repair. Between 1632 and 1635, Scudamore restored the building, forming the parish church from the crossing and choir of the abbey. He added a new roof, south porch, belfry, a new bell and a churchyard wall. The church was fitted out in full Laudian style, with an altar, new woodwork and stained glass. The total cost was more than £425 – a great sum in those days. The restored church was the model of Scudamore's high church or Laudian beliefs, emphasising the beauty of holiness, the central place of the Eucharist and the role of ceremony in worship. The church was consecrated on 22 March 1635, in a service which lasted all day. In his lifetime Scudamore was held up as 'a Worthy Copy for others to write after'. And it is not just religion in which he was interested. A noted agricultural improver, he discovered, grafted and developed the 'redstreak' apple, which became known as the best cider apple in Herefordshire. Scudamore is also credited with introducing from the Low Countries the ancestors of the famous white-faced Hereford cattle. A man of generosity, he looked after the interests of poor clergy, especially those disadvantaged by ejection at the Commonwealth, and by 1662 he had disbursed more than £1,650 to about 80 clerics, some of them obscure country ministers, but others nationally known figures like Matthew Wren.

The via media *of true Anglicanism and its encouragement of decent ceremonial in worship was espoused by William Laud and some of his contemporaries in the 17th century:*

As for the Rites and Ceremonies of Divine Worship, they do highly approve that virtuous mediocrity which our Church observes between the meretricious gaudiness of the Church of Rome and the squalid sluttery of fanatic conventicles. Devotion is so overclad by the Papists that she is oppressed and stifled with the multitudes of her own garments ... Some of our modern Reformers, to make amends, have stripped her stark naked, till she is become in a manner cold and dead. The Church of England only hath dressed her as befits an honourable and virtuous matron. There are few men so abstractly intellectual but that their devotion had need to be advanced with something that may strike upon their outward senses and engage their affections; and therefore, while we live in this region of mortality, we must make use of such external helps, and recommend religion to the people by those ornaments which the Church hath according to her prudence thought fittest for those ends. The Church of Rome is a luxuriant vine, full of superfluous branches and overrun with wild grapes from whence many a poisonous and intoxicating potion is pressed forth; but the greatest part of Reformers have done like the rude Thracian in the Apologue, who instead of moderate pruning and dressing his vines, as his more skilful Athenian neighbours did, cut them up by the roots. But the Church of England is the only well ordered vineyard.

Simon Patrick 1626–1707, *An Account of the New Sect of Latitude-Men* (1662)

William Gilpin 1724–1804

Champion of the Picturesque

The difficulties of travel in Europe, due to the French Revolution and other turbulence, led many to consider England's earliest tourist pastime – the Wye Tour. Its popularity at the end of the 18th century was due largely to this man. Born in Cumbria, William Gilpin retained his love of the Lake District, but his professional life took him south where he became a school-master in Cheam in Surrey. During summer holidays he made extensive tours around Britain, sketching and writing about the landscape as he went. In 1770 his summer excursion was to the Wye valley and South Wales. In his writings, Gilpin developed his theories of the Picturesque. He extolled the wild and rugged in scenery but was very prescriptive as to what constituted the Picturesque – the view from the Prospect at Ross did not qualify; it was merely 'amusing'. However, further down the Wye, near Goodrich, the scenery improved, until arrival at Tintern, which he saw as the ultimate in Picturesque. The presence of a ruined castle or abbey added 'consequence', although even here he was not completely satisfied – Tintern Abbey would, he felt, be improved by 'a mallet, judiciously used' on some of the protruding stonework! Gilpin's *Observations on the River Wye* was not published until 1782, although it had been circulating in manuscript among the cognoscenti for a decade. Certainly, his books were published at the right time – road improvements led to the explosion of domestic tourism during the 1780s and 1790s and Gilpin's volumes proved ideal companions for the traveller.

The poetry of Wordsworth often reflects the descriptions of Gilpin:

If this
Be but a vain belief, yet, oh! how oft –
In darkness and amid the many shapes
Of joyless daylight; when the fretful stir
Unprofitable, and the fever of the world,
Have hung upon the beatings of my heart –
How oft, in spirit, have I turned to thee,
O sylvan Wye! Thou wanderer thro' the words,
How often has my spirit turned to thee!
... for I have learned
To look on nature, not as in the hour
Of thoughtless youth; but hearing oftentimes
The still, sad music of humanity,
Nor harsh nor grating, though of ample power
To chasten and subdue. And I have felt
A presence that disturbs me with the joy
Of elevated thoughts; a sense sublime
Of something far more deeply interfused,
Whose dwelling is the light of setting suns,
And the round ocean and the living air,
And the blue sky, and in the mind of man;
A motion and a spirit, that impels
All thinking things, all objects of all thought,
And rolls through all things.

William Wordsworth 1770–1850, 'Lines Composed a Few Miles Above Tintern Abbey'

John Davies 1565–1618

Teacher of handwriting & poet

Handwriting can tell us much about character and personality, and is sometimes used in the detection of crime. It certainly once formed an important part of the primary school curriculum. Today we remember one known in his lifetime as a great exponent of handwriting. Born in Hereford, (his birthplace was always noted on his title-pages – 'John Davies of Hereford'), he was educated at Hereford Cathedral School and became, according to Thomas Fuller in his *Worthies of England,* 'the greatest master of the pen that England in her age beheld', and his renown reached as far as Germany. His book *Writing Schoolmaster* or *The Anatomy of Fair Writing* (earliest surviving edition 1633) exhibits specimen-copies of his handwriting, together with practical advice for learners. His students included royalty, members of the nobility and many famous people, including John Donne, Ben Jonson and Inigo Jones – but for all his connections he appears to have pleaded poverty at every opportunity.

Perhaps Davies ought to have limited himself to his superb skill as a writing master but he saw his future as a poet and published vast quantities of poetry – religious and moral – and one of his works, *Microcosmos* (1603) runs to 6,000 lines. He gained little recognition for his poetry; as a contemporary put it: 'the master of fast, fair, close, and various handwriting was as a poet slow, laborious, diffuse and flat.' Indeed, in one of his many sonnets he asks, perhaps with irony:

> Busie Invention, whie art thou so dull
> And yet still doing?

Even in his poems on plague-stricken London, he appears to have continued his rather laborious and unmemorable style. Among all Davies's works, only his volume of epigrams *The Scourge of Folly* (1610) is mentioned today, mainly as he addresses many of the 292 examples to the greatest figures of the age – the king, Francis Bacon, Ben Jonson, William Shakespeare, John Fletcher. Maddeningly, however, his cryptic lines on Shakespeare, telling him that:

> Hadst thou not played some kingly parts in sport
> Thou hadst been a companion for a king

have found no reasonable explanation among generations of Shakespeare scholars.

Amazingly, I won the Look and Learn *handwriting competition in about 1964, which those who know my handwriting today will find difficult to believe. Since, then, my handwriting has got worse and worse. Is this because of carelessness, lack of time or because we all write so little today, relying instead on the keyboard of the computer? Clearly, God knows how to use handwriting which is instantly understood and recognised. Here, the Old Testament king, Belshazzar, after stripping the Temple of sacred ornaments, is carousing with his court, when there is a mysterious happening:*

Immediately the fingers of a man's hand appeared and wrote on the plaster of the wall of the king's palace, opposite the lamp-stand; and the king saw the hand as it wrote. And this is the writing that was inscribed: MENE, MENE, TEKEL, PARSIN. This is the interpretation of the matter:
MENE, God has numbered the days of your kingdom and brought it to an end.
TEKEL, You have been weighed in the balance and found wanting.
PARSIN, Your kingdom is divided and given to the Medes and Persians.

Daniel 5:25–28

Junabius *c.*6th–7th century
Early Celtic saint

Herefordshire cannot compete with Cornwall in the number of its indigenous saints, but it does have several who lived in this area, preached the gospel here and gave their names to local churches. Junabius is one such saint. In the *Book of Llandaff,* the name appears 12 times in different spellings, with one reference to 'Iunapeius episcopus'. He appears to have been a bishop in the Archenfield area and to have been linked with St Dubricius. It seems that in the 6th century Pepiau was king of Ergyng, a tiny Welsh-speaking kingdom bounded by the rivers Wye, Monnow and Worm. The king gave to his relative or friend, Dubricius, a grant of land to endow the church of Junabius the priest. The name Junabius became, in Welsh, Dinabo, and so the church was called Llandinabo, church of Dinabo. There is still a church at Llandinabo, but beside the busy main road near Harewood End. The *Book of Llandaff* charmingly describes the boundaries of the land concerned: 'From the ford above the church, downwards over the honeysuckle, to the breast of the hill, straight across the Cecg, till it descends above the old ford which is on the stream in the great wood, through the wood, straight on to the top of the crooked pool. From the crooked pools straight on to the Guy [Wye]. Of the clergy are witnesses Arguistil, Iunabui the priest, Cinguari, Cimmeired, Iudnou, Elharnn. Of the laity, Pepiau a witness, Cinuin, Colt, Guobrir, Guidcon, Cintmit, Cingint. Peace upon those who shall keep it, but on those who shall violate it a malediction. Amen.'

These tantalising fragments of early church life in Herefordshire are remarkable for their emphasis on tiny details – 'ford', 'crooked pool' and, most delightful of all, 'honeysuckle':

The fragrant Honeysuckle spirals clockwise to the sun
And many other creepers do the same.
But some climb anti-clockwise; the bindweed does, for one,
Or *Convulvulus,* to give her proper name.

Rooted on either side a door one of each species grew
And raced towards the window-ledge above;
Each corkscrewed to the lintel in the only way it knew,
Where they stopped, touched tendrils, smiled, and fell in love.

Said the right-handed Honeysuckle
To the left-handed Bindweed:
'Oh, let us get married
If our parents don't mind; we'd
Be loving and inseparable,
Inextricably entwined; we'd
Live happily ever after,'
Said the Honeysuckle to the Bindweed.

'Misalliance' from *The Songs of Flanders and Swann* (1977)

Saint Ruthen 9th century?

Obscure Shropshire saint

There is only one church in England dedicated to this saint and it is at Longden, near Shrewsbury. This mysterious saint is unknown in both the Roman and Celtic calendars, but the proximity of Longden to the Welsh border and to Denbighshire may give a clue. In this neighbouring county there is a town bearing the same name, though spelt Ruthin – might our Ruthen be a Welsh saint? Another possibility is that in Longden we have a dedication to a Mercian bishop – Rethun or Reathun. He flourished in the first half of the 9th century and his name, under the form of Rethunus, may be found in the list of the bishops of Lincoln, in the days when that immense diocese had its headquarters in Leicester. Among the stories surrounding this saint is that, for some unknown reason, he was driven out of his bishopric and forced to take refuge in the monastery of Abingdon in Oxfordshire, where he was honourably received and where he later became abbot. Curiously, opposite St Ruthen's church in Longden is the Tankerville Arms, for by coincidence, not far from Abingdon was the castle of Shirburn, once the seat of the Tankerville family. Might this connection of the Tankervilles with Abingdon possibly account for their interest in the persecuted bishop Rethun and give us a clue to do him honour on their Shropshire property? Perhaps we will never know, but the links are tantalising!

While we know little of Ruthen's life, we may assume that he possessed qualities as a Christian that marked him off from others – patience, wisdom, self-giving – all marks of the saint in every generation. These words were written centuries after Ruthen:

In the early days of the Church, in the times of persecution, many people were so wonderfully and unexpectedly touched by grace that, without any previous spiritual experience, craftsmen threw down their tools and children their slates, and ran to be martyred with the saints. That being so, why should not we who live in peaceful times believe that God may, can, will and, indeed, does touch different people just as suddenly with the grace of contemplation? And this I believe he willingly does to chosen souls by the bounty of his grace. For ultimately he will be known for what he is, to the wonderment of the whole world. Such a soul, lovingly reducing itself to nothing and making God everything, is protected from all physical and spiritual foes by the fullness and goodness of God's grace, and not by any effort of its own. For common sense demands that God should keep safe all who for love of him forsake themselves and become indifferent to their own welfare.

Anonymous (*c.*1370), *The Epistle of Privy Counsel*

The writer of words in the Apocrypha *extols those who are famous – but also celebrates those about whom little is known:*

Let us now praise famous men, and our fathers that begat us.
Such as did bear rule in their kingdoms, men renowned for their power.
Leaders of the people by their counsels, and by their knowledge.
Such as found out musical tunes and recited verses in writing:
All these were honoured in their generations, and were the glory of their times.
And some there be which have no memorial;
Who are perished as though they had never been.
Their bodies are buried in peace;
But their name liveth for evermore.

Ecclesiasticus 44

Henry Peach Robinson 1830–1901

Photographer & writer on photography

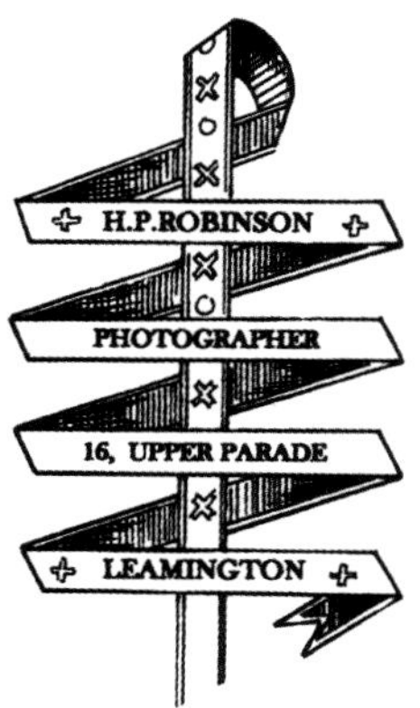

One of the greatest influences on the emerging art of photography, Henry Robinson was born on this day in 1830, at Linney, Ludlow. Educated locally, he studied drawing privately and was apprenticed to Richard Jones, a printer and bookseller in Ludlow. His interests turned to photography, then in its infancy, and he was instructed by an itinerant daguerreotype portraitist. Meanwhile he continued his studies in art and, in 1852, exhibited an oil painting, *On the Teme near Ludlow,* at the Royal Academy. In 1856 Robinson opened a photographic studio in Leamington Spa, Warwickshire and was achieving success when he was forced to discontinue his business through ill health due to exposure to photographic chemicals. He turned instead to writing for a variety of photographic journals, and his treatise *Pictorial Effect in Photography* (1869) was one of the first serious treatments of photography as a fine art. His books explain to amateurs and professionals alike the basic techniques of photography and give clear aesthetic principles to follow. In his own professional photography, he was acknowledged master of the combination printing technique by which several images from different negatives were combined into a photographic ensemble. Famous pictures like *Fading Away* (1858) and *The Lady of Shalott* (1860–1) often used amateur or professional models, arranged in fictional settings to suggest a narrative. His philosophy was entirely guided by an insistence that photography should bow to art rather than nature and that subjects which had been 'created' were preferable to the natural. His work may be found in major museum collections throughout the world.

Robinson, like all photographers, dealt in images. At first sight, the photograph takes away from the image the subjective – such an important part of a portrait. However, as we have seen, Robinson's photographs were by no means all 'true to life' and were subject to the photographer's art and distortion. In a similar way, we make our own images of God. Some of these are good, some are distortions. The Jesuit priest and writer Gerard Hughes challenges some of these false images:

The particular image we have of God will depend very much on the nature of our upbringing and how we have reacted to it, because our ideas and our felt knowledge derive from our experience. If our experience has taught us to think of God as a policeman-like figure, whose predominant interest is in our faults, and if our encounters with him have been mostly in cold churches where we are bored out of our minds with barely audible services and sermons presenting God as he who disapproves of most of the things we like, then we are not likely to want to turn to him, no matter how many people may tell us that prayer is a necessity.

To become aware that we have a distorted notion of God is to have made progress on our journey towards him. As the journey continues, we shall discover other distortions of which we were not aware. Such discoveries can be very painful at first, but it is like the pain we feel when our limbs are at last free after being constricted; it is the pain of freedom. The journey to God is a journey of discovery and it is full of surprises.

Gerard W Hughes, *God of Surprises* (1985)

Richard Barnfield bapt.1574 d.1620

Shropshire's poetic link with Shakespeare

The poetry of Richard Barnfield is relatively unknown but some scholars have seen in it links with the great William Shakespeare. Indeed, it has been suggested that several poems once attributed to Shakespeare are in fact by Barnfield.

Baptized in 1574, Barnfield was born at Norbury in Shropshire. He attended Brasenose College, Oxford and there studied law as well as continuing his poetic writing. Perhaps the most famous of his poems is *The Affectionate Shepheard Sick for Love* or *The Complaint of Daphnis for the Love of Ganymede.* While enthusiastically received at the time of its publication, the work was subsequently disapproved of because of its homoerotic nature and the explicit attraction between the two principal characters. Indeed, while the 18th-century writer Thomas Warton praised Barnfield's poetic achievements in *The History of English Poetry* (1774-81), he found the subject matter often objectionable and distasteful.

Perhaps we can do no better than judge for ourselves, comparing love poems by Shakespeare and Barnfield himself:

Not marble, nor the gilded monuments
Of princes shall outlive this powerful rhyme,
But you shall shine more bright in these contents
Than unswept stone, besmeared with sluttish time.
When wasteful war shall statues overturn,
And broils root out the work of masonry,
Nor Mars his sword, not war's quick fire shall burn
The living record of your memory.
'Gainst death, and all-oblivious enmity
Shall you pace forth, your praise shall still find room,
Even in the eyes of all posterity
That wears this world out to the ending doom.
So, till the judgement that your self arise,
You live in this, and dwell in lovers' eyes.

William Shakespeare 1564–1616, Sonnet 55

Two stars there are in one faire firmament,
(Of some entitled *Ganymede's* sweet face),
Which other stars in brightness doe disgrace,
As much as *Po* in clearenes passeth *Trent.*
Nor are they common natur'd stars: for why,
These stars when other shine vaile their pure light,
And when all other vanish out of sight,
They adde a glory to the world's great eye.
By these two stars my life is onely led,
In them I place my joy, in them my pleasure,
Love's piercing Darts, and Nature's precious treasure
With their sweet foode my fainting soule is fed:
Then when my sunne is absent from my sight
How can it chuse (with me) but be dark night?

Richard Barnfield

Sarah Alston, 4th Duchess of Somerset 1631–92

Benefactor & philanthropist

Both Hereford Cathedral and its school have been recipients of the generosity of benefactors through the centuries, and none more generous than the woman we commemorate today, whose provision in the 17th century has influenced for good many lives – and continues to do so. Sarah Alston came of a professional and wealthy London family, and made the first of her three marriages, in 1652, to George Grimston. Widowed at the age of 24, she married Lord John Seymour, later fourth duke of Somerset. The marriage was not a happy one, her husband often being in debt. On his death, Sarah was granted the right to continue to enjoy the precedence of a duchess 'notwithstanding any marriage she may hereafter contract'. She married for the third time Henry Hare, Lord Henry Coleraine, but it is as a widow – and a wealthy one at that – that Sarah is especially remembered. In her will she made provision for the support of scholars at Brasenose College, Oxford and at St John's College, Cambridge. In both bequests, special mention was made to benefit boys from Herefordshire and from the Cathedral School. It is thought that her interest in the county came through her agent, Sir William Gregory of How Caple (see 9 May), himself an old boy of Hereford Cathedral School. Sarah's generosity extended to support for churches, including Tottenham Parish Church and St Margaret's, Westminster, as well as schools and the endowment of almshouses at Froxfield in Wiltshire. Certainly, her generous legacy bore much fruit and those who became 'Somerset Scholars' include many famous people, among them Fred Weatherly (1848–1929) (see 7 September), the famous song-writer, and E J Rapson (1861–1937) (see 13 May), perhaps the greatest Sanskrit scholar of his day. Sarah was buried in Westminster Abbey, her monument designed by Grinling Gibbons – a fitting memorial to a magnanimous Christian lady.

A poem by George Herbert weaves together the themes of life, death, virtue and generosity – themes which are seen in such rich measure in the life of Sarah Alston:

Sweet day, so cool, so calm, so bright,
The bridal of the earth and sky,
The dew shall weep thy fall to night;
For thou must die.

Sweet rose, whose hue, angry and brave,
Bids the rash gazer wipe his eye,
Thy root is ever in its grave,
And thou must die.

Sweet Spring, full of sweet days and roses,
A box where sweets compacted lie,
My music shows ye have your closes,
And all must die.

Only a sweet and virtuous soul,
Like season'd timber, never gives;
But though the whole world turns to coal,
Then chiefly lives.

George Herbert 1593–1633, 'Virtue', from *The Temple* (1633)

Susanna Hopton 1627–1709

Devotional writer & friend of Traherne

Often cited as a leading member of Thomas Traherne's (see 10 October) circle, Susanna Hopton was a writer and poet herself. Born and brought up in London, she espoused the Royalist cause in the Civil War and by 1654 had converted to Roman Catholicism. Her marriage in 1655 to Richard Hopton had a major influence on her life. His family hailed from Canon Frome and he became a chief justice of the North Wales circuit. Susanna wrote that she loved him 'truly and passionately' and their marriage was a long and happy one. Richard Hopton devoted 'laborious studies and indefatigable pains' to enticing Susanna back into the Church of England and he encouraged her to study the various claims of the two churches 'with the best Divines of the Church of England which our parts afford'. She returned to the Anglican fold in 1660 and wrote a long letter justifying this change of heart. This was published in 1710 by George Hickes, the non-juror bishop as *A letter written by a gentlewoman of quality to a Romish priest.* Susanna was a great reader and wrote her own books of devotion. In 1673 her *Daily Devotions* was published, followed in 1700 by her *Devotions in the Ancient Way of Offices*, a reformed version of the Roman Catholic John Austin's popular book of daily offices of 1668. She also left a manuscript of her own religious poetry. Most of her works are substantially collections from other writers, including material from unpublished manuscripts of Thomas Traherne.

During the 1660s and 1670s, Susanna lived with her husband at Gattertop, Hope-under-Dinmore, and during the 1680s they moved to Kington, where Richard Hopton died in 1698. During her widowhood, Susanna led a life of great devotion, rising for matins at four, worshipping five times a day, fasting and giving alms, and was well known for her controversial turn of mind. During the last years of her life, she was an ardent non-juror, supporting those who could not, in conscience, take the oath to William and Mary, and she was a close friend of Bishop George Hickes, who spent time hiding at her home. By 1708 Susanna had moved to the parish of St Peter, Hereford and there she died on 12 July 1709. Two days later she was buried in the chancel of Canon Frome church, close to her husband. Her bequests included money left in trust for non-juror clergy and many religious books to her friends.

Susanna's devotion to the Sacraments of the Church is especially seen in her writings, among which is this thanksgiving to be said at home after receiving Holy Communion. Her vocabulary is clearly much influenced by the words of the Book of Common Prayer*:*

Blessed art thou, O Lord God, and blessed be thy holy name for ever, who hast now vouchsafed to feed me with the Bread of Life, and hast given me to drink the Cup of Eternity, the holy and heavenly Mysteries of the Body and Blood of my Saviour, thereby assuring my Soul of thy Favour and Goodness towards me, for the increase of my Faith, for the Pardon of my Sins, for the obtaining of my Peace, and all other Benefits of Christ's blessed Passion.

I now most humbly beseech thee to assist me with thy heavenly Grace, that I may continue thine for ever, and be made a Temple of thy Holy Spirit; and that having now Christ dwelling in me by Faith, I may accomplish the rest of my Life in Repentance and Godly Fear, in mortifying my own sinful desires, and in keeping thy holy Commandments; for which end, guide me with thy Power, enlighten me with thy Word, quicken me with thy Spirit, elevate my Senses, compose my Memory, and order my Conversation aright; for thou art able to do abundantly above what I can ask or think; by which thy great and bountiful Goodness towards me, thou wilt glorify thy Name in me, and bring me at last to thine eternal Kingdom of Glory, through him who is the King of Glory, my blessed Lord and Saviour Jesus Christ. Amen.

A Collection of Meditations and Devotions (1717)

Silas 1st century

Companion to St Paul

The little Victorian church at Bollingham outside Kington is dedicated to this little-known figure from the early church. Silas, or Silvanus, was the companion of St Paul, chosen to take a letter from the Council of Jerusalem to the Christians of Antioch (Acts 15). Afterwards he stayed with Paul at Antioch until Paul separated from Barnabas, then accompanying him to Syria, Cilicia, and eventually Macedonia. Silas may also be identified with Silvanus the scribe of 1 Peter (5:12) and tradition relates that he died in Macedonia. With so little background, Silas understandably has no medieval dedications and most in England are associated with Victorian churches. This is certainly true of Bollingham, a church with a medieval foundation but largely rebuilt in the Victorian era. Sometimes churches were dedicated to give honour to a generous benefactor (a church near to where I grew up was dedicated to St Jerome in the 1930s, not because there was a local devotion to this doctor of the Church but because the land on which the church was built was given by the local landowner, Jerome de Salis!) Sometimes, in the 19th century, churches were given new, more popular dedications, removing obscure Celtic saints and replacing them with more 'mainstream' ones. I like to think that a dedication to St Silas celebrates the gift of friendship – for certainly, without the support of friends like Silas, Barnabas and Timothy, Paul's great missionary endeavours would have been greatly compromised.

Words celebrating the gift of friendship:

I wonder sometimes if I have been unfaithful in my friendships; so many have come and gone, not through any active breach or loss of kind feeling, but from the fact that we have each become different people; and as we became different our points of intimate contact have diminished. It was Emerson, I think, who maintained that for sincerity in friendship, change must be recognized – and accepted; and the real test of the genuineness of a friendship, when circumstances have brought about separation, is whether one does or does not regret that the friendship was ever formed. In very few of my friendships has that sense of regret followed; over all the rest, when the period of intimacy has ended, I have retained a lively feeling for benefits received, and to some, whom I never now meet or even hear from, my thoughts go constantly, still registering the old affection of the days when meeting was an exciting pleasure and parting always a regret.

Laurence Housman 1865–1959, *The Unexpected Years*

A prayer of thanksgiving for friendship

May the God of love who is the source of all our affection for each other formed here on earth take our friendships into his keeping, that they may continue and increase throughout life and beyond it, in Jesus Christ our Lord.

William Temple 1881–1944

Caroline Clive 1801–73

Sensational novelist & poet

Born Caroline Wigley, at the age of two she contracted a disease, possibly poliomyelitis, which left her permanently disabled. She was educated by governesses and after the death of her mother and brother became a wealthy heiress. In 1840, Caroline married the Reverend Archer Clive, rector of Solihull, Warwickshire, and they had two children. In 1845, following the death of his father, Clive inherited Whitfield, the family estate in Herefordshire, and the family moved here.

Caroline Clive's first book was a volume of religious meditations entitled *Essays on the Human Intellect as Constructed by God,* but it was poetry in which she was chiefly interested and her first book of verse, *IX poems by V,* made its appearance in 1840. It was well received and established Caroline as one of the leading female poets of her day. Over the next 12 years she had five long poems published, as well as *Saint Oldooman: a Myth of the Nineteenth Century* (1845), a prose satire on Newman's *Lives of the Saints*. All her works were proclaimed as written by 'V', short for Vigolina, Archer Clive's Latin translation of Wigley, her maiden name. In 1855 her first novel was published – *Paul Ferroll: a Tale by the Author of 'IX Poems by V'.* A forerunner of the modern sensational and romantic novel, it shocked many readers by its apparent amorality. In the book, the hero not only murders his wife, with seemingly no qualms of conscience, but also shoots a workman in cold blood – events which appear to elicit no shock or condemnation from the author. The book's sequel *Why Paul Ferroll Killed his Wife* was published in 1860 and was followed by further novels and collections of poetry. Accidents in 1860 and 1863 left Caroline permanently confined to a wheelchair and in 1865 she suffered a stroke. She died on 14 July 1873 from injuries received two days before, when her dress caught fire in her library at Whitfield.

One of Caroline's poems takes its subject from her imagining a letter she received telling her that 150 people (who were actually dead) had been invited to the queen's ball:

How soon forgotten are the Dead!
A splendid throng the Palace calls
To meet and revel in its halls;
And of the names that thus are sped,
Seven score and ten of them are dead.

Caroline goes on to imagine that the ghosts of some of the dead accept their invitations to Buckingham Palace. Whether they are forgotten or remembered it is equally painful. A girl seeks out her fiancé:

Her fond fantastic arms she wound,
Beseechingly, his form around
Her airy lips his visage kiss'd;
In vain, in vain; no thought he cast
Back on the memory of the past,
And she must let it go at last,
The cherish'd hope that she was miss'd.

Serlo, Abbot of Gloucester 11th century

Founder of St Peter's Abbey

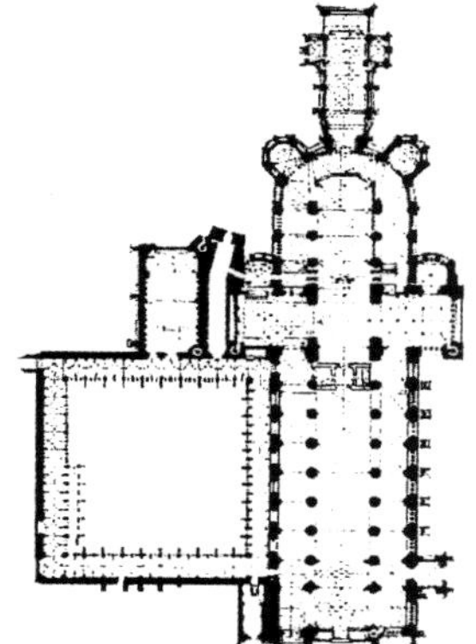

Hereford has an important part in the foundation of what is now Gloucester Cathedral. A local contemporary account gives details of the laying of the foundation stone of St Peter's Abbey: 'In 1089, on the day of the festival of the Apostles Peter and Paul [29 June], in this year were laid the foundations of the Church of Gloucester, the venerable man Robert, Bishop of Hereford, laying the first stone, Serlo, the Abbot being in charge of the work'. Serlo was a chaplain to William the Conqueror and was appointed by him to be abbot of Gloucester in 1072. He was a supporter of the reforms ordered by Archbishop Lanfranc and he set about implementing them at St Peter's Abbey. He increased the number of monks in the abbey community and built up its estate. In 1088 a fire destroyed the old monastic buildings and seizing this opportunity Serlo cleared the ground and marked out foundations for what was to be a new church.

St Paul speaks of the importance of firm foundations:

According to the grace of God given to me, like a skilled master builder I laid a foundation, and another man is building upon it. Let each man take care how he builds upon it. For no other foundation can any one lay than that which is laid, which is Jesus Christ. Now if any one builds on the foundation with gold, silver, precious stones, wood, hay, straw – each man's work will become manifest; for the Day will disclose it, because it will be revealed with fire, and the fire will test what sort of work each one has done. If the work which any man has built on the foundation survives, he will receive a reward. If any man's work is burned up, he will suffer loss, though he himself will be saved, but only as through fire.

1 Corinthians 3:10–15

Just 40 years after Serlo's laying of the foundation stone of Gloucester Abbey, Abbot Suger wrote these words on the west door of the great abbey church of St Denis near Paris when it was consecrated in 1144. They remind us of the vital importance of great buildings in pointing us to Christ:

Bright is the noble work; but being nobly bright, the work
Should brighten the minds, so that they may travel, through the true lights,
To the True Light where Christ is the true door.
In what manner it be inherent in this world the golden door defines:
The dull mind rises in truth through that which is material
And, in seeing this light, is resurrected from its former submersion.

Abbot Suger *c.*1081–1151

John Grandison 1292–1369

Hereford supplies Exeter's most famous bishop

The influence of Bishop John Grandison on the worship and life of Exeter Cathedral in the 14th century was enormous – and he hailed from Herefordshire. Born at Ashperton, he became a protégé, friend and chaplain of Pope John XXII and he was rewarded with various church positions, culminating in his being made bishop of Exeter in 1328. He gave his life to the diocese and endowed the cathedral richly with books, metalwork, jewellery and textiles – all making great use of his Grandison coat of arms. He was a great scholar and wrote in depth on liturgy and the saints. Above all, he endowed Exeter Cathedral with a detailed *ordinale,* regulating liturgy, ceremonial and polyphony. During his episcopate of 42 years, he rarely left his diocese but attended to the needs of the clergy – his episcopal registers strictly enforce discipline and deal with clerical offenders. He was a great episcopal builder, raising funds for the completion of the nave of Exeter Cathedral and providing his own chantry chapel at the west end of the building as well as the unique minstrels' gallery on the north side of the nave, used in the annual Palm Sunday ceremonies. Outside Exeter, he founded the collegiate church of Ottery St Mary in 1337. This was his most lavish project and he took pleasure in linking this great church with Exeter Cathedral, in design and fittings. The lives of the saints held a great fascination for him – he had great devotion to the Blessed Virgin Mary and contributed towards historical study on the life of St Thomas of Canterbury. He encouraged a local interest in St Sidwell of Exeter as well as recording the lives of Cornish saints. Grandison died on this day in 1369. On his tomb, he directed that these words of humility be written: 'piteous bishop, most piteous servant of the Mother of Mercy'.

The minstrels' gallery is a unique feature of Exeter's liturgical architecture and had a particular use on Palm Sunday, when the procession returned to enter the cathedral and seven boys sang from the gallery. Palm Sunday, with its paradoxical presentation of the lowly king, is a reminder of the God who turns our human values upside down – a paradox seen well in the life of Grandison, who strove to combine his earthly office and its duties of state with the humility of a lowly pastor:

Christ came to establish a Kingdom, not to proclaim a set of opinions. Every man entering his Kingdom becomes interested in all its relations, members and circumstances. He cannot separate himself in any wise apart from them.

My business, because I am a theologian, and have no vocation except for my theology, is not to build but to dig, to show that economy and politics must have a ground beneath themselves. Our task consists in proclaiming society and humanity to be divine realities, as they stand, not as they may become.

We do not suppose that success will necessarily attach to any particular system of human contrivance, but that it will depend on the degree in which we keep close to the true law of human society, which God has ordained. Society is not to be made anew by arrangements of ours, but is to be regenerated by finding the law and ground of its order and harmony, the only secret of its existence, which is God himself. There will be discovered beneath all the politics of the earth, sustaining the order of each country, upholding the charity of each household, a city which has foundations, whose builder and maker is God.

F D Maurice 1805–1872, *Politics for the People* (1848/9)

John Bradford 1750–1805

Anglican & Nonconformist combined

In an age reckoned to adhere strictly to denominational boundaries, John Bradford tried to find ways of combining Anglicanism with newly emerging traditions – not always successfully! Born in Hereford, the son of a clothier, he was educated at the Cathedral School and then at Wadham College, Oxford. He was ordained and became a curate in Berkshire but found that in doctrine he tended to the heresy of Arianism (a denial of the divinity of Christ). A conversion to greater orthodoxy followed and he embraced Calvinistic theology. In this spirit of openness he began to preach in several chapels belonging to the Countess of Huntingdon's Connexion (an 18th-century variant of Methodism) but this was frowned upon by the church authorities and he was dismissed from his church position. Bradford then joined the Countess's Connexion and for several years preached in chapels in South Wales and the west Midlands. He regularly preached at the old playhouse in Birmingham, using a pulpit positioned at the front of the stage. From all accounts he was a popular speaker and the theatre was often crowded. However, desiring a more settled ministry, he accepted leadership of the newly opened Paradise Chapel in Bartholomew Street, Birmingham. There he continued his literary interests, publishing in 1792 *A Collection of Hymns,* some of them by himself. His other notable literary work, also published in 1792, was his set of notes to Bunyan's *Pilgrim's Progress.* Bradford married in 1779, had a family of 12 children, and later moved to the more lucrative position of minister at the City Chapel, in Grub Street, London. He died on 16 July 1805.

Selina, countess of Huntingdon gathered around her a number of ministers, like John Bradford, and used them as preachers in the chapels which she opened and maintained. She had a volatile personality and was prone to bouts of impulsiveness and introspection. Few had the courage to challenge her, but one friend, Thomas Barnard, clearly recognized her need to work at her spiritual life! His prescription was:

- That your Ladyship would observe moderation in all things; nor be hurried on with too much eagerness in the spiritual combat; nor fall into discouragement and despondency for any slips you may make.
- That your Ladyship would admit but very few to any knowledge of the business you have in hand, not make any discovery of it by any violent changes in outward appearances.
- That you would hold all your passions, as joy, grief, desire, fear etc out of extremes.
- That your exercises of prayer & meditation be not too laborious, nor bear too hard upon your strength.

Thomas Barnard to Lady Huntingdon, 28 July 1739

Fix thou our steps, O Lord, that we stagger not at the uneven motions of the world, but steadily go on to our glorious home; neither censuring our journey by the weather we meet with, nor turning out of the way for anything that befalls us.

The winds are often rough, and our own weight presses us downwards. Reach forth, O Lord, thy hand, thy saving hand, and speedily deliver us.

Teach us, O Lord, to use this transitory life as pilgrims returning to their beloved home; that we may take what our journey requires, and not think of settling in a foreign country.

John Wesley 1713–91

Adam Orleton *c.*1275–1345

Bishop of Hereford unjustly linked with Edward II?

When Edward II was murdered at Berkeley Castle in 1327, many fingers were pointed. Adam Orleton, bishop of Hereford was certainly a member of a delegation sent to the king at Kenilworth to solicit his abdication. His reputation has not been helped by the chronicler Geoffrey Baker, who put about the story of an ambiguous letter sent by Orleton to seal Edward's fate – slanders that Orleton robustly rejected. Whatever his role in the tragic events of 1327, Orleton was a bishop of great influence in the Church of his day. Born probably not in Orleton but in Hereford, he had a brilliant career in the Church, becoming, successively, bishop of Hereford, Worcester and finally, Winchester. Before this, he had come to public attention through his work as a canon lawyer and church diplomat, first through his part in the mission to promote the canonisation of Thomas Cantilupe and then in many embassies to Europe – to secure the rescinding of the excommunication of Piers Gaveston and acting as the agent of King Edward II at Rome. His career was not without its setbacks. In 1322 he was taken to task by the king at Hereford for assisting the resurgent barons in the Welsh Marches, and the following year he was implicated in the escape from the Tower of London of Roger Mortimer (see 29 November). All this might suggest that Orleton was far from being a holy man, but despite his political and diplomatic activities, he is thought to have been a conscientious bishop, performing his episcopal duties whenever possible, until old age and blindness prevented him. He died on this day in 1345 at Farnham Castle, the palace of the bishop of Winchester.

Successive historians and writers have sought to discredit the hapless Edward II, and eminent churchmen like Orleton have been part of the smear campaign. Often his weak government has been unfairly linked with his perceived sexuality, and a writer like Marlowe fully exploits this in his play. In this passage, Gaveston suggests that the king is a weak character, easily led:

I must have wanton poets, pleasant wits,
Musicians, that with touching of a string
May draw the pliant king which way I please:
Musicke and poetry is his delight,
Therefore ile have Italian maskes by night,
Sweete speeches, comedies, and pleasing shows,
And in the day when he shall walke abroad,
Like Sylvian Nimphes my pages shall be clad,
My men like Satyres grazing on the lawnes,
Shall with their Goate feete daunce the antick hay.
Sometime a lovelie boye in Dians shape,
With hair that gilds the water as it glides,
Crownets of pearle about his naked armes,
And in his sportfull hands an Olive tree,
To hide those parts which men delight to see,
Shall bathe him in a spring, and there hard by,
One like Actaeon peeping through the grove,
Shall by the angrie goddesse be tranformde,
And running in the likeness of an Hart,
By yelping hounds puld downe, and seeme to die.
Such things as these best please his majestie.

Christopher Marlowe 1564–93, *Edward II*

Humphry Repton 1752–1818

Self-styled landscape gardener

Herefordshire gentry of the 18th century were often intent on 'improving' their country estates and many turned to Humphry Repton to assist them in their aspirations. After he had tried his hand at several careers – as a textile manufacturer, journalist, dramatist, artist and political agent – Repton hit on the idea of combining his sketching skills with his limited experience of laying out grounds. With supreme confidence, he coined the term 'landscape gardener'. Since the death of Capability Brown, no one had replaced the great master as *doyen* of landscape development and Repton gladly filled the gap, sending circulars advertising his services to the upper classes. To help clients visualise his design, Repton produced 'red books' with text and watercolours and a system of overlays to show 'before' and 'after' effects. In this way he produced over 400 designs, although only a fraction of these were completed. He defended Capability Brown against attack from contemporaries Richard Payne Knight (see 11 February) and Uvedale Price (see 25 September), who extolled the Picturesque – rugged and natural as against Brown's (and, to some extent Repton's) greater use of artifice and elegant design. Working with contemporary architects like John Nash, Repton had notable successes and in Herefordshire is best known for his work at Old Hill (Dr John Matthew's Belmont, outside Hereford), New Weir at Kenchester, Garnons and Stoke Edith.

In 1811 Jane Austen decided to draw on the services of Humphry Repton, not to plan a garden, but as providing material for the novel she had just embarked upon – Mansfield Park. *Ridiculing the fashions of her time, Austen would immortalise Repton as the relentless 'improver' of gardens and nature. Can one 'improve' nature? For centuries, humankind has worked with the raw material of creation to modify and make more efficient – but improve? The discussion will always continue.*

'It wants improvement, Ma'am, beyond anything. I never saw a place that wanted so much improvement in my life; and it is so forlorn that I do not know what can be done with it.'

'Smith has not much above a hundred acres altogether in his grounds, which is little enough, and makes it more surprising that the place can have been so improved. Now, at Sotherton, we have a good seven hundred, without reckoning the water meadows; so that I think, if so much could be done at Compton, we need not despair. There have been two or three fine old trees cut down, that grew too near the house, and it opens the prospect amazingly, which makes me think that Repton, or anybody of that sort, would certainly have the avenue at Sotherton down.'

Jane Austen 1775–1817, *Mansfield Park*

'Whoe'er from Nature takes a view,
Must copy and improve her too.
To heighten every work of art,
Fancy should take an active part:
Thus I (which few I think can boast)
Have made a Landscape of a Post.'

William Combe 1741–1823,
'The Tour of Doctor Syntax in Search of the Picturesque' (1812)

Arilda date unknown

Martyr in Gloucestershire

An obscure note on the fly-leaf of a book in Hereford Cathedral library is one of the few allusions we have to this Gloucestershire saint. (The book belonged to Thomas Bredon, abbot of Gloucester 1224–28, and was confiscated from Gloucester at the Dissolution of the Monasteries.) The name Arilda is Anglo-Saxon and little is known about her. Tradition associates her with Kington near Thornbury, in the parish of Oldbury-on-Severn in Gloucestershire. Here she is said to have been murdered by 'Muncius a tiraunt, who cut off her heade becawse she would not consent to lye with him'. In the same place we find St Arilda's church and well. A local tradition that the water runs red with blood is well founded, as the stones in the well's outflow are stained red, not with the iron associated with chalybeate springs, but with freshwater algae having the name *Hildebrandia rivularis*. After the Norman Conquest, Arilda's relics were translated to St Peter's Abbey, Gloucester, where her shrine was famous for miracles and 20 July was proclaimed as her feast day. She is possibly depicted in the east window of the cathedral, where she appears to share a light with St Lawrence, to whom Didmarton church, neighbour to Oldbury, is dedicated. There is evidence for a statue of her in the reredos of Gloucester's Lady Chapel.

St Arilda appears in the English Benedictine liturgical calendar as 'Virgin and Martyr' and these themes are very much found in her hymn:

O Mother Church, today proclaim
The honour of Arilda's name.
And grant that we may have a share
In that great sound of praise and prayer.

With flesh unstained and pure of mind,
Untouched by sin of humankind,
Your mind was turned to Christ above,
On him alone you fixed your love.

She gave her life to Christ below
And in his strength she smote the foe.
Three times she fought the power of sin
And walked with Christ made pure within.

O Arild, of this holy place
The guardian, and our hope of grace,
O Mother, hear your children's prayer,
That we the peace of Heaven may share.

Pray now for us to Christ your Lord,
Whom by the angels is adored,
That we at last with you may come
To greet Him in our heavenly home.

Walter Map d.1209/10

Royal clerk & medieval humorist

Clergy are often in demand as after-dinner speakers. This cleric may well have been the first in such an honoured line! Walter Map came from a border family and may have been related to the Lord of Wormsley near Hereford. Certainly his nephew was a canon of Hereford Cathedral. Map spent much of his early career in royal service, representing Henry II on numerous occasions. He then became a canon of Lincoln and although, in his writing, he severely criticised religious orders, the monk-bishop, Hugh of Lincoln promoted him and he became archdeacon of Oxford. In 1199 the cathedral chapter of Hereford petitioned Richard I to ask permission to elect Map as their bishop, but the king died before their petition could be answered and his successor, King John (see 11 June), appointed Giles de Briouze. Walter Map from then on is known not so much for his work as a cleric but as a writer. He is best known for his *De nugis curialium* (Courtiers' Trifles), a work which survives only in a single late 14th-century copy in the Bodleian Library, and which became widely known only in the 19th century. The work contains some serious elements (especially his celebrated diatribe against the Cistercians), but much of it comprises a gathering of disparate elements – humorous and satirical stories, some sophisticated, some crude; ghost stories; and fragments of history – just the material for after-dinner speeches! Other works develop the Round Table Legends of King Arthur while another, the humorous *Golias Episcopus*, attributed to Map, speaks of an imaginary prelate who speaks candidly of his life and clearly enjoys his drink! Thought to reflect the writer's own experiences, such works gained for Map the probably undeserved title of 'the drunken archdeacon of Oxford'.

Two short extracts, translated from the Latin, give a flavour of Walter Map's wit and humour. First, a passage from his Dissuasio, *derived in part from Cicero:*

Pacuvius, weeping, said to his neighbour Arrius: 'Friend, I have a disastrous tree in my garden: my first wife hung herself on it, so did my second later on, and now my third has done the same.' Said Arrius, 'I wonder that after so many strokes of luck you find it in you to weep.' And again, 'Good gods, what expenses has that tree suspended for you!' And a third time: 'Friend, give me some cuttings of that tree to plant.'

Map's so-called Drinking Song*:*

I propose to end my days in a tavern drinking,
May some Christian hold for me the glass when I am shrinking;
That the cherubim may cry, when they see me sinking,
God be gracious to a soul of this gentleman's way of thinking.

A glass of wine amazingly enlighteneth one's internals,
'Tis wings bedewed with nectar that fly up to the supernals,
Bottles cracked in taverns have much the sweeter kernels,
Than the sups allowed to us in the College journals.

Sir John Oldcastle 1360–1417

Lollard leader

Often associated with the character of Falstaff in Shakespeare's *Henry IV*, and as boon companion of the future Henry v, Sir John Oldcastle was, in fact, very different from the wine-bibbing, overweight playboy with whom we have come to link his name. Indeed, in real life he appears to have been associated with one of the strictest and most austere religious movements of the late 14th century.

His place of birth is disputed, but one theory suggests Almeley in Herefordshire, where certainly there are strong family connections. He married twice, his second wife being Joan de la Pole, through whom he took the title Lord Cobham. He was well thought of as a soldier and as 'a man of grave and uncompromising character, and a friend of the king'. However, he is chiefly known for his connection with the Lollards, by whom he was regarded as champion and protector. The Lollards spoke out against the orthodox clergy, with their wealth and often immoral life. While Richard ii favoured the new sect, his successor, Henry iv, owing his elevation to the clerical party, fiercely persecuted them, seizing lands and property. Church and state combined to crush the heresy and some were tried, condemned and burned at the stake. While Oldcastle escaped censure during Henry iv's reign, on his son's accession Oldcastle's position became untenable and he was handed over to the Church authorities for trial. Condemned as a heretic and sent to the Tower, he managed to escape and lead an ill-planned and easily suppressed attempt to seize the king. He fled to the Marches and evaded capture for three years before being finally taken and returned to London. On Christmas Day 1417 he was hung at Tyburn. Popular rumour records that on the scaffold he is said to have begged Sir Thomas Erpingham to intercede for the Lollards 'if within three days he should rise from the dead'.

Oldcastle's story is one of betrayal and isolation – themes which come over clearly in this tragic poem, written centuries afterwards:

I am – yet what I am, none cares or knows;
    My friends forsake me like a memory lost:
I am the self-consumer of my woes –
    They rise and vanish in oblivions host,
Like shadows in love frenzied stifled throes
    And yet I am, and live – like vapours tost

Into the nothingness of scorn and noise,
    Into the living sea of waking dreams,
Where there is neither sense of life or joys,
    But the vast shipwreck of my lifes esteems;
Even the dearest that I love the best
    Are strange – nay, rather stranger than the rest.

I long for scenes where man hath never trod,
    A place where woman never smiled or wept,
There to abide with my Creator God,
    And sleep as I in childhood sweetly slept,
Untroubling and untroubled where I lie
    The grass below, above, the vaulted sky.

John Clare 1793–1864, 'I am'

Richard Godfrey Parsons 1882–1948

Bishop of Hereford & hymn writer

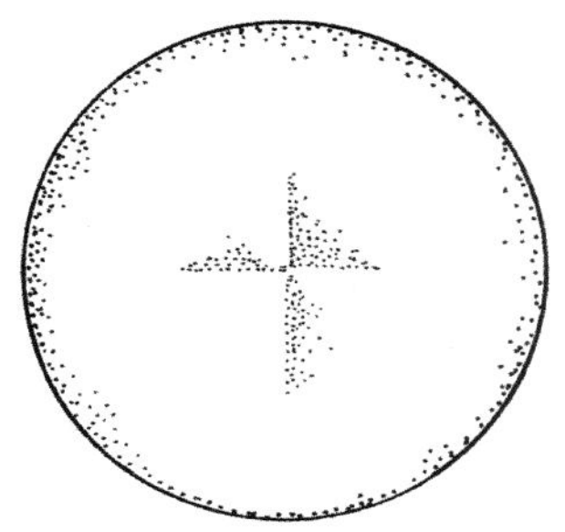

Bishop Parsons' portrait in the Great Hall of the Bishop's Palace shows him to be a kindly and pastoral man, and yet, at first sight, his background seemed to fit him for a very different diocese than Hereford. A brilliant academic, he was educated at Durham School and Magdalen College, Oxford, serving later as principal of Wells Theological College. However, he had a great love of the poor and those on the margins and served two incumbencies in the north-west before becoming bishop of Middleton in Manchester diocese in 1927. During this time he was much involved in the controversy surrounding Prayer Book revision. He went on to become bishop of Southwark and was translated to Hereford in 1941. For all his academic and urban background, Parsons was a much-loved pastoral bishop, delighting in the Clee Hills and Long Mynd. He knew great sadness, too, as his son was killed during the Second World War at Tobruk, North Africa.

For all his great learning, Richard Parsons was a man of great humility – a quality so clearly seen in his face in his portrait in the Bishop's Palace. Here, another bishop, writing 300 years before, speaks of the importance of humility in learning:

Our learning is then best when it teaches most humility; but to be proud of learning is the greatest ignorance in the world. For our learning is so long in getting, and so very imperfect, that our greatest clerk knows not the thousandth part of what he is ignorant; and knows so uncertainly what he seems to know, that he more uncertainly guesses at some more unnecessary thing than many others who yet know all that concerns them, and mind other things more necessary for the needs of life and commonwealth.

Jeremy Taylor 1613–67

Whether as theological college principal, parish priest, urban or rural bishop, Richard Parsons held the same devotion to the God who sustained him throughout his ministry. He writes movingly about the Sacrament at the heart of his faith, in one of his most famous and well-loved hymns:

We hail thy Presence glorious,
O Christ our great High Priest,
O'er sin and death victorious,
At thy thanksgiving feast:
As thou art interceding
For us in heaven above,
Thy Church on earth is pleading
Thy perfect work of love.

Through thee in every nation
Thine own their hearts upraise,
Offering one pure Oblation,
One sacrifice of praise:
With thee in blest communion
The living and the dead
Are joined in closest union,
One Body with one Head.

O Living Bread from heaven,
Jesu, our Saviour good,
Who thine own self hast given
To be our souls' true food;
For us thy body broken
Hung on the Cross of shame:
This bread, its hallowed token
We break in thy dear name.

O stream of love unending,
Poured from the one true Vine,
With our weak nature blending
The strength of life divine;
Our thankful faith confessing
In thy life-blood out poured,
We drink this Cup of blessing
And praise thy name, O Lord.

Richard Tomson late 17th century

Benefactor to the Cathedral School & Choir

In the porch to St John's door in Hereford Cathedral is a benefaction board with the following inscription:

> RICHARD TOMSON
> Left in trust to the Dean and Chapter of this Cathedral
> certain lands for the purpose of Distributing Bread and Money
> to 12 poor persons who shall attend the Choir Service
> on the Vigils of Sabbaths and certain holy days
> to the Deacon having charge of such distributions
> for copying music for the Choir – for clothing certain poor persons
> for obtaining discharge for some poor debtor from prison
> and for binding in apprenticeship some poor boy
> brought up a chorister in this Cathedral.

Richard Lane, alias Tomson, by his will of 24 July 1619, directed his executors to purchase land which would yield an annual income of £20, and to vest it in the dean and chapter. By 1835 the allowances to the 12 poor on the dean and chapter's list consisted of six pence a week, two four-penny loaves every Tuesday and Saturday and six pence on each of the 12 annual vigils per person. In 1977 a new scheme was approved whereby all the income from the charity was to be applied to the provision and maintaining of choral scholarships for choristers at Hereford Cathedral School. While we know little of Richard Tomson's life, his bequest all those years ago still provides a substantial income, and Tomson's Charity remains an important means of supporting the cathedral choristers.

How we use our money does have a lasting effect – for good and for ill – as this passage by an 18th-century writer makes clear:

If a man had eyes, hands and feet that he could remove to give to those who wanted them, if he should then lock them up in a chest, or please himself with some needless or ridiculous use of them, instead of giving them to brothers in need, wouldn't we have every justification in calling him an inhuman beast? If he chose rather to amuse himself with furnishing his house than to entitle himself to an eternal reward by giving those in need the eyes and hands they require, would we not justly class him mad?

Now money is very much in the same category as eyes and feet. If we lock it up in chests or waste it in needless and ridiculous expenses while the poor and the distressed are in great need of it, or if we consume it on ridiculous ornaments or clothes while others are starving in nakedness, we are not far from the cruelty of the man who chooses wastefully to dispose of his hands and eyes rather than give them to those who need them. If we choose to indulge ourselves in the kind of expensive enjoyments which have no real value, things which aren't really necessary, rather than to gain for ourselves an eternal reward by disposing our money well, we are guilty of the same madness.

Once we have satisfied our own reasonable needs, all the rest of our money is like spare eyes or spare hands. It is something that we cannot keep for ourselves, foolishly wasting it, but is something that can only be used well by giving it to those who need it.

William Law 1686–1761, *A Practical Treatise upon Christian Perfection* (1726)

Oliver de Merlimond 12th century
Pilgrim to Santiago de Compostela

On this day, the feast of St James, thousands converge on Santiago de Compostela, in north-west Spain, to visit the shrine of the saint, where it has stood since the 8th century. A pilgrimage to Santiago during the Middle Ages was thought to convey great grace to the pilgrims, and many well-worn routes were travelled from all corners of Europe. Among the English pilgrims who made the journey was one we commemorate – Oliver de Merlimond. The Chronicle of Wigmore Abbey recounts that Hugh de Mortimer chose Oliver as his chief steward and entrusted him with the building of a new church at Shobdon. Having begun to build, Oliver felt called to make the pilgrimage to Santiago – probably between the years 1125 and 1130. On his return journey from Spain, he stayed at the Abbey of St Victor in Paris – an important visit, as it led not only to a link between the abbey and Shobdon, but also to Oliver's introduction to the architectural styles seen in churches in western France. Indeed, a comparison between engravings of the carved doorways at Poitou, Santiago and Shobdon shows a common style with marked similarities in their use of carved beasts and other decorative features. The Romanesque church of Shobdon was demolished in 1752 by Lord Bateman and was replaced with the present unique 'Rococo Gothic' structure. However, the chancel arch and north and south doorways of the old church were re-erected in the park about a quarter of a mile to the north of the church as a folly, with the addition of gables, pinnacles and crockets according to the fashion of the day. Most of the detail is now lost, but we can see from earlier engravings and plaster casts exhibited at Crystal Palace until 1936, that the stylistic link with churches on the Santiago route in France is very apparent. Shobdon thus takes its place with Kilpeck and other local churches as an example of the Herefordshire School of sculpture, with its international roots and significance.

Two centuries after Oliver's visit to Spain, an English mystic wrote these words, extolling the virtue of pilgrimage, as a model of the interior spiritual life:

A real pilgrim going to Jerusalem leaves behind his house and land, his wife and children; he divests himself of all that he possesses, so that he can travel light. Similarly, if you wish to be a spiritual pilgrim, you must strip yourself of all your spiritual possessions; your good deeds as well as your bad deeds must be left behind. You must regard yourself as so spiritually poor that you have no confidence in your own actions; instead you must desire only the presence of Jesus, and his profound love. In this way you will be setting your heart on reaching Jerusalem; on obtaining the love of Jesus and such vision of him as he sees fit to give you.

You are now on the road, and you know the way. But beware of enemies who will try to obstruct you if they can. Their intention is to uproot from your heart your desire for the love of Jesus, and to turn your heart back to earthly desires.

You are now fast approaching Jerusalem. You have not yet arrived, but you are able to see the city in the distance before you arrive because of the rays of light shining from it. Remember that, although your soul is untroubled by thoughts of this world, you are not yet at the end of the journey, for your soul is not yet clothed in light and set aflame with the fire of love.

Jerusalem symbolizes the perfect love of God, set upon the hill of contemplation. To a soul that has no experience of it, it can seem quite small. But as you continue towards the city, it appears far greater – greater that anything that you could possibly have conceived. And the reward awaiting you in Jerusalem transcends the highest human desire.

Walter Hilton *c.*1340–96, *The Ladder of Perfection*

Anne and Joachim

Parents of the Blessed Virgin Mary

If it is true that the county of Herefordshire has a particularly high proportion of retired residents and, no doubt, by implication, a large number of grandparents, then today's saints should certainly be venerated and celebrated! In the *Protogospel of James,* written in the middle of the second century, the parents of Mary the mother of Jesus are named as Anne and Joachim. Neither character appears in the Bible itself, and their story appears to be heavily based on that of Hannah, the mother of Samuel in the Old Testament. A church was built in honour of Anne in Constantinople by Justinian and by the 10th century her feast was growing in popularity. In art she is often represented teaching the Virgin to read and she is also shown with her husband Joachim at their betrothal or marriage. There is a fine depiction of this scene in Great Malvern Priory – indeed, St Anne gives her name to the former well on the hills close to the Herefordshire border. The most famous shrine in Anne's honour in England was at Buxton and she was patron of various religious guilds in England. Her cult was bitterly attacked by Luther, especially the images representing her with Jesus and Mary, scenes so favoured by Renaissance painters. But her cult survived, and is still hugely popular in Brittany and in Canada. In England, churches dedicated to Anne continued to be built after the Reformation, but these are often a saintly compliment to Queen Anne, in whose reign these churches were often built or restored. The diocese of Hereford has just one dedication to St Anne – at Thornbury (here known as Anna). The feast day is kept today both to emphasise God's plan from the beginning to send his Son, born of a woman, to redeem fallen humanity, and also to show God's faithfulness in keeping his covenant with all generations.

Of the many passages about marriage, perhaps these words of Kahlil Gibran speak of the paradox of marriage and, indeed, of all loving relationships:

Love one another, but make not a bond of love:
Let it rather be a moving sea between the shores of your souls.
Fill each other's cup but drink not from one cup.
Give one another of your bread but eat not from the same loaf.
Sing and dance together and be joyous, but let each one of you be alone,
Even as the strings of a lute are alone though they quiver with the same music.

Give your hearts, but not into each other's keeping.
For only the hand of Life can contain your hearts.
And stand together yet not too near together:
For the pillars of the temple stand apart,
And the oak tree and the cypress grow not in each other's shadow.

Kahlil Gibran 1883–1931, *The Prophet* (1926)

Francis Tebbs Havergal 1829–90

Historian of Hereford Cathedral

Hereford's Havergal was one of a large dynasty. His father was a priest and, after trying his vocation as a missionary, he devoted himself to church music, writing, among other compositions, an anthem-like setting of Reginald Heber's *From Greenland's icy mountains*. His sister, Frances Ridley Havergal, was also famous for her hymn-writing. Francis himself was a Bible clerk of New College, Oxford. He served as vicar choral in Hereford Cathedral, at the same time serving in the parish of Pipe-cum-Lyde (1861–74). He was later incumbent at Upton Bishop (1874–90), while at the same time serving as a prebendary of Hereford Cathedral (1877–90). As an historian he wrote a number of books on Herefordshire and its cathedral as well as collecting all the obituaries of Ouseley, founder of St Michael's College, Tenbury (see 6 April).

From Havergal we can gain a great deal of the history and background of an English provincial cathedral. However, for glimpses of its real life, we have to look to other sources. Trollope enables us to see the foibles of ecclesiastical life, in microcosm. Here, Francis Kilvert, in his diary, similarly opens our eyes to some of a cathedral's hilarities!

'The little games that go on in Cathedrals'

Wednesday, 21 December 1870

Coming into the Vicarage from the school I found Sir Gilbert Lewis pacing round the gravel walk round the lawn in gloves and stick and great coat trying to get warm before starting on his cold journey to Harpton. He told me a good deal about Maria Kilvert of Worcester whom he knew, as he is a Canon of Worcester. He said she was tall and thin. She used to come rapidly into Church (into the Cathedral) to receive the sacrament two or three times a month, but for the last three years she had not attended the other services. She used to come in a respirator. She shut herself up almost entirely ever since he had been Canon of Worcester, 15 years. Lady Lewis used to call and was sometimes admitted, Sir Gilbert had not called for three years. The house looked most melancholy and dreary, like a house of the dead, no movement, the blinds never drawn up, no carriage ever stopping at the gate, scarcely any one ever going out or in at the door. Sir Gilbert does not believe she had the slightest acquaintance with Lord Lyttleton, or that she even knew him by sight. He said mad people are apt to come to Cathedrals. There was a mad woman who came to Worcester Cathedral to give him a great deal of trouble by screeching out. There was a Mr Quarrell who used to make antics at the time of the Communion.

At a certain point in the service this man would bow down till he got his head on the pavement and his movements were so extraordinary that all they could do was to look at him and watch him. The authorities did not know what to do with him. They could not say, 'You shall not be a Communicant,' but they let him know directly that they thought his proceedings very ridiculous. 'Ah,' said Sir Gilbert, 'you don't know all the little games that go on in Cathedrals.'

Francis Kilvert 1840–79, *Diaries*

John Constable early 19th century

College butler who perished in the fire of 1828

By the beginning of the 19th century, the number of vicars choral had dropped to below 12, but the members continued their task of singing in cathedral services, of community living and of assisting in neighbouring parishes. The vicars were often in trouble with the dean and chapter, not least for infrequent attendance and for inappropriate behaviour. They were assisted in their duties by a group of servants who lived in the college. Among these were the college butlers, the most famous of whom was John Constable, in service during the 1820s. During this period there were several fires in the cloister, the most serious being on 26 July 1828 when 'a great portion of the building was materially injured and the buttery, cellar, larder, kitchen and servants' bedrooms totally consumed'. It appears that fire started in the buttery, and by half-past two in the morning:

> presented a terrific appearance; the offices in the south-east angle of the square and the roof of the centre part of the southern side, were enveloped in flames and burning furiously whilst the destructive element appeared spreading with fearful rapidity.

Many townsfolk helped the various fire engines and by 5 o'clock the fire had been brought under control. But John Constable died as a result of the injuries he received when he tried to rescue property from the building during the fire.

Constable's role was that of a servant, and in the discharge of his duties he met his death. Service is surely at the heart of the life of a cathedral, indeed of any Christian community and it is a salutary reminder to all clergy, be they bishop, dean or canon that they are always deacons – servants – of Jesus Christ. The bishop's words to those to be ordained deacon at an ordination deserve to be read and re-read by all:

Deacons are called to work with the bishop and the priest with whom they work as heralds of Christ's kingdom. They are to proclaim the gospel in word and deed, as agents of God's purposes of love. They are to serve the community in which they are set, bringing to the Church the needs and hopes of all the people. They are to work with their fellow members in searching out the poor and weak, the sick and lonely and those who are oppressed and powerless, reaching into the forgotten corners of the world, that the love of God may be made visible.

Deacons share in the pastoral ministry of the church and in leading God's people in worship. They preach the word and bring the needs of the world before the Church, in intercession. They accompany those searching for faith and bring them to baptism. They assist in administering the sacraments; they distribute communion and minister to the sick and housebound.

Deacons are to seek nourishment from the Scriptures; they are to study them with God's people, that the whole Church may be equipped to live out the gospel in the world. They are to be faithful in prayer, expectant and watchful for the signs of God's presence, as he reveals his kingdom among us.

Ordination of Deacons, *Common Worship* (2000)

Offa d.796

Wicked king of Mercia

King Offa is probably best known for his famous dyke, a military earthwork on a huge scale, stretching from the north coast of Wales to the mouth of the Wye. It was clearly intended to counter insurgent raids from the Welsh and to aid his own attacks on them. The gaining of lands through force formed an important part of Offa's rule. Becoming ruler of Mercia in 757, by the end of his reign he had become the dominant ruler in England and a force to be reckoned with on the European stage, treated as a near equal by Charlemagne. Indeed, while in some documents he is styled *rex anglorum*, 'king of the English', in others he is titled *rex totius Anglorum patriae*, 'king of the whole fatherland of the English'. During the 770s, Offa began a series of campaigns to remove local kings and absorb their territories into a Mercian empire. The South Saxons and the Hwicce were thus incorporated and the independent power of Kent greatly reduced. Offa's designs on the kingdom of East Anglia are much connected with the story of King Ethelbert (see 20 May) and his subsequent beheading at the hands of Offa, though later sources lay the blame on Offa's wife, Cynefritha.

Offa appears to have experienced great guilt as a result of Ethelbert's death and his later founding of the monastery at St Albans is sometimes seen as his reparation for the crime. Other opinions suggest that he founded and endowed St Albans after his miraculous discovery of the remains of the proto-martyr there. His enthusiasm for Christianity may be seen in his founding of many religious houses during his reign and his support for the creation of a second archbishopric in southern England, in addition to Canterbury, with the new archbishop's seat at Lichfield, in the heartland of Mercia. Offa died on this day in the year 796 and his son Ecgfrith succeeded him. His actual place of burial is unknown.

The story of the death of Ethelbert at the hands of King Offa and his queen has many resonances with the account in the gospels of the death of St John the Baptist:

King Herod heard of it; for Jesus's name had become known. Some said, 'John the baptizer has been raised from the dead; that is why these powers are at work in him.' But others said, 'It is Elijah.' And others said, 'It is a prophet, like one of the prophets of old.' But when Herod heard of it he said, 'John, whom I beheaded, has been raised.' For Herod had sent and seized John, and bound him in prison for the sake of Herodias, his brother Philip's wife; because he had married her. For John said to Herod, 'It is not lawful for you to have your brother's wife.' And Herodias had a grudge against him, and wanted to kill him. But she could not, for Herod feared him, knowing that he was a righteous and holy man, and kept him safe. When he heard him, he was much perplexed; and yet he heard him gladly. But an opportunity came when Herod on his birthday gave a banquet for his courtiers and officers and the leading men of Galilee. For when Herodias' daughter came in and danced, she pleased Herod and his guests; and the king said to the girl, 'Ask me for whatever you wish and I will grant it.' And he vowed to her, 'Whatever you ask me, I will give you, even half of my kingdom.' And she went out and said to her mother, 'What shall I ask?' And she said, 'The head of John the baptizer.' And she came in immediately with haste to the king, and asked, saying, 'I want you to give me at once the head of John the Baptist on a platter.' And the king was exceedingly sorry; but because of his oaths and his guests he did not want to break his word to her. And immediately the king sent a soldier of the guard and gave orders to bring his head. He went and beheaded him in the prison, and brought his head on a platter, and gave it to the girl; and the girl gave it to her mother. When his disciples heard of it, they came and took his body, and laid it in a tomb.

Mark 6:14–29

STANLEY GOWER bapt.1600? d.1660

Arch-puritan & parish priest

WE OFTEN hear of clergy ejected at the Commonwealth for their refusal to espouse the new Presbyterian religion insisted on by Cromwell and the Puritans. Stanley Gower was one of a generation who benefited from such ejections. Trained from an early age as a Puritan, he was eventually ordained and served as a chaplain to James Ussher, archbishop of Armagh. Moving to England in 1643, Gower became rector of Brampton Bryan, a parish in the gift of Sir Robert Harley. Here, Gower had a successful career, protected by Harley. He even named two of his children Robert and Brilliana, after his patron and his wife. Certainly, he was a preacher of renown – and endurance! It is said that on fast days he entered the pulpit at 8 or 9 o'clock in the morning to pray and preach extempore until 5 o'clock, 'if daylight continue so longe'. He insisted on Puritan practices, and was criticised by some for neglecting parts of the liturgy, for not wearing the surplice or for not using the sign of the cross at baptism. Gaining in reputation, he prepared a survey on the state of the ministry in Herefordshire. In this Gower blamed episcopal ministry for many abuses in the Church of his day, favouring the abolition of what he regarded as an anti-Christian institution. He also acted as a spy for the Puritan camp, forwarding to his patron notes of Royalist sermons preached in Hereford Cathedral and denouncing Royalist clergy as the 'devill's orators'. Moving from Herefordshire, he became preacher at the staunchly Presbyterian parish of St Martin, Ludgate Hill, in London and was invited to preach before Parliament on several occasions. His sermon to the Commons of 31 July 1644 was printed as *Things Now-a-Doing* (1644), in which he predicted that the year 1650 would see the downfall of the Church of Rome. By 1649, he had become rector of Holy Trinity, Dorchester in Dorset, described by some as 'the most Puritan place in England'. There he became what amounted to the great Puritan patriarch of England, not only writing in support of Puritanism but also authorising himself to ordain clergymen of his persuasion.

Preaching was at the very heart of Gower's work. Here, a later writer, Jonathan Swift, speaks of the importance of this ministry:

I take it for granted, that you intend to pursue the beaten Track, and are already desirous to be seen in a Pulpit; only I hope you will think it proper to pass your Quarantine among some of the desolate Churches five miles round this Town, where you may at least learn to Read and to Speak before you venture to expose your Parts in a city-Congregation; not that these are better judges, but because, if a Man must needs expose his Folly, it is more safe and discreet to do so, before few Witnesses, and in a scattered Neighbourhood. And you will do well, if you can prevail upon some intimate and judicious Friend to be your constant Hearer, and allow him with the utmost Freedom to give you notice of whatever he shall find amiss, either in your Voice or Gesture; for want of which early Warning, many Clergymen continue defective, and sometimes ridiculous, to the End of their Lives; neither is it rare to observe among excellent and learned divines, a certain ungracious Manner, or an unhappy Tone of Voice, which they never have been able to shake off.

I should likewise have been glad if you had applied yourself a little more to the study of the English Language, than I fear you have done; the neglect whereof is one of the most general Defects among the scholars of this Kingdom, who seem to have not the least conception of a Style, but run on in a flat kind of Phraseology, often mingled with barbarous Terms and Expressions and the frequent Use of obscure Terms.

Jonathan Swift 1667–1745, 'Letter to a young gentleman lately entered into Holy Orders', in *Satires and Personal Writings*

Didwg 5th century?

Celtic missionary

The little settlement of Dixton a mile north of Monmouth is named after a saint about whom very little is known. The old Celtic name of the site was Llandidwg, meaning the Llan, or enclosure of Didwg, probably a monk who evangelised this district in the 5th century. The Normans rededicated the church to St Peter in the 12th century, but retained the founder's name. Didwg was one of many Celtic holy men who set up places of worship near the river Wye or who focused their ministry on a holy well. Interestingly, Dixton has links not only with its founder, Didwg, but also with the better known St Oudoceus. In Celtic times Oudoceus founded an important monastery at Llandogo, further down the Wye. His cult seems to have spread over the whole neighbourhood, for a document of about 1190 mentions a *Fontem Sancti Eudaci* in the parish of Dixton. So, this little settlement on the Wye has links with three saints – two almost unknown Celtic holy men and Peter, the Prince of the Apostles (see 29 June). Dixton itself has a fascinating history. By 1100 Archenfield, including Dixton, had been seized from the Welsh church by the bishop of Hereford. The parish remained in the diocese of Hereford until 1844 when it was returned to Llandaff. In 1914 it was one of the border parishes which was allowed to vote whether it wished to stay in the Church of England or be part of the soon to be disestablished Church in Wales. By 209 votes to 29, it opted to be in the Church of England and joined 14 other Welsh parishes cared for by the diocese of Hereford.

As we remember that Dixton was re-dedicated to St Peter in the 12th century, 31 July would seem an appropriate date on which to remember the great saint, being the eve of his other feast day, St Peter-ad-Vincula, or St Peter in Chains, which is celebrated on 1 August. This feast speaks of Peter's release from the clutches of King Herod. Peter experienced release several times in his lifetime, not least when he received the release of forgiveness from Jesus after he had denied his Master. These words speak powerfully of that forgiveness:

If you think inwardly of the good things God has done for you and will do for you, and if you would love him entirely, then you will be stirred to love him more heartily. For when you were nothing, he made you out of nothing; when you were lost, he found you; when you were perished, he sought you; when you were sold to sin he bought you; and when you were lost eternally, he saved you. When you were born in sin, he baptised you, and often afterwards when you sinned he bore with you generously and waited your amendment, receiving you sweetly, and through his grace placing you in his sweet fellowship. Each day when you fall, he reproves you; and when you repent, he forgives you. When you err, he amends you; when you doubt, he teaches you; when you hunger, he feeds you; when you are cold, he warms you; when you are hot, he cools you; when you sleep, he saves you; and when you get up, he beholds you; and always when you are ill at ease, he comforts you.

These good things and many more has our Lord Jesus Christ done for you. Consider the sweetness of his heart, and evermore speak of it; and, if you know anything of love, thank him both day and night.

Edmund of Abingdon *c.*1175–1240, *The Mirror of St Edmund*

August

Richard Atkins 1559?–81

Protestant martyr

The story of Richard Atkins is a terrible tale of dark days of religious intolerance and cruelty. A native of Ross-on-Wye, Atkins was a Roman Catholic until the age of 19, but became a zealous Protestant – so much so that he travelled to Rome in 1581 to speak out against his former faith. Often considered to be mad because of his raving style of preaching, so convinced was he that he would suffer martyrdom that he wore a 'figurative' garment with gallows sewn in red cloth on front and back. In Rome, even though he publicly stated his intention 'to charge the Pope with his sinnes', he was cared for, as a madman, in the English College. Even this care was rewarded by a railing against the college students there, for their homage to 'that filthy Sacrament, which is nothing else but a foolish idol'. Contemporary writers also mention Atkins' unsuccessful attack on the host as it was carried in the street, for which he was excused as merely 'catching at the holinesse' coming from the Sacrament. When, later in 1581, he deliberately knocked the consecrated chalice from a priest's hand during mass, he was delivered to the Inquisition, refused to give up his heretical beliefs and was put in prison near the English College. On 2 August, stripped to the waist, Atkins was set on an ass and taken to be burned. At the place of execution, his right hand was cut off and his legs burned first to prolong the torture. Contemporary accounts differ in their view of Atkins' reaction to his death – a Catholic writer spoke of his 'impatience and pucillanimitie' under torture, while a Protestant account presents a serene Atkins who 'suffered all cheerfully', leaning into the torches and sometimes seizing them to burn himself.

I spent some time at the English College in Rome in 1981–2 and as one of two Anglican students among over 70 Roman Catholic seminarians, could not have met with greater kindness and generosity. In the college church are graphic paintings of the martyrdoms of the 16th century – rightly preserved as reminders of a darker history and as a warning that religious intolerance is something against which we must always guard. Atkins' death is not without similarities to that of the first Christian martyr, Stephen, here described by a 17th-century writer:

And as a little before his execution, he had the comfort of seeing heaven open before him, and Jesus standing at the right hand of his father; so he gave proof of being his disciple, in praying for those that stoned him; they had malice in their hearts, and he perfect charity in his; they threw stones and death at him, he sent up prayers to heav'n for them; he kneeled down and cried with a loud voice, Lord, lay not this sin to their charge, and so expir'd. All these: I say, look on as evil Christians, who live without charity, and are in evident danger of dying so. These have not learnt St Stephen's lesson, in receiving the stones thrown at them with his patience and charity, but still endeavour to throw them back again with the passion of that hand, with which they were cast at them; and truly, considering the great number of Christians that thus, in rendering evil for evil, are throwing stones at one another, 'tis to be fear'd, so many lose the patronage of Jesus, who thus unduly undertake to vindicate themselves.

John Goter 1650–1704, *Instructions of the Epistles and the Gospels of the Whole Year* (1696)

August 2

Hugh Broughton 1549–1612

Great Hebrew scholar

טברמון
טהרה
טוב

ONE OF THE greatest contributors to knowledge of the Hebrew language in his generation, Hugh Broughton was born at Oldbury, Bridgnorth in Shropshire, although he referred to himself as 'of Welsh descent'. A disagreement with John Whitgift, archbishop of Canterbury, over the interpretation of scripture persuaded Broughton to go to Germany, where he lived for most of his life. His first book, *A Concent of Scripture* (1588), insisted that all parts of the Bible were equally authoritative. As a Hebraist he was unsurpassed, not only able to read the Old Testament in the original, but conversant with post-biblical Jewish authors. He was also insistent that vowels were a part of the original text – a view in which he differed greatly from contemporary Catholic scholars. His great linguistic skills led him to translate the New Testament into Hebrew. For the last 20 years of his life, Broughton sought in vain to gain the support of the authorities for a new English translation of the Bible, to supersede versions then in vogue – the Bishops' Bible (1568) and the Geneva version (1560) – translations which Broughton regarded as highly suspect. All his attempts to gain support failed, and eventually, in 1604, James I entrusted the new translation to leading Puritans, among them Rainolds, an old adversary. Broughton was not included in the 54 scholars appointed as translators of what became known as the Authorised Version, and he spent years criticising the new work. 'Tell his Majesty', he wrote, 'that I had rather be rent in pieces with wild horses, than any such translation, by my consent, should be urged upon poor churches.' Much of Broughton's other work was critical in tone and content – he castigated the bishop of Winchester for his interpretation of the clause in the apostles' creed which refers to Jesus' descent into hell, while he made further enemies by roundly criticising Bancroft, archbishop of Canterbury as 'a deadly enemy to both testaments' and 'an assistant to the unbelieving Jews'. Despite his frequent outbursts, Broughton was a popular teacher, loved by his students. On his deathbed he lamented his bad humour and regretted that he was so easily provoked. He died in London on 4 August 1612 and was buried at St Antholin's church.

Words which speak of the wonder and complexity of language:

No civilisation but has its version of Babel, its mythology of the primal scattering of languages. There are two main conjectures, two great attempts at solving the riddle via metaphor. Some awful error was committed, an accidental release of linguistic chaos, in the mode of Pandora's box. Or, more commonly, man's language condition, the incommunicados that so absurdly divide him are a punishment. Why did certain languages effect a lasting grip on reality? Did Hebrew, Aramaic, Greek and Chinese (in a way that may also relate to the history of writing) have distinctive resonances? Or are we, in fact, asking about the history of particular civilisations, a history reflected and energized by language in ways so diverse and interdependent that we cannot give a credible answer? I suspect that the receptivity of a given language to metaphor is a crucial factor. That receptivity varies widely: ethno-linguists tell us, for example, that Tarascan, a Mexican tongue, is inhospitable to new metaphors, whereas Cuna, a Panamanian language, is avid for them. An Attic delight in words, in the play of rhetoric, was noticed and often mocked throughout the Mediterranean world ... By contrast other civilisations seem 'speechless', or at least, as may have been the case in ancient Egypt, not entirely cognizant of the creative and transformational powers of language. In numerous cultures blindness is a supreme infirmity and abdication from life: in Greek mythology the poet and seer are blind, so that they may, by the antennae of speech, see further.

George Steiner b.1929, *After Babel*

August

Weonard date unknown

Hermit & woodsman

Little is known of this saint who gives his name to the village and parish of St Weonards, south-west of Hereford. His name also appears as 'Gwainerth' (AD 450) and as 'Waynard' (1291). He may have been a Celtic monastic saint connected with Dubricius (see 14 November), while a local tradition associates him with being a hermit and woodcutter. Thomas Blount, the antiquarian, writes in 1675 of the church at St Weonards: 'I find in the North Window of the Chancel the Picture of an Ancient Man with a long Beard, holding a book in one hand and an axe in the other and under written in old characters – S.Wenardus Heremyta. I suppose he was a British Saint and that the church is dedicated to him.' The figure in the present window (1875) seems to derive from this description. The church at St Weonards is his only dedication in England, although Llanwenarth in Gwent may also preserve his name.

Taking up the theme of Weonard as a woodsman, we read in words by Thomas Hardy of the dark and complex life of the woodland – from within which, according to the author, comes the possibility of the human:

The casual glimpses which the ordinary population bestowed upon that wondrous world of sap and leaves called the Hintock Woods had been with these two, Giles and Marty, a clear gaze. They had been possessed of its finer mysteries as of commonplace knowledge; had been able to read its hieroglyphics as ordinary writing; to them the sights and sounds of night, winter, wind, storm, amid those dense boughs which had to Grace a touch of the uncanny and even of the supernatural, were simple occurrences whose origin, continuance and laws they foreknew. They had planted together, and together they had felled; together they had, with the run of the years, mentally collected those remoter signs and symbols which seen in few were of runic obscurity, but altogether made an alphabet.

'He ought to have married you, Marty, and nobody else in the world!' said Grace with conviction, after thinking in the above strain.

Marty shook her head. 'In all our outdoor days and our years together ma'am,' she replied, 'the one thing he never spoke of to me was love; nor I to him.'

'Yet you and he could speak in a tongue that nobody else knew – not even my father; though he came nearest knowing – the tongue of the trees and fruits and flowers themselves.'

'Now, my own, own love,' she whispered, 'you are mine and only mine; for she has forgot 'ee at last, although for her you died! But I – whenever I get up I'll think of 'ee, and whenever I lie down, I'll think of 'ee again. Whenever I plant the young larches I'll think that none can plant as you planted; and whenever I split a gad and whenever I turn the cider wring, I'll say none could do it like you. If ever I forget your name let me forget home and heaven! ... But no, no, no, my love, I can never forget 'ee; for you was a good man, and did good things.'

Thomas Hardy 1840–1928, from *The Woodlanders*

Laura Knight 1877–1970
Painter of the Nuremberg trials

One of the great artists of the 20th century spent much of her life in this area and was born on this day in 1877 in Derbyshire. She entered the Nottingham School of Art when she was 14 and there she met the prize student, Harold Knight, whom she eventually married. Like Harold, Laura was much influenced by the naturalistic methods taught at Nottingham as well as by their time in Amsterdam, studying the 17th-century masters. In 1906 they moved to Newlyn in Cornwall and there they joined a colony of artists led by Stanhope Forbes. This group rejected the idealized subjects of Victorian paintings, but instead insisted on 'the simple truth of nature' in art, with an emphasis on painting out of doors; certainly the marvellous quality of the Cornish light was a constant inspiration to them. Moving to London, Harold concentrated on portrait painting while Laura was attracted to drawing and painting scenes with much movement – performers for Bertram Mills circus, gypsies at Epsom and Ascot, ballet dancers and actors. By the late 1930s the Knights were living at Colwall and Laura became involved in work for the War Artists' Advisory Committee. Her most notable canvas was for the Ministry of Munitions, and depicted a woman munitions worker called Ruby Loftus screwing the breech ring in a Bofors gun, a delicate operation thought impossible for a woman to do. Laura's photographic eye for details and command of technique brought a great reality to the painting, one of the best she ever completed. After the war came a unique assignment – in 1946, at the age of 68, Laura went to Nuremberg to paint what was to become a pictorial record of the war criminals' trial. She regularly wrote to Harold, then living in the Park Hotel, Colwall, describing the scenes in court. She made many sketches and her final pictures of the prisoners in the dock were unusual for her, in that they were surrounded by vivid impressions of their crimes. Both Harold and Laura received many honours for their work – Laura became a Dame Commander of the British Empire and, in 1936, became the first woman elected as a full member of the Royal Academy.

The Nuremberg trials gripped the world for months after the Second World War. How could such terrible crimes be judged? What vocabulary did we have to articulate what had been done in the Holocaust? These words, from a prayer found in a Concentration Camp, approach the whole subject from a different angle:

Let there be an end to all vengeance,
to all demands for punishment and retribution.
Crimes have surpassed all measure,
they can no longer be grasped by human understanding.
There are too many martyrs.
Let all this, O Lord, be laid before thee
for the forgiveness of sins,
as a ransom for the triumph of righteousness;
let the good and not the evil be taken into account.
And may we remain in our enemies' memory
not as their victims, not as a nightmare, not as haunting spectres,
but as helpers in their striving
to destroy the fury of their criminal passions.
There is nothing more that we want of them.

William Pardoe 1631–92

'John Bunyan of the Marches'

Just as the great John Bunyan wrote his *Pilgrim's Progress* while in gaol, so this lesser known Baptist preacher was often persecuted and wrote his books in prison. William Pardoe was originally from Tenbury, Worcestershire and seems to have begun evangelizing in about 1660. His career as a 'General Baptist messenger' carried him extensively around Worcestershire and he travelled as far as Yorkshire on his preaching missions. Excommunicated from the Church of England in 1662, he suffered many years of imprisonment as a 'conscientious objector' – seven years in Worcester gaol, four years in Hereford and shorter spells in Lichfield and Leicester prisons. It was in Worcester gaol that Pardoe began writing *Antient Christianity revived: being a description of the doctrine, discipline and practice, of the little city Bethania* (1688). This work, eventually completed in Leicester prison, accounts for Pardoe's doctrinal positions as regards salvation and church discipline. Other writings include *The Mariner's Compass* (1675) and a series of letters, offering spiritual advice to converts.

Pardoe's views on Christian salvation were close to those of his more famous contemporary, John Bunyan. Here, Bunyan reflects on God's judgement when the soul stands before the judgement seat:

I was much about that time tempted to content myself, by receiving some false Opinion; as that there should be no such thing as a Day of Judgement, that we should not rise again, and that sin was no such grievous thing; the Tempter suggesting thus, *For if these things should indeed be true, yet to believe otherwise, would yield you ease for the present. If you must perish, never torment yourself so much before-hand, drive the thoughts of damning out of your mind, by possessing your mind with some such conclusions that* Atheists *and* Ranters *use to help themselves withal.*

But Oh! When such thoughts have passed through my heart, how, as it were within a step hath Death and Judgement been in my view! methought the Judge stood at the door; I was as if 'twas come already: so that such things could have no entertainment; but methinks I see by this that Satan will use any means to keep the Soul from Christ. He loveth not an awakened frame of spirit; security, blindness, darkness, and error, is the very kingdom and habitation of the Wicked one.

I found it a hard work now to pray to God, because despair was swallowing me up; I thought I was as with a Tempest driven away from God, for always when I cried to God for mercy, this would come in, *'Tis too late; I am lost, God hath let me fall, not to my correction, but condemnation: My sin is unpardonable, and I know, concerning* Esau, *how that, after he had sold his Birth-right, he would have received the Blessing, but was rejected.*

John Bunyan 1628–88, *Grace Abounding to the Chief of Sinners* (1666)

A prayer of John Bunyan

Fullness to such a burden is
That go on pilgrimage;
Here little, and hereafter bliss,
Is best from age to age.

August

Richard Conyngham Corfield 1882–1913

Peace maker in Somaliland

The little village of Cardington in the Shropshire hills has links with this man of peace and courage. Richard Corfield went out to Somaliland when he was only 23, and in 1912 was put in charge of the 150-man Somaliland camel corps, charged with maintaining peace among friendly tribes and avoiding hostile contact with the dervishes, led by the so-called Mad Mullah. In eight months, Corfield had established peace and order, and had encouraged the resumption of caravans and traders. However, in 1913 there was a major uprising by the dervishes, during which 36 British troops, including Corfield, were killed and 21 others sustained wounds. The setback, known as the 'Somaliland disaster', was a severe blow to British prestige and influence throughout the region. The Mad Mullah celebrated Corfield's death by writing a poem, gloating over his victory. A Corfield memorial fund was set up under the chairmanship of Lord Dundonald who, in December 1913, presented Corfield's mother with a bound album of letters received from all parts of the empire expressing admiration for Corfield's gallantry. He was certainly remembered as a headstrong officer, whose career was cut short by his recklessness, and yet he also had a reputation for treating Somalis fairly, a trait that was by no means common but which gained their loyalty and admiration.

A contemporary writer speaks of the importance of understanding the depth of our own anger before preaching the gospel of peace:

Anger, righteous and unrighteous, is a feature of human existence. In the past fifty years we have seen too much of destructive anger, too close to hand, both through personal experience of war and through the media. In consequence, many of us have become desensitised to what is going on in us and in all around us. It is not surprising that some of us, who do not recognise the extent of the problems arising out of human aggression, are tempted to avoid getting entangled in any action that might bring violence into our own lives. We may still be wanting to avoid looking at our own anger or its physical effects on us and other people. Those of us who are Christians, however, really have no option.

God has give us as Christians the ministry of reconciliation. He has 'entrusted to us the ministry of reconciliation', and he has called us to be 'ambassadors for Christ' (*cf.* 2 Corinthians 5:18–20). In order to fit ourselves for that work we need to face the size and extent of our own pugnacity before embarking on any attempt at peacemaking.

Una Kroll b.1929, *Vocation to Resistance* (1995)

A prayer for peace

Show us, good Lord,
the peace we should seek,
the peace we must give,
the peace we can keep,
the peace we can forgo,
and the peace you have given in Jesus our Lord.

From *Contemporary Prayer for Public Worship*, ed. Caryl Micklem

HUGH FOLIOT *c.*1150–1234

Founder of St Katherine's Hospital, Ledbury

THE PORTRAIT of Hugh Foliot in the chapel of St Katherine's in Ledbury reminds us of a visionary bishop with a great care for the poor and those in need. First recorded in the entourage of his kinsman, Bishop Robert Foliot of Hereford, Hugh was probably a canon of Hereford and later became archdeacon of Shropshire. Although commended by King John (see 11 June) as a candidate for the see of St Davids, he became instead bishop of Hereford in 1219, succeeding Hugh de Mapenore. In 1221 he made a pilgrimage abroad – some accounts suggest this was to Rome, others that his destination was Santiago de Compostela. Certainly, his experience as a pilgrim stayed with him, and was influential in his later charitable work. In his diocese, Hugh showed great interest in the foundation of St Ethelbert's Hospital at Hereford by Elias of Bristol, a canon of Hereford, at some point shortly before 1225. Elias placed his hospital under the charge of the dean and chapter. The foundation almost certainly encouraged Hugh to set up his own hospital, St Katherine's at Ledbury, in the late 1220s – in 1233 he likewise placed it under the control of the dean and chapter of Hereford. Ledbury was an important episcopal manor, and by the late 12th century had become a market town on the main road between Worcester and Hereford. Hugh declared that the hospital was intended to benefit pilgrims and the poor. He also assisted the Grandmontine order, helping to found Alberbury Priory in Shropshire in the early 1220s and confirming a grant to the order's other priory at Craswall. In 1228 he issued an indulgence on behalf of St Paul's Cathedral to encourage gifts for the priory fabric – similarly, he allowed Much Wenlock Priory to appropriate Clun parish church to its fabric fund. He was a great organizer and developed the prebendal endowments at Hereford Cathedral to increase their revenues, as well as endowing two chaplains at Hereford to serve in the episcopal chapel. He was the first bishop to appoint an episcopal official and seems to have issued an early set of diocesan statutes, known as *Constitutiones cuisdam episcopi* which date from the late 1220s. Hugh was taken ill in the spring of 1234, and was unable to attend the consecration of Edmund Rich as archbishop of Canterbury on 2 April. He died on this day in 1234 and was buried in Hereford Cathedral.

Although today hall and chapel at St Katherine's Hospital at Ledbury are divided, when Hugh Foliot planned the foundation, the beds of the sick would doubtless have been in the same room as the chapel and the sick would have been able to see the altar and hear prayers said and sung on their behalf. These words express beautifully the prayer of those in need and sickness:

In the hour of my distress,
When temptations me oppress,
And when I my sins confess,
Sweet Spirit comfort me!

When I lie within my bed,
Sick in heart and sick in head,
And with doubts discomforted,
Sweet Spirit comfort me!

When the house doth sigh and weep,
And the world is drowned in sleep,
Yet mine eyes the watch do keep,
Sweet Spirit comfort me!

Robert Herrick 1591–1674, 'Litany to the Holy Spirit'

Dominic 1170–1221

Founder of the Order of Preachers

The preaching cross in public gardens off Widemarsh Street in Hereford and the ruins of a cloister are all that remain of the house of the Friars Preachers, otherwise known as the Dominicans or Blackfriars. Their monastic settlement was founded in 1322 after endless quarrels with the cathedral chapter, who doubtless regarded the introduction of another religious house into the city as something of a threat. The order's founder, Dominic, died on 8 August 1221 at Bologna. He had been born in Castile and became an Augustinian friar, leading a disciplined life of prayer and penance. He became prior in 1201 but, three years later, while travelling through France, his settled life was placed in turmoil by his introduction to the Cathars or Albigenses. They claimed to be Christian, but held the unorthodox belief that flesh and material things were evil, that the spirit only was of God and that flesh and spirit were in permanent conflict. Dominic formed an Order of Preachers to combat such beliefs, although he would have nothing to do with the vengeful Crusade that began to be waged against the Cathars. His communities were to be places of sacred learning, with members devoted to study, teaching and preaching. He retained the divine office, but it was chanted more simply than in monasteries. Dominicans were to be more mobile, and were to have a special concern for the poor and needy. The Dominican Order spread to many countries in a short period of time and did much to maintain orthodoxy in later medieval Europe.

Dominic is often depicted in art by a lily or by a black and white dog, a pun (*Domini canis*) on the name of Dominic. Later artists depict him with a rosary, a devotion he was erroneously believed to have invented.

A late medieval source charts the history of the Order of Preachers and says this about its founder:

So noble in character, so ardently on fire with divine love was Dominic that there can be no doubt that he was a chosen vessel of grace. Except when he was moved to pity and compassion he always displayed great firmness of mind. A joyous heart is reflected in the countenance, and Dominic revealed his tranquillity of soul by the joyful kindliness of his look.

Everywhere, in word and in deed, he showed himself to be a herald of the gospel. By day no one was more affable, more friendly than he with his brethren and companions, no one more fervent than he in vigils and prayer at night. His conversation was always either with God or about God; rarely did he speak on other matters, and this practice he commended to his disciples.

Dominic's frequent and special prayer for himself was to beg from God true and efficacious charity for the salvation of men, for he was convinced that just as our Saviour, the Lord Jesus, gave himself totally for our salvation, only when he, Dominic, had devoted himself to the winning of souls would he truly be a member of Christ. When he had pondered the matter long and deeply he founded the Order of Friars Preachers for this very purpose.

He often exhorted the friars, both in his writing and by his words, to study constantly the sacred scriptures, in the old and new testaments. He always carried a copy of the gospel according to Saint Matthew and the epistles of Saint Paul; these he had studied to such an extent that he almost knew then off by heart.

Several times Dominic was chosen as bishop, but he always refused the office, preferring to live in poverty with his brethren, than to possess any bishopric. All his life long he preserved his purity intact. He longed ardently to be beaten, to be cut in little pieces, to die for his faith. Gregory IX declared: 'I knew him as a wholehearted follower of the apostolic way of life, and there is no doubt that he shares in heaven the glory of the apostles themselves.'

Mary Sumner 1828–1921

Founder of the Mothers' Union

The world-wide Mothers' Union, with a membership of millions, has connections with the diocese of Hereford through its founder. When aged just four, as the young Mary Elizabeth Heywood, she moved with her parents to Colwall. There, her mother, a woman of great devotion, began mothers' meetings and this may well have influenced Mary. No doubt the sudden death of her six-week old brother would have affected her greatly, too. Mary was educated at home, learned three languages and developed her musical talent. While travelling to Rome, she met George Sumner, a young curate and son of the bishop of Winchester, and the couple were married at St James Church, Colwall on 26 July 1848. When her husband moved to be vicar of Alresford, near Winchester, Mary, by then a mother of three children, called a meeting in 1876 at which the Mothers' Union was founded. This provided a forum in which to unite mothers of all classes with the aim of bringing up children in the Christian faith. At first a parochial organisation, it grew steadily into an international concern, encouraging the ideal of a Christian home. Mary's husband became suffragan bishop of Guildford in 1888 and Mary herself died on this day in 1921.

A reading from the Bible sums up much of Mary Sumner's aspirations for the place of family life in church and society:

A good wife who can find? She is far more precious than jewels. The heart of her husband trusts in her, and he will have no lack of gain. She does him good, and not harm, all the days of her life. She seeks wool and flax, and works with willing hands. She is like the ships of the merchant; she brings her food from afar. She rises while it is yet night and provides food for her household and portions for her maidens; she considers a field and buys it; with the fruit of her hands she plants a vineyard. She girds her loins with strength and makes her arms strong ... she opens her hands to the poor, and reaches out her hands to the needy. She is not afraid of snow for her household, for all her household are clothed in scarlet ... Strength and dignity are her clothing, and she laughs at the time to come. She opens her mouth with wisdom, and the teaching of kindness is on her tongue ... her children rise up and call her blessed; her husband also, and he praises her: 'Many women have done excellently, but you surpass them all.'

Proverbs 31

A prayer used by Mary Sumner

All this day, O Lord,
let me touch as many lives as possible for thee;
and every life I touch, do thou by thy spirit quicken,
whether through the word I speak,
the prayer I breathe, or the life I live.

Laurence d.258

Deacon & martyr

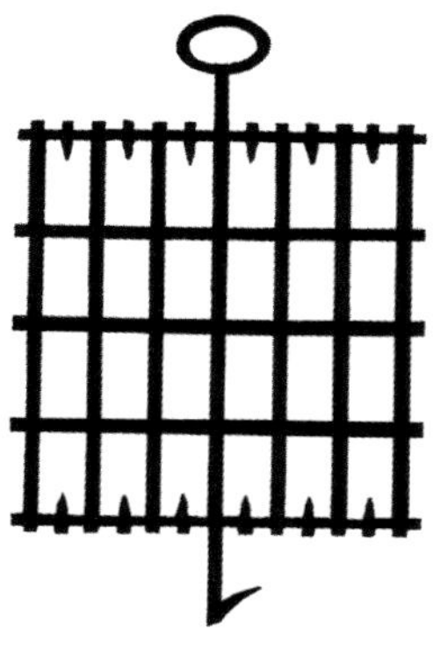

The great central tower of Ludlow parish church bears witness to this great saint – patron not only of Ludlow but also of four other churches in our part of Shropshire and of five in Herefordshire. The great east window of St Laurence's, Ludlow contains 27 scenes from his life and posthumous miracles, but most of these stories come from medieval legend and embellishment of the basic facts. Laurence was certainly one of the seven deacons of Rome and closely associated with Pope Sixtus II – indeed he was martyred just a few days before him. His examiners insisted that he produce the church's treasures, as booty. He promptly did so – assembling all the poor, he is reputed to have said, 'These are the treasures of the Church.' Other details are less reliable, including the famous roasting of Laurence on a gridiron, as the contemporary instrument of capital punishment was more likely to have been the sword. In Rome, five ancient basilicas are dedicated to him, while in England, there are 228 pre-Reformation dedications, including the famous Anglo-Saxon church at Bradford-on-Avon, Wiltshire. The most complete cycle of his life was painted by Fra Angelico for the chapel of Nicholas V in the Vatican and, in addition to Ludlow, there are notable stained-glass windows of his life in the cathedrals of Bourges and Poitiers. With St Stephen, he is patron saint of deacons, and his emblem is the gridiron and occasionally a purse, to recall his generous almsgiving.

St Augustine shows us a parallel between Laurence's administering of Christ's blood in the Sacrament and the shedding of his own blood in martyrdom:

On this day Blessed Laurence earned his triumph when he trod underfoot the noisy world and rejected its blandishments, thereby defeating the devil who sought his soul. Accordingly the Church of Rome commends this day to our observance. Laurence carried out the office of deacon in the Church, as you know. In that office he administered Christ's sacred blood to the faithful; and for Christ's sake he shed his own blood. The blessed apostle John clearly expounded the mystery of the Lord's Supper when he said: 'Just as Jesus laid down his life for us, so should we lay down our life for our brother.' Saint Laurence understood this and acted accordingly. His self-sacrifice was similar in kind to that which he received at the altar. He loved Christ in his life and imitated him in death.

Brethren, let us imitate Laurence if we truly love Christ. We cannot show a better proof of our love than by imitating him. 'Christ suffered for us, leaving us an example that we might follow in his footsteps.' It is clear from these words that the apostle Peter understood that, since Christ suffered on behalf of those who follow his footsteps, his passion is of no avail to those who do not imitate him. The holy martyrs imitated him even to the point of shedding their blood in emulation of his passion. But it was not only the martyrs who imitated him. When they passed into eternity, the bridge was not broken down, nor did the fountain dry up after they drank from it.

Indeed the garden of the Lord contains not only the roses of martyrdom but also the lilies of virginity, the ivy of marriage, and the violets of widowhood. So no one, my dear brethren, need despair of his vocation. Christ suffered for all. Truly it is written: 'He wills all men to be saved and to come to the knowledge of the truth.'

Augustine of Hippo 354–430, *Sermon 304*

Edward William Lane 1801–76

Orientalist

Hereford Cathedral School helped to provide the education of one the leading scholars of oriental languages. Born in Hereford, the son of a prebendary of the cathedral, Lane was expected to follow his father to Cambridge and to become a clergyman. Instead he became an engraver, and during the 1820s his imagination was captured by Egypt, then a subject of popular fascination. He decided to make the Egyptian people and their language his life's work. Arriving in Egypt in 1825, Lane lived in Muslim areas of Cairo, adopted local dress and soon spoke Arabic fluently, moving freely in Egyptian society and recording all his observations. His studies were eventually published in 1836 as *An Account of the Manners and Customs of the Modern Egyptians* and the two-volume work was a huge success. Other literary works included a translation of the Arabic classic *The Thousand and one Nights* (1839–41) and *Selections from the Koran* (1843). Perhaps Lane's greatest work began in 1841 when he accepted an offer from his friend Algernon Percy to support the compilation of a definitive Arabic-English lexicon. Assisted by his sister, Sophia Poole (see 11 January) and her two sons, Lane collected material for the lexicon – a daunting task, turning him into a near recluse, not leaving his house for months at a time. Returning to England in 1849, Lane completed work on the lexicon while living in Worthing, Sussex and the first volume appeared in 1863, followed by succeeding volumes at regular intervals. Lane was working on the sixth volume at the time of his death. His nephew, Stanley Lane-Poole completed the work, the eighth and final volume appearing in 1893. The *Arabic-English Lexicon*, a monumental work of 19th-century scholarship, remained an indispensable resource for scholars throughout the 20th century, and, as late as the year 2000, his work was still being hailed as ground-breaking. Not until that year was his *Description of Egypt*, an early collection of his Egyptian geographical and historical studies, published. Lane's eminence was recognised by his being honoured by many academic institutions, although he is said to have refused a knighthood. He died on 10 August 1876 and was buried in Norwood cemetery, London.

Edward William Lane, although a staunch Christian, came to realise the value of Islam, its teaching and writings. Indeed, many features are common to both religions. Here, two passages, both from the Qur'an, give us material which might be used by all people of integrity and spiritual openness:

In the Name of God, the merciful Lord of mercy.
Praise be to God, the Lord of all being,
the merciful Lord of mercy,
Master of the day of judgement.
You alone we serve: to You alone we come for aid.
Guide us in the straight path,
the path of those whom You have blessed,
not of those against whom there is displeasure,
nor of those who go astray.

O my Lord, make me minded to thankfulness for Your grace towards me and my parents, and to deeds of righteousness acceptable to You. Make me, in turn, blessed in my children. To You have I come in penitence. Here I am as one of the surrendered.

Brian Hatton 1887–1916

Hereford artist & soldier

Born on this day in 1887, Brian spent most of his childhood and early adult life with his family in Hereford, first at Whitecross and later at Broomy Hill. As a young child he made remarkable drawings which showed his natural artistic ability. In 1898, at the age of 11, he was awarded the 'Gold Star' of the Royal Drawing Society. Following this, the artist G F Watts took a keen interest in his artistic development and became his mentor. He travelled extensively at home and abroad, including an expedition to Egypt in 1908 – on these travels, and later, as a soldier, he recorded the people and places around him. Brian had a studio in London where he began his professional career as a portrait painter, but he continued to love his native Herefordshire where his work was inspired by local people and places. During his short life he created over 1,000 works, including oil paintings, watercolours and pastel and pencil drawings. His subjects included landscapes, horses and other animals, agricultural activities and country people, together with imaginative subjects inspired by literature. On the outbreak of the First World War, Brian served with the Worcester Yeomanry and was killed in action in Egypt in April 1916. He left a wife, Lydia May, and a baby daughter, Mary Amelia.

The 20th-century writer and historian Nikolaus Pevsner reflects on what makes a portrait 'English':

Thus the English portrait also keeps long silences, and when it speaks, speaks in a low voice, just as the Englishman does to this day, and as indeed, the muffled sound of the English language seems to demand. Or, to put it differently, the English portrait conceals more than it reveals, and what it reveals it reveals with studied understatement. These men and women illustrate what Jane Austen in *Emma* calls 'the true English style' by 'burying under a calmness that seems all but indifference, the real attachment'. 'Dr Livingstone, I presume?' is the *locus classicus* of this aspect of Englishness, and if that assertion is countered by a reminder of Shakespeare and the passions raging in his plays, one ... can equally refer to the words which he put into the mouth of Hamlet: 'In the very torrent, tempest, and, as I may say, whirlwind of passion, you must acquire and beget a temperance that may give it smoothness.' He also warns that what is 'overdone ... cannot but make the judicious grieve.'

There would be no better way of characterizing the portraits of Reynolds and Gainsborough: temperance, smoothness, judiciousness, moderation ...

A decent home, a temperate climate, and a moderate nation. It has its disadvantages in art. There is no Bach, no Beethoven, no Brahms. There is no Michelangelo, no Titian, no Rembrandt, no Dürer or Grünewald. There are no vast compositions in the churches, and only bad if vast compositions in the palaces, but there are exquisite watercolours and miniatures, things on a small scale, and there are in the Middle Ages exquisitely carved bosses and capitals rather than the superhuman *dramatis personae* of French church portals. England also produces a nice crop of amateur painters from maiden aunts to prime ministers, and what the amateur painter must be lacking in, in order to remain an amateur, is a violent compulsion towards a single-minded self-expression. The amateur is altogether characteristic of England, and not the specialist.

Nikolaus Pevsner 1902–83, *The Englishness of English Art*

William Penny Brookes 1809–95

Reviver of the Olympic Games

Although we remember this man for his great contribution to the modern celebration of the Olympic Games, he was a polymath, with a huge number of interests. Born in Much Wenlock on this day in 1809, he spent most of his life there. In the town, he was not only an eminent doctor and surgeon, but was also fluent in French, Greek and Latin and was a nationally respected botanist. Appointed a justice of the peace in 1841, he took an active role in civic life – he instigated the building of the Corn Exchange in Much Wenlock and was instrumental in bringing gas lighting and the railway to the town. He set up the Wenlock Agricultural Reading Society and from this emerged, in 1850, annual games, 'for literary and fine-art attainments, and for skill and strength in athletic exercise'. Initially, the sports were a mixture of athletic events and old country sports but they were certainly popular and, building on their success, Brookes founded the Shropshire Olympian Games (1861) and the National Olympian Society (1865). The latter sought to bring some organization to the many athletic associations springing up around the country and the first national games were held at the Crystal Palace in 1866, an event which attracted over 10,000 spectators. From 1859, Brookes petitioned the Greek government to re-establish Olympic-style games and while political unrest prevented this at the time, the cause was taken up by Baron Coubertin. The latter's Congress of the Sorbonne for the establishment of an Olympic revival duly acknowledged Brookes' influential role, but although the first modern Olympics were held in Athens in April 1896, Brookes did not live to see them. He died in December 1895 and was buried at Much Wenlock parish church.

The Olympic Games, whether in ancient Greece or in modern times, bind together competitors and spectators in an extraordinary way. A revealing story is told about the Olympic Games of 212 BC, when the champion boxer Clitomachus of Thebes was matched against Aristonicus, a protégé of King Ptolemy IV of Egypt. The large audience, according to the report of a contemporary historian:

... immediately cheered him on, because they were pleased that someone had the courage to stand up to Clitomachus. As the bout continued, Aristonicus showed himself equal to it. When he landed a well-placed punch, there was a burst of applause and shouts of 'Keep up your courage, Aristonicus.' Clitomachus then stepped back, caught his breath, turned to the audience and asked them why they were cheering Aristonicus and supporting him as hard as they could. 'Have I committed a foul or broken the rules? Do you not know that I am fighting for the glory of Greece, Aristonicus for that of King Ptolemy? Would you prefer an Egyptian to carry off the Olympic wreath by beating Greeks, or a Theban and a Boetian to be the world's boxing champion?' When the spectators heard these words of Clitomachus, it is reported, they suffered such a change of heart that Aristonicus was eventually beaten, more by the temper of the crowd than by Clitomachus.

St Paul uses the image of an athlete to represent the Christian life:

Do you not know that in a race all the runners compete, but only one receives the prize? So run that you may obtain it. Every athlete exercises self-control in all things. They do it to receive a perishable wreath, but we an imperishable. Well, I do not run aimlessly, I do not box as one beating the air; but I pommel my body and subdue it, lest after preaching to others I myself should be disqualified.

1 Corinthians 9:24–27

Samuel Sebastian Wesley 1810–76

Firebrand of a cathedral organist

One of Hereford Cathedral's most famous, perhaps infamous, organists was born on this day in 1810. Samuel Sebastian Wesley was the fourth child of the celebrated organist and composer Samuel Wesley and grandson of Charles Wesley the hymn writer. Despite his distinguished lineage, the circumstances of his birth and upbringing were anything but conventional, as he was born to his father's teenage housemaid and spent his childhood under the shadow of strong family disapproval. Samuel Sebastian's father succumbed to debt and depression and was committed to an asylum – circumstances which led to his son being sent to London as Child (chorister) of the Chapel Royal, St James's Palace. Later, as an adult in London, Wesley became involved in the capital's theatrical and operatic life as a pianist and conductor, being introduced to the music of composers like Weber, Spohr and Mendelssohn. Encouraged by the dean of Hereford, John Merewether (see 4 April) (who had previously been curate of Hampton Parish Church in Middlesex, where Wesley had been organist), the 22-year-old Wesley became cathedral organist at Hereford on a salary of £60 *per annum*.

Wesley found at Hereford a choir in dire need of care and attention, with its vicars choral frequently reprimanded for absence and poor standards of musicianship. Famously, a performance of his anthem *Blessed be the God and Father* one Easter Day had to be rendered with trebles and only one adult voice, that of the dean's butler! The Hereford musical scene did, however, give scope for his compositional skills – the fine verse anthem *The Wilderness* (called by contemporary critics 'a clever thing, but not Cathedral Music') was written for the opening of the rebuilt cathedral organ in 1833, and the Three Choirs Festival certainly gave scope for his wider orchestral and choral interests. However, Wesley was not happy with the dean and chapter, nor they with him, and he left Hereford in 1835 to become organist at Exeter Cathedral, accompanied by his new wife, sister to Dean Merewether (who apparently disapproved of the marriage). He went from one cathedral and great church to another (Leeds parish church, Winchester Cathedral, Gloucester Cathedral), never settling to the routine and necessary discipline of life in a provincial cathedral city. He died on 19 April 1876 and was buried in Exeter.

Wesley was not alone is his disagreements with successive deans and chapters. Clergy and musicians often have different priorities and fail to find common ground. In this passage, Dean Inge of St Paul's Cathedral expresses his distaste for church music – an attitude which is hardly likely to have endeared him to his musician colleagues:

My diary abounds with petulant and almost profane lunges against the dreary and interminable musical services which I had to attend. I can and do pray when I 'enter my chamber and shut the door'; but in the midst of howling and caterwauling I cannot. 'Melodies heard are sweet, but those unheard are sweeter. Quite right, John Keats; they are.' 'Music hath charms to soothe the savage breast. It has the opposite effect on me who am not a savage.' 'If I believed that I shall listen through all eternity to the seraphim blowing their loud uplifted trumpets, it would almost deter me from the practice of virtue.' 'They turned the Nicene Creed into an anthem; before the end I had ceased to believe anything.' 'Use not vain repetition. For ten minutes today the choir repeated the words "I wrestle and pray".' 'Are we quite sure that the Deity enjoys being serenaded?' Such were the groans of a much suffering unmusical man.

W R Inge 1860–1954, *Diary of a Dean* (1949)

Robert Crowley 1517/19–88

Archdeacon & prophet of sustainable agriculture

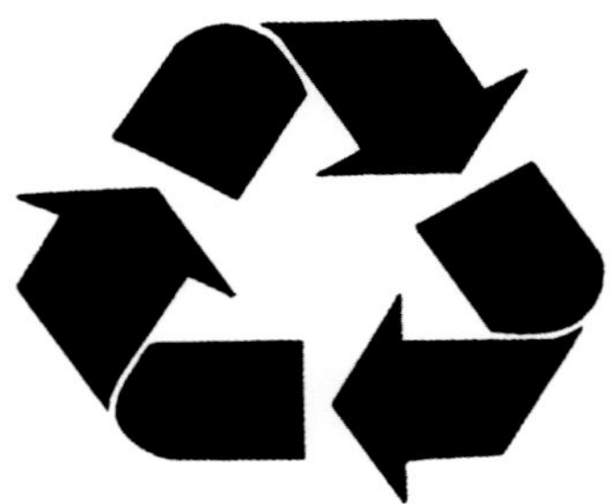

We think of exhortations to use the resources of the planet responsibly as something which began in the 20th century. Today we recall one whose much earlier visionary approach to land ownership and agriculture might be seen as highly prophetic. As a newly converted Protestant, Robert Crowley came into contact with other radicals at Oxford, and on moving to London printed important tracts criticising those who had benefited unfairly from the endowments of the former monasteries. He spoke out against 'engrossers of farms, rack-renters, enclosers, leasemongers, usurers and owners of tithes', who, in his opinion, failed to practice good stewardship in their ill treatment of the poor. Along with Hugh Latimer and Thomas Lever, Crowley expressed 'the social conscience of Edwardine England' and had the imagination to see the possibilities afforded by the press to mould popular opinion. The stewardship theory of property ownership was at the heart of his thinking and he felt that only a reorganized Church could bridle the greed and exploitation that was ravaging the land. In addition to editions of Wyclif and Tyndale, Crowley published in 1550 the first complete edition of Langland's *The Vision of Piers Plowman* (see 6 May) – a work which has enough anti-clericalism to have come to be regarded as a Protestant work, and may have been previously unprinted for that reason. With the accession of Mary Tudor, Crowley was exiled to the Continent but by 1559 he was back in England and was made archdeacon of Hereford in March of that year. He now practised an even more radical Protestantism, providing an important source for the martyrology of John Foxe, and contributing greatly to the later unfavourable image of Mary's reign. Fiercely opposing Archbishop Parker's regulations on clerical vestments, he led about a third of London's beneficed clergy to oppose the archbishop on this issue. His refusal to wear the surplice led to his being deprived of his preferments and placed in the custody of the bishop of Ely. He later returned to favour and became incumbent of several London churches, including St Lawrence Jewry and St Giles, Cripplegate, where he was buried after his death in 1588.

Crowley's words, written during the 1550s are strangely prophetic as the world today grapples with greed and exploitation:

... To a temper nurtured on such ideas, the new agrarian regime, with its sacrifice of the village – a fellowship of mutual aid, a partnership of service and protection, a 'little commonwealth' – to the pecuniary interests of a great proprietor, who made a desert where men worked and prayed, seemed a defiance, not only of men, but of God. It was the work of 'men that live as though there were no God at all, men that would have all in their own hands, men that would leave nothing for others, men that would be alone on the earth, men that be never satisfied'.

The Way to Wealth (1550)

A prayer of thanksgiving for Harvest

Almighty God, Lord of heaven and earth, in whom we live and move and have our being; who doest good unto all men, making thy sun to rise on the evil and the good, and sending rain on the just and on the unjust: favourably behold us thy servants, who call upon thy name, and send thy blessing from heaven, in giving us fruitful seasons, and satisfying us with food and gladness; that both our hearts and mouths shall be continually filled with thy praise, giving thanks to thee in thy holy church; through Jesus Christ our Lord.

John Cosin 1594–1672

John Allen 1789–1829

Tragic bookseller & antiquary

John Allen's name is associated with the history of his native county, Herefordshire, and with the systematic collecting of material relating to it. The son of a leading bookseller in Hereford, Allen was baptized at St Peter's church. He showed an early interest in antiquarianism and visited the famous Richard Gough in London. He hoped to write a history of the county; this never materialised but he did complete a bibliography of Herefordshire books, pamphlets and printed ephemera, entitled *Bibliotheca Herefordiensis,* published in 1821 – this is perhaps the earliest county bibliography published in England. He translated and printed in 1820 the royal charter granted to the city by William III, and later published a miscellany of local material entitled *Collectanea Herefordensia* (1825). During the 1820s he became involved in a libel suit which ruined him and forced him to leave Hereford for London. Here he spent time in Clerkenwell prison and in 1827 he was admitted to Bethlem Hospital, a lunatic asylum. On discharge he was admitted to Hereford Asylum, where he died on this day in 1829.

The harsh treatment afforded to John Allen and his lack of recognition in his time contrasts vividly with the praise heaped on another, earlier antiquary, Henry Spelman (c.1555–1641):

There's none I know hath written heretofore,
Who hath obliged this Church and Kingdome more.
Thou hast deriv'd, nay prov'd, our Church as high
As Rome can boast, and giv'n her pride the lie.
Thou hast the series of her story shown,
So hast o'er us her Hierarchy o'er thrown.
I read thy books, and I admire thy soule,
Thy daring soule that durst proud Rome controule:
Thou with their own Authorities, dost prove
That which they would, but never shall remove.
Thou prov'st to us the mighty power of Kings
In calling Councells even in spirituall things;
And temporall rights the Churches Pedigree,
Her frequent Councells even in Brittany;
As a choice piece of evidence a story
Which we may style great Brittaines chiefest glory,
The British Church, our Kings owe this to thee;
Shall we not reverence then thy memory?
Hadst thou been Romes, thy supererogation
Had raised a stock of merits for our Nation.
But thou art ours, I joy I live to know
I had a friend good men shall reverence so.

Francis Wortley 1591–1652, *Characters and Elegies* (1646)

John William Fletcher 1729–85

Shropshire follower of Wesley

John Fletcher was born in Switzerland and after education in Geneva, was set upon a career in the army. An accident prevented this, and instead he settled in England and became tutor to a Shropshire family. Here he came under the influence of Methodist preachers and in 1757 was ordained by the bishop of Bangor. Fletcher became a staunch ally of John Wesley, often preaching with him and for him. In 1760 he accepted the living of Madeley, in Shropshire, where for 25 years he lived and worked with great devotion. In theology, Fletcher upheld the Arminian position, adopted by Wesley himself, writing powerfully in support of Wesley and against the Calvinistic position of his opponents. He himself summarized this theological position, with its insistence on compromise:

> The error of rigid Calvinists centres in the denial of that evangelical liberty, whereby all men, under various dispensations of grace, may without necessity choose life ... and the error of rigid Arminians consists in not paying a cheerful homage to redeeming grace, for all the liberty and power which we have to choose life, and to work righteousness since the fall ... to avoid these two extremes, we need only to follow the Scripture-doctrine of free-will restored and assisted by free-grace.

Fletcher's insistence on courtesy and fairness was seen many times during his lifetime. A parting of the ways with the countess of Huntingdon over her training college at Trevecca in Breconshire left no antipathy and the poet Southey said of him that 'no age ever provided a man of more fervent piety or more perfect charity'. Even Voltaire, when challenged to produce a character as perfect as that of Christ, at once mentioned Fletcher of Madeley.

In 1781 Fletcher married Mary Bosanquet, who became the first woman authorized by John Wesley to preach. Their marriage was to be short-lived, for Fletcher died on 14 August 1785. Wesley preached at his funeral on the words 'Mark the perfect man' and characterized him as the holiest man he had ever met, or ever expected to meet 'this side of eternity'. Mary Fletcher continued her husband's work in the parish for 30 years until her own death in 1815.

Two prayers by John Wesley

Thou art never weary, O Lord, of doing us good. Let us never be weary of doing thee service. But, as thou hast pleasure in the prosperity of thy servants, so let us take pleasure in the service of our Lord, and abound in thy work, and in thy love and praise evermore. O fill up all that is wanting, reform whatever is amiss in us, perfect the thing that concerneth us. Let the witness of thy pardoning love ever abide in all our hearts.

Do all the good you can,
By all the means you can,
In all the ways you can,
In all the places you can,
As long as ever you can.

Roger William Bede Vaughan 1834–83

Leader of Australia's Roman Catholic community

THE STRUGGLES between the monastic and parochial approaches to Catholic life in 19th-century England were reflected in similar struggles in Australia, where disagreements between the original Irish settlers and Benedictines emigrating from England were to rage for years. At the heart of this controversy was Roger Vaughan, born in Ross-on-Wye, one of 14 children. His father belonged to one of the oldest recusant families in England and his brother became Cardinal Herbert Vaughan, archbishop of Westminster. After education at Downside, Roger Vaughan became a Benedictine and assumed the name Brother Bede. He was ordained priest in 1859, and after a further period at Downside was appointed professor of metaphysics and moral philosophy at Belmont Abbey, and, a year later, was elected prior of the diocesan chapter of Newport and Menevia and superior of Belmont. During his ten years at Belmont he contributed to leading reviews and published his most important literary work, his *Life of St Thomas Aquinas.* In 1866 he met Archbishop Polding of Sydney, then on a visit to England. The archbishop persuaded Vaughan to become his co-adjutor bishop in Sydney, a post which he eventually took up in 1873.

In Sydney, Vaughan devoted himself to two important movements, the provision of education for Catholic children and the completion of the building of St Mary's Cathedral. He became archbishop of Sydney on the death of Archbishop Polding in 1877 and worked tirelessly for the promotion of Catholic education, vigorously opposing the government in its plans to terminate aid to denominational schools. The resentment felt by Irish-educated clergy towards their new Benedictine archbishop continued throughout his episcopate and was not settled until his successor, Cardinal Moran, a great supporter of Vaughan's, was appointed.

Archbishop Vaughan died on this day in 1883. First buried in England, during the 1950s Vaughan's body was exhumed and is now buried in the crypt of St Mary's Cathedral in Sydney – the church he did so much to complete.

Vaughan's ministry was, in some ways, overshadowed by controversy occurring because of different understandings of church discipline. Sometimes in its history the Christian faith has been consumed by matters which, in the end, have proved inessential. Perhaps it is the native inhabitants of the great continents – such as the Australian aborigines, with their emphasis on the wonder of nature – who can, once again, teach us simplicity:

Each of the Ancients (now basking in the sunlight) put his left foot forward and called out a second name. He put his right foot forward and called out a third name. He named the waterhole, the reed-beds, the gum trees – calling to right and left, calling all things into being and weaving their names into verses.

The Ancients sang their way all over the world. They sang the rivers and ranges, salt-pans and sand dunes. They hunted, ate, made love, danced, killed: wherever their tracks led they left a trail of music.

They wrapped the whole world in a web of song; and at last, when the Earth was sung, they felt tired. Again in their limbs they felt the frozen immobility of Ages. Some sank into the ground where they stood. Some crawled into caves. Some crept away to their 'Eternal Homes', to the ancestral waterholes that bore them.

All of them went 'back in'.

Bruce Chatwin 1940–89, *The Songlines* (1987)

Sukey Harley 1780–1853

Zealous Shropshire evangelist

Born Susan Overton at Prolley Moor in the shadow of the Long Mynd, her father died when she was three. Hunger and ignorance made her 'a very wild, unruly child'. As soon as she was old enough, Sukey served in a farmhouse, where her willingness to work hard made her popular with her employers. She married, gave birth to a daughter and moved to Dorrington. In seeking to find meaning in her life, she tried the religion on offer in her local church, but was unconvinced. She then experienced a religious conversion, which she described in her own words: 'I had a desire to read; I longed to read the blessed Word for myself. I got my little wench to teach me the letters; she used to grow sleepy, so I would give her two suppers of a night to encourage her, all the while I was praying to my God to enable me to learn. She brought me as far as this – God is love, God is light. He can teach me himself. From that time I would take my book, and go down on my knees and look up to my Heavenly Father, and beg of Him to teach me ... and He did teach me.'

Sukey and her family moved to the outskirts of Pulverbatch, where her lively faith met with opposition and resentment: 'I used to attend the church. They used to pelt me with books from the gallery and the farming men used to throw their sticks from the gallery at me below, so I left the church.' Such behaviour was not the only problem for the Pulverbatch rector, the Reverend William Gilpin. Several members of his congregation, including his daughters Jane and Mercy, began meeting with Sukey and her family in a cottage or farmhouse on the Sabbath. 'My poor, pious children are all bigots,' the rector complained. Sukey, however, was always ready to fight for her religion, and during her lifetime her village witnessed many battles and disagreements over her approach to faith. She died on this day in 1853 and was buried in Pulverbatch churchyard, her grave becoming the focus of visits from those who admired her courage and persistence in the face of opposition from the established church.

Many have come to Christian faith through other channels than those provided by established denominations. In England, from the mid 1950s, many who may not have entered a church building nevertheless found conversion through the preaching of the American evangelist, Dr Billy Graham – his approach not very different from that of Sukey Harley, some 200 years earlier:

It is important that you make your decision and your commitment to Christ now. 'Now is the accepted time ... now is the day of salvation' (2 Corinthians 6:2). If you are willing to repent of your sins and to receive Jesus Christ as your Saviour, you can do it now. At this moment you can either bow your head or get on your knees and say this little prayer that I have used with thousands of persons on every continent:

'O God, I acknowledge that I have sinned against Thee. I am sorry for my sins. I am willing to turn from my sins. I openly receive and acknowledge Jesus Christ as my Saviour. I confess Him as Lord. From this moment on I want to live for Him and serve Him. In Jesus' name, Amen.'

If you are willing to make this decision, if you have to the best of your knowledge received Jesus Christ, God's Son, as your Saviour, then according to the preceding statements of Scripture, you have become a child of God in whom Jesus Christ dwells. Altogether too many people make the mistake of measuring the certainty of their salvation by their feelings. Don't make this serious mistake. Believe God. Take Him at His Word.

Billy Graham, b.1918, *World Aflame* (1965)

James Wathen 1751–1828

Artist & walker

The drawings of the ruins of the west end of Hereford Cathedral after the collapse of 1786 are perhaps the best known examples of James Wathen's skill as a draughtsman and artist. Known as 'Jemmy the Sketcher', he was born in the city of Hereford, apprenticed as a glover, but spent most of his life drawing and painting. As early as 1787 he contributed to the *Gentleman's Magazine* a 'View of Aconbury Chapel', and his sketches of the Wye helped to popularise its beauties in an age of increasing tourism. He was a fast worker, often completing 20 views in a day, on each noting the time of the sketch – sometimes as early as 5 o'clock in the morning! In 1811 an opportunity arose for Wathen to travel further afield and he accompanied a friend on a voyage to India and back. He published an account of the journey, including a visit on the return voyage to St Helena. Here, he made a number of sketches of views of the island. A few years later, when the island became famous as Napoleon's prison, the sketches became of even greater interest.

Back in England, many of Wathen's sketches were made on his walking tours in various parts of the country. He averaged some 30 miles each day and attributed his good health to his diet – he 'never ate meat, nor drank wine, beer or spirits – tea being his principal refreshment'. In 1821 he undertook a walking tour of the Lake District and, although 62 years old, out-walked all his companions. His walking also took him abroad – in 1816 he completed a tour of the Netherlands, Switzerland, Italy and France – as always, publishing an account of his walk together with many drawings and sketches.

The year 1827 saw an extraordinary excursion, with a fortnight's trip to Heligoland – a journey which he boasted cost him only 14 guineas – and on his return he wrote a description of this little-known island off the coast of Germany on which he found but 'two houses of any importance'. His passion for walking continued to the end of his life. In the spring of 1828, and in his 77th year, Wathen completed his 40th walk to London, but it was to be his last, and returning to Hereford, he died there on 20th August, 'deeply regretted by a most numerous acquaintance in all parts of the United Kingdom'.

The early 19th-century writer William Hazlitt speaks of the joys of walking:

Give me the clear blue sky over my head, and the green turf beneath my feet, a winding road before me, and a three hours' march to dinner – and then to thinking! It is hard if I cannot start some game on these lone heaths. I laugh, I run, I leap, I sing for joy. From the point of yonder rolling cloud I plunge into my past being, and revel there, as the sun-burnt Indian plunges headlong into the wave that wafts him to his native shore. Then long-forgotten things, like 'sunken wrack and sumless treasuries', burst upon my eager sight, and I begin to feel, think, and be myself again. Instead of an awkward silence broken by attempts at wit or dull commonplaces, mine is that undisturbed silence of the heart which alone is perfect eloquence. No one likes puns, alliterations, antitheses, argument, and analysis better than I do; but I sometimes had rather be without them. 'Leave, oh, leave me to my repose!' I have just now other business in hand, which would seem idle to you, but is with me 'very stuff of the conscience'. Is not this wild rose sweet without a comment? Does not this daisy leap to my heart set in its coat of emerald? Yet if I were to explain to you the circumstance that has so endeared it to me, you would only smile. Had I not better then keep it to myself, and let it serve me to brood over, from here to yonder craggy point, and from thence onwards to the far-distant horizon? I should be but bad company all that way, and therefore prefer being alone.

William Hazlitt 1778–1830, 'On Going a Journey', *Table Talk* (1822)

Thomas Cole 1628–97

Fiercely independent minister

Brampton Bryan in Herefordshire has often been a place where radical views in both religion and politics have been expressed. The siege in the Civil War and the courage of Brilliana Harley (see 29 October) are well attested. Less well-known are the quiet ministries of clergy who may have been persecuted elsewhere but who, in this small village, found acceptance and understanding. Thomas Cole was baptized at St Giles, Cripplegate in London and attended Westminster School. After a period of persecution in London he was ordained deacon and priest and became minister at Brampton Bryan. In November 1660 Thomas Harley wrote that he had preached there and 'the whole parish are well satisfied with him'. However, he refused the tests laid down by the Act of Uniformity of 1662 and resigned, although, returning the kindness shown by the Harleys, he deferred his resignation in order to allow his patron sufficient time to find a successor. He seems to have maintained a connection with his former benefice, for in April 1666 a member of the Harley family was 'at Aulam, where preaches one Mr Cole affectionately and to edification'. Cole opened a Dissenting academy at Nettlebed in Oxfordshire, but this was not a great success – Cole was criticised as 'too remiss in matters of morality and religion'. On the closure of the academy, he moved to London as an Independent minister – and was fiercely independent it seems, refusing to join the 'happy union' between Presbyterians and Congregationalists and being one of three London ministers who refused to advocate sacramental communion with the Church of England. He was, by all accounts, a strict and unbending Calvinist and in one of his last writings insisted, 'God hath made me a man of contention; but I would have all the world know, that the doctrine I have been preaching, I can comfortably die in.' He preached his last sermon on 22 August 1697 and died in September of that year.

The 17th-century divine Jeremy Taylor, who himself knew the pain of disunity in the Church in Ireland where he served, wrote these wise words, encouraging toleration in matters of faith:

It is a hard case that we should think of all Papists and Anabaptists and Sacramentaries to be fools and wicked persons. Certainly, among all these sects, there are very many wise men and good men as well as erring. And although some zealots are so hot and their eyes so inflamed with their ardours that they do not think their adversaries look like other men, yet certainly we find by the results of their discourses and the transactions of their affairs of civil society that they are men that speak and make syllogisms, and use reason, and read Scripture; and although they do no more understand all of it than we do, yet they endeavour to understand as much as concerns them, even all that they can, even all that concerns repentance from dead works and faith in our Lord Jesus Christ. And, therefore, methinks this also should be another consideration distinguishing the persons. For, if the persons be Christians in their lives and Christians in their profession, if they acknowledge the eternal Son of God for their Master and their Lord and live in all relations as becomes persons making such professions, why then should I hate such persons whom God loves, and who love God, who are partakers of Christ and Christ hath a title to them, who dwell in Christ, and Christ in them, because their understandings have not been brought up like mine, have not had the same masters, they have not met with the same books nor the same company, or have not the same interest, or are not so wise, or else are wiser; that is, for some reason or other, which I neither do understand nor ought to blame, have not the same opinions that I have and do not determine their school-questions to the sense of my sect and interest?

Jeremy Taylor 1613–67, *A discourse of the Liberty of Prophesying, in Works* (1648)

John Kemble 1599–1679

English Catholic martyr

John Kemble was born at Rhydicar Farm, St Weonards, in 1599, the son of John and Anne Kemble, prominent local recusant Catholics. There were four other priests in the family. John was ordained priest at Douai in 1625 and returned to England as a missionary in Monmouthshire and Herefordshire. Here, he cared faithfully and discreetly for his Catholic flock. The uneasy tolerance within which Kemble operated was shattered by the anti-Catholic hysteria which swept the country as a result of Titus Oates' plot in 1678. Oates concocted a plot suggesting that Charles II was to be assassinated and his Catholic brother (later James II) installed as king in his place. Kemble was arrested by Captain John Scudamore at Pembridge Castle and although 80 years old was taken to London to be interviewed about the plot. He was found to have no connection with it but was found guilty of treason as a Catholic priest, and was sentenced to be hanged, drawn and quartered.

Kemble was returned to Hereford for the sentence to be carried out – which happened on this day in 1679. Before he was led out to his execution, Kemble insisted in saying his prayers and finishing his drink, and the assembled party joined the elderly priest in a final smoke and a drink. To this day the sayings 'Kemble pipe' and 'Kemble cup', meaning a parting pipe or cup, are used in Herefordshire. Before his death on Widemarsh Common, Kemble addressed the crowd, insisting that no association with the 'plot' had been charged to him. He went on to say, 'The failure of the authorities in London to connect me to the plot makes it evident that I die only for professing the Catholic religion, which was the religion that first made this kingdom Christian.' After his execution, he was buried in the churchyard of St Mary's, Welsh Newton – a place now often visited in pilgrimage by local Catholics. One of Kemble's hands is preserved in the church of St Francis Xavier in Hereford. Miracles were soon attributed to the saintly priest. Scudamore's daughter was cured of throat cancer and his wife recovered her hearing whilst praying at Kemble's grave. John Kemble was beatified in 1929 by Pope Pius XI and canonised on 25 October 1970 as one of the Forty Martyrs of England and Wales by Pope Paul VI.

A Hymn in Honour of Saint John Kemble, Priest and Martyr

O trusty shepherd, John,
Whose maimed and lifeless hand
Draws blessing yet upon
Your loved and faithless land;
Through you we praise
The Lord for whom
You met your doom
In hate-marred days.

Within this western shire
Where England climbs to Wales,
You fed the faith's bright fire,
That, all untended, fails,
And, year by year,
Come storm or shine,
One friend divine
You held most dear.

Then, like the Lord you served,
Without the city gate
You suffered, undeserved,
A hard and cruel fate;
For us you plead,
Who chose to die
And not deny
Your boyhood creed.

Our years, without return
Retreating to the past,
That endless lodging earn
Which must be ours at last;
As best we can,
May we, like you,
In all we do
Love God and man.

Michael Oakley, *Verses & Versions* (1988)

RICHARD HAKLUYT *c.*1552–1616

Chronicler of the sea

THOMAS FULLER (see 31 August), the 17th-century historian, insists that Richard Hakluyt was born in Herefordshire, though other writers suggest London as his birthplace. Certainly, he was educated at Westminster School, where he became interested in geography and cosmology, studying descriptions of voyages and discoveries in many languages. He lectured on the subject, showing both the 'old imperfectly composed and the new lately reformed mappes, globes, spheres, and other instruments of this art'. On ordination he was selected to accompany Sir Edward Stafford, the English ambassador to Paris, as chaplain, in order that he might be able to report on the progress of French and other discoveries in the New World. The results of his researches were published in 1584. More important was his 1589 work, said by some to be the 'prose Epic of the modern English nation'. It is entitled: *The Principall Navigations, Voyages, Traffiques, and Discoveries of the English Nation, made by sea or over land, to the most remote and farthest quarters of the earth, at any time within the compasse of these 1500 years.* The book includes an account of great voyages by Raleigh, Davies, Drake and Greville, and extols the spirit of adventure in explorers, known and unknown, who 'setting forth from the banks of the Thames and the Avon, the Plym and the Dart, self-taught and self-directed ... went out across unknown seas, fighting, discovering, colonizing, and giving out channels, paving them at last with their bones, through which the commerce and enterprise of England has flowed out over the world'. In later life, Hakluyt was made a prebendary of Westminster and, on his death, in 1616, was buried in Westminster Abbey.

Richard Hakluyt writes about the courage of Elizabethan sailors:

To harp no longer upon this string and to speak a word of that just commendation which our nation do indeed deserve; it cannot be denied, but as in all former ages they have been men full of activity, stirrers abroad and searchers of the remote parts of the world, so in this most famous and peerless government of her Most Excellent Majesty, through the special assistance and blessing of God, in searching the most opposite corners and quarters of the world, and to speak plainly, in compassing the vast globe of the earth more than once, have excelled all the nations and people of the earth. For which of the kings of the land before her Majesty had their banners ever seen in the Caspian Sea? Which of them hath ever dealt with the Emperor of Persia, as her Majesty hath done, and obtained for her merchants large and loving privileges? Whoever saw, before this regiment, an English Ligier [Ambassador] in the stately porch of the grand Signor at Constantinople? Whoever found English consuls and agents at Tripolis in Syria, at Aleppo, at Babylon, at Balsara, and, which is more, whoever heard of Englishmen at Goa before now? What English ships did heretofore ever anchor in the mighty river of Plate? Pass and repass the unpassable (in former opinion) Straits of Magellan, range along the coast of Chile, Peru, and all the backside of Nova Hispania, further than any Christian ever passed, traverse the mighty breadth of the South Sea, land upon the Luzones in despite of the enemy, enter into alliance, amity, and traffic with the Princes of the Moluccaes and the Isle of Java, double the famous Cape of Bona Speranza, arrive at the Isle of Santa Helena, and, last of all, return most richly laden with the commodities of China, as the subjects of this now flourishing monarchy have done?

The Principall Navigations, Voyages, Traffiques, and Discoveries of the English Nation (1589)

Owen *c.*600–84

Patron of a Hereford church long demolished

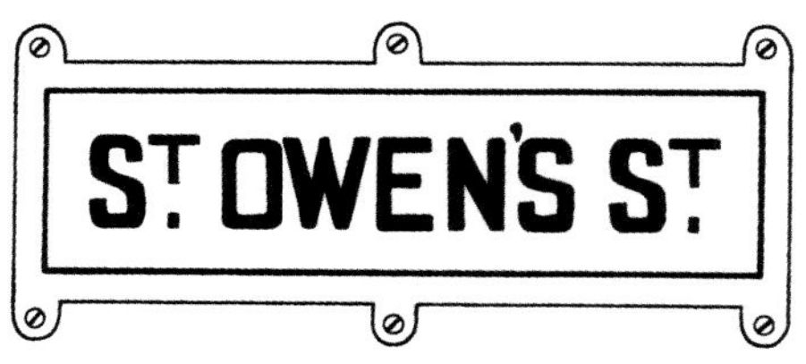

His name is variously given as Audoen or Ouen in France, and Owen or Ewen in England. He was brought up at the Frankish court and became chancellor to two kings. He later became a monk and was consecrated bishop of Rouen in 641, gaining a high reputation for sanctity during his long episcopate. Owen sent missionaries to many parts of his diocese and founded monasteries and places of learning. He died on 24 August 684, his relics being claimed both by Rouen and Canterbury. The latter claimed that during the reign of King Edgar, four clerics arrived at court bearing the bones of Owen. Edgar's suspicions were allayed by the miraculous cures performed, all approved by Oda, archbishop of Canterbury (940–60). The bones were placed in a reliquary with those of Saints Blaise and Wilfrid and a chapel in the south-east transept was dedicated in Owen's honour. A similar, and probably more reliable cult, was continued at Rouen.

There are only five dedications to this saint in England – three to Owen and two to Ewen. His church in Hereford was destroyed in the Civil War siege of 1645 and never rebuilt, although its name still survives in the title of the parish and in St Owen's Street.

To the church in Saxon and medieval times, the possession of relics meant power and riches and there were frequent raiding parties from one monastery to another to capture valuable relics. But such criminal behaviour at shrines was often detected, as this description suggests:

In our own lifetime a miracle very similar to this happened in Bury St Edmunds. A poor woman used to visit the Saint's shrine, ostensibly to pay her devotions. She came not to give, but to take away. It was her habit to steal gold and silver offered by others. The way she took it was extremely clever, for she would kiss it, suck it into her lips as she did so, and then carry it away hidden in her mouth. One day she was actually doing this, such being her custom, and her lips and tongue stuck fast to the altar. She was caught in the act by divine intervention, and she spat out the piece of silver which she had in her mouth. A great crowd of people came running to gape at this, some of them Jews and some of them Christians. There she remained, fixed and motionless, for the greater part of the day, so that the miracle was clear for all to see and there could be no doubt about it in anyone's mind.

Gerald of Wales *c.*1146–1220, *A Journey through Wales*

A 20th-century archbishop of York (and a descendant of James Garbett, see 11 October) speaks of the importance of integrity in our Christian lives:

The Church will not be able to meet the great claims of tomorrow unless in its own life there is holiness. It is the holiness of a Church which proves the authenticity of its claims to be the Catholic and Apostolic Church. There is a great need for the deepening of the spiritual life of both clergy and laity. Soundness of theology, efficiency in organisation, the external splendour of worship will count for little with the world if holiness is absent. But if shining through the life of our Church men see something of the holiness of God, shown in justice, self-sacrifice and love, they will be the more ready to acknowledge that the Church of England is indeed the true and authentic representative in this land of the Catholic Church of Jesus Christ.

Cyril Garbett 1875–1955, *The Claims of the Church of England* (1947)

Thomas Cantilupe *c.*1218–82

Hereford's medieval saint

Most saints have to be content with one feast day, several saints have two, but Hereford's own St Thomas has a grand total of three! Born into a noble family, Thomas Cantilupe was a bright child and studied at Oxford and Paris. Entering the world of politics he became Chancellor during the reign of Henry III and served in Edward I's Council, acting with others as regent during Edward's absence in 1279. In 1275, Cantilupe was consecrated bishop of Hereford. From all accounts he was a faithful and hard-working pastor in this diocese. But he was feisty (he is said to have had red hair!) and he fell into an argument with John Peckham, archbishop of Canterbury over jurisdiction and precedence in the diocese of Hereford. The dispute became so fierce that Peckham excommunicated Cantilupe – a terrible punishment, as it denied to the person so sentenced the benefits of Church and Sacrament, and worse still, denied any chance of bliss in the hereafter. Cantilupe, determined to clear his name, set off in March 1282 to plead his cause with Pope Martin IV. With his entourage, he travelled from Hereford, via Paris, Nimes and Genoa, arriving at the pope's court in Orvieto in June, and later moving with the court to nearby Montefiascone. Here he is said to have been well received by the pope and received absolution. But his health rapidly deteriorated – he contracted a fever and died on this day in 1282. His body was boiled, to remove the flesh from the bones, and the flesh was buried at the monastery of San Severo, outside Orvieto. Cantilupe's heart was brought back to England and placed in the care of a college of canons at Ashridge in Hertfordshire, while his bones were brought back to Hereford, for interment in his cathedral.

Cantilupe's death, far from his own native land would have been a great bereavement to his people in far-off Hereford. Here, in a 20th-century poem, the sadness, yet hope of death is recalled:

When I lie where shades of darkness
Shall no more assail mine eyes,
Nor the rain make lamentation
    When the wind sighs;
How will fare the world whose wonder
Was the very proof of me?
Memory fades, must the remembered
    Perishing be?

Look thy last on all things lovely,
Every hour. Let no night
Seal thy sense in deathly slumber
    Till to delight
Thou have paid thy utmost blessing;
Since that all things thou wouldst praise
Beauty took from those who loved them
    In other days.

Walter de la Mare 1873–1956, 'Fare Well' in *Collected Poems*

Horatio, Lord Nelson 1758–1805

Famous British admiral

Nelson's column in Trafalgar Square in London is perhaps the most famous memorial to this great seafarer, but there are others throughout the land – in Liverpool, Norwich, and on Salisbury Plain to name but three. Hereford has its own 'Nelson's Column' on Castle Green. Erected in 1809, four years after Nelson's death, a statue of the great man was planned for the summit of the column, but money ran out so there is merely an urn at the top. The enthusiasm for Nelson in Hereford reminds us that he was made a Freeman of the city in 1802, and in the same year visited Ross-on-Wye in the company of Emma, Lady Hamilton. Nelson was on a tour of the west country, *en route* to visiting Milford Haven in an attempt to promote its equality with the great naval dockyards of Chatham, Portsmouth and Plymouth. On 24 July, having spent the night in Gloucester, Nelson and his party visited the Forest of Dean, from where wood was often obtained as a source of timber for the Navy's ships. On arrival in Ross, the Nelson party breakfasted at the Swan Inn and, watched by a great crowd of Ross citizens, strolled beside the river Wye. They then embarked on a boat garlanded with laurels and drifted downstream, reaching Monmouth by the afternoon and taking in the picturesque scenery of the Wye Tour on the way. On the return journey from Milford, Nelson and his party again visited Monmouth and Ross, and, when staying at nearby Rudhall Manor, were regaled with a grand ball and a firework display – again, with hundreds of spectators in attendance. Not to be outdone, the mayor of Hereford arrived, inviting the party to visit his city – which, obligingly, they did, before travelling to Ludlow and Worcester.

The cult of celebrity, such as was courted by Nelson, is reflected in every generation, whether it be the Beatles during the 1960s or Big Brother *in the early years of the 21st century. The seriousness of these cults has often needed tempering with humour, and the libretti of W S Gilbert, tackling a number of issues, do this magnificently:*

When I was a lad I served a term
As office boy to an Attorney's firm.
I cleaned the windows and I swept the floor,
And I polished up the handle of the big front door.
I polished up the handle so carefullee
That now I am the Ruler of the Queen's Navee!
He polished up the handle so carefullee
That now he is the Ruler of the Queen's Navee!

Now, landsmen all, whoever you may be,
If you want to rise to the top of the tree,
If your soul isn't fettered to an office stool,
Be careful to be guided by this golden rule –
Stick close to your desks and never go to sea,
And you all may be Rulers of the Queen's Navee!
Stick close to your desks and never go to sea,
And you all may be Rulers of the Queen's Navee!

W S Gilbert 1836–1911, *HMS Pinafore*

DAVID LEWIS 1616–79

Jesuit martyr

FOR MORE THAN 30 years this Jesuit priest was known as the 'father of the poor'. He was principal of St Francis Xavier's College at the Cwm near Llanrothal, a Catholic farmhouse hideaway in the Monnow Valley which ministered to the English and Welsh borders and where men were trained as priests before being sent to the Continent. Although it was illegal for a Catholic priest to say mass, Father Lewis and his fellow priests worked quietly and discreetly, and often the authorities 'turned a blind eye'. However, in 1678 anti-Catholic hysteria swept the country as a result of the so-called 'Popish Plot' in which Titus Oates made claims of a Catholic plot to kill King Charles II. Many priests were hunted down. Fr Lewis fled the Cwm just before it was raided by government officials and went into hiding in Wales, but he was betrayed by the wife of a former servant and arrested by soldiers acting on the orders of local 'priest-hunter' John Arnold. The priest was charged with treason for practising the old religion, was tried and convicted in Monmouth and sentenced to be hanged, drawn and quartered. While awaiting execution, he was taken to London and interrogated by the Privy Council and was offered his life if he gave information and conformed to the Protestant faith. As the plot was an invention of Titus Oates, he had no information to give and refused to give up his religion.

Brought back to Usk, he was hanged on this day in the year 1679. People who gathered to watch the execution prevented the blacksmith executioner from drawing and quartering the priest and pulled on his body, to ensure a quicker death for a man they greatly admired, whatever their own religion. On the scaffold he said: 'My religion is Roman Catholic. If all the good things of the world were offered me to renounce it, all should not remove me one hair's breadth from my Roman Catholic faith. I was condemned for reading mass, hearing confessions and administering the sacraments, and therefore, dying for this, I die for religion.'

Both Catholics and Protestants were martyred for their faith – and often reasons for those martyrdoms on both sides were entwined with political argument. Whatever their backgrounds, martyrs like David Lewis often met their death with great courage. These words, by the Anglican martyr William Laud (see 10 January), remind us that denominational differences are of little or no account in the face of death – that all place themselves at God's mercy:

But I have done; I forgive all the world; all and every of those bitter enemies which have persecuted me. And I humbly desire to be forgiven – of God first, and then, of every man, whether I have offended him or not, if he do but conceive that I have. Lord, do Thou forgive me, and I do beg forgiveness of him. And so, I heartily bid you join in prayer with me. I am coming, O Lord, as quickly as I can. I know I must pass through death before I can come to see Thee. But it is only the mere shadow of death; a little darkness upon nature. Thou, by Thy merits, hast broken through the jaws of death. The Lord receive my soul, and have mercy upon me, and bless this kingdom with peace and plenty, and with brotherly love and charity, that there may not be this effusion of Christian blood among them: for Jesus Christ's sake, if it be Thy will.
Lord, receive my soul.

Archbishop William Laud, Tower Hill, 10 January 1645

Roger Cadwallader 1568–1610

Leominster's Catholic martyr

The execution of Roger Cadwallader on 27 August 1610 was a most shameful and cruel act of barbarism – a terrible reminder of what fanaticism and suspicion can achieve. Born in Stretton Sugwas, Cadwallader trained as a priest in Rheims in France, and later at the English College in Valladolid in Spain. As a recusant priest, he returned secretly to England and for 16 years celebrated mass in private houses in Herefordshire. Eventually he was imprisoned in the Forbury Prison at Leominster, tried and sentenced to death. His execution was to have taken place at Hereford, but was moved to Leominster as Hereford was then in the throes of a major epidemic. Even the professional executioner was unable to reach Leominster, so two masons were employed for the task. As a result, eye-witness accounts speak of Cadwallader's terrible and prolonged suffering. Today, this martyr is remembered at the Catholic church of St Ethelbert in Bargates, Leominster.

A similar sectarian murder in 17th-century France reminds us of the horror and pointlessness of religious strife:

If mere fanaticism had been their motive, the men who were most active in the massacre would not have spared so many lives. While Guise was galloping after Ferrières and Montgomery, who had taken horse betimes, and made for the coast, his house at Paris was crowded with families belonging to the proscribed faith, and strangers to him. A young girl who was amongst them has described his return, when he sent for the children, spoke to them kindly, and gave orders that they should be well treated as long as his roof sheltered them. Protestants even spoke of him as a humane and chivalrous enemy. Nevers was considered to have disgraced himself by the number of those whom he enabled to escape. The Nuncio was shocked at their ill-timed generosity. He reported to Rome that the only one who had acted in the spirit of a Christian, and had refrained from mercy, was the King; while the other princes, who pretended to be good Catholics, and to deserve the favour of the Pope, had striven, one and all, to save as many Huguenots as they could.

The worst criminals were not the men who did the deed. The crime of mobs and courtiers, infuriated by the lust of vengeance and of power, is not so strange a portent as the exultation of peaceful men, influenced by no present injury or momentary rage, but by the permanent and incurable perversion of moral sense wrought by a distorted piety.

Lord Acton 1834–1902, *History of Freedom and Other Essays*

Edward Littleton 1589–1645

Lawyer & 'friend' of Charles I

Sometimes ties of friendship can be at variance with loyalty to the state. Edward Littleton found this. Born at Munslow in Shropshire, he came of a family of judges and all his life was spent in the service of Parliament and the law. Member of Parliament at different times for Bishop's Castle and Leominster, he was active on many committees and in 1628 was instrumental in emphasising the rights of the individual of whatever station, when arrested. He proceeded to a career in law, becoming Solicitor-General in 1634 and, in 1640, Chief Justice of the Court of Common Pleas, in which post he enjoyed a close friendship with Charles I. However, when appointed as Lord Keeper of the Great Seal, he came into conflict with the king, refusing to put the great seal to the proclamation for the arrest of the five members in January 1642. His hopes that his actions would preserve peace were misplaced and he ended his career a broken and disappointed man. His last years, were, however, productive; he wrote a major treatise on law. Only parts of the manuscript survive but it was clearly intended to be a major encyclopaedia to cover international and ecclesiastical as well as private and constitutional law. On Littleton's death on 27 August 1645, he was buried in Christchurch Cathedral, Oxford.

Two themes emerge from Littleton's life – the importance of faithfulness in friendship and the loneliness which high office can entail:

So then to your question, how far a dear and perfect friendship is authorized by the principles of Christianity? The answer is ready and easy. It is warranted to extend to all mankind; and the more we love, the better we are and the greater our friendships are, and the nearer we are to God; let them be as dear and let them be as perfect, and let them be as many as you can; there is no danger in it; only where the restraint begins, there begins our imperfection; it is not ill that you entertain brave friendships and worthy societies; it were well if you could love and if you could benefit all mankind; for I conceive that is the sum of all friendships.

Jeremy Taylor 1613–67, *Friendship*

Unthinking heads, who have not learned to be alone, are in a prison to themselves, if they be not also with others; whereas on the contrary, they whose thoughts are in a fair, and hurry within, are sometimes fain to retire into company, to be out of the crowd of themselves. He who must needs have company, must needs have sometimes bad company. Be able to be alone. Lose not the advantage of solitude and the society of thine own self, nor be only content, but delight to be alone and single with omnipresency. He who is thus prepared, the day is not uneasy nor the night black unto him. Darkness may bound his eyes, not his imagination. In his bed he may lie, like Pompey and his sons, in all quarters of the earth, may speculate the universe and enjoy the whole world in the hermitage of himself. Thus the old ascetic Christians found a paradise in a desert, and with little converse on earth held a conversation in heaven; thus they astronomized in caves, and, though they beheld not the stars, had the glory of heaven before them.

Sir Thomas Browne 1605–82, *Christian Morals* (1716)

John Hoskins 1566–1638

Poet, judge, friend of Raleigh

Born near Llanwarne, it is said that the young Hoskins did not learn to read until he was ten, but then, 'at the year's end entered into his Greek grammar'. He was certainly highly intelligent and proceeded to Oxford, where he showed great aptitude for Latin verse – a skill he continued when entering the legal profession. In his early days he wrote his most substantial work *Directions for Speech and Stile, a treatise on rhetoric.* Through his connections with William Herbert, earl of Pembroke, he was appointed deputy steward or recorder of Hereford, where he purchased a substantial house and was returned to Parliament in 1604. However, his fiery temperament sometimes got the better of him and, after outbursts against royal policy, he was imprisoned in the Tower, displaced from his recordership, and stripped of other royal favours. During his imprisonment he became friendly with a fellow prisoner, Walter Raleigh, with whom he was allowed to discuss literary matters. On release, he became mayor of Hereford in 1616 and regained former royal favour, becoming a respected judge on the Carmarthen circuit and purchasing a substantial estate at Moorhampton in Herefordshire. In his retirement, he was able to pursue other interests, even composing an anthem for Hereford Cathedral – thereby offending, it is said, the puritanical Sir Robert Harley. Despite failing health, Hoskins continued to ride the circuits and travel to London, until at the Hereford assizes 'a massive country fellow trod on his tow', which caused gangrene. He died on 27 August 1638 at Moorhampton and was buried in nearby Dore Abbey.

Hoskins used his time in prison to continue his writing and to consult with others like Raleigh. Others, in the same way, have found ways of turning their captivity into a creative experience:

I now write to you from my confinement in Newgate, where I have been ever since Monday last, and where I enjoy myself with much more tranquillity than I have known for upwards of a twelve-month past; having a room entirely to myself, and pursuing the amusement of my poetical studies, uninterrupted, and agreeably to my mind. I thank the Almighty, I am now all collected in myself; and though my person is in confinement, my mind can expatiate on ample and useful subjects with all the freedom imaginable. I am now more conversant with the Nine [Muses] than ever; and if instead of a Newgate Bird, I may be allowed to be a Bird of the Muses, I assure you, Sir, I sing very freely in my cage; sometimes indeed in the plaintive notes of the nightingale; but at others in the cheerful strains of the lark.

Richard Savage, letter to a friend, 30 January 1743 in Samuel Johnson's *Life of Savage* (1744)

Stone walls do not a prison make,
  Nor iron bars a cage;
Minds innocent and quiet take
  That for an hermitage:
If I have freedom in my love,
  And in my soul am free,
Angels alone, that soar above,
  Enjoy such liberty.

Richard Lovelace 1618–57, 'To Althea, from Prison' (1649)

Thomas Fuller 1608–61

Man of tolerance & vision

THOMAS FULLER in his great work *History of the Worthies of England* (1662) wrote: '[Herefordshire] doth share as deep as any [county] in the alphabet of our English commodities, through exceeding in W for Wood, Wheat, Wood and Water. And seeing God hath blessed this county with so many Ws, we wish the inhabitants the continuance and increase of one more –Wisdom.' In the book he describes each county's distinctive features, including commodities and proverbial expressions, and he provided biographies of its noteworthy inhabitants. His description of Herefordshire is surely still relevant! Educated at Cambridge, Fuller was ordained and served first in the diocese of Salisbury. He soon showed himself as an able historian, writing the first modern history of the Crusades in English. On moving to London as minister at the Savoy Chapel, he was tireless in preaching for peace, encouraging King and Parliament to resolve their differences. The Civil War saw his appointment as chaplain to the Royalist Sir Ralph Hopton and later as chaplain to the infant Princess Henrietta, but his career was shattered by the defeat of the Royalist cause and the remainder of his life was spent in quiet ministry at Waltham Abbey and at Cranford, in Middlesex. Here he wrote *The Church History of Britain* (1655) and, on the Restoration of Charles II, sought to encourage an established church that included Episcopalians and Presbyterians, with toleration for other sects.

Some saw Fuller as one who was able to 'accommodate himself rather too easily to men of all parties', and who 'steered rather too skilful a course, perhaps, through revolutionary times'. On the contrary, his actions and writings show him to be one who took considerable risks to support the institutions he most cherished: a constitutional monarchy and a tolerant established church, under episcopal leadership. A contemporary, Sir Robert Shirley, showed similar courage in building the magnificent church at Staunton Harold in Leicestershire – one of the few to have been built during the Commonwealth. Indeed, we may hear echoes of Shirley in Fuller's own work Good Thoughts in Worse Times *(1647). Over the west door of Staunton Harold church is this inscription:*

In the yeare 1653
When all things sacred were throughout ye nation
Either demolisht or profaned
Sir Robert Shirley, Baronet,
Founded this church;
Whose singular praise it is,
to have done the best things in ye worst times,
and
hoped them in the most callamitous

Giles of Provence d.c.700

Healing hermit

In England, 162 ancient churches are dedicated to this saint, with ten such dedications in the diocese of Hereford. However, despite his huge popularity in the Middle Ages, we know little about Giles except that he was born in the early 7th century and founded a monastery at the place later called Saint-Gilles in Provence. His shrine became an important stopping place for pilgrims en route to Compostela or Jerusalem. Various legends later surround the scantily recorded details of his life. In one, the local king, while out hunting, aimed at a hind, but the arrow wounded and crippled Giles with whom the hind had taken refuge. According to another legend, Giles was given great powers of perception of the sins of others. From Provence his cult spread to other parts of Europe, partly due to the Crusades. His patronage of cripples, lepers and nursing mothers (based on the story of his giving shelter to the hind) gave him particular popularity with those seeking healing. Giles is patron of at least 24 ancient hospitals in England, including one in Hereford. His association with the healing of those suffering from leprosy led to his hospitals being placed at some distance from the centre of towns – from which lepers were excluded. His churches are also often found at road junctions (as at St Giles in Oxford), which travellers could visit while their horses were being shod in nearby smithies, of which Giles was also patron. He is often portrayed as an abbot with staff, or seen protecting the hind. Perhaps the most famous of his churches are in Edinburgh (St Giles Cathedral or High Kirk) and at Cripplegate in the City of London – another reminder of his association with the sick and injured.

Giles is associated with places of prayer and healing. Here, a major encourager of the healing ministry in the Church speaks of the vital part that prayer has to play in true and deep healing:

I have always maintained that one of the major contributions being made by the healing movement to the life of the churches is deep prayer. Prayer is placing one's whole self at the disposal of God the Father through Jesus Christ in the power of the Holy Spirit. Prayer is itself a gift from God who enables us to make this self-surrender. It is therefore also the response to the prevenient grace of God in which we seek to align our wills with the divine will, to attune our being to the music of heaven, so that we may resonate in harmony with the continual adoration of God offered by the saints and angels. Prayer is thus being caught up into *le milieu divin*; it is a space for adoration with the whole company of heaven and a time when we are enabled to bring our requests with confidence before the throne of grace (Hebrews 4:16). ... Without deep and persistent prayer we set limits to our effectiveness in our work for the Kingdom and to our usefulness in God's plan for his healed creation. Without prayer we only heal the hurt of God's people lightly (Jeremiah 6:14).

It is surely a fact that Jesus' unbroken communion with his heavenly Father was the secret of his whole ministry of preaching and healing – his example has been followed by all the saints and people of God down the ages. This was the testimony of Theophan the Recluse (815–94):

> Prayer is the test of everything;
> Prayer is also the source of everything;
> Prayer is the driving force of everything;
> Prayer is also the director of everything.
> If prayer is right, everything is right.
> For prayer will not allow anything to go wrong.

Morris Maddocks 1928–2008, *The Christian Healing Ministry* (1981)

Thomas Telford 1757–1834

'Colossus of roads'

When we look at the splendid late 18th-century church of St Mary Magdalene at Bridgnorth, we may find it difficult to associate this elegant building with a man whose skills in canal and road building led to his reputation as one of the greatest civil engineers of all time. Born in Scotland, Thomas Telford was apprenticed to a stonemason and later, on coming south to London enjoyed the patronage of Robert Adam and William Chambers, both then working on Somerset House. He became county surveyor of public works for Shropshire, living in and practising as an architect from Shrewsbury Castle. It was during the 1790s that he tried his hand at a number of church commissions – in addition to Bridgnorth, he was involved in restoration work at St Mary, Shrewsbury and the new church of St Michael at Madeley. Pevsner calls Bridgnorth 'a remarkable design, of great gravity inside and out, apparently done in full awareness of recent developments in France'. From 1793, Telford's career developed on his appointment as 'General agent, Surveyor, Engineer, Architect and Onlooker' to the 68-mile Ellesmere Canal. Although he was working at the end of the great period of canal building, Telford's skills were widely called upon – for the Caledonian Canal in Scotland, for canals in Sweden, as well as for the Welland Canal in Canada and the Panama Canal. His main achievements in road making were the London to Holyhead and Bangor to Chester roads. These long-distance arteries of the heyday of coaching declined in use from the 1840s as the railway network developed, but they were resurrected in the 20th century as Telford's vision of mechanical propulsion was fulfilled by the motor vehicle. In Scotland he provided over 1,200 miles of new or improved roads in the Highlands, with 1,100 bridges. These works opened up Scotland north and west of the Great Glen. Bridges, too, were a speciality – over the Severn at Gloucester and at Montford and, later, using cast-iron, at Buildwas. Perhaps his greatest achievement was the Menai suspension bridge, with its unprecedented span of nearly 580 feet, opened in 1826. He was no supporter of the railways, however, proposing instead steam carriage transport on the roads – an enthusiasm that never came to fruition. In addition to all his engineering prowess, Telford found time to indulge his interest as a poet, being a friend of the Reverend Archibald Alison (see 17 May). He was highly respected by all, becoming first President of the Institution of Civil Engineers. Southey wrote of him, 'there is so much intelligence in his countenance, so much frankness, kindness and hilarity about him flowing from the never-failing spring of a happy nature, that I was upon cordial terms with him in five minutes'. Telford died on this day in 1834 and was buried in Westminster Abbey. The new town of Telford was named after him.

Robert Adam dubbed Telford 'Colossus of Roads' and 'Pontifex Maximus'. But bridges have humbler functions, too – and speak of the importance of linking, whether it be between countries or peoples or between God and humankind. This human element comes over well in a song I remember from my youth:

When you're weary, feeling small
When tears are in your eyes, I'll dry them all.
I'm on your side, oh, when times get rough
And friends just can't be found,
Like a bridge over troubled water,
I will lay me down.
Like a bridge over troubled water,
I will lay me down.

Paul Simon and Art Garfunkel (1970)

Putta d.*c*.688

First bishop of Hereford

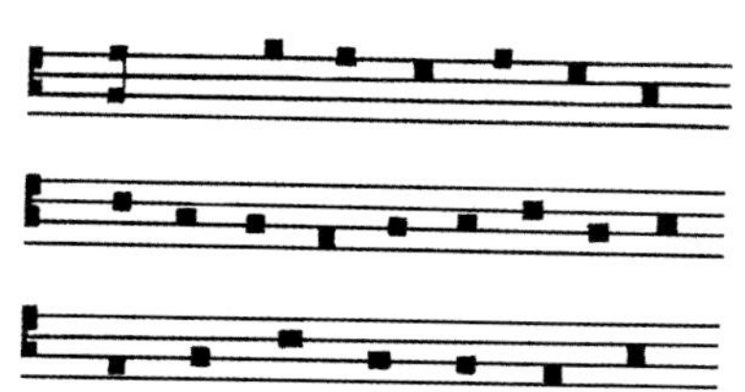

Hereford is 'neck and neck' with Canterbury when it comes to the number of bishops holding the office. Thus, in 2012 both Rowan Williams and Anthony Priddis are the 104th holders of their respective sees. But if Canterbury can trace its roots to Augustine, sent from Rome by Gregory, to whom does Hereford go back? The carved stone tablets in the retro-choir of Hereford Cathedral tell us that the first bishop was named Putta. Ethelred, king of Mercia set out on a plundering mission, got as far as Kent and attacked and burnt Rochester. Putta, then bishop of Rochester, was a peace-loving man with a fondness for Gregorian chant. He fled. But where could he go? Clearly, the one place Ethelred would not attack was Mercia, his own country. So Putta made his way to Mercia and made contact with Mercia's bishop, Saxulf of Lichfield. Saxulf gave Putta a church where he could minister, and a small piece of land. It is generally assumed that this was the site of the future Hereford Cathedral in a diocese carved out of Mercia, for the historian Florence of Worcester speaks of Putta as the first bishop of Hereford, recording his death in AD 688. The Anglo-Saxon Chronicle, however, states that Putta was still styled as bishop of Rochester at a synod in Hatfield in AD 680, so the date 676 as that of the foundation of the diocese may be more traditional than accurate! We celebrate Putta today as this is the feast of St Gregory the Great, the traditional 'inventor' of the chant to which he gives his name – a saint often pictured as having a dove cooing into his ear the divinely-inspired strains of the chant.

The timeless sounds of Gregorian chant were clearly the way to God for Putta as they have been for countless others since his time. Music can transport us to the courts of Heaven itself, as these words of a much later writer assure us:

When music sounds, gone is the earth I know,
And all her lovely things even lovelier grow;
Her flowers in vision flame, her forest trees
Lift burdened branches, stilled with ecstasies.

When music sounds, out of the water rise
Naiads whose beauty dims my waking eyes,
Rapt in strange dreams burns each enchanted face,
With solemn echoing stirs their dwelling-place.

When music sounds, all that I was I am
'Ere to this haunt of brooding dust I came;
And from Time's woods break into distant song
The swift-winged hours, as I hasten along.

Walter de la Mare 1873–1956, 'Music' in *Motley* (1918)

Thomas Eyton 1809–80

Shropshire's 'bird man' & Hereford's 'bull man'

Hereford's enduring symbol – the Hereford bull – owes much to this man, but it is for his great interest in the bird life of the world that he is chiefly remembered. Born at Eyton Hall, near Wellington in Shropshire, Thomas Eyton was educated at Cambridge, but while he left without a degree he nevertheless became an authority on ornithology and natural history, regularly in touch with some of the great naturalists of the time, including Charles Darwin and Alfred Russel Wallace (see 8 January). In 1836 Eyton published the first volume of his *History of the Rarer British Birds*. He built a spacious museum at Eyton Hall, in which he formed one of the finest collections of skins and skeletons of birds in Europe. Although the contents of the museum were sold after Eyton's death, many have survived in museums in England and in the United States. Eyton named several birds after himself, including the *Dendrocygna eytoni,* the plumed whistling duck from Australia, also called 'Eyton's tree duck'. Spending much of his life on the family estates in Shropshire, Eyton did much to improve the Hereford cattle breed and in 1842 instituted the *Herd Book of Hereford Cattle*, which was published until 1860. A friend of Darwin since undergraduate days, he helped Darwin prepare the descriptions of birds collected on the *Beagle* voyage. His interest in natural history was not confined to birds – at his own expense, he conducted an investigation for the government into the oyster fisheries of the British Isles. He was also a keen fisherman and wrote on methods of fishing.

A poet reminds us that birds can teach us much about the fleeting nature of life:

When a dream is born in you
    With a sudden clamorous pain,
When you know the dream is true
    And lovely, with no flow nor stain,
O then, be careful, or with sudden clutch
You'll hurt the delicate thing you prize so much.

Dreams are like a bird that mocks,
    Flirting the feathers of his tail.
When you seize at the salt-box
    Over the hedge you'll see him sail.
Old birds are neither caught with salt nor chaff:
They watch you from the apple bough and laugh.

Poet, never chase the dream.
    Laugh yourself, and turn away.
Mask your hunger, let it seem
    Small matter if he come or stay;
But when he nestles in your hand at last,
Close up your fingers tight and hold him fast.

Robert Graves 1895–1985, 'A Pinch of Salt' from *Fairies and Fusiliers* (1917)

Private Robert Jones 1857–98

Tragic holder of the Victoria Cross

A simple gravestone in the churchyard at Peterchurch bears witness to an age when however courageous someone was in war, they could not be forgiven the perceived sin of suicide. Born in Clytha, Monmouthshire, Private Robert Jones was serving with the Second Battalion of the 24th Regiment of Foot when he became one of 11 soldiers to win the Victoria Cross in the Battle of Rorke's Drift, Natal, on 22/23 January 1879. A force of around 100 British soldiers defended a small mission station from an attack of over 3,000 Zulus, before being relieved by a column commanded by Lord Chelmsford. Hundreds of Zulus surrounded the mission hospital where a handful of soldiers including Robert Jones and dozens of patients were barricaded. Jones used his bayonet to defend a doorway into a hospital ward until it was almost filled with dead and wounded Zulus. Despite suffering four assegai (spear) wounds and being struck by a bullet he helped evacuate six patients through holes in the walls during a desperate retreat through the blazing building. Robert Jones was the last to leave the building before it collapsed.

Following his distinguished army service, Robert Jones settled in Herefordshire and worked as a farm labourer. Throughout the summer of 1898 he was unwell and, on 6 September, then aged 41, he borrowed his employer's gun to go crow shooting. A shot was later heard and Jones was found dead with gunshot wounds. A verdict of 'suicide while temporarily insane' was recorded, after the coroner heard evidence that Jones suffered nightmares following his traumatic struggles at the South African mission station at Rorke's Drift. Although suicides were generally excluded from burial in consecrated ground, Private Jones' distinguished war record and his holding of the VC meant that his body was allowed to be interred in Peterchurch churchyard, but not before the coffin was forced to enter the churchyard over a wall, and his headstone to this day faces away from the direction in which all the other tombs are placed. In 1998 an article appeared in *The Sunday Telegraph* suggesting that it was time that Jones' headstone be reversed, even if this meant the overturning of the coroner's original verdict.

It may seem heartless and cruel to us that the trauma which may (or may not) have led to a suicide should be treated so unsympathetically. It is not only suicide to which such a terrible stigma was attached. Here, a dead child, born out of wedlock, is not allowed a full Christian burial, though the plight of Tess is understood by the parson. She is desperate to know whether the baby's fate will be 'just the same as if he had been baptized':

How the Vicar reconciled his answer with the strict notions he supposed himself to hold on these subjects it is beyond a layman's power to tell, though not to excuse. Somewhat moved, he said in this case also – 'It will be just the same.'

So the baby was carried in a small deal box, under an ancient woman's shawl, to the churchyard that night, and buried by lantern-light, at the cost of a shilling and a pint of beer to the sexton, in that shabby corner of God's allotment where He lets the nettles grow, and where all unbaptized infants, notorious drunkards, suicides, and others of the conjecturally damned are laid. In spite of the untoward surroundings, however, Tess bravely made a little cross of two laths and a piece of string, and having bound it with flowers, she stuck it up at the head of the grave one evening when she could enter the churchyard without being seen, putting at the foot also a bunch of the same flowers in a little jar of water to keep them alive. What matter was it that on the outside of the jar the eye of mere observation noted the words 'Keelwell's Marmalade'? The eye of maternal affection did not see them in its vision of higher things.

Thomas Hardy 1840–1928, *Tess of the D'Urbervilles* (1891)

Philip Bisse bapt.1666 d.1721

High Tory bishop of Hereford

The 18th century is sometimes, rather unfairly, characterised as one of indolent slumber for the Church of England, and a period when political connections counted if one wished to 'get on' in the Church. Certainly the contacts Philip Bisse established did him no harm – a cousin of Robert Harley, he married Bridget Osborne, daughter of the first duke of Leeds and widow of the earl of Plymouth, an illegitimate son of Charles II. Described by Harley as 'my urbane and socially-minded cousin, whose talents as a genial matchmaker for the aristocratic young were unsurpassed', Bisse became bishop of St Davids and later, in 1713, bishop of Hereford – no doubt proposed by Harley in return for political support. He was a favourite of Queen Anne and many saw him as a likely successor to the archbishop of York, John Sharp, on his death in 1714. For all his political angling, Bisse was an exemplary diocesan bishop. He undertook his episcopal duties efficiently and with great care. His visitation articles were very thorough and he was a great supporter of diocesan charities. In particular, he supported his brother, Thomas (see 22 April), in his aim to make the fledgling Three Choirs Festival into a significant means of support for poor clergy and their dependants. At a time when most bishops were enthroned using a proxy, Bisse attended in person and, also unusual for the time, conducted most of the ordinations in his own cathedral. He was a great supporter of Hereford Cathedral and made substantial alterations to the quire, providing panelling, galleries for his family and prebendaries and a huge reredos, with realistically painted curtains with tassels. The central tower was causing anxiety, and Bisse ordered two supports to be inserted, but these were worse than ineffectual and actually weakened the structure by lateral pressure. On arrival in the diocese, he had found the bishop's palace 'incommodious and unwholesome' and practically rebuilt it at a cost of about £3,000 of his own money. He divided the great hall into five compartments and re-faced the walls with stone from the ruinous chapter house. Philip Bisse died on this day in 1721.

Bisse was zealous in his diocesan visitations, using them to uncover slackness among clergy and diocesan officers. The following passage, from a recent book on 18th-century church life, reminds us that often bishops and archdeacons had an uphill struggle:

Other churchwardens were presented for not fulfilling their task of providing suitable furnishings to the church or vestments for the clergy. The wardens of Discoed in 1687 were ordered to provide a new surplice, the old one being 'not large enough'. Two years later, Richard Holder of Coddington was presented for providing a pint of communion wine on Good Friday 'which was neither pure nor was it fit for that purpose by reason it was mingled with perry or cider so that the communicants knew not what to make of it'. Again, in 1690 Edward Pritchard, churchwarden of Colwall, was accused of providing 'dead ill-tasted sherry wine altogether unfit for the sacrament'; he was admonished. Sometimes a presentment under this heading resulted from a feud between the incumbent and his wardens. On one occasion when Thomas Buckley, incumbent of Linton, was faced with a congregation of 20 Whitsun communicants, but without wine which the churchwarden had failed to provide, he was forced to use 'some metheglin I had by chance at home'.

William Marshall, *Church life in Hereford and Oxford, 1660–1760* (2009)

Frederick Edward Weatherly 1848–1929

'Roses of Picardy' came from his pen

One of my earliest childhood memories is of sitting round the piano in our family home – father playing the piano, mother singing. And one of the songs the family regularly sang was *The Holy City*, a sentimental religious text with its rousing chorus 'Jerusalem, Jerusalem, lift up your voice and sing'. Little did I know then of the hymn's Hereford connections! It was written by Frederick Weatherly – born in Somerset and educated at Hereford Cathedral School. He went on to study classics at Brasenose College, Oxford and on graduating in 1871 became a university 'coach'. He began to practise law in the late 1880s and was appointed king's counsel in 1925. Alongside his professional work, he was an author of more than 50 children's books and wrote a book of verse – *A Happy Pair*. But it is as a songwriter that he is best remembered. At school and university he had started writing poems – winning poetry prizes in the sixth form and reciting his own congratulatory ode on the installation of the marquis of Salisbury as chancellor of Oxford University. He wrote the haunting and poignant ballad *Danny Boy* in 1912, after his sister-in-law sent him, from America, the Irish tune *Londonderry Air*, and it became a favourite inclusion in many song books throughout the 20th century. He never forgot his school days – 'My love of music,' he wrote, 'found a genial soil at Hereford.'

Witnessing the horrors of the First World War, Weatherly wrote, in 1916, the ballad 'Roses of Picardy', which expresses so well the sense of longing and isolation experienced by many families during that conflict:

She is watching by the poplars
Colinette with the sea-blue eyes,
She is watching and longing and waiting
Where the long white roadway lies.
And a song stirs in the silence,
As the winds in the boughs above,
She listens and starts and trembles,
'Tis the first little song of love:

Roses are shining in Picardy,
in the hush of the silver dew,
Roses are flowr'ing in Picardy,
but there's never a rose like you!
And the roses will die with the summertime,
and our roads may be far apart,
But there's one rose that dies not in Picardy!
'Tis the rose that I keep in my heart!

Edward Cornwall late 16th century

Burford's giant

In the lovely church of St Mary in Burford, near Tenbury, is the most extraordinary monument. It is a painted triptych, 11ft high. Painted and signed by the Italian artist Melchior Salabuss and dated 1588, it has two panelled doors, painted outside with the 12 apostles and inside with coats-of-arms. The doors open to show life-size portraits of three of the Cornwall family – Richard and Jenet in long gowns and ruffs and their son Edmund resplendent in coloured armour, his plumed helmet at his feet. Edmund is said to have stood 7 feet 3 inches tall. Two doors at the foot of the triptych open to reveal Edmund lying full length, ghostly and shrouded, and an inscription tells not only of his great stature but also of his sweet nature, the great strength of his body, and his dainty touch upon the lute.

Although a giant – and one whose stature must have been extremely unusual in the 16th century – Edmund Cornwall also had a gentle side. Giants are often portrayed in fairy stories as cruel ogres (we all remember Jack and the Beanstalk*!) but they are not all so, and the lovely story* The Selfish Giant *ends movingly when the giant, who has denied his lovely garden to the children, sees Winter turned into Spring:*

Downstairs the Giant ran in great joy, and out into the garden he hastened across the grass, and came near to the child. And when he came quite close his face grew red with anger, and he said, 'Who hath dared wound thee?' for on the palms of the child's hands were the prints of two nails and the prints of two nails were on the little feet.

'Who hath dared to wound thee?' cried the Giant; 'tell me, that I may take my big sword and slay him.'

'Nay!' answered the child; 'but these are the wounds of Love.'

'Who art thou?' said the Giant, and a strange awe fell on him as he knelt before the little child.

And the child smiled on the Giant, and said to him, 'You let me play once in your garden, today you shall come with me to my garden, which is in Paradise.'

And when the children ran in that afternoon, they found the giant lying dead underneath the tree, all covered with white blossoms.

Oscar Wilde 1854–1900, *The Selfish Giant*

Some words from a psalm, which liken God to a giant:

In them hath he set a tabernacle for the sun: which cometh forth as a bridegroom out of his chamber, and rejoiceth as a giant to run his course.
It goeth forth from the uttermost part of the heaven, and runneth about unto the end of it again: and there is nothing hid from the heat thereof.

Psalm 19

I.D. A Native of Africa d.1809

A slave in Bishop's Castle?

In the churchyard at Bishop's Castle lies an unusual gravestone. The inscription reads:

Here lieth the Body of I.D.
a Native of Africa,
who died in ths [*sic*] town
Sept 9th 1801.
God hath made of one blood all
Nations of men. Acts 17:26

We have no certain information about the person commemorated by this headstone. Who was I.D.? The burial register records the interment of one John Davies on 12 September 1801, so it may well be that I.D. refers to him (I being the Latinized J). But who was he? Was he a slave who came to live in Bishop's Castle? Shropshire was not notable for its links with the West Indies and the slave trade, but it may be that I.D. came to the town or to one of the nearby country houses as a servant. The quality of the headstone, with its elegant inscription and decoration, suggests that the person commemorated held a certain status, whether a servant or not. The biblical quotation is one sometimes used by abolitionists and its levelling sentiments suggest that the person responsible for erecting the memorial was sympathetic to the movement. The positioning of the tomb is curious, it being turned away from the other graves in the area.

Shropshire had, in the person of Archdeacon Joseph Plymley (see 4 January), an ardent supporter of the anti-slave trade movement of the late 1700s. Is it fanciful to see his benign influence in the support of this African, who, through the efforts of local people of compassion, was given an honoured burial? We may recall the famous words of William Pitt as he brought to a climax his speech in favour of abolition:

We may live to behold the natives of Africa engaged in the calm occupations of industry, in the pursuits of a just and legitimate commerce. We may behold the beams of science and philosophy breaking in upon their land which, at some happy period in still later time, may blaze with full lustre; and joining their influence to that of pure religion, may illuminate and invigorate the most distant extremities of that immense continent. Then may we hope that even Africa, though last of all the quarters of the globe, shall enjoy at length, in the evening of her days, those blessings which have descended so plentifully on us in a much earlier period of the world.

Just as the first rays of sunlight shone through the windows above him, Pitt chose two lines from Virgil's Aeneid *to illustrate the coming of dawn to Africa:*

And when the rising sun has first breathed on us with his panting horses,
Over there the red evening star is lighting his late lamps.

A prayer for racial harmony

God, the Father of all, who in your great love made all the peoples of the world to be one family; help those of different races and religions to love, understand and accept one another – take away all hatred, jealousy and prejudice so that all may work together for the coming of your kingdom of righteousness and peace; through Jesus Christ our Lord.

Burnett Hillman Streeter 1874–1937

Biblical scholar & champion of Hereford's chained library

We associate the name of B H Streeter with his great work *The Chained Library* (1931), written when he was a canon of Hereford (1915–34). It is the more astonishing a work of scholarship when we recall that the world of medieval books and manuscripts was a world away from the subject which he originally studied. Streeter's academic career was brilliant and he became a highly respected New Testament scholar through his work on *The Synoptic Problem* (1911), giving weight to the case for the priority of St Mark's gospel and the existence of the source 'Q'. In particular he developed two hypotheses of great importance – he argued in favour of an early Caesarean text of the gospels and of an original source behind St Luke's gospel in its present form. The great value of his work lies in its first-hand character – whether he was dealing with chained libraries or with gospel manuscripts, he went direct to the sources and owed very little to the work of other scholars. As a priest, he had a great pastoral sense, always concerned to communicate the faith to others. He was often attacked as a modernist, especially after his contribution to *Foundations: a Statement of Christian Belief in Terms of Modern Thought* (1912). He was a regular speaker and a popular figure at Student Christian Movement conferences and made many journeys abroad, lecturing in China, Japan, India and the United States – always seeking new ways of communicating the age-old questions of life and religion. He had a great interest in other religions and his Bampton Lectures, *The Buddha and the Christ* (1932), paved the way for later studies in comparative religion. In his last years, he became Provost of Queen's College, Oxford and was hailed as a scholar with a world-wide reputation. In September 1937, he and his wife were staying in Switzerland, joining other members of the so-called Oxford Group founded by Dr Frank Buchman. It was while they were returning from this visit, on 10 September, that their aeroplane crashed into a mountain at Waldweide, Waldenburg, near Basel, in fog, and he and his wife were killed.

Books were at the heart of Streeter's life, whether they were chained in Hereford Cathedral Library or freely available to purchase or to be borrowed from public libraries. Books have provided the corporate sense of history in many communities and we are greatly impoverished without them:

It is not possible to have the true pictures or statues of Cyrus, Alexander, Caesar, no nor of the kings or great personages of much later years; for the originals cannot last, and the copies cannot but lose of the life and truth. But the images of men's wits and knowledges remain in books, exempted from the wrong of time and capable of perpetual regeneration. Neither are they fitly to be called images, because they generate still, and cast their seeds in the minds of others, provoking and causing infinite actions and opinions in succeeding ages: so that, if the invention of the ship was thought so noble, which carrieth riches and commodities from place to place, and consociateth the most remote regions in participation of their fruits, how much more are letters to be magnified, which, as ships, pass through the vast seas of time, and make ages so distant to participate of the wisdom, illuminations and inventions, the one of the other?

Francis Bacon 1561–1626, *The Advancement of Learning* (1605)

Words by B H Streeter himself on the conquest of pain and evil:

Pain, we have seen, even though wrongly borne at the time, may yet be transformed in retrospect, and defeat turned into victory in later days. If then, we believe that the growth of souls will continue after this life, we can see a way in which even that suffering, which, because it was not rightly borne, has been wholly unprofitable and demoralising in this life, may one day be changed in quality and made the condition of a richer, deeper, nobler life in the Beyond.

Deinst or Deiniol 6th century

Inspiration for Gladstone's great library

WHILE THERE are several church dedications to this saint in his native Wales, there is only one in England, at Llangarron, where tradition suggests that the saint himself founded a chapel. Reputedly a descendant of Coel Godebog, a Celtic chieftain of north Britain, Deiniol helped his father, Duawd, to found the monastery of Bangor Is-coed on the banks of the Dee in Flintshire, and another at Bangor Fawr, on the Menai Straits. The former became, according to Bede, the most famous monastery of British Christianity, numbering over 2,000 monks before it was routed at the battle of Chester by Aethelfrith, king of Northumbria in the early 7th century. Later, Deiniol was regarded as first bishop of Bangor, being consecrated by St Dubricius (see 14 November). He is said to have been present at the Synod of Llanddewi Brefi in Flintshire – the great meeting concerned to stem the spread of the heresy of Pelagianism – and to have spent some time in Ireland and Brittany. He died in about 584 and was buried on Bardsey Island, 'the island of saints'. His cult was widespread in North Wales, where there are churches and holy wells dedicated to him – there are also several in South Wales and one in Monmouthshire at Itton (formerly called Llandeiniol). W E Gladstone's famous library at Hawarden in Flintshire was eventually re-housed in a new building, named after the saint.

Whether or not Gladstone himself was familiar with Deiniol's life and piety, certainly prayer was at the heart of both men's discipline and spirituality. In this passage, we learn a little of Gladstone's own routine in this:

On 26 December 1888, when the Gladstones were staying for two months with the George Rendels at their villa in Naples, Gladstone argued after dinner that occasional drunkenness, when it was solely due to 'social feeling and temptation', deserved to be treated with indulgence. Later that evening, Gladstone sat alone, reading a theological book in German by Dollinger, in a small study which had been fitted up for him by his host. Stuart Rendel, watching his brother's guest through a chink in the door, could see the book firmly held up in the candlelight. Unwilling to go to bed before the guest, Rendel was making up his mind to disturb Gladstone, when he suddenly noticed the great arch of Gladstone's head so situated that it was obvious that he had dropped on to his knees, and was deep in prayer, bending low over the seat of the arm-chair in which he had been reading. Ten minutes passed, while Rendel waited, and then the light suddenly disappeared. Gladstone has slipped out by another door, 'shunning, I suppose,' Rendel noted, 'any break in his thoughts and acts by his usual bidding of me goodnight.'

Philip Magnus 1906–88, *Gladstone* (1954)

A prayer by Gladstone

Go forth with us, O Lord, from this Thy holy house; cast about us a fence which the evil one cannot pass, and clothe us in the armour which his darts cannot pierce. Send down upon us Thy love and light and calm, wherein, as in a cloud, we may continually dwell and worship Thee for evermore: through Jesus Christ our Lord.

Peter Mark Roget 1779–1869

Medical man with a love of words

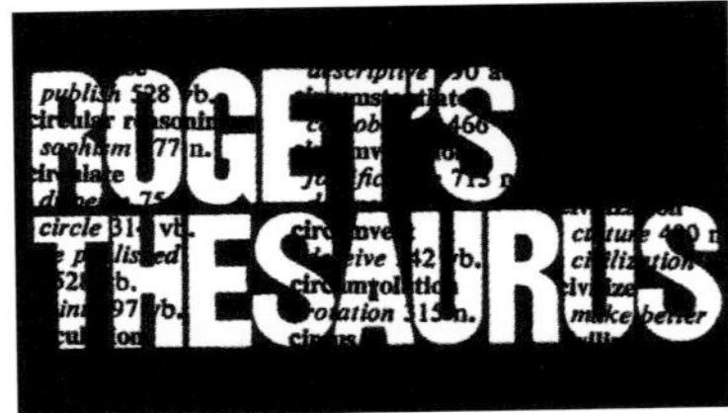

Roget's *Thesaurus* was first published in 1852 and since then it has never been out of print. After several revised editions, and now also being produced in electronic form, it is still an indispensable tool for serious cross-word solvers and compilers, writers, poets and journalists. Its original compiler, Peter Mark Roget was a local, inasmuch as he made an annual visit to West Malvern, and died there on this day in 1869; there is a memorial to him in the churchyard looking out over Herefordshire. A fascination with words was only one area in which Roget excelled. By training a medic, he lectured and practised in Manchester and London, specializing in anatomy. He co-operated with Jeremy Bentham in a scheme to reduce diseases in the capital through a proper sewage scheme, and later became physician to the Spanish embassy. But he had many other interests. Always fascinated by mechanics, in 1814 he invented a logarithmic slide rule. This and other inventions led to his becoming a Fellow of the Royal Society in 1815, and later its secretary, a post he held for 21 years. In his later years Roget attempted to construct a calculating machine, but perhaps more influential for the future was his work with kaleidoscopes and other forms of optical illusion. First adapted to creating amusing toys for children and adults, his work in this area led to the first motion pictures, and the centenary of Roget's discovery in 1825 was celebrated by the motion picture industry. Roget took an active part in the establishment of the University of London in 1837 and was a prolific writer, contributing to the *Encyclopaedia Britannica*. He even constructed and solved countless chess problems, publishing these in the *Illustrated London News*. But it is for his *Thesaurus* that he will always be remembered – a work that would make him a household name a century and a half later. He had an idea for a 'treasury of words' early in his career – a compendium of English words and phrases, classified and arranged so as to facilitate the expression of ideas and assist in literary composition. He worked on it full-time between 1849 and 1852 and completed it aged 73.

Words influence us for good or ill:

Words are deeds. The words we hear
May revolutionize or rear
A mighty state. The words we read
May be a spiritual deed
Excelling any fleshly one,
As much as the celestial sun
Transcends a bonfire, made to throw
A light upon some raree-show.
A simple proverb tagged with rhyme
May colour half the course of time;
The pregnant saying of a sage
May influence every coming age;
A song in its effects may be
More glorious than Thermopylae,
And many a lay that schoolboys scan
A nobler feat than Inkerman.

William Charles Wentworth 1790–1872, 'Words'

Sir John Hoskins 1634–1705

Lawyer & natural philosopher

Born in Herefordshire, John Hoskins was eldest son of Sir Benet Hoskins, first baronet of Harewood and Moorhampton Park. As MP for Hereford (1685–7), he became an eminent lawyer, serving at the Middle Temple. It was not his skill in politics or the law, however, but his interest in natural philosophy that distinguished Hoskins among his contemporaries. From an early age he showed an interest in the new experimental philosophy and became one of the original Fellows of the Royal Society when it was incorporated in 1663, becoming, in 1682, president in succession to Sir Christopher Wren. Outside the Royal Society, Hoskins was a noted conversationalist and a favourite dinner companion. He frequently dined with the likes of Robert Hooke and John Aubrey and it was noted that 'these often go to supper together', and the conversation was 'intirely upon experimentall philosofye, astronomy, etc.' In his description, the contemporary writer Granger reports of Hoskins that 'there was nothing at all promising in his appearance: he was hard-favoured, affected plainness in his garb, walked the street with a cudgel in his hand, and an old hat over his eyes. He was often observed to be in a reverie: but when his spirits were elevated over a bottle, he was remarkable for his presence of mind, and quickness of apprehension, and became an agreeable and instructive companion.' Hoskins died on 12 September 1705.

Seeing God in the world around us and using nature as raw material for our meditation upon life – these were at the heart of some of the philosophical arguments proposed by Hoskins. Writing a generation earlier, another writer and poet had similar thoughts:

Now for my life, it is a miracle of thirty years, which to relate were not a history, but a piece of poetry, and would sound to common ears like a fable; for the world, I count it not an Inn, but an Hospital; and a place not to live in, but to die in. The world that I regard is my self; it is the microcosm of mine own frame that I cast mine eye on: for the other, I use it but like my globe, and turn it round sometimes for my recreation. Men that look upon my outside, perusing only my condition and fortunes, do err in my Altitude, for I am above Atlas his shoulders. The earth is a point, not only in respect of the Heavens above us, but of that Heavenly and Celestial part within us: that mass of flesh that circumscribes me, limits not my mind; that surface that tells the Heavens it hath an end, cannot persuade me I have any; I take my circle to be above three hundred and sixty; though the number of the arc do measure my body, it comprehendeth not my mind; whilst I study to find how I am a Microcosm, or little world, I find myself something more than the great. There is surely a piece of Divinity in us; something that was before the elements, and owes no homage unto the Sun. Nature tells me I am the Image of God, as well as Scripture: he that understands not thus much hath not his introduction or first lesson, and is yet to begin the Alphabet of man. I am the happiest man alive: I have that in me that can convert poverty into riches, adversity into prosperity: I am more invulnerable than Achilles; Fortune hath not one place to hit me. In brief, I am content, and what should Providence add more? Surely this is what we call Happiness, and this do I enjoy: with this I am happy in a dream, and as content to enjoy a happiness in a fancy as others in a more apparent truth and reality.

Sir Thomas Browne 1605–82, *Religio Medici* (1642)

Frank Weston 1871–1924

Historic link with Tanzania

For many years, the life of Hereford diocese has been enriched through links with the church in Tanzania (see also 28 November). The bishop we commemorate today – born on 13 September 1871 – was a great supporter of the church in East Africa, not least through his work in the diocese of Zanzibar. Educated at Dulwich College and Trinity College, Oxford, Frank Weston was ordained and, after two curacies, joined the Universities' Mission to Central Africa (UMCA) which sent him to Zanzibar. Here his work was mainly educational and here he established St Mark's Theological College. In all this work, he insisted that missionaries should identify themselves with Africans' own ideals, lifestyles and traditions. Consecrated as bishop of Zanzibar in 1908, he energetically reorganized his diocese, speaking out against not only the expansion of Islam and the practices of traditional religion but also the corrupting impact on African family life of the commercial society of the coastal towns. He was in many ways a visionary bishop, establishing in 1910 the Community of the Sacred Passion with its female membership, designed above all to contact African women in their own homes. Weston was also highly controversial. In 1913 the Kikuyu missionary conference proposed an ecclesial federation, to foster common cause against Roman Catholicism and Islam. Weston, as a prominent Anglo-Catholic, denounced the scheme, fearful that it would alienate Roman Catholics and compromise the historic claims of the Church of England. His response caused a great stir and he was summoned to England to explain himself. Returning to Zanzibar at the start of the First World War, Weston recruited a carrier corps of his own – opposed to the current practice of forced recruitment – and, incredibly, his 2,500 men suffered no casualties and he himself was appointed OBE.

In 1920 he attended the first Anglo-Catholic Congress – tall and imposing, he was a brilliant speaker, equally capable of holding an audience of several thousand in the Albert Hall as of fascinating a handful of African children. However, he was regarded with suspicion by the establishment. Archbishop Randall Davidson spoke of him as 'a source and centre of real danger to the Church at present owing to the unguarded way in which he writes and speaks' – this attitude no doubt exacerbated by his telegram of greetings from the 1923 Anglo-Catholic Congress to the pope. Returning to Zanzibar for the last time in 1923, he continued his administration of the diocese, much admired for his dedication, sense of service and fair-mindedness.

Today, Holy Cross Day – so near to the date of his birth – seems ideal to celebrate one so devoted to the Cross of Christ. Certainly, Weston's great powers of oratory and love of Christ are clearly seen in his writings:

You will bear me out that Gethsemane and Calvary are most real in Africa; that Christ is brutally crucified here, crucified in the persons of Africans, by his professing followers ... God in manhood, God on the Cross, God of the empty tomb. Now into the glory of our Calvary breaks the voice of prelatical and priestly liberalism. And its message, what is it? It is that Africans cannot possibly understand the Gospels, Church or Sacraments until they re-interpret them in the light of modern European thought! Poor Africans: not yet among the wise of European thought.

The Christ and the Critics (1919)

John Clayton 1819/20–61

Writer on architecture

John Clayton was born in Hereford but moved to London to study, entering the Royal Academy Schools at the age of 18. He exhibited designs and was awarded a prize for his detailed drawings of the church of St Stephen Walbrook in the city of London. In 1842, Clayton was elected an Associate of the Institute of British Architects, contributing several papers on bridges and viaducts. It was at this time that his design for Hereford Central Station and of the Newport and Hereford Railway was exhibited and this signalled his return to live in the place of his birth. Clayton is best known for his architectural publications and his *A Collection of the Ancient Timber Edifices of England* (1846) is unsurpassed in its field, giving a valuable record of many buildings which have now disappeared. His later book, *The Works of Sir Christopher Wren* (1848/9) contains elevations, plans and sections of 46 of Wren's city churches and was regarded by the Wren Society as his 'great enterprise'.

Great buildings give us glimpses of Heaven itself. The west fronts of cathedrals, with their depictions of the heavenly Jerusalem, were intended to raise minds and spirits, while great stone depictions of the Last Judgement were meant to instil fear, terror and repentance. Here, a 20th-century poet reflects on the wonders of our great churches and cathedrals and the men who created them:

We have graven the mountain of God with hands,
As our hands were graven of God, they say,
Where the seraphs burn in the sun like brands
And the devils carry the rains away:
Making a thrift of the throats of hell,
Our gargoyles gather the roaring rain,
Whose yawn is more than a frozen yell
And their very vomiting not in vain ...

We have graven the forest of heaven with hands,
Being great with a mirth too gross for pride,
In the stone that battered him Stephen stands
And Peter himself is petrified:
Such hands as have grubbed in the glebe for bread
Have bidden the blank rock blossom and thrive,
Such hands as have stricken a live man dead
Have struck, and stricken the dead alive ...

Fold your hands before heaven in praying,
Lift up your hands into heaven and cry;
But look where our dizziest spires are saying
What the hands of a man did up in the sky:
Drenched before you have heard the thunder,
White before you have felt the snow;
For the giants lift up their hands to wonder
How high the hands of a man could go.

G K Chesterton 1874–1936, 'For Four Guilds: Stone-Masons' (1922)

EDITH 10th century

Patron of Stoke Edith

THERE ARE, confusingly, several Anglo-Saxon Ediths who were given the title saint. The best known is Edith of Wilton (961–84). She was the illegitimate daughter of King Edgar by a nun of Wilton Abbey, near Salisbury. She was brought up at Wilton and became renowned for her learning, charity and piety. The king wished to appoint her abbess of Barking and of other abbeys but Edith refused and remained at Wilton until her early death at the age of 23. Miracles took place at her tomb and she became patroness of the great abbey of Wilton. She built an oratory in honour of St Denys which was decorated with murals of the passion of Christ and the martyrdom of Denys. At the dedication, Dunstan is said to have prophesied her approaching death and, for some reason, the incorruption of her thumb. Edith was tireless in her service for the poor and for her love of wild animals. Another Edith given the title of saint was foundress of an abbey at Polesworth in Warwickshire, but the St Edith apparently commemorated at Stoke Edith was the wife of Edward the Confessor (see 13 October) and sister of King Harold. Certainly there has long been confusion. The historian Blount, writing of Stoke Edith, refers to 'the dedication of the church to St Edytha, but which St Edytha I know not'. Today, Stoke Edith is dedicated to St Mary. The 18th-century historian Duncumb writes: 'The original church was dedicated to St Edith (daughter of King Edgar) although, as is often found, with the new church the dedication was altered to St Mary.' In any case, there is, near to the church, a 'St Edith's Well' to which people came for healing until the 19th century. St Edith's feast is traditionally kept today.

For all the mystery of St Edith, two themes seem clear. Certainly, in the case of Wilton's Edith, there is a great love of the natural world and a focus on the miraculous. These two themes – the natural and the miraculous – come together in a wonderful piece of prose:

But what after all is one night? A short space, especially when the darkness dims so soon, and so soon a bird sings, a cock crows, or a faint green quickens, like a turning leaf, in the hollow of the wave. Night, however, succeeds to night. The winter holds a pack of them in store and deals them equally, evenly, with indefatigable fingers. They lengthen; they darken. Some of them hold aloft clear planets, plates of brightness. The autumn trees, ravaged as they are, take on the flash of tattered flags kindling in the gloom of cool cathedral caves where gold letters on marble pages describe death in battle and how bones bleach and burn far away in Indian sands. The autumn trees gleam in the yellow moonlight, in the light of the harvest moons, the light which mellows the energy of labour, and smooths the stubble, and brings the wave lapping blue to the shore. It seemed now as if, touched by human penitence and all its toil, divine goodness had parted the curtain and displayed behind it, single, distinct, the hare erect; the wave falling; the boat rocking, which, did we deserve them, should be ours always. But alas, divine goodness, twitching the cord, draws the curtain; it does not please him; he covers his treasure in a drench of hail, and so breaks them, so confuses them that it seems impossible that their calm should ever return or that we should ever compose from their fragments a perfect whole or read in the littered pieces the clear words of truth. For our penitence deserves a glimpse only, our toil respite only.

Virginia Woolf 1882–1941, *To the Lighthouse* (1927)

Sir John Darnall bapt.1673 d.1735

Wise judge in difficult cases

We often hear high profile cases of child custody in the divorce courts. Who is best placed to bring up children? Cases are long and complex. But it is no new dilemma. Today we remember John Darnall, baptized on this day in 1673 at Canon Pyon. He was called to the bar in 1695 and soon became known for his wisdom in cases of sensitivity and difficulty. In 1717 Darnall was asked his opinion on whether the king (George I) was entitled to the custody of his grandchildren when the Prince of Wales appealed to have his children returned to his care after he had been expelled from court. Although he advised that everyone had the right to custody of his own children, the decision went against the prince, and it was ruled that according to English law royal grandchildren belonged to the Crown. In another difficult case, in 1719, Darnall appeared for the Crown in the case of the Reverend William Hendley, who had been accused at Rochester of using children to collect money for the Pretender (James Stewart) during a church service, by purporting to be raising money for a charity school. In another case, Darnall defended Thomas Bambridge, warden of the Fleet Prison, who was tried at the Old Bailey in 1724 for murdering a prisoner by putting him in a cell with a man suffering from smallpox, so that he would catch the infection and die. Bambridge was acquitted. Darnall moved from Herefordshire with his wife and daughters, and lived in a large house in Petersham, Surrey. There he is buried in the churchyard.

Darnall dealt in the language of accusation and acquittal – legal terms of clarity. As we remember today not Darnall's birthday but his baptism-day, it is good to recall the benefits given to us in baptism – our new relationship before God – our sins forgiven and a new start assured. These words are by a contemporary of Darnall:

Our baptism is to signify our seeking and obtaining a new birth. And our being baptized in or into the name of the Father, Son and Holy Ghost, tells us in the plainest manner, what birth it is that we seek, namely, such a new birth as may make us again what we were at first, a living, real image or offspring of the Father, Son, and Holy Ghost.

It is owned on all hands that we are baptized into a renovation of some divine birth that we had lost. And that we may not be at a loss to know what that divine birth is, the form in baptism openly declares to us, that it is to regain that first birth of Father, Son and Holy Ghost in our souls, which at the first made us to be truly and really images of the nature of the Holy Trinity in unity. The form in baptism is but very imperfectly apprehended, till it is understood to have this great meaning in it. And it must be owned, that the scriptures tend wholly to guide us to this understanding of it. For since they teach us a birth of God, a birth of the Spirit, that we must obtain, and that baptism, the appointed sacrament of this new birth, is to be done in the name of the Father, Son, and Holy Ghost, can there be any doubt, that this sacrament is to signify the renovation of the birth of the Holy Trinity in our souls?

What an harmonious agreement does there thus appear, between our creation and redemption! and how finely, how surprisingly do our first and our second birth answer to, and illustrate one another!

William Law 1686–1761, *A Practical Treatise upon Christian Perfection* (1726)

Thomas Brewster 1705–*c.*1757

Physician & translator

This son of Eardisland combined great skills both in medicine and in translation of classical languages. Educated at Merchant Taylors' School in London and at St John's College, Oxford, he was in his late 20s when he published his first translation, the second *Satire* of Persius. Contemporaries noted the poet's 'uncommon delicacy of ear', though whether the lively rendering of some lines would find appreciative audiences today is another matter:

> What of these lines, Sir ... if you can't admire 'um,
> Grant me, at least, they equal *Arma Virum*.
> Nay *Virgil's* sure, are spungier still than these;
> *His* empty lines! Like Limbs of dodder'd Trees,
> Puft up with fungous, fat excrescencies!

After leaving university, Brewster practised medicine at Bath – indeed, it is probable that he was the Dr Brewster mentioned at the end of Fielding's *Tom Jones* as being in attendance on the philosopher Mr Square during his last illness at Bath. Fielding certainly quotes from Brewster's translation of Persius, which he describes as 'thus excellently rendered by the late ingenious translator of that obscure author'.

Classical writers often speak of the unity of a person and the contribution that good health of body may make to a well-ordered mind. Here, in translation, another classical author speaks of the importance of knowledge to our whole being:

Your every separate action should contribute towards an integrated life; and if each of them, so far as it can, does its part to this end, be satisfied; for that is something which nobody can prevent. 'There will be interferences from without,' you say? Even so, they will not affect the justice, prudence, and reasonableness of your intentions. 'No, but some kind of practical action may be prevented.' Perhaps; yet if you submit to the frustration with a good grace, and are sensible enough to accept what offers itself instead, you can substitute with some alternate course which will be equally consistent with the integration we are speaking of.

You have perhaps seen a severed hand or foot, or a head lying by itself apart from its body. That is the state to which a man is doing his best to reduce himself, when he refuses to accept what befalls him and breaks away from his fellows, or when he acts for selfish ends alone. Then you become an outcast from the unity of Nature; though born a part of it, you have cut yourself away with your own hand. Yet here is the beautiful thought: that it still lies in your own power to reunite yourself. No other part of creation has been so favoured by God with permission to come together again, after once being sundered and divided. Behold, then, his goodness, with which he has dignified man: he has put it in his power, not only initially to keep himself inseparate from the whole, but afterwards, if separated, to return and be reunited and resume his membership as before.

Marcus Aurelius 121–180 AD, *Meditations*

John Stanhope Arkwright 1872–1954

'O Valiant Hearts' came from his pen

Many a service on Remembrance Sunday includes the hymn *O Valiant Hearts*. Some today find it unsuitable, suggesting that it glorifies war and conflict, while others are uneasy about its references to 'lesser Calvaries'. But it is, in many ways, one of the few hymns that directly link human suffering and sacrifice to the sacrifice of Christ. The writer of the hymn, John Stanhope Arkwright, was born in Herefordshire at Hampton Court near Leominster and died on this day in 1954, at Kinsham Court. As a schoolboy at Eton, Arkwright had shown a talent for poetry but it was not until the First World War, when private secretary to a member of the War Cabinet, that his skills were seen as creative in bringing together a nation in grief for its war dead. 'O Valiant Hearts' was first sung in Colwall at a service to mark the unveiling of a plaque in memory of the rector's son, killed in Mesopotamia, in April 1917, and indeed, the tune to which Arkwright's hymn was – and still is – sung, was by the rector of Colwall himself, Charles Harris (1865–1936). The hymn was brought to wider notice when it was included at a service of solemn intercession attended by George v and Queen Mary in Westminster Abbey on 5 August 1917, to mark the war's third anniversary. Arkwright was also active in Herefordshire affairs, as freeman and chief steward of the city of Hereford. He was a noted gardener, producing a popular hybrid, *Lychnis arkwrightii,* and experimenting with the propagation of daffodils. But when he was knighted in 1934 it was for the authorship of 'O Valiant Hearts' that he was best known. The theme of sacrifice in war came very close to him later, when one of his own sons was killed in the Second World War.

O valiant hearts who to your glory came
Through dust of conflict and through battle flame;
Tranquil you lie, your knightly virtue proved,
Your memory hallowed in the land you loved.

Proudly you gathered, rank on rank, to war
As who had heard God's message from afar;
All you had hoped for, all you had, you gave,
To save mankind – yourselves you scorned to save.

Long years ago, as earth lay dark and still,
Rose a loud cry upon a lonely hill,
While in the frailty of our human clay,
Christ, our Redeemer, passed the self-same way.

Still stands his Cross from that dread hour to this,
Like some bright star above the dark abyss;
Still, through the veil, the victor's pitying eyes
Look down to bless our lesser Calvaries.

O risen Lord, O Shepherd of our dead,
Whose cross has bought them and Whose staff has led,
In glorious hope their proud and sorrowing land
Commits her children to Thy gracious hand.

Owain Glyn Dwr *c.*1354–1415

Champion of the Welsh buried at Monnington?

About the year 1680, the church at Monnington was rebuilt, in the churchyard of which stood the trunk of a sycamore, in height about nine feet, and two and a half in diameter, which, being in the workmen's way, was cut down: a foot below the surface of the ground was laid a large grave-stone without any inscription; on its being removed there was discovered at the bottom of a well lined grave the body (as it is supposed) of Owen Glendower, which was whole and entire and of goodly stature, but there was no appearance of any remains of a coffin; where any part of it was touched, it fell to powder ...

So wrote an 18th-century author. It's a lovely story but unlikely to hold any truth. However, the legend that the great Welsh rebel died at Monnington on this day in 1415 is curiously reluctant to disappear entirely! Certainly his family had connections in Herefordshire, not least with Croft Castle. In 1400, partly in response to the deposition of King Richard II and (as they saw it) the usurpation of the throne by Henry Bolingbroke, the Welsh began an uprising at Glyndyfrdwy and proclaimed Glyn Dwr as Prince of Wales. Four years later, after fighting many battles, Glyn Dwr was at the height of his campaign and in control of the greater part of Wales. In an open air ceremony at Machynlleth, he was crowned 'by the grace of God, Prince of Wales', before the envoys of France, Scotland and Castile. By adopting the coat of arms of Gwynedd, he linked his cause with the two Prince Llywelyns of the 13th century. Undoubtedly he was a man ahead of his time with a political vision of a free Wales with an independent senate; universities in the south and the north to train Welshmen to the service of Wales; a Welsh Church independent of England and himself as the ruling prince. But success was followed by a series of defeats and by 1410 Glyn Dwr had become a hunted outlaw who disappeared into the mists of time to be remembered as a Welsh patriot whose exploits were comparable to those of the mighty King Arthur. Did this great champion live and die in Herefordshire? Who knows? Perhaps we are wiser to follow the counsels of the copier of a manuscript of about 1560 who notes: 'Many say that he died; the *brudwyr* [the prophetic poets] say that he did not.'

Leadership is a rare quality and we know it when we see it. For all his failings, Owain Glyn Dwr provided a leadership in which ordinary people could believe, as this marvellous prose passage makes clear:

Owain Glyn Dwr's career can be summed up in two phrases – defender of the common people, and the incarnation of love of country. Love of country prepared him for his life's work; the common people's love for him, and their faith in him, gave him strength to pursue it from day to day. He drew his inspiration from the history of Wales; he saw the splendour, half imagined it is true, of her ancient kings. His letters to the king of Scotland and to the Irish princes are redolent of the dreams of a student of history. He saw the common people of his country writhing under oppression, enduring the tyranny of a lordling and official, and with a keener edge on their suffering for having had a glimpse of a better life. He gave them a nobler ideal than merely that of hanging stewards and burning manorial rolls, the pedigree charts of their subjection. He gave a direction to blind resentment – national unity and a university. And no one has ever been loved as the common people of Wales loved Owain Glyn Dwr. Llywelyn is a figure in history, but Owain Glyn Dwr is as if he were still alive with the nation, and it is no wonder that like Moses and Arthur, the location of his grave is not known. The poets sang their longing for his return, and the common people awaited his coming.

Sir Owen M Edwards 1858–1920, *Y Llynnoedd llonydd*, translated from the Welsh by D M Lloyd

Robert Etheridge 1819–1903

Fossil expert

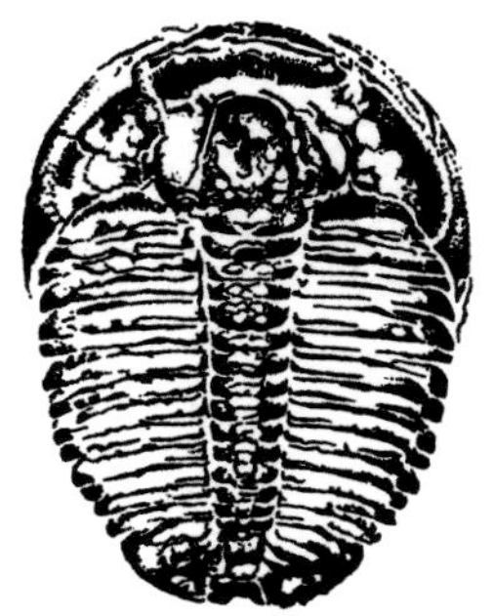

How indebted we are to teachers, friends and relatives when we are young for encouraging us and laying the foundations for future interests in our lives. Robert Etheridge, born at Ross-on-Wye, appears to have been largely self-educated, but his grandfather, harbour master at Bristol, encouraged him to form a 'museum' of local specimens and this small and insignificant start led to Etheridge's life work and passion. He attended lectures at the Bristol Philosophical Institution and through these developed an interest in geology. His extensive knowledge of Jurassic fossils and Cotswold geology caught the attention of T H Huxley, whom he assisted at the Royal School of Mines as a demonstrator of palaeontology. Etheridge became assistant keeper of geology at the British Museum where he worked on his influential catalogues of British fossils and published *Palaeozoic Fossils* in 1888. Etheridge became a Fellow of the Royal Society in 1871 and was influential in the work of the Geological Society of London. Perhaps his greatest contribution to the knowledge of fossils was his study of rocks in north Devon. His geological interests were supplemented by an extensive knowledge of the coalfields of southern Britain and he was involved as consultant geologist for the development of water supplies in Bristol, Plymouth and London.

Poets and writers often speak of the wonders of the heavens or of the beauty of the natural world as leading us to God. But what is under the earth is of great significance, and Etheridge and others like him have helped us to see that subterranean beauty. Norbert Casteret, the explorer, speaks of his experiences:

If I had been alone when I saw these marvels, I would hardly dare to describe them now for fear of sceptical smiles. But the absolute stupefaction of my companions is a sign that I am not exaggerating. And there were yet more astonishing things to come.

The white sea narrowed to a winding fjord between beetling cliffs; then the surface rose to the foot of a petrified waterfall. Beyond, the gallery continued narrow; its walls were covered with a spiny deposit which hooked and scratched the passer-by. We scrambled up an abrupt rise into a spacious chamber.

Here we stood speechless. Just when we thought we had exhausted our powers of admiration, we stepped into a fairy palace. Hundreds of caverns and countless strange stories and pictures had not prepared me for marvels like these.

Stalactites and crystals sparkled everywhere; their profusion, their whiteness, their shapes were fantastic beyond belief. We were inside a precious stone; it was a palace of crystal. But that is a mere cliché for what we saw. I will not pile up superlatives by attempting a general description. Even in colouring and delicacy the formations surpassed the most gorgeous flowers of nature.

There were microscopic stalactites and flawlessly transparent giant crystals. There were shiny formations, dull formations, smooth formations, spiny formations, milky, red, black, crude green formations. The colours came from mineral infiltrations, of which the mountain has a rich and varied store. Finally, there were two entirely new phenomena, still unexplained: huge needles as fine as cobwebs, which trembled and broke at a breath, and silver strings with the brilliance of silk yarn, which dangled from roof and walls.

Norbert Casteret 1897–1987, *Ten Years Under the Earth,* translated by Barrows Mussey (1939)

George Bentham 1800–84

Humble botanist

Popular knowledge of many plants only became possible during the 19th century through the industry and skill of this man. Although Herefordshire held a place dear to his heart, it was in Devon that he was born on this day in 1800. George Bentham came of a famous family – his uncle was Jeremy Bentham (1748–1832), the renowned philosopher and social reformer. George studied for the bar and published several legal tracts but it is as a horticulturalist that he is best known. In 1833 he came into an inheritance and this, together with his marriage to Sarah Brydges at Kentchurch, led him towards the life of a leisured and dilettante botanist. In 1842 the Benthams moved to Pontrilas Court and there George continued his botanical work, writing on many of the new species collected by his friend, Richard Spruce, on his journeys to the Amazon. Moving to London, he began an association with Kew Gardens, where he worked in the herbarium each day from ten till four. His publications were substantial. In 1858 his *Handbook of British Flora* appeared. It was the result of several years' work – on one occasion he even shaved by candlelight to have an hour to study his plants before breakfast. The handbook remained in print until the Second World War. Later he co-authored the *Genera plantarum*, beginning the work in 1862 and ending it in 1883 – a great work, much admired by the whole botanical world, and indeed its three volumes are still in almost daily use at large herbaria worldwide. Bentham received many honours for his work – the royal medal of the Royal Society in 1859 and a doctorate of laws from Cambridge in 1874. Despite all of this he was a very humble man – on being made a companion of the Order of St Michael and St George he characteristically noted that he had 'no claims to the distinction – it much annoys me and I have written to remonstrate'.

Bentham clearly loved Nature in all its aspects. But it is not so with all:

Cyril: (coming in through the open window from the terrace) My dear Vivian, don't coop yourself up all day in the library. It is a perfectly lovely afternoon. The air is exquisite. There is a mist upon the woods, like the purple bloom upon a plum. Let us go and lie on the grass and smoke cigarettes and enjoy Nature.

Vivian: Enjoy Nature! I am glad to say that I have entirely lost that faculty. People tell us that Art makes us love Nature more than we loved her before; that it reveals her secrets to us; and that after a careful study of Corot and Constable we see things in her that had escaped our observation. My own experience is that the more we study Art, the less we care for Nature. What Art really reveals to us is Nature's lack of design, her curious crudities, her extraordinary monotony, her absolutely unfinished condition. Nature has good intentions, of course, but, as Aristotle once said, she cannot carry them out. When I look at a landscape I cannot help seeing all its defects. It is fortunate for us, however, that Nature is so imperfect, as otherwise we should have no art at all. Art is our spirited protest, our gallant attempt to teach Nature her proper place. As for the infinite variety of Nature, that is pure myth. It is not to be found in Nature herself. It resides in the imagination, or fancy, or cultivated blindness of the man who looks at her.

Cyril: Well, you need not look at the landscape. You can lie on the grass and smoke and talk.

Oscar Wilde 1856–1900, *The Decay of Lying* (1891)

Francis Kilvert 1840–79

Diarist of the Marches

He being dead yet speaketh – words on the grave of the Reverend Francis Kilvert, at Bredwardine. Born into a clerical family, he was educated at Oxford and, after ordination, served as his father's curate in Wiltshire, and then as curate in Clyro, Radnorshire. After a year as vicar of St Harmon, in 1877, he was appointed vicar of Bredwardine. He was a popular clergyman who wrote conventional verse and made a collection of Radnorshire folklore, some of which was published in local newspapers. Kilvert kept diaries from the beginning of 1870 until his death, but he remained unknown to the public until the publication of a selection from these in a three-volume edition edited by William Plomer in 1938–40. Some of the manuscript diaries had already been destroyed by his wife and others were destroyed by family members during the 1950s. But what remains is enough to see why his work endures and why 'he being dead yet speaketh'. The diaries give a picture of life in mid-Victorian rural society, painted by Kilvert with sharp observation, wit and compassion. The diaries show his love of nature – he walked miles in all weathers, visiting the sick and local schools – his poetic skill and his love of the Greek classics, and his ability as a pastor to mix with people of all classes and backgrounds. He had no gift for self-analysis but records in his diaries, sometimes with alarming candour, his propensity for falling in love. The public events of Kilvert's time find little place in the diaries, and apart from descriptions of visits to London, Oxford and Cornwall, his record hardly strays beyond rural Radnorshire and Wiltshire, but what he has bequeathed to us is a vividness and simplicity shared by few similar journals.

Kilvert married Elizabeth Anne Rowland on 26 August 1879, but, on returning from honeymoon, he succumbed to peritonitis and died on this day the same year. In 1948 the Kilvert Society was formed on the initiative of William Plomer 'to foster an interest in the Rev. Francis Kilvert, his work, his diary, and the country he loved'.

There are so many passages of the diary that might be quoted. Instead, here is one of Kilvert's poems with its multi-layered biblical allusions, complete with shades of Wordsworth, Byron and Tennyson. Kilvert deploys the natural world as a springboard for prayer:

Oft in the Advent night I think of Thee,
And then Thou com'st in dreams, dear Lord! to me.

I hear the faint cock-crow from farm to farm,
And then I watch and pray for help from harm.

I see the winter dawn break o'er the hill;
Lord! stay my soul on Thee as calm and still.

On one red lingering leaf the sun has shone;
Let Thy face shine on me when left alone.

The morning wind blows sweet on tower and tree;
So let Thy Spirit flow, dear Lord, on me.

I hear the wakening birds at their sweet laud;
So let my rising heart sing praise to God.

'Advent' in *Musings in Verse* (1882)

Joseph Murray Ince 1806–59

Presteigne's painter

Born in London, Ince was brought up in Presteigne, Radnorshire after his father joined a medical practice there shortly after the start of the Napoleonic wars. The young Joseph became a pupil of David Cox in Hereford (see 7 June) and worked under him until 1826, when he went to London. He exhibited in that year for the first time at the Royal Academy and was also an occasional exhibitor at the British Institution, the Society of Arts and other galleries. In later life he lived in Cambridge where he made many architectural drawings, five of his paintings being given to Queen Victoria when she visited the city. In about 1835 he returned to Presteigne where he spent much of the rest of his life. His watercolours depict local harvest scenes, maritime scenes, castles and ruins as well as country houses, many of which were commissions for wealthy patrons. Ince died on this day in 1859 and was buried in Kensal Green Cemetery. There is a plaque in his memory in St Andrew's church, Presteigne, which speaks thus of him:

But although acquainted with the noblest scenes in Europe
he returned from foreign travel
to love anew the charms of this valley.
'Those fields, those hills – what could they less! had laid
strong hold on his affections, were to him
a pleasurable feeling of blind love,
the pleasure which there is in life itself.'

This passage sees many parallels between creativity in art and in human relationships. To the artist there is a true order, broken up into shards of light by everyday existence, which can be pieced together and made sense of by art:

Good art teaching (and creativity itself) is dependent on a greater than usual tolerance of anxiety because of the need to work through one's total personality. This requires a more than average strength of the ego. It is wrongly thought that creative people thrive on neurotic illness. This is not so. The philistine can ignore his illness by living with only a part of his personality and can keep his illness from showing. The creative person faces his illness and its attendant anxieties so that they noisily dominate his behaviour. And he is not more neurotic for this reason: rather the reverse is true. If satisfactory human relationships are proof of mental health, as is universally accepted, then the creative mind is healthy through establishing at least one good object relationship: with his own work acting as an independent being. He is able to accept what Adrian Stokes has called the 'otherness' of the work of art. This acceptance requires the whole apparatus of projection, integration and introjection, which is part of any good relationship. The link between creativity and good object relations also works in the reverse direction. The continuous growth and nursing of a human bond requires a modicum of creative imagination, the receptive watchfulness needed in creative work ... If he allows his work to talk back to him as an independent being, his work will also be capable of talking to others with the same eloquence. But the communication between the artist and his work comes first.

Anton Ehrenzweig 1908–66, *The Hidden Order of Art*

Sir Uvedale Price 1747–1829

Champion of the Picturesque

Uvedale Price was born into a Herefordshire family, and inherited his father's estate at Foxley near Mansell Lacy. Here he indulged his interests in horticulture and landscape gardening and was a close friend and colleague of the Knights of Downton (see 11 February and 22 May). He was something of a polymath, writing on archaeology and classical languages but it is as an exponent of the Picturesque that he is chiefly remembered. In his book *Essay on the Picturesque as compared with the Sublime and Beautiful*, Price maintained that there are many objects which give delight to the eye and yet are fundamentally different from one another. Some objects are intrinsically beautiful – Greek ruins and great gothic edifices. Others are highly interesting from an artistic point of view – he mentions hovels, cottages, mills, insides of old barns, stables, etc, wherever these have any marked and peculiar effect of form, tint, light or shadow. He insists, however, that in these, 'grandeur and beauty are out of the question'. Such objects, he argues, are neither beautiful nor ugly but 'picturesque' and he continues this distinction in the animal and vegetable world – 'The ass (amongst animals) is generally thought more picturesque than the horse ... and amongst our own species, objects merely picturesque are to be found among gypsies and beggars.'

'Beauty is in the eye of the beholder' – a wise maxim but one which Uvedale Price found hard to accept with his rigorous understanding of what can truly be called beautiful. A more detached and magnanimous view is found in these words:

We carve and paint, or we behold what is carved and painted, as students of the mystery of Form. The virtue of art lies in detachment, in sequestering one object from the embarrassing variety. Until one thing comes out from the connection of things, there can be enjoyment, contemplation, but no thought. Our happiness and unhappiness are unproductive. The infant lies in a pleasing trance, but his individual character and his practical power depend on his daily progress in the separation of things, and dealing with one at a time. Love and all the passions concentrate all existence around a single form. It is the habit of certain minds to give an all-excluding fullness to the object, the thought, the word, they alight upon, and to make that for the time the deputy of the world. These are the artists, the orators, the leaders of society. The power to detach, and to magnify by detaching, is the essence of rhetoric in the hands of the orator and the poet. This rhetoric, or power to fix the momentary eminency of an object, – so remarkable in Burke, in Byron, in Carlyle, – the painter and sculptor exhibit in colour and in stone. The power depends on the depth of the artist's insight of that object he contemplates. For every object has its roots in central nature, and may of course be so exhibited to us as to represent the world.

Ralph Waldo Emerson 1803–82, *Essays* (1841)

Cosmas and Damian 4th century

Patron saints of doctors

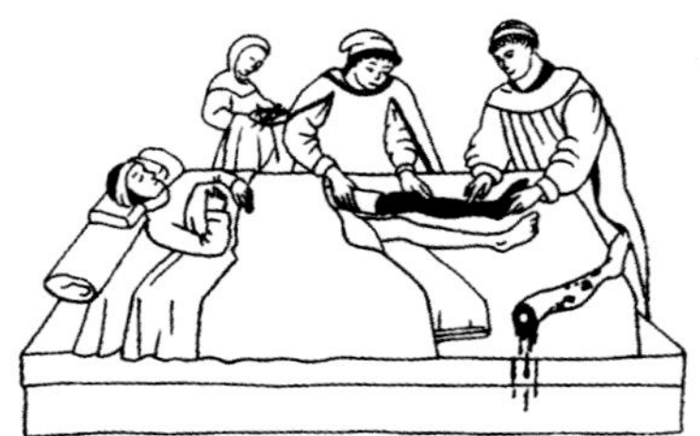

There are only five churches in England dedicated to these little known saints of the early Church. One of the churches is near Leominster at Stretford. Tiny and isolated in a farmyard, the church is now in the care of the Churches Conservation Trust. It is full of interest, not least for the shrine at the entrance to the chancel which is said to have held relics of Cosmas and Damian. So popular was the shrine that, in 1538, offerings there were estimated to bring in just over £2 annually – half the total income of the rector of Stretford. There are also records of a healing well at the church, but the site of this is now lost.

But who were these little known saints who now have an honoured place in Herefordshire? Legend describes them as two young Arabs, possibly twin brothers, who lived at Cyrrhus and were martyred there for refusing to sacrifice to idols. Later legends made them doctors, who practised their art without asking for fees. Many cures were effected at their intercession and they gained a high reputation for healing both humans and animals. Their stories appealed to artists, who depicted not only individual portraits but also whole cycles of their lives. One of the most notable is painted by Fra Angelico, while another is in a 15th-century north Italian Antiphoner. This includes their most remarkable (some would say picturesque) achievement – the grafting of a new black leg on to the body of a white man suffering from cancer. Their cult spread throughout the Christian world and was given encouragement by the Medici family, a number of whom were called Cosmo (an ironic connection, perhaps, remembering the saint's reputation for lack of interest in financial gain). Cosmas and Damian are certainly remembered today and there is an annual service in their little church at Stretford, around the time of their September feast, attended, among others, by local doctors.

These little known saints found a place among the great ones. Their cult spread far and wide and notable churches were built in their honour at Constantinople (5th century) and Rome, where a 6th-century example survives near the Forum, with mosaics of the saints inside. One of the Eucharistic Prayers used today in the Roman Catholic church dates back to the 4th century, and contains an invocation of the prayers of the saints, among them lesser known ones who were greatly venerated at that time in Rome:

In union with the whole Church
we honour Mary,
the ever-virgin mother of Jesus Christ our Lord.
We honour Joseph, her husband,
the apostles and martyrs,
Peter and Paul, Andrew,
James, John, Thomas,
James, Philip,
Bartholomew, Matthew, Simon and Jude;
We honour Linus, Cletus, Clement, Sixtus,
Cornelius, Cyprian, Lawrence, Chrysogonus,
John and Paul, Cosmas and Damian
and all the saints.
May their merits and prayers
gain us your constant help and protection.

Thomas Thornton *c.*1541–1629

Champion of the Chained Library

Hereford Cathedral is unique in possessing two chained libraries. The larger of the two and the more famous is now in a new building (1996) dedicated to its display. This library houses 1,450 books ranging in date from the 8th to the 19th centuries, including 227 manuscript books, many of which are illuminated. The present chained bookcases were designed and donated by Thomas Thornton and appear to be based on the three-shelf design installed by Sir Thomas Bodley in the Bodleian Library, Oxford in about 1600. Thornton was an enthusiastic reformer and formidable scholar, being a canon of Christ Church, Oxford, of Worcester Cathedral and of Hereford Cathedral from 1583 to 1629. He was also vice-chancellor of Oxford University in 1583 and 1599, and while at Oxford was tutor to Sir Philip Sidney and Robert Dudley. In addition to his gift of the book-presses, Thornton reorganised the cathedral library, encouraging donations and purchases, doubling the number of books during his time at Hereford, and leaving many books to the cathedral in his will. From 1612 Thornton was also master of St Katherine's Hospital, Ledbury – he is buried in the parish church there, where there is a fine memorial to him.

Books were precious objects – often having the value of a whole year's wages for a medieval worker. No wonder they were chained for security. Chains speak of slavery and confinement and yet the objects they chain in the library speak of freedom – books remind us of the ability of the human mind to be expanded and liberated by reading and learning. Freedom is a precious quality to be guarded. The breadth of human freedom is constantly being revised and expanded. This passage, for instance, speaks of the freedom, discovered many years after Thornton, of being able to fly:

I held the stick forward, nosing down and towards the road to counteract the drift of the wind. It was marvellous. I was aware, because of the nearness of the earth, of the roaring machine, headlong hurtling, racing over the surface of the earth. Sometimes I brought her really very low, and then as I saw trees looming up ahead, lifted her.

At Hilton, I did two turns round the house. I had no eyes for possible members of my family, but only for the elms as I roared off about twice their height.

With the wind behind us on the way back, we were going at the hell of a lick – about 120 miles an hour over the ground, so it was not long before hideous Girton heaved in view. I took her up a bit as I cut across Chesterton. I shut off and brought her round perfectly to a good landing. 'Time for one more circuit.'

We took off all right, but over the elms the engine missed. Marshall throttled back, took over and lifted her up so steeply that I spoke my thought: 'What are you up to?'

He was gaining height for a conk out. Then he did a right-hand turn, shut the throttle and sang out: 'You've got her.'

I took her in and landed. I was drunk with air. I was wild, and driving home sang and shouted, full of realization that we have found a new freedom – a new Ocean. For thousands of years we have crawled or run on the earth, or paddled across the seas, and all the while there has been this great ocean just over our heads in which at last we sail with joy. The longing for the sea: the call of the sea, one has heard of that, and that was the natural adventure in the past. But now it is a longing for the air, to go up. The air is more marvellous than any sea, it holds more beauty, more joy than any Pacific swell or South Sea lagoon.

David Garnett 1892–1981, *A Rabbit in the Air* (1932)

Sergeant Hugh Carter 1931–56

Brave Herefordshire policeman

In 2009 I had the privilege of dedicating a new plaque placed in Hereford Police Station. The plaque is in memory of a brave member of the Herefordshire Constabulary who became caught up in the Cypriot troubles of the 1950s. A native of Lyonshall, Hugh Carter was educated at Leominster Grammar School, served in the King's Shropshire Light Infantry from 1949 to 1951 and saw service with his regiment in Korea. By 1955 British foreign policy was focused on Cyprus. Here, the Greek Cypriot nationalist organisation, Ekoa, was fighting for the expulsion of British troops from the island. In March 1956 Archbishop Makarios was forcibly detained by the British and exiled to the Seychelles. This so enraged the Greek Cypriots that the Ekoa campaign gained momentum. The British government decided that the civil force – the police – had to be strengthened from outside and up to 600 British policemen and women volunteered and saw service in Cyprus. But they were a vulnerable group, being seen, along with the local Cypriot police, as representing the colonial authority, and became an early target. Police stations were bombed and individual Cypriot officers were intimidated by threats of execution if they did not sympathise with Ekoa's aim – *enosis,* or the union of Cyprus and Greece. Among those who volunteered were Sergeant Hugh Carter and Sergeant William Webb of the Worcester Constabulary. These two, along with Sergeant Cyril Thorogood from Leicester and Rutland Constabulary, were on Nicosia's 'Murder Mile' on this day in 1956. They were all shot from behind by a sniper. Carter and Thorogood were killed, while Webb survived. Sergeant Carter's body was flown back to Herefordshire for burial at Kingsland. By the end of the conflict Ekoa had been responsible for murdering seven British police officers and wounding nine of them. Nico Sampson, a 25-year-old Greek Cypriot, later admitted killing the officers. In February 1959 the London Agreement was signed which promised Cypriots independence but not *enosis.* The island was proclaimed a self-ruling republic in August 1960.

The story of Sergeant Hugh Carter is found in many other periods of our history – young men, full of hope and idealism, grasping the opportunity to fight for freedom and justice. This poem is by John Cornford, a talented young poet, who was killed in Spain fighting against Fascism:

Heart of the heartless world,
Dear heart, the thought of you
Is the pain at my side,
The shadow that chills my view.

The wind rises in the evening,
Reminds that autumn is near.
I am afraid to lose you,
I am afraid of my fear.

On the last mile to Huesca,
The last fence for our pride,
Think so kindly, dear, that I
Sense you at my side.

And if bad luck should lay my strength
Into the shallow grave,
Remember all the good you can;
Don't forget my love.

John Cornford 1915–36, 'Huesca'

Michael
Archangel

I had to include my own patron saint! Not that he is a saint in the accepted sense for he is a heavenly being but if a saint is 'a holy one' then I imagine that the captain of the heavenly armies qualifies! He was certainly popular as a choice for the dedication of churches – by the end of the Middle Ages, 686 English churches were dedicated to him, with 32 in Herefordshire (second only to the Blessed Virgin Mary in popularity) and over 20 in south Shropshire. Michael was a popular dedication in Wales, with local examples at Discoed and Michaelchurch-on-Arrow, and, close to Hereford, Belmont Abbey is dedicated to St Michael. It is often said that churches with Michael as patron are on hill-tops, perhaps because of his heavenly activity, and there are indeed some spectacular examples such as St Michael's Mount in Cornwall and Glastonbury Tor, but hill-top sites are certainly not common in Herefordshire. Michael is often depicted as the winged captain of the spiritual forces of the church against the powers of darkness, trampling the dragon underfoot – perhaps the most magnificent example of this, in recent years, is the Jacob Epstein bronze figure at the entrance to Coventry Cathedral. Also popular were depictions of Michael holding the scales of justice at the Day of Judgement – there is a magnificent stained glass image of Michael weighing souls at Eaton Bishop, as seen in our illustration.

A prayer for angelic company, guidance and protection on the pilgrimage of life

O Michael Militant, thou King of the angels,
Shield thy people with the power of thy sword.

Spread thy wing over sea and land,
East and west, and shield us from the foe.

Brighten thy feast from heaven above,
Be with us in the pilgrimage, and in the twistings of the fight.

Thou chief of chiefs, thou chief of the needy,
Be with us in the journey, and in the gleam of the river.

Thou chief of chiefs, thou chief of the angels,
Spread thy wing over sea and land,
For thine is their fullness, thine is their fullness.

Alexander Carmichael 1832–1912, translated from the Gaelic

The collect for the feast of Michaelmas

Eternal God,
you have ordained and constituted the ministries
of angels and mortals in a wonderful order:
grant that as your holy angels
always serve you in heaven,
so, at your command,
they may help and defend us on earth;
through Jesus Christ our Lord.

Ernest Ballard 1870–1953

Champion of the michaelmas daisy

Michaelmas-tide is surely the right time to celebrate this horticulturalist, who lived in our midst and who did more than any other to promote the beauty and variety of the michaelmas daisy. The youngest of the children of Stephen Ballard, the civil engineer (see 12 June), Ernest briefly attended Malvern College before studying chemistry at Birmingham, in preparation for work in the family business. He brought his scientific training to bear on his hobby, gardening, and became known as a breeder of michaelmas daisies, autumn-flowering hardy perennials which had long been neglected by the horticultural world. In 1906 he started his own business and achieved early success with his double flowered plant, 'Beauty of Colwall'. During the First World War he began to make his hybrids available from his Old Court Nursery in Colwall. Over the next decades he developed a huge number of varieties, many named after family members – Marie Ballard was named after his second wife and had a double flower of dark lavender, the closest he achieved to the strong blue he particularly sought. He gathered his thoughts and experiences in books, including *Days in My Garden* (1919). The work of Old Court Nursery declined during the Second World War, but revived afterwards under Percy Picton, head gardener. Ballard moved to Staplow, where he died in 1952. His speciality of flowering asters is maintained at Old Court Nursery, which now holds the national collection of michaelmas daisies. On a personal note, I greatly value, in the deanery garden, a small collection of michaelmas daisies, propagated in the 1920s and all with clerical titles – 'The Chorister', 'The Sexton', 'The Rector', 'The Dean', 'The Bishop', 'The Archbishop' and finally 'The Cardinal'.

Flowers are symbols of mortality but this poem reminds us of their pointing to immortality. After the show of colour in June, it's tempting to see the rest of the year as an anti-climax. The coming of michaelmas daisies in late September says otherwise, and reminds us of the hope which is always present in life:

So, some tempestuous morn in early June,
When the year's primal burst of bloom is o'er,
Before the roses and the longest day –
When garden-walks and all the grass floor
With blossoms red and white of fallen May
And chestnut-flowers are strewn –
So have I heard the cuckoo's parting cry,
From the wet field, through the vext garden-trees,
Come with the volleying rain and tossing breeze:
The bloom is gone, and with the bloom go I!

Too quick despairer, wherefore wilt thou go?
Soon will the high Midsummer pomps come on,
Soon will the musk carnations break and swell,
Soon shall we have gold-dusted snapdragon,
Sweet-William with his homely cottage-smell,
And stocks in fragrant blow;
Roses that down the alleys shine afar,
And open, jasmine-muffled lattices,
And groups under the dreaming garden-trees,
And the full moon, and the white evening-star.

Matthew Arnold 1822–88, 'Thyrsis'

Mary Webb 1881–1927

Shropshire novelist & poet

Hailed as 'The Shropshire Lass' by her biographer, Thomas Moult, Mary Webb's love for the county shines through her poetry and novels. Born Gladys Mary Meredith at Leighton in Montgomeryshire, she spent much of her childhood at Much Wenlock. Her father encouraged her love of nature and introduced her to the traditions and folklore of Shropshire. Also reflected in her poetry is her own character – she was a person of great generosity and compassion, loathed cruelty, especially blood-sports, and was a vegetarian from childhood. She bore much pain in her life, succumbing to Graves' disease, a disorder which marred her features, and she wrote of physical pain and suffering in a series of philosophical lectures, published as *The Spring of Joy* (1917).

Moving to Meole Brace, she became interested in pantheistic nature mysticism and this informed much of her writing. In 1912 she married Henry Webb, a schoolmaster and writer – their unconventional wedding was typical of Mary, for most of the guests were old people from the workhouse. After a period in Weston-super-Mare, Somerset the Webbs returned to Shropshire, spending two years in Pontesbury. Here, the border country was the inspiration and setting of her six novels, including *The Golden Arrow* (1916) and *Gone to Earth* (1917), both greatly admired by Rebecca West, John Buchan and other writers. A move to London was a tragic mistake and Mary was deeply unhappy there, although being in the capital brought her into contact with literary figures and while there she reviewed for *The Spectator* and *The Bookman*. Mary died on 8 October 1927. She did not win popular success in her lifetime, although a contemporary assessed her as 'a novelist of great and growing ability ... with more than a touch of genius'. She became famous after her death when Prime Minister Stanley Baldwin praised her novel *Precious Bane* (1924) and acclaimed her work at a Royal Literary Fund dinner. A belated *Times* obituary declared 'she was probably at her death on the verge of making a great reputation'. There are stage, radio and television adaptations of Mary Webb's novels and a film of *Gone to Earth* (1950), shot in Shropshire locations. Perhaps the most fitting memorial is the Shropshire landscape, now designated 'Mary Webb Country'.

In this month, when many will be celebrating Harvest Festivals, Mary Webb's poem presents a blissful local harvest scene, with a suggestion that the Eucharist is found in our very midst:

The noise of bells has sunk to rest;
The low grey clouds move swiftly on.
The land is still as Avalon,
Deep-breathing in its sleep, and blest.

For us the holy corn is spread
Across the quiet, misty dales
Towards the hyacinth hills of Wales,
To give our souls their daily bread.

For us that starling flock took wing,
And, like a silken banner blown,
Across the rippling corn has flown,
To teach our spirits how to sing.

'Harvest Song', in *51 Poems*

Thomas Cantilupe 1218–1282

Hereford's own saint

This is the second of the three feasts of Thomas of Hereford (see also 25 August and 25 October), and the most important. On 3 April 1287, the bones of Thomas Cantilupe were moved by his successor, Bishop Swinfield, to the north transept of Hereford Cathedral and soon after this began a series of miracles of healing. During April 1287, 71 miracles were recorded, and between 1287 and 1312, over 500 were noted – the second greatest number recorded at any English shrine, after that of Thomas Becket at Canterbury (see 29 December). There were healings recorded of mental and physical ailments – drowned children were brought back to life after prayers were offered to Thomas. Sometimes a coin would be bent over the sick person and prayers said, and at other times the person was 'measured' to the saint – a candle of the person's height was made and left at the tomb in intercession and thanksgiving. There were even miracles of healing involving animals and birds and, perhaps the most dramatic of all, the claims that a hanged man was restored to life after his distraught parent prayed to Thomas. Driven by Swinfield, there was a move to have Thomas canonized – a long, costly and cumbersome business (see 15 March). In 1307 commissioners from London embarked on the process of enquiry, when those who had been healed or who had other evidence were questioned. Thanks to royal influence and to the persistence of Swinfield, Thomas was declared a saint in 1320 with a Bull of Canonization. Prayers and readings were provided for a new feast (2 October) to be celebrated throughout the church, many of which bear close resemblance to those used for the feast of St Thomas of Canterbury. This link takes us back to Cantilupe's childhood when, it is said, on being asked what he wanted to be in adulthood, the young Cantilupe declared that he wished to be a soldier, following in the footsteps of the blessed Thomas Becket.

When Thomas was canonised by Pope John XXII, these words were used in the declaration:

At length, the saint from being an innocent lamb was made a good shepherd in the church of Hereford, and ever studying to advance from virtue to virtue from the time when he was placed in so high a position in the Temple of God, so shone as to be called the very jewel of Bishops. He went before his sheep to the pastures, defended them from fierce wolves, and led them back to Christ's sheepfolds, fed them by word and example. He stoutly defended the rights of his church, having put on justice as a breastplate. Thus this blessed man, in committing his soul to God, from being a stranger and pilgrim became an illustrious citizen of heaven.

Words in honour of Thomas by a 20th-century hymn writer:

God, Creator, wise and loving,
God, mysterious, past all proving,
    Father of all souls that be;
May we share in love and giving
With Saint Thomas hope of living
    In one caring family.
Trinity, whose love has brought us
Pilgrims here, where Thomas taught us,
    Humble healer, bishop, sage;
All with him your faith confessing,
Send us with your daily blessing
On our Christian pilgrimage.

H C A Gaunt 1902–83

William Swinderby fl.1382–92

Thorn in the side of the bishop of Hereford

Here is Hereford's great heretic! His origins, date of birth and education are unknown, but he is first recorded in Leicester, and had been a preacher and a hermit associated with Leicester Abbey. Although he saw himself as 'only simply lettered', in his writings he makes great use of biblical and patristic quotations, both Latin and English. In the 1380s he began preaching 'Wycliffite' doctrines, criticising the eucharist, absolution, tithes and preaching – indeed the whole structure of medieval religion. Immediately unpopular with authority, attempts were made to silence him and the bishop of Lincoln ordered an enquiry into his preaching. He was found guilty of heresy but, it is said, his punishment was mitigated through the influence of John of Gaunt. Swinderby's next certain appearance was in the diocese of Hereford, when in 1390, Bishop John Trefnant summoned Swinderby to appear before him. This he repeatedly failed to do, much to the frustration of the bishop. In October 1391 the accused heretic submitted a defence of the charges brought against him – again he was condemned for these, but, again, managed to escape from custody. By early March 1392 he was being sought in Wales and no more is heard of him.

Swinderby was, for much of his life, an outcast – one wandering in the wilderness, pursued by the establishment and having little or no settled existence. The image of wilderness is an important one in the spiritual life. We often associate it with the life of John the Baptist and with the season of Lent. Indeed, this next passage speaks of the wilderness of the Lenten experience, but it could well be applied to so much of life:

This then is our Lent, our going with Jesus into the wilderness to be tempted. And we might apply to it some words from the First Epistle of St Peter: 'Beloved, do not be surprised at the fiery ordeal which comes upon you to prove you, as though something strange were happening to you. But rejoice, in so far as you share Christ's sufferings, that you may also rejoice and be glad when his glory is revealed.'

Christ's glory is His full and satisfying communion with all that is. It is the opposite of being isolated. All things are His and He fills all things. This complete communion springs from a love which is able to give to the uttermost, a love which doesn't give in order to get, but which finds in the act of giving itself its own perfect satisfaction. To love is to give. To give is to be. To be is to find yourself in communion with all about you. And this communion is glory. Christ's glory and yours. You don't have to wait for it until you die or the world comes to an end. It can be yours now. Accept your wilderness. From the story of the Son of Man realize what your Lent really means, and then the angels will minister to you as they did to Him. In other words, you'll find moments when giving for love's sake really satisfies you, really makes you feel alive and in contact. And at such moments Christ's glory is revealed, and we rejoice and are glad. We look at the travail of our soul and are satisfied. Lent, we discover, is Easter in disguise.

H A Williams 1919–2006, *The True Wilderness* (1965)

Francis of Assisi 1181–1226

Bearer of the marks of Christ

St Francis is a saint with whom it is easy to identify, living as we do in a wonderful corner of God's creation. The window at Brinsop church, showing Francis surrounded by animals and birds, is a popular image of the saint but so also is that of Francis and the stigmata – the marks of Christ's crucifixion, placed on Francis' own body. These two elements – nature and suffering – endear Francis to Christians throughout the world. He was the son of a wealthy Italian cloth merchant, and joined his father's business, but he was taken prisoner in a local war and suffered a serious illness. This had a great effect upon him and he decided to renounce all material comforts and to lead an ascetic life. Gradually a group of like-minded disciples gathered around him and Francis drew up a simple rule for them, and this was approved by the pope in 1210. The order increased in numbers, the brothers going out on preaching missions and returning to their mother house at Assisi. By 1220 the order had grown to over 5,000 friars, with houses throughout Italy and further afield in Europe. This led to the formation of Tertiaries – laymen who followed the Franciscan ideal but who lived with their families and engaged in everyday life.

Franciscans came to England in 1224, and within a century they had established 50 houses in towns throughout the land, including Bridgnorth and Hereford – in each case only the name 'Greyfriars' survives. Few medieval churches are dedicated to Francis, but his name appears as a saint to be observed in the ancient 'Uses' of Hereford and York. Local Franciscans attained fame, including William Herbert (d.1333/1337) who, after an academic career in Paris and Oxford, retired to Hereford where he died at the Franciscan convent. He wrote commentaries on books of the Bible as well as English translations of Latin hymns, including *Vexilla regis* (The royal banners forward go) and hymns to the Blessed Virgin.

Oscar Wilde, in public disgrace and serving a prison sentence, wrote these words, drawing out the meaning of some of his suffering. In them, Wilde writes of the graciousness of Christ's 'poetic' nature and of his sympathy and love towards all. For Wilde, only the life of St Francis truly mirrored these qualities of Christ:

There is something so unique about Christ. Of course just as there are false dawns before the dawn itself, and winter days so full of sudden sunlight that they will cheat the crocus into squandering its gold before its time, and make some foolish bird call to its mate to build on barren branches, so there were Christians before Christ. For that we should be grateful. The unfortunate thing is that there have been none since. I make one exception, St Francis of Assisi. But then God had given him at his birth the soul of a poet, as he himself when quite young had in mystical marriage taken poverty as his bride: and with the soul of a poet and the body of a beggar he found the way to perfection not difficult. He understood Christ, and so became like him. We do not require the *Liber Conformitatum* to teach us that the life of St Francis was the true *Imitatio Christi*, a poem compared to which the book of that name is merely prose.

Indeed, that is the charm about Christ, when all is said: he is just like a work of art. He does not really teach one anything, but by being brought into his presence one becomes something. Once at least in his life each man walks with Christ to Emmaus.

Oscar Wilde 1854–1900, *De profundis* (1897)

Raphael
Hereford's archangel

As in the case of Michael, the archangel Raphael is in a difficult position – certainly not a sinner and, as an angel, hardly a human saint! But there are reasons why this great archangel should find a special place in Hereford. Raphael is one of the three archangels mentioned in the Bible, notably in the book of Tobit. He has been venerated from early times, especially in the East, as a healer, being sometimes identified with the angel who moved the waters of the healing pool in Jerusalem (John 5:1–14). Although no churches were dedicated to him in England, Edmund Lacy, bishop of Exeter 1420–55 had a special devotion to the archangel and wrote an office in his honour. Lacy had been bishop of Hereford (1417–20) and it seems that his successor at Hereford, Thomas Spofford (1422–48) shared Lacy's devotion, for he introduced Raphael's feast into the calendar of the Use of Hereford – Hereford's own liturgical sequence. With great precision, Spofford specifies not only the day of Raphael's feast in Hereford (5 October), but also that the office and mass were to be those used at Exeter. In many ways, 5 October was not a convenient day for such an observance at Hereford – the great feast of Hereford's own saint, Thomas, occurs on 2 October and this was honoured with a week's celebrations, so Raphael would rather have got in the way. Indeed, in the 1505 breviary of the Use of Hereford, Raphael's observance has become optional. But it's interesting to note how some of the saints achieved their local status, and Hereford should be proud of its own archangel of healing!

A prayer to the guardian angels

Thou angel of God who has charge of me
From the dear Father of mercifulness,
The shepherding King of the fold of the saints
To make round about me this night.

Drive from me every temptation and danger,
Surround me on the sea of unrighteousness,
And in the narrows, crooks and straits,
Keep thou my coracle, keep it always.

Be thou a bright flame before me,
Be thou a guiding star above me,
Be thou a smooth path below me,
And be a kindly shepherd behind me,
Today, tonight, and forever.

I am tired and I a stranger,
Lead thou me to the land of angels;
For me it is time to go home
To the court of Christ, to the peace of heaven.

Celtic Prayer

Faith 3rd century
Herefordshire patron?

There is some confusion here. Two churches in the Golden Valley are dedicated to St Faith – Bacton and Dorstone — but is this the French St Faith or the more local St Foy, a Celtic disciple of St Dubricius? If the former, we should remember today the famous virgin martyr, born in south-west France and said to have been roasted to death on a bedstead. Her cult in the Middle Ages became popular, because her shrine at Conques was on the pilgrim route to Santiago de Compostela. Here her reliquary survives – a masterpiece of art from the so-called Dark Ages. No fewer than 23 ancient English churches are in her honour and there are chapels dedicated to her in Westminster Abbey and St Paul's Cathedral. Our two Golden Valley churches may, alternatively, owe their dedications to the Celtic Foi, or Tyfoi. Certainly, according to the *Book of Llandaff*, the church at Lanntiuoi (now Foy) was consecrated by bishop Herwald 'at the time of Edward the Confessor' (see 13 October), but by the 12th century the dedication is described as St Faith. To add to the confusion, at some stage, Foy's dedication was changed to St Mary. Perhaps this is a day to remember both Faith and Foy – whoever they were!

Whatever the confusions of church dedications, the Christian message of constant faith overrides changes in fashion and doctrine.

The priority of faith

Finally there is the mark of a deep-seated moralism, which to those who know it best, is perhaps the most distinctive feature of Anglicanism ... of the three supreme qualities, goodness, truth, and beauty, the Anglican has no doubt that the first is the most important. 'By their fruits ye shall know them' is a favourite text, and an accepted aphorism is: 'It is character and character alone that can truly save us'. The hardest doctrine to bring home to an Anglican is the priority of faith over works. Even his religious revivals are strongly moralistic. The Evangelical Revival soon found its most popular expression in works of charity, and the supreme object of the Catholic Revival is not churchliness, but holiness. Above everything the Anglican wants to be good, and his strongest temptation is to regard his religion as a mere means to that end.

J W C Wand 1885–1977, *The Anglican Communion: A Survey* (1948)

When Bishop John Robinson wrote Honest to God *in 1963, he was severely criticised for daring to challenge the simple faith of millions. But that was not his purpose. He was trying to encourage 20th-century Christians to review their faith and to find new ways of expressing it:*

The ancient myth was saying something true. But such language today would not convey the truth to modern man. It would be much more likely to conceal it.

So with Christian truth. The reality is that in Jesus we see the clue to all life. To say that he was the Son of a supernatural being sent to earth from heaven may help to bring this home.

But for others it may take it out of their world altogether – so that the events of Christmas and Holy Week seem to belong to a religious fairy story. If the traditional way of putting it makes Christ real for you – the most real thing in the world – well and good. I don't want to destroy anyone's imagery of God. I wrote my book for those who have increasingly come to feel that it makes him unreal and remote.

John Robinson 1919–83, quoted in Eric James, *A Life of Bishop John A T Robinson* (1987)

Katherine of Ledbury 14th century

Recluse

The Chapel and Hospital of St Katherine of Alexandria in Ledbury was founded in 1232 by Bishop Hugh Foliot (see August 7) and the foundation has always occupied an important place in the life of the town. Off the north aisle of St Michael's church in Ledbury there is a chapel dating from the first half of the 14th century, usually known as St Katherine's Chapel. This is usually thought to refer to Lady Katherine Audley, sometimes called St Katherine or Catherine of Ledbury. We know little about her – nothing of her appearance, almost nothing of where she lived during most of her life, except that towards the end of her life she was a recluse or anchoress at Ledbury. Of the legends associated with her, perhaps the most famous is that she was bidden to wander till she heard church-bells ring without ringers. It was at Ledbury that she heard this sign and from that time on, she stayed there with her maidservant, Mabel, at the Farm or Mill of the Hazels, about a mile from the church. There are certain features in the town with names such as 'Mabel's Furlong' and 'Katherine's Stone' which suggest that she caught the popular imagination. She was never canonised but, by popular acclaim, was thought to be a good and holy woman. There has certainly been confusion between her and Katherine of Alexandria (see 25 November) – the latter's feast day is 25 November and in at least one book of English saints, this date is given as one on which to commemorate Katherine of Ledbury. Her story became more popular when she became the subject of a long poem and the heroine of a play in the 19th century. We can glean various happenings in her life, including one, a grant of land, made by her on this day in 1313 – one of the few dates we can associate with her.

Katherine was made famous by William Wordsworth. In his later years the poet spent many months at different times at Brinsop Court, in the folds of the quiet, rolling and wooded hills near Hereford. The Story of Katherine of Ledbury clearly fascinated him:

When human touch (as monkish books attest)
Not as applied nor could be, Ledbury bells
Broke forth in concert flung adown the dells,
And upward, high as Malvern's cloudy crest;
Sweet tones, and caught by a noble lady blest
To rapture! Mabel listened at the side
Of her loved mistress: soon the music died
And Catherine said, Here I set up my rest.
Warned in a dream, the wanderer long had sought
A home that by such miracle of sound
Must be revealed: she heard it now, or felt
The deep, deep joy of a confiding thought;
And there, a saintly Anchoress, she dwelt
Till she exchanged for heaven that happy ground.

A hymn celebrating the Call of the Bells

Let bells peal forth the universal fame,
Creator Lord, of thy mysterious name;
Conscience within, the boundless heavens above,
Disclose to faith the hidden name of Love.

Peter Baelz 1923–2000

Keyne or Cein 6th century?

Another link with Cornwall

KEYNE WAS A DAUGHTER of the great King Brychan, the father of many saints, including Clydog (see 3 November). Like many of her brothers and sisters – the legendary number of whom varies from 11 to 62 – she migrated to Cornwall, where she is commemorated by the church, holy well and village of St Keyne. A popular legend about her is found in a ballad by Southey called *The Well of St Keyne.* The tradition suggests that if husband or wife is the first to drink of its waters, he or she will thereby 'get the mastery'. It is said that a Cornishman left his bride at the church porch in order to be first at the well, but he was outwitted by her as she had already taken a bottle of the well-water to church! In Herefordshire, Keyne was the patron or founder of the church at what is now Kentchurch, though the dedication was at some time changed to St Mary. In early days the parish was known as Llancein or St Keyneschurch, and this name is given so in the Bishop's Register for 1302. This became Keynchurch then Kenchurch. There is a story that an early 19th-century squire insisted on the insertion of the letter 't' because his letters were often misdirected to Kenchester – but this story may well be fanciful! There is a chapel dedicated to St Keyne in Brecon Cathedral.

There is a humanity in the story of St Keyne – the legend of the well – her humanity no doubt developed in coming from such a large family. This passage is about another woman saint, Elizabeth of Hungary, but it points in the same direction:

... that we ... should see so few really great, convincing Christians amongst us is, I venture to say, due to one simple but sufficient cause: we are not human enough to be saints. No, right from the outset, from an utterly false notion of piety, we dare not let ourselves become human beings. A human being is made, not born. We don't let our children grow up into real, healthy men and women, we wish them to be simply and solely Christians – and forget that grace needs a deep, reliable, healthy, natural ground if it is to take root and bear a hundred-fold; that otherwise the 'supernatural' remains in the air, is unnatural, a phantom without strength or life-blood, and will therefore disappear before the first onslaught of a real power, springing from strong, natural roots.

And Elizabeth? The essence of her humanity is that she is a great lover, a generous heart of incomparable capacity for self-giving. And the essence of her Christianity is that she is a saint – and that means literally the same thing, a great lover, a heart with an incomparable capacity for self-giving.

... Not 'love' then, of the idyllic, pathetic and 'poetical' sort, but that great love in which passion burns, unmeasured, dangerous. A loving soul: that means that in her love there lived that spiritual element which raises it, so to speak, to a higher dimension, and gives it a new quality of danger and finality, because it lifts it into the sphere of the permanent, indestructible, irrevocable, inalienable. Do you begin to see how perilous it is, when courage is needed to risk such love?

Ida Coudenhove 1901–71, *The Nature of Sanctity*

Denys d.*c*.250

'La belle 'France' in Herefordshire

Why the patron saint of France in the Marches? It is said that Denys was born in Italy in the 3rd century and was sent by the pope with five companions to convert France. He established a Christian centre where Paris now stands, on an island in the river Seine, and suffered martyrdom by beheading. Over his tomb was built the Abbey of St Denis, later the burial place of French kings. He is claimed as the first bishop of Paris and in medieval art is depicted as a bishop, holding a crozier in one hand and a severed head in the other. The cult of Denys became popular in England where no fewer than 41 ancient churches are dedicated in his honour, probably because of post-Conquest Norman influence. There are two such dedications in Herefordshire, at Harewood (the church is no longer used) and Pencoyd.

There may seem little connection between Denys and the words in the piece of prose that follows, apart from its association with the river Seine, but in these words we see the tension of 'being' and 'doing' – a tension with which all the saints will have been familiar!

There were mornings when, casting off at dawn, I drifted through long cool shadows, watching the sunlight on the trees creep down to meet the water, hearing no sound but the tremolo of the aspens, seeing no one but a chance sportsman and his dog. There were noons with cooling breezes and flocculent clouds high in the sky, and evenings when the forest rang with bird song and the river was a sheet of moving glass. There were nights when, looking skywards, the passing clouds seemed like new continents and islands marked on the inside of a mighty globe.

Hereabouts there was just enough current to keep me moving through the stretches of restful, unexciting landscape. I could relax and let fancies flitter through my brain as inconsequentially as a lady-bird or a drowsy moth might rest a moment on the gunwale.

The trouble with just 'being' is that you get nothing done. The trouble with 'doing' is that it makes you unconscious of 'being'. Nothing is worth doing unless you concentrate your thoughts upon it, yet if you do that you miss the consciousness of the doing, and enjoy only the having done.

Robert Gibbings 1889–1958, *Coming Down the Seine* (1953)

A prayer for unity from the liturgy of the French Reformed Church

O God, whose will it is that all your children should be one in Christ; we pray for the unity of your Church. Pardon all our pride and our lack of faith, of understanding and of charity, which are the cause of our division. Deliver us from narrow-mindedness, from our bitterness, from our prejudices. Save us from considering as normal that which is a scandal to the world and an offence to your love. Teach us to recognise the gifts of grace among all those who call upon you and confess the faith of Jesus Christ our Lord.

Thomas Traherne *c.*1636–74

Hereford's poet of ecstasy & inclusion

The stained glass windows in the Audley Chapel at Hereford Cathedral (by Tom Denny, 2007) commemorate the life of one of the city's greatest sons and one whose prose and poetry have made a huge contribution to the life and spirituality of many, not least in recent years. Traherne was born in Hereford in about 1636, the son of a shoemaker, and here he was baptized in All Saints church, going on to study at Brasenose College, Oxford. Traherne returned to Hereford and became incumbent at Credenhill. The windows depict four key areas of Thomas Traherne's life: first, we see Traherne running across a cornfield, the hills of Herefordshire surrounding him, with the city in the distance. This scene recalls his oft-quoted phrase, 'The corn was orient and immortal wheat which never should be reaped nor was ever sown' – a lovely image of Traherne's delight in the created world. The second light of the window shows a cross 'set on fire with invisible flame – the flame is love', a reminder of Traherne's emphasis throughout his writings on Christ and on his inclusive love. A little church (Credenhill) is seen in the third window, which has an image of Traherne himself, bathed in light, the river Wye snaking into the distance. This scene for Denny was inspired by Traherne's lovely phrase – 'You are as prone to love as the sun to shine'. Finally, in the fourth light, Denny depicts a scene in Hereford – 'The city seemed to stand in Eden, or to be built in Heaven. The streets were mine, the temple was mine, the people were mine.' Traherne published very little during his lifetime, and many of his manuscripts were not signed so that they were lost until a chance purchase in 1896 led to the publication and widespread appreciation of some of his poems and the *Centuries.* Further unpublished manuscripts were identified as recently as 1997. Traherne himself, although he spent most of his life in the environs of Hereford, moved to London in 1672 as Chaplain to Sir Orlando Bridgeman. There he died in 1674 and was buried in that year, on this day, in the chancel of St Mary's church, Teddington.

Here we read of Traherne's emphasis on the power of love and the God who is seen in Nature and in human lives:

That violence wherewith sometimes a man doteth upon one Creature, is but a little spark of that love, even towards all, which lurketh in His Nature. We are made to love: both to satisfy the necessity of our Active Nature, and to answer the Beauties in every Creature. By love our souls are married and soldered to the creatures: and it is our Duty like GOD to be united to them all. We must love them infinitely but in God, and for God: and God in them: namely all His Excellencies Manifested in them. When we dote upon the Perfections and beauties of some one Creature: we do not love that too much, but other things too little. Never was anything in this World loved too much, but many things have been loved in a false Way: and all in too short a Measure.

Centuries of Meditations, II.66

A prayer of thanksgiving by Traherne

Is not sight a jewel? Is not hearing a treasure? Is not speech a glory? O my Lord, pardon my ingratitude and pity my dullness who am not sensible of these gifts. The freedom of my bounty hath deceived me. These things were too near to be considered. Thou presented me with thy blessings and I was not aware. But now I give thanks and adore and praise thee for thine inestimable favours.

EDWARD GARBETT 1817–87

Feisty evangelical

THE FORBIDDING portrait of James Garbett (1775–1857) frowns down on us in College Hall at Hereford Cathedral. He was a vicar choral and prebendary of the cathedral and produced a large family of clergy including James (1802–79) who became archdeacon and who officiated at his father's second marriage, and Edward, whom we commemorate today. Edward was educated at Hereford Cathedral School and won a Somerset scholarship to Brasenose College, Oxford. Ordained in 1841, he became curate to his father and later moved to Birmingham as curate to a cousin. He soon entered the world of religious writing, becoming editor of *The Record*, a position he held until 1867. Under Garbett the journal became less militantly evangelical and shifted its controversial attention from the high to the broad church, especially after the appearance of the liberal *Essays and Reviews* (1860). Garbett believed that evangelical and high-churchmen should join forces to counter the threat of encroaching liberalism. Apart from his life in journalism, Garbett was active as a lecturer, delivering the Boyle lectures in 1860 – and those for 1861 were published as *The Bible and its Critics*, an attack on *Essays and Reviews*. His conservative stance continued with *The Pentateuch and its Authority* (1862) – an attack on Bishop Colenso. He played a key role in the establishment of the Evangelical Union of Clerical and Lay Associations throughout the country and, from 1866, was one of the first evangelicals to participate in regular church congress meetings, drawing together churchmen of various schools of thought. He became vicar of Christchurch, Surbiton, in Surrey and later rector of Barcombe in Sussex, where he died on this day in 1887.

In many ways, Edward Garbett and Bishop David Jenkins (bishop of Durham 1984–94) are poles apart – the former attacking liberalism, the latter one of its greatest exponents. Yet in these words by David Jenkins, we see a challenge to religion to be open to the signs of the times and to this, Garbett would have added a hearty 'Amen':

In these times we live in we are plainly facing the spread of fundamentalism, simplified ideologies and the peddling of solutions to problems at both the world level and for the individual which can be expressed in slogans and slick, instant moralisms. The current controversies about faith, authority and meaning going on in Christian churches are mirrored in Judaism and Islam. In secular politics we are seeing the degeneration of debate, compromise and consensus in favour of the adoption of dogmatic theories. Humanity is being threatened on both religious and secular fronts by the effects of infantile simplicity and the old, cruel demons of dogma. Reaction to the discovery that neither the Enlightenment nor science and technology have turned out to be as promising as we supposed, and that, indeed, they have led to the production of many threatening things, is leading to a variety of recommendations that we should return to the attitudes and methods of the Dark Ages. We are facing a crisis within the whole Western intellectual and cultural tradition. It becomes ever more vital that worship of the One True Living God be reinstated as a crucial resource in exposing and challenging the false and destructive limitations of all philosophies, theories, and religious interpretations raised to the status of dogma.

David Jenkins b.1925, and Rebecca Jenkins, *Free to Believe* (1991)

Miles Smith 1554–1624

Translator of the Authorised Version

Among the learned scholars employed by King James I to translate what has become known as the 'King James' or 'Authorised Version' of the Bible, Miles Smith stands pre-eminent. Born in Hereford, the son of a fletcher, after Oxford and ordination he became a prebendary of Hereford Cathedral, then, in 1584, vicar of Bosbury and, in 1587, rector of Hampton Bishop and a canon residentiary at the cathedral. Smith gained a high reputation as a classical scholar and as a student of oriental languages and was an obvious candidate to join the team of translators assembled by the king for the great revision of the English Bible – one of the few outside the universities to be included. He worked on the prophetic books of the Old Testament and shared with the bishop of Winchester the final review before being given the task of writing the preface.

In 1612 Smith was consecrated bishop of Gloucester, a period of some unhappiness as he came into conflict with William Laud (see 10 January) who became dean of Gloucester in 1616 and who set about a liturgical re-ordering of the cathedral with which Smith greatly disagreed. Certainly, Smith's theological views tended to the conservative and at his funeral he was extolled for his opposition to 'papists, Arminians and carnal gospellers'. He continued to write and published books of sermons – a task which he felt highly important; as he wrote in one work, 'he that speaketh profiteth his owne congregation, but he that writeth profiteth all'. Smith died on 20 October 1624 and is buried in the Lady Chapel of Gloucester Cathedral, along with members of his family.

The Preface to the Authorised Version, *penned by Miles Smith, speaks of the richness of the Bible and its central place in Christian life and thought:*

[The Bible] is not only an armour, but also a whole armoury of weapons, both offensive and defensive; whereby we may save ourselves and put the enemy to flight. It is not an herb, but a tree, or rather a whole paradise of trees of life, which bring forth fruit every month. And the fruit thereof is for meat, and the leaves for medicine. It is not a pot of Manna, or a cruse[1] of oil, which were for memory only, or for a meal's meat or two, but as it were a shower of heavenly bread sufficient for a whole host, be it never so great; and as it were a whole cellar full of oil vessels; whereby all our necessities may be provided for, and our debts discharged. In a word, it is a Panary[2] of wholesome food, against fenowed[3] traditions; a Physician's shop (Saint Basil calls it) of preservatives against poisoned heresies; a Pandect[4] of profitable laws, against rebellious spirits; finally, a fountain of most pure water springing up unto everlasting life. And what marvel? The original thereof being from heaven, not from earth; the author being God, not man; the editor, the Holy Spirit, not the wit of the Apostles or Prophets; the Penmen such as were sanctified from the womb, and endued with a principal portion of God's spirit; the matter, verity, piety, purity, uprightness; the form, God's word, God's testimony, God's oracles, the word of truth, the word of salvation, etc.; the effects, light of understanding, stableness of persuasion, repentance from dead works, newness of life, holiness, peace, joy in the Holy Ghost; lastly, the end and reward of the study thereof, fellowship with the Saints, participation of the heavenly nature, fruition of an inheritance immortal, undefiled, and that never shall fade away. Happy is the man that delighteth in the Scripture, and thrice happy that meditateth in it day and night.

1. A small bottle
2. A breadbasket
3. Corrupted
4. A collection of texts

Edward the Confessor 1003–66

Saintly & humble king

The existence of two Shropshire churches in the diocese of Hereford dedicated to this saintly king – Dorrington and Hopton Castle – encourages us to remember him today, the day on which, in 1163, his relics were translated to a new shrine in Westminster Abbey, the great church which he had founded. Son of King Ethelred the Unready, Edward was educated first at Ely, then in Normandy. He became king of England in 1042. Some have viewed him as a weak monarch, who paved the way for the Norman Conquest; others have seen him as shrewd, preserving his land in peace for over 20 years. Certainly, he had a reputation for holiness, being seen as accessible to his subjects and always generous to the poor. Perhaps the most famous image of Edward is seen in the Wilton Diptych (*c.*1380), where he is depicted holding a ring.

Edward was seen as patron of England, a position he held until the 15th century, by which time this title was being ascribed to St George. After the 1163 translation of his body, there was a further translation in 1269, when Henry III's rebuilding of the east end of Westminster Abbey was complete, and to this day, the Confessor's shrine remains, undisturbed, behind the high altar of the abbey. There are at least 17 ancient churches in England dedicated to the Confessor and in our area there is a fine depiction of him in a 15th-century stained glass window in St Laurence's, Ludlow.

Edward was known in his day for his humility. Despite his royal background and connections, his life was turned towards God – a practice here described by a much later Christian. As one quite hopeless at any kind of sport, I find William Temple's confidence about catching balls over-optimistic, but I take the point!

The source of humility is the habit of realizing the presence of God. Humility does not mean thinking less of yourself than of other people, nor does it mean having a low opinion of your own gifts. It means freedom from thinking about yourself one way or the other at all. It may be quite right that a person conscious of certain powers given him or her by God should desire the opportunity to exercise these powers for God. It may be quite right that under certain circumstances we should insist that we are more capable than another of doing something that must be done ...

Humility means that you feel yourself, as a distinct person, out of count, and give your whole mind and thought to the object towards which they are directed, to God himself in worship, and to the fulfilment of His will in Christian love; and humility, in that sense, is quite plainly a source of effectiveness. The humility which consists in being a great deal occupied about yourself, and saying you are of little worth, is not Christian humility. It is one form of self-occupation and a very poor and futile one at that; but real humility makes for effectiveness because it delivers one from anxiety, and we all know that in all our undertakings, from the smallest to the greatest, the chief source of feebleness is anxiety. Even in a game we all know that nothing so much paralyzes good play as anxiety. If you once begin to wonder whether you are going to catch the ball you will drop it, but if you just catch it without thinking about anything but catching it – probably you will hold it. That goes through everything from such a simple act to the greatest. But there is nothing big enough to hold your soul in detachment from the centre of yourself through all the occupations of life except the majesty of God and His love; and it is in worship, worship given to God because He is God, that we will most learn the secret of real humility.

William Temple 1881–1944, *Christ in his Church* (1925)

Callixtus d.222

Pope in the Shropshire countryside

The little church at Astley Abbotts, near Bridgnorth has a very rare dedication and one which takes us back to the days of the early church in Rome. Callixtus was born as a slave, but when entrusted with financial responsibility, he lost a great deal of money, fled from Rome, was caught at Porto and sentenced to the treadmill. His creditors obtained his release but he was soon arrested again for brawling in a synagogue. Sentenced to work in the mines of Sardinia, he was released through the influence of the Emperor Constantine and was put in charge of what is now called the cemetery of Callistus, a burial ground with a crypt where most of the bishops of Rome were buried. This he administered well and became a deacon. Eighteen years later, in 217, Callixtus became pope. He had a short but controversial reign. He attempted to act as mediator between two rival parties with different theories of the Incarnation – and ended by pleasing neither! He also allowed the readmission to communion of those who repented of murder and adultery, and for this he was accused of laxity. His generous approach was also seen in his determination to allow the validity of marriages between free people and slaves – then against Roman civil law. The result of all this controversy was a schism in the Roman Church, led by a rival of Callixtus, Hippolytus. Callixtus himself died in a popular riot, although the popular tradition of his being killed by being thrown down a well is probably apocryphal.

Callixtus' qualification for being pope may seem a little unorthodox! But he had lived life to the full and, no doubt, he brought this to his great ministry. His experience of life led to his being willing to forgive and be forgiven – to know himself as he really was. Perhaps that was what enabled him to see God and to lead others to God? Sometimes, above all, we need the courage to love:

We are somewhere very frightened of love without recognizing at all clearly that we are. For absolute love, God's love, makes us fully ourselves, instead of the half people we generally are. And to become fully yourself is a terrible risk. It would commit you to God knows what and lead you God knows where. If I open my heart in simplicity to God's love I might soon find myself in Bangladesh or something of that sort, or I might find myself disagreeing or even agreeing with Mrs Whitehouse. Or letting in God's love might prompt me to join the Campaign for Homosexual Equality, or the Tory party, or it might lead me actively to support the Tribune Group, or it might make me concerned about the oppressed peoples of the Third World or even about my neighbour next door who is lonely. And God's love has been known to make the most respectable people enjoy a pub crawl. And letting in God's love is no guarantee at all that I will necessarily remain an enthusiastic member of the Church of England or even of the Anglo-Catholic set-up. And so, not so much in our minds consciously as in our bones unconsciously, we see to it that when we pray we keep ourselves tied up in knots. It is much safer. Let us keep on the armour of our sophistication and plump for security.

But then of course we miss the glorious liberty of the children of God. We remain half dead, too afraid to know what life is. And missing out on the splendour and warm intimacy of God's love, we become hooked on some compensatory activity like overwork or keeping up with the Joneses, or drink, or sex, or it might even be religiosity and church going. Such compensatory activities don't in practice compensate at all.

H A Williams 1919–2006, *Becoming What I am*

Joseph Leycester Lyne (Father Ignatius) 1837–1908

Eccentric monk & preacher

The magnificent scenery of the Black Mountains provided the setting for one of the strangest experiments in monastic living – at its heart was its founder, Joseph Lyne. After ordination as a deacon, Lyne became fascinated by the monastic life and, at Plymouth, founded the Society of the Love of Jesus, calling himself 'Brother Joseph'. After a period of parish work in London's east end, he made new attempts to found monastic communities, often falling foul of episcopal authority and being refused priestly ordination by the archbishop of Canterbury. In 1869, now calling himself Father Ignatius, he purchased a property at Capel-y-ffin in the Black Mountains. The choice of place, not far from the ruins of the 12th-century Augustinian priory at Llanthony, was motivated by his sense of, and identification with, the history of pre-Reformation monasticism in Wales and he used the Welsh language in services. On St Patrick's Day 1870, the foundation stone of a new monastery was laid. Ten years elapsed before the choir was completed and the nave was never started – practically all the money was raised by Ignatius himself on his many preaching tours around the country. Llanthony Abbey became known for its eclectic style of Benedictine observance and for its exotic ceremonial – there were reports of miracles and heavenly visions. Because of Ignatius' frequent absences and his questionable status within the Anglican church, though the venture lasted 38 years it did not succeed. Unable to receive orders in his own church, Ignatius was ordained priest in 1898 by Mar Timotheos, a Syrian archbishop and metropolitan for the Old Catholic church in America and, for a time, Ignatius dreamed of establishing a British Old Catholic church. Towards the end of his life, as well as championing Welsh culture, his views became even more eccentric and he became a Zionist, a British Israelite and a believer in the flat-earth theory. Father Ignatius died on 16 October 1908 and was buried at Llanthony Abbey on 23 October. The property passed into the hands of the Anglican Benedictines of Caldey Island, Pembrokeshire, in 1911. Later, Eric Gill (see 9 June) took on the buildings as the focus of a community for his own family and work.

For all his eccentricity, Father Ignatius was seen as a holy and humble man. Francis Kilvert (see 23 September) visited Capel-y-ffin in 1870:

Mr and Mrs Lyne came up out of their dingle and Mrs Lyne brought up Father Ignatius and introduced us. He struck me as a man of gentle simple kind manners, excitable, and entirely possessed by the one idea. He always spoke to his father and mother as 'Papa' and 'Mamma', and called me 'Father'. I could not persuade him that my name was not Venables. His head and brow are very fine, the forehead beautifully rounded and highly imaginative. The face is a very saintly one and the eyes extremely beautiful, earnest and expressive, a dark soft brown. When excited they seem absolutely to flame. He wears the Greek or early British tonsure all round the temples, leaving the hair of the crown untouched. His manner gives you the impression of great earnestness and single-mindedness ...

Father Ignatius wore the black Benedictine habit with the two loose wings or pieces falling in front and behind, two violet tassels behind, the knotted scourge girdle, a silver cross on the breast, and a brazen or golden cross hanging from the rosary of black beads under the left arm ...

We shook hands and departed. 'Goodbye, Father,' he said with an earnest kindly look, 'and thank you for your good wish. You must come and see us again when we have our guest house ready.' When we had parted a little way and our roads had diverged he called out through the half screen of a hazel hedge, 'Father! Will you remember us the next time you celebrate the Holy Communion?' 'Yes,' I replied, 'I will.'

Francis Kilvert, *Diaries*, Friday 2 September 1870

Daniel Rowland 1711?–1790

Founder of Welsh Methodism

After early studies in Cardiganshire, Daniel Rowland spent some time at Hereford Cathedral School and then went on to be ordained by the bishop of St Davids. In the year of his becoming a priest, he underwent a spiritual conversion, possibly as a result of hearing a sermon by the great Griffith Jones. The conversion certainly changed his life and he became known as the 'angry cleric' from his frequent chastisement of sinners. Indeed, at his funeral, he was hailed as Boanerges, the 'son of thunder'. In later life his sermons focused less on God's judgement and more on the saving power of Christ. In 1737 Rowland met Howel Harris, and this meeting marked the foundation of the Methodist movement in Wales. Although they were united by their common concern to save souls, the two men had very different personalities. Despite Rowland's reputation for seriousness in preaching, he had a good sense of humour and Howel clearly disapproved of this, often accusing his colleague of unbecoming levity. A split came in 1750, with many joining Rowland, who then became the effective leader of Welsh Methodism. Rowland often went on preaching tours but also spent much time in pastoral care for his parish at Llangeitho in Cardiganshire. Later, through the influence of the countess of Huntingdon, he was appointed chaplain to the duke of Leinster. However, his ministry was not without its sadness – because of his frequent preaching tours he was deprived of his curacies. In order to retain his services, his parishioners built a chapel for his use at Llangeitho, which was often full to overflowing on communion Sundays. While remaining an Anglican clergyman, he was devoted to the Methodist cause and, along with Howel Harris and William Williams, hugely influenced the future of Methodism in Wales. Rowland died on this day in 1790.

George Whitefield, the great Methodist, was appointed as moderator of the newly-founded Association of Methodists in Wales in 1743. Like Rowland and Harris he was a powerful preacher and letter-writer, focusing on Christ's redemptive love:

How inconsistent is the devil! How artfully does he strive to keep poor souls from Christ! Sometimes he labours to drive the poor souls into despair; sometimes to presumption. These are the two rocks against which he would fain have poor souls to make shipwreck of faith and a good conscience. I pray God to enable you to steer a middle course.

May you see your misery, and at the same time see your remedy in the cross and wounds of Jesus Christ. He calls to all weary, heavy-laden souls; consequently He calls you. Your coming to Him will be a proof of your election. The devils know nothing of God's decrees. If ever [Satan] should tempt you so again, say, 'If I do perish, I will perish at the feet of Christ.' He is willing to save, to save to the uttermost. He sees, He feels your anguish. He longs to rejoice over you. Venture therefore upon Him.

Thomas, be not faithless, but believing. Christ shall yet show you His hands and His feet. He is the same now as He was yesterday, full of love and graciousness to self-condemned sinners. That you may experience the full power and efficacy of the Redeemer's blood is the ardent prayer of, dear Thomas,

Your sincere friend,

GW

George Whitefield 1714–70, *Letter to Thomas Webb*

Robert Fills *c.*1521–78

John Calvin comes to Herefordshire

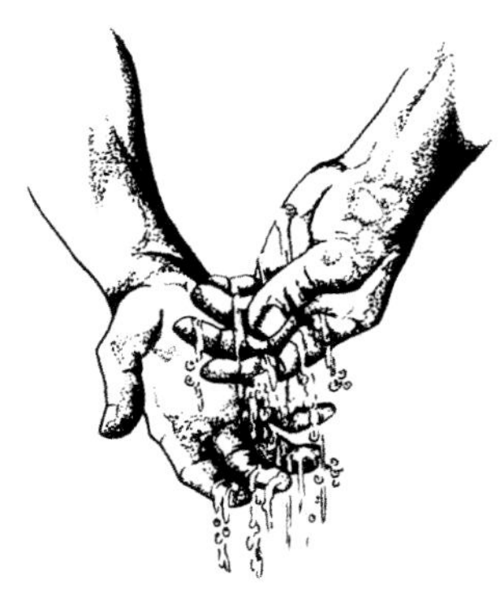

It is thanks to Robert Fills that the works of John Calvin and other leading figures of the Reformation were able to be read in English translations. After ordination, and on the accession of Mary Tudor, Fills and his wife fled to the Continent where they became members of a congregation in Geneva. On returning to England he was presented by the bishop of Hereford, John Scory, to the living of Bromyard. In 1562 he published his first translation, from the French, of a text inspired by Calvin, *The laws and statutes of Geneva, as well concerning ecclesiastical discipline, as civill regiment.* The following year Fills became rector of Kingsland and continued his publishing work with a translation by another reformer – Theodore Beza's *A brief and pithie summe of the Christian faith.* The dedication of this work, to the Puritan earl of Huntingdon, complains of the state of religious life in England as a 'myngle mangle of spirituall and temporall regiment', and he draws particular attention to the state of the cathedrals – many, in his opinion being 'only a very refuge and denne of idell, igonoraunt and unpreaching lubbers'. From 1570 Fills also held the living of Pembridge and, with that of Kingsland, he was earning an annual income of at least £67 – a fairly substantial figure for that time. In 1576 he was appointed by Edmund Grindal, archbishop of Canterbury, as a commissioner for his visitation of the cathedral, city and diocese of Hereford. Attended by his surgeon on 16 October, he died on that same day and was buried in Kingsland on this day in 1578.

Translation is an important means of communication, and meanings in an original language can be radically altered by a less than sensitive translation. Sometimes, however, a phrase is so well-known that its translation into any number of languages will not lessen its impact:

PILATE: Claudia, Claudia, tell me – what was this dream of yours?

CLAUDIA: I was in a ship at sea, voyaging among the islands of the Aegean. At first the weather seemed calm and sunny – but presently the sky darkened – and the sea began to toss with the wind ... (*Wind and waves*) Then, out of the east there came a cry, strange and piercing – "Pan ho megas tethneke – Pan ho megas tethneke". And I said to the captain, "What do they cry?" And he answered, "Great Pan is dead." And I asked him, "How can God die?" And he answered, "Don't you remember? They crucified him. He suffered under Pontius Pilate." Then all the people in the ship turned their faces to me and said: "Pontius Pilate."

(*Voices, some speaking, some chanting, some muttering, mingled with fragments of Greek and Latin liturgies, weaving and crossing one another:* "Pontius Pilate. ... Pontius Pilate ... he suffered under Pontius Pilate ... crucified, dead and buried ... sub Pontio Pilato ... Pilato ... he suffered ... suffered ... under Pontius Pilate ... under Pontius Pilate ...)

... in all their tongues and all voices ... even the little children with their mothers ....

(Children's voices: "Suffered under Pontius Pilate ... sub Pontio Pilato ... crucifié sous Ponce Pilate ... gekreuzigt unter Pontius Pilatus ... *and other languages, mingling with the adult voices*)

... your name, husband, your name continually – "he suffered under Pontius Pilate."

PILATE: The gods avert the omen.

Dorothy L Sayers 1893–1957, *The Man born to be King* (1947)

Joshua Cristall 1768–1847

Artist in search of Arcadia

WHAT CAUSED an artist at the height of his career to abandon London and live in a remote Herefordshire village? Joshua Cristall first fell in love with the Wye valley in 1803 when he was introduced to the area by John and Cornelius Varley. (Cornelius painted Cristall sketching a Wye scene under an umbrella.) The visit left its mark on him, for 20 years later, aged 56 and after a rather struggling career, he moved to Goodrich, living from 1823 till 1841 in Granton Cottage, close to the church, where the smaller cottage is thought to have been his studio. His wife had run a school for young ladies in Paddington, her pupils including the Lovett sisters who now lived with their father at Hellens, in Much Marcle, and it seems to have been their presence and that of Sir Samuel Meyrick, a patron of Cristall, that brought the artist back to the Wye. Indeed, the Lovett sisters became like the Cristalls' own daughters. From his cottage Joshua looked across at Coppet Hill and it was these local scenes that he made his own. He was in pursuit of his vision of an Arcadia where people lived in harmony with each other and with Nature and many of his scenes are of pastoral life – *The Gleaners; Girl Harvesting Bracken; Cottages near Symonds Yat with country figures.*

Although he loved the Wye valley, he also had a national profile – with the Varleys he co-founded, in 1803, the Society of Painters in Water-colours, with which he exhibited for the rest of his life. He was president of the society four times. His early work shows an affinity with that of Samuel Prout and David Cox (see 7 June), but he soon developed his own style which combined neat draughtsmanship with stylized, classical treatment of form. In his latter years he lived and worked in London and died there, on this day, in 1847. His body was taken back to Herefordshire and buried 12 days later beside his wife's in the churchyard at Goodrich.

A 20th-century author writes of the importance of experience in the artist's work:

All great drawing is drawing by memory. That is why it takes so long to learn. If drawing were transcription, a kind of script writing, it could be taught in a few years. Even before a model, you draw from memory. The model is a reminder. Not of a stereotype you know by heart. Not even of anything you can consciously remember. The model is a reminder of experience you can only formulate and therefore only remember by drawing. And those experiences add up to the sum total of your awareness of the tangible, three-dimensional, structural world ... Make a mark on (a blank white page) ... and the edges of the page ... have become the borders of a microcosm. Make two marks of uneven pressure and the whiteness ... becomes opaque three-dimensional space that must be made less opaque and more and more lucid by every succeeding mark. That microcosm is filled with the potentiality of every proportion you have ever perceived or sensed. That space is filled with the potentiality of every form, sliding plane, hollow, point of contact, passage of separation you have ever set eye or hand on. And it does not stop even there. For, after a few more marks, there is air, there is pressure, and therefore there is bulk and weight. And this scale is then filled with the potentiality of every degree of hardness, yieldingness, force of movement, activeness or passiveness that you have ever buried your head in or knocked your head against. And from all this you must select in a few minutes, as nature did through millennia, in order to create a human ankle, a human arm-pit with the pectoral muscle burying itself like an underground stream, or the bough of a tree. From all this you must select the one lock and one key.

John Berger b.1926, *A Painter of Our Time*

Thomas Swift d.1658

Grandfather of the great Dean Swift

We remember Jonathan Swift as the author of *Gulliver's Travels* – the Anglo-Irish satirist, essayist, political pamphleteer, poet and cleric, who became dean of St Patrick's Cathedral, Dublin. Perhaps less well-known are his roots in our area. His paternal grandfather, Thomas Swift was the Royalist vicar of Goodrich who was removed from his church and imprisoned. The church still possesses the chalice given to it by Dean Swift himself. The story is told that Thomas Swift journeyed to Raglan Castle, where Charles I had retired after the battle of Naseby, where the governor asked the vicar what he wanted with the king. 'To give him my coat,' was the reply. 'It is of little worth,' remarked the Governor, smilingly. 'Why, then,' said the vicar, 'take my waistcoat also,' and this, being ripped open, was found to contain 300 pieces of gold which Swift had collected by mortgaging his estate. Lord Clarendon remarked that no relief for the king was more seasonable or acceptable than Swift's great gift. We remember Thomas Swift today, not on his own death day, but on the day his famous grandson died in 1745.

Jonathan Swift's writings include these maxims for the Christian life:

I am in all opinions to believe according to my own impartial reason; which I am bound to inform and improve, as far as my capacity and opportunities will permit.

Violent zeal for truth hath an hundred to one odds to be either petulancy, ambition, or pride.

God's mercy is over all his works, but divines of all sorts lessen that mercy too much.

I am not answerable to God for the doubts that arise in my own breast, since they are the consequences of that reason which he hath planted in me, if I take care to conceal those doubts from others, if I use my best endeavours to subdue them, and if they have no influence on the conduct of my life.

I never saw, heard, nor read, that the clergy were beloved in any nation where Christianity was the religion of the country. Nothing can render them popular but some degree of persecution.

Although reason were intended by providence to govern our passions, yet it seems that, in two points of the greatest moment to the being and continuance of the world, God hath intended our passions to prevail over reason. The first is, the propagation of our species, since no man ever married from the dictates of reason. The other is, the love of life, which, from the dictates of reason, every man would espy, and wish it at an end, or that it never had a beginning.

Jonathan Swift 1667–1745, *Thoughts on Religion*

A prayer for Stella in her last sickness

Almighty and most gracious Lord God, extend, we beseech Thee, Thy pity and compassion towards this Thy languishing servant: Teach her to place her hope and confidence entirely in Thee; give her a sense of the emptiness and vanity of all earthly things; make her truly sensible of the infirmities of her past life, and grant to her such a true sincere repentance as is not to be repented of. Preserve her, O Lord, in a sound mind and understanding, during this Thy visitation: Keep her from both the sad extremes of presumption and despair. If Thou shalt please to restore her to her former health, give her grace to be ever mindful of that mercy, and to keep those good resolutions she now makes in her sickness, so that no length of time, nor prosperity, may entice her to forget them ...

'Three prayers used by the Dean for Mrs Johnson' (1727)

James Beauclerk 1709–87

Bishop of Hereford linked to Nell Gwyn

If Nell Gwyn really was born and lived in a cottage adjoining the bishop's palace in Hereford (and this is doubtful), she would never have dreamed that one day her grandson would be bishop 'over the wall'. But it is true. The famous romance between Charles II and Nell Gwyn resulted in the birth of a son, Charles Beauclerk, first duke of St Albans. The duke's eighth son, James (said to resemble his royal grandfather) became bishop of Hereford in 1746 at the early age of 36 and remained so until his death 41 years later. With his royal and aristocratic roots, one might be forgiven for assuming that Bishop Beauclerk would be the archetypal absentee, always in London and neglectful of his distant diocese. This was not the case. In fact, Beauclerk made every effort to raise standards in the diocese and, until a year before his death, personally conducted almost all ordinations in Hereford Cathedral – not in London, as was often the case with other bishops at the time. In fact, when compared with most of his predecessors, his attendance in the House of Lords was quite scanty, suggesting his preference for being in his diocese. He demanded the highest standards – ordinands, especially non-graduates, came to fear the tests he set them. He was often at odds with the dean and chapter – there were disputes about patronage rights, the disposal of canons' houses, and a right of way for a carriage through the palace grounds to the chapter timber yard. It seems that all were so engrossed in these legal matters that they had little time to attend to the cathedral fabric. Beauclerk was in office when the tower and west end collapsed on Easter Monday, 1786. However, there was little time for the bishop to take the matter in hand – he died on this day the following year, and was buried in the choir near to the bishop's throne. There is a memorial to him in the bishop's cloister.

A devotional work, written during Beauclerk's lifetime speaks eloquently of the high calling of a clergyman – an attitude Beauclerk would have emphasised in his frequent charges to those about to be ordained:

The profession of a *Clergyman*, is an holy profession, because it is a ministration in holy things, an attendance at the *Altar*. But worldly business is to be made holy unto the Lord, by being done as a service to him, and in conformity to his divine will. Men of worldly business therefore must not look upon themselves as at liberty to live to themselves, to sacrifice to their own *humours* and *tempers*, because their employment is of a worldly nature. But they must consider, that as the world and all worldly professions as truly belong to God, as *persons* and *things* that are devoted to the *Altar*, so it is as much the duty of men in worldly business to live wholly unto God, as 'tis the duty of those, who are devoted to divine service. As the whole world is God's, so the whole world is to act for God. As all men have the same *relation* to God, as all men have all their *powers* and *faculties* from God, so all men are oblig'd to act for God with all their powers and faculties. As all things are God's, so all things are to be used and regarded as the things of God.

William Law 1686–1761, *A Serious Call to a Devout and Holy Life* (1729)

George Frederick Bodley 1827–1907

Restorer of Kinnersley church

One of the greatest architects of the Victorian and Edwardian era had his home in our midst. Studying first under George Gilbert Scott, Bodley went on to be a pupil of G E Street and William White – leaders of a more *avant garde* style of gothic revival architecture. Influenced by the Tractarian movement and the writings of John Ruskin, Bodley completed his first church at Llangrove in Herefordshire (1854–6) and went on to design many other churches. In 1872 he married Minna Frances Reavely, a daughter of Thomas Reavely of Kinnersley Castle, and Herefordshire became an important part of his life. Other important churches followed – the great Holy Angels, Hoar Cross, in Staffordshire and churches for the aristocracy, including the chapel at Clumber Park in Nottinghamshire and the magnificent parish church at Eccleston in Cheshire for the first duke of Westminster. Unlike some contemporary architects who favoured the individuality of craftsmen alongside their own designs, Bodley wished every element of the design, including furnishings, to be part of the architect's vision. Perhaps the greatest disappointment in his life was his failure in 1879 to win the competition to design the new Truro Cathedral, but in 1906 he was asked to design a new cathedral for the American Episcopal Church at Washington, DC, and parts of this were completed to his design. Bodley was closely involved with many English cathedrals – he became assessor, with Norman Shaw, in the second competition for Liverpool's Anglican cathedral, and was architect at York Minster, and Peterborough, Exeter and Manchester Cathedrals. He was responsible for numerous church restorations, including that of his own home church, St James, Kinnersley – the design of his stencilling in the chancel is seen on this page. Bodley died on this day in 1907 and was buried in Kinnersley churchyard.

Bodley's pupils included several eminent names closely involved in church architecture and in the Arts and Crafts movement, including C R Ashbee, F C Eden, Sir Walter Tapper and Sir Ninian Comper. The latter's philosophical writings on church architecture speak eloquently of the place of the church building in Christian worship:

A church built with hands, as we are reminded at every Consecration and Dedication Feast, is the outward expression of that spiritual Church built of living stones, the Bride of Christ, *Urbs beata* Jerusalem, which stretches back to the foundation of the world and onwards to all eternity. With her Lord she lays claim to the whole of His Creation and to every philosophy and creed and work of man which His Holy Spirit has inspired. And so the temple here on earth, in different lands and in different shapes, in the East and in the West, has developed or added to itself fresh forms of beauty and, though it has suffered from iconoclasts and destroyers both within and without, and perhaps nowhere more than in this land, it has never broken with the past: it has never renounced its claim to continuity.

To enter therefore a Christian church is to enter none other than the House of God and the Gate of Heaven. It is to leave all strife, all disputes of the manner of Church government and doctrine outside – 'Thou shalt keep them secretly in Thy tabernacle from the strife of tongues' – and to enter here on earth into the Unity of the Church Triumphant in Heaven. It cannot be otherwise, since He himself, who is the Temple of it, the Lamb slain from the foundation of the world, is there also. Such a conception of a church, however faintly realized, must put to shame the quarrels of Catholic Christians, who profess the same creeds but set up Church against Church.

Ninian Comper 1864–1960, *Of the Atmosphere of a Church* (1936)

William Seward 1702–40

First Methodist martyr

Born at Badsey in Worcestershire, William Seward worked at the Treasury in London and succeeded his father as steward to Lord Windsor. Among the first converts of the evangelical revival, Seward came under the influence of Charles Wesley in 1738 and the following spring he became the travelling companion of the great preacher, George Whitefield. In just two years, 1738–40, Seward travelled throughout South Wales and the border country and went further afield, joining Whitefield on his visit to the American colonies. There, he provided money to finance ventures such as a school for slave children in Pennsylvania. In 1740 he accompanied Howel Harris, the great Methodist preacher, on a tour of South Wales. They were mobbed by a hostile crowd at Newport and similarly treated at Caerleon, where Seward received severe injuries. Worse was to come – on 15 October Seward reached Hay, where an angry crowd, supported by local clergy and magistrates, quickly gathered. There, while preaching, he was stoned by the mob and, it is said, fell praying for his assailants. He died on this day in 1740 and is buried in the churchyard of St Mary, Cusop. The plaque in the church quotes words of St Paul – 'for me to live is Christ and to die is gain'.

One of the most important prayers of Methodism is the Covenant Prayer, recited in most Methodist churches on the first or second Sunday of the New Year. Used in worship by Wesley as early as 1755, it appears in his Directions for Renewing our Covenant with God *(1780). Although probably unknown to William Seward, the prayer's powerful words with their emphasis on doing Christ's will, even if it leads to suffering, were clearly understood – and made a reality by Seward as he faced the angry mob:*

I am no longer my own, but thine.
Put me to what thou wilt, rank me with whom thou wilt.
Put me to doing, put me to suffering.
Let me be employed for thee or laid aside for thee,
exalted for thee, or brought low for thee.
Let me be full, let me be empty.
Let me have all things, let me have nothing.
I freely and heartily yield all things to thy pleasure and disposal.
And now, O glorious and blessed God, Father, Son and Holy Spirit,
thou art mine, and I am thine.
So be it.
And the covenant which I have made on earth,
let it be ratified in heaven.

Book of Offices of the British Methodist Church (1936)

KING STEPHEN 1104–54

Occupier of a royal seat at Hereford?

IN THE SANCTUARY of Hereford is an ancient wooden seat composed of 57 separate pieces, with traces of the original vermilion and gold still recognisable. Tradition has it that King Stephen sat in this seat when he attended mass in Hereford Cathedral on Whitsunday 1138. It is unlikely that there is a great deal of truth in this assertion, although the seat is undoubtedly from a very early period and King Stephen clearly had close links with the Marches (see 16 April and 23 May). The son of William I's daughter, Adela and the Count of Blois, Stephen, despite his weak claim to the throne, was chosen king by the people of London and was immediately crowned.

His claim to the throne was challenged by his cousin, the Empress Matilda (daughter of Henry I), and the whole country became embroiled in civil war. Hereford became involved – the city was seized first for Matilda but a few weeks after the siege, the castle was captured by Stephen who celebrated his victory by attending the cathedral. His triumph was short-lived – the next year Milo, constable of Gloucester, deserted Stephen, attacked Hereford and took possession of the cathedral. The clergy were expelled, the cathedral nave used as stables and the tower converted into a launching site for missiles against the castle. A trench with a rampart was cut across the burial ground, now the Close. Stephen failed to relieve Hereford though he advanced as far as Leominster. In 1141 he was taken prisoner and Matilda, temporarily queen, rewarded Milo with the earldom of Hereford. The pendulum swung again and Matilda was herself besieged in Oxford Castle. Eventually, by the treaty of Wallingford, Matilda's son, the future Henry II, was acknowledged as heir apparent to the throne.

Although King Stephen may never have sat in the ancient seat bearing his name, it certainly has a revered place in the life of Hereford Cathedral. It has been used on royal visits and is sat upon by the bishop during ordination services. Seats and thrones have a solemn significance in church and state. Perhaps this solemnity needs to be balanced by a little tongue-in-cheek humour – would that the co-operation suggested here had been practised by Stephen and Matilda!

Said the table to the chair,
'You can hardly be aware
How I suffer from the heat
And from chilblains on my feet!
If we took a little walk
We might have a little talk.
Pray, let us take the air,'
Said the table to the chair.

Said the chair unto the table,
'Now you know we are not able:
How foolishly you talk
When you know we cannot walk!'
Said the table with a sigh,
'It can do no harm to try.
I've as many legs as you:
Why can't we walk on two?'

So they both went slowly down,
And walked about the town,
With a cheerful bumpy sound
As they toddled round and round.
And everybody cried
As they hastened to their side,
'See! the table and the chair
Have come out to take the air!'

But, in going down an alley,
To a castle in a valley,
They completely lost their way,
And wandered all the day
'Till, to see them safely back,
They paid a ducky-quack,
And a beetle and a mouse,
Who took them to their house.

Edward Lear 1812–88, 'The Table and the Chair'

24 October

United Nations Day

Saints & Sinners of Hereford's Mappa Mundi

The day on which we remember the unity of our world and its peoples seems a good day to focus on Hereford's own image of the world and what it tells us about the infinite variety of humanity – and indeed of its own collection of saints and sinners. *Mappa Mundi* is not a geographical map but more a theological and philosophical compendium to teach and amaze. *Mappa Mundi* certainly has its saints – the Blessed Virgin Mary appears at the top of the map, bare-breasted, beseeching her son, the judge, for mercy for his people. Elsewhere is seen the legend of St Brendan, an Irish monk of the 6th century and, in another place, Zosimas, a 5th-century monk. Then there are characters from the Old Testament – Adam and Eve in the act of eating the forbidden fruit, Abraham, Mr and Mrs Noah, Lot's wife and Moses. There are classical figures – Alexander the Great, Hercules and the Emperor Augustus, enthroned and wearing a papal tiara, delivering a mandate for the survey of the world. There are legendary human races – the Psylii, the Troglodytes, the Blemyes, the Sciapods; and strange creatures reported by returning travellers. And there is the author – we are bidden on the map to 'pray to Jesus in His divinity to have mercy on the soul of Richard of Haldingham and Lafford, and grant him happiness in heaven' – although recent research has challenged this authorship and sees the map as having greater links with Richard Swinfield's campaign for the canonisation of Thomas Cantilupe (see 2 October). *Mappa Mundi* reminds us of the inextricable link between heaven and earth, between saint and sinner, and encompasses all the bewildering variety of human and animal life, under the kingship of Christ who sits enthroned above all.

At the centre of Mappa Mundi *is Jerusalem, focus of unity for the whole earth, to which so many religions look for their origin and inspiration. Jerusalem is often used in a metaphorical, rather than literal sense, as a perfect state to which all should aspire and which encompasses all – saints and sinners.*

Is this not plain and manifest to the thought? Can you think at all and not pronounce heartily: That to labour in knowledge is to build up Jerusalem: and to despise knowledge is to despise Jerusalem and her builders. And remember: He who despises and mocks a mental gift in another; calling it pride and selfishness and sin: mocks Jesus the giver of every mental gift, which always appear to the ignorance-loving hypocrite as sins, but that which is a sin in the sight of cruel Man, is not so in the sight of our kind God. Let every Christian as much as in him lies engage himself openly and publicly before all the world in some mental pursuit for the building up of Jerusalem.

William Blake 1757–1827, *Jerusalem* (1804)

The Jerusalem referred to in the following passage is Jerusalem Chamber at Westminster Abbey:

King Henry:	Doth any name particular belong Unto the lodging where I first did swoon?
Warwick:	'Tis called Jerusalem, my noble lord.
King Henry:	Laud be to God! Even there my life must end. It hath been prophesied to me many years, I should not die but in Jerusalem; Which vainly I suppos'd the Holy Land But bear me to that chamber; there I'll lie; In that Jerusalem shall Harry die.

William Shakespeare 1564–1616, *Henry IV, part 2*, Act IV, Scene 5

Translation of Thomas of Hereford

Celebration of the physical presence of saints

THE THIRD and final annual celebration of Hereford's saint (see 25 August and 2 October). Following the proclamation of Thomas Cantilupe as a saint in 1320, work on a new shrine was begun in the Lady Chapel, richly endowed with gifts of gold and marble, but it was not until 1349, on this day, that the relics of the saint were moved to their new resting place. In fact, even after canonization St Thomas never regained the popularity among pilgrims that he had enjoyed in the late 13th century, and after the dramatic death of Edward II in 1327, many pilgrims were diverted to Gloucester. It may be that the arrival of the Black Death in 1348/9 gave impetus to new honour for the saint and the hope that his intercession would help to halt the dreadful pestilence. In any case, the splendid ceremony of translation took place in the presence of Edward III, and the offerings of pilgrims, although much reduced, continued to provide funding for the embellishment of parts of the cathedral. Previous bishops were 're-housed' in tombs in each choir aisle, no doubt to exalt the office of bishop and to proclaim to pilgrims and visitors, on their way to the Lady Chapel shrine, that at least one of the company of bishops had achieved sainthood! At the Reformation, the Lady Chapel shrine was destroyed but the relics found their way into the hands of devout Catholics, in whose homes they became the focus for veneration. In the early 17th century, a local priest, William Ely, became their custodian, and, through his influence, in 1610 they were even carried in a private procession by night to ask the saint's intercession in averting the plague which threatened the city. The subsequent history of the relics is fascinating and complex – the skull found its way to the abbey of Lambspring in Germany, where it was discovered in 1881 and brought back to England; it now rests at Downside Abbey. The tibia, or right shin bone, is now at Holywell in North Wales, in a reliquary made by the great Victorian craftsman, Hardman of Birmingham. Other smaller relics are at Belmont Abbey and in the reliquary within the saint's restored shrine in the north transept of Hereford Cathedral.

The Anglican Church has always had an ambivalent attitude towards the relics of saints and has found them difficult to accommodate within its theology and worship. Yet, even Thomas Traherne, often fiercely opposed to Roman Catholicism, could write thus about the importance of the remains of the saints:

In a qualified sense, the very bodies of saints are held sacred by us and used venerably of us, being gathered to their fathers and honourably disposed of into quiet graves.
For they were once temples of the living God
The storehouses of his holy word
The earthen vessels of heavenly treasures
The living conduit-pipes of the Holy Ghost
The members of our Saviour's body
The relics of celestial kings
The seeds of eternity
Whom nature teacheth us to handle with respect.
As we see in the very heathen, who scarce knew the immortality of the soul yet thought it very dreadful not to cover the members of the dead, and with sacred reverence deposited their ashes in honourable urns.

Thomas Traherne *c.*1636–74, *Church's Year Book*

Edfrith 7th century

Celtic founder of Leominster

In about the year 660, the Northumbrian monk Edfrith, influenced by Iona and the tradition of St Columba, journeyed to Mercia having received a heavenly vision to convert the king of the Mercians, Merewahl (see 2 January). On arrival, he prayed and, so the legend goes, a huge lion with bristling mane appeared. Unperturbed, Edfrith offered the lion bread, which it ate at his feet, like a lamb. Edfrith was invited into Merewahl's presence to interpret a dream which troubled the king and which no one could explain. Edfrith successfully interpreted the dream and Merewahl was converted and baptized. On the site where Edfrith had received his vision, a church was built, dedicated to St Peter, and the king richly endowed it. Although the 'leo' of Leominster may refer to the Old English word for a low-lying, watered district, the lion described in the Edfrith legend found its way into the ancient tradition of the town and priory. A later description of Edfrith's life, possibly written for Bishop Adam de Orleton (bishop 1317–27; see 18 July), expands the legends surrounding him, and in the 1290s Leominster's great autumn fair, which attracted people from as far afield as central Wales, was held on the vigil and feast of St Edfrith, 26 October. The saint's cult survived the Dissolution and Reformation, and another *Life* of the saint, in the vernacular, was published in 1605. However, unlike earlier stories, this was designed not to attract pilgrims, but to foster civic pride by stressing the antiquity of the borough to which Queen Mary had granted a charter in 1554.

Leominster's tradition of the lion reminds me of this wonderful image of resurrection, as Aslan breathes life into the stone lion:

I expect you've seen someone put a lighted match to a bit of newspaper which is propped up in a grate against an unlit fire. And for a second nothing seems to have happened; and then you notice a tiny streak of flame creeping along the edge of the newspaper. It was like that now. For a second after Aslan had breathed upon him the stone lion looked just the same. Then a tiny streak of gold began to run along his white marble back – then it spread – then the colour seemed to lick all over him as the flame licks all over a bit of paper – then, while his hindquarters were still obviously stone, the lion shook his mane and all the heavy, stone folds rippled into living hair. Then he opened a great red mouth, warm and living and gave a prodigious yawn. And now his hind legs had come to life. He lifted one of them and scratched himself. Then, having caught sight of Aslan, he went bounding after him and frisked around him, whimpering with delight and jumping up to lick his face.

C S Lewis 1898–1963, *The Lion, the Witch and the Wardrobe*

A similar theme of exultation in the Resurrection of Christ is found in this prayer

Going down to death, O Life immortal, thou hast slain hell with the dazzling light of thy divinity. And when thou hadst raised up the dead from their dwelling place beneath the earth, all the powers of heaven cried aloud: 'Giver of Life, O Christ our God, glory to thee.'

Hymn for Holy Saturday, Orthodox tradition

Robert Burnell d.1292

Son of Shropshire in Bath & Wells

At the same time as Thomas Cantilupe was ministering as Hereford's most famous bishop, the diocese of Bath and Wells was being served by one of the greatest churchmen and politicians of his day. Like Cantilupe, Robert Burnell became chancellor to Edward I. He came from a family which had given its name to Acton Burnell in Shropshire. Robert was hugely wealthy with lands throughout the Marches and with his wealth he extended his estates, building the castle at Acton Burnell, the ruins of which still survive. As chancellor he was much involved in the making of new laws, overseeing the overhaul of the legal system and the enforcement of royal writs. Under his direction the Statutes of Westminster (1275–90) developed royal prerogative in the realm – indeed, many have seen him as the most influential politician of the 13th century. As bishop of Bath and Wells, to which he was appointed in 1275, he oversaw major developments in the cathedral fabric and built the chapel in the bishop's palace. He went on numerous foreign and diplomatic missions to Scotland, Wales and France and was, for a time, governor of Gascony. Several times the king nominated him as archbishop of Canterbury but his personal life appears to have counted against him – he is said to have kept a mistress who bore him four sons, although Burnell always denied this. He died on 25 October 1292 – his body was buried in Wells Cathedral and his heart in Bath.

One could not think of two more different bishops of Bath and Wells than Robert Burnell and Thomas Ken (bishop 1684–89) – the former worldly and easily accommodating his life and career to the politics of the time, while the latter was deprived of his bishopric precisely because he was unable to hold to the political settlements of the day. Thomas Ken's hymn Awake my soul *is well known, but the verses we sing are part of a much longer hymn, some of whose verses are rarely sung:*

Had I your wings to heaven I'd fly,
But God shall that defect supply;
And my soul wing'd with warm desire,
Shall all day long to heaven aspire.

Heav'n is, dear Lord, where e'er thou art,
O never then from me depart:
For to my soul, 'tis hell to be
But for one moment void of thee.

Lord, I my vows to thee renew;
Disperse my sins as morning dew:
Guard my first springs of thought and will,
And with thyself my spirit fill.

Praise God from whom all blessings flow,
Praise him all creatures here below,
Praise him above ye heavenly host,
Praise Father, Son and Holy Ghost.

Thomas Ken 1637–1711, from *Exposition of the Church's Catechism* (1685)

Thomas Taylor Lewis 1801–58

Expert on fossils

A wonderful example of a clergyman who had time and leisure to pursue his interests and scientific enthusiasms! Thomas Taylor Lewis became curate of Aymestrey in 1826, then of Leinthall Earls in 1832, moving to Bridstow, near Ross-on-Wye, as vicar in 1841. While at Aymestrey he developed his reputation as a geologist, forming a large collection of fossils from the area. His contemporaries hailed him as conferring upon Aymestrey what Gilbert White had done for Selborne. He spent all his leisure hours on geology, researching the rocks and fossils of the Ludlow anticline. He did not publish any of his findings but his memory is preserved in the names of local fossils, such as the *Lingula lewisii*, *Spirorbis lewisii* and *Cephalaspis lewisii.* He also edited the letters of Lady Brilliana Harley (see 29 October) in 1854 for the Camden Society. Lewis died, aged 58 on this day in 1858, at the vicarage in Bridstow.

One of the great preachers of the 20th century speaks of the grave lessons which ammonite fossils can teach us:

Consider the ammonites ... they are the fossils of a shellfish of a kind that was very common indeed in all the seas of the world between 70 and 170 million years ago. And this shellfish had a peculiar habit which explains the spiral shape of its shell. So anxious was it to be right up to date and in the forefront that every year it built on to the front of its shell a new room or compartment. And when the new room was ready it moved its whole body into it, and then built behind it a wall of mother-of-pearl, thus completely shutting itself off from the room it had left behind. The ridges made by these annual partitions can be clearly seen in the fossils, and by counting them you can calculate the age of the creature ... but they are one of nature's washouts. In the struggle for existence they have failed to survive – and for this reason: that wherever they went they had to lug around on their backs shells or houses of empty, useless rooms, houses sometimes of dozens of empty, useless rooms. Wherever they went they were burdened with a cumbrous shell of which they made no use – and indeed could make no use. When danger threatened they could not get back inside into the safe depths and recesses of their shells. The way back was blocked, blocked by wall after wall of mother-of-pearl, walls which they themselves had made. Putting it another way: they crawled about with their past on their backs but they made no use of it. They lived only *in* the present, and *for* the future. But in fact they had no future, *because they had cut themselves off from their past* ... Forget not. Forget not the past. History is not bunk. You cannot cut yourself off from it without impoverishing and weakening yourself – and risking extinction. ...

It will not do to have done with remembering. We have our history and we cannot escape from it. We are what we are because of it; and to try to forget it, not to be aware of it, not to make use of it, not to celebrate it – this is to court extinction too ... what everyone does not recognize is that we must also keep in touch with the past, with our origins – and that if we don't we shall not have any future to look to. That is why Christians still make a point of reading the old Scriptures. That is why Jesus made a point of telling his followers to do certain things with bread and wine – and to go on doing them 'in remembrance of me', as he put it.

So now thank we all our God ... and be warned by the example of those ammonites of what happens if you think only of the present and the future and wall yourself off from the past – you become extinct, just a fossil.

'Consider the ammonites' , a sermon by the Very Reverend Michael Stancliffe, dean of Winchester, 1969–86, in *Jacob's Ladder* (1986)

Brilliana, Lady Harley bapt.1598 d.1643

Woman of courage in the Civil War

Brilliana Harley's courageous stance in holding Brampton Bryan Castle against the Royalists in the English Civil War must be one of the most endearing and well-known episodes in 17th-century Herefordshire history. Brilliana was the third wife of Sir Robert Harley and, while little is known of her life before her marriage, the survival of about 375 letters, written mainly to her husband from 1623 and to her eldest son, Edward, from 1638 provides a rich illustration of her married life. Her letters show her to have been a literate woman, able to write in French, and give us glimpses of life in the county. While her husband attended Parliament, Lady Harley kept him informed about his family and estates as well as local political affairs. She also used her letters to pass on her own Puritan beliefs to her children and in some of them she showed her disapproval of innovations in ceremonial then being encouraged by Archbishop Laud (see 10 January). From the outbreak of the Civil War in 1642, Herefordshire remained largely under Royalist control and Lady Harley had to protect her family and dependants. In March 1643 she received a demand from the sheriff to surrender Brampton Bryan Castle to the Royalists and she refused – an action which led to the siege of the castle, begun under the command of Sir William Vavasour in July 1643. Throughout the siege, Brilliana conducted a series of negotiations by letter, and she also gave refuge at Brampton to local Parliamentarians, taking over 50 soldiers into the house for her own defence. Eventually, the siege was withdrawn, but Brilliana, although advised to leave the castle by her absent husband, took decisive action to prevent a renewal of the siege. She ordered her troops to level the earthworks raised by the Royalists and sent them on forays to attack a Royalist camp at Knighton, four miles away. In one of her last letters, in October 1643, Lady Harley described her resistance as an earnest desire to defend Harley property and to preserve religious freedom in Herefordshire. She died at Brampton Bryan on this day in 1643.

Women of courage, like Brilliana Harley, have made huge differences to society in every generation. In this passage, a 19th-century champion of freedom speaks of the role of women in changing the attitudes of society:

I will say then to the women here one word. Dear women, I recall a scene: you will understand me. The night of the memorable debate in April, lasting many hours, there were meetings of women not far from the House of Commons, where I was in the Ladies' Gallery, and joined those meetings for a few minutes. It was a sight I shall never forget. At one meeting there were the poorest, most ragged and miserable women from the slums of Westminster on their knees before the God of Hosts with tears and groans pouring out the burden of their sad heart. There were women who had lost daughters; there were sad-hearted women; and side by side with these poor souls, dear to God as we are, there were ladies of high rank, in their splendid dresses – Christian women of the upper classes kneeling and also weeping. I thank God for this wonderful solidarity of the women of the world before God. Women are called to be a great power in the future, and by this terrible blow which fell upon us forcing us to leave our privacy and bind ourselves together with our less fortunate sisters, we have passed through an education – a noble education. God has prepared in us, in the women of the world, a force for all future causes which are great and just.

We shall not stop, our efforts will not cease when this particular struggle is at an end. God has called us out, and we must not go back from any warfare to which he will call us in the future.

Joseph Williamson, *Josephine Butler – The Forgotten Saint* (1977)

William Wolfe Capes 1834–1914

Walker, canon & classical scholar

It's amazing the number of clergy who appear to enjoy walking! The character we remember today started regular walking when a boy, making the journey on foot daily from his home in Norwood to school in the city of London. William Capes went on to much greater challenges, once walking from the Netherlands to Rome. At Oxford, he became a fellow of The Queen's College, and began a career in teaching classics for the newly-instituted examinations in the subject. Capes was ordained in 1865 and served in the diocese of Winchester, first at Abbot's Ann and then as rector of Bramshott, a living he held for 32 years. Here he was heavily involved in pastoral work, sometimes having as many as 14 meetings or services on a single Sunday! As well as his parish ministry, he continued his teaching career at Oxford, published editions of Livy and Sallust and wrote several influential books, including *The Early Roman Empire* (1874) and *The Age of the Antonines* (1877).

In 1904 Capes became a canon residentiary at Hereford Cathedral and turned his attention to historical research – in 1908 he published *The Charters and Records of Hereford Cathedral* which, in its long introduction, contained a valuable account of the constitution of the cathedral. Under his leadership, the Cantilupe Society was formed, and this succeeded in a few years in printing all the pre-Reformation registers of the bishops of Hereford. Capes was also a generous benefactor to Hereford Cathedral School, enabling the purchase of several properties. Towards the end of his life, he began arranging and cataloguing the cathedral library, a work unfinished at his death, on this day in 1914. He and his wife were both buried at Bramshott.

William Capes was able to combine his Christian faith and ministry with a teaching career in classics at Oxford. Perhaps he also found resonances between Christianity and classical thought. Many early Christian writers like Justin (c.165) felt it their duty to explain Christianity in a way which was compatible with contemporary classical philosophy. Plato, especially, was seen as a 'Christian before Christ' and in this passage we see reflections of the Epistle to the Hebrews, *with its ideas of the earthly as a pale reflection or copy of the heavenly reality:*

Socrates is saying that the wise man will pay much more attention to his soul than to his body. Glauco assents, and Socrates continues:

'Again as to honours he will keep to the same point of view. With some he will gladly take his share and have a taste, of those, that is, which he thinks will make him better; but others which he thinks will demoralize him, he will avoid both in his private and in his civic life.'

'If that is what he is to care about, he will be unwilling to take a part in politics,' he said.

'No, no,' I said, 'he will be very willing indeed in his own city, but not perhaps in the place he is sprung from, unless by some remarkable piece of good fortune.'

'I understand,' he said. 'You mean he will go in for politics in the city which we have been engaged in founding, one that is situated in the realms of thought, or at least, I think, nowhere on earth.'

'Perhaps,' I said, 'there is a pattern of it laid up in heaven for anyone with eyes to see it, and seeing it to shape the constitution within him on the same lines. But it makes no difference whether it actually exists anywhere or ever will. He would take part in the politics of this city only and of no other.'

Plato (*c.*429–347 BC), *Republic* (388 BC)

HALLOWE'EN 1837–1915

Saints & Sinners on the eve of their great day

On 31 October 2010, the people of Hereford were treated to an extraordinary sight – a procession of some 400 people walking down Broad Street between All Saints church and the cathedral, led by a jazz band playing *When the saints go marching in*. Some in the procession were dressed as local saints – all of them in this book. The whole occasion was designed to make the point that Hallowe'en, associated in the minds of most these days with witches and ghouls, is in fact much more about the saints and their battle with the forces of evil which are said to be out in force on this night. Hallowe'en does, all the same, remind us of the intangible world of the spirit, and the folk tradition of Herefordshire is rich in such associations. Certain villages were feared for their witches. 'There'll always be nine witches from the bottom of Orcop to the end of Garway Hill as long as water runs' was the firm belief in this remote area of the county. Some characters are best known for their ghostly form. A Saxon nobleman called Edric, who owned land in Shropshire and five manors in Herefordshire, fiercely resisted the Norman invasion in alliance with the Welsh kings, Bleddyn and Rhiwallon. Only in 1070 did he make peace with William the Conqueror. Ever since then 'Wild Edric' and a ghostly army of horsemen are said to pass in procession across the sky whenever catastrophe threatens. A more recent ghostly appearance concerns the composer E J 'Jack' Moeran, who lived in Kington for a number of years and often stayed at the rectory with his brother (incumbent 1945–50). Jack died in Ireland on 1 December 1950. At that very time, it is said, a woman who knew Jack and his family very well was convinced she saw him in Ledbury High Street, instantly recognising him by his familiar and unique gestures. Minutes later she was told that, at this very time, his dead body was being brought ashore from the waters of the Kenmare river into which he had fallen after a fatal heart attack. A coincidence? Or should we be agnostic about the spirit world, for in the end, surely we do not *know* ...

The Bible is very aware of the existence of spirits and ghosts and of the dangers of meddling in the world of the occult. In this passage, King Saul has gone to consult the witch-medium of Endor about his future, hoping to discover this from the dead prophet, Samuel:

Then the woman said, 'Whom shall I bring up for you?' He said 'Bring up Samuel for me.' When the woman saw Samuel she cried out with a loud voice; and the woman said to Saul, 'Why have you deceived me? You are Saul.' The king said to her, 'Have no fear; what do you see?' And the woman said to Saul, 'I see a god coming up out of the earth.' He said to her, 'What is his appearance?' and she said, 'an old man is coming up; and he is wrapped in a robe.' And Saul knew that it was Samuel, and he bowed with his face to the ground, and did obeisance. Then Samuel said to Saul, 'Why have you disturbed me by bringing me up?'

1 Samuel 28:11–15

As Hallowe'en gives way to All Saints Day, our thoughts turn from the world of spirits and ghosts to human beings whose saintliness is seen in ordinary, compassionate ways:

We thank you, God, for the saints of all ages, for those who in times of darkness kept the lamp of faith burning, for the great souls who saw visions of larger truths and dared to declare them, for the multitude of quiet gracious souls whose presence purified and sanctified the world; and for those known and loved by us, who have passed from this earthly fellowship into the fuller life with you. Accept this, our thanksgiving, through Jesus Christ, to whom be praise and dominion for ever.

1

November

William Brewster 1665–1715

Hereford physician & benefactor of All Saints chained library

All Saints Day is a feast for remembering the great host of men and women through the centuries who, in lives of kindness and generosity, have encouraged the kingdom of God in their day. The chained library of All Saints, Hereford, now in Hereford Cathedral, is an example of kindness and generosity shown by a 17th-century Hereford doctor, William Brewster. Baptized on 9 November 1665 at Eardisland, Brewster came of a medical family, his father being an apothecary in London for much of his life. William was educated at Hereford Cathedral School and St John's College, Oxford, where he studied anatomy and became a physician, settling in Hereford and living in what is now Widemarsh Street. On his death he left his valuable collection of books to the Bodleian Library, St John's College and All Saints church. From the list of books it is clear that Brewster was a man of considerable learning, conversant with the progress of science in the 17th century – indeed, it may be that his physical disability (he was lame) made for long periods in his study, in what contemporaries described as 'the most elegant house in Hereford'. In the 18th century the following was written by Thomas Withers, MD, physician to York County Hospital. It might well apply to William Brewster:

> The character of a physician ought to be that of a gentleman, which cannot be maintained with dignity but by a man of literature ... If a gentleman engaged in the practice of physic be destitute of that charge of preliminary and ornamental learning, which is requisite ... if he do not speak on any subject of history or philosophy [he] is immediately out of his depth ... which is a real discredit to his profession.

During Brewster's own life, goodness was persecuted and religious intolerance ran rife – saints were made as one denomination killed another. Here in a poem translated from the Welsh, the heroic dying and living of the saints – especially the Catholic martyrs of Wales – is celebrated as a joining with Christ's own sacrifice and resurrection:

They are at one with the light, where peace masses and gathers
In the infinities above my head; and where the sky moves into the night,
Then each one is a spyhole for my darkened eyes, lifting the veil.

Oh, they ran swift and light. How can we weigh them, measure them,
The muster of their troops, looking down into damnation?
Nothing, I know, can scatter those bound by the paying of one price,

The final, silent tariff. World given in exchange for world,
The far frontiers of agony to buy the Spirit's leadership,
The flower paid over for the root, the dying grain to be his cradle.

Their guts wrenched out after the trip to torment on the hurdle,
And before the last gasp when the ladder stood in front of them
For the soul to mount, up to the wide tomorrow of their dear Lord's Golgotha.

Waldo Williams 1904–71, from 'After Silent Centuries', translated by Rowan Williams

Jenny Lind 1820–87

The 'Swedish Nightingale' in Malvern

When the 'Swedish Nightingale' came to London in 1847 she caused a sensation – her performance at Her Majesty's Theatre in Haymarket was the most overwhelming operatic performance the capital had ever experienced, and even Queen Victoria threw down her bouquet from the royal box to land on stage at Jenny Lind's feet. She had been brought up in Sweden and from an early age impressed all with her vocal agility and style. Her tours took her to Paris and Berlin, and great composers like Meyerbeer wrote operatic roles specially for her. Later in her career she turned to singing sacred oratorios and to raising money for worthy causes. Devastated by the death of Mendelssohn in 1847, she waited more than a year before she felt able to sing the soprano part in *Elijah*, which he had written specially for her. Her performance raised £1,000 to fund a Mendelssohn scholarship, the first holder of which was Arthur Sullivan. In 1852 Jenny Lind married Otto Goldschmidt and they settled in Dresden. Her reputation continued and she continued to raise vast sums of money by singing without fee for the benefit of hospitals throughout Great Britain, including £1,872 to help Florence Nightingale's Nursing Fund at the end of the Crimean War. In 1858 the Goldschmidts made their permanent home in England and further honours were showered upon Jenny – she was appointed by the Prince of Wales as the first professor of singing at the newly founded Royal College of Music in 1883. Her final public appearance was at a concert given for the Railway Servants' Benevolent Fund at the Spa Hall, Malvern Hills in 1883. She and her husband spent their last years there at Wynd's Point, where she died of cancer on this day in 1887. Otto Goldschmidt lived until 1907 – they were buried together under a simple stone of Swedish granite in Great Malvern cemetery. Jenny Lind is honoured in Poets' Corner, Westminster Abbey, with a plaque placed under the statue of Handel.

The dulcet tones of the nightingale – that bird of exquisite melody – are here recalled by a 17th-century poet:

The arching boughs unite between
The columns of the temple green;
And underneath the wingèd Quires
Echo about their tunèd fires.
The nightingale does here make choice
To sing the trials of her voice;
Low shrubs she sits in, and adorns
With music high the squatted thorns.
But highest oaks stoop down to hear
And listening elders prick the ear.
The thorn, lest it should hurt her, draws
Within the skin its shrunken claws …
Thus I, easy philosopher,
Among the birds and trees confer,
And little now to make me wants
Or of the fowls, or of the plants …
Already I begin to call
In their most learn'd original;
And where I language want, my signs
The bird upon the bough divines.

Andrew Marvell 1621–78, 'Upon Appleton House'

CLYDOG 6th century

Martyr in the shadow of the Black Mountains

THE LITTLE church at Clodock, looking towards the Black Mountains, is well known for an extraordinary interior with its 17th-century pulpit – at least 'six feet above contradiction' – and its carved box pews, with a range for the 'lesser orders' in the very centre of the nave. Less well-known is the life of the saint after whom church and village are named. Clydog was one of the family of Brychan who ruled in Ewyas (the Hereford and Monmouth area). His legend, first recorded in the *Book of Llan Dâv* about six centuries after his death, relates that a nobleman's daughter fell in love with King Clydog and said she would marry nobody but him. One of Clydog's comrades, who had himself decided to marry her, killed the king while hunting. Clydog's body was placed in a cart and driven to a ford in the river Monnow, but then the yoke broke, the oxen refusing to be driven further, and a church was built on the spot, ever since called Clodock or Merthir Clitauc, where the king was buried. Richard Whytford, the 16th-century historian, described him as 'a kynges son of strayte justice, a lover of peace, and of pure chastity, and of strayte and perfect life, who was cruelly slayne by a false traytor at whose death were shewed many miracles and at his tombe after many more'. He is represented in art wearing a crown and bearing a sword and a lily.

Clydog's life is surrounded in myth and mystery, and yet the goodness of his life shines through. In this poem, translated from the Welsh, the writer speaks of the risen Christ, who, after his own suffering, was raised to new life. The parallels between the suffering and triumphant Christ and martyrs like Clydog are found time and time again:

Under the dark trees, there he stands,
there he stands; shall he not draw my eyes?
I thought I knew a little
how he compels, beyond all things, but now
he stands there in the shadows. It will be
Oh, such a daybreak, such bright morning,
when I shall wake to see him
as he is.
He is called Rose of Sharon, for his skin
is clear, his skin is flushed with blood,
his body lovely and exact; how he compels
beyond ten thousand rivals. There he stands,
my friend, the friend of guilt and helplessness,
to steer my hollow body
over the sea.
The earth is full of masks and fetishes,
what is there here for me? are these like him?
Keep company with him and you will know:
no kin, no likeness to those empty eyes.
He is a stranger to them all, great Jesus.
What is there here for me? I know
what I have longed for. Him to hold
me always.

Ann Griffiths, 1776–1805, 'I Saw him Standing',
translated from the Welsh by Rowan Williams

Sir David Stirling 1915–90

Founder of the Special Air Service Regiment

The name of David Stirling will forever be associated with Hereford – the place where the Special Air Service Regiment has found its home and where many important links with the community have been made over the years. David Stirling was born in Scotland and educated at Ampleforth College, Yorkshire. Courage was in his veins – in his early years he spent time climbing in the Swiss Alps and the Canadian Rockies. At the outbreak of war in September 1939, he joined the Scots Guards Supplementary Reserve. On active service in the Middle East he soon saw the need for new strategies in the desert campaign and the potential for sending well-equipped raiding parties to strike at targets far behind the enemy's front line. In one of his early raids, 90 enemy aircraft were destroyed on the ground in two weeks. Stirling possessed great gifts as a leader, carrying those he led with his confidence. He was promoted to major and then to lieutenant-colonel in 1942. Under his leadership, the value of the SAS and its contribution to military thinking became recognized, and the regiment went on to play an important part in the Mediterranean and later in the European theatres of war. Taken prisoner in January 1943, Stirling escaped from prison in Germany four times and was eventually imprisoned in Colditz. On his return to Britain in May 1945, his first thought was to offer SAS operations in the war against Japan, but before these plans could be put into operation, the war there had finished and by the end of 1945 the SAS had been disbanded. In due course the regiment was reconstituted in the shape of one regular and two territorial regiments. After the war, Stirling's work was focused on Africa – he settled in Southern Rhodesia and in 1947 became president of the newly founded Capricorn Africa Society, set up to help find a solution to Africa's many racial, economic, social and political problems. With the advent of independence for African countries, he returned to Britain again and organised GB75, which could run essential services such as power stations in the event of a general strike. Thus, his courage and determination found their place in peace time campaigns as well as in a distinguished war record. Stirling was appointed OBE in 1946 and was knighted in 1990. He was a large man in all senses – in his personality and in his stature, being 6 feet 6 inches tall. He died on this day in 1990.

The quest for freedom and the imperative for courage were at the heart of Stirling's work and these are among the core values of the regiment today:

The most tremendous thing granted to man is choice, freedom. And if you want to save it and keep it, there is only one way: in the very same second to give it back to God, and yourself with it. If the sight of what is granted to you tempts you, and you give way to the temptation and look with desire of your own on your freedom to choose, you lose your freedom.

Soren Kierkegaard 1815–55

Words often spoken at services attended by the Regiment:

We are the Pilgrims, Master; we shall go
Always a little further: it may be
Beyond the last blue mountain barred with snow,
Across that angry or that glimmering sea.

James Elroy Flecker 1884–1915, from the Epilogue of
The Golden Journey to Samarkand

Sir John Hawkins 1532–95

Shipbuilder, naval commander, merchant, navigator, slave trader

In the entrance hall to Lady Hawkins' School in Kington hangs a portrait of Lady Margaret Hawkins, a lady of Elizabeth I's chamber and second wife of Sir John Hawkins. On her death in 1619 she bequeathed £800 to maintain a school in Kington 'for the teaching of youths and children in literature and good education'. Lady Hawkins' generosity, it seems, was only made possible through the fortune her husband made in slave trading. Born in Plymouth in 1532, John Hawkins became a seafarer at an early age, and in 1562 he sailed with three small vessels to the west coast of Africa where he captured 500 Africans to sell as slaves. In what must have been terrible conditions, this human cargo was then transported to the West Indies, where the slaves worked on the sugar plantations. Hawkins' second journey, two years later, was equally profitable, but this time had royal approval and his ship was able to sail under the royal standard. The voyage brought back more wealth for the Crown but it increasingly antagonised Spain, and his third slaving expedition, in 1568, accompanied by his cousin, Francis Drake, was attacked by the Spanish fleet – only his vessel and that of Drake were able to escape. Hawkins' trade in slaves ended with this third voyage, but for a further 20 years he loyally served the Crown as treasurer and controller of the navy, building up the fleet that defeated the Spanish Armada. He died on 12 November 1595 while on an expedition with Drake hoping to rescue his son, Richard, who was held captive by the Spanish in Lima. Hawkins came to public attention in June 2006, when his descendant, Andrew Hawkins, publicly apologized for the role his ancestor had played in the slave trade.

Money is hardly ever completely without taint, but we have it within our power to use it for good or for ill. Despite the dubious source of Lady Hawkins' fortune, she did, at least, use it for the well-being of others, and her generosity is still being enjoyed by young people today.

John Wesley preached many times about money and its godly use. In this passage we are reminded of Jesus' words on the matter:

I tell you, use worldly wealth to gain friends for yourself, so that when it is gone, you will be welcomed into eternal dwellings.

Luke 16:9

The right use of money is of the utmost importance to the Christian, yet it is a subject given too little attention. Wealth has often been regarded by poets and philosophers as a source of evil and yet the fault lies, not with money, but with those who use it. Indeed, money should be regarded as a gift of God for the benefits that it brings in ordering the affairs of civilization and the opportunities it offers for doing good. In the hands of God's children, money is food for the hungry, clothing for the naked and shelter for the stranger. With money we can care for the widow and the fatherless, defend the oppressed, meet the need of those who are sick or in pain.

It is therefore most urgent that God's people know how to make use of their money for his glory. All the necessary instructions can be condensed into three simple rules:

- Gain all you can
- Save all you can
- Give all you can

John Wesley 1703–91, *Sermon No. 44*

Leonard 6th century

Bridgnorth's hermit landmark

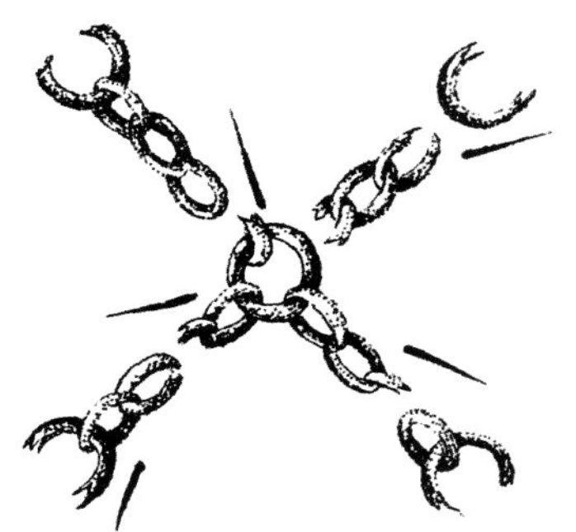

The rocky outcrop which supports the town of Bridgnorth is punctuated by two memorable church towers – that designed by Telford (see 2 September) set on the church of St Mary Magdalene and the Victorian red sandstone tower of St Leonard's, now vested in the Churches Conservation Trust. Leonard's patronage is found in other churches in Shropshire and Herefordshire and in the whole of England there are no fewer than 177 churches dedicated to him. For all this, he is thought to be a rather unhistorical figure. According to an 11th-century *Life,* Leonard was a Frankish noble converted to Christianity by Remigius. He became a monk and retired to a hermitage in the forest of Noblac near Limoges. One day his godfather, Clovis, king of France, was hunting in the forest with his pregnant wife, who was suddenly overtaken with labour pains. They took refuge in Leonard's hermitage, where, thanks to his prayers and assistance, the child was safely delivered. In gratitude, Clovis offered Leonard as much land as he could ride around on a donkey in a single night. With this endowment, Leonard founded the abbey of Noblac, of which he was abbot until his death. He used his influence with the king to secure the release of many well-known prisoners. Because of his service to the queen, he is hailed as patron saint of pregnant women. He is also patron of prisoners, being usually represented as an abbot holding a broken chain or fetters.

Leonard represents different aspects of solitariness. As patron of prisoners he speaks of the loneliness of the prisoner – a loneliness not self-chosen but imposed by others. As a hermit, he speaks of the solitariness which is a vital part of the spiritual life:

One may not be so given to contemplation as to forget the good of one's neighbour, not so given over to action as to forget divine speculation.

Our saviour Jesus lived a life in public, sociable, humane, charitable, free and common. And yet, for opportunity of special devotion, retired to prayer and contemplation. It was in solitude that he kept his fasts. Rocks and mountains heard his prayers. Among beasts was he born, and in the wilderness he fed his thousands. Upon a mountain he prayed, upon a mountain he was transfigured, upon a mountain he died, to a mountain in Galilee he invited his disciples, and from a mountain he ascended. In which retirements his devotions received a great advantage of freedom from distractions. So that solitude is a good school to learn piety and virtue in, and the world the best theatre to practise it.

Thomas Traherne c.1636–74, *The Church's Year Book*, 39

A prayer in loneliness by Dietrich Bonhoeffer

In me is darkness,
But with you there is light;
I am lonely, but you do not leave me;
I am feeble in heart, but with you there is help;
I am restless, but with you there is peace.
In me there is bitterness, but with you there is peace.

John Kyrle 1637–1724

'The Man of Ross'

Those who enjoy the wonderful views of the Wye from the churchyard in Ross-on-Wye may not be aware of the debt the town owes to this great benefactor. Born in Dymock, John Kyrle spent all his life in Ross, living in a three-storeyed timber-framed house adjoining the market place. In politics he was a staunch loyalist and had a monogram cut into the wall of the new market hall which read, 'Love Charles to the Heart'. The only public office he held was that of high sheriff in 1683 and he declined the office of justice of the peace.

Kyrle owes his fame largely to the eulogy of him in Alexander Pope's third 'Moral Epistle', published in 1732, eight years after Kyrle's death. It was Kyrle's great reputation for philanthropy that caught Pope's attention – he provided portions for poor brides, ensured the poor had decent funerals, enabled debtors to re-establish themselves in trade, paid the fees of poor apprentices and provided simple medicines for the sick. Not everybody was as impressed as Pope with Kyrle's good character. One contemporary spoke of him as the 'vainest man living' who 'always hated his relations'. Pope was also attracted to Kyrle because of his delight in horticulture, architecture and urban improvement. Beyond Ross churchyard, on the sandstone cliff above the Wye, Kyrle acquired land from Lord Weymouth which he planted and laid out as an ornamental promenade. The Prospect, as the town end of the walk became known, was enhanced by a fountain and made accessible to the public. His taste for what became known as the Picturesque in landscape, helped establish Ross as a centre of the Wye Tour in the late 18th century. He supervised the replacement of the top of the spire of Ross church, and the vicarages at Foy and Much Marcle were rebuilt under his direction. Kyrle died on this day in 1724, at the age of 88. There was an extended period of mourning and he was not buried until 20 November. In his will he asked to be buried in the chancel of Ross church, at the feet of the late rector, Dr Whiting, his friend and the founder of the town's Bluecoat School. His grave was marked with a simple stone inscribed with the initials J.K. Later, in 1776, with the increase of his fame as a result of the Wye Tour, a pyramid in marble was erected with his bust in relief. After a period in private hands, in 1860 the Prospect was given in perpetuity to the inhabitants of Ross-on-Wye. The Kyrle Society was founded in 1877 to promote gardening 'among the industrious classes'.

Pope writes of the virtues of this most-remembered inhabitant of Ross:

Whose Causeway parts the vale with shady rows?
Whose Seats the weary Traveller repose?
Who taught that heav'n-directed spire to rise?
'The Man of Ross,' each lisping babe replies.
Behold the Market-place with poor o'erspread.
The Man of Ross divides the weekly bread.
He feeds yon alms-house, neat, but void of state,
Where Age and Want sit smiling at the gate.
Him portion'd maids, apprentic'd orphans blest.
The young who labour, and the old who rest.
Is any sick? The Man of Ross relieves,
Prescribes, attends, the med'cine makes and gives.
Is there a variance? enter but his door,
Balk'd are the Courts, and contest is no more.
Despairing Quacks with curses fled the place,
And vile Attornies, now an useless race.

Alexander Pope 1688–1744, 'Ode to the Man of Ross'

John Eagles 1783–1855

Art critic & poet

The date when we remember John Eagles is the one on which he was baptized in 1783 and also the one when he died in 1855 – a reminder that life and death are closely linked and that our baptism gives us a glimpse of eternal life. John Eagles glimpsed glory in the world of art – he greatly admired the work of Poussin and Rosa and intended to become a professional landscape painter. Instead, he trained for ordination, and after curacies in his native Bristol, he served in the parish of Kinnersley. Alongside his pastoral work, Eagles contributed to several leading journals of the day, not least *Blackwood's Magazine*, a periodical whose narrow conservatism accorded with his own stance in politics and art. Many of his articles on art were subsequently collected as a book, *The Sketcher*, in 1856.

Eagles also wrote poetry and many of his poems are published in *The Sketcher*. His friend John Gutch made a selection of these and, after Eagles' death, published them as *A Garland of Roses* (1856). The volume contained a poem which had appeared at intervals in the columns of Felix Farley's *Bristol Journal* and which had been written to expose the abuses which had existed for years in several public bodies in Bristol, especially in the Corporation. Eagles also published *The Bristol Riots* (1832), a response to local disturbances over the Reform Bill.

John Eagles sounds a rather serious individual, with his learned discourses and critical publications, yet he clearly had a more humorous side as the opening of one of his poems suggests:

Come all ye jolly dogs, let us take a cup of tea
Gunpowder Hysop, Souchong and Bokea,
Your simple water drinkers will never last it long
Unless to every pint they add an ounce of good Souchong.
[Versatur omnicum Versa], tea urn is it not
Which means that every mortal man alive must go to pot.
But we like true philosophers philosophise aright
Our pot shall always ready be both morning noon and night.
I love a jolly bumper, and when I'm in my cups
I do not care a fig for life with all its downs and ups,
My wit like a *teetotum* spins round the more I drink
'Tis glorious Congo sets my brain to work and makes me think.
Why should we prate of Bacchus, and call him God divine
To me his grapes are sour, and sour grapes make sorry wine
Don't talk to me of Sherry Port or French Fronteriac
Nor barbarous Barbardoes' rum nor Brandy Cogniac.

'A right merry, jolly song proposed to be sung by all true drinkers of tea' (1826)

Joyce Jefferies c.1570–1650

Moneylender & diarist

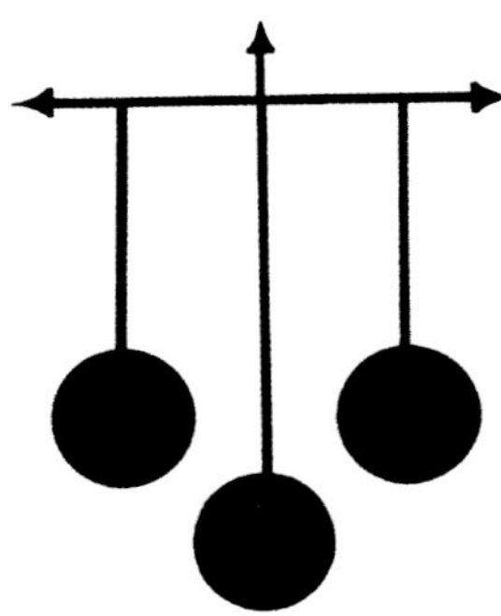

On this day we remember a most enterprising woman of the early 17th century who made her living by lending money and who recorded her transactions with enormous care. Joyce Jefferies was born at Clifton-upon-Teme in Worcestershire, and inherited large sums of money from several relatives. It was this wealth that she used to provide income for the rest of her life. Her financial diary, now in the British Museum, shows that she made loans for as much as £800 – loans made to friends and relatives and sometimes to perfect strangers. By 1634 Joyce was living in Hereford – first in a rented house and then, from 1640, in one she bought on Widemarsh Street, near the city gate. When this house was torn down in efforts to defend the city during the Civil War, she lived in another that she had built herself in 1643–4. Hereford was a dangerous place to live at this time, and Joyce spent much of the period in self-imposed exile, seeking safety with relatives in nearby villages and in Worcestershire.

Joyce's diary reveals interesting aspects of her life – she maintained a household and small staff, had a wide circle of friends and tended to do business with other women. She was highly literate, keeping the diary herself, except when too ill, purchased books and paintings and followed the news of the day closely. Something of her political and religious interests may be inferred from her purchases. She bought two pamphlets on the death of Ben Jonson, which event she lamented in her diary, and a book on the 'untimely death' of Mary, queen of Scots. She also purchased pictures, and when almost 80 years old and in poor health, she paid to have a pair of shoes mended. Joyce died in 1650, between 3 April, when she made a codicil to her will, and this day, when her will was proved. She was buried, at her own request, in her home village of Clifton-upon-Teme. (See also 19 November.)

Joyce Jefferies clearly executed the business of money-lending with care and discretion but it has not always been so and in the Bible usury – the taking of interest on a loan – is certainly seen as a sin:

Lord who shall dwell in thy tabernacle: or who shall rest upon thy holy hill? Even he that leadeth an uncorrupt life: and doeth the thing which is right, and speaketh the truth from his heart. He that hath used no deceit in his tongue, nor done evil to his neighbour: and hath not slandered his neighbour. He that setteth not by himself, but is lowly in his own eyes: and maketh much of them that fear the Lord. He that sweareth unto his neighbour, and disappointeth him not: though it were to his own hindrance. He that hath not given his money upon usury: nor taken reward against the innocent. Whoso doeth these things: shall never fall.

Psalm 15

Another and more famous diarist, writing later than Joyce Jefferies, takes a poor view of being asked to lend money when it shows a lack of judgement and strategy:

So with my wife to Mile End and there drank of Bides ale, and so home. Most of our discourse is about our keeping a coach the next year, which pleases my wife mightily; and if I continue as able as now, it will save us money. This day comes a letter from the Duke of York to the Board to invite us, which is as much to fright us, into lending the King money; which is a poor thing and most dishonourable, and shows in what a case we are at the end of the war to our neighbours. And the King do now declare publickly to give 10 per cent to all lenders; which makes some think that the Dutch themselves will send over money, and lend it upon our publick faith, the Act of Parliament. So home and to my office, wrote a little, and then home to supper and to bed.

Samuel Pepys 1633–1703, *Diary,* 24 August, 1667

Robert Devereux, 2nd Earl of Essex 1565–1601

Poet, favourite of Elizabeth I & traitor

This flamboyant character was born on this day in the year 1565 at Netherwood, near Bromyard. His maternal great-grandmother was Mary Boleyn, sister to Anne Boleyn and thus, Devereux was a cousin to Elizabeth I. He inherited the earldom of Essex at the early age of 11 on the death of his father, and found himself under the care of his stepfather Robert Dudley, earl of Leicester, who introduced him to military service in the Netherlands. In 1590 Essex married Frances Walsingham, becoming well known at Court, and by the 1590s he was known as a favourite of Elizabeth I. The queen seems to have been captivated by his lively mind, eloquence and skills and by his reputation as a showman and an exponent of 'courtly love'. Their relationship was, however, very stormy and at one Privy Council meeting the queen is said to have cuffed Essex for his impertinence, for which indignity Essex is said to have drawn his sword against the queen. In 1589 he took part in Drake's Armada to the Iberian coast and undertook many voyages of exploration and adventure. He fell from grace, however, through his ill-fated time in Ireland – he was appointed Lord Lieutenant and led an expedition of 16,000 to quell a rebellion there. This ended in failure and Essex found himself on trial. He was convicted but eventually pardoned. Pursued by enemies, he gathered his own followers around him and attempted to hold out against the forces of the Crown. He was tried again – this time for treason – was found guilty and beheaded on Tower Green in February 1601.

For all his notoriety, he was much admired by succeeding generations and much represented in art, perhaps the most famous portrait being a miniature by Nicholas Hilliard. His poetry was set to music by the 16th-century composer John Dowland, and succeeding generations have found him an attractive subject in opera (including works by Donizetti and Britten) and on stage and television. In his own day, two treatises on the sport of fencing were dedicated to him.

The tragedy of Robert Devereux – his yearning for love and yet his inability to combine his love with loyalty and discretion – is a story all too familiar in history. His own words in this sonnet are poignant indeed:

To plead my faith where faith had no reward,
To move remorse where favour is not borne,
To heap complaints where she doth not regard, –
Were fruitless, bootless, vain, and yield but scorn.

I lovéd her whom all the world admired,
I was refused of her that can love none;
And my vain hope, which far too high aspired,
Is dead, and buried, and for ever gone.

Forget my name, since you have scorned my love,
And woman-like do not too late lament;
Since for your sake I do all mischief prove,
I none accuse nor nothing do repent.

I was as fond as ever she was fair,
Yet loved I not more than I now despair.

Martin of Tours 4th century

Soldier, monk, bishop

Today is Remembrance or Armistice Day, when thoughts of war, faith and thanksgiving for the departed combine. The person we remember today combined in his life all these different elements. We remember Martin as a soldier in the Roman army and one who realised that his Christian calling prevented him from so continuing – an early example of a 'conscientious objector'. During this part of his life occurred the famous incident when he cut his cloak in half to clothe a nearly naked beggar at Amiens – an episode which was followed by a dream in which Christ appeared to him, wearing the cloak he had given away. Martin became a disciple of Hilary at Poitiers, was baptized and eventually became a monk. Others joined him in his monastery until, in 372, he was acclaimed as bishop of Tours. As bishop, he continued to live as a monk, visited his diocese on foot, by donkey or by boat, and founded numerous monasteries. He was credited with many miraculous acts and after his death in 397 his tomb became a place of pilgrimage. In France, 500 villages and 4,000 parish churches are dedicated to him. In Britain, by the end of the Middle Ages 173 churches bore his name. In view of his great popularity it is surprising that there is now only one dedication to him in Herefordshire – St Martin's church south of the Wye in Hereford city, an appropriate dedication considering that church's links with the SAS regiment. The first mention of this church is *c.*1200, but the medieval church was destroyed during the siege of the city in 1645 and was replaced in 1845 by the present church half a mile to the south. There was also a chapel of St Martin in Hereford Castle, described by Hugh de Lacy in 1154 as 'the chapel which my ancestors founded', but during the reign of Henry II its endowments were transferred to St Guthlac's priory and it is not heard of again. The old church at Marstow (known as *Lann Martin* in 1130 and as *Martinstow* in 1277) was dedicated to Martin, but the new church is dedicated to St Matthew.

11 November brings together many thoughts and memories. Here, two contemporary accounts speak of the burial, on 11 November 1920, of the remains of the Unknown Warrior in Westminster Abbey. This burial spoke of the wish to honour the war dead, but also of the futility of war and of the earnest desire to work for peace – prayers found in the life of Martin and in numerous others after him:

Most impressive of all was the night scene in Whitehall. The vast sweep of the road was almost silent save for the ceaseless murmur of footsteps. Under the brilliant glare of the lamps that were softened by the foggy air the long, dark lines of people stretched from Trafalgar Square to the Cenotaph from whose base they could be seen vanishing in the distance, two narrow lines of slowly moving people separated by a wide pathway on which stood here and there vague figures of policemen on horseback.

Daily Mail 12 November 1920

One policeman spoke of old women who had come from remote country villages to pay homage to the dead. 'One lady came from the far north of Scotland. She carried a bunch of withered flowers, and told me with tears in her eyes that the flowers came from a little garden which her boy had planted when he was only six.'

Daily Telegraph 12 November 1920

Tysilio 7th century

Welsh monastic saint

Tysilio was a brother of Cynon, king of Powys and cousin and successor of St Asaph as abbot of Llanelwy (now St Asaph's). Against his father's will, he became a member of the religious community established by Gwyddfarch at Meifod. Tysilio succeeded Gwyddfarch as abbot of Meifod and under his leadership it became the most important religious centre in Powys. St Beuno (see 21 April) spent 40 days there with Tysilio, after Berriew was overrun by the Saxons. The cluster of church dedications to him in Montgomeryshire and Denbighshire reflects his influence in the area. On Anglesey, there is a chapel of his beautifully situated at Llanfairpwllgwyngyll, while other dedications in Pembrokeshire suggest that, as well as being a saint of Powys, Tysilio also travelled to other parts of Wales. The *Book of Llandaff* records the consecration of the church at *Llansulus*, now Sellack, although since there is no record of his having visited Herefordshire, the reason for the Sellack dedication is obscure.

A Welsh poet, writing many years after Tysilio, speaks of the power of poetry in glimpsing God:

We have no certainty the soul but dreams
When it arises far above this life,
Above man's journey from cradle to the grave,
Whispering of things that words will not reveal
Though we may force them far beyond their limits
Like stars into the vast eternal space.
Has not the soul a story of its own?
A dark ebb strangely murmurs in its depths
On distant shores we cannot reach, on shores
Where Memory was lost in wrecks stupendous
Of some great world or worlds.
Are the stars above
As splendid and divine as poets sing?
Their power sublime on our responding spirit
May it not be the hold of memories dim
Of far diviner scenes, radiant of God?
The stars are in us! And all poetry
Is but the recollection of our past,
Or premonition of what we shall be.
Our imaginings, who can
Prove or disprove that they are fragments strewn
On a deep sea, the wreck of a nobler life,
And that the soul in stupor lies, until
Restored by the ever-seeking, living breath
Of poetry? O blessed hour, when God
Appears, a Sun in Majesty, above
Earth's many days, and the Holy Spirit's path
A ray of light on the world's broken tracks
Lighting the way back to those heights Divine.

William Thomas 1832–78, trans. from the Welsh by D M Lloyd

November

Paul Foley 1645–1699

Speaker of the House of Commons

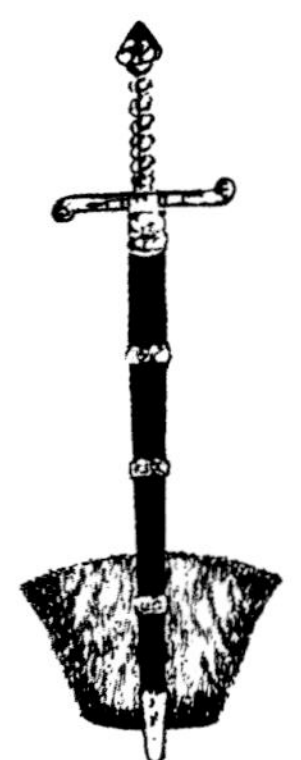

Here is a 'committee man' *par excellence!* At one stage in his parliamentary career he served on 128 committees, and was chairman of seven. Paul Foley had both a local and a national profile. In 1670 he bought the Stoke Edith estate, outside Hereford, from the widow of the Royalist Sir Henry Lingen. This established him in the area as did his purchase of the living of St Peter's, Hereford. By all accounts he was a generous man, purchasing for the Corporation of Hereford a new sword and a cap of maintenance. In national politics he was a staunch Whig, holding extreme Protestant views. He was at the forefront of attempts in the 1670s to exclude from the throne the Catholic duke of York, and he was much involved in speaking out against Catholics at the time of the Popish Plot. In many ways he provided a credible Protestant opposition to the pro-Catholic leanings of many in government at that time, and insisted, 'I shall rather exclude the duke of York from Succession than lose the Protestant religion.' In 1695 the Commons chose Foley as Speaker, a position he held in several parliaments until 1698, when he retired to Hereford, building a new house at Stoke Edith. This remained until the 20th century, when it was burned down. Foley died of gangrene in the foot on this day in 1699 and was buried at Stoke Edith. His will established trustees for tithes gathered from Herefordshire and Gloucestershire lands to dispense to ministers in need and particularly to the vicar of St Peter's, Hereford.

If Paul Foley had chosen bishops with whom to associate he is unlikely to have chosen Thomas Ken, bishop of Bath and Wells, or William Sancroft, archbishop of Canterbury. These were 'non-jurors' who, having made their oath to James II, felt unable to take the oath of allegiance to William and Mary. Many like them were expelled from their livings. Foley would have been more comfortable with Gilbert Burnet, who became a friend of William and Mary and who ardently supported the Glorious Revolution. Burnet became bishop of Salisbury in 1689. His advice on preaching, though written over 300 years ago, bears repeating!

The shorter sermons are, they are generally both better heard, and better remembered. The custom of an hour's length forces many preachers to trifle away much of the time, and to spin out their matter, so as to hold out. So great a length does also flat the hearers, and tempt them to sleep; especially when, as is usual, the first part of the sermon is languid and heavy. In half an hour, a man may lay open his matter in its full extent, and cut off those superfluities which come in only to lengthen the discourse: and he may hope to keep up the attention of his people all the while. As to the style, sermons ought to be very plain; the figures must be easy; not mean, but noble, and brought in upon design to make the matter better understood. The words in a sermon must be simple, and in common use; not savouring of the schools, nor above the understanding of the people. All long periods, such as carry two or three different thoughts in them, must be avoided; for few hearers can follow or apprehend these: niceties of style are lost before a common auditory. It is certain that a sermon, the conclusion whereof makes the auditory look pleased, and sets them all a-talking with one another, was either not right spoken, or not right heard; it has been fine, and has probably delighted the congregation, rather than edified it. But that sermon that makes everyone go away silent and grave, and hastening to be alone, to meditate or pray over the matter of it in secret, has had its true effect.

Gilbert Burnet 1643–1715, *A Discourse of the Pastoral Care* (1692)

Dyfrig or Dubricius 6th century

He brought the faith to Herefordshire

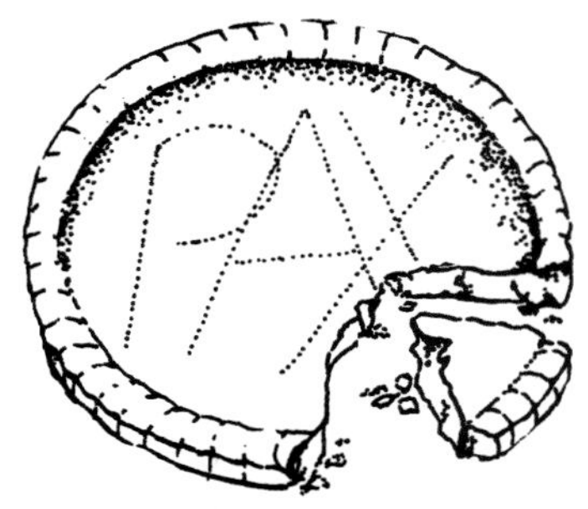

Dyfrig (Latin – Dubricius, French – Devereux) evangelised the kingdom of Archenfield (Ergyng) – the southern part of Herefordshire – in the 6th century. Much of our knowledge of him comes from the much later *Book of Llandaff.* This relates his birth at Madley. According to legend, one day Pepiau, king of Ergyng, noticed that his daughter Ebrdil was pregnant. In anger, he ordered her to be tied in a sack and thrown into the Wye. Each time she was thrown into the river she was miraculously swept back to the bank, so in frustration the king ordered her to be burnt alive on a pyre. This attempt also failed, for the girl would not catch alight. The next day, Ebrdil was found nursing a new-born baby, whom she named Dyfrig or 'water baby'. Pepiau, full of remorse, took the infant in his arms. The child stretched up and touched his grandfather's face, thereby curing him of a condition from which he suffered – a perpetual foaming at the mouth. Little is known of Dyfrig's early life, but he founded a number of churches, monasteries and schools, most famously the colleges at Hentland and Moccas, from which he and his disciples were active in spreading Christianity throughout Archenfield and Gwent. He is said to have been the first bishop of Llandaff and also archbishop of Caerleon, in which office he was succeeded by St David, who moved the see to Menevia (St Davids). Dyfrig spent his last years as a hermit on Bardsey Island and died there in about 546. In 1120, in order to substantiate Llandaff's rather dubious claim that Dyfrig was its first bishop, his remains were translated to the cathedral there. There are five Herefordshire churches dedicated to Dyfrig – Hentland, Ballingham, Whitchurch, St Devereux and Hamnish (a 19th-century foundation). However, others of his churches have had their dedications changed – Llanwarne, originally dedicated to saints Dyfrig and Teilo (see 9 February) and Madley, which is said to have been originally dedicated to Dyfrig's mother Ebrdil, then to Dyfrig himself.

The story of Dubricius speaks of love – a love found between grandfather and grandson after a period of great trauma, and the love of Dubricius for his disciples and the communities he founded. That spirit of love is fostered today in some of the churches dedicated to him. Hentland and Sellack, for instance, continue the ancient custom of distributing Pax Cakes to the congregation on Palm Sunday. These are small biscuits, each with the image of an Easter lamb and the words 'Peace' and 'Good Neighbourhood'. A poem reminding us of the cost of love and generosity:

If love should count you worthy, and should deign
One day, to seek your door and be your guest,
Pause! Ere you draw the bolt and bid him rest,
If in your old content you would remain.
For not alone he enters; in his train
Are angels of the mist, the lonely quest
Dreams of the unfulfilled and unpossessed,
And sorrow and life's immemorial pain.

He wakes desires you never may forget,
He shows you stars you never saw before,
He makes you share with him, for evermore,
The burden of the world's divine regret.
How wise you were to open not! And yet
How poor if you should turn him from the door.

Sidney Royse Lysaght 1860–1941, 'The Penalty of Love'

Thomas Parr d.1635

England's oldest-ever man?

According to his tombstone in the south transept of Westminster Abbey, Thomas Parr died in 1635 aged 152 years – 'he lived under 10 princes: Edward 4, Edward 5, Richard 3, Henry 7, Henry 8, Edward 6, Mary, Elizabeth, James 1, Charles 1'. He was said to be the son of John Parr, of the parish of Alberbury in Shropshire. According to later accounts he remained a bachelor until he was 80, when he married. At the age of 105 he did penance in Alberbury church for adultery and, after the death of his wife and remaining a widower for ten years, he is said to have re-married, at the age of 122. In 1635, blind and with only one tooth, he was taken to London by Thomas Howard, 14th earl of Arundel. The journey was made in easy stages, admiring crowds turning out *en route* to gape at the old man. In London, Parr was put on show. His portrait was painted by Rubens and presented to Charles 1. Six weeks after his arrival in London he died suddenly, on this day in 1635. At the king's command, the royal physician, William Harvey, conducted an autopsy. This uncritically accepted that Parr really had been 152 and that he only died because he was suddenly exposed to the effects of London's atmosphere and to rich food and strong drink after so many years of a simple Shropshire diet!

Parr's legend lived on; portraits of him were widely reproduced and the story of his longevity entered popular folklore. In Alberbury, 'Old Parr's Cottage' remained an object of curiosity until it was burned down in 1959. In 1841 a biography was published as *The Extraordinary Life and Times of Thomas Parr* – its main purpose was to promote an all-purpose herbal medicine called *Parr's Life Pills,* said to be made from a recipe found in Parr's will. As late as 1906, the 73rd edition of this booklet was still advertising *Parr's Life Pills for Health, Strength and Beauty.* Other 19th-century accounts were more sceptical and searches of local records threw doubt on the veracity of the story. In a semi-literate society, the exaggeration of age was a common practice, particularly when it brought people attention and respect.

Many insisted that Parr had only died because he was encouraged to question his station in life – moving from the simplicity of Shropshire to the fleshpots of the metropolis! But whatever the truth of the story of Old Parr, perhaps it is a lesson that sometimes it is important to trust the spirit rather than the letter and that, when it comes to old age, we do well to appreciate and celebrate the benefits of experience!

When you are old and grey and full of sleep,
And nodding by the fire, take down this book,
And slowly read, and dream of the soft look
Your eyes had once, and of their shadows deep;

How many loved your moments of glad grace,
And loved your beauty with love false or true,
But one man loved the pilgrim soul in you,
And loved the sorrows of your changing face.

And bending down beside the glowing bars,
Murmur, a little sadly, how Love fled
And paced upon the mountains overhead
And hid his face amid a crowd of stars.

W B Yeats 1865–1939, 'When you are old'

Thomas Chaundler c.1417–90

Humanist scholar

A book in the library of Trinity College, Cambridge, shows Thomas Chaundler kneeling before his patron, Bishop Beckington of Wells, and presenting the bishop with a copy of his own book. One of the leading scholars of his day, Chaundler was educated at Winchester and at New College, Oxford, becoming a protégé of William Waynflete, bishop of Winchester. He became the dominant academic influence at Oxford from about 1457 to 1479, years in which he encouraged the growth of humanist teaching and learning. His *Liber Apologeticus* is reckoned to be the earliest academic drama in England and seems to be a morality play, adapted for performance by students in a college hall, while his *Collocutiones* is a compendium of teaching ideas and methods of the mid-15th century. Many of his works are illustrated, possibly by Chaundler himself. He held many important posts in church and university and was canon chancellor of Wells and of York and chancellor of Oxford University, finally, in 1482, becoming dean of Hereford. In his time at Oxford, Chaundler is thought to have had considerable influence in the building and furnishing of Duke Humphrey's library. This library had standing lecterns and it is possible that, as a result, he introduced such lecterns into the library at Hereford, in the upper room of the old west cloister. From there they may have been removed to the Lady Chapel, to be replaced by the present cases in 1611. Chaundler died at Hereford on 2 November 1490 and is buried in the cathedral, where his memorial brass survives, though without head and feet. We can, however, make out, on the brass, his cope, decorated with pomegranates.

Thomas Chaundler was one of the earliest humanists of his age, stressing the importance of a return to Latin authors and the revival of ancient philosophical schools. He was succeeded by better-known humanists, the most famous of whom was Desiderius Erasmus, 1466–1536. His writings communicate a great deal of common sense:

I consider as lovers of books not those who keep their books hidden in their store chests and never handle them, but those who, by nightly as well as daily use thumb them, batter them, wear them out, who fill out all the margins with annotations of many kinds, and who prefer the marks of a fault they have erased to a neat copy full of faults.

Letter to an unidentified friend (1489)

The most disadvantageous peace is better than the most just war.

Adagia (1508)

A constant element of enjoyment must be mingled with our studies, so that we think of learning as a game rather than a form of drudgery, for no activity can be continued for long if it does not to some extent afford pleasure to the participant.

Letter to Christian Northoff (1497)

For what is life but a play in which everyone plays a part until the curtain comes down?

The Praise of Folly (1511)

John Varley 1778–1842

Prodigious artist

By the time of his death, on this day in 1842, John Varley had exhibited over 700 watercolours in various exhibitions, making him one of the most prolific artists of his day. First apprenticed to a silversmith in London, Varley turned to sketching, and by the age of 20 had exhibited at the Royal Academy. His first tour to Wales in 1798 laid the foundation of his art, and Wales and the Marches became his inspiration and subject matter for the rest of his life. He produced watercolours of topographical views and many of these, depicting Hereford, Leominster and Chester, are now in Hereford Art Gallery. His Welsh mountain views capture the awe-inspiring nature of the scenery while his landscape views follow William Gilpin's advice in 'adapting' nature to the requirements of the composition. Varley played a prominent role in the establishment of the Society of Painters in Water Colours in 1804, and his ability to produce numerous fresh drawings for each opening earned them the nickname of 'Varley's hot rolls'. He was a sought-after teacher and produced many teaching manuals – among his pupils was the Hereford artist, David Cox (see 7 June).

As well as being an artist, Varley was a keen astrologer and believed in the importance of signs of the zodiac for determining the differing physical characteristics, abilities and temperaments of mankind. It was his belief in visions that cemented his friendship with William Blake, whom he encouraged to draw portraits of historical and imaginary figures during their evening sessions at Varley's house in London. Varley also shared Blake's interest in J C Lavater's theories of physiognomy, which sought to demonstrate that a man's innate qualities determine his outward appearance. In later years, Varley's work became less popular and he turned to new styles, influenced by the glowing, mystical landscapes of Samuel Palmer.

Varley certainly enjoyed discussing art and astrology with William Blake, but perhaps the two men also shared a common interest in poetry. Blake's work often encourages compassion in others:

Can I see another's woe,
And not be in sorrow too?
Can I see another's grief
And not seek for kind relief?

Can I see a falling tear,
And not feel my sorrow's share?
Can a father see his child
Weep, nor be with sorrow fill'd?

Can a mother sit and hear
An infant groan, an infant fear?
No, no! Never can it be!
Never, never can it be!

William Blake 1757–1827, 'On Another's Sorrow'

Richard Munslow ?–1906

Shropshire's last 'sin-eater'

In the churchyard at Ratlinghope, high up on the Long Mynd, is the grave of Richard Munslow, said to be the last 'sin-eater' in England. The term 'sin-eater' refers to a person who, through ritual means, would take on, by means of food and drink, the sins of a deceased person, thus absolving his or her soul and allowing that person to rest in peace. Traditionally the ritual was performed by a beggar, but certain villages maintained their own 'professional' sin-eater. The sin-eater would be brought to the dying person's bedside, where a relative would place a crust of bread on the breast of the dead person and pass a bowl of ale to the sin-eater over the corpse. After praying or reciting the ritual, he would then drink and remove the bread from the breast of the corpse and eat it, the act of which would remove the sin from the dead person and take it into himself. Richard Munslow, far from being a beggar, was a well-established farmer in the area. He appears to have revived the practice of sin-eating following personal tragedy. In May 1870, within the space of one week, three of his children died of scarlet fever, an older child also having died in 1862.

His grave had fallen into disrepair and it was restored in 2010. On it is the inscription 'Suffer little children to come unto me, and forbid them not' (Mark 10:14). Did Munslow somehow feel that his own sin had led to this family tragedy? This was certainly what Viscount Scudamore had thought under similar circumstances (see 4 July).

The taking on the sins of others is a key concept in much theology of the Old and New Testaments. The Scapegoat, as described in the book of Leviticus, *shows how the community of Israel attempted to deal with its corporate sin, while all Christian denominations have seen the death of Christ as having a propitiatory significance in taking away 'the sins of the world'. The forgiveness of sins is yearned for, passionately, in this poem:*

Wilt Thou forgive that sin where I begun,
Which is my sin, though it were done before?
Wilt Thou forgive those sins, through which I run,
And do run still: though still I do deplore?
When Thou hast done, Thou hast not done,
For I have more.

Wilt Thou forgive that sin by which I have won
Others to sin, and made my sins their door?
Wilt Thou forgive that sin which I did shun
A year, or two, but wallowed in a score?
When Thou hast done, Thou hast not done,
For I have more.

I have a sin of fear, that when I have spun
My last thread, I shall perish on the shore;
But swear by Thyself, that at my death Thy Son
Shall shine as He shines now, and heretofore;
And, having done that, Thou hast done,
I fear no more.

John Donne 1572–1631, 'Hymn to God the Father'

Humfrey Coningsby 1567–1611

Collector of poems & adventurer

Humfrey Coningsby was described by a contemporary as 'A perfect scholar by education and a great traveller by his own affections'. He was a great collector and the compiler of an important Elizabethan poetic miscellany. It consists of courtly poems by writers such as Queen Elizabeth, Walter Raleigh and Philip Sidney, with many poems unique to this collection. Coningsby was also a traveller – he left England in April 1594 and during the next four or more years visited much of Europe, including France, Germany, Sicily and Italy. A second journey took him to Bohemia, Poland and Hungary, where he served under the Emperor Rudolph II at the siege of Strigonium. He then went on to Greece, into Asia and stayed for 13 months in Turkey. He set off on his final journey on 10 October 1610, bound for Venice, but was never heard of again and was pronounced dead in 1611. In his will made on 10 November 1608 he left his lute and his pictures to his relative, Thomas Coningsby of Hampton Court (see 30 May). Other bequests included 'a white hower glasse of sea horse tooth' and 'Three greate Venetian looking glasses'.

Coningsby is commemorated by a fine cenotaph in the church at Neen Sollars on the Clee Hill, set up in 1624 by his half-sister, Joyce Jefferies (see 9 November). This shows the adventurer in armour, resting his head on one hand and grasping a sword with the other. There are carved figures of Father Time on each side of him, one with an hourglass and the other with a sickle.

Coningsby's demise was sad and mysterious and yet he is magnificently remembered by those who loved him. Love conquers all and endures forever, long after a person's death. This enduring love is reflected in a sonnet by one of Coningsby's most famous contributors to his poetic collection:

Leave me, O Love, which reachest but to dust;
And thou, my mind, aspire to higher things;
Grow rich in that which never taketh rust;
Whatever fades but fading pleasure brings.
Draw in thy beams, and humble all thy might
To that sweet yoke where lasting freedoms be;
Which breaks the cloud and opens forth the light,
That doth both shine and give us sight to see.
O take fast hold; let that light be thy guide
In this small course which birth draws out to death,
And think how evil becometh him to slide,
Who seeketh heaven, and comes of heavenly breath.
Then farewell, world; thy uttermost I see;
Eternal Love, maintain thy life in me.

Sir Philip Sidney 1554–86, *Splendidis Longum Valedico Nugis*

John Trillek *c.*1308–60

Bishop of Hereford at the time of the Black Death

Unlike some of his predecessors as bishop of Hereford, who had no knowledge of the area, John Trillek was born and bred in the Marches and served all his ministry here. He came from Trelleck in Monmouthshire and was from an early age a member of the household of Bishop Orleton of Hereford (see 18 July). After education at Oxford, he returned to the diocese as incumbent of Bromyard and became bishop of Hereford at the early age of 36. He set about enforcing clerical discipline, insisting on personal residence in parishes and dealing with clerical abuses. Pastoral and educational standards among the clergy were raised by his granting of licences for absence for study, perhaps at Trillek's Inn at Oxford, a hall which the bishop and his brother maintained.

The catastrophe of the Black Death greatly affected the whole diocese and Trillek prohibited theatrical plays in churches as 'contrary to the practice of religion', but very likely with the idea of checking infection. Despite the ravaging of the population by the plague, Trillek maintained pastoral care – benefices were quickly filled, ordinations continued and in the aftermath of the epidemic he tried to prevent clergy leaving their posts in search of larger stipends. In Hereford Cathedral, Trillek was partly responsible for the wooden choir stalls and the bishop's throne, but his principal achievement was the enhancement of the cult of St Thomas of Hereford. On 25 October 1349, in the presence of King Edward III, the saint's remains were translated from the north transept to a new, richly decorated shrine in the Lady Chapel and a new feast, the Translation of St Thomas, was instituted (see 25 October). Trillek's last years were blighted by poor health and by a power struggle for the episcopal succession between his brother, the dean of Hereford and Thomas Shipton, archdeacon of Shropshire. During this struggle, Trillek was imprisoned for a time at Bishop's Castle. He died on this day in 1360 and was buried in the centre of the choir. The brass commemorating him was moved by Bishop Bisse (see 6 September) in the 18th century and is now on the north side of the choir. The brass depicts him fully vested, with ring, mitre and crozier. Its inscription describes him as wise and pious.

John Trillek showed great love and devotion to his flock in a time of enormous stress and sadness. The source of his compassion – a following of the way of Christ – is reflected in words by a contemporary who died in the year the Black Death ravaged Hereford:

I was more astonished than I showed the first time I felt my heart burn with fire. The sensation was not imaginary: I felt real warmth. I was amazed at the way the fire burst up in my soul and gave me unexpected comfort, and I kept touching my breast to see if there was some physical cause. Once I knew that the fire had been spiritually kindled within me and was nothing to do with earthly love or material cause, then I was assured that it was the gift of my Maker. And so I am glad to melt into a desire of greater love; and especially I rejoice at the wonderful delight and spiritual sweetness of this holy flame which so comforts my mind.

Before this moment I had no idea that we exiles could know such comfortable and sweet devotion: for truly my heart was as inflamed as if a real fire were burning there.

Let us seek the love of Christ burning within us, rather than involve ourselves in unprofitable disputes, for when we argue and discuss amongst ourselves we cannot feel the sweetness of eternity. So many people nowadays seek knowledge rather than love; they seem hardly to know what love is or to feel its delights. Yet really all their work and discourse should lead them to the fire of God's love. They should be ashamed of themselves. An old woman can know more of God's love, and less of worldly pleasures, than the brilliant theologian whose study is in vain.

Richard Rolle *c.*1300–49, *The Fire of Love*

Samuel Romilly 1757–1818

Advocate of criminal law reform

The French Revolution of 1789 inspired great fear in many in England, but some saw its political reform as capable of being transferred to this country. Among these radicals was Samuel Romilly. Born in London, he embarked on a career as a solicitor but later turned to politics and modern political theory. While he was critical of the atheism of the revolutionary regime in France and with the violence and anti-clericalism that subsequently erupted, he wrote widely in its favour and his *Thoughts on the probable influence of the French Revolution on Great Britain*, published in 1790, was widely acclaimed. In 1798 he married into the Garbett family of Knill Court in Herefordshire and much of his later life was spent in the county. As a lawyer he was in great demand in the highest circles – he served on the committee investigating allegations of misconduct against Caroline, princess of Wales, and conducted the impeachment of Henry Dundas for financial irregularity. Romilly is chiefly remembered as a champion of criminal reform, especially in the areas of corporal punishment, incarceration and capital punishment. He railed against a system which enforced the death penalty for 200 offences, including pick-pocketing, stealing from bleaching grounds and for sailors and soldiers wandering without an effective pass. He supported attempts to abolish the pillory and to stop flogging in the military. He also encouraged the government to build prisons on more humane, Benthamite principles in preference to transporting criminals to penal colonies or confining them in prison ships or common gaols. Romilly was active in opposition to the slave trade and in 1787 he joined Wilberforce on the committee, writing and speaking on the subject. His later years were blighted by mental health problems and on the death of his wife, Anne, on 29 October 1818, the strain proved unendurable and he cut his throat and died at his home in London. He was buried, with his wife, in the parish church of St Michael and All Angels, Knill. While he achieved only limited success in his quest for penal reform, his work did focus public and parliamentary attention on the subject and his views found expression in the programmes of subsequent Tory and Whig governments.

At the heart of all Romilly's thinking was a belief in the imperative of justice tempered with mercy:

The quality of mercy is not strain'd,
It droppeth as the gentle rain from heaven
Upon the place beneath: it is twice blest;
It blesseth him that gives, and him that takes:
'Tis mightiest in the mightiest: it becomes
The throned monarch better than his crown;
His sceptre shows the force of temporal power,
The attribute to awe and majesty,
Wherein doth sit the dread and fear of kings;
But mercy is above this sceptred sway;
It is enthroned in the hearts of kings,
It is an attribute to God himself;
And earthly power doth then show likest God's
When mercy seasons justice.

William Shakespeare 1564–1616, *The Merchant of Venice,* Act IV, Scene I

William Chelle fl.1524–56

Musician & composer

Today is a day to remember musicians as we recall St Cecilia, patron saint of music. Famous musicians were born on this day – Henry Purcell in 1659 and Benjamin Britten in 1913. It has been celebrated with music by many of the great composers and there is an annual festival on this day in London. Locally, we remember today a lesser known musician, William Chelle. Born probably in the diocese of Worcester, he was ordained acolyte on 21 May 1513 and subdeacon on 7 March 1516. As a priest, he became a bachelor of music at Oxford on 14 December 1524, submitting the composition of six mass settings and other antiphons. He was later engaged to lecture in music at Oxford and during this time is known to have composed a setting of the antiphon *Stella caeli*. Chelle had a long association with Hereford Cathedral. In 1518 he was appointed vicar choral and, in 1526, succentor. In February 1533 Chelle was collated to a canonry of Hereford Cathedral and to the prebends of Eign, then Ewithington. His preferment did not end there, for he later became incumbent of parishes in Hereford as well as becoming rector of Colwall in 1551 or 1552. When Bishop Charles Booth died in 1535, Chelle is described in the bishop's will as succentor and was the recipient of six silver spoons. In 1554 he became precentor and held this post till his death in 1556. He was succeeded by John Purfey who was deprived of this office in 1559, being unable to take the oath of supremacy to the new queen.

The later Middle Ages saw a huge increase of devotion to the Blessed Virgin Mary, who was seen as a source of mercy and succour for Christians in the face of an often stern and judgemental Father and Son. The words of the antiphon Stella Caeli *reflect this reliance on Mary's mercy – they were set to music by Chelle and by other composers in the early 16th century:*

The star of heaven who suckled the lord
Has rooted out the plague of death which the first parent of men planted.
May that very star now deign to restrain the constellations
Whose wars kill people with the sore of terrible death.
O glorious star of the sea, save us from the plague.
Hear us, for thy Son honours thee, refusing thee nothing.
Save us, Jesus, on whose behalf the Virgin mother beseeches thee.

Words celebrating music for the feast of St Cecilia:

When whispering strains do softly steal,
With creeping passion through the heart;
And when at every touch we feel
Our pulses beat and bear a part;
When threads can make
A heart-string shake,
Philosophy
Can scarce deny
The soul consists of harmony.

William Strode 1598–1645, 'In Commendation of Musick'

Clement Barksdale 1609–87

Translator of Grotius the Dutch war apologist

Today the church celebrates Clement, a pope of the early church and one remembered by generations of children in 'Oranges and Lemons'. Locally, we remember another Clement – Clement Barksdale – born on this day in 1609 at Winchcombe in Gloucestershire. After education at Oxford and ordination he moved to Hereford, where he was appointed master of the Cathedral School and later, in 1641, vicar choral and rector of St Nicholas in the city. A firm Royalist, he retained his position until Parliamentary forces occupied Hereford in 1646. At this time the Chandos family, served by Barksdale as chaplain, took him in at Sudeley Castle, close to his birthplace. Later, Barksdale moved to Hawling, in the Cotswolds, where he taught at a private school and was rector. While there, he began an ambitious programme of writing and translating. During his lifetime he published over 30 books, including biographies, poetry and sermons. His greatest significance lay in his work as a translator of Hugo Grotius, the 17th-century Dutch writer and apologist for the Christian principles of war. Between 1650 and 1670 Barksdale translated much of Grotius' work, including *De iure belli ac pacis* (Of the law of war and peace) and *De veritate religionis Christianae* (Of the Truth of the Christian Religion). He helped to popularize the Dutchman by producing a collection of his 'judgements' on such diverse subjects as predestination, the pope, Calvin, the sacraments and the saints. To Barksdale, Grotius was 'the wisest Scholar of his age'. In his later years he was appointed rector of Naunton and Stow-on-the-Wold, a position he held until his death in 1687. He was buried at Naunton in Gloucestershire.

Grotius' work discusses the legal status of war and is regarded as a foundational work in international law. He began the work while in prison and completed it in 1623. The conclusion speaks powerfully of the vital importance of fairness and justice in any settlement:

Even for the stronger party, when flushed with victory, peace is a safer expedient, than the most extensive successes. For there is the boldness of despair to be apprehended from a vanquished enemy, dangerous as the bite of a ferocious animal in the pangs of death.

If indeed both parties are upon an equal footing, it is the opinion of Caesar, that it is the most favourable moment for making peace, when each party has confidence in itself.

On whatever terms peace is made, it must be absolutely kept. From the sacredness of the faith pledged in the engagement, everything must be cautiously avoided, not only savouring of treachery, but that may tend to awaken and inflame animosity. For what Cicero has said of private friendships may with equal propriety be applied to public engagements of this kind, which are all to be religiously and faithfully observed, especially where war and enmity have ended in peace and reconciliation.

And may God, to whom alone it belongs to dispose the affections and desires of sovereign princes and kings, inscribe these principles upon their hearts and minds, that they may always remember that the noblest office, in which man can be engaged, is the government of men, who are the principal objects of the divine care.

Hugo Grotius 1583–1645, *De iure belli et pacis* (1625), ch.25, trans. A C Campbell (1814)

Hugh Despenser 1286–1326

Hereford's tragic link with Tewkesbury

When I moved from Tewkesbury Abbey to become dean of Hereford in May 2002, in my installation sermon I reminded the congregation of the many links between Tewkesbury and Hereford: Richard de Capella, bishop of Hereford was present at the consecration of Tewkesbury Abbey in 1121, and manuscripts once in Tewkesbury Abbey library are now in the cathedral library at Hereford. On a darker note, I recalled that Hugh Despenser, son of the great Tewkesbury family and favourite of Edward II, was on this day in 1326 dragged through the streets of Hereford on a cart, then hanged, drawn and quartered in the Market Place – afterwards, his remains were collected and returned to Tewkesbury. In my sermon, I thanked the present-day inhabitants of Hereford for welcoming this arrival from Tewkesbury rather more enthusiastically than they had Hugh Despenser! Despenser was much involved in the intrigue surrounding the court of Edward II and his queen, Isabella, and he and his wife, Eleanor de Clare, became extremely powerful, holding lands and manors in Wales and in Herefordshire. Despenser was hated by the barons, who resented his influence with the king and, opposed by a group of Marcher lords including Roger Mortimer of Wigmore (see 29 November) and Humphrey de Bohun, earl of Hereford, he was exiled for a time. Returning from exile, his fortunes again rose, but when the queen formed a liaison with Roger Mortimer, Despenser quickly fell from grace. On a lighter note (or a darker note, depending on how you view it), Hereford was thrashed by Tewkesbury in 1971 in the final of the BBC competition, *It's a Knockout!*

The story of Hugh Despenser is one of tragedy – the tragedy of an overbearing ambition, the tragedy of a passion and love for Edward which led to resentment and death. The sadness of that love is reflected in this poem:

Thou knowest, love, I know, that thou dost know
that I am here more near to thee to be,
and knowest that I know thou knowest me:
what means it then that we are sundered so?

If they are true, these hopes that from thee flow,
If it is real, this sweet expectancy,
break down the wall that stands 'twixt me and thee;
for pain in prison spent hath double woe.

Because in thee I love, O my loved lord,
what thou best lovest, be not therefore stern:
souls burn for souls, spirits to spirits cry!

I seek the splendour in thy fair face stored;
yet living man that beauty scarce can learn,
and he who fain would find it, first must die.

Michelangelo 1475–1564, 'To Tommaso dei Cavalieri', trans. J A Symonds

Catherine (Katherine) of Alexandria 4th century

Hilltop saint

Many of the 62 English churches dedicated to St Catherine of Alexandria are placed on hilltops. Herefordshire has one – Hoarwithy – and that amazing Italianate Victorian church is most certainly set at the top of a steep bank. These hilltop positions are said to have been adopted because of Catherine's association with Mount Sinai. She is said to have been of royal birth, and having made a vow of chastity, to have rejected the advances of the Emperor Maxentius. For this impudence, she was tortured on the spiked wheel which has become her emblem in art. Catherine was then beheaded, and her body was miraculously transported to a monastery on Mount Sinai. Her cult built on this legend and, under the influence of the Crusades, spread all over Europe. Catherine is the patron saint of nurses (because milk instead of blood flowed from her severed head) and of craftsmen whose work was based on the wheel – wheelwrights, spinners and millers.

She is frequently depicted in art – there are early mural paintings of her life in Winchester Cathedral and many depictions of her life in stained glass, including examples at St Laurence, Ludlow and Old Radnor. St Katherine's Hospital in Ledbury is dedicated to this saint, reflecting the founder, Bishop Foliot's personal devotion to her (see 7 August). The bishop also founded another chantry to Catherine in the Romanesque double chapel built between the palace and the cathedral in Hereford by Bishop Robert Losinga (see 26 June). Hereford's devotion to the saint spread to other parts of Europe – in 1255 the Savoyard bishop Aquablanca (see 27 November) dedicated a hospital to her in his home town of Aigueblanche, where services continued to be performed according to the Use of Hereford.

The writer of the Letter to the Hebrews *in the New Testament extols the example of martyrs who gave their life in the cause of what they believed to be right and true. Catherine's own example of courage and fortitude echoed throughout Europe and inspired many in their own sufferings:*

And what more shall I say? For time would fail me to tell of Gideon, Barak, Samson, Jephthah, of David and Samuel and the prophets – who through faith conquered kingdoms, enforced justice, received promises, stopped the mouths of lions, quenched raging fire, escaped the edge of the sword, won strength out of weakness, became mighty in war, put foreign armies to flight. Women received their dead by resurrection. Others were tortured, refusing to accept release, that they might rise again to a better life. Others suffered mocking and imprisonment. They were stoned, they were sawn in two, they were killed with the sword; they went about in skins of sheep and goats, destitute, afflicted, ill-treated – of whom the world was not worthy – wandering over deserts and mountains, and in dens and caves of the earth.

And all these, though well attested by their faith, did not receive what was promised, since God had foreseen something better for us, that apart from us they should not be made perfect.

Hebrews 11:32–40

Radegund 518–87

Thuringian princess in Ledbury

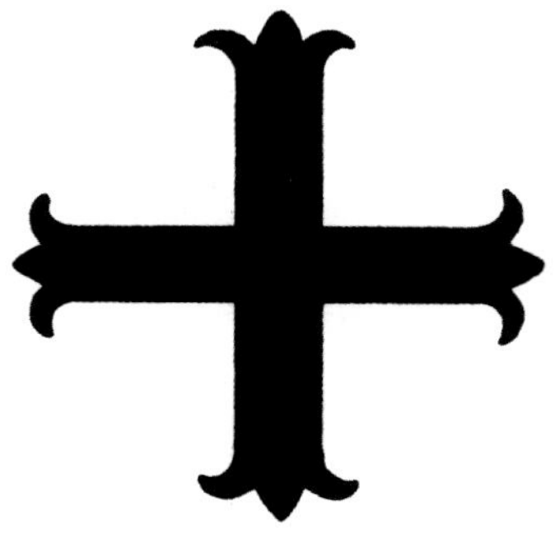

The medieval church of St Michael in Ledbury once contained a chapel dedicated to St Radegund, probably the ornate north-east chapel. Who was this unusual saint and what is she doing in east Herefordshire? She was born in about 520, a princess of pagan Thuringia, in what is now Germany. She had a violent childhood and at the age of 12 was captured by the Franks under King Clothar and carried off to France. There she became a Christian and embraced the faith with enthusiasm. Forced to marry Clothar, she eventually took the veil at Noyan and became a deaconess. Later she founded the monastery of the Holy Cross at Poitiers. There she welcomed the hymn writer Venantius Fortunatus, who was enchanted by her physical and spiritual beauty and wrote verses to her. Venantius also wrote the hymn 'The royal banners forward go' to celebrate the arrival at Poitiers of a relic of the true cross sent by the Byzantine emperor, whom Radegund had asked for relics for her abbey. After her death in 587, Radegund's cult spread widely in France and reached England by the mid-12th century when a priory at Cambridge (now Jesus College) was dedicated to St Mary and St Radegund. By the end of the century another priory and chapel in Charlecote in Warwickshire had been dedicated to her. Radegund also had chapels in Gloucester Abbey and at Usk Priory. The only English *Life of St Radegund*, a late medieval compilation based on a French source, is usually attributed to Henry Bradshaw, who lived and wrote in Chester in the early 16th century. Perhaps this is evidence for the special attraction Radegund's cult had for the people of the Welsh borders – including the people of Ledbury!

The famous hymn of Venantius Fortunatus is, of course, for Passiontide, but reading it today as we approach the season of Advent reminds us that the message of the cross is for all times and seasons:

The royal banners forward go,
The Cross shines forth in mystic glow,
Where He in flesh, our flesh Who made,
Our sentence bore, our ransom paid.

Fulfilled is all that David told
In true prophetic song of old,
The universal Lord is He,
Who reigns and triumphs from the tree.

O Tree of beauty, Tree of light,
O Tree with royal purple dight,
Elect on whose triumphal breast
Those holy limbs should find their rest.

O Cross, our one reliance, hail!
So may thy power with us prevail,
To give new virtue to the saint,
And pardon to the penitent.

Venantius Fortunatus 530–609, 'Vexilla Regis'

Peter d'Aigueblanche (Aquablanca) d.1268

Savoyard bishop & politician

Here is a bishop who, it is said, spoke no word of English. Deriving his name from his birthplace in Savoy, he came to England in the retinue of Eleanor of Provence who married Henry III. By 1240 Peter had become bishop of Hereford, and although the king and archbishop tried to secure for him the more lucrative sees of Durham and London, he remained at Hereford until his death. Not that he was very often in his diocese, as he was frequently on the king's business, in embassies and in political intrigue. During his frequent absences he appointed proctors in the diocese – mainly foreigners who were greatly resented. Indeed, in 1252 violence over this erupted and his proctor, Prior Bernard, was murdered while saying mass in St Mary Magdalene's chapel in the palace precinct. After one long absence, Peter returned to a confrontation with a group of barons, who carried him off to imprisonment in Eardisley Castle. Released from prison, Peter went to his native Savoy, completed his collegiate church at Aiguebelle, and drew up statutes for its administration, directing that the services should be according to the Use of Hereford. Although this bishop had many activities which took him abroad, he did not neglect the cathedral. In his time the north transept was re-modelled, having similarities to contemporary work in Westminster Abbey, with twin straight-sided arches, and purbeck marble shafts. After his death, on this day in 1268, he was buried in a tomb already completed for him in the north transept – a magnificent memorial, with effigy and a canopy surmounted by a crucifix. The canons of Aiguebelle exhibited a rival tomb, with a bronze 15th-century effigy, said to contain his heart, a tomb destroyed at the Revolution. Here, then, a man disliked by many. Matthew Paris was one of his sternest critics, accusing him of 'fox-like cunning' and claiming that 'his memory exudes a sulphurous stench'. While he undoubtedly played his part in a widening breach between the king and the barons, he may be remembered for much more than this – not least for his magnificent additions to his cathedral church.

The tomb of Aigueblanche in Hereford Cathedral is undoubtedly one of the finest in the building, with its noble effigy, its crucifix and traces of original colour. Perhaps, in planning his tomb, the bishop was influenced by the great examples of funerary art in Westminster Abbey – a church so lavishly endowed by his master, Henry III. Here, a later author writes of what we can learn of life and death from the tombs in Westminster Abbey:

For my own part, though I am always serious, I do not know what it is to be melancholy; and can therefore take a view of nature in her deep and solemn scenes, with the same pleasure as in her most gay and delightful ones. By this means I can improve myself with those objects, which others consider with terror. When I look upon the tombs of the great, every emotion of envy dies in me; when I read the epitaphs of the beautiful, every inordinate desire goes out; when I meet with the grief of parents upon a tombstone, my heart melts with compassion; when I see the tomb of the parents themselves, I consider the vanity of grieving for those whom we must quickly follow. When I see kings lying by those who deposed them, when I consider rival wits placed side by side, or the holy men that divided the world with their contests and disputes, I reflect with sorrow and astonishment on the little competitions, factions, and debates of mankind. When I read the several dates of the tombs of some that died yesterday, and some six hundred years ago, I consider that great day when we shall all of us be contemporaries, and make our appearance together.

Joseph Addison 1672–1719, *The Tombs in Westminster Abbey*

EDWARD STEERE 1828–82

Pioneering bishop in Africa

Baba yetu

Baba yetu uliye mbinguni,
Jina lako litukuzwe,
Ufalme wako uje,
Mapenzi yako yatimizwe,
hapa duniani kama huko mbinguni.
Utupe leo riziki yetu.
Utusamehe deni zetu,
kama sisi nasi tuwasamehevyo wadeni wetu.
Na usitutie majaribuni,
lakini utuokoe na yule mwovu.
[Kwa kuwa ufalme ni wako, na nguvu, na utukufu, hata milele.]

Amina.

THE STRONG ANGLICAN presence in what is now Tanzania owes much to this man and, with the many links between the church in Tanzania and in Hereford diocese, we celebrate his memory (see also 14 September). From an early age, Edward Steere showed great compassion for the poor and needy. Ordained in 1856, he served curacies in Devon and in Lincolnshire – as curate in Skegness, he made his reputation among the fisherman as a 'downright shirt-sleeve man and a real Bible parson'. In 1862 he joined his friend William Tozer, the new missionary bishop of the Universities' Mission to Central Africa (UMCA), and the following year he landed at the mouth of the Zambesi, to then set up missionary headquarters on Zanzibar. Steere soon realised that little headway would be made until there was teaching in Swahili, and very soon he had compiled a Swahili grammar and inaugurated a mission on the mainland. In 1872, because of Bishop Tozer's ill health, Steere was left to run the mission single-handed. He pressed on with the foundation of an English cathedral on the site of what had been the Zanzibar slave market, and re-established the mission on the mainland at Lagila. In 1874 Steere was consecrated bishop in Westminster Abbey and, on returning to Africa, founded a new mission station at Masasi. He continued his translation work, including a complete translation into Swahili of the New Testament and of the prayer book. Eventually his health broke down, and he died on 27 August 1882 and was buried in his cathedral at Zanzibar.

Steere was an uncompromising high-churchman, but his breadth of view won the esteem of all. He shared the concern, common among UMCA clergy, to preserve where possible the cultural identity of different African communities, and did a great service to the African church by providing translations not only in Swahili but in other languages and dialects, including Yao, Nyamwezi and Makonde.

Working in Tanzania many years after Edward Steere, Edmund John was born at Muheza. His brother, John Sepeku later became the first archbishop of the church of the province of Tanzania. After a career in education and working for Radio Tanzania, Edmund had a vision which resulted in his starting to minister in the streets and beer halls of Dar-es-Salaam. His ministry included a great emphasis on healing and exorcism:

Guidance for prayer groups in fasting and praying for the sick:

1. It is desirable that the leader be a pastor wherever possible.
2. In order that the group receive the power of the Holy Spirit and have much blessing in its efforts, it must keep the following conditions:
   (a) Beginning with the pastor himself, the leader of the group and every member in the group must repent of all his sins to the Lord Jesus before climbing into his bed at night and before prayers.
   (b) He should not drink alcohol, or smoke cigarettes or tobacco.
   (c) He should pray every day, morning and evening.
   (d) Beginning with the pastor, the leader of the group and every member of the group must fast on the day of intercessions for the sick, as well as the sick people themselves and their helpers. Even the sick who are far away should fast on the day of intercessions.
   (e) The sick people must be given conditions to observe, that is, to pray, to fast, and to repent of their sins.
3. It is good for the pastor who leads the group (rather than the members of the group) to testify on Sundays in the congregation about the blessings and results of their prayers.

Edmund John 1922–75

Roger Mortimer 1287–1330

Ruthless Marcher lord

The name of Roger Mortimer is synonymous with ruthless greed, and contemporary and modern historians have dealt harshly with him. Most would regard him as most definitely in the 'sinner' category! He had power thrust upon him at an early age, gaining lands and manors in the Marches, including Ludlow Castle, which became the most important stronghold of the Mortimers. He became lord lieutenant of Ireland and did much to bring the Irish in line with English law, but soon his disaffection with his king, Edward II, led him to disloyalty. He formed an alliance of Marcher lords in a revolt sometimes known as the Despenser war – a reference to Hugh Despenser, Edward II's hated favourite (see 24 November). Escaping to France, Mortimer was joined by Isabella, Edward's queen, who became his mistress and chief ally, and in 1328 he declared himself first earl of March. After the murder of Edward II in Berkeley Castle, Mortimer became, in effect, ruler of England before being overthrown by Edward's eldest son, who became Edward III. Accused of assuming royal power and other crimes, he was tried and, on this day in 1330, was hanged, drawn and quartered at Tyburn as a common criminal – the first execution to take place at what became a notorious place of execution in succeeding centuries. He was buried alongside his widow, Joan, at Wigmore, but the site of their grave was later destroyed. The Mortimer Trail, a long distance path, runs from Ludlow to Kington taking in key sites associated with Mortimer, his ancestors and descendants, and acknowledging this important family which left such a mark on the geography and history of this area.

Medieval carols often challenge their listeners to turn away from sin to new life in Christ. We may well imagine how contemporary preachers and singers might challenge Mortimer, and others, for their often ruthless lifestyle:

Pride is out and pride is in,
And pride is root of every sin,
And pride will always fight to win,
    Till he has brought a man to woe.
    Man, beware, or fall in woe:
    Consider pride, and let it go.

If you think that swear-words roared
Or fashionable clothes afford
You rights to be a king or lord,
    Little shall avail you so. Man beware, etc.

When to church at last you glide,
Worms shall burrow through your side,
And little shall avail your pride
    Or any other vice you show. Man, beware, etc.

Pray to Christ with bloody side
And other gashes cruel and wide,
That so he may forgive your pride
    And all your sinning here below. Man, beware, etc.

MS Sloane 2593, early 15th century

Andrew d.*c.*60

Apostle in Wales

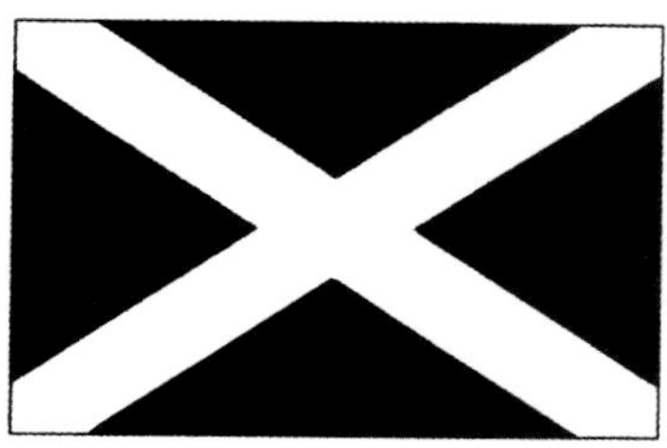

Llanandras – the church of Andrew – is the Welsh name for the town of Presteigne in Radnorshire. The fine church there is dedicated to the saint, along with 17 others in the diocese of Hereford. Andrew's popularity among the apostles in medieval English dedications was second only to St Peter (see 29 June). He was a fisherman by trade and brother of Simon Peter. He does not play a prominent part in the gospel narratives, but is specially remembered for his part in the feeding of the five thousand. Later legends associate him with Greece where he is said to have met his death by crucifixion. In the 8th century some of his relics were said to have been taken to Scotland, where St Andrews became a religious centre and a place of pilgrimage. Andrew was adopted as the patron saint, not only of Scotland, but also of France and Russia. In early art, Andrew is depicted with a normal Latin cross, but the saltire cross, commonly called 'St Andrew's Cross' was associated with him from the 10th century. His other symbol is a fishing net – seen to great effect in the east window of St Andrew's church, Presteigne, where Andrew is shown, with Christ, in John's description of the call of the disciples (John 1:40–1).

The Old English poem Andreas *portrays Andrew as an heroic figure similar to Beowulf, who sails the ocean to rescue his fellow-apostle Matthew from prison – a story based on the apocryphal* Acts of Andrew and Matthew. *In this excerpt, Andrew is on this voyage as the ship meets a terrible storm. In the second part, Andrew praises the ship's captain, unaware that the vessel is being piloted by God himself:*

The depths were troubled.   The horn-fish darted,
Gliding through ocean;   the gray gulls wheeled,
Searching for carrion.   The sun grew dark;
A gale arose,   and great waves broke;
The sea stirred.   Halyards were humming,
Sails were drenched.   Sea-terror grew
In the welter of waves.   The thanes were adread,
Who sailed with Andrew   on the ocean-stream,
Nor hoped with life   ever to come to land.
Nor yet was it known   Who guided their bark
Through the breaking seas ...
Sixteen voyages   early and late
It has been my lot   to sail in my sea-boat,
With freezing hands   as I smote the sea,
The ocean-streams.   Now this is another.
Never have I known   one like to thee
Of the sons of men,   steering over stem.
The roaring billows   beat on the strand;
Full swift this bark   and most like a bird
Foamy-necked faring   over the waves.
Well I know   that I never have seen
In any sailor   wondrous sea-craft.
Most like it is   as if on land
The boat stood still   where wind and storm
Could stir it not.

From *Andreas,* Old English, *c.* late 9th century, trans. Charles W Kennedy

I

December

John of Bridlington d.1379

Yorkshire saint in Herefordshire

In 1405 an indulgence was promised to all who visited the church of Llanwarne to honour St John of Bridlington and who contributed to church funds. In the same year, an image of the saint was erected at Llanwarne. How is it that this Yorkshire saint found a place in the Welsh borders? He was born at Thwing, near Bridlington and studied at Oxford, returning to Bridlington Priory as precentor, cellarer, and lastly prior (1362). In an age when monastic slackness was widespread, John gave an example of faithfulness to his order and vocation and was greatly revered. Some of his words have been preserved, among them a recommendation to study the fourth gospel. After his death, many miracles were reported at his tomb and he was canonised by Pope Boniface IX in 1401, the last Englishman to be so honoured before the Reformation. As a saint he was greatly revered – the English success at the battle of Agincourt was attributed by Henry V to the intercession of two Yorkshire saints, John of Beverley and John of Bridlington. And Llanwarne? It is probable that John's cult was brought to the Welsh borders by the Augustinian brothers of Llanthony, patrons of Llanwarne. He is also attributed as author of several contemporary prophecies foretelling the end of the world.

John of Bridlington's devotion to St John's gospel and his reputation for prophecy are symbolised in these verses, when Jesus challenges Peter's natural desire to peer into the future:

Peter turned and saw following them the disciple whom Jesus loved, who had lain close to his breast at the supper and had said, 'Lord, who is it that is going to betray you?' When Peter saw him, he said to Jesus, 'Lord, what about this man?' Jesus said to him, 'If it is my will that he remain until I come, what is that to you? Follow me!' The saying spread abroad among the brethren that this disciple was not to die; yet Jesus did not say to him that he was not to die, but 'If it is my will that he remain until I come, what is that to you?'

John 21:20–24

Today, Llanwarne has no evidence of the medieval devotion to St John of Bridlington, but with its ruined church, it remains a place of great atmosphere and mystery, especially in the winter gloom:

Ruined it stood, by time's neglect undone,
    In lonely shame; beneath grey walls a stream
    Caught on its gliding face a wintry gleam,
Halting awhile the westward-fleeting sun.
About the wreck of many a lurching tomb
    Rose in an ebbless tide the mounting brier;
    Drearily slow, the brook by sedgy mire
Crept with a lisping gurgle through the gloom.
So desolate a place to seek by dusk
    Under the dark and star-bejewelled sky –
    Roofless old walls that men in days gone by
Made loud with song, now but a voiceless husk.
And we stood silent, knowing we must share
No other bed than theirs who slumber there.

Michael Oakley, *Verses & Versions* (1988)

John Percival 1834–1918

Bishop famed for education & discipline

A giant of the Victorian age, John Percival established one public school (Clifton College, Bristol) and reformed another (Rugby). At first, he seemed an unlikely bishop of Hereford – a staunch supporter of temperance in a county of cider-makers; a liberal in a fiercely Tory county; a Protestant in a diocese with high-church leanings; and a known supporter of Welsh disestablishment. He was also a rather puritanical disciplinarian – a reformer and controversialist – and whether from pulpit or in the press, castigated the forces of inertia and reaction. However, he proved a pastorally-hearted bishop – always enthusiastic about education (he founded the Workers' Educational Association) and encouraging literacy in the parishes through the giving of prizes in parish schools. At heart, however, his interests were more national than local – he chaired the 1897 Lambeth Conference's committee on industrial problems and became increasingly involved in educational reform. There was also a deep loneliness – partly through the death of a son and of his first wife, partly as he felt out of the thick of national events in Hereford and partly through being passed over when the archbishopric of York became vacant in 1908. Percival died on 3 December and was buried in the crypt of the chapel at Clifton College, but he is remembered in Hereford by a fine marble plaque beneath the central tower.

Percival's sense of right is clearly reflected in this passage, thoroughly supporting the cause of the allies in the First World War – an attitude which is not so far from contemporary views of British foreign policy:

We meet today under heavy clouds: anxiety and sorrow, sacrifice and bereavement, are casting their shadow over so many lives. It is in the hope that we are contributing in some degree to the upraising of the life of nations a little nearer to the standard of Christ's Kingdom and to the promise of happier days for the generations in front of us that we bear unflinchingly, and as a call of God, each of us our individual share of the sure and heavy burden of sacrifice and bereavement in our darkened homes.

Strengthened by such reflections, and feeling that along with our Allies we are the predestined instruments to save the Christian civilisation of Europe from being overcome by a brutal and ruthless military paganism, we should make it our primary duty to prosecute this warfare at all costs till the victory is won and the law of Christ is firmly established as the paramount authority in all national and international affairs.

Sixth Visitation Charge, 1915

However, the bishop also had a more human side, as this letter from an incumbent in the diocese at the time shows:

First, I held the living of Donnington, near Ledbury. It was one of the poor livings in the Hereford diocese. It was a little country parish with a small church. The Friday before a Sunday in Lent, I was taken suddenly ill. I telegraphed at once to the Bishop's Secretary, whom I knew, and asked him if he could find me a helper for the Sunday. On Saturday morning I received a letter from Dr Percival saying that he would be very pleased to take the services in my Church himself.

The Bishop arrived at 10 o'clock on the Sunday morning, having driven all the way from Hereford. He took my services himself, at 11 o'clock and at 3.30 pm. He would not partake of any food in the Rectory, because he knew that the living was a poor one, but he brought his own sandwiches with him. When the afternoon service concluded, he drove back to Hereford.

Letter from the Revd Maxwell F Webb

Francis Xavier 1506–52

Jesuit missionary

The Roman Catholic church of St Francis Xavier on Broad Street in Hereford surprises the visitor to the city. Looking like a Greek temple, it is modelled on the Treasury of the Athenians at Delphi. Its unashamed classical style with ionic columns reminds us that when the church was built in 1838–9, anti-Catholic feeling was still prevalent and the classical style was thought to be more acceptable than the 'ecclesiastical' and emerging gothic revival. Even so, the windows of the church are placed high up, lest stones should be thrown. The dedication of the church to Francis Xavier reminds us that for many years the church was staffed by Jesuits, and Francis was one of the great Jesuit missionaries of his age. Born at the castle of Xavier in Navarre, he was educated in Paris with Ignatius Loyola and became one of the seven who took vows as the first members of the Society of Jesus. Since preaching the gospel overseas was an integral part of the Jesuit vocation, Francis sailed for Goa on the west coast of India in 1541. He travelled all over the East Indies, preaching and teaching and established the church in Ceylon, Malacca, Malaya and Japan, where he left behind 2,000 converts. He was on his way to China when he died on board ship in December 1552. His body is enshrined at Goa, and there are relics of his at the church of the Gèsu at Rome. He was canonised by Gregory xv in 1622 and declared Patron of Foreign Missions by Pius xi in 1927.

Francis Xavier was sometimes criticised for his methods. Like most of his Catholic and Protestant contemporaries, he believed that all who died unbaptized would be damned. This gave both urgency to his activity and a lack of understanding of some of the great religions of the east. But perhaps today he would be more inclined to see in all religions a spark of the divine? Certainly this prayer from Japan seeks to draw together all people in an appeal to their common humanity:

Have us born anew and let us possess our being through the Providence of Light.
Teach us to respect the essence of all religions, and lead us to learn the One Ultimate Truth.
Have us perform our duties out of penitence, and do all our work with gratitude.
Enable us to perfect the way of our living by completely submitting to the Laws of Nature.
Grant that we may return to the land of heavenly flowers and so tread in the Paradise of Light.

Ittoen – The Garden of the One Light

Even in the early days of the life of St Francis Xavier's church in Hereford, there were glimpses of the warm ecumenical fellowship that we were to enjoy in the city many years later. The reporter of The Hereford Times, *describing the opening ceremony in August 1839, wrote:*

O that this scene of harmony might last forever! O that we could all at this moment swear an eternal, inviolable friendship, one with another, which might stand unbroken in spite of the powers of the demon of discord! And why should it not be so? Why should not our hearts and souls be one, as were the hearts and souls of all the Primitive Christians?'

Thomas Wolsey *c.*1473–1530

Very briefly dean of Hereford

Today we recall the powerful Cardinal Wolsey, not on the date of his birth or death but on the day in 1512 when he resigned the deanery of Hereford. He publicly announced his conditional resignation in St Paul's Cathedral, 'desiring for just reasons to be relieved of the burden, care and rule of the deanery, hoping, however that a pension may be assigned to me from the revenue of the said deanery, otherwise I do not resign.' Wolsey probably never even visited Hereford! Said to be a butcher's son from Ipswich in Suffolk (the occupation of his father is now questioned), he was clever, ambitious and industrious and he soon rose through the ranks in church and state. Possibly through the influence of Richard Mayhew, President of Magdalen College, Oxford (later bishop of Hereford), Wolsey (also a Magdalen man) accepted the Hereford prebend of Pratum Minore and in 1509 there is a reference to his becoming dean. He held this post with many others including a canonry of Windsor and the deanery of York, besides being chaplain to the king. Wolsey persuaded the authorities and was granted the pension he desired – £45 *per annum* for three years and then £40 for life – both sums a great deal of money in 1512. Wolsey went on to even greater heights in church and state, becoming bishop of Lincoln and archbishop of York in 1514 and later adding the bishopric of Durham to his list. As Lord Chancellor to Henry VIII he held a huge amount of power both in foreign and domestic policy, becoming key in the negotiations to secure Henry a divorce from Catherine of Aragon so that he could marry Anne Boleyn. His fall came in 1529, when he was accused of high treason. However, he never answered the charges brought against him as he died at Leicester on his way to London to face trial, and was buried at Leicester Abbey. His short time at Hereford was remembered 500 years later, when, in 2009, the dean received a letter from Ipswich Town Council, seeking donations towards a new statue of their most famous son. The town authorities had clearly done their homework, seeking help from cathedrals and dioceses where Wolsey had held office. Hereford replied by offering to pay one year's pension – £45 – insisting that this was to be at 2009 and not 1512 values!

Thomas Wolsey was, frankly, little use as dean of Hereford – he never visited the place and clearly held it solely for the income! A later dean – of Carlisle – received some useful advice before he took up the appointment. Such a job description would have been all too much for Wolsey!

'I do hope that, in your hands the post of Dean will prove not to be a completely useless office. For, indeed, it seems to me that if a man had judgement and courage, a Dean might indeed prove an invaluable person in a Cathedral town. Not only might he take the lead in the works of mercy and in the business of education, but he might also be the foremost man in preaching the gospel to the people. But this last will require that he should step out of the beaten path by instituting some such thing as an Evening Service, or a service at some suitable time for the poor. Again, may I ask you to forgive me if I suggest another serious subject for serious thought? Cannot you as Dean be kind to some of the poorer clergy? It is quite painful to see how great people forget our Lord's command to invite those who cannot repay them and if the Whigs carry you up higher, and make you a Bishop, never forget the advice of a truly affectionate friend, who does long to see you breaking through the miserably unchristian customs of most Cathedral dignitaries, and proving yourself to be one who is willing, not to make a show in society, but by simple-minded preaching of the Gospel, by self-denying simplicity of habits and tastes, by self-humbling endeavours, to show kindness to the poor of all classes, to earn from your Master the name in your Deanery of a good and faithful servant.'

Samuel Waldegrave 1817–69, *Life of Archbishop Tait* (1891)

William Felton 1715–69

Composer & vicar choral

In the bishop's cloister at Hereford Cathedral is a large stone to the memory of this man. It describes him as 'Vir animose, Justus et rerum musicarum peritissimus' ('A just and courageous man, supreme in the art of music'). We see his portrait in College Hall, holding the manuscript of one of his compositions. William Felton was born at Market Drayton in Shropshire, was educated at Manchester Grammar School and was ordained at Hereford Cathedral in 1742, becoming a vicar choral in the following year. As with many of the vicars choral, he combined his cathedral duties with parish responsibilities and in 1749 he became rector of Norton Canon. Felton was a gifted keyboard player and published sets of concertos for organ or harpsichord. Handel knew of them but suggested that a clergyman would be better employed writing sermons than concertos! His compositions were certainly popular. An 'andante with variations' by Felton was performed at a subscription concert in Manchester in 1744 and is said to have been played when the Young Pretender, Bonnie Prince Charlie, fled from Manchester in 1745.

In 1749 Felton revived the Musical Society in Hereford, which, founded in 1723, had ceased activity ten years later because of the poor state of College Hall. Felton gave the society new impetus by establishing its meetings in 'Frank Woodcock's house' (in what is now St John Street). These concerts were so successful that in 1750 fund-raising was begun and the hall was entirely rebuilt by 1753, ready for the concerts of the Three Choirs Festival in Hereford that year. Felton was a driving force behind the fund-raising and was disappointed not to be made custos or senior vicar choral when the post became vacant in 1754. For this he had to wait until 1769, when 'the Vicars offered the first-fruits of their freedom to Mr. Felton' and he at last became custos. In the same year he was appointed to the vacant benefice of Preston and Blakemere. He died at Hereford on 6 December 1769.

Felton would have experienced many kinds of church music – that performed in the cathedral by the professional choir and the rather simpler offerings of the parish churches in the villages he served. A contemporary writer speaks of one of the distinctive features of parochial worship in the 18th century:

The good old practice of psalm-singing is, indeed, wonderfully improved in many country churches since the days of Sternhold and Hopkins; and there is scarce a parish clerk who has so little taste as not to pick his staves out of the New Version. This has occasioned great complaints in some places, where the clerk has been forced to bawl by himself, because the rest of the congregation cannot find the psalm at the end of their prayer-books; while others are highly disgusted at the innovation, and stick as obstinately to the Old Version as to the old style. The tunes themselves have also been new set to jiggish measures; and the sober drawl, which used to accompany the two first staves of the hundredth psalm, with the *gloria patri*, is now split into as many quavers as an Italian air. For this purpose there is in every county an itinerant band of local musicians, who make it their business to go round to all the churches in their turns, and, after a prelude with the pitch-pipe, astonish the audience with hymns set to the new Winchester measure, and anthems of their own composing. As these new-fashioned psalmodists are necessarily made up of young men and maids, we may naturally suppose that there is a perfect concord and symphony between them: and, indeed, I have known it happen that these sweet singers have more than once been brought into disgrace, by too close an unison between the thorough-bass and the treble.

William Cowper 1731–1800, *Essay on Country Congregations*

Nicholas of Myra 4th century

Bishop & Santa Claus

Hereford maintains the ancient tradition of the Boy Bishop. A senior chorister is appointed on or near the feast of St Nicholas and holds office until Christmas. At his installation in the cathedral, he gives a sermon, pronounces the blessing and holds the bishop's crozier as a symbol of his authority. During *Magnificat,* while the bishop himself takes a lower seat, the Boy Bishop ascends to the bishop's throne as these words are being sung – 'He hath put down the mighty from their throne and hath exalted the humble and meek'. These words remind us of the central message of the tradition – that of the vital importance of child-like humility in the Christian life. The linking of the ceremony with the feast of St Nicholas reminds us of this saint's patronage of children, and he is a popular figure when, on this day in the Low Countries, he appears as Santa Claus, distributing presents to all. Nicholas was bishop of Myra in Turkey and was revered in his lifetime, but most of what we know of him comes from exotic legends of a later date. He is patron of countries like Russia, villages such as Sutton St Nicholas near Hereford, and of sailors, unmarried girls, merchants, pawnbrokers, apothecaries and perfumiers. He was a popular saint in the dedication of churches – 400 in England claim him as patron, and there are many depictions of his life in stone and glass, notably a fine window at Great Malvern Priory.

In his installation sermon, a recent Boy Bishop preached on the meaning of blessedness and described scenes painted by the 13th-century artist Lorenzetti:

The final panel shows St Nicholas standing humbly before an altar, wearing what is perhaps a familiar red robe with fur lining. It portrays him confirming his faith as he is given the office of bishop of Myra. Today, as I have been given the office of Boy Bishop of Hereford, perhaps we too, like St Nicholas, should confirm our faith in the love of God, by trying to follow these Christian principles to follow a good life.

So, is to have a mixture of faith, charity, hope and kindness (as depicted in these four pictures) the general meaning of blessedness? Or can all of these things be simplified further to love alone? The genius Mozart, who died on this day in 1791, is once alleged to have said 'Neither a lofty degree of intelligence, nor imagination, nor both together go to the making of genius. Love, love, love – that is the soul of genius.'

And so perhaps the words Love and Friendship are the closest we can get to defining Blessedness and, as we think about those who have shown us love and friendship, either directly through help or indirectly by example, we thank God for these gifts.

Rory Turnbull, *Installation Sermon*, 5 December 2010

The Choristers' Prayer

Bless O Lord, us thy servants who minister in thy Temple. Grant that, what we sing with our lips we may believe in our hearts, and what we believe in our hearts we may show forth in our lives; through Jesus Christ our Lord.

Sir Humphrey Edwin 1642–1707

Local boy made good

There are similarities here with the story of Dick Whittington and our neighbouring Gloucestershire. Humphrey Edwin was the son of a Hereford felt-maker and hatter. His father prospered in the city, becoming an alderman and twice mayor. It was expected that son Humphrey would follow his father and he was apprenticed to a tailor, but soon he set his sights on the big city and established himself as a wool merchant in the city of London. Edwin was involved with several of the city livery companies – as a freeman of the Barber-Surgeons and later as a member of the Skinners' Company, of which he became master in 1691. As a committed Nonconformist, Edwin came to the notice of James II, who was anxious to court the Dissenters to assist him in relaxing the penal laws against Roman Catholics. Edwin was rewarded for his help and was knighted by James in 1688. Later that year he found favour with the new king, William of Orange, attending him as sheriff on his entry to London and taking part in the proclamation of the new king and queen. Edwin held to his dissenting views, although he received the sacrament in order to hold civic office. Once installed, he openly proclaimed himself a Dissenter by attending one of their places of worship in full civic state, preceded by the city sword and mace. Somehow he managed to preserve his office and maintain his religious views – no mean feat in those days! In many ways he was a 'Vicar of Bray' character, happy to serve successive sovereigns and modify his views accordingly.

In 2011, the Friends of Hereford Cathedral visited the capital for a 'Hereford in London' experience – visiting places linking the two cities. Did Edwin look back to his early days in Hereford with affection? Some find the bustle of the city irksome and long for rural solitude – others long for the bright lights. One 17th-century poet could not wait to return to the metropolis from 'dull Devonshire':

From the dull confines of the drooping west,
To see the day spring from the pregnant east,
Ravisht in spirit, I come, nay more, I flie
To thee, blest place of my Nativitie!
Thus, thus with hallowed foot I touch the ground,
With thousand blessings by thy fortune crown'd.
O fruitfull Genius! that bestowest here
An everlasting plenty, yeere by yeere.
O place! O people! Manners! Fram'd to please
All Nations, Customes, Kindreds, Languages!
I am a free-born Roman; suffer then,
That I amongst you live a Citizen.
London my home is; though by hard fate sent
Into a long and irksome banishment;
Yet since call'd back; henceforth let me be,
O native country, repossest by thee!
For, rather than Ile to the West return,
Ile beg of thee first here to have mine Urn.
Weak I am grown, and must in short time fall;
Give thou my sacred Reliques Buriall.

Robert Herrick 1591–1674, 'His Returne to London'

Cyndir 8th century?

Saint of Kenderchurch

Cyndir now has no church dedicated to him in Herefordshire, but Kenderchurch, now dedicated to St Mary, preserves his name (Kenderchurch/Llangyndir), and he must originally have been its patron and probably founder. Some sources suggest that he was, like Clydog (see 3 November), a son or grandson of King Brychan, while others claim that he was descended from Gwynllyw and Gwladys and thus the brother of Cadoc (see 24 January). His most important foundation was at Glasbury, where he was buried. Cyndir is sometimes described as a bishop, and Kenderchurch was possibly the seat of a bishopric between the 6th and 10th centuries. He also established a hermitage on an island in the Wye near Winforton. Blount (see 16 December), writing in 1675, says: 'Bishop Hugh Foliot with Walter, a Canon of Wormsley Priory, betook himself to an Eremetical Life in a little island upon the River Wey [*sic*] ... (which Island is called by the Inhabitants 'Hermit Island') wherein ... he built a Chappel dedicated *deo beatae Mariae, beato Kenedro* – a Saxon saint as I suppose – and afterwards it usually bore the name of St Kendred's Chapel.' Blount lists several important benefactors of this chapel. He continues, 'The church [Winforton] I suppose is also dedicated to the before-mentioned St Kendred, for they keep their feast of dedication at an unusual time, viz: a little before Christmas. The place where St Kendred's Chapel stood is yet called the Chapel Close, where the foundation stones have been lately digged up, and where yet stands an Yew tree, and the place is only surrounded by the River Wey in the Tyme of a flood.'

Although we know little about Cyndir, he is clearly associated with a place of peace and retreat, to which later generations could withdraw to find seclusion and renewal. That sense of peace – which we seek so much as the frantic preparations for Christmas surround us – is captured well by a 17th-century poet, who, like Cyndir, worked and ministered in Breconshire, where Llangyndir is named after him:

My Soul, there is a Countrie
  Far beyond the stars,
Where stands a wingèd Sentry
  All skilfull in the wars,
There, above noise and danger
  Sweet peace sits crown'd with smiles,
And One born in a manger
  Commands the beauteous files.
He is thy gracious friend
  And (O my Soul awake!)
Did in pure love descend
  To die here for thy sake.
If thou canst get but thither,
  There growes the flower of Peace,
The Rose that cannot wither,
  Thy fortresse, and thy ease;
Leave then thy foolish ranges;
  For none can thee secure,
But one, who never changes,
  Thy God, thy life, thy Cure.

Henry Vaughan 1622–95, 'Peace' in *Silex Scintillans* (1650)

William Powell 1736–69

Master of tragedy

Many who saw William Powell acting judged him to be the best interpreter of tragic parts in his generation. Born in Hereford, he was educated at the Cathedral School and on moving to London soon embraced the career of an actor. He came to the attention of David Garrick (see 19 February), who coached him and helped him in his career. Powell was soon drawing vast crowds – all impressed by his great ability to hold audiences and by his skill in interpreting extreme states of mind or feeling. Whether it was *Othello* or *Cymbeline* or *Henry IV* – in all his roles he was praised for 'great feeling', 'tenderness', 'pathos' and 'strong emotions'. After 1766 Powell tried his hand at theatre management, but he never made a great success of this, being criticised by Garrick and others for his lack of culture and qualifications. He continued his acting, especially at Bristol, until his early death at the age of 33 in July 1769. His funeral at Bristol Cathedral was attended by huge crowds. The *Bristol Journal* commented that 'the spectators were too numerous to observe silence and decorum' and were impatient 'to take a final look at him, to whom they had been indebted for so many hours of elegant entertainment'.

Powell's greatest performances were as King Lear – that Shakespearean character who, perhaps above all others, so expresses grief, rage, tragedy and betrayal – those powerful emotions which are shown to tear apart Lear's family. Here Lear speaks of the darkness which can so often envelop human life:

O, reason not the need! Our basest beggars
Are in the poorest thing superfluous.
Allow not nature more than nature needs,
Man's life is cheap as beast's. Thou art a lady;
If only to go warm were gorgeous,
Why, nature needs not what thou gorgeous wear'st,
Which scarcely keeps thee warm. But, for true need –
You heavens, give me that patience, patience I need.
You see me here, you gods, a poor old man,
As full of grief as age; wretched in both.
If it be you that stirs these daughters' hearts
Against their father, fool me not so much
To bear it tamely; touch me with noble anger,
And let not women's weapons, water-drops,
Stain my man's cheeks! No, you unnatural hags,
I will have such revenges on you both
That all the world shall – I will do such things –
What they are yet I know not; but they shall be
The terrors of the earth. You think I'll weep.
No, I'll not weep.
I have full cause of weeping; but this heart
Shall break into a hundred thousand flaws
Or 'ere I'll weep. O fool, I shall go mad.

William Shakespeare 1564–1616, *King Lear*, Act II, Scene 4

George Coke 1570–1646

Bespectacled bishop

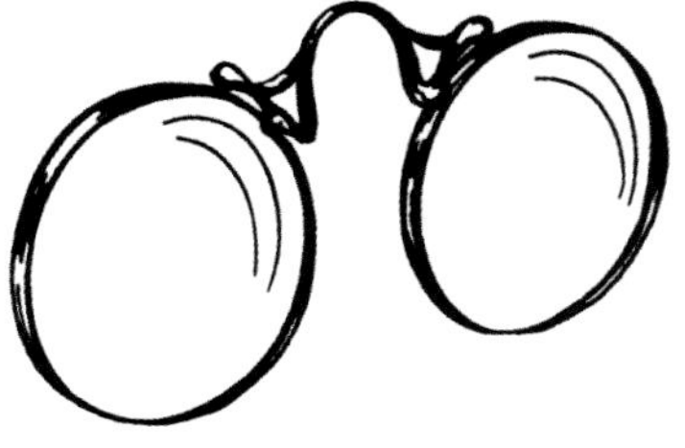

George Coke was bishop of Hereford at a time of great crisis for the city and country. He moved to Hereford from Bristol where he had been bishop and probably owed his preferment to Archbishop William Laud (see 10 January). By all accounts his time at Hereford was not a happy one. He described the city in February 1640 as 'this place of trial, under so much variety of business and among such men, as are too strong and cunning for me'. He estimated that among all the justices in the county, only four were his staunch supporters and he sensed a great deal of opposition. Added to this, he experienced personal and family difficulties – by 1637 his eyesight was failing, and in dim light he was forced to wear spectacles. In October 1638 he was censured by Archbishop Laud for presenting one who was insufficiently learned to a cathedral post. Apparently one of Coke's sons had deserted his apprenticeship and had run away to sea, but seeing in the storms that battered his vessel a sign from heaven, he had turned back, and sought ordination. His indulgent father, Bishop Coke, made him precentor of Hereford Cathedral! Coke was certainly of the high-church party and championed all that the Church of England stood for. When, in 1641, a bill for excluding bishops from the House of Lords was passed by the Commons, 12 bishops, including Coke petitioned Parliament, for which he was impeached and imprisoned for 17 weeks. Retiring to his see, he was in Hereford in April 1643 when it fell to Parliament, but under the articles of surrender of the town, escaped further persecution. However, when Hereford fell for the second time, in December 1645, Coke was taken prisoner and sent to Gloucester and thence, in August 1646, to London. He was allowed to return to his house at Eardisley and here he died on this day in 1646. Coke was buried in Eardisley church and there is a cenotaph in his memory in the south-east transept of Hereford Cathedral.

The high-church party and the Puritans disagreed on many matters. They would certainly have differed in their definition of 'a saint'. The Puritan party would have focused on saints as the 'living people of God', while others, like Coke, would have been happy to proclaim and honour saints after their death. A contemporary of Coke's writes powerfully of the importance of saints as deserving of honour in each generation:

Now, as these are the saints of the church of Christ, from whence they were called the 'churches of the saints' (1 Corinthians 14:33) so there was never any church of God, but there were such persons in it as were saints. We read in the Psalms of 'the congregation and the assembly of the saints' (Psalm 89:5,7) and Moses assured the people of Israel, that all the saints of God were in his hand (Deuteronomy 33:3): we read in the prophets of 'the saints of the Most High' (Daniel 7:25) and at our Saviour's death 'the bodies of such saints which slept arose'. (Matthew 27:52). Where again we may observe, that they were saints while their bodies were in the grave; as Aaron in the time of David kept the name of 'the saint of the Lord'. (Psalm 106:16). Such as are holy in their lives do not lose their sanctity, but improve it at their deaths; nor can they lose the honour of that appellation, while that which gives it doth acquire perfection.

Hence grows that necessary distinction of the saints on earth, and the saints in heaven; the first belonging to the militant, the second to the triumphant church. And all those which were spoken of as saints then in the earth, if truly such, and departed so, are now, and shall for ever continue, saints in heaven.

John Pearson 1613–86, *An Exposition of the Creed* (1659)

Alexander Clogie 1614–98

Biographer & peace-maker

This Scotsman made his home in Herefordshire, at Wigmore, and there served faithfully as a parish priest and champion of peace. He moved at an early age from his native Scotland and studied at Trinity College, Dublin. On ordination he served in the diocese of Kilmore and assisted the bishop, William Bedell, in his translation of the scriptures into Irish. On the outbreak of the Civil War he travelled to England with troops dispatched by the marquess of Ormond to serve the King, acting as chaplain to the cavalry. By September 1646 he was minister at Beoley in Worcestershire and by the following year was officiating minister at Wigmore, a living in the hands of the Parliamentarian Harley family. Clogie remained at Wigmore for the rest of his life. On his being threatened with deportation back to Scotland, his parish successfully petitioned in his favour. As well as being a faithful parish priest, he turned his hand to biography and wrote, during the 1670s, *Speculum episcoporum* or *The apostolique bishop, being a brief account of the lyfe and death of the reverend father in God, D. William Bedell* – this work was not published until 1862. He also published *Vox corvi* or *The Voice of a Raven* (1694), a sermon prompted by an incident where his grandson heard a raven 'that thrice spoke these words distinctly: "Look into Colossians the 3rd, and 15th",' a command which Clogie related to a family dispute in the parish. He died in 1698 at Wigmore, where he is buried.

A contemporary of Clogie's, who himself learned to work for peace and concord in the turbulent Ireland of his day, speaks of the importance of a daily rule of life in seeking to engage with God:

Suppose every day to be a day of business; for your whole life is a race and a battle, a merchandize, and a journey: every day propound yourself a rosary or a chaplet of good works, to present to God at night ...

Read not much at a time; but meditate as much as your time and capacity and disposition will give you leave: ever remembering, that little reading, and much thinking: little speaking and much hearing: frequent and short prayers, and great devotion, is the best way to be wise, to be holy, to be devout.

Receive the blessed sacrament as often as you can: endeavour to have it once a month, besides the solemn and great festivals of the year.

Confess your sins often, hear the word of God, make religion the business of your life, your study and chiefest care; and be sure that in all things a spiritual guide take you by the hand.

Thou shalt always rejoice in the evening, if thou dost spend thy day virtuously.

Jeremy Taylor 1613–67, *The Golden Grove* (1655)

The words – passed on to Clogie by his grandson – which inspired him to write and work for peace in his neighbourhood:

Let the peace of Christ rule in your hearts, to which indeed you were called in the one body. And be thankful.

Colossians 3:15

John Boydell 1720–1804

Engraver par excellence

One of my earliest memories is seeing on a relative's wall an engraving of 'The Laughing Cavalier'. These mass-produced engravings were hugely popular in the early 20th century, and enabled famous paintings to become known to a wider constituency. Influential in the history of engraving is a local man, John Boydell, who was born in Dorrington in Shropshire on 19 January 1720. Like others of his day, he was disinclined to lose a year of his life to the change in calendar and so always gave the year of his birth in 'old style', as 1719. It was while staying at Hawarden in North Wales that he discovered artistic gifts and was especially drawn to the medium of engraving. Moving to London, he quickly cornered the market in the production of foreign prints, then much in vogue, learned French and often visited Parisian printsellers. Boydell gained a reputation for historical prints, taking the works of the great masters and 'translating' them into a form which could be purchased by a great variety of connoisseurs. His shop became a tourist attraction and he soon became an esteemed figure in the city of London, becoming an alderman and, in 1790, lord mayor. Perhaps his most famous work is a series of prints illustrating the works of Shakespeare. To house these and to attract customers, a new gallery was built in Pall Mall, and when it was opened, 20,000 people visited, 6,600 catalogues were sold and many names added to the subscription. Boydell's last years were dogged by financial problems and ill health, and he died on this day in 1804 at his house in Cheapside.

The image of engraving is nowhere more movingly described than in Job's answer to his accusers:

O that my words were written!
O that they were inscribed in a book!
O that with an iron pen and lead they were graven in the rock for ever!
For I know that my Redeemer lives,
and at the last he will stand upon the earth;
and after my skin has been thus destroyed,
then from my flesh I shall see God,
whom I shall see on my side,
and my eyes shall behold, and not another.

Job 19:23–27

Boydell's reproductions of the great masters were peerless in their time. But do reproductions keep faithfully to the original, or do they attempt to 'improve' and 'correct'? It is always a temptation! Shakespeare knew all about such temptations:

Therefore, to be possess'd with double pomp,
To guard a title that was rich before,
To gild refined gold, to paint the lily,
To throw a perfume on the violet,
To smooth the ice, or add another hue
Unto the rainbow, or with taper-light
To seek the beauteous eye of heaven to garnish,
Is wasteful and ridiculous excess.

William Shakespeare 1564–1616, *King John*, Act IV, Scene 2

December

Sir James Rankin, baronet 1842–1915

Politician & benefactor

A stained glass window in the south aisle of Hereford Cathedral depicts the visit to the city by Charles I in 1645. The window is given in memory of Sir James Rankin, a man at the heart of Herefordshire life for over 30 years in the late 19th and early 20th centuries. A shipping and trade magnate, he inherited Bryngwyn Manor at Wormelow and there built a magnificent manor in 1868 designed by Frederick Kempson (see 20 June). This served as a base for his political activities – as chief steward for the city of Hereford 1878–1915 and as Member of Parliament for Leominster and north Herefordshire three times between 1880 and 1912. His memorial in St David's church, Much Dewchurch, describes him thus: 'Through life his law was duty and his end was peace'. Created a baronet (of Bryngwyn) in 1898, the title passed to his son on Rankin's death. Lt Col Reginald Rankin achieved notoriety as a big-game hunter, shooting and killing the largest snow leopard recorded in India. He also survived being frozen solid after falling asleep on an expedition in the Andes!

James Rankin's qualities are enshrined not only in his epitaph at Much Dewchurch but also by his family motto – Prudentia et Virtute *– words seen in the apex of the window he gave to commemorate Charles I. Perhaps Rankin was drawn to Charles I as one who, despite huge opposition from others, sought in his life to embody these principles – principles found in his last speech:*

So, Sirs, I do wish with all my soul, and I do hope there is some here [turning to some gentlemen that wrote] that will carry it further, that they may endeavour the peace of the kingdom.

Now, sirs, I must show you both how you are out of the way and will put you in the way.

First, you are out of the way, for certainly all the way you have ever had yet, as I could find by anything, is by way of conquest. Certainly this is an ill way, for Conquest, sirs, in my opinion, is never just, except that there be a good just cause, either for matter of wrong or just title. And then if you go beyond it, the first quarrel that you have to it, that makes it unjust at the end that was just at the first. But if it be only matter of conquest, then it is a great robbery, as a pirate said to Alexander the Great, that he was the great robber, he [the pirate] was just a petty robber. And so, sirs, I do think the way that you are in, is much out of the way.

Now, sirs, to put you in the way. Believe it, you will never do right, nor God will never prosper you, until you give God his due, the King his due (that is, my successors) and the people their due. I am as much for them as any of you.

You must give God his due by regulating rightly His Church according to the Scripture, which is now out of order. For to set you in a way particularly, now I cannot, but only this. A national synod freely called, freely debating among themselves, must settle this, when that every opinion is freely and clearly heard.

Speech of Charles I from the scaffold, Whitehall, 30 January 1649

Lennox Bertram Lee 1864–1949

Textile magnate & benefactor

The generosity of this man did much to enrich and beautify Hereford Cathedral during the 20th century. Lennox Lee was educated at Eton and, years later, he commemorated this through his support for new stained glass for the Stanbury Chapel, showing Bishop Stanbury's links with Eton (see 11 May). He joined the family textile firm which, after amalgamations in 1899, became the Calico Printers' Association, thus forming the country's largest company. As chairman of the board, a post he held until 1947, he developed the textile industry worldwide, successfully challenging foreign competition, especially from India and Japan. With keen foresight, Lee pioneered direct investment abroad, with printworks in China and Egypt during the 1930s followed by Java, Australia and South Africa during the Second World War. Lee and his associates were also in the vanguard of new scientific developments in the textile industry, and in the early 1940s developed the potential of Terylene, discovered in the company's laboratories. Much of his work was focused in the north and he became an outspoken defender of Lancashire traditions and interests, with their important role in the national textile industry. He preferred, however, to retreat to Herefordshire and to his estate at How Caple, where he had lived since 1901. He played an active part in county society, reared pigs and took a keen interest in the Church of England and the architectural beauty of its buildings. He gave generously towards the restoration of How Caple church and of the cathedral's Lady Chapel, where there is a memorial tablet to him. In 1932 he was instrumental in setting up the Friends of Hereford Cathedral. He died on this day in 1949.

The book of Exodus *is full of references to the importance of textiles in the offering of worship. Here, God gives instructions for the furnishing of the tabernacle in the wilderness:*

Moreover you shall make the tabernacle with ten curtains of fine twined linen and blue and purple and scarlet stuff; with cherubim skilfully worked shall you make them. The length of each curtain shall be twenty-eight cubits, and the breadth of each curtain four cubits. Five curtains shall be coupled to one another; and the other five curtains shall be coupled to one another. And you shall make loops of blue on the edge of the outmost curtain in the first set; and likewise you shall make loops on the edge of the outmost curtain in the second set. You shall make the robe of the ephod all of blue. It shall have in it an opening for the head, with a woven binding around the opening, like the opening of a garment, that it may not be torn. On its skirts you shall make pomegranates of blue and purple and scarlet stuff, around its skirts, with bells of gold between them, a golden bell and a pomegranate, round about on the skirts of the robe.

Exodus 6 & 28

A poem, written many years later, uses the image of beautiful fabrics to express love and devotion:

Had I the heavens' embroidered cloths,
Enwrought with golden and silver light,
The blue and the dim and the dark cloths
Of night and light and the half-light,
I would spread the cloths under your feet.
But I, being poor, have only my dreams;
I have spread my dreams under your feet;
Tread softly, because you tread on my dreams.

William Butler Yeats 1865–1939, 'Aedh wishes for the Cloths of Heaven'

John Newton 1621–78

Priestly mathematician

John Newton was passionate about the place of mathematics in life and education and used his training in this discipline to support himself by teaching when ejected from his living during the Commonwealth. At the Restoration, he became vicar of Ross-on-Wye, a living which he held until his death. In addition he was, for a time, rector of Stretton Sugwas and prebendary at Hereford Cathedral. But alongside his pastoral ministry, Newton continued his work as a mathematician and astronomer. He wrote a series of books advocating the use of decimal arithmetic, insisting that it was his 'chief aim to show how much of trouble may be avoided in computing the motions of heavenly bodies, if only the form of our Tables were changed from Sexagenery into Decimall'. As vicar of Ross, Newton argued strongly for the teaching of mathematics in the English language and in his illustrated *School Pastime for Young Children* (1669) he wrote: 'Let this book be given to Children, to delight themselves withal as they please, with the sight of the Pictures, and making them as familiar to themselves as may be, and that even at Home, before they be put to School.' Newton died on 26 December 1678 at Ross and was buried two days later in the chancel of the parish church of St Mary.

Mathematics and the Christian faith are closely linked, not least in notions of the perfection of God, and this is especially seen in the way in which the medieval mind insisted on the perfection of geometry in its buildings:

The relationship between sacred space and geometry is vital in thinking about medieval sacred space. Today we tend to think of beauty as in the eye of the beholder. For Augustine of Hippo and those who followed him, beauty was rather more objective. Something could be beautiful if it exactly mirrored the geometric regularity of the divine order, and if it did, it had by definition to be beautiful. Chartres is the supreme example, where the builders embraced the sacredness of geometry and the aesthetic consequences of exposure to it. They believed that geometry was a means of linking human beings to God, that mathematics was a vehicle for revealing to humankind the innermost secrets of heaven. This could lead to disastrous consequences, of course. Because builders aspired to model their structures on divine order they assumed that, as long as they kept to strict geometric principles, their buildings would be structurally safe and sound. Some assumed that, even when buildings were showing signs of instability, one had only to keep building until geometric regularity was achieved for all to be well. We take warning from William Golding's terrifying novel *The Spire* (see 17 April). Geometry was vital in any consideration of medieval sacred space, but it could also be dangerous!

For us today, the geometry and mathematical perfection of medieval buildings are hugely awe-inspiring. 'How did they do it in those days?' is a frequently asked question in our cathedrals. Indeed, the perfection, balance and proportion of the finest of our cathedrals and sacred spaces may well speak to us about God: these images of beauty, balance and proportion surely feed our contemporary society with much-needed images of that God of perfection. But equally, for us today, it is important to place into these perfect areas elements which help us to see images of God that are not perfect. If God is to be made sense of amid the horrors of the twentieth century with its world wars and of the twenty-first century with its terrorism, then surely our sacred spaces must reflect this; otherwise we will simply associate God with grandeur, perfection and inaccessibility. This is why contemporary art is so important ... such art [in cathedrals] challenges and often shocks us into re-thinking our images of God.

Michael Tavinor b.1953, from *Sacred Space: House of God, Gate of Heaven* (2007)

Thomas Blount 1618–79

Hereford's Dr Johnson

WORDS

We associate early dictionaries of the English language with the name of Dr Samuel Johnson. One hundred years before Johnson, Herefordshire was making its mark in this through the work of Thomas Blount. His *Glossographia* (1656) was the first dictionary to give sources for definitions and to attempt etymologies. In 1670 he published *Nomolexikhon* – a dictionary of legal terms, which, like his earlier work, was plundered by plagiarists and issued under other names. It is, however, as an antiquarian that Blount is chiefly remembered today. In his latter years he embarked on a history of Herefordshire. He visited a large number of churches and in about 1677 compiled the history in two volumes, arranged alphabetically by parish. Although never published, it has been used by every subsequent historian of the county. The first volume, relating to parishes A to K, was lost in the mid-18th century, but the second volume was acquired by Hereford City Library in 1956. Blount was a Catholic and suffered persecution as a result of the wave of anti-Catholic sentiment in the wake of the Popish Plot of 1678/9. During that time he wrote to a friend that he was sick with 'a spice of the palsey, from what occasion you may conjecture' and that he had 'quitted all books except of devotion'. He died at Orleton Manor on 26 December and was buried in the chancel of the parish church.

Like Blount, Dr Johnson was not only a writer of dictionaries! He was a man of deep religion and his compassion for others shines through in this sermon:

Wherever the eye is turned it sees much misery, and there is much which it sees not; many complaints are heard, and there are many pangs without complaint. The external acts of mercy, to feed the hungry, to clothe the naked, and to visit the sick and the prisoners, we see daily opportunities of performing; and it may be hoped, they are not neglected by those that abound with what others want.

But there are other calls upon charity. There are sick minds as well as sick bodies; there are understandings perplexed with scruples, there are consciences tormented with guilt; nor can any greater benefit be conferred, than that of settling doubts, or comforting despair, and restoring a disquieted soul to hope and tranquillity.

The duty of commiseration is so strongly pressed by the gospel, that none deny its obligation. But as the measures of beneficence are left undefined, every man necessarily determines for himself, whether he has contributed his share to the necessities of others; and amidst the general depravity of the world, it can be no wonder if there are found some who tax themselves very lightly, and are satisfied with giving very little.

Samuel Johnson 1709–84. From a sermon on the text 'Finally be ye all of one mind, having compassion one of another, love as brethren, be pitiful, be courteous.' (1 Peter 3:8)

A prayer of Dr Johnson 'before any new study'

Almighty God, in whose hands are all the powers of man; who givest understanding, and takest it away; who, as it seemeth good unto Thee, enlightenest the thoughts of the simple, and darkenest the meditations of the wise, be present with me in my studies and enquiries.

Enable me, by Thy Holy Spirit, so to shun sloth and negligence, that every day may discharge part of the task which Thou hast allotted me; and so further with Thy help that labour which, without Thy help, must be ineffectual, that I may obtain, in all my undertakings, such success as will most promote Thy glory, and the salvation of my own soul, for the sake of Jesus Christ. Amen.

Richard Reece 1775–1831

Apocalyptic physician

Richard Reece was a celebrated medical writer and a native of Colwall, where his father was curate. After a time as apprentice to a country surgeon and as assistant at the Hereford Infirmary, he moved to London and practised in Covent Garden. In 1814 Reece became involved in the controversy surrounding the case of Joanna Southcott. Born in Devonshire, she became persuaded that she possessed supernatural gifts, wrote and dictated prophecies in rhyme and announced herself as the woman spoken of in Revelation 12. Coming to London at the age of 64, she affirmed that she was pregnant and would be delivered of the New Messiah, the Shiloh of Genesis 49:10. Southcott consulted a number of medical men on the subject, including Richard Reece, who gave a guarded diagnosis that her belief was well founded. The birth date was fixed for 19 October 1814 and so great was the excitement that the streets leading to her residence were thronged with sightseers. The day arrived and passed, and the expected birth did not happen – indeed the pronounced pregnancy turned out to be dropsy and the unfortunate Southcott died on 17 December. The reputation of Richard Reece suffered and although he tried to vindicate himself in a pamphlet entitled *A Plain Narrative of the Circumstances attending the last Illness and Death of Joanna Southcott*, his professional work was severely affected. As for the Southcott prophecies, they continued, as Joanna had left a sealed box of prophecies and her followers, known as Southcottians (they numbered 100,000 at her death), guarded this, with its instruction that it be opened only at a time of national crisis – and then only in the presence of all 24 bishops of the Church of England. Attempts were made to persuade the episcopate to open it during the Crimean War and again during the First World War. Eventually, one reluctant prelate, the bishop of Grantham, was persuaded to be present at the box's opening in 1927, but it was found to contain only a few oddments, among them a lottery ticket and a horse-pistol – a strange story indeed!

Richard Reece became involved in Joanna Southcott's strange notions of the second coming and the advent of the Messiah. It is a theme much in evidence in the season of Advent but, while the last judgement may be a theme on which to ponder, we may be better directed to search for the advent of God not in the spectacular, but in the here and now:

Advent should admonish us to discover
in each brother or sister that we greet,
in each friend whose hand we shake,
in each beggar who asks for bread,
in each worker who wants to use the right to join a union,
in each peasant who looks for work in the coffee groves,
the face of Christ.
Then it would not be possible to rob them,
to cheat them,
to deny them their rights.
They are Christ,
and whatever is done to them
Christ will take as done to himself.
This is what Advent is:
Christ living among us.

Oscar Romero 1917–80, 'Advent'

Israel Tonge 1621–80

Spy & informer

The Popish Plot of 1678 led to a wave of anti-Catholic sentiment throughout the land and to the deaths of many innocent people. We associate the plot with the name of Titus Oates, but he was, in turn, encouraged by Israel Tonge – by all accounts a rather shady character. Tonge was clearly an accomplished man, being skilled in gardening, alchemy and chemistry. He was ordained and turned his hand to schoolmastering. In 1661, through the patronage of Edward Harley, he became incumbent at Leintwardine and later, in 1666, he was given the rectory of St Mary Stayning in London, but this burnt down during the Great Fire of London and with this catastrophe Tonge's mind appears to have become permanently disturbed. Tonge became obsessive about the Jesuits, whom he blamed for his own losses as well as those of the nation. After a period abroad, he returned to Herefordshire as rector of Pipe Aston, a post he held from 1672 to 1677. In 1677 Tonge met Titus Oates, whom he fed with anti-papal propaganda. Together they wrote pamphlets and hatched the rumours of Jesuit intrigue and treason which issued in the famous plot of 1678. When interviewed about the plot, Tonge's motives were suspected and he was dismissed as a man only 'making discoveries ... [in the hope that he would] get himself to be made a dean'. Tonge was himself brought before the Privy Council to relate his tale but his rambling style disturbed the Council and they put more credence in Oates, who now became the 'saviour of the nation' and who took the main reward for revealing his spurious plot. Tonge wrote a huge number of tracts including *Jesuit Assassins* (1680) and *New Design of Papists Detected* (1679) in which he continued his anti-Jesuit ramblings. He persisted on his deathbed in his belief in the plot's truthfulness and died in London on this day in 1680.

I wonder if Israel Tonge ever read any works by the great Jesuit authors? If he had, perhaps he would have come to realise that their spirituality was not to be feared but, on the contrary, made an important contribution to our understanding of God in ways which can be approached and understood by Christians of all denominations:

It belongs to God and his angels to bring true happiness and spiritual joy to the soul and to free it from all the sadness and disturbance which the enemy causes. It is the nature of the enemy to fight against such joy and spiritual consolation by proposing false reasons, subtleties, and continual deceptions.

Also, it is characteristic of the evil one to transform himself into an angel of light, to work with the soul in the beginning, but in the end work for himself. At first he will suggest good and holy thoughts, and then, little by little he strives to gain his own ends by drawing the soul into his hidden deceits.

In those who are making spiritual progress, the action of the good angel is gentle, light and sweet, as a drop of water entering a sponge. The action of the evil spirit is sharp, noisy, and disturbing, like a drop of water falling upon a rock. In those souls that are going from bad to worse, the action of these two spirits is the reverse.

The cause of this difference of action is the disposition of the soul which is either contrary or similar to the spirits mentioned above. When the disposition of the soul is contrary to that of the spirits, they enter it with noise and disturbances which are easily perceived. When the disposition of the soul and that of the spirits are similar, they enter silently as one coming into his own house through an open door.

Ignatius of Loyola 1491–1556, *Spiritual Exercises*

David Griffiths 1792–1863
Missionary in Hay & Kington

When David Griffiths returned from the mission field in 1842, he settled as pastor of the Congregational church at Hay and formed a new meeting at Kington. What stories of his earlier life he must have shared with his congregations! He had been appointed, in 1820, as a missionary to Madagascar and here he spent over 20 years. With his colleague, David Jones, he established congregations and schools, and a chapel was annexed to Griffiths' house which could hold 1,000 people. In 1824 King Radama allowed the missionaries to preach in the Malagasy language for the first time, and by 1828 Griffiths had completed and published a catechism, hymn book and some schoolbooks, all in Malagasy. In July 1828 King Radama, who had been a great friend of the missionaries, died. A period of political upheaval followed and the missionary work was disrupted. The new monarch, Queen Ranavalona, did not support preaching or hymn singing but she approved of education and so the work of translation could continue. By 1831 the whole of the New Testament and a large part of the Old Testament had been published in the vernacular. The queen's liberal attitude was not mirrored by her ministers and in 1836 Griffiths and his colleagues were expelled and they returned to England. However, two years later Queen Ranavalona suggested that Griffiths might return, but as a merchant rather than a missionary. This he did, but Christians were still being persecuted and Griffiths was found guilty of helping some native Christians to escape to Mauritius. He was given a death sentence, later commuted to a fine. On his final return to Britain, as well as his work in Hay and Kington, he continued his work of translation, producing a Malagasy grammar and a book, *The Persecuted Christians of Madagascar* (1841). He died on 21 March 1863 at Machynlleth and was buried there.

A contemporary of Griffiths, Bishop Reginald Heber (with strong Shropshire connections) wrote, famously, on the importance of missionary work in a hymn sung by many in former years. We may well find some of its sentiments hard to take today, yet these words bear witness to the zeal and courage of many of our early missionaries:

From Greenland's icy mountains,
    From India's coral strand,
Where Afric's sunny fountains
    Roll down their golden sand.
From many an ancient river,
    From many a palmy plain,
They call us to deliver
    Their land from error's chain.

Waft, waft, ye winds, His story,
    And you, ye waters, roll,
Till, like a sea of glory,
    It spreads from pole to pole;
Till o'er our ransom'd nature
    The Lamb for sinners slain,
Redeemer, King, Creator,
    In bliss returns to reign.

Reginald Heber 1783–1826, *Hymns Ancient and Modern* (1861)

Richard Gardiner 1591–1670

God's planter

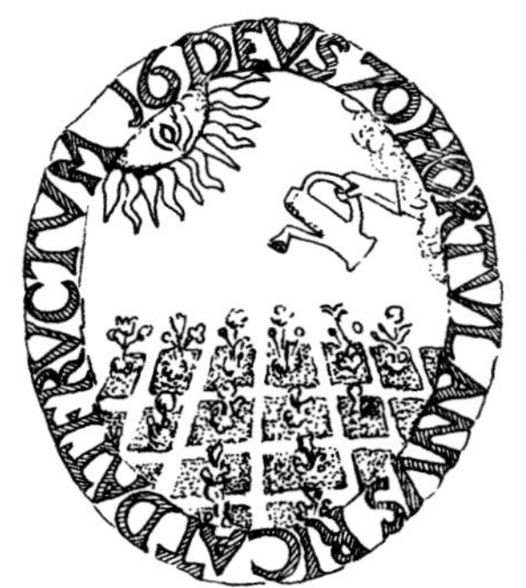

The unusual plaque in Hereford's College Hall shows a garden planted with flowers, being watered by a hand emerging from a cloud above. The inscription – *Hortulanus rigat dat fructum Deus* ('the gardener plants but God gives the growth') – is a rebus or pun on the name of the man we commemorate today. Richard Gardiner, a canon of the cathedral was probably responsible for the restoration of College Hall and the date on the plaque – 1670 – gives a clue to this. Thomas Dingley (see 7 May), writing in 1684, makes mention of 'a very fair and square refectory or hall looking into their garden and towards the river Wye. Over the screen whereof it carried this rebus painted carved and gilded.' The college accounts for 1670–1 seem to confirm this, with their mention that a 'balcony on pillars' had been constructed in College Hall. Gardiner was born and bred in Hereford, studied at Christchurch, Oxford and became 'a quaint preacher and orator'. He was presented to a Christchurch canonry by James I, before whom he had delivered a Latin oration 'in the scotch tone', which clearly pleased the Scottish king! Ejected from his canonry at the Commonwealth, he was reinstated at the Restoration. Although most of his life revolved around Oxfordshire, Gardiner clearly had a great affection for Hereford, not least in the generosity he showed towards the college of vicars choral.

Gardiner clearly found God in the gardens surrounding his hall, running down to the river Wye. Gardens often give us glimpses of God – the Garden of Eden is central to the story of Man's fall and it is in a garden that the risen Christ is first glimpsed by Mary Magdalen. In this poem, the garden of Gethsemane provides the setting for the agonies and desolation of Christ on the eve of his crucifixion:

O, what a desolate garden that enfolds your grief and despair
Agony replacing an Eden; darkness replacing the light.
The trees of life groan under the weight of impending death.
In the tomblike stillness you bring Peter, James and John
– The same disciples who were eyewitnesses to your dazzling transformation –
Beseeching them to bear witness to your prayers
To stay with you during this, your night of deep distress.
Yet huddled together under a tree they sleep on, whether in tiredness or grief you know not
Their eyes heavy and weary, sorrowful yet not fully understanding.
But while they slumber, to your anguish the garden is brutally awake,
The moonlight creates a suspicious spotlight across the floor, casting foliage into an eerie half-light.
The very leaves of the shady olive grove act as ears to your moment of terror and dread.
Lying face-down in the dust you pray for courage to conclude your earth-enclosed life.
Grieved and agitated, fearful and despairing, you cry tormented tears of blood.
Clinging to the soil with clenched fists, you ask the question while already knowing the answer,
For you plead with your heavenly father to dissolve this death-filled cup from your lips.
Yet you yearn to fulfil God's will; to summon the strength to surrender to your Passion,
And you will – resolutely resolved that the road from Gethsemane to Golgotha is yours to walk alone.
'Awake!' Thrice you cry to your disciples, 'could you not stay awake one hour?'
'How little you comprehend; for your spirit is willing but your flesh is weak,
For the hour is at hand for the Son of Man to be betrayed to the hands of sinners.'
You hear them approach, trespassing the garden, and the time has come
To be handed over to death with a kiss.

Kirsty Clarke b.1981, 'Gethsemane' (2009)

Philip Clissett 1817–1913

Bosbury chair-maker

As the Christmas festival draws near, our thoughts turn to the various characters in that great story and to Joseph – so often 'on the margins'. We remember his humble background – his life as a carpenter, a craftsman. Today, we remember a local man who, many years later, followed the same profession as Joseph. Philip Clissett was born in Birtsmorton, Worcestershire and moved to Bosbury on his marriage in 1840. Here he set up business as a chair-maker – a craft he had learned from his father, who had, in turn, inherited his skills from his father. Clissett became well-known for making chairs in the traditional way, splitting green wood and shaping it with a draw-knife on a pole lathe, and his ladder-back and spindle-back chairs became much sought after. He came to the attention of the Arts and Crafts Movement in the mid-1880s, when the architect James MacLaren came upon Clissett's workshop by chance. MacLaren introduced Clissett to key people in the movement, among them Ernest Gimson, who came to Bosbury to be taught by the master. Gimson produced several famous designs based on Clissett's ladder-back. In addition to his work in chair-making, Clissett was parish constable in Bosbury between 1844 and 1849, as well as being a keen gardener – he won prizes in the Colwall Flower Show for many years in succession. He passed on his craft to his son and grandsons and was still making chairs well into his 90s. He died in January 1913 and his funeral took place in the Wesleyan Chapel in Bosbury, where he was a keen member. Clissett's chairs may be found in collections and museums throughout the world and 50 of them still grace the Great Hall of the Art Workers' Guild in London.

Through his relationship with Joseph, Jesus has always been seen as a carpenter and as having an affinity with those who work with their hands. In this poem, we see woodworking as an image of integrity:

What is he?
– A man, of course.
Yes, but what does he do?
– He lives and is a man.
Oh quite! But he must work. He must have a job of some sort.
– Why?
Because obviously he's not one of the leisured classes.
– I don't know. He has lots of leisure. And he makes quite beautiful chairs.
There you are then! He's a cabinet maker.
– No, no!
Anyhow a carpenter and joiner.
– Not at all.
But you said so.
– What did I say?
That he made chairs, and was a joiner and carpenter.
– I said he made chairs, but I did not say he was a carpenter.
Alright then, he's just an amateur.
Perhaps – but would you say a thrush was a professional flautist or just an amateur?
I'd say it was just a bird.
– And I say he is just a man.
All right! You always did quibble.

D H Lawrence 1885–1930, 'What is he?', *Collected Poems*

Thomas Banks 1735–1805
Sculptor

Thomas Banks, regarded as a founding father of the British school of sculpture, was born in London on this day in 1735 and educated at Ross-on-Wye. He first studied under his father, who worked for the famous architect William Kent, and went on to study sculpture in London under Peter Scheemakers. He came to the attention of the London art world through his sculpting of classical scenes and developed this skill during his time in Rome and St Petersburg. He gained greater fame with his church memorials, which included the recumbent effigy of Penelope Boothby in Ashbourne church, Derbyshire, which depicts the six-year-old child sleeping. Other important memorials include one to Isaac Watts in Westminster Abbey. In his later years, Banks specialised in portrait busts – his last exhibited work, a bust of Oliver Cromwell, was ordered to be withdrawn from the exhibition of 1803 to avoid embarrassment to the Royal Academy. In spite of this, he retained his reputation as the doyen of late 18th-century sculptors and was called on to advise by the highest in the land. Today, his work may be seen in many museums and in the entrance halls of country houses such as Stowe in Buckinghamshire and Holkham Hall in Norfolk. Above all, Banks showed that Britain could produce sculpture of the highest order, and was the first of his native land to seriously challenge works of the earlier generation of immigrant sculptors like Roubiliac, Rysbrack and Scheemakers. He is buried in the churchyard of St Mary, Paddington and there is a tablet to his honour in Westminster Abbey – the first erected to a sculptor in that great church.

Thomas Banks specialised in producing great images of famous people and scenes. These he 'brought to life', enabling viewers to feel as if they were part of the scene. One of the great Christmas messages is about Christ as our great 'image' of God. When we look on Christ, we see the most perfect image of God that we could ever imagine or want and through that image we are drawn into the being of God himself.

A writer from earlier in the 18th century speaks powerfully of this:

But now, was there any wonder ever comparable to this! To behold Divinity thus clothed in flesh! The Creator of all things humbled not only to the company, but also to the cognation of His creatures! It is as if we should imagine the whole world not only represented upon, but also contained in one of our little artificial globes; or the body of the sun enveloped in a cloud as big as a man's hand, all which would be looked upon as astonishing possibilities and yet as short of the other as the greatest finite is of the infinite, between which the disparity is immeasurable. For that God should thus in a manner transform himself, and subdue and master all his glories to a possibility of human apprehension and converse, the best reason would have thought it such a thing as God could not do, had it not seen it actually done. It is, as it were, to cancel the essential distances of things, to remove the bounds of Nature, to bring Heaven and Earth, and (what is more) both ends of the contradiction, together.

Robert South 1634–1716, *Sermons* (1692)

ROWLAND WATKYNS *c.*1614–64

Longtown's Christmas poet

THE MOST famous poem of this son of the Welsh borders is on the theme of Christmas, and so we remember him today. Born in Longtown, Rowland Watkyns attended Jesus College, Oxford, was ordained and became vicar of Llanfrynach, near Brecon, in 1635. A loyal Anglican, during the Commonwealth he was deprived of his living, returning to his parish on the Restoration of Charles II. His high-church leanings are reflected in his poetry, in which he is contemptuous of Presbyterians whom he regards as 'the new illiterate lay-teachers'. He was a neighbour of the better-known Henry Vaughan, but they appear to have been rivals, often disagreeing with one another. Like Vaughan, Watkyns also had medical skills and these are reflected in his most famous poem *Flamma sine fumo* (Smoke without fire) which contains medical terms, and in *A Looking-Glasse for the Sicke* (1662). Indeed, it may well be that Watkyns practised as a physician while he was deprived of his living. In relation to contemporary medical controversy, Watkyns and Vaughan seem to have taken opposing positions. Watkyns advocated herbal cures, while Vaughan practised Paracelsian or 'chymical' medicine. In any case, Watkyns' remedies are most unappealing – his herbal remedies suggest crow's dung applied directly for the toothache, goat's dung for the fistula and 'dog's toords' for the 'flux'. Watkyns' will was drawn up on 18 October 1664 and proved on 8 November of the same year. His estate amounted to about £24, more than half of it in corn – his books were valued at £1.

Like Henry Vaughan, Watkyns wrote a poem on Christ's Nativity, the feast disliked by many Puritans. He published none of his poetry until 1662, when the Commonwealth was over and it was safe to do so:

From three dark places Christ came forth this day:
From first His Father's bosom, where He lay,
Concealed till now; then from the typic law,
Where we His manhood but by figures saw;
And lastly from His mother's womb He came
To us, a perfect God and perfect Man.

Now in a manger lies the eternal Word:
The Word He is, yet can no speech afford;
He is the Bread of Life, yet hungry lies;
The Living Fountain, yet for drink He cries;
He cannot help or clothe Himself at need
Who did the lilies clothe and ravens feed;
He is the Light of Lights, yet now doth shroud
His glory with our nature as a cloud.
He came to us a Little One, that we
Like little children might in malice be;
Little He is, and wrapped in clouts, lest He
Might strike us dead if clothed with majesty.

Christ had four beds and those not soft nor brave:
The Virgin's womb, the manger, cross, and grave.
The angels sing this day, and so will I
That have more reason to be glad than they.

Rowland Watkyns, 'Upon Christ's Nativity'

James Atlay 1817–94

Bishop who died at Christmas

The death of Bishop James Atlay on Christmas Eve 1894 must have cast gloom on both cathedral and diocese. Atlay had been a much loved bishop and his loss was keenly felt. After Cambridge and ordination, he served in parish ministry in Nottinghamshire and near Cambridge, but it was as a tutor at his old college, St John's, that he showed his particular skills as an educator of the young. This skill he extended in his next post as vicar of Leeds. Here, Atlay continued the distinguished ministry of his predecessor, Walter Hook, training many curates and running his parish with huge care and efficiency. In 1867 he refused the bishopric of Calcutta, but the following year he accepted Disraeli's offer of the bishopric of Hereford, in succession to Renn Dickson Hampden (see 24 April). Atlay brought to the diocese the same thoroughness which had been so successful at Leeds and Cambridge. Except for his times of duty in the House of Lords, he rarely left the diocese, but spent all his time focused on his clergy and their parishes. He is said to have visited every church in the diocese and certainly worked tirelessly for the improvement of clergy incomes and accommodation. Education was of great importance to him – he supported its extension in the diocese and was a great champion of girls' schooling – an area often neglected in his rural diocese. His own family – he had 11 children – gave him a great sympathy for young people and Archbishop Benson summed up the views of both young and old when he described Atlay as 'the most beautiful combination of enthusiasm, manliness and modesty'. He is buried in the Lady Arbour of Hereford Cathedral and there is a fine marble recumbent effigy of him in the north transept of the cathedral.

Reading Atlay's Visitation Charges to his clergy today, one might be forgiven for thinking him a stern disciplinarian. However, he had a gentler side:

I read a passage in a book the other day which exactly illustrates what was in my mind. You are acquainted, I dare say, with Overbeck's picture of Christ blessing little children. There is one figure in it which strikes some people more than all the rest. Some are gazing in reverent wonder and attention; one kisses His robe; a fond mother seems anxious to draw His attention to her own little one; but at His right side, as it were under the shadow of His wing, one little calm-faced child is standing as close to the Saviour as possible, and appears to wish for nothing more than to be close to Him. O! The blessedness of thus simply coming to, and abiding under the All-holy Presence; surely it is good for us to be there.

Stir up, we beseech Thee, O Lord, the wills of thy faithful people, that, loving Thee above all things, in Thee we may find rest and peace. Amen.

Visitation Charge April 1879

A passage which shows Atlay's abiding love for his cathedral:

Think of the Cathedral in which we are now assembled; if the spirits of the departed could walk the earth once more; if Athelstan, and Lozing, and Raynelm, and Stanbury, and Audley, my honoured predecessors in this See; if the spirit of that man to whom mainly, under God, the present restoration is due, Dean Merewether, could revisit the earth, would they not rejoice, think you, with exceeding great joy, at the condition in which we now see the fabric, so deservedly the pride of the County and the Diocese?

Visitation Charge April 1870

December

Christmas Day

Saints & Sinners unite

In so many ways, Christmas Day is the day *par excellence* for saints and sinners as both are drawn together by the Christ-Child, who came to bring peace and forgiveness for all. The Hereford Cathedral Crib shows, in a dramatic way, how both saints and sinners take part in the story. The figures were all made by local schools. The first group (Aylestone School, 2003) shows the 'saints' – the holy family of Mary, Joseph and the Christ-Child and the angel Gabriel, towering over the scene (Whitecross School, 2004). Nearby are the 'sinners' – the rustic shepherds shield their eyes at the angel's brilliance (Hereford Cathedral School, 2004) and the wise men (Bishop's School, 2006) give an air of mystery to the scene. Finally, neither saint nor sinner, but serving both is an enormous camel (St Mary's RC School, 2007) which provides amusement for the many who come to the cathedral at the Christmas season.

Thomas Traherne imagines the whole community of Hereford – saints and sinners – coming together in unity on Christmas Day:

Hark how remoter parishes do sound!
Far off they ring
For Thee, my king,
Even round about the town:
The churches scattered over all the ground
Serve for Thy praise, who art with glory crowned.
This city is an engine great
That makes my pleasure more complete;
The sword, the mace, the magistrate,
To honour Thee attend in state;
The whole assembly sings;
The minster rings.

Thomas Traherne *c.*1636–74, 'On Christmas Day' – *Centuries*

Shortly before Christmas 1907 while they were holidaying in Rome, Lady Elgar, wife of Sir Edward, wrote this carol especially for 'Dr Sinclair and the choristers of Hereford Cathedral'. The theme of the carol likewise reminds us that Christmas Day breaks down barriers of rich and poor, saint and sinner:

Bowered on sloping hillsides rise
In sunny glow, the purpling vine;
Beneath the greyer English skies,
In fair array, the red-gold apples shine.
To those in snow,
To those in sun,
Love is but one;
Hearts beat and glow
By oak or palm
Friends, in storm or calm.

C Alice Elgar 1848–1920, 'A Christmas Greeting'

Stephen d.*c.*35

First Christian martyr

The magnificent church of St Stephen in Old Radnor possesses several great treasures. First, a beautiful rood screen reminiscent of many in Devon and Cornwall, which stretches across the entire church. Then, in the chancel, we see the ornate organ case dating from the late 16th century, possibly given by John Bull (see 13 March), the famous musician and noted son of this community. Finally, there is the ancient font close by the main door, over four feet across and almost big enough for baptism by total immersion! That 'going down into the waters of death' has always been a feature of Christian baptism – a reminder that the Christ Child was born to suffer and that he calls his followers likewise to suffer so that they may know his glory. That vocation was first embraced by St Stephen, patron of Old Radnor. One of the first deacons appointed by the apostles to serve the poor and needy, Stephen was persecuted by the Jewish Sanhedrin and was stoned to death. He became the first Christian martyr. His cult spread far and wide, and in England 46 ancient churches are dedicated to him, most of them being built after the Norman conquest.

The paradox, which runs through this book – that of saint and sinner – is reflected in the bitter-sweet theme of Christmas. Many artists have represented this – the Christ-child born with the shadow of the cross above the manger – and it is a paradox reflected in many carols:

Sing lullaby!
Lullaby baby, now a-sleeping,
Sing lullaby!
Hush, do not wake the Infant King,
Soon will come sorrow with the morning,
Soon will come bitter grief and weeping:
Sing lullaby!

Sing lullaby!
Lullaby baby, now a-dozing,
Sing lullaby!
Hush, do not wake the Infant King,
Soon comes the cross, the nails, the piercing,
Then in the grave at last reposing
Sing lullaby!

Sing lullaby!
Lullaby! Is the babe awaking?
Sing lullaby!
Hush, do not stir the Infant King,
Dreaming of Easter, gladsome morning,
Conquering Death, its bondage breaking:
Sing lullaby!

Basque noel, trans. S Baring-Gould 1834–1924

John the Evangelist

Beloved disciple

John the Evangelist – 'the beloved disciple' – is remembered on this day as we link him with 'the Word made Flesh', so wonderfully celebrated in the fourth gospel, attributed to John. After the resurrection, John is described in *Acts* as playing, with Peter and James, a leading part in the church at Jerusalem. Many later stories of the saint are legendary, such as the story of how John was challenged to drink a poisoned cup. He rendered the poison harmless with a blessing and drank the draught unscathed, and hence is often shown holding a chalice with a snake. As one of the four evangelists, his better known emblem is that of the eagle, and he must have been a familiar figure to medieval congregations through being represented on rood screens, standing with Mary at the foot of the cross. John is commemorated by several church dedications in Shropshire (including Newcastle, near Clun) and in Herefordshire (including Shobdon and Storridge). In all there are over 180 Johannine dedications throughout the country. Today we remember especially our sister cathedral at Brecon, dedicated in honour of St John the Evangelist.

The great theme of the Incarnation – the Word made Flesh – is reflected in this poem:

The heart could never speak
But that the Word was spoken.
We hear the heart break
Here with hearts unbroken.
Time, teach us the art
That breaks and heals the heart.

Heart, you would be dumb
But that your Word was said
In time, and the Echoes come
Thronging from the dead.
Time, teach us the art
That resurrects the heart.

Tongue, you can only say
Syllables, joy and pain,
Till Time, having its way
Makes the Word live again.
Time, merciful Lord,
Grant us to learn your Word.

Edwin Muir 1889–1959, 'The Heart Could Never Speak'

Henry Stanley Newman 1837–1912

Protector of orphans

On the day when we recall the scheming King Herod and the children put to death on his orders, we remember one whose attitude to the young and vulnerable was the complete opposite, and whose legacy of care continues today. Henry Stanley Newman was an influential Quaker in the Marches and helped to revive the Meeting at the Pales near Llandegley, Radnorshire, with its beautiful meeting house. He was a great supporter of education in the area and also established a day school at the Pales. In 1873 Newman founded the Orphans Printing Press, a business aimed at supporting the recently founded Leominster Orphans Homes. It was intended that the Press should serve three main functions – to provide training for at least some of the orphans in its care, to generate support for the homes, and to publish material which would act as a force for good. With a gas-powered press valued at £100 the children set to work for three hours in the morning, with the afternoon set aside for schooling. By 1874 Newman noted that 'there seems to be a more healthy tone about them, now they feel they are earning their own bread and learning a useful trade'. Soon after this the Elementary Education Act was to prohibit the employment of children. Nevertheless the seeds had been planted and several of the children went on to work within the business. Newman was also a prolific writer, being editor of *The Friend*, the Quaker weekly journal from 1892 until his death in 1912.

Newman showed his Christian faith and ministry through his work in education and in encouraging the young – a reminder that we can be such an influence for good when we encourage rather than criticise:

Children learn what they live

If a child lives with criticism – he learns to condemn.
If a child lives with hostility – he learns to fight.
If a child lives with ridicule – he learns to be shy.
If a child lives with shame – he learns to feel guilty.

If a child lives with tolerance – she learns to be patient.
If a child lives with encouragement – she learns confidence.
If a child lives with praise – she learns to appreciate.
If a child lives with fairness – she learns justice.

If children live with security – they learn to have faith.
If children live with approval – they learn to like themselves.
If children live with acceptance and friendship – they learn to find love in the world.

Anon.

Thomas Becket *c.*1118–70

'The other Thomas'

In the little church of Credenhill is a tiny stained glass window dating from about 1420, and showing two bishops named Thomas, side by side. One is Thomas of Canterbury, who died on this day in 1170, struck down by four knights in his own cathedral in Canterbury. The other is Hereford's own Thomas Cantilupe (see 25 August, 2 October and 25 October). From early days, these two Thomases were linked. As a boy, Cantilupe, when asked what he wanted to be when he grew up, replied that he wished to be a soldier, following in the footsteps of Becket. Although Cantilupe was not martyred, his life showed many similarities to his more famous forebear – like Becket he was involved in court service and was a notable politician. On his canonisation, the liturgies devised for the feast day of the new saint bear many resemblances to those already in use at Canterbury, and in art, the two Thomases are often linked. The window at Credenhill was possibly made for the centenary of Cantilupe's canonisation, and near to Cantilupe's shrine in the north transept of Hereford Cathedral there were, according to historical records, painted murals of both saints. The new canopy over Cantilupe's shrine, in its depiction of the 'saints of Hereford', shows both Thomases kneeling before the Virgin and Child – Cantilupe with his 'lupus' or wolf and Becket with a sword through his mitre – a symbol of his death. But whereas Becket's canonisation was 'rushed' through and declared by 1170, Cantilupe had to wait much longer – for 38 years.

Becket was revered as a 'red martyr' – one who shed his blood for Christ. Cantilupe was regarded as a 'white martyr' – one who knew great suffering and yet did not suffer a martyr's death. In both, the element of self-giving is pre-eminent:

Beloved, we do not think of a martyr simply as a good Christian who has been killed because he is a Christian: for that would be solely to mourn. We do not think of him simply as a good Christian who has been elevated to the company of the Saints, for that would be simply to rejoice: and neither our mourning nor our rejoicing is as the world's is. A Christian martyrdom is never an accident. Saints are not made by accident. Still less is a Christian martyrdom the effect of a man's will to become a Saint, as a man by willing and contriving may become a ruler of men. Ambition fortifies the will of man to become a ruler over other men: it operates with deception, cajolery, and violence, it is the action of impurity upon impurity. Not so in Heaven. A martyr, a saint, is always made by the design of God, for His love of men, to warn them and to lead them, to bring them back to His ways. A martyrdom is never the design of man; for the true martyr is he who has become the instrument of God, who has lost his will in the will of God, not lost it but found it, for he has found freedom in submission to God. The martyr no longer desires anything for himself, not even the glory of martyrdom. So thus as on earth the Church mourns and rejoices at once, in a fashion that the world cannot understand; so in Heaven the Saints are most high, having made themselves most low, and are seen not as we see them, but in the light of the Godhead from which they draw their being.

T S Eliot 1888–1965, *Murder in the Cathedral* (1935)

Charles Dickens 1812–70

The great novelist visits Ross-on-Wye

We smile at the number of times we hear 'Elizabeth I stayed here' and indeed, many ancient country houses build their reputation on such legends. The Royal Hotel in Ross-on-Wye likewise frequently uses its famous associations – not with Elizabeth I but with Charles Dickens, the most popular novelist of the Victorian period. Dickens stayed in the building when it was a private house owned by George Dolby, his business manager and proof reader. He certainly stayed there for a weekend in January 1869 when he was planning his American Book Reading Tour, and, while we can by no means claim Dickens for the Marches, we can confidently celebrate his affection for Herefordshire in general and for Ross in particular. Born in Portsmouth, Dickens moved to London at an early age, and when his father was imprisoned for debt, went to work in a 'blacking' or shoe polish factory. This had a profound effect on the young Charles and gave him a life-long sympathy with the poor and marginalised. He started his professional writing life as a reporter and published short stories, but his first success was *Pickwick Papers* (1836–7). This was, like most of its successors, published in instalments in magazines. The practice lent his stories rhythm and the frequent 'cliff-hangers' kept the public interested. His novels have given to us some of the most memorable characters in English literature and they undoubtedly brought him fame and success. Dickens was in frequent demand to travel abroad (he made a celebrated visit to the United States) and he gave many public recitals of his works. On his death on 9 June 1870 he was buried, not in Rochester Cathedral (as had been his wish), but in Poets' Corner in Westminster Abbey. On his tombstone are inscribed the words: 'He was a sympathiser to the poor, the suffering and oppressed – and by his death, one of England's greatest writers is lost to the world'.

Dickens is associated with the development of Christmas as a family festival and a season of goodwill and conviviality. Our focusing on a passage celebrating Christmas Day reminds us that the great festival does not end on 25 December but continues for the whole 'twelve days' until Epiphany on 6 January and, in some traditions, until the feast of Candlemas on 2 February:

Running to the window, he opened it, and put out his head. No fog, no mist; clear, bright, jovial, stirring, cold; cold, piping for the blood to dance to; Golden sunlight; Heavenly sky; sweet fresh air; merry bells. Oh, glorious. Glorious!

'What's today?' cried Scrooge, calling downward to a boy in Sunday clothes, who perhaps had loitered in to look about him.

'Eh?' returned the boy, with all his might of wonder.

'What's today, my fine fellow?' said Scrooge.

'Today!' replied the boy. 'Why, CHRISTMAS DAY.'

'It's Christmas Day!' said Scrooge to himself. 'I haven't missed it. The Spirits have done it all in one night. They can do anything they like. Of course they can. Of course they can. Hallo, my fine fellow!'

'Hallo!' returned the boy.

'Do you know the Poulterer's, in the next street but one, at the corner?' Scrooge inquired.

'I should hope I did,' replied the lad.

'An intelligent boy!' said Scrooge. 'A remarkable boy! Do you know whether they've sold the prize Turkey that was hanging up there? Not the little prize Turkey: the big one?' ... Go and buy it, and tell 'em to bring it here. Come back with the man, and I'll give you a shilling. Come back with him in less than five minutes, and I'll give you half-a crown! ... I'll send it to Bob Cratchit's!' whispered Scrooge, rubbing his hands and splitting with a laugh.

Charles Dickens, *A Christmas Carol* (1843)

Fabian Stedman 1640–1713

Father of 'change-ringing'

Tonight, many bell-ringers will ring out the old year and ring in the new. In many towers, the last half hour of the old year will be mourned by bells rung 'half-muffled' and then, just before midnight, the leather muffles will be removed and the new year joyfully welcomed with the clashing of unsheathed bells. In England, church bells are not rung in melody, but in permutations or 'changes', and this practice has spread to Australia, Canada and the United States. While most campanologists will be aware of the many different 'methods' of change-ringing, many will be unaware that one of the most well-known methods – Stedman Triples – celebrates one born in Herefordshire. Fabian Stedman, a son of the Reverend Francis Stedman of Yarkhill, was baptized there on 7 December 1640. At the age of 15 he was apprenticed to a master printer in London and joined the Scholars of Cheapside, a bell-ringing society, serving as its treasurer in 1662. In 1664 he joined the Society of College Youths, which had been founded in 1637. Renamed the Ancient Society of College Youths in the 19th century, this bell-ringing society is still active today.

Stedman seems to have moved from London to Cambridge, where he worked as a printer and served as parish clerk at St Benet's Church. In 1677 he became Steward of College Youths and five years later, Master. Returning to London he changed profession, becoming a clerk in the Customs and Excise office. He died in 1713 and was buried at St Andrew Undershaft. His main claim to fame is as one of the 'fathers of change-ringing', setting out his scientific approach to the subject in two books – *Tintinnalogia* (1669) and *Campanalogia* (1677) – a full century before Joseph Lagrange, the French mathematician, wrote his treatise *Reflexions* (1770) with its mathematical approach to campanology.

There can be none better than Tennyson's words to 'ring out the old and ring in the new':

Ring out wild bells to the wild sky,
The flying cloud, the frosty light:
The year is dying in the night;
Ring out wild bells and let him die.

Ring out the old, ring in the new,
Ring, happy bells, across the snow:
The year is going, let him go;
Ring out the false, ring in the true.

Ring out the grief that saps the mind,
For those that here we see no more;
Ring out the feud of rich and poor,
Ring in redress to all mankind.

Ring in the valiant man and free,
The larger heart, the kindlier hand;
Ring out the darkness of the land,
Ring in the Christ that is to be.

Alfred, Lord Tennyson 1809–92, from 'In Memoriam' (1849)

Index of Names

Where a person has a day entry the page number is given in red

Index of Places

Index of Sources

Select Index of Themes